FABRICATING WOMEN

Fabricating Women

The Seamstresses of Old Regime France, 1675–1791

CLARE HARU CROWSTON

DUKE UNIVERSITY PRESS *Durham & London* 2001

© 2001 Duke University Press
All rights reserved
Printed in the United States of
America on acid-free paper ∞
Designed by Amy Ruth Buchanan
Typeset in Bembo by Tseng
Information Systems, Inc.
Library of Congress Cataloging-in-
Publication Data appear on the last
printed page of this book.

For my parents, Taka and Wallace Crowston

The Lackey: Miss, here is your seamstress.

Colombine: Ah! Margot, have you brought my mantua?

Margot: Yes, miss; I think it will suit you perfectly well. Since I started working, I've never seen an outfit so well-cut.

Arlequin: Now, there's a charming little creature. My dear, how would you like to make me a shirt and some leggings?

Margot: If you please, sir; we don't work for men at our place.

Colombine: But it seems to me, Margot, that this dress comes up very high; you can't see my bosom at all.

Margot: It's perhaps not the fault of the dress, miss.

Colombine: Be quiet, Margot, you stupid thing. Take back your dress, I look like I don't know what in it.

Arlequin: The more I see that child, the more she pleases me . . . a word with you: I need a chamber maid; I think that you would suit me well; can you shave?

Margot: Me, shave? I can see you're a kidder; I'd die of fear just touching a man with the tip of my finger. Goodbye, miss; I'll bring your mantua back in a quarter of an hour with some bosom.

—REGNARD, *La Coquette* (1691)

Contents

List of Figures and Tables

Figures

Tables

List of Abbreviations

AC	Archives communales
AD	Archives départementales
AN	Archives nationales
AN MC	Archives nationales Minutier Central
BA	Bibliothèque de l'Arsenal
BN	Bibliothèque nationale
BN MSS	Bibliothèque nationale manuscript collection

Money and Measurements

1 livres = 20 sous
1 sol = 12 deniers
1 écu = 3 livres
1 louis = 6 livres
1 aune = 1.18 meters or 46.5 inches

Note on French language usage: Unless otherwise indicated, quotations in the text from French language sources have been translated into English by the author.

Acknowledgments

In the course of this project, I have incurred innumerable debts in France, Canada, and the United States, which I am very happy to acknowledge here. This project received funding from a number of institutions over the years. The Einaudi Foundation and the Council of European Studies each funded a summer of research in France during the predissertation stage. A Social Sciences and Humanities Research Council of Canada fellowship and a Bourse Châteaubriand allowed me to spend three years in France researching and writing my dissertation. The Andrew W. Mellon Foundation sponsored another year of dissertation writing, allowing me to remain happily at my desk in Paris. At the University of Illinois at Urbana-Champaign, I received a semester of leave funded by the university's Research Board. Publication of the book was made possible in part by a grant from the UIUC Research Board. I am very grateful to all of these institutions for their generosity.

A cadre of highly competent and diligent staff members at the archives and libraries I visited in France guided me through the research process. I am particularly indebted to Mme Bimbinet and M. Boudignon of the Archives nationales who helped me negotiate the Y series and the Minutier central. My knowledge of the material culture of clothing was greatly enriched by Jean-Paul LeClerc, curator of eighteenth-century garments at the Musée de la Mode in Paris, who decked me out in white gloves and booties to visit the museum's collection of Old Regime dresses, skirts, shirts, corsets, men's suits, and sample books. At the Musée Galliera, I was welcomed by director Mme Join-Detierle, and I received invaluable infor-

mation from Françoise Vittu-Téart, historian and curator of eighteenth-
and nineteenth-century clothing.

My longest-standing debts are to the faculty and staff of the Cornell
University History Department, who provided the supportive home in
which this project was conceived and nurtured. Steven L. Kaplan has been
and continues to be an extraordinary mentor. He has offered the insights
of his profound immersion in French history and culture and provided an
exemplary model of intellectual curiosity, discipline, and imagination. I
am deeply grateful for his generosity and friendship. I would also like to
thank Isabel Hull for her close attention to my work and for her encouragement over the years. She has been an inspiring model of scholarship and
pedagogy. My graduate seminars with her and with Dominick LaCapra
were tremendously helpful in opening my thinking to new questions and
approaches to history. I also benefited on several occasions from presenting
my work to the history department's European Colloquium.

While undertaking research, writing the dissertation, and completing
revisions, I benefited from the encouragement and advice of many historians in France. Gilles Postel-Vinay reviewed many of the book's arguments—often smuggled into our discussions of eighteenth-century apprenticeship—and helped me to shape and refine them. Philippe Minard
has been a very supportive friend and mentor. I also learned an enormous
amount from seminars and discussions with Simona Cerutti, Christian
Jouhaud, Jacques Revel, and Daniel Roche. These historians helped me to
think about history in a new way and they also aided me in designing
my project, locating important sources, and interpreting my results. Jean
Jetzsch offered important contributions from his own research, including
the discovery of the P series, where records of the reception of post-1776
masters and mistresses had been hiding for two hundred years. I am obliged
to Maurice Aymard for inviting me to present my work to his seminar at
the Ecole des Hautes Etudes en Sciences Sociales in Paris in 1993.

A group of scholars working on women and guilds, including Daryl
Hafter, Janine Lanza, Carol Loats, and Cynthia Truant generously shared
archival information and commentary on my ideas, and I benefited a great
deal from reading their published and unpublished work. Almost as much
as their research, their example gave me an understanding of women's corporate solidarity. During revisions of this manuscript, I made presentations
at the Society for French Historical Studies conferences, the Conference
on Family History, the conference Women, Work, and the Breadwinner

Ideology, in Salzburg, Austria, and to the Economics Department of the University of Chicago and the History Department of the University of Michigan. I would like to thank Judith Bennett, David Galenson, Christopher Johnson, Laura Lee Downs, and Peter Scholliers for their thoughtful comments on these papers.

While revising my manuscript I was lucky to find another supportive academic home. I am grateful to my colleagues at the Department of History at the University of Illinois at Urbana-Champaign, who took a chance on an untested scholar and have since provided me with unwavering enthusiasm and encouragement. The history department provided a congenial environment for undertaking my revisions and, almost as important, allowed me a year's leave of absence to finish them. In particular, I benefited from suggestions and comments by members of the History Workshop and the Early Modern Europe Group, to whom I presented my work. I would especially like to thank Frederic Jaher and Tony Ballantyne, who bravely tackled the entire manuscript and gave me excellent suggestions for rewriting, as well as Antoinette Burton, Diane Koenker, Craig Koslofsky, John Lynn, Meagan McLaughlin, and Dana Rabin, who read individual chapters. The students in my graduate seminars on women's and gender history and material culture and consumption inspired and stimulated me as I completed the manuscript. Another midwestern institution, the Wabash Valley French History Group, provided expert readers for my work. Its members include Brad Brown, Jim Farr, Paul Hanson, David Kammerling-Smith, Rene Marion, Kevin Robbins, and Matthew Vester.

Over the years, a group of friends and fellow historians has provided invaluable support, insight, and camaraderie. Janine Lanza has been a constant friend and colleague from our first days of graduate school at Cornell University, through research in France, dissertation writing, and the tribulations of the job market and our first faculty positions. Fellow Cornellians Martin Bruegel, Tina Campt, Michael Wilson, and Sydney Watts have been stimulating intellectual *compagnons* and wonderful friends. Posterity may never enjoy our e-mail correspondence, but it gave me a much-needed community and some very funny stories. I am also grateful to Cynthia Koepp for her friendship, wise advice, and hospitality in Ithaca. In France, Catherine de l'Arc and Emmanuelle Sruh were admirable friends, listening patiently to my academic and nonacademic exploits and sharing with me their insiders' knowledge of French culture and language. My cohort in the archives and libraries—Paul Cohen, Cynthia Cupples, Lisa

DiCaprio, Nicole Dombrowski, Jeff Horn, Lynn Sharp, Judith Sirkus, and Victoria Thompson—formed another source of intellectual and moral support, as well as welcome diversion and distraction.

In the final stages of preparing this manuscript I was lucky to have Melissa Salrin as my research assistant. She not only checked my references scrupulously but she also knew when to order me sternly to send in the final manuscript. Lil Morales kindly assisted me in preparing photographs for the book. I have been blessed in my dealings with Duke University Press. I am very grateful to its editorial board and in particular to my editor Valerie Millholland for her enthusiastic support and for agreeing to publish a long manuscript from a first-time author. Miriam Angress and Jonathan Director have cheerfully and skillfully guided the book through the long obstacle course of production. I thank Duke's anonymous readers for their encouragement and their helpful suggestions. I also thank my copyeditor, Jean Brady, for her painstaking and masterful work on the manuscript, and Amy Ruth Buchanan for her fabulous design.

Finally, I would like to thank the people who have helped me on a daily basis over the years. The friendly and helpful staff of Micro-Université generously accorded me a place to write my dissertation and, later, my book. My little office in the corner upstairs was a wonderful haven from the outside world. The Banihashem and Sachs families extended their homes and hearts to me when I was far from my own home. I am grateful to them for their warmth and hospitality. Ali Banihashem provided first-rate technical skills and support; he continues to sustain me with infinite patience, generosity, and love. Amir Banihashem was a constant source of energy and fun and has turned out to be a model of academic achievement. In North America, my brother Kevin and sister Catherine provided regular moral boosts. Last but not least, I am profoundly grateful to my parents, Taka and Wallace Crowston, to whom this book is dedicated, for their unfailing encouragement and assistance. Without their help—and their persistent inquiries into the progress I was making—this project would have never reached UMI, let alone the printing press. I am extraordinarily pleased to affirm to them in writing that I have at long last finished the book that they have been worrying about since it was a term paper.

Introduction

"The needle and the sword cannot be manipulated by the same hands. If I were sovereign, I would permit sewing and the needle trades only to women and to cripples reduced to occupying themselves like them." Writing *Emile* in 1762, Jean-Jacques Rousseau dismissed the centuries-old male trade of tailoring, recasting needlework as an essentially feminine activity. An emasculating occupation for men, needlework was a natural and appropriate vocation for women. For Rousseau, women's affinity to the needle stemmed from their innate love of clothing and finery, itself a product of their biological need to seduce men in order to produce children. As a toddler, his fictional character Sophie was drawn to needlework as a means to decorate her doll, a stand-in for the grown woman she would become. The pen and the sword held scant interest for her, being futile to her reproductive needs. Rousseau thus pitied the Italians their sad streets and shops, where gross male hands traded in delicate fabrics and lace. Each sex, he declared, should wield only the tools appropriate to it.[1]

What Rousseau did not acknowledge was that women's capacity to work in the needle trades was not a universally enshrined aspect of French life. For centuries, male tailors' guilds enjoyed a monopoly over the fabrication of custom-made clothing in French towns and cities. Women breached this preserve for the first time in 1652 when the tailors' guild of Aix-en-Provence started accepting female members, and more decisively in 1675 when seamstresses in Paris and Rouen acquired independent, exclusively female guilds. After this date, seamstresses in numerous cities across France entered tailors' guilds as subordinate members. Until they joined the guild system—and in the many cities where they did not—women were legally forbidden from making and selling clothing, despite the proclamations of social commentators such as Rousseau. This book is about the seamstresses of late seventeenth- and eighteenth-century France, and the process by which their trade became both a major actor in the urban economy and a quintessentially feminine occupation.

The French word for seamstress is *couturière,* often translated as "dressmaker" or "milliner." These choices are misleading, because the word was derived from the fact that they were women who sewed for a living, not from the specific articles of clothing they made. *Couturière* comes from *coudre,* to sew, while the French *tailleur,* or tailor, derives from *tailler,* to cut.[2] Given the risks involved, cutting was considered the most difficult and most noble element of the garment trades. One could easily remove and restitch a faulty seam, but an error in cutting might ruin an entire piece of valuable cloth. The statutes of the thirteenth-century Parisian tailors' guild reserved cutting cloth for established masters, leaving sewing to subordinate workers called *valets cousturiers.*[3] The origins of their trade appellations thus reflect disparities in privilege and reputation between tailors and seamstresses, which persisted throughout the Old Regime.

The male form of *cousturier* appeared occasionally during the sixteenth century, but it faded from usage by the end of the next century.[4] In 1680, Richelet's *Dictionnaire françois* defined the word as a provincial term for tailor: "This word means Tailor. It is said in some Provinces, but in Paris one does not make use of it."[5] By 1694, the dictionary of the *Académie française* was succinct: "Whose trade is sewing . . . It is hardly used anymore."[6] The *couturier* did not reemerge until the end of the nineteenth century, when the predominance of mechanized mass production accorded new glamor to the bespoke trade. In this period, the *couturier* lost his medieval humility to become the creative genius of fashion, the driving force behind the luxury and prestige of custom-made clothing. In late-twentieth-century France, a *couturière* is a modest female artisan who performs mending and alterations for a neighborhood clientele, while the *couturier* is a world-famous artist and businessman.

As the male form of the word declined in the seventeenth century, the female version gained ground. The female term had come into use in medieval times to describe a woman who sewed, either professionally or for private purposes.[7] With the growth of women's participation in the trade and their attainment of guild privileges in 1675, *couturière* acquired stricter professional and gender connotations. In 1680, Richelet defined the term as "she who earns her living sewing linen or cloth."[8] By 1694, the Académie française had arrived at the conclusion that a *couturière* was defined not only by her own sex, but by the sex of her clients: "Who works in sewing, either linen, or dresses . . . who makes women's and children's dresses."[9] By the mid-eighteenth century, the notion of corporate privilege was intrinsically associated with the term. The *Encyclopédie* thus opened its definition of *couturière* in 1754 with "woman authorized to work in different garments, as a member of a guild established in 1675."[10]

These definitions reflected a sexual division of labor within the garment trades, which was enshrined by the seamstresses' guild statutes. When they entered guilds, seamstresses in Aix-en-Provence, Paris, and Rouen acquired the right to make articles of clothing for women and children, but not for men or boys over age eight. This sexual division of labor reappeared in every French town or city where seamstresses joined guilds. The eighteenth-century *couturière* thus emerged from the intersection of three distinct forces: first, from cultural conceptions of femininity that cast needlework as an appropriate female trade and encouraged women to work for clients of their own sex; second, from a practical sexual division of labor in the garment trades that intensified over the seventeenth century; and, finally, from the legal and institutional reification of this situation with the creation of the seamstresses' guild in 1675. Drawing on these origins, seamstresses played a crucial role in the economic, social, and cultural production of eighteenth-century France, creating goods, social relations, and cultural meaning.

Within their trade limitations, the seamstresses' empire ranged from mending to *modes*. Seamstresses performed simple darning and alterations, raising hems and patching petticoats for women of the middling and lower orders. They also made fine dresses of delicate silk or plush velvet for members of the royal family and the court aristocracy. In twelve-hour workdays in ateliers scattered across the urban landscape, they fabricated garments for prominent noblewomen, rich bourgeois ladies, and masters' wives, garments that later circulated down to the humblest washerwoman or street hawker through networks of gift giving, resale, and theft. Seamstresses stood at one end of a complex process of production and distribution, which started with the importation of cloth or its domestic manufacture, passed through the hands of Parisian wholesale and retail merchants, and drew on the services and products of an array of ancillary trades, including merchant mercers, linen-drapers, ribbonmakers and lacemakers, fashion merchants, embroiderers, and peddlers of pins and needles.

Individual seamstresses were usually modest artisans, operating out of their own households with a handful of workers at most. Together, they formed a vast and highly effective labor force. Once they had acquired legal standing, they quickly became one of the largest skilled crafts in France, numbering up to ten thousand women and girls in Paris by the end of the eighteenth century. Mistress seamstresses were major employers in a huge, specialized labor market. They offered jobs to thousands of working women, allowing them to accumulate a dowry or support their families. Across the century, the trade offered strong stimulus to French economic development, encouraging the growth of cloth production, the expansion and diversification of the garment trades, and the flourishing of the accessory trades on which they depended.

With the dresses, corsets, and hoopskirts they made, seamstresses helped produce, reproduce, and ultimately change the gender ideologies of their society. These articles of clothing were highly visible markers of femininity, serving to transform their clients from a state of imperfect nature, with all its bulges, boniness, and wrinkles, to a culturally sanctioned feminine appearance comprised of molded breasts, tightly restrained waists, and copious skirts. By highlighting a bustline or skillfully concealing a flawed figure, the seamstress endowed her client with the seductive charms recognized by French men and women as a form of particularly female power. Within their own social world, seamstresses transmitted to their workers and apprentices the professional and cultural skills they acquired through work. With hundreds of new apprentices in Paris and the provinces each year, Old Regime seamstresses trained generations of girls not only to be skilled needleworkers but to be French women. They taught teenage girls the female comportment, self-restraint, delicacy, and taste they learned from their elite clients, thereby helping to convey the civilizing process from the nobility to the working women of Paris. For both client and apprentice, therefore, the mistress seamstress provided one of the most important rites of passage from rough nature to civilized culture.

These different aspects of their trade—size, institutional organization, economic weight, and the "gendered" definition of their work—place the seamstresses at the heart of a range of issues important to historians of early modern Europe. One of these issues is the ongoing reappraisal of the guild system and its place in Old Regime economy and society. French guilds dated from the early Middle Ages at least, and they persisted until their abolition in 1791 under the French Revolution. They were called *communautés* or *corps de métier* in the Old Regime and have been known since the nineteenth century as "corporations," a word I will use interchangeably with "guild" throughout this book.[11] Corporations were formal, trade-based associations, whose members drafted regulations for their craft or commerce and set criteria for admission. Royally approved statutes enshrined the guild's collective legal personality as well as its monopoly over a carefully defined economic or commercial sector. Artisans who belonged to guilds held the status of master or, more rarely, mistress. Masters' workers and apprentices were not guild members, although they participated in the aura of corporate prestige and honor to a certain extent.

Guilds received surprisingly little attention from the proponents of the new labor and social history of the 1960s and 1970s. One reason for their reticence was the consensus that had congealed—in a line from Turgot to contemporary economic liberals—that the guilds were antimodern and antieconomic institutions. Accepting this assumption, many historians dismissed Old Regime corporations as backward, exclusionary, and resistant to new technology. As doomed relics of medieval society, guilds held little attraction for historians more interested in the progressive narratives of industrial and political revolution. Moreover, the fascination the guilds exercised over late-nineteenth-century Social Catholics and proto-fascist economists of the 1930s offered further proof of their essentially pathological character. The self-declared "corporate" nature of the Vichy regime finally cast them beyond the pale of historical research during the postwar period.[12]

In the last fifteen years, however, scholars have returned to the guilds, seeking to understand their functions and significance in a manner unburdened by the teleology of the Revolution and subsequent corporatist revivals.[13] Their reassessment of the guilds has vividly demonstrated the close relationship between the regulation of work and wider systems of social classification and control, and the depth of knowledge that a study of work can offer about the society and culture in which it is performed. As this scholarship has shown, guilds were numerically inferior in the world of work, yet they organized and oversaw many forms of urban production and commerce, including rich luxury trades involved in national and international distribution networks. They provided training for generations of French youths, overseeing the transmission of practical skills and imparting social values of self-discipline, respect, and hard work. Guild masters delivered finished products to meet the myriad needs and desires of city dwellers, they supervised jostling urban labor markets, and they provided an anchor amidst the floating working population of large cities.

Corporations did not operate solely in narrow economic domains, but were an essential part of the fabric of municipal life. Guild leaders engaged in a constant process of negotiation with royal officials regarding the imposition of taxes, production rights, and corporate financial administration. Along with other corps, they formed a link in the chain of credit that supplied the crown with a substantial portion of its income. When royal financial credibility waned in the late seventeenth and eighteenth centuries, ministers passed the burden to corporate institutions, whose members acquired loans based in part on their collective credentials. This service in turn provided the trade corps with a form of moral obligation over the king, giving them leverage to extract protection, sympathetic arbitration, and indirect financial recompense for their expenditures.[14] Individual corporations were more or less equipped to succeed in these negotiations, depending on their privileges and prestige, their economic force, their leaders' savvy, and their lawyers' skill. We know less about the ways guilds cooperated and competed with the multitude of nongovernmental institutions that shared an intense interest in urban social order. Parish foundations sponsored orphaned children's apprenticeship, hospitals offered forms of vocational training and sometimes mastership for the poor, and some convents or monastic orders allowed artisans to sell goods freely on their territory. The role of these institutions in urban networks of craftsmanship and commerce remains to be elucidated.

If recent studies have clarified the crucial place of guilds in urban communities, they have also emphasized the distance between the daily lives of individual guilds and the corporate vision of a harmonious order of mutual solidarity and social integration. Trade corporations were characterized by a high degree of internal strife, between the elite and the rank and file and among factions of masters divided by wealth, specialization, or family ties. Guild masters continually transgressed the legal and ideological barriers that ostensibly separated them from the outside world, maintaining complex relations with competing corporations, illegal workers, and inhabitants of suburban areas free from guild control. Steven Kaplan's work on the faubourg Saint-Antoine emphasizes the wide-ranging economic ties between Parisian masters and the inhabitants of that unincorporated suburb. Michael Sonenscher has characterized preindustrial systems of production and distribution as a "bazaar economy," far from the highly regimented and segmented template envisioned in guild statutes.[15]

One issue on which scholars have not always agreed has been the social and cultural aspects of corporate organization. Steven Kaplan has argued that the guilds' social significance preceded and surpassed their economic functions. According to Kaplan, guild membership conveyed a fixed and privileged status within the Third Estate. A guild master's place in the social taxonomy was as important as his economic or commercial privileges.[16] Others have found that relations between master and guild included as much cynicism, opposition, and strategic self-interest as they did loyalty and self-identification. Michael Sonenscher has thus drawn the counterportrait of a guild system characterized by high rates of failure among apprentices, an extremely mobile and transient labor force, and widespread recourse to the law to settle endemic conflicts between masters and journeymen. In a study of guilds in eighteenth-century Turin, Simona Cerutti argued that membership in the tailors' guild fulfilled economic and familial strategies that had almost nothing to do with the trade of tailoring itself.[17]

It is no doubt true, as Cerutti and Sonenscher insist, that guild membership did not convey a simple or singular identity on these privileged artisans. The memoirs of the Parisian glazier Jacques-Louis Ménétra offer vivid testimony to the antipathy and indifference ordinary masters might feel toward overbearing corporate elites.[18] It would be a mistake, however, to reduce the social and cultural weight of guild membership to mere self-interest or to dismiss guilds as hollow institutions. Masters and mistresses of Old Regime corporations consistently identified themselves as such to notaries, policemen, judges, and other interlocutors. Their status carried economic force, enabling them to operate in specialized labor and product markets, to train apprentices, and to participate fully in their sphere of trade. While people argued about the respect due to members of different corps, it is clear that guild membership was also an important source of honor in the urban context. Masters' and mistresses' conception of their place in the city, of their rights and duties, and of their relationship to other social actors and institutions were fundamentally affected by guild membership.

This complicated interaction of institutions, individuals, and external forces defies any singular or linear chronology. The corporate system did not follow a simple downward path from the High Middle Ages to the Revolution, but rather a series of different trajectories that waxed and waned over time. Guilds varied a great deal from trade to trade, from city to city, and from region to region. They endured waves of adhesion or alienation among their members, caused by economic conjunctures, royal legislation, internal politics, wars, and a host of other conditions. There is no way to predict the accessibility of a particular guild, the efficacy of its regulations, or the loyalty of its members, certainly not by its place on a teleological path of downward degeneration. In these shifting tides, one event nonetheless stands out sharply. Turgot's abolition of the guilds in 1776, and their reestablishment shortly thereafter, marked a crucial moment of rupture. These events profoundly changed and destabilized the corporate system in ways that historians are only beginning to understand.

A final aspect of the reassessment of the guilds has been a new interest in women's place in the corporate sphere. Historians such as Daryl Hafter, Cynthia Truant, Judith Coffin, and Carol Loats have drawn attention to the possibilities available to women in corporate life, either as wives of male masters, as apprentices, or as members of a small number of independent female guilds. This literature has successfully challenged the neglect of women and gender in revisionist studies of the guilds, emphasizing the social and legal advantages women acquired through guild membership.[19] As these historians have pointed out, guildswomen gained the right to conduct independent businesses and defend their trade prerogatives in court. They also held exceptional prominence among women by sponsoring public guild ceremonies and negotiating with royal and municipal officials.[20]

Building on previous studies, this study is on one level a close examination of the vicissitudes of an individual guild. It is the first to scrutinize a women's corporation and to analyze its organization and function both synchronically and across time. It investigates the process by which a women's corporate body came into being and the means by which it governed and reproduced itself, and it examines the relationship between the corporation, the royal government, and other urban institutions. The female nature of the guild offers both advantages and disadvantages for a study of eighteenth-century corporatism. The Parisian seamstresses were clearly exceptional. One of only four women's guilds in the city, their experiences differed to a significant extent from those of their male colleagues.[21] Moreover, their trade prerogatives were explicitly defined by gender, a fact that placed them in a unique position among Parisian guilds. Nevertheless, the distinctive nature of this corporation is also helpful for a general understanding of the system, highlighting the underlying elements deemed essential regardless of gender as well as the variables that could and did change with the introduction of women. The comparative aspect of gender history thus reveals as much about the "normal" case as it does about the "exceptional." In order to bolster this comparative approach, throughout this book I have used the tailors as a foil for the seamstresses.

Apart from asking general questions about corporate organization, in this book I investigate the effects of gender on this female trade and the possible relationship between women and guilds. Approaching the guild system from the perspective of women and gender, I examine the place envisaged for women in the corporate world, on the part of royal and municipal governments, male guild members, and female artisans themselves. Could a woman be a master? Or, in other words, what kind of master was a mistress? Under what circumstances was the creation of a woman's guild seen to be possible? What inspired women, at different periods in different cities, to demand incorporation, and why did the official responses vary over time and space? Finally, how did women's new guild privileges intersect with existing ones that women held as members of guild families or other corporate groups?

By placing women at the center of the analysis, I draw heavily on previous scholarship in women's and gender history. Previous work in female labor history by Natalie Zemon Davis, Olwen Hufton, Louise Tilly, Joan Scott, Tessie Liu, and Gay Gullickson documented the wide range of women's economic activities in the eighteenth and nineteenth centuries. The notion of the "family economy" described in their studies provides a crucial starting point for understanding women's role in the early modern economy. As argued by these scholars, women's—and men's—work took place within the context of family orientations and strategies, rather than as a solitary activity performed to meet individual needs or aspirations. Women's decisions about work and career were thus fundamentally shaped by the demands of male family members. While this book offers new perspectives on women's work and the family economy, it would have been impossible without the foundations established by earlier historians.[22]

The concept of "gender" as developed by feminist theorists and historians has also been central to my research and writing. In this volume I use gender to refer to culturally and socially constructed notions of the characteristics associated with sexual difference. My definition assumes that conflicts, disagreements, and misunderstandings regarding these characteristics and appropriate male and female behavior coexist within any given culture. Subject to change over time, gender ideologies are by nature unstable, contradictory, and in a constant process of negotiation. Their contents do not change at a uniform pace but unevenly, with certain elements undergoing rapid transformation while others endure. My definition of gender also presumes that historians must attend to male and female experiences, to concepts of both masculinity and femininity, in order to elucidate its meaning and change over time. Men's and women's lives cannot be understood in isolation from each other because they have lived most often in societies and households composed of both sexes. Gender definitions operate as interdependent binaries rather than distinct or autonomous notions. As a result, their nuances emerge most clearly in the interaction between men and women or between symbolic representations of masculinity and femininity.[23]

For all its debts to previous scholars of women and gender, my work in this book rubs against the grain of at least two tenets of existing historiography. One is the widespread impression of an essential discord between women and corporate organization. Women's work has been characterized as essentially informal and heavily influenced by family and reproductive functions and thus as incompatible with the formal training and hierarchical career ladder enshrined in guild statutes. Moreover, historians have often agreed that the consolidation of corporate control over urban trades in the sixteenth and seventeenth centuries led to women's exclusion from skilled work. According to this argument, male guilds formed one element of an unholy triumvirate whose two other branches were encroaching centralized government and the patriarchal family, with the church offering its ideological blessing on them all. Over the early modern period, the argument goes, these forces colluded to submit women's lives to ever greater male control. Historians who have focused on late-medieval guilds, such as Martha Howell, Lyndal Roper, or Merry Wiesner, have generally confirmed a narrowing of women's economic opportunities with the rise of the corporate system. Given these preconceptions, studies of European women in the seventeenth and eighteenth centuries have tended to turn away from the guilds, focusing instead on spheres of activity coded as feminine and dominated by women, such as domestic service, midwifery, wet-nursing, and prostitution.[24]

This study demonstrates, by contrast, that women could thrive in corporate organization and that authorities did not uniformly discriminate against female labor. In contrast to the accepted narrative, the seamstresses of France acquired new access to the guild system at the moment when absolutizing power in France reached an apex under Louis XIV. In this case, the centralizing and unifying tendencies of the royal state acted to extend women's economic and legal privileges, not to curtail them. Moreover, French women proved extremely willing and eager to profit from their new corporate prerogatives. Over its history, more women joined the seamstresses' guild every year than any other male or female corporation; the number of apprentices who began training every year also outstripped male trades. Incorporation offered mixed results to women—particularly to those who could not or would not join the corporate sphere—but clearly women had much greater access to formal structures of trade organization and training than previous studies have suggested.

The second issue I challenge in this book is the notion that modern gender ideologies emerged in the late Old Regime as a result of Enlightenment philosophes and political criticism of the absolutist state. The idea that the world is best explained and run according to binary distinctions centered on an essentialized male-female opposition may indeed be a development of the late eighteenth century, but this book will argue that a long history in the seventeenth and early eighteenth centuries paved the way for that change. The seamstresses demonstrate very clearly that cultural ideas about masculinity and femininity shaped a sexual division of labor during the seventeenth century. A seamstress was a woman who sewed clothing for other women and children, not merely one who sewed for a living. Gender did not await the arrival of the Enlightenment or the Revolution to manifest itself in the garment trades.

Indeed, I suggest in this study that seamstresses not only reflected existing ideas about gender, they were themselves important contributors to changing gender ideologies. Their guild offered a concrete and highly visible symbol of the affinity between women and needlework, transforming a customary affiliation into a set of state-sponsored legal privileges. After 1675, the example of the guild encouraged a growing "feminization" of the garment trades, as new forms of commerce and craft were taken up mostly by women, and men's participation in needlework was increasingly stigmatized as unnatural and undesirable. By the end of the eighteenth century, partly through their example, needlework was hailed not as an appropriate female trade but as a biologically innate feminine skill. Rousseau's dogmatic proclamations would become the received wisdom of the nineteenth century, as all sides agreed that women were naturally made for sewing.

In addition to calling attention to sexual difference as a means of structuring work in the garment trades, seamstresses also played a central role in disseminating the notion that fashion was a particularly feminine concern. Seventeenth-century observers criticized male fops almost as frequently as female fashion addicts, in a social and political context in which ostentatious dress could be equally important for men and women. The link drawn between the female seamstresses and their female customers encouraged the notion of a natural connection between women and clothing that transcended the division between humble needleworker and illustrious client. As abundant and cheap female labor streamed into the seamstresses' trade, women's consumption of clothing quickly began to outpace men's, giving visible support to this idea. Women became privileged consumers of whimsy, caprice, and choice, all furnished by the many hands of the seamstresses. By the end of the eighteenth century, therefore, the seamstresses' labor had helped implant three interrelated notions in French conceptions of gender: a sexual division of labor based on essentialized gender characteristics, an innate and exclusive connection between women and fashion, and an emphasis on learning and displaying femininity through clothing and appearances.

Defined by their own gender and that of their clients, the seamstresses' trade also provides an important perspective on debates regarding the origins of consumer culture in France.[25] Daniel Roche has shown that a "clothing revolution" took place in eighteenth-century Paris as wardrobes grew in size and value across a wide social spectrum, particularly among women. According to Roche, the most important symbol of this revolution was the dress, which moved from being a noble women's monopoly in 1700 to become by 1789 a commonplace of all Parisian women's wardrobes.[26] A closer look at the garments produced by seamstresses reveals that this development more likely took place between the 1670s and 1700, suggesting that crucial changes in mentalities and attitudes may have occurred a century earlier than Roche and others have argued. More profoundly, the seamstresses also underline the constant interrelation between production and consumption. The very definition of their trade identified female producers of clothing with the female consumers who purchased and wore it. An examination of the seamstresses' trade therefore suggests that evolving attitudes toward the material world, the self, and gender ideologies cannot be separated from evolving techniques of production, the creation of corporate institutions regulating work, or the sexual division of labor.

In a similar vein, a final area of historiographical debate I address in this book is the relationship between social and cultural history, a subject of strong interest in both France and the United States in recent years.[27] Joining scholars with similar ambitions, this study strives to overcome the gap that has grown between the two fields, bringing together the methods and problems of social history with the insight and innovation of the new cultural history. To do so, I start with a close examination of seamstresses' techniques of production and distribution—the manner by which they made and sold dresses, skirts, and other female garments—and the social relations that grew out of their labor. I discuss the hierarchy of work within the trade and the characteristics of the female labor market, composed of thousands of women of varying backgrounds, competencies, and ambitions. I also examine the process by which the guild reproduced itself, through the apprenticeship of young girls and the recruitment of new mistresses.

While viewing seamstresses as makers of goods and social relations, in this study I also investigate the cultural meanings associated with them. This effort requires, first of all, understanding and reconstructing as far as possible the seamstresses' cultural habitus. As we have learned, all historical subjects lived within cultures and apprehended "reality" through culturally constructed filters. Culture limits, shapes, and ultimately makes possible social actors' conception of the world. Seamstresses thus drew on and shared collective notions about women and femininity, appropriate female labor, honor, and family life. They formed their perceptions of themselves, their trade, and guild identities from available ideas, which were shaped by discourses constructed within unequal power relations. To understand the seamstresses or other social groups, historians must situate them within the context of their own cultures. In the absence of first-person memoirs or journals, one way to approach this question is through the significance assigned to the *couturière* in contemporary almanacs, plays, engravings, satirical literature, and in eighteenth-century debates about fashion, femininity, and women's work.

A second step in assessing seamstresses' "cultural meaning," however, is to investigate needleworkers as creators of culture. This study begins with the assumption that men and women create meaning, fabricate culture, and produce significance in the work they perform in their ateliers, and indeed in all the mundane gestures of their everyday lives. They are not only subject to culture but are subjects of it, collectively producing and reproducing their worlds of meaning, of social relations, and of goods. This perspective informs my understanding of seamstresses' influence on changing perceptions of fashion and femininity. It also has important methodological implications. While insisting on connections between texts written by seamstresses and broader debates about "femininity" or "women in the public sphere," I also view their documents as strategic statements aimed at achieving goals in specific situations of conflict or competition. An important element of my task has been to uncover and explain those goals and the particular stakes attached to them. I have also tried to use archival documents, in a sensitive and self-critical manner, as a means to access the nuances of culture and social life that went without saying, that were expressed in gestures, looks, laughter, and the hard sweat of physical labor. For these purposes, material culture and visual images offer an intriguing alternative to written sources. The techniques employed for making a dress—and the dress itself hanging in a museum vault—may say as much about seamstresses as the legal briefs written by their lawyers. By taking equally seriously the problems posed by social and cultural history, and informing them with a strong interest in material culture, I offer one attempt at synthesis between the two fields.

My work in this volume is based on archival research in Paris and two French provinces. In order to address the seamstresses in the broadest possible perspective, I offer a limited geographic comparison. To be sure, Paris dominates this book in many ways. The ideological and practical importance of the Parisian guilds—not to mention the abundance of source material on them—argued for a primary focus on the capital city. However, I also devote significant attention to the cities of Aix-en-Provence and Marseilles in Provence and Caen in Normandy. These cities straddled the imaginary line that divided southern and northern France into two distinct cultural, legal, and even linguistic zones, with very different histories of corporate organization. Provincial examples help illuminate the specificity of the Parisian experience and underline the way in which seamstresses evolved in similar ways in very different regions.

The sources for this study consist of notarial, police, and government documents as well as engravings and printed materials. Notarized contracts offered perhaps the most important source of information. In Paris, archives of the notarial office (*étude*) that served the guild for much of the period constituted a crucial set of documents. These include minutes from the guild's assembly meetings, spanning fifty years of the eighteenth century. Given the destruction of the Parisian guilds' archives in the 1871 Hôtel de Ville fire, to my knowledge this study is the first to make use of assembly minutes from a Parisian guild. Although the notarial filter eliminates the seamstresses' actual voices, these minutes offered valuable insight into the guild's internal administration and its interaction with the royal government. They stand in sharp contrast to the loquacious minutes from the

Aix tailors' guild assembly, which exist for a 120-year period in the city's communal archives.[28]

The guild's notary also preserved a large number of seamstresses' apprenticeship contracts, including over four hundred from the year 1716 as well as scattered samples from the 1710s to the 1740s. I supplemented this group with a sample of apprenticeship contracts encompassing all Parisian notaries from the years 1751 and 1761, generating a total of approximately eight hundred contracts. These documents allowed me to investigate practices of apprenticeship and to reconstruct the socioeconomic characteristics of the trade, based on their information regarding apprentices' geographic origins and fathers' professions as well as mistresses' addresses and marital status. A group of seventeenth-century apprenticeship contracts helped clarify the nature of the seamstresses' trade prior to the guild's creation in 1675.

Outside of guild-related documents, notarial contracts provided vital information about seamstresses at two major life events: marriage and death. Marriage contracts included important details about seamstresses and their families, including their fathers' and their grooms' names and professions, brides' and grooms' geographic origins, and the fortunes each partner brought to marriage. This information called for cautious interpretation, because marriage negotiations are not conducive to honesty or transparency. Nevertheless, the contracts offered important insight into marriage strategies among seamstresses and their grooms, including the role of female guild membership in creating matrimonial alliances.

If marriage contracts revealed seamstresses as they established families, probate inventories listed the objects and individuals present in their apartments when they died. The inventories thus provided a summary of the seamstresses' lives, albeit at moments of illness or old age. They allow the historian to glimpse the interior of their homes, meet their family members, and delve into their commercial and personal affairs. The professional gaze of the notary, with its lacunae and distortions, imposes limitations on this glimpse, yet it is extremely valuable nonetheless. The inventories showed me seamstresses' workshops, tools, and something about the kind of garments they made. They also revealed the composition of seamstresses' households and their employment of workers. Personal papers provided information about clients and income, while clothing, books, and engravings indicate cultural preoccupations. Calculating seamstresses' fortunes from these documents was an extremely risky business; however, the rarity of information regarding working women's fortunes made the risk worthwhile.

Police documents provided a second set of crucial sources. Many of these documents emanated from the office of the king's procurator at the Châtelet of Paris. After 1658, this royal official held jurisdiction over the Parisian guilds, including the responsibility for receiving oaths of loyalty from all new guild members. Records from the procurator's office named the men and women accepted to the Parisian guilds from 1735 to 1791 and their path of entry. This source permitted me to draw conclusions about patterns of trade transmission as well as the accessibility of the seamstresses' and tailors' guilds over time. The king's procurator at Châtelet also acted as magistrate for guild affairs. From the late seventeenth century to the end of the Old Regime, guild leaders brought offenders before his court for judgment, testifying to the corporation's role in policing its own members along with outsiders who illegally practiced the trade.

Neighborhood police *commissaires* offered another vital source of information. In their districts, the police *commissaires* filled the joint functions of police officer, ombudsman, and magistrate. Their records illustrated the daily life of the trades, including conflicts among mistresses, workers, and apprentices. Seamstresses shared the common tragedies of working men and women: they quarreled with their neighbors and spouses; they were robbed; they stole; they committed suicide; and they died suddenly in extreme poverty. Police records also highlighted the prevalence of sexually related difficulties. Seamstresses experienced sexual harassment in the workshop; they were seduced and impregnated by fickle lovers. When misery—or temptation—pushed them to it, they joined the swelling ranks of prostitutes.[29]

Another important group of sources came from the royal government itself, including royal edicts, tax records, surveys, and other documents. This material contained valuable information about the guilds, including their size, assets, and the fiscal contributions they made to the crown. Given the nature of the sources, they also provided crucial insight into the interaction between guild and royal government. Audits conducted by a royal commission created to liquidate guild debts constituted another major source for this investigation. These audits offered a wealth of financial information about the seamstresses' guild and documented the extent of royal control over corporate administration.

A variety of different sources supplied information about the ways seamstresses actually made and sold garments, and the way their labor was perceived by contemporaries. Bankruptcy records contained precious detail about the daily practice of the trade, including the purchase of supplies, cycles of production, and relationships between seamstresses and their clients. Contemporary technical literature, such as François de Garsault's 1769 *L'Art du tailleur,* the *Encyclopédie,* and the *Encyclopédie méthodique,* also helped me understand the different types of garments manufactured and the precise steps followed to produce them. Published almanacs listed the most famous members of the garment trades, sometimes indicating the particular specialties for which they were known. Social commentators like Louis-Sébastien Mercier or Nicolas-Edmé Restif de la Bretonne, as well as philosophers and medical writers, all conveyed vivid impressions of the cultural and social weight of clothing in Old Regime France and the place that garment trades occupied in discourses about the female body, fashion, and appearances.

In the realm of nondiscursive sources, contemporary engravings furnished precious images of the division of space in artisanal workshops and the tools and gestures employed by men and women at work, filtered, of course, through the artists' perceptions and biases. Surviving garments held in museum collections, kindly explicated by museum curators, did much to kindle my imagination and make concrete what might have been far too abstract. These dresses, corsets, hoopskirts, petticoats, and jackets offered poignant testimony to the many hours of painstaking labor furnished by individual seamstresses. Close examination of them aided me a great deal in understanding how seamstresses worked.

The nine chapters of this book are divided into three parts. The first part, "Making the Goods," focuses on the seamstresses as producers of clothing by examining the types of garments they made, the composition of the workforce that made them, and the concrete techniques they employed to do so. The first chapter investigates the evolution of women's clothing from the late seventeenth to the eighteenth century, relating changing styles of fashion to discourses about fashion and femininity and the vicissitudes of the garment trades over the same period. This chapter draws a strong connection between the rise in women's consumption of clothing over the late seventeenth and eighteenth centuries and the seamstresses' organization and success as a guild. Chapter 2 explores different forms of specialization in the trade, vertical hierarchies dividing success and failure, and the seamstresses' labor market. This chapter emphasizes the diversity of the trade population, the informal nature of hiring processes, and the cyclical problems of unemployment. Finally, Chapter 3 focuses on seamstresses' and tailors' techniques of production and distribution. It examines the tools they used, the division of labor in the workshop, their interaction with clients and credit systems, and the steps they followed to produce dresses, skirts, and corsets.

The second part, "Making the Guild," addresses the institutional organization of the seamstresses' trade in Paris, Normandy, and Provence. Chapter 4 is an investigation of the origins of the Parisian seamstresses' guild in 1675 and the process by which provincial seamstresses attained membership in provincial tailors' guilds. In order to clarify the significance of these events, I place the seamstresses within the context of the broader principles underlying the guild system as well as the evolving attitudes of the royal government toward corporate structures and the possibility of incorporating women's labor. Chapter 5 explores the conflict between seamstresses' new guild privileges and the preexisting prerogatives of master tailors and their female relatives in the cities of Paris, Caen, and Marseilles. Drawing on these disputes, I reveal the consequences of women's inclusion in guilds both for their own legal and social identities as well as for the men and women who had belonged to the guild system before them. Chapter 6 focuses on the administration of the Parisian seamstresses' guild during the eighteenth century. In it I analyze the composition and recruitment of the guild elite and assess the extent to which the closed circle of corporate leaders was able to intervene in the trade. I also provide a close examination of the relationship between the royal government and the guild in order to assess royal control over this female corporation and over the guilds in general.

The final part, "Making the Mistresses," turns to an examination of the trade population itself and the lives of the women who composed it. Chapter 7 examines the production and reproduction of the trade through a study of guild admissions and apprenticeship. In this chapter I document the overwhelming demand for access to the trade and the gender-specific patterns of trade transmission that existed among tailors and seamstresses. Chapter 8 sketches a portrait of family life and marriage patterns among seamstresses. I find that trade qualifications featured prominently in matrimonial and life strategies and enabled a substantial group of women to survive outside of marriage. This chapter also explores seamstresses' lifestyles, examining their cultural interests, wardrobes, and widely varying levels of fortune. As I make clear, their private and professional lives were virtually inseparable because they lived and worked in the same space, often with the same people.

The final chapter of the book takes the seamstresses' story through the French Revolution and to the turn of the twentieth century, seeking to explain continuity and change in the trade after the fall of the Old Regime. With the rise of mass production in ready-to-wear clothing and the accompanying processes of consolidation and proletarianization, the garment trades underwent fundamental change. Nonetheless, certain aspects of production persisted. This was particularly true of forms of specialization and the fact that workers felt loyal toward their trade affiliations, rather than to their gender or class as a whole. Professional association also recurred among seamstresses, but this must be read as a result of the Old Regime feminization of the garment trades, rather than a direct product of corporate experience. The strongest legacy eighteenth-century seamstresses offered their successors was the conceptual association of femininity with needlework and fashion, an ambivalent inheritance that we continue to share today.

PART ONE

Making the Goods

ONE

Seamstresses and the Culture of Clothing

in Old Regime France

Eighteenth-century France witnessed a dramatic rise in the consumption of clothing, particularly in Paris and other cities. Daniel Roche has documented a "clothing revolution" between 1700 and 1789, characterized by a substantial growth in the size and value of Parisian wardrobes as well as a new level of diversity in garments and accessories, colors, and fabrics. For the first time, elements of personal taste, choice, and superfluity entered the attire of the middling orders and the working people. Across Parisian society, women significantly outconsumed men, acquiring larger and more expensive wardrobes than their husbands, brothers, and fathers. A new fashion industry sprang to life to meet increasing demand, staffed by legions of female artisans and merchants working for a predominantly female clientele. The realm of fashion, it was increasingly agreed, was a woman's land in which citizenship was acquired by birth alone.[1]

Contemporaries and modern observers have both often accepted this conclusion, tacitly agreeing that women are drawn by their very nature to clothing and consumption. Beginning in the eighteenth century, however, critics began to refute this view by arguing that the femininity of fashion was a cultural and social phenomenon, called into being by the very prevalence of such ideas about women. According to burgeoning feminists such as Mary Wollstonecraft, women invested more than men in money and attention to their clothing because they had been taught that appearances were their female destiny.[2] This argument found echoes in sociological and historical studies of the consumption of material goods in early modern Europe. In his classic study of the leisure class, Thorstein Veblen interpreted women's disproportionate consumption of clothing and other goods as a function of the social role they filled in displaying family wealth and status.³ Many historians followed Veblen's lead in analyzing women's role in the rise of consumer culture in eighteenth-century Europe. Recently, scholars have taken this analysis further by focusing on the ways in which new practices of shopping and fashionable dressing were coded as "feminine" by contemporary observers, and they have even suggested that the construction of a "modern female subject" was fundamentally tied up with the emergence of a gendered consumer culture.⁴

This gendered examination of consumption is part of a wider effort to uncover the cultural and social origins behind European economic transformation. Pioneering studies of consumer culture in the 1980s complained about the excessive attention accorded to technological innovation and economic production in accounts of the Industrial Revolution. In particular, they criticized the reigning assumption that demand for finished goods naturally expanded with a growth in supply. In developing cultural explanations for rising consumption, their studies focused on shifts in attitudes toward material goods and on the commercial techniques adopted to incite demand. This cultural turn was a necessary corrective but it may have moved too far, encouraging historians to focus on the meaning and dynamics of material culture and consumption to the exclusion of production. The seamstresses' trade provides an important example of the need to balance these factors and to reconstruct the complex imbrication among production, consumption, and the specific nature of the goods themselves.

The very definition of the seamstresses' trade underlines the close ties that existed between production and consumption in contemporaries' minds. According to the 1675 statutes, a seamstress was a woman who made articles of clothing for other women and for children. Producer and consumer were thus united by their sex and their privileged relation to clothing. The timing of the guild's creation further supports the link between production and consumption. From 1675 on, the seamstresses' guild attracted legions of new participants eager to profit from the social and economic privileges it offered in a labor market with restricted opportunities for women. The result was a large, skilled, and relatively inexpensive labor force keen to make and sell articles of female clothing. A push from the production side thus acted as a major catalyst for women's capacity to acquire new, custom-made garments in the latest styles and fashions. It was not merely new ways of conceiving of consumption or femininity that encouraged them to do so. Seamstresses acquired their trade niche as a result of cultural associations of femininity with needlework, yet once they gained legal status their swelling numbers inspired a growth in consumption, which ultimately reinforced and subtly transformed existing ideas about women's work and femininity.[5]

Another factor intervening between the forces of production and consumption was the clothing itself. To some degree, fashion was an independent variable, generated neither by changes in the organization of production nor by cultural ideas about femininity, consumption, and clothing. The origins of new fashions were often as mystifying for contemporaries as they presently are for historians. Nevertheless, the introduction of new styles in clothing and accessories could have a major impact on production and consumtpion. This was particularly true of novelties that did not conform to existing guild monopolies, as we will see below. Fashion generated conflict and competition in the garment trades even as it stimulated discussion and debate among observers. Together, these three factors—the practice and organization of labor; cultural concepts of gender, consumption, and fashion; and the objects of fashion itself—shaped, influenced, and informed each other over time. They did not always operate in synchronicity, but their evolution cannot be understood separately and no absolute causal primacy may be assigned among them.

In this chapter, I will develop these arguments by examining three moments in the history of fashion. Located from the 1670s to the 1780s, each of these moments witnessed a striking change in women's styles of apparel, accompanied by a flurry of published debates about fashion as well as significant developments in the garment trades. The first moment took place in the 1670s, when the seamstresses of Paris acquired an exclusively female guild with the right to make clothing for women and children but not for men. At the same time, a crucial transformation was taking place in the female wardrobe, as the expensive and cumbersome two-piece formal ladies' dress was replaced by a simpler, one-piece gown. Seamstresses soon monopolized the new *manteau* dress, which they produced for women from a surprisingly wide social spectrum. Not coincidentally, the 1670s also witnessed the birth of the first contemporary periodical to focus on fashion, which reported on the spread of the *manteau* and the growing role of fashion professionals outside the royal court.

The second break occurred some fifty years later in the 1720s, with the emergence of hoopskirts, which were worn under the loose *robe volante,* or "sack dress" as it was known in England. With flowing back pleats and voluminous skirts, women now appeared in a shockingly new silhouette.

The garments quickly generated a stir among observers who condemned them from a religious point of view or mocked them from a satirical one. In 1725, this debate entered the world of work with a violent raid by tailors' officials on a mistress seamstress. In the subsequent legal battle, tailors and seamstresses disputed the right to make the hoopskirts and whaleboned stays worn under the new dresses. Together, debates about women's fashions and legal conflicts among tailors and seamstresses helped to propagate the growing notion that the sphere of fashion and appearances was an essentially female domain, despite the persistence of male production rights.

The final moment is located in the 1770s and 1780s, with a third major change in the female wardrobe. Instead of ushering in a new dress standard, this period witnessed a proliferation of different styles of female attire and accessories. It was also marked by a new insistence on "natural" forms of dress and a turn away from heavy stays or hoopskirts. This transition echoed wider cultural developments in which medical writers and social critics increasingly insisted on a deference to nature in human society. In the late 1770s, women gained extended guild prerogatives in the production of female clothing, as the legal rights women had acquired in this sector were strengthened by the idea of a "natural" female role in needlework. The French Revolution formally consecrated innate labor rights in 1791, abolishing all guilds and permitting men and women to work freely in whatever trades they chose. From being a tacit or underlying force that informed, supported, or even contradicted law, "nature" thus emerged in the second half of the eighteenth century as the most important standard for judging society and culture, including women, fashion, and work.

This chapter begins with a reflection on the social and cultural role of clothing in Old Regime France, which serves as a background for the three moments discussed in detail. I then turn to an overview of the major developments in French women's fashion in each of the three time periods chosen. This review of fashion history is followed by an examination of the interplay in each period between discourses and representations of fashion on the one hand, and the vicissitudes of the garment trades on the other. As we will see, seamstresses usually did not create new styles. In all likelihood, they cannot lay claim to the *manteau* dress, the hoopskirt, or the many new styles of the 1770s. Nonetheless, it was seamstresses' capacity to make and sell such fashions in large quantities that made their diffusion possible. In turn, developments in the consumption and production of clothing together helped to change cultural ideas about clothing, fashion, and women's relation to them. The seamstresses were particularly important in this interplay because of their strong gender identity and the explicit link their trade drew between female creators and consumers of clothing.

The Social Role of Clothing

Clothing has long been recognized by anthropologists, sociologists, and historians as a key social and cultural signifying system. From the embroidered patterns on Indonesian betel-nut purses to the Old Regime nobleman's gold-embroidered suit and sword to the blue jeans of the late-twentieth century, styles of dress emit strong signals. First, they serve as visual markers that express and reinforce social taxonomies and their wearer's place within them. Even in today's apparently casual Western societies, a person's social status, economic situation, cultural values, and even political engagements can often at a glance be read in his or her attire. Clothing also conveys a visual interpretation of the ostensibly "natural" distinctions of age and gender, providing strictly delimited vocabularies within which men and women fashion their identities. It is the most vivid symbol of our transition from nature to culture, from biological male and female to men and women in society.[6]

As Georg Simmel insisted, dress furnishes a meeting point between the collective and the individual, a place where social structures and hierarchies intersect with personal choices and tastes. As anyone who has hesitated in front of the mirror can attest, the act of dressing oneself each day is a complicated negotiation between the norms and judgments of the social world and the expression of a private identity, itself forged through a lifetime of such encounters. In a given context, more or less room for individual choice and the elaboration of a personal style exists depending on wealth, the rigidity of social hierarchies, the circulation of information, and the availability of different types of garments and accessories. With the daily choices they make, men and women send important signals to the outside world and to the self.[7]

Of course, the interpretation of these messages is not straightforward; the possibility of intentional or accidental obscuring, misuse, or masquerading of social dress codes always exists. One constant anxiety is that individuals will take advantage of recognized codes to pass themselves off as something they are not. Literature is full of ambitious outsiders who ape the costume of their betters to gain illicit entry to the group. Like Molière's bourgeois gentleman, however, the bounder's constant failure to deceive, and the ridicule he or she attracts, reassuringly demonstrate that true nobility is in the blood and not in the suit. The same moral results from the unfailingly valiant character of the noble foundling dressed in peasant's clothing. Garments may serve to reflect and display one's superior status, these stories tell us, but they cannot substitute for it. The frequency of such tales, however, betrays strong misgivings about the possible discrepancy between appearances and social categories and the fear of outsiders who might successfully infiltrate the elite. The rise of a fashion system in fourteenth-century Europe has thus been explained as an attempt to secure the tools of social and cultural distinction. Following a "trickle-down" logic, fashion originated as courtiers introduced swift changes in their styles of apparel to reconfirm their social distance from wealthy commoners.[8]

The social weight of fashion, however, is not exhausted by strategies of upward social aspiration. In societies with a wide range of styles, a considerable play within and against established dress codes is possible. Marie-Antoinette bore very little resemblance to a real shepherdess when she dressed up at the Trianon in Versailles, but she acted out a broader, elite discourse preaching a return to "natural" ways of living. In contrast to the linguistic systems to which it is often compared, clothing permits its wearer to resist established hierarchies and traditions without manifesting overt defiance. If, for example, the rules regarding male and female attire at the court of Versailles were intended to ensure the visual prestige and honor of the absolutist monarchy, courtiers could exploit nuances within the established code to express their greater attachment to or alienation from the king. A circle of young aristocrats thus expressed their frustration with the tradition-bound court of the aging Louis XIV with an exaggeratedly fashionable, foppish way of dressing. Their dress choices allowed them to display a form of cultural resistance, without engaging in open political opposition.[9]

It is also doubtful that any society harbors a unitary clothing system that is transparent and meaningful to all its members in the same way. An article of clothing like a corset or a pair of pants could signify quite different things to different groups of people. If an aristocrat's strikingly luxurious attire emitted a clear message of superiority to those below him on the social scale, it also contained nuances of detail, such as the pattern of his lace sleeve cuffs or the design of his silver shoe buckles, which could only be read and appreciated by members of his own milieu. A number of distinct taxonomies of clothing could thus coexist, clash, and overlap within one city or across multiple spaces constructed socially, visually, or politically. Choices of apparel could aim to fulfill aspirations apart from simple socio-economic emulation, including much more subtle and localized struggles over cultural or social power and self-identity.

As the proliferation of studies on French fashion attest, few societies have accorded as much explicit attention to clothing and appearances as Old Regime France.[10] From the seventeenth century to the Revolution, France was known by subjects and by foreigners as a place where one's exterior aspect counted more than anything else. As Jean-Jacques Rousseau declared in disgust, Paris was the city where "everything is judged on appearances."[11] Clothing formed a central part of the social and self-identity of an aristocrat, a Frenchman, a Parisian, a man, or a woman. The nobleman was instantly recognizable by his powdered wig, breeches, and jacket of fine cloth decorated with rich embroidery and precious stones, along with his hat and sword. By contrast, the working man's long pants were so well known that they would serve as a symbol of antiaristocratic fervor for the revolutionary sans-culottes.[12]

In addition to its social functions, clothing held a particular political importance in Old Regime France. Given the nature of absolutist monarchical ideology—in which the king literally embodied the nation—the royal body constituted the focal point of France. The king's appearance held enormous political symbolism as a visual display of the vitality and glory of his nation. His clothing accordingly occupied a crucial place in the representation and exercise of absolutist power, as portraitists depicted his sumptuous robes and courtiers vied for the right to participate in royal dressing and undressing ceremonies. In this monarchical society that overlapped politics, social status and cultural representation, appearances could be a potent political tool.[13] Fine attire not only distinguished the nobleman from the commoner, it also provided a means to win notice and favor at court. In 1636, Nicolas Faret's etiquette manual advised ambitious courtiers to invest in the most expensive clothing possible: "It is one of the most useful expenditures made at Court. It is almost the only one followed by those who know how to make use of it, and it opens doors which are often closed to high condition, and even more often to virtue."[14]

Beyond its borders, France's political and cultural domination of Europe manifested itself through the influence of its fashion. From Louis XIV on, the French set clothing styles for all the courts of Europe and even the American elite, first through the dispatch of fashion dolls dressed in the latest styles and later through a commercialized fashion press. As the *Mercure galant* boasted in 1672: "Nothing pleases more than Fashions born in France . . . everything made there has a certain air that Foreigners cannot give to their Works."[15] The importance of clothing to Old Regime society and politics was further emphasized by the attention it received under the French Revolution. In their efforts to break completely with the Old Regime, revolutionary leaders accorded serious consideration to installing an entirely new dress code. French citizens, they esteemed, could not forget the aristocratic and monarchic society of the past while surrounded by visual reminders of it. Social equality was impossible if citizens' dress constantly evoked differences in wealth and status. These projects were never realized, but the debates around them demonstrate the perceived social and political importance of attire.[16]

Women's clothing in particular formed the focus of heated debate in eighteenth-century France, with philosophers from Montesquieu to Rousseau criticizing women's vestimentary extravagance. As recent historical studies have shown, the delegitimization of the Old Regime in the 1770s and 1780s occurred at least in part through an attack on female courtiers, and in particular through an assault on the queen's supposedly extravagant and corrupt lifestyle. In addition to a long list of political and sexual crimes, Marie-Antoinette was accused of bankrupting the state with outrageously expensive purchases from her fashion merchants. This heated political criticism reproduced on a magnified scale accusations that had been leveled at women for decades. Social observers ridiculed women for their selfish vanity, their devotion to superficial appearances, and their provocative sexuality. Female luxury is, of course, an ancient trope, but eighteenth-century France produced an uncommonly lively commentary on women's fashions and on the power and influence women might acquire through a beautiful and seductive appearance.[17]

As we will see, the perceived meaning and function of the "fashion system," and women's place in it, altered significantly across time. From the seventeenth to the eighteenth century, commentators offered an evolving and ambiguous interpretation of the dynamics of fashion and its relation to gender and to systems of social distinction. Their ideas about fashion were shaped by the evolution of the garment trades and by the creation of a seamstresses' guild with rights over women's and children's clothing. Before we turn to these debates, however, let us take the simpler step of examining the evolution of styles of female clothing in France from the

1670s to the end of the Old Regime. This discussion will illuminate the different garments being made and worn as well as the shifting economic territory occupied by the seamstresses after 1675. This discussion is also necessary background to understand the intricate relations among concrete styles of clothing, the expansion of the garment trades, and debates about fashion and femininity in the Old Regime.

Seamstresses and Women's Clothing

When they acquired guild status in 1675, the seamstresses' statutes outlined a precise set of garments that they were entitled to make. They also placed two explicitly off-limits. As they stated:

> The mistress Seamstresses will have the faculty to make and sell Dressing Gowns [robes de chambre], Skirts, Justaucorps, Manteaux, Hongrelines, Camisoles, Bodices [corps de jupes] and all other Items of all kinds of fabric to clothe Women and Girls, with the exception of Dress Bodices [corps de robes] and Dress Skirts [bas de robes] only; in all of these Items that they are permitted to make, they will be able to make use of Whalebone and other things that will be appropriate for making and perfecting these Items.[18]

These garments included the most common elements of the female wardrobe of the late seventeenth century. Outside of the nobility, most women donned a combination of skirt, shirt, and bodice for everyday wear. Their full skirts reached to the floor, fastening at the waist with ribbons or hooks. Pockets were sewn onto a string tied around the waist and accessed through gaps in the side seams. Women might don several layers of skirts, depending on the season and their resources, including quilted or padded ones for extra warmth in the winter months (figure 1.1).

Men and women wore loose and ample shirts of white linen, or a linen-cotton blend, that descended past their hips. These shirts had wide, scooped necklines and full sleeves gathered just below the elbow, both of which could be decorated with lace or cloth ruffles. They belonged to the category of personal linen and were usually sold by linen-drapers. Seamstresses did, however, make the sleeveless corps de jupe, or skirt bodices, which many women wore over their shirts. These garments fastened with laces and ended at the bottom in scalloped or serrated edges. Some bodices contained strips of whalebone for extra stiffness and support (see figure 1.1).

FIGURE I.I A woman in skirt and bodice (*corps de jupe*), showing the bodice laced in front and in back, as depicted in "A" and "B." Images "C" and "D" show the *robe à la française* of the 1760s. Image "E" shows a woman in skirt and *juste*. The latter corresponds to the *justaucorps* jacket mentioned in the seamstresses' 1675 statutes. Engravings From François de Garsault, *L'Art du tailleur* (1769)

Working women commonly wore a jacket over their shirt and bodice for warmth and protection from the elements. Bourgeois and noble ladies wore a similar ensemble for active endeavors such as hunting or traveling. The *justaucorps* named in the seamstresses' statutes was cut like the men's jacket of the same name, fitting tightly to the waist and flaring over the hips (see figure 1.1). The *hongreline* was another type of jacket, described in Antoine Furetière's 1690 dictionary as a "type of women's apparel made in the manner of a short-sleeved shirt [*chemisette*] which has large tabs." Both of these jackets disappeared from Parisian wardrobes during the eighteenth century.[19] At night, women wore *camisoles* to bed, which fit like loose bodices and tied in the back. Dressing gowns were long, loose, one-piece garments resembling the Japanese kimono with the sleeves cut as part of the front and back pieces. Both men and women of high social status wore dressing gowns in the morning before donning formal attire. As Furetière's 1690 dictionary explained: "A dressing-gown is what one wears [while] at ease and which serves while one combs one's hair, one grooms oneself, one keeps to one's room."[20]

The seamstresses were also permitted to make clothing for girls, and for boys up to age eight. As their absence from the statutes suggests, few specialized garments existed for children in this period. Mothers and wet nurses wrapped infants in swaddling cloth to protect their fragile bodies. They dressed small children in long, one-piece cotton or linen gowns called *fourreaux,* which laced down the back. Underneath these gowns, boys and girls of high social status often wore stiff whaleboned bodices. Both parents and medical authorities believed that the child's body was like "soft wax," highly vulnerable to injury and improper growth.[21] They thus relied on bodices to prevent deformities and even to correct congenital spinal defects. Like many concerned grandparents, Madame de Sévigné advised her daughter to dress her grandson in a pair of stays, writing: "For his waist, that's another affair . . . you must put little stays on him, a bit hard, that hold his waist."[22] Roughly at the age of eight, the upper limit for male clothing established by the seamstresses' statutes, boys and girls adopted the dress styles of their elders. Like their fathers, boys wore short pants, a waistcoat and a jacket. Young girls continued to wear bodices, along with a skirt and jacket. For formal occasions, around age fifteen or sixteen girls of the upper classes began to wear dresses and skirts like their mothers.[23]

If the seamstresses' statutes permitted them to make virtually all elements of women's and children's everyday wear, they prohibited them from making two specific articles of clothing: the dress bodice (*corps de robe*) and the dress skirt (*bas de robe*). These garments composed the formal ladies' attire of the 1670s. The dress bodice was heavily whaleboned, lined with fine cloth, and covered with the same material as the dress skirt. The bottom half of the outfit consisted of a long trained skirt that hooked or buttoned onto the bodice. On very formal occasions, a servant carried the long train; otherwise it could be folded up and hooked or buttoned at the back.[24] Women usually wore the dress skirt open in the front to reveal a matching underskirt. The bodice with trained skirt and matching underskirt together formed the *habit,* which was called a *grand habit* when made for wear at court. This dress remained the official female attire of the French court until the Revolution (figures 1.2 and 1.3).[25]

Reinforced by numerous strips of whalebone and tightly laced down the back, the dress bodice held the spine erect, pulled the shoulders back, compressed the stomach and the waist, and molded the breasts. Cut low over the chest and shoulders, it did not serve to hide the woman's body, but to impose a rigid silhouette on it. In contrast to the informal skirt bodice (*corps de jupe*) that had shoulder straps, the dress bodice cut horizontally across the chest and shoulders, exposing the upper arms and chest and ending in short sleeves. Although the skirt bodice ended at the waist, the dress

FIGURE I.2 Court dress of the late seventeenth century, including dress bodice ("a"), dress skirt ("b"), and matching underskirt ("c"). From François de Garsault, *L'Art du tailleur* (1769).

bodice descended to a long point over the abdomen. Women inserted a "busk," a thin strip of wood, metal, or whalebone, in a pocket down the front of the dress bodice to further compress the breasts and stomach.

Dress bodices were complicated creations, requiring hours of specialized labor to cut, fit, and stuff with whalebone. Their price, and the immobility they imposed, put them out of the reach of all but the most privileged women. The whaleboned bodice thus formed a key element of distinction in women's dress, conferring a "noble and majestic bearing" on the wearer.[26] Its rigid form was a visual reminder of the self-discipline and self-control imbuing contemporary notions of female honor, signalling the moral as well as social and economic superiority of noble and upper-bourgeois ladies. Madame de Maintenon insisted that the impoverished young noblewomen raised under her patronage at Saint-Cyr always wear the dress bodice and skirts. Lacking the wealth of their caste, she reasoned, they would at least retain its honorable appearance.

What motivated the royal government to forbid seamstresses from

FIGURE 1.3 Court dress of the late eighteenth century. *Cahiers des costumes français,* courtesy of the Cabinet des estampes, Bibliothèque nationale.

making dress bodies and dress skirts in 1675? Although the statutes offered no explanations, it is clear that questions of skill or technique can supply only part of the answer. Dress bodices required a high degree of proficiency, which officials may have believed to be lacking among seamstresses; however, the dress skirts were quite easy to make and did not require special training. Instead of technical concerns, the royal government appears to have been motivated by the desire to retain some element of the tailors' centuries-old privileges in the face of the new female corporation. With this ruling, the king and his ministers assigned the seamstresses' guild to a secondary position in the garment trades. Guildswomen would produce common elements of the female wardrobe, but the most expensive and prestigious ones remained in the tailors' hands.

These stipulations were based on a false but reasonable assumption that the basic attire of noblewomen was not subject to fashion and that it would not change over time. This was an understandable error, for the king imposed strict rules governing apparel at court, leaving male and female courtiers little room for vestimentary maneuver. He and his ministers did not realize, however, that at precisely this moment the female wardrobe was undergoing a profound transformation, which would create a new form of elite female dress and an unexpected opportunity for seamstresses. Within a few short years, a new dress—worn by noblewomen outside of the most formal court ceremonies—opened the world of aristocratic consumption to Parisian mistress seamstresses. In turn, female needleworkers exploited this fashion to its fullest potential, turning it into a staple of elite and even common women's wardrobes.

A Revolution in Women's Apparel: The manteau

The *manteau* named in the seamstresses' statutes stood at the origins of this transformation. In the late seventeenth century, *manteau* could refer to at least three different garments. One sense of the word was the one that it carries today, that of an overcoat worn outdoors. Furetière offered this as the first definition of the word in his 1690 dictionary. His second definition referred to an informal female garment worn indoors: "*Manteau* is also a type of dressing gown that women wear over their skirt bodices [*corps de jupes*]." In 1694, the dictionary of the Académie française furnished a third definition, explaining that "women also call *Manteau* a sort of pleated dress that they close with a belt." Other sources confirm the Académie's hint that French women had begun to adapt the *manteau* in the 1670s from a

FABRICATING WOMEN

casual housegown into a more formal dress, which they wore over a skirt and a bodice outside the home.[27]

In this form, the *manteau* initiated a fundamental transition in women's apparel in which casual one-piece gowns were transformed into formal garments for public outings. This development was not limited to France but spread across Europe, including England where the *manteau* was known as a "mantua." The dress was tied at the waist with a cord or ribbon and often pinned at the neck. Made of fine silk, richly decorated, and worn with a matching underskirt, it soon became elegant attire suitable for social visits and strolling in the boulevards and parks of Paris. Women also wore the mantua more casually as a form of *deshabillé,* binding up the voluminous sleeves and front pleats with ribbons and pinning the long trained skirts over their hips (see figures 1.4 and 1.5).[28]

During the 1670s, the mantua gradually replaced the heavy two-piece dress among noble and rich bourgeois women, except for very formal occasions. By 1678, *L'Extraordinaire du Mercure galant* would comment, with reference to an image of a two-piece dress, that "this is not what is presently the most ordinary for [women]." Instead, the author explained that "as one lives today very comfortably in France, one dresses rather rarely there, & one no longer wears almost anything but what are called *Manteaux.* Dresses are only for ceremonial visits, or for those which we pay to People of a higher rank than the one we hold, & and one does not make use of them to see one's [female] Friends familiarly nor for Walking Parties."[29]

The spread of the new dress demanded a new type of underwear to preserve women's stiff silhouette. Whereas the old dress bodice contained internal whalebone supports, the mantua was made simply of cloth. Women now began to wear a separate whaleboned bodice—which I will refer to as "stays"—under the long mantua. These stays fell halfway between the informal skirt bodice and the formal dress bodice, combining the rigid whaleboning of the latter with the plain cloth and sleeveless pattern of the former. If the mantua was worn open between the waist and collar, women usually covered the stays with a decorated, triangular piece of cloth, known as a "stomacher" (*pièce d'estomac*).

Perhaps because so few examples of the mantua survive today, fashion historians have neglected the implications of its adoption and focused on later versions of the one-piece gown. A closer consideration of the mantua, however, reveals its potential for transforming existing patterns of clothing consumption. The mantua was much easier and less expensive to make than the two-piece dress, which required complicated and time-

Habit d'Esté

Agraphe de
Piereries.

gans de point
d'Angleterre.

Manchettes doubles.

Manteau de gaze.

Iupe de point
d'Angleterre Sur
en fons de Couleur.

d'entelle d'Angleterre
plissée.

FIGURE I.4 Summer dress of 1678, showing a *manteau* dress by Jean LePautre. From the *Mercure galant,* courtesy of the Cabinet des estampes, Bibliothèque nationale.

Deshabillé
d'Hyuer

Coeffé de Soye .ecruë
Coeffe noire.
Palatine de Point.

Manche Serée de pluche.
Manche de Chemise.
Menchettes de point.
Ceinture de tissu d'Or.
Manteau de brocart
a fleurs d'Or doublé
de pluche couleur
de feu.

Manchon
de pluche
couleur de feu

Iupe de pluche
couleur de feu.

trois rangs de
grande dentelle
Or et Argent —
vollante.

Iupon de brocart a fleurs d'argent
borde d'ermine.

FIGURE 1.5 Informal winter dress of 1678, showing a *manteau* dress by Jean LePautre. From the *Mercure galant,* courtesy of the Cabinet des estampes, Bibliothèque nationale.

consuming techniques of production and very large quantities of fabric. A small number of specialized master tailors dominated production of the *corps de robe,* demanding high prices for their labor. By contrast, the simple kimono-shaped *manteau* called for no great technical skill. It required less cloth than the formal dress and could be made by less qualified artisans. Moreover, instead of having an expensive new whaleboned bodice made for every dress, women could wear one pair of stays with many different mantuas. Sheer considerations of price thus made this dress more accessible than the two-piece ensemble.

The social connotations of the dress were also important. Adapted from the informal dressing gown, the mantua did not carry the same significance as the two-piece dress, which signaled a visual claim to high social status. A new type of apparel, the mantua offered comfort, affordability, and an increasingly accepted form of elegance. Ambitious bourgeois women could thus adopt the new fashion without attracting the outrage or mockery they would have in the formal dress. For their part, noblewomen must have been thrilled to dispense with the heavy and constricting dress bodice, if only for visits and walks during the day. They probably did not anticipate the popularity of the dress among their social inferiors, or the potential for social confusion it implied.[30]

The final, and perhaps most important, catalyst for the adoption of the mantua was the timing of its birth. In the 1670s, as the mantua appeared on the streets of the capital, the Parisian seamstresses emerged from long years of illicit labor with the status of an independent guild. Needleworkers who had formerly engaged in clandestine work could now openly seek female clients. They took up the mantua eagerly, as a garment they were authorized to produce and one which was not too difficult to create. Producing thousands of these gowns in workshops across Paris, the seamstresses propagated a novel form of dressing for women, using it to establish a niche in the high-end of the garment trades and to spread the new taste to other social groups. Like Coco Chanel in her day, seamstresses prospered by rendering casual, comfortable garments into a new style for elite women and their social inferiors.

The results were apparent to observers. As early as 1672, the *Mercure galant* reported that the popularity of the mantua had spread not only among Parisian elite society, but to women of the working classes (*grisettes*), who had started wearing mantuas made from inexpensive printed cotton.[31] Probate inventories reveal that the mantua had indeed achieved a broad social adherence by 1700 at least. In a sample of one hundred probate inventories from that year, Daniel Roche found that approximately 90 percent of all Parisian women, from domestic servants to aristocrats, possessed at least one *manteau*.[32] While we cannot be sure of the exact nature of these garments, in all likelihood the majority were the mantua dress described and illustrated by the *Mercure galant*. If noble and rich bourgeois women owned custom-made gowns, women lower on the social scale inherited second- or third-hand castoffs or had them made from cheaper cloth.

The female wardrobe thus underwent a startling change in the 1670s. Previous distinctions between elite and common apparel began to break down, as women of all social groups adopted a similar style. A noblewoman's mantua obviously looked very different from a shopgirl's, but the two women now might share a common type of apparel. Women of humble social origins had gained access to the basic styles of their betters and could more closely approximate a fashionable appearance. The mantua offered a new conceptual and visual terrain in which women could experiment with self-presentation in ways that challenged traditional social hierarchies.

With the adoption of the mantua, the future of women's clothing passed into the seamstresses' hands. The *Mercure galant* directed women desiring the most fashionable mantuas to a seamstress: "Those who wish to have them made like they make them at Court, only have to address themselves to Madame du Creux, Rue Traversine who dresses the largest part of the people of the first quality." By contrast, the small trade in court dresses remained largely with male tailors. The *Mercure* accordingly sent women to a tailor to obtain the best dresses of this kind: "Sieur de la Vallée, Court Tailor, who lives in the place of the Palais Royal, will be able to further inform People who address themselves to him."[33] The strong association between the new dress and the female workforce appeared most explicitly in England, where the name for a seamstress throughout the eighteenth century was "mantua maker." A new female labor force and its most important item of production thus emerged hand in glove onto the cultural and material marketplaces of the late seventeenth century.

A Second New Look: The robe à la française *and the Hoopskirt*

By the early 1720s, French women had adopted a new and radically different silhouette consisting of a loose gown worn over wide, bell-shaped hoopskirts. Originally called the *robe à battante*, the *robe volante*, or the "sack dress" in English, the new dress originated in the 1690s as a second deriva-

FIGURE 1.6 Hoopskirts and the *robe volante*. This engraving shows the *robe volante* worn over the bell-shaped hoopskirts of the 1720s. Courtesy of the Cabinet des estampes, Bibliothèque nationale.

tive of the dressing gown. The *robe volante* had full pleats in the front and back like the *manteau,* but was left untied at the waist, with its back pleats falling freely. (figure 1.6). As with the mantua, women wore the gown over whaleboned stays, which preserved their stiff figures underneath the hanging back pleats. From approximately 1718, the new dress was worn over another innovation of the early eighteenth century, the hoopskirt, or *panier.* It was formed of stiff hoops of whalebone, cane, or metal and held together by strips of linen or other cloth. Originally bell-shaped (see figure 1.6), during the 1730s the hoopskirt flattened in the front, giving the dress a wider, oval shape.

Over time, the *robe volante* gradually acquired a more precise shape for formal wear. During the 1730s, the loose back pleats evolved into two neatly folded double box pleats, and the front of the dress became fitted through the torso. In this form, the dress became known as the *robe à la française.*[34] Sewn from brightly patterned cloth and decorated with ribbons and ruffles, it was the dominant dress style across Europe from the 1730s to the 1760s. Noble and bourgeois women wore lavish silk versions with expensive decorations, while domestic servants and shopgirls wore modest ones of cheaper linen or cotton cloth. In the 1780s, court etiquette accepted the dress for daily wear in lieu of the two-piece *grand habit*.[35] As the gown transformed, so did the hoopskirts worn under it. Through the 1740s they grew increasingly wide, an evolution that took on particularly exaggerated dimensions in England. To create extra width at the sides, women began to wear two side pouches instead of a single hoopskirt, using the pouches for extra storage space during walks or visits. By the 1770s, Parisian women outside court circles wore the dress over a modest hoopskirt or none at all (see figure 1.1, "C" and "D").

The Third Moment: The Diversification of Fashion in the 1770s and the "Natural" Look

With the growth of clothing consumption and the expansion of the garment trades, new styles of women's apparel proliferated during the second half of the eighteenth century. The period of the 1770s and 1780s was characterized by a growing diversity in women's garments and accessories. No longer would one dress style dominate the female wardrobe as the mantua or the *robe à la française* had done. In common with fashions in landscape design and leisure activities, English styles often served as a model for more practical and simpler modes of dressing. In the 1770s, the *robe à l'anglaise*, a descendant of the mantua, became popular in France. It had a series of fitted back seams that curved together toward the tailbone and opened in pleats over the buttocks. Frenchwomen also adopted the English dress known as the *rédingote*. Modeled on the man's riding jacket, it had a male jacket collar, a row of buttons sewn down the front, and long, tight sleeves. The *polonaise* dress was a continental style, in which the dress skirts were divided into three pouches at the back by two cords drawn up under the fabric and hooked at the back of the waist (figure 1.7). These and other new styles gradually replaced the *robe à la française,* which did not appear outside of court after the 1780s.[36]

Elegant women also adopted the skirt-jacket ensemble as a type of semiformal day wear during the 1770s. The *caraco* jacket, which had belonged to the working-class wardrobe, was now taken up by women of high society. It fit tightly to the waist and flared over the hips, with the long, tight sleeves that had served practical purposes for working women (figure 1.8). The *casaquin* jacket was a mid-thigh-length version of the *robe à la française,* with its box pleats in the back. The front of the *casaquin* could be fitted or loose.

FIGURE I.7 The *polonaise* dress, characterized by three back pouches created by two cords drawn up under the dress and buttoned at the back. Courtesy of the Cabinet des estampes, Bibliothèque nationale.

FIGURE I.8 Woman in a *caraco* jacket. Courtesy of the Cabinet des estampes, Bibliothèque nationale.

FIGURE 1.9 Portrait of Emilie Sériziat and her son, by Louis David (1795), showing the simple muslin shift of the 1780s and 1790s. Courtesy of the Musée du Louvre.

In a move toward an ostensibly more "natural" silhouette in the early 1780s, women began to wear simple white muslin shifts, which they tied at the waist with colored ribbons. Elizabeth-Louise Vigée Lebrun exhibited a portrait of Marie-Antoinette in such a dress at the Salon of 1783. The hostile reaction of the Parisian public at the sight of their queen in such a simple and flimsy dress lead to its removal from public view. Despite this critical response, the queen's choice helped popularize and disseminate the style, which was dubbed the *chemise à la reine*. Women's fashion in dresses remained self-consciously understated through the 1780s and 1790s, with the rise of neoclassicism in the last years of the Old Regime and through the Revolution. The common dress of this period was a shift cut close to the body, with the high waist still known as the "empire style" from the period of Napoleon's imperial rule (figure 1.9). Napoleon's efforts to create a new court society fostered a revival in expensive and luxurious textiles, which belied the simple form of these dresses.[37]

Perhaps the most striking shift of the second half of the eighteenth century occurred in women's hats and underwear. In the 1770s and 1780s, women's hats grew increasingly tall and complex, being composed of an artful mix of feathers, ribbons, and flowers, perched on a support of pins and fake hair. Commentators joked about women being unable to enter their carriages; they protested at the blocked views in the theater; and they marveled at the steady stream of new creations, often modeled on current events or popular theater productions. In women's underwear, the trend was reversed. Starting from the 1760s, women increasingly abandoned the hoopskirt outside of court, usually in favor of two small hip pouches that they attached under their dresses. Similarly, a lighter half-boned corset began to replace the rigidly boned stays during the last decades of the eighteenth century. Children's clothing moved in the same direction. Under the urging of medical reforms and philosophes such as Rousseau, a movement arose in favor of breast-feeding and against tight swaddling of infants. As mothers abandoned fully boned stays for lighter corsets, they stopped strapping their daughters and sons into stays as well. Girls began to wear simple white muslin shifts, similar to the *chemise* dress popularized by Marie-Antoinette. Boys began to wear clothing adapted from sailors' outfits, with long pants and straight jackets. For the first time, distinct articles of clothing appeared for children's wear.

The Fashion System in the 1670s: Tensions between
Court and City

The evolution of fashion described above did not take place in a vacuum, driven merely by the whims of rich ladies and their seamstresses. Fashion engaged in a complicated relationship with larger cultural shifts and debates, and with changes in the organization and practice of economic production. In the late seventeenth century, for example, the mantua dress style defied the king's nominal control over noble fashions at court. Noble-women began to wear the new dress at all occasions where they were not explicitly required to appear in court attire. In the same period, observers expressed an ambivalent understanding of the contemporary fashion system, which was ostensibly controlled by court nobles, but which seemed to be influenced by outside factors as well. Although the adoption of the hoopskirt in Europe in the first decades of the eighteenth century has never been adequately explained, the abandonment of hoopskirts and stays had much to do with cultural valorization of "nature" and natural dressing. The remaining sections of this chapter will examine the ways in which these three fashion moments witnessed a complex interplay between material object, cultural representation, and the organization and practice of production.

In 1690, Antoine Furetière's dictionary offered an intriguing definition of the fashion system in the period of transition to the one-piece dress. In explaining the meaning of the word *mode,* Furetière declared that "[it] is said more particularly of styles of dressing oneself following the received usage of the Court. The French change fashions everyday. Foreigners follow the fashions of the French, except for the Spanish, who never change fashions. The most extravagant are those who invent fashions. Merchants profit from changes in fashion." [38] This definition offers two contradictory understandings of fashion. On the one hand, Furetière viewed the French court as its sole source and arbiter, the unmoved mover in matters of style and elegance; on the other hand, however, he could not help but notice the rapidity with which fashions changed under the influence of anonymous innovators and a burgeoning mercantile sector, both beyond the control of the king and his courtiers. [39]

Two decades earlier, Jean Donneau de Visé had expressed similar uncertainties. Founded in 1672, his *Le Mercure galant* became the first journal to publish articles on fashion and to illustrate them with pictures. Between 1672 and 1678, Donneau wrote regular reports on men's and women's fashions, hiring the engraver Jean Le Pautre to furnish engravings of the latest styles. [40] He was the first to remark in print on the spread of the new mantua dress in the 1670s. In his articles, Donneau presented a "trickle-down" model of fashion, in which new styles passed from the pinnacle of the court to a series of social groups in a downward cycle of imitation and adaptation:

> And it was then said that Fashions pass from the Court to the Ladies of the City, from Ladies of the City to rich Bourgeois women, from rich Bourgeois women to *Grisettes,* who imitated them with lesser cloth; and that when the Ladies of the Court and the City put on gemstones [*pierreries*], the Bourgeoises put on fake ones and the *Grisettes* Silversmiths' Buttons; and that when the *Grisettes* could not wear fine ones, they put fake ones in the same places. [41]

As soon as fashions had spread beyond the court aristocracy, Donneau continued, they were quickly abandoned: "All People of quality have hardly begun to follow a fashion when the Monkeys of the Court make them abort, because the great Lords leave them as quickly to take new ones; and that is why the Bourgeois who think they are in fashion never are."[42] In this schema, the reins of fashion lay in the hands of the king's courtiers, who switched courses continually in order to outrun bourgeois emulation. The efficacy of fashion as a tool of social distinction thus lay in its swiftly changing nature. When discarded by the court, a style of lace, a sleeve length, or a turn of phrase became a fatal error, betraying its owner's outsider status.

Like Furetière, Donneau offered a number of complications to this apparently straightforward model of social emulation. First of all, he positioned his fashion system at the center of a series of concentric geographic circles, placing the provinces and foreign countries at the outer limits of style: "It was added that Fashions passed from these *Grisettes* to Ladies of the Provinces, from Ladies of the Provinces to Bourgeois women of the same places; and that from there they passed to Foreign Countries; in such a way that when they started their runs there, those which had been invented at court in the meantime had already begun to grow old."[43]

Fashionability thus relied on the possession of visual information, which was unequally accessible and which might pass through circuits other than social status or wealth. Fashion was an urban, particularly Parisian form of cultural capital, in which the *grisette* could be "richer" than a provincial noblewoman. Donneau explicitly presented his fashion reports as a means to redress this imbalance and to permit provincial elites quicker access to new styles: "I have not ceased making rather curious Research and which will be of a great utility for all the Ladies of your Provinces, and for all the Men, who without being at Paris, nor at the Court, want to pride themselves on being dressed with a good air."[44]

The origins of the term *grisette* further highlight the ambivalence of Donneau's model. *Grisette* originally referred to a type of inexpensive grey woolen cloth worn by women who could not afford better. It was then used to describe the poor women who wore such cloth. Furetière defined *grisettes* as "women or young girls dressed in gray. One says it in contempt of those [women] who are of low condition, in whatever cloth they are dressed. People of quality often amuse themselves by frequenting *grisettes.*" This passage suggests that the *grisettes* as a social group may have existed primarily in the imagination of the elites who made use of the term. Their supposed fondness for associating with *grisettes* hints that elites were as fascinated by their social inferiors as the latter were with them. The notion of poor women dressing up as court ladies perhaps arose more from the fantasies of aristocratic men than the actual practices of the women themselves.[45]

The final complication to Donneau's trickle-down model lay in the role that he explicitly accorded to merchants and manufacturers. In the *Mercure galant* it was not court aristocrats who imposed new colors or textile designs on producers, but Parisian merchant mercers. Each season they decreed the new mode with the items they sold in their Parisian boutiques or through their ties to silk producers in Lyons. Donneau's reports served the dual purpose of disseminating fashion information and publicizing the talents of the Parisian merchants and artisans to whom he constantly referred. Moreover, instead of referring to court nobles or Parisian great ladies, Donneau consistently used the anonymous pronoun *on* (the equivalent of "one" or "we") to describe who was wearing current fashions. Commerce and the consensus of the Parisian boulevards apparently ruled fashion as much as the king's courtiers.

For commentators of the late seventeenth century, therefore, the court of the Sun King had come to occupy a reactionary rather than an innovative place in fashion. It served as the safeguard of normative standards, a regulated and traditional *mode,* increasingly bypassed by an urban, mercantile system of innovation and rapid change. To observers, particularly those based in court society, these novelties threatened traditions of social deference and submission. Bourgeois "exaggeration" of fashion thus drew the condemnation of numerous authors and artists. In 1671, Antoine de Courtin recommended that in order to avoid the "awkward strangeness" (*bizzarerie incommode*) of new and extravagant fashions, "one must go back to the source of fashion which is the Court." In contrast to later periods, nature had no role in late seventeenth-century accounts of fashion. The tug-of-war between the court and the city opposed tradition and innovation; neither side appealed to natural appearances or to an underlying human nature as justification for its claims.[46]

The seamstresses' role in this fashion system was, on the surface, quite limited. Apart from the seismic changes noted above, the basic styles of men's and women's clothing did not alter a great deal from year to year. Fashion consisted not in nuances of cut or style as it does today, but in the colors and motifs of textiles, in accessories, and in the design and placement of decorations, all of which changed from season to season. As a result, fashion belonged to merchant mercers who sold fabrics and accessories, rather than seamstresses who assembled garments.[47] Nevertheless, rather than its invention, seamstresses played a crucial role in the dissemination of fashion. With their cheap and abundant labor, they made it possible for more women to acquire new dresses in cheap versions of the latest textile patterns and to adapt current fashions to their limited means. De Courtin's battle would be lost not only as a result of the influence of powerful merchants and manufacturers but because of the creation of the seamstresses' guild four years later in 1675.

The Hoopskirt Debate of the 1720s

With the adoption of the voluminous sack dress and the bell-shaped hoop-skirt in the 1720s, French women appeared in a shockingly new guise. These styles attracted immediate and intense attention from contemporaries, most of it critical. Religious commentators condemned hoopskirts as an offense to decency, complaining that they exhibited an excessive devotion to the world of appearances and a provocative lack of modesty. Accepting the common explanation that loose dresses and hoopskirts had originated to disguise unwanted pregnancies, they exhorted pious women to set a good example by refusing to wear them.[48]

Secular observers also attacked hoopskirts. The author of the *Satyre sur les cerceaux, paniers, criardes et manteaux-volans de femmes* (Satire on women's hoops, hoopskirts, shriekers [*criardes*] and manteaux-volans) agreed on the problems raised by the hoop-skirt: the ease of disguising pregnancies, the expense for women's husbands, and the open access they offered to women's genitals in an age with no female underpants. In addition to these dangers, the author also emphasized the skirts' sheer physical awkwardness, and offered comical stories of the pratfalls of women encumbered by them. He worried about the revelations caused by a sudden fall in public, and he speculated on the sexual repercussions of so much fresh air on a woman's private parts. He also posed a question that has troubled modern observers: "I cannot conceive how, with this get-up [*bricolage*], a woman can move or make use of her body; because in certain pressing needs everyone moves in one's own fashion; what do they do in those moments?" According to this author, ambitious women of the bourgeoisie were responsible for the excesses of the new fashion. Instead of copying the modesty of real court aristocrats, they exaggerated elite styles of dress in the vain hope of acquiring "the airs of nobility." With their constantly changing desires and self-indulgent expenses, he concluded, these women were "slaves of fashion," one of the first printed uses of a phrase that would soon become a cliché.[49]

In criticizing the new fashions, the author drew an explicit contrast between the elegant, streamlined torso imposed by the dress bodice and the loose, unformed pleats of the sack dress. As he urged his readers: "One must imitate the Nobility of the Dress Bodices of the Court. There is nothing as gracious as this charming method; and with this majestic air a woman is always in fashion." While the *corps de robe* showed how a woman was made "in the mold of Nature," the new dress served merely to hide the body's natural contours. The author's complaints about hoopskirts and the dresses worn over them focused on the disjuncture they created between reality and appearances. Women used their voluminous skirts to disguise natural conditions of age, pregnancy, and social status, and by doing so caused social disorder, sexual profligacy, and the impoverishment of families. Nature was not, however, an unquestioned good for this author; illicit pregnances were "Nature's disgrace" and it was a characteristic of "undisciplined Nature to always turn toward evil." Unchecked, the natural body threatened social hierarchy and harmony.

This author's negative view of hoopskirts was tempered by a document that accompanied it into print, the *Réponse à la critique des femmes sur leurs manteaux-volans, paniers, criardes ou cerceaux* (Response to the critique of women on their manteaux-volans, hoopskirts, shriekers, and hoops). Written in the voice of a woman, ostensibly the noble muse to whom the author had dedicated his work, this text presented a defense of the hoopskirt, albeit in a briefer and less strident manner than the previous document. Men's and women's fashions were equally ridiculous, the author stated, a fact that women had hitherto politely overlooked. Fashion, she added, had its owns laws and dominion. To ignore them was to become ridiculous; adhering in moderation to the whims of fashion was the only reasonable route for both sexes. The purity of women's hearts, she concluded, had no connection with the dimensions of their skirts, and her interlocuter's "trial" against them had no justification. The fact that this exchange may well have been the work of a single author underlines the ambivalent view of women's fashions that characterized the debate.[50]

Another pair of documents appeared in 1719, both written in the form of royal proclamations. Like the earlier texts, these pamphlets presented opposing sides of the question. In the *Ordonnance burlesque de la reine des modes* (Burlesque ordinance of the queen of fashion), Arethuse de Radamante, the "queen of fashion," conceded that because women were born imperfect, they were obliged to turn to clothing "to make themselves loved and to introduce themselves in the world." Now, however, fashion had gone too far. Radamante denounced the "vain ornament, the magnificence and the excess of dresses which are more appropriate for the Actresses who invent them than for modest and virtuous women." The queen also deplored the spectacle of women running around "the streets and public promenades in tucked-up dresses, with Chest and Shoulders entirely uncovered." To prevent these abuses, she forbade the wearing of hoopskirts, setting a fantastic fine of three thousand livres for infractions. She also prohibited: "Mistress Seamstresses and Apprentices from making or having made any Hoops or Hoop-Skirts under penalty of corporal punishment."[51] The second document, the *Lettres patentes en faveur du royaume des modes et provinces en dependant* (Letters patent in favor of the kingdom of fashion and its dependent provinces), was presented as an explicit response to the royal ordinance. In this document, Venus, the goddess of pleasure, formally annulled the queen's ordinance in order to preserve the liberty of "the Sex" to hide congenital or temporary bulges. She not only ordered seamstresses to continue making hoopskirts and inventing new fashions, she also called for a public celebration of their work, stating: "On the contrary, of what praise and what recompense are not worthy those who apply themselves to inventing these outfits [*ajustements*] by which defects are so well hidden. Posterity should take great care to conserve their memory."[52]

A satirical writer continued this mock legalistic genre in 1727 with *L'Apologie ou la défense des paniers* (The apology or the defence of hoopskirts). This document presented a facetious "assembly of women," convoked by "letter in the accustomed manner." After establishing rules of discourse, which included the right of three or four women to speak at a time so that all could have their say, the assembly passed to substantive discussion. Like the previous pamphlets, this text presented an ambivalent view of women's relationship to clothing. At the same time that it mocked the foolishness of female talk and apparel, it developed a defense of fashion as the only arena remaining for women in a male-dominated world. As the President of the Assembly declared: "You know Mesdames that dissension has made us lose our credit among men. They have made Laws which are disadvantageous to us. They have taken over our fortune, our liberty and our will. The only good which remains to us is the despotic power we have over our clothing, our decisions in this regard have always prevailed, and no one has ever appealed our court."[53]

Criticism of hoopskirts, she claimed, constituted an attack on the sole remaining sector of female authority. She urged assembly members to riposte with arguments about the utility, the affordability, and the convenience of hoopskirts, as well as the precedents for them in previous eras. In such debates, she declared, women had a traditional and innate authority, while men's attempts to arbitrate in the sphere of apparel deserved only contempt. Reiterating arguments made in previous pamphlets, she emphasized the absurdity of different male fashions and decried the hypocrisy of male satirists.

As these documents suggest, the new female wardrobe of the 1720s provoked mixed sentiments among observers. Religious commentators agreed on the utter sinfulness of hoopskirts. This fashion was a shameful display of women's attachment to the sensual world and an abandonment of proper female modesty and decorum. More worldly observers, however, were less sure of their opinions. On the one hand, they clearly perceived hoopskirts as ridiculous and wholly impratical. On the other hand, they also resented the claims on public space that women made in hoopskirts. It seems that they could not help but admire the sheer audacity of women's sartorial invention and their devotion to appearances. Hoopskirts were a vigorous assertion of women's intention to wear whatever pleased them—or the stylemakers of the day—despite the reaction of onlookers. Such female obstinacy dismayed, bemused, amused, and titillated observers, helping to convince them that fashion was an utterly female domain, where rational man could have no say.

As in the 1670s, nature was not a central trope in the literature. The pamphlets described the conflict over hoopskirts as a battle between men and women, using images of law, empire, and organized assemblies. This was a question of social and cultural authority, focusing on women's control over their appearances, rather than an inquiry into the nature of the female body itself or the overall relation between nature and society. Women's voices played a vivid part in the debate, whether written by male or female pens. Even the religious text that hotly condemned hoopskirts was written as a dialogue between a woman—one strongly tempted to follow the new fashion—and her confessor. She presented a series of arguments in favor of bowing to the dictates of style, but finally accepted her confessor's condemnation of the garments. Such pamphlets called on women to explain their adherence to the new fashions, which they did for the most part through age-old stereotypes of female licentiousness, irrationality, and self-indulgence.

Despite their misogynist vein, however, these pamphlets left a door open to the potentially subversive possibilities of female appearances. In a society where men dominated legal, economic, and social privileges, fashion was the only sector where women might assume the throne. Far from being trivial or ridiculous, women's capacity to seduce men through their appearances was recognized as a potentially disruptive power. It formed a constant topic of discussion and disquiet among French social observers throughout the Old Regime. For writers of the 1720s, the threatening nature of women's seductive powers was perhaps only too well symbolized by the gargantuan and grotesque nature of their new dresses. They were threatening not because they mimicked pregnancy, but because they allowed women too much ability to conceal pregnancies. In hoopskirts women made a provocative declaration of control over their own appearances. The physical space they occupied could be read as a dangerous invasion of the male public arena, making visible to all the influence women were feared to wield in private. This was a subject of anxiety and debate in the 1720s, but it also sparked a certain admiration and a defense of women's authority over the realm of fashion.

The Battle over Whalebone in the Garment Trades

At the same time that secular and religious moralizers debated the appropriateness of women's fashions, the needle trades divided into sharp conflict over the right to fabricate the new garments. The battle erupted on June 21, 1725, when the Parisian tailors' guild raided the home of a mistress seamstress, Marie Thérèse Sermoise. The tailors seized several pieces of clothing she had made with whalebone, on the grounds that such items fell within their corporate monopoly. According to the seamstresses' account, the raid was executed in a particularly brutal manner: "These officials [*petits jurez*] without considering Demoiselle Sermoise's pregnant state, tore away from her with violence these Children's Stays or stitched garments and persisted in wishing to take them away." As a result of this treatment, Sermoise suffered blood loss, vomiting, and the stillbirth of her child.[54] The brief portrayed Sermoise as a skilled female worker who was at the same time a (future) mother operating within her home. It painted a strong image of feminized domestic sanctity forcefully invaded by a crowd of loud, violent men. It is tempting to read the attack as an inversion of the female invasion of male public space represented by the new hoopskirts.

The seamstresses' guild successfully appealed this attack, which endangered both a mistress of the corporation and their collective economic prerogatives. On July 6, 1725, the king's procurator at the Châtelet of Paris issued a sentence condemning the faulty procedures followed by the tailors' officials, who by law could not inspect mistress seamstresses without being accompanied by female guild officials. On July 10, the tailors appealed this sentence in their turn.[55] They succeeded in obtaining a favorable ruling from the king's procurator at the Châtelet, which the lieutenant general of police confirmed on August 17, 1725. This judgment stated that "we permit Mistress Seamstresses to make all Works included in the first article of their statutes, of all sorts of cloth only and with Whalebone: we prohibit them, however, from making any Whalebone *emboutissures* . . . as also we forbid them in the future from making *Vertugadins* and hoopskirts [*paniers*]." The language of this sentence indicates that the king's procurator had accepted the logic of the tailors' arguments, available to us in several legal briefs commissioned by their guild.[56]

The tailors based their case on definitions of specific techniques of production, and in particular on one they called *emboutissure*. According to the tailors, *emboutissure* was a procedure used to embed whalebone within a bodice or a set of stays. The tailor created a pocket for each strip by sewing parallel rows of stitches through two layers of cloth and then inserted specially honed strips of whalebone (see figure 3.22). If the royal government had refused the dress bodice to the seamstresses in 1675, they argued, it was because the women were incapable of properly employing this technique. Fifty years later, the tailors claimed, seamstresses had made no progress. They painted a pathetic picture of poor masters being exploited by successful seamstresses, who paid them meager wages to make whaleboned garments. To support these claims, they produced several pairs of stays and corsets, which had been made using different techniques:

> First, the supplicants represent and produce to the court a dress bodice [*corps de robe*] which was made by a tailor and has been made with embedded [*emboutie*] whalebone, which one sees is encrusted in the cloth, and which makes a firm and solid base of work, and [which is] worked with art and science, which the seamstresses would not know how to do with the same industry, their knowledge not extending thus far.
>
> In the second place, they represent a child's bodice of string made by a seamstress with whalebone, it is a common work in which they dress the whalebone which they attach with string; and which does not lack a certain consistency, with which some women and girls would be content, and which is not sold so dearly to the public, but which does

not have the solidity and the quality [*bonté*] of the embedded whale-bone bodice, which is a work infinitely superior that only the tailors can construct with art and science.[57]

The tailors thus contrasted the "art and science" of their production with the seamstresses' lowly skills, setting the luxurious dress bodice above the child's cheap skirt bodice. Seamstresses might attach whalebone to bodices with string or cord, but they could not (and should not be allowed to) work the whalebone into the garment itself. The tailors further claimed that the hoopskirt was merely a revamped version of the old *vertugadin* used to bolster women's skirts in the sixteenth century, and which featured in their 1660 trade monopoly.[58] To counter these arguments, the seamstresses issued legal briefs pointing to the stipulations of their guild statutes, which explicitly permitted them to use whalebone in any garments except dress bodices. They did not refer to specific techniques used to make the garments, but insisted that the objects of the conflict were clearly not dress bodices or *vertugadins.* Instead, the seamstresses claimed, they were entirely new types of garments, which therefore fell within the parameters of their statutes.

Apart from these technical and legalistic arguments, both sides also appealed to more ideological concerns. Although they never made the claim explicitly, the tailors' arguments rested on an unspoken assumption of their opponents' inherent technical inferiority. They gave no explicit reason why members of the seamstresses' trade would be unable to perform the same techniques as tailors; they did not discuss, for example, apprenticeship practices or discrepancies of physical strength that might have prevented women from cutting whalebone. Instead, they asserted the seamstresses' technical inferiority as a simple fact, trusting their readers to accept the plausibility of inferior female skill. They also augmented the stakes of the debate by stressing the therapeutic uses of stays. They claimed that surgeons and other members of the medical profession often called on them to fabricate stays for children with skeletal malformations. Thus tailors were not concerned with the trivial world of fashion but with grave problems of public health.

If the tailors used gender as a tacit means to denigrate the seamstresses, their opponents made explicit use of their gender as an argument in their favor. They argued that women should have the "liberty" to employ female artisans if they desired. Female modesty and decency, they insisted, called for women's participation in this sphere, because hoopskirts and stays had to be fit on the nearly naked female body (see figures 3.20 and 3.22). The results of this legal battle therefore held implications for the sexual honor of the entire female population. The seamstresses' legal brief also made strong arguments regarding the female identity of their trade population and its vulnerability to male competition. According to the brief, the tailors' lawsuit represented merely the latest in a series of male attacks on female labor. They characterized the tailors' arguments as "the vain pretexts with which they daily authorize themselves to harass and fatigue a guild of Women and Girls, the majority of whom are totally ignorant of their Rights and Privileges."[59] We may imagine an assembly meeting similar to the one that the pamphlet writer evoked, in which the officers of the corporation urged their members to resist the tailors' attack on their small oasis of female privilege.

The tailors' response to this charge also echoed the pamphlet literature. Joining in with the satirists, they declared that the time had passed when "decency and modesty were the part and virtue of Women," adding that if there were any virtuous women left they would certainly not wear hoopskirts. The tailors thus cast the seamstresses' appeal to female modesty as a rhetorical strategy and one open to derision. Because women were so eager to defy conventional standards of decency, they suggested, there could be no need to protect them with female artisans. The tailors did not comment on the ramifications for their own corporate honor of making a living from such indecent garments.[60]

Despite their initial success, the tailors ultimately failed to convince the magistrates of the Parisian Parlement. In August 1727, the Parlement overturned the police ordinance of 1725. Refusing to become enmeshed in technical semantics, the magistrates' ruling stated merely that "it will be permitted to the said Mistress Seamstresses to use whalebone in the works of their profession." On the question of hoopskirts, they declared that seamstresses held the right to make "skirts, petticoats and hoop-skirts."[61] With this ruling, the seamstresses achieved a new inroad into the tailors' remaining monopolies on women's clothing. The dress bodices and skirts prohibited by the 1675 statutes belonged to a small, specialized market of court women. Hoopskirts and stays had greater economic importance because they were worn by women outside of court society.

Conflicts in the world of print and in the world of work clearly informed and inflected each other. Satirical commentators were inspired by the seamstresses' role in the garment trades and by the female guild that held assemblies and launched court cases. The seamstresses' numbers and their institutional status encouraged contemporaries to imagine a self-contained female world of fashion, encompassing both producers and consumers. In turn, printed debates about the new styles of apparel furnished seamstresses and tailors with arguments to defend and extend their trade prerogatives. Instead of relying on legal rights and privileges alone, the seamstresses could appeal to cultural concerns about female modesty and to the widespread acceptance of women's special role in fashioning female appearances. The tailors responded with contemporary tropes of extravagant and indecent femininity. Cultural debates thus furnished tactics of legitimization for male and female guilds, while the world of work furnished grist for the satirists' mill.

The Medicalization of the Debate

Stays and hoopskirts formed crucial elements of fashion from the 1720s through the 1760s, but they began to disappear outside of court circles during the 1760s. An important catalyst of this development was the intervention of medical experts into the debate over women's apparel. Often viewed as a phenomenon of the 1760s and 1770s—and in particular as a result of the influence of Rousseau and his views about female attire—doubts about the physiological effects of stays were in fact raised at least two decades earlier. The first to raise the alarm was the prominent anatomist Jacques-Bénigne Winslow. In 1741, he published a report to the Royal Academy of Science, entitled "On the Bad Effects of the Use of Whaleboned Stays." In this document, Winslow indicated that his concerns about these garments were first aroused by noting the high incidence of malformations of the rib cage among elite women, problems absent in women of the laboring classes. The anatomist concluded that the disfigurement resulted from the stays elite women wore as children and adults. On examining the garments more closely, he found that they formed a complete opposite to the natural shape of the human body. While the torso is thinnest at the top and widens toward the hips, the stays were widest at the top, becoming thinner and tighter through the waist and hips. This discrepancy was exacerbated by the practice of lacing the stays very tightly.[62]

Winslow's article graphically described the harmful effects on the female body that he ascribed to stays. As the first holes were threaded, he postulated, the strips of whalebone began to compress and force the intestinal organs upward, including the small intestines, kidneys, colon, rectum, bladder, and the membrane lining the abdominal cavity. In turn, the pressure of these organs pushed up the liver, stomach, spleen, and diaphragm. As the stays tightened over the mid-torso, the lower ribs were incapacitated, resulting in greatly reduced lung capacity and shallow breathing. When the stays were fully laced, two long strips of whalebone running down the back eliminated the natural curvature of the spine, forcing it into an abnormally erect posture. The woman's chest and stomach were further compressed by the insertion of the busk.

Winslow concluded that the compression, immobility, and unnatural posture imposed by this undergarment were responsible for a wide range of female medical complaints. These included lingering diseases and chronic conditions such as jaundice, stomachaches, nausea, vomiting, poor digestion, and pale color. In addition, he believed that many obstructions and tumors were caused by pressure on the pancreas, liver, ovaries, and other organs in the lower stomach.[63] Finally, Winslow decided that numerous upper-body ailments must also result from restricted breathing, ranging from chest pains, difficult respiration, and lung afflictions to heart palpitations, heart attacks, and disorders of the mucus glands.[64] The shoulder straps, which appeared to be the softest and least dangerous element of the garment, were in themselves quite harmful. They pulled the collar bones and shoulder blades back so far that the latter almost touched, forcing the sternum and chest forward. The narrow arm openings and tight shoulder straps squeezed the shoulder and upper arm, producing swelling and a violet hue down the length of the arm. The formal dress bodice was the worst of its kind, for its straps cut horizontally across the upper arm rather than over the shoulder, inhibiting any movement of the upper arms and shoulders.

Far from preventing deformities, Winslow concluded, stays damaged children's skeletal structure in the long term. He reasoned that a child restrained by stays would only use his or her strongest arm to reach for objects, thereby stretching the fabric on that side. The strong arm would continue to grow in its extra space, while the weaker arm withered progressively. Despite this host of dangers, Winslow did not advocate the entire abandonment of stays. He thought that properly constructed stays might be the only solution for some orthopedic problems developed in adulthood. He also suggested that women could avoid the worst dangers by lacing their stays less tightly. Winslow held firm, however, on the absolute inappropriateness of stays for children, advising mothers and fathers to trust nature for the proper development of their children's spines. As he argued, observation of Native American tribes and poor peasants did not reveal any more skeletal deformities than among the French aristocracy.

Winslow's claims in his brief text became the most influential—and plagiarized—statement against stays in eighteenth-century France. Over the next decades, consensus grew in his favor both within the medical community and among interested observers. In 1772, Alphonse LeRoy published *Recherches sur les habillemens des femmes et des enfants* (Research on women's and children's clothing), a much longer text that took up many of Winslow's arguments, without citing the earlier document. In addition to reiterating the physical horrors produced by the stays, LeRoy pointed out that women's supposedly innate tendency toward the vapors must result from damage to the heart. Taking Winslow's medical arguments one step further, he also insisted on the antiaesthetic qualities of the stays. According to LeRoy, the *robe à la française* worn over whaleboned stays hid the "most powerful" of women's charms, the "admirable hollow [*voûte*]" under the breasts, which highlighted the breasts and the slenderness of the waist. Stays molded the female torso into a straight line, rendering chest and waist indistinguishable from each other: "Where then is the beauty of this firm and massive breast-plate? What agreeable positions can a woman thus armored take? A negligent air suits beauty much better; the charm is even stronger in appearing more natural."[65] LeRoy recommended that French women imitate Asian courtesans, who enflamed men's imaginations by allowing their natural contours to be obscurely observed through their veils. This spectacle, he urged, offered an infinitely more alluring sight than the stiff uncovered chest and shoulders of his compatriots. This was a distinct contrast to the celebration of the nobility and graciousness of the dress bodice by the pamphlet writer of the 1720s.

A small minority in a crowd of critics, two tailors took up the task of responding to Winslow and his followers. In 1758, D'Offemont was a master tailor specializing in the fabrication of stays on the rue de la Verrerie, just down the street from the seamstresses' guild offices. In his *Avis très important au public* (Very important notice to the public), he announced the results of his "large number of Observations and experiences," which he proudly declared to have been approved by the Faculty of Medicine of the University of Paris and by the corps of master surgeons. Focusing on children's stays, D'Offemont emphasized the fragility of the infantile skeleton and the necessity of stays for correct development. Most children were born, he acknowledged, with proper bone structure, but he insisted that many lost it as they grew. To prevent deformities, children should wear whaleboned stays from the moment they donned their first gown through the age of puberty or "until the perfect solidity of the bones." According to the author, the stays would protect the children's chests and vital organs, in addition to shielding their bones from everyday dangers such as falls, convulsions, or colic.[66]

D'Offemont implicitly answered Winslow's critique by insisting that the stays should be turned inside out every day to prevent one side from being stretched. He also advocated the use of a special set of stays at night, arguing that failure to maintain proper protection during sleep would obviate any good done during the day. D'Offemont's proudest contribution to his craft was his new "health stays" (*corps de santé*), which fell somewhere between a corset and a set of stays. To avoid discomfort he made the top very flexible, with the top quarter being only lightly boned. The tailor proposed an even more supple version for grown men, which he recommended particularly for fat men, office workers who spent long hours hunched over their desks, and elderly men whose spines had lost their youthful vigor.

Another master tailor, a German-born immigrant to Lyons named Reisser, published a second defense of stays in 1770, titled *Avis important aux sexe, on essai sur les corps baleinés* (Important notice to the sex or essay on whaleboned stays). This text revealed its author's combined anxiety and ambition in publishing his work. Drawing on Enlightenment ideals, Reisser claimed to be inspired not by glory or the vanity of publication, but by the "good of humanity." Despite his avowed respect for both Rousseau and Winslow, he maintained that the medical dangers ascribed to stays all stemmed from faulty craftsmanship or overly tight lacing. He implicitly agreed with his colleague D'Offemont that properly constructed stays played an essential role in blocking the progression of skeletal deformities and in camouflaging those deformities that could not be treated.

If many stays failed to alleviate these problems, or even aggravated them, the fault lay not in their design but their improper construction. According to Reisser, this was the work of ignorant and lazy tailors who blindly followed routine instead of respecting each client's individual needs. He therefore directed his message not only to the community of medical and social commentators, but to his fellow tailors as well. Reisser hoped that those who had been unable to complete an apprenticeship or had been taught by incompetent masters could profit from his technical advice. Above all, he urged that tailors work in accordance with the new ruling principle, "nature": "Woe then to those who contradict Nature in Her functions; it is She who an ingenious Tailor should always have in view, without ever subjugating himself to an idiotic routine, which is always the rule of the crowd of men incapable of having views and who will remain eternally blind slaves of their masters' lessons."[67]

In the 1720s, a critic of hoopskirts underlined the tension between reality and appearances, positing a need for social controls over potentially disorderly natural impulses. In 1740, Winslow located nature within the physiology of the human body. Winslow trusted the innate tendencies of the body, believing that freed from human interference nature would achieve in most cases a proper development. Practices that respected the physical needs and characteristics of the body were healthy and desirable, while those that defied the body inevitably led to disease and ill health. In the 1770s, LeRoy and Reisser disagreed on the effects of stays, but they concurred on a view of nature as essentially wise, beautiful, and good. They took Winslow's faith in the untrammeled human body one step further by ascribing aesthetic and moral connotations to nature, personified by Reisser as a woman. In so doing, they followed wider cultural developments expressed most forcefully by philosophers such as Rousseau.

With the turn to nature in debates over female fashions, religious beliefs and social conventions lost their primacy as criteria for judgment. Instead, nature and health—as interpreted by male experts—furnished a secular and ostensibly objective response to questions about appropriate female apparel. Debates about fashion lost much of their religious content, but not their moralistic tone. Defying one's innate characteristics would soon become as much of a sin as defying God had once been. The chief difference lay in the fact that writers no longer believed women had interesting answers to furnish regarding their choice of apparel. Where the problem had consisted of an outrage to convention, pamphlets and broadsides solicited women's voices to explain their behavior. Although the inclusion of female voices usually served a misogynist rhetoric, it left room for the evocation of an alternate, "feminine" form of social and sexual power. Now, when the fault lay in harming their own bodies, women's failure to conform to outside experts became an inherently self-destructive act. Their words appeared only to report symptoms of distress or to mouth a stubborn devotion to their looks, as the outspoken queen of fashion was dethroned by an abstract goddess of nature. Women's moral failure now lay not in their outrage of God or social conventions, but in the equally serious crime of disobeying the dictates of their own bodies.

Inspired by medical discussions of stays, Jean-Jacques Rousseau became one of their most outspoken and influential critics. Writing *Emile* in 1762, he complained about the practice of wearing stays as unhealthy and an assult on good taste. He urged women to discard whaleboned corsets in favor of comfortable and simple garments, convinced that their continued use must result in a degeneration of the species.[68] Rousseau would go much further than other writers, however, in advocating not only the innate goodness of nature or the need to remove artifice from human society, but in deriving the essential principles of human nature and social organization from the mechanics of biological procreation. Based on their role in the reproductive sex act, he concluded that women's purpose in life was the essentially passive one of pleasing and attracting men. By contrast, the active male role consisted of acquiring female acquiescence in the sex act. This was a view of nature reduced to the mechanics of heterosexual reproduction, which became the basis of gender roles, the family, and all social and political activity.

Rousseau used these views to formulate a new understanding of women's age-old association with clothing and appearances. Destined by birth to seduce men, it was only natural that women love the dresses and finery that enabled them to do so. This was not a self-indulgent failing on women's part, but an expression of their biological imperative, found even in the youngest of the sex: "Little girls, almost from birth, love finery: not content with being pretty, they want to be found to be so: one sees in their little airs that this care preoccupies them already; and as soon as they are in a state to understand what they are told, one should govern them in speaking of what others think of them." With heterosexual attraction serving to anchor Rousseau's vision of social and political organization, women's love of clothing was not only inevitable, it was appropriate and desirable.[69]

According to Rousseau, girls were innately drawn to sewing and other forms of needlework as an extension of this primary impulse to adorn themselves. In *Emile,* he declared that sewing was one of the first activities that a little girl would learn, inspired by a desire to make clothes for her doll and, one day, for herself: "Almost all little girls learn to read and write with repugnance; but, as for holding the needle, that is what they always learn voluntarily. They imagine in advance being grown-up, and think with pleasure that these talents will one day serve to attire them."[70]

With these arguments, Rousseau explained the long-standing association between women's desire to wear clothes and their role in making them as part of a system of social relations grounded in the biological and sexual differences between men and women.

In keeping with his system of sexual differentiation, Rousseau insisted on a disregard for appearances among men. He wished his imaginary pupil Emile to be clean and attractively dressed, but not overly interested in his attire. In direct contrast to the court etiquette manuals of Faret or de Courtin, Emile was never to use clothing as a display of status or wealth: "He will take no recourse in a golden frame, and the signs of wealth will never soil his outfit." With women consigned by birth to the realm of appearances, men were explicitly banished from it. They were to occupy themselves instead with assertive action in society and politics.[71] Rousseau also rejected with horror male participation in the needle trades, considering it a crime against nature: "A young boy would never aspire of himself to become a tailor; it takes art to bring to this women's trade [*métier de femmes*] the sex for which it was not made."[72] For Rousseau, male tailors were no better than eunuchs, having voluntarily castrated themselves.[73]

In 1725, Parisian tailors opposed their male skill in needlework to inherent female incompetence, a formula that Rousseau inverted by positing an innate female affinity for the needle and thread that was foreign to men. If the tailors of the early eighteenth century had imagined—in some unconscious manner—wielding their needles like expert "pricksman," Rousseau would reply that for a man to hold his needle in his hand meant that he had none between his legs. Only female fingers should manipulate the phallic needle, using their skills to awaken and satisfy male desire. Given the role of needlework and clothing in the Rousseauian (hetero)sexual economy, men must renounce both the needle trades and the practice of wearing striking and seductive garments, at the risk of a polluting confusion of male sexual desire.

This social critic, who has been viewed by some scholars as the strongest voice arguing for women's seclusion in the home, thus issued a call for women to monopolize the commerce and fabrication of clothing and accessories. As he described his experiences in Italy:

> Seeing these [male] fashion merchants sell women ribbons, pompons, lace, chenille, I found this delicate finery quite ridiculous in large hands, made to blow the forge and strike the anvil. I said to myself: In this country the women should, in reprisal, open shop as metal-

workers [*fourbisseurs*] and gunsmiths [*armuriers*]. Eh! let each sex make and sell the arms of its sex. To know them, one must make use of them.[74]

The Rousseauian naturalization of women as consumer and producer of clothing drew on a long history of developments in the garment trades. In the first half of the seventeenth century, seamstresses created an economic niche for themselves as women making clothing for other women and children. The royal government enshrined this situation in 1675 with the creation of the seamstresses' guild. One hundred years later in 1762, Rousseau offered a new and powerfully formulated explanation of the connection between female producers and consumers of clothing as arising from the natural laws of procreation. Where corporate regulations had been a question of debate, discussion, and legal arbitration in the 1720s, henceforth the sexual division of labor was based on essentialized notions of gender. Obeying one's innate gender characteristics became a moral and social imperative. Ideological claims made for men's and women's work and their lifestyles in the second half of the eighteenth century had a strong impact on gender ideologies and labor in the late Old Regime and into the nineteenth and twentieth centuries; their acceptance was made possible by a century of evolution in the garment trades.

Seamstresses in the Last Decades of the Old Regime

Rousseau's wish for female domination of the garment trades was in many ways realized during the last decades of the Old Regime. In 1781, the seamstresses' guild obtained a set of revised statutes, which confirmed their victory over the tailors in the sphere of female clothing. With these statutes, the guild gained important new privileges, including a monopoly on the fabrication of women's clothes and the right to make some articles of clothing for men. As the statutes declared, the seamstresses "will enjoy alone, and at the exclusion of all others the right to undertake, cut, sew, trim and sell all kinds of dresses and new clothing for women, girls and children."[75] One hundred years after their guild was established, with only limited rights to clothe women in competition with the tailors, the seamstresses had succeeded in eliminating men from the production of made-to-measure female clothing. There is no better mark of the seamstresses' success over the eighteenth century.

According to the new statutes, the seamstresses would compete with the newly united tailors' and used-clothes dealers' guild in three sectors. One was in the fabrication of ball costumes and dressing gowns for both men and women. A second sector of competition was the "right to repair, re-cut, and sew old dresses and other old clothes for women, girls, and children for people who order them and without being able to conduct a commerce in them." Finally, the statutes accorded the seamstresses definitive victory in a battle they had fought with the tailors since the 1720s by allowing them to make whaleboned stays, corsets, and hoopskirts in competition with tailors. The statutes also allowed for competition with the new fashion merchants' guild. The newcomers were permitted to make dress decorations alongside seamstresses, but only when using material different from that of the dress itself.[76]

Despite its portentous implications, the new legal division of the garment trades endured only fifteen years. In 1791, the National Assembly fulfilled Turgot's legacy by abolishing the guild system throughout France. This time the destruction was definitive; despite sporadic interest across the nineteenth century, guilds were never again reestablished in France. This did not mean, however, that the sexual division of labor established in the garment trades was repudiated. Women's association with needlework and the garment trades was viewed by the turn of the nineteenth century as a form of natural law, rather than as a product of human laws and regulations. What had required royal legislation to enforce in 1675 was increasingly perceived as an expression of women's innate capabilities.

Fashion in the Eighteenth-Century: The marchandes de modes

Seamstresses were not the only female professionals to benefit from the expansion of the female wardrobe in the second half of the eighteenth century. Increased consumption led to an overall expansion and proliferation of the garment trades, with many new forms of specialization being practiced by women. The most important figures in this development were the female fashion merchants (*marchandes de modes*), who emerged from the shadows of the mercers' guild around in mid-century and soon overshadowed the seamstresses in commercial status and prestige. Fashion merchants started out by renting their privileges from the mercers' guild or working as the wives or daughters of merchant mercers. Their rise in the Parisian garment trades culminated in the attainment of an independent guild in August 1776, when the guilds were reestablished after the fall of the reformist minister Turgot.[77]

In his *Tableau de Paris,* the social commentator Louis-Sébastien Mercier repeatedly expressed a fascination with the fashion merchants, whom he credited with the central role in inventing and commercializing the amazing variety of new styles that characterized the 1770s and 1780s. As he stated: "Nothing equals the gravity of a fashion merchant combining *poufs,* and giving a hundred-fold value to gauze and flowers. Every week you see the birth of a new form in the construction of bonnets. Invention in this area makes a celebrated name for its author. Women have a profound and heartfelt respect for the happy geniuses who vary the advantages of their beauty and their face."[78]

The fashion merchants' domain consisted of a range of articles associated with the female head and shoulders, including hats, headdresses, shawls, mantles, and bonnets. They also furnished and assembled the ribbons, lace, rhinestones, feathers, and other items used to decorate women's dresses. According to François de Garsault, these women referred to their trade neither as a "profession" or a "skill," but as a "talent" that "consist[ed] principally of mounting and garnishing headdresses, dresses, skirts, etc., that is to say to sew and arrange, following daily styles, the decorations which Ladies and themselves are perpetually imagining." Like the mercers before them, the fashion merchants endowed stylishness on their clients' dresses by selecting the right color and pattern of ribbons, lace, or decorations.[79]

Fashion merchants also went beyond the traditional boundaries of the mercers' activities by making or contracting the production of some articles of women's clothing. Whereas the mercers were known as those who "sell everything and make nothing," these women undertook the fabrication of loose-fitting shawls and capes that did not require custom fitting, selling them ready-made in their fancy shops. In some cases, fashion merchants also furnished new, custom-made dresses to their clients putting out the sewing work to a needleworker and furnishing the dress decorations from their own stock. These cases, however, appear to have been exceptional arrangements for special clients, rather than part of everyday commercial practices. In the second half of the eighteenth century, fashion merchants' boutiques flourished in the new commercial areas of Paris, primarily on the rue Saint-Honoré, around the place des Victoires, and in the galleries of the Palais Royal, the new center of fashion (see figure 1.10).[80]

With the rise of fashion merchants, new techniques for inciting con-

FIGURE I.10 Fashion merchant's shop. From the *Encylopédie méthodique,* courtesy of the University of Illinois at Urbana-Champaign

sumption came to the fore. The celebrity of practitioners such as Rose Bertin—known as the "minister of fashion" for her services to Marie-Antoinette—and the visibility of their shops did a great deal to encourage the purchase of new garments and accessories among elites and a wider female population. Fashion merchants not only sold new styles to their customers, they transmitted the very notion of fashion to a wider public. The ingenuity of the individual Parisian woman, who imitated noble clothing based on first-hand observation, now gave way to the fashion merchant's shop, which specialized in displaying and selling the latest looks. Fashion was generated by professionals, whose livelihood depended on fostering their clients' constant desires for renewal. Writing *Emile* in 1762, Rousseau did not write the fashion merchants into existence, nor did he simply respond to a self-evident reality; instead, he articulated and gave ideological meaning to movements already under way, which were created by a combination of economic, social, and cultural forces.

The rise of these specialized tradeswomen accompanied the emergence of a new fashion press. The year 1785 saw the birth of one of the first journals entirely dedicated to fashion, *Le Cabinet des Modes,* which lasted under different titles and editors into the French Revolution. The editorials in the journal highlighted the important changes that had occurred in attitudes toward fashion since the 1670s. If the *Mercure galant* had offered an ambivalent reading of the court's dominance of fashion, the *Cabinet des Modes* ascribed the court a scant role in dictating fashion. Instead, it was created by Parisian elegants and professional fashion merchants, whose imagination and creativity were lauded in the pages of the journal.[81]

The *Cabinet des Modes* reflects important transitions in the distribution and marketing of clothing and accessories, but its claims should not be taken at face value. The journal existed in large part to publicize fashion professionals, and it naturally exaggerated their utter dominance of the world of style. In the 1770s and 1780s, royal influence over fashion had, if anything, increased since the early eighteenth century. Marie-Antoinette wielded an influence over fashion that had not been felt since the days of the marquise de Pompadour, the mistress of Louis XV. Her role in popularizing the *chemise* dress testifies to the attention and authority her wardrobe commanded in the last years of the Old Regime. Indeed, the fashion merchants Rose Bertin and Mademoiselle Eloffe became famous precisely because they worked for the queen. Like these outstanding members of their profession, fashion merchants, cloth dealers, and other ambitious entrepreneurs drew on their services to the royal family and the court aristocracy to attract new customers, naming their illustrious clients on printed billing forms.[82] The court had always relied on commerce for new fashions, and commerce never broke free of the court during the Old Regime. Elite Parisian merchants continued to derive prosperity and prestige from the ostentatious consumption required by court life.

It is also important to note that men by no means disappeared from the sphere of fashion in the *Cabinet des Modes*.[83] Despite Rousseau's commands, men continued to follow fashion, and the journal demonstrated a keen interest in masculine apparel. Its first issue offered an ethnological explanation for men's and women's interest in clothing, accepting a "natural" impulse towards sartorial display, but defying Rousseau's attempts to exclude men from this inclination: "In all times, in all places, the two sexes, in the view of mutually pleasing each other, have sought to adorn themselves. The Savage, to attract the look of the women he loves, or to make himself noticed among his companions, paints his body in different colors, decorates his head with feathers or with the hides of animals he has killed in the hunt: it is the same need to please and to make oneself noticed that brings the polite man to choose the cleanest or the richest garments."[84] Subsequent issues provided detailed information and images regarding changing fashions in male garments and accessories. Indeed, some issues were devoted almost entirely to men's apparel, while others gave equal play to men and women.[85] Rousseau's arguments in *Emile* had enormous influence on childrearing practices, fashion, and ideas about gender. They did not, however, lead French men to abandon wearing or making clothing in the last decades of the eighteenth century. Women had gained a powerful place in the garment trades, but men continued to play a strong role in making and buying fashions, a fact that the *Cabinet des Modes* acknowledged and encouraged. From the seventeenth to the eighteenth century, fashion was driven by an ambiguous mixture of masculine and feminine, court and city, consumption and production.

Conclusion

In 1675, Parisian seamstresses acquired an exclusively female guild with the right to make limited articles of clothing for women and children. They quickly enlarged their territory with the *manteau* dress, whose comfort and accessibility attracted court women as well as a broad cross section of the female population. In the 1720s, fashionable women began to wear loose "sack" gowns over hoop-skirts and stays, leading to conflicts between seamstresses and tailors over the right to make these undergarments. Finally, in the 1770s and 1780s, the female wardrobe expanded to include an impressive array of dresses, jackets, hats, and other accessories. The diversification of clothing, along with the substantial rise in its production and consumption, sparked a "clothing revolution" in which women stormed the barricades.

The clothing revolution attracted numerous commentators across the late seventeenth and eighteenth centuries, who were struck by the novelty of women's fashions, the expense they required, and the fact that women were engaged in buying and making clothing on an unprecedented scale. In 1675, observers noted the rise of fashion systems outside the court and blamed bourgeois women for aping the costumes of their betters. In the 1720s, commentators wrote of a feminine world of fashion in which women created and wore outrageous garments in defiance of all standards of female modesty. Their pamphlets used religious precepts, or mock laws and royal decrees, to induce women to abandon these shocking fashion statements. In the real world, law courts upheld women's position in the garment trades, judging that seamstresses' statutes allowed them to make the whaleboned garments that stirred such controversy. In the second half of the eighteenth century, nature emerged as a new standard of judgment, with medical experts, social critics, and some tailors adopting new ideals of health and comfort in women's attire, based on a newfound respect for the needs of the "natural" body. Rousseau took these notions further by linking women's predominant role in consuming and producing clothing to their innate biological characteristics.

Seamstresses played an important role in all of these changes. Their numbers and economic territory expanded along with the female wardrobe. When Donneau noted the arrival of the *manteau,* he attributed its production to seamstresses. In the 1720s, pamphlet literature depicted mistress and apprentice seamstresses as key figures in producing the garments they criticized. In 1781, seamstresses won new legal privileges, including a monopoly over the production of women's clothing. In one century, seamstresses had run the gamut from being illegal workers to establishing control over the female half of the garment trades.

In tracing in this chapter the intertwined destinies of fashion, production and discourse, I have posited an alternative chronology to previous historical studies. Historians seeking the roots of modern gender ideologies have largely focused on the second half of the eighteenth century and on the notions of femininity that emerged from Enlightenment social and political criticism. Similarly, studies of consumer culture have viewed the mid-eighteenth century as the turning point for new habits of consumption, with the rise of a fashion industry and the proliferation of finished goods for a broad market. This chapter has suggested that crucial developments for gender, clothing production, and the rise of consumption occurred as early as the 1670s. While the creation of the seamstresses' guild may have drawn on changes in consumption prior to 1675, its establishment drew many more hands to the task of fabricating dresses for elite and, increasingly, middling and lower groups of women. It also created a labor force defined by the gender of its practitioners and its clients, with the capacity to use legal action to defend and advance its trade prerogatives. The result was a new incentive for women to consume clothing and a new visibility of women as producers and consumers of appearances. The realignment of the garment trades in 1675 produced not only dresses, skirts, and other articles to clothe women and children, it helped to generate new notions of femininity and the possibility for new forms of female self-presentation and ways of appropriating the material world.

In this chapter I have also insisted on the complexity of ties between material objects, work, and discourses. While they influenced each other profoundly, fashion, production, and representation also maintained a degree of independence; their intersection produced unexpected and unpredictable results. If seamstresses seem to have taken the initiative in popularizing and propagating the mantua dress in the 1670s, they most likely did not invent it. They were clearly surprised by the sudden spread of other new fashions, such as the hoopskirt in the 1720s. Indeed, the rising demand for hoopskirts and stays created conflict in the garment trades precisely because neither the tailors' nor the seamstresses' statutes had anticipated their arrival.

Finally, I have pointed out connections between late-eighteenth-century ideas about "nature" and "gender" and the trajectory of the garment trades and fashion. In his articulation of natural principles for human society, Rousseau surely drew on women's privileged role in making and consuming fashions in the society around him. In turn, his ideas reinforced the notion that needlework and appearances belonged to women as a naturally female sphere. With the turn to nature as a supreme principle for ordering society, however, the potentially subversive power of female appearances disappeared. Women were indeed naturally talented to make, purchase, and display dresses and finery, Rousseau declared, but this predilection was merely an expression of their innate submission to men. He thus defused the political or social threat posed by women's appearance by interpreting it as an outcome of their subordinate position in the patriarchal family. The particular female power of seduction and entrancement was thus diverted to the mundane task of maintaining conjugal relations and soliciting male desire.

In the world of work, first Turgot and then the French Revolution would operate a similar turn away from law toward innate characteristics. With the abolition of the guilds in 1791, women's place in the garment trades would no longer be guaranteed by statutes and legal privileges, but by inborn predilections and an ostensibly "natural" sexual division of labor. The discourse on nature and the biological grounding of feminine characteristics in some ways protected women's rights in this sector, but they ultimately served to confine women to ill-paid labor as homeworkers in the new putting-out industries of the nineteenth century. Armed with this knowledge of the products seamstresses made and the representations others formed of their labor, the next chapter will examine the composition and division of labor within this workforce.

TWO

From Mending to modes: *Trade Hierarchies and the Labor Market*

Together, the garment trades composed the largest group of incorporated artisans and merchants within Paris. The guild system established a series of boundaries in this industry: between male and female trades, among custom-made, ready-to-wear, and used clothing, and among outerwear, underwear, and accessories. The centuries-old tailors' guild specialized in the manufacture of custom-made clothing for men, women, and children. After 1675, they were forced to compete with the seamstresses in made-to-measure women's and children's clothing, but they maintained exclusive rights over men's apparel. Among tailors, the trade was divided among a small minority who worked for women, and a much larger group who made men's clothing. The *fripiers'* guild sold used garments and furniture, competing with market women who hawked second-hand clothes. *Fripiers* also possessed the right to sell prefabricated garments made from cheap fabric, resulting in an endless battle with the tailors over the precise value of cloth they could use. The female linen-drapers' guild dominated the sale of linen cloth and finished goods such as aprons, shirts, bed sheets, and tablecloths. Merchant mercers sold the different types of cloth used for men's and women's clothing, as well as accessories and decorations. After the middle of the eighteenth century, fashion merchants sold articles for the female head and shoulders including hats, bonnets, and shawls. Other accessories, such as shoes, fans, purses, umbrellas, and stockings, fell under the manufacturing and commercial monopolies of separate guilds.[1]

These trade boundaries represented a guild ideal that often faltered in practice. Guild masters and mistresses violated corporate statutes in countless ways. They produced and sold forbidden goods, they employed illegal workers in their own workshops or through the putting-out system, they rented their trade privileges to nonguild artisans, and they formed associations with workers in the independent faubourg Saint-Antoine. Extensive production and commerce networks existed both across guild boundaries and across the frontier between the corporate and noncorporate worlds of work. Cross-gender hiring constituted another frequent violation of guild rules. Corporate regulations often forbade masters from employing women, but many masters relied on hired female labor, particularly in the clothing and textile trades.[2]

This chapter examines the labor market in the seamstresses' trade, one of the largest in eighteenth-century Paris. The first section estimates the size of the trade and describes its divisions, horizontally into distinct forms of specialization and vertically into steep hierarchies of prestige and fortune. Given the wide diversity of workers' ages and skill levels, as well as the highly cyclical nature of the trade, labor conditions varied dramatically. Unemployment and underemployment were chronic, with begging or prostitution looming as a recourse for those who failed to find jobs. In contrast to male guilds, the seamstresses' corporation offered remarkably little guidance for mistresses' or workers' behavior in the labor market. Guild leaders did not impose control over hiring practices and seem to have intervened only rarely in disputes between workers and mistresses.

The Size of the Trade Population

The seamstresses' guild quickly grew in size after its creation in 1675. According to the records of the royal procurator at the Châtelet of Paris, 82 new mistresses joined the guild between May and December 1675; these pioneers were followed by another 75 women in 1676. Around 1691, a government study reported the total population of the guild to be around 1,000 mistresses.[3] By the 1720s, the corporation reported its population to be 1,700 mistresses, a figure published by Jacques Savary des Bruslons in 1741. This number made the seamstresses' guild the fourth largest of the 124 trade corporations in Paris.[4]

The first-place merchant mercers' guild, with twenty different forms of specialization, was not much larger, with slightly over 2,000 members. The tailors occupied second place with 1,882 masters. A second exclusively female corporation, the linen-drapers, ranked tenth with 659 mistresses. With a total Parisian population of approximately 500,000 people in this period, there would have been 1 mistress seamstress for every 150 women or girls, and a similar distribution of tailors among the male population.[5] By the 1770s, the population of Paris had grown considerably, and the size of the guild along with it. A guild memoir written in 1776 gives the population as approximately 3,000 mistresses.[6] Around 1770, leaders of the tailors' guild also declared its size to be almost 3,000.[7]

At the bottom of the professional hierarchy, the seamstresses' trade attracted a very large number of apprentices. Between 300 and 400 young women entered apprenticeship each year, most of them for a period of three years. At any given moment a total of, 900 to 1,200 young women must have been engaged in vocational training. Apprenticeship figures also offer insight into the number of skilled workers in the trade. Given the high rate of failure among apprentices, it is likely that no more than one-half of the 300 or 400 who began training succeeded in completing it. The city would have thus gained 150 to 200 skilled journeywomen each year. If each woman worked for at least ten years before marrying and possibly abandoning the trade, there would have been up to 2,000 finished apprentices working at all times. This figure probably did not change over the eighteenth century, because of the relatively stable pool of new apprentices who began training each year.[8]

These skilled journeywomen apart, the trade must have included an even greater number of workers who had not finished apprenticeship in Paris. Some were failed apprentices, while many others had immigrated to Paris from the provinces, bringing whatever skills they had acquired in their home towns. In all, these workers probably numbered between 3,000 and 4,000 women in the first half of the eighteenth century, rising above 5,000 by the Revolution, with the significant growth of immigration after 1750. Many of these workers shuttled between active and inactive periods depending on their family responsibilities, and between legitimate and illegal labor depending on the availability of jobs. Adding these figures together, the total number of women working in the seamstresses' trade in the first half of the century as mistresses, workers, or apprentices was probably between 7,500 and 8,500. By the end of the eighteenth century, this number rose well over 10,000.[9] These figures do not include women who sewed in the employ of tailors, linen-drapers, or fashion merchants.

The Distribution of Mistress Seamstresses

Parisian seamstresses did not live in a single district, but were scattered across the city. A group of almost 830 mistresses, named in apprenticeship contracts, lived in forty-two of the capital's forty-eight parishes, in apartments that doubled as workshop and dwelling. Some areas, however, attracted more seamstresses than others. Of the forty-two parishes represented, eight accounted for two-thirds of the women. In order of importance, these parishes were Saint-Eustache, Saint-Sulpice, Saint-Paul, Saint-Nicolas-des-Champs, Saint-Roch, Saint-Germain-l'Auxerrois, Saint-Jean-en-Grève, and Saint-Gervais. With the exception of Saint-Sulpice, all were located on the right bank of the Seine.

Saint-Eustache and Saint-Germain-l'Auxerrois covered the central market area of the city, known as the Halles. As the traditional working center of Paris and home to many artisans and merchants, its commercial importance remains visible today in street names such as the rues de la Lingerie, de la Coutellerie, de la Ferronerie, and de la Tannerie. The parishes of Saint-Nicolas-des-Champs, Saint-Gervais, and Saint-Paul together constituted the Marais quarter. This area included both a declining aristocratic center and a large working-class section. On the left bank of the Seine, the parish of Saint-Sulpice contained the relatively new aristocratic residential area of the faubourg Saint-Germain.[10] Seamstresses were thus well integrated into the working population of Paris, clustering in neighborhoods with high proportions of artisanal and commercial trades. Their homes also lay in close proximity to the rich inhabitants of the Marais, the faubourg Saint-Honoré, and the faubourg Saint-Germain. They were not particularly numerous in the parish of Saint-Jean-en-Grève, where the guild's office was located. The guild as an institution had apparently little effect on seamstresses' residential choices.

Although apprenticeship contracts encompassed a substantial cross section of the guild, two Parisian almanacs, the 1692 edition of the *Livre commode des adresses de Paris* and the 1772 edition of the *Tablettes royales de renommé,* reveal the geographical distribution of the trade's elite.[11] In both 1692 and 1772, the best-known seamstresses did not significantly depart from the residential patterns of their colleagues. Like them, they clustered around the Halles district, close to the garment and luxury trades concentrated on and around the rue Saint-Honoré. While most of the 1692 seamstresses lived near the place des Victoires, the 1772 group had moved south, closer to rue Saint-Honoré, reflecting the street's rising commercial importance. Only a handful of the 1772 seamstresses lived on the left bank. Their homes were grouped around the aristocratic hotels of the rue de Varenne, all located in the faubourg Saint-Germain.

Trade Specialization

A report written in the 1770s offered the following account of trade specialization among seamstresses: "The Guild of seamstresses is very numerous. It contains four sorts of Estates: 1. Dress workers; 2. those in stays, corsets, camisoles and children's gowns; 3. those who make all kinds of hoop-skirts; 4. the skirt stitchers and [those] who make hoods."[12]

The first type of specialization constituted by far the largest group, consisting of women who made dresses, dressing gowns, skirts, and other items of outerwear for their clients. They often went by the title of "dress seamstress" (*couturière en robes*) or seamstresses *en habits,* the term referring to the formal woman's ensemble composed of a dress and matching petticoat. A smaller number of seamstresses concentrated on undergarments, including whaleboned stays and corsets. Originating in the last decades of the seventeenth century, this specialization constituted a diminutive but important group within the trade. Working for rich noble and bourgeois clients, they competed with the "ladies' tailors," a more powerful and older presence. An even smaller group focused on the production and sale of the hoopskirts that appeared in French fashion around 1718, making their way from the highest social levels down to masters' wives and elegant shopgirls. These two types of specialization took on increasing importance during the first half of the eighteenth century, as the use of stays and hoop-skirts spread among Parisian women. A fourth group of seamstresses made quilted skirts and performed the decorative stitching that became fashionable for skirts during the second half of the eighteenth century.[13]

Provincial seamstresses divided in similar ways. A dispute in Marseilles in the 1720s and 1730s pitted a small number of women producing whaleboned stays against a much larger group who made dresses, skirts, and other articles of female outerwear. In neighboring Aix-en-Provence, at least 10 out of 127 seamstresses accepted into the tailors' guild from 1751 to 1789 declared a specialization in the production of women's stays and corsets. Another two concentrated on children's clothing. One made stays for girls and boys up to the age of seven, while the other described herself as a seamstress of children's gowns. The remaining women most likely concentrated on dresses and skirts.[14]

The second half of the eighteenth century witnessed the emergence of a new category of specialization, when a small group of seamstresses began to make the *dominos* worn by men and women to costume balls. *Domi-*

nos were loose, hooded robes that did not require precise fitting. These seamstresses usually held a stock of premade gowns that they rented or sold to male and female clients. They acquired display space for their wares by forming commercial agreements with merchants who owned public shops. The rue Saint-Honoré was the center for this trade, which attracted used clothes dealers and merchant mercers as well as seamstresses. As the frequent raids conducted against these boutiques made clear, however, the production and distribution of *dominos* belonged officially to the tailors' guild. The seamstresses' persistent defiance of this monopoly bore fruit in 1781, when their new statutes awarded them the capacity to make and sell *dominos* for men and women in competition with tailors and *fripiers*.[15]

Seamstresses were not the only women in eighteenth-century Paris who earned their living through needlework. Linen workers (*ouvrières en linge*) formed a large trade population, sewing the finished goods sold by mistress linen-drapers, such as undergarments, table linen, and bedding. Fashion workers (*ouvrières en modes*) sewed dress decorations, headdresses, aprons, dressing gowns, and other articles for fashion merchants and merchant mercers. They were sometimes known as *agréministes*, from the word *agrément* or decoration. They formed a growing trade population, and were set apart from the better-paid shopgirls who served clients in fashion merchants' boutiques (see figure 1.10).

Trade specialization began for a seamstress at the time of her vocational training. A young woman who apprenticed with a dressmaker would be unable to make stays or hoopskirts without further training. In 1744, for example, a finished apprentice seamstress named Jeanne Dubosq lodged a formal complaint with the Caen police regarding the masterpiece (*chef d'oeuvre*) that officials of the tailors' guild had assigned her. According to records of the lieutenant general of police, the tailors had asked Dubosq to make stays filled with whalebone and decoratively stitched to the measurements of a twenty-year-old girl. Dubosq asked to be allowed to make a woman's dress instead, declaring that her previous training had been in this area and that she had no experience in making stays. As she explained:

> In the seamstresses' profession each worker attaches herself to the work which seems to her the most advantageous, some making only stays and nothing else, others working for common people, others for people of a middling estate, and others for the most distinguished people, without it being possible for any of these workers to succeed in making articles other than those which they have practiced.[16]

Workers expressed their adherence to a particular branch of the trade when they described their occupations to notaries and police officials. They called themselves "dress workers" (*ouvrières en robe*), "children's clothes workers" (*ouvrières en habits d'enfants*), or "corset workers" (*ouvrières en corsets*). Others employed more generic terms such as "sewing worker" (*ouvrière en couture*) or "girl seamstress" (*fille couturière*). The word *fille* referred to dependent workers who were not married. Unlike the male term *garçon,* which could be used by married journeymen, *fille* did not apply to married women.

Vertical Hierarchies

As the Caen seamstress suggested, a needleworker's business was shaped to a large extent by her clientele. The ideal client had a noble title, a substantial fortune, and a reputation to maintain at court. A large clientele of humbler women could provide a decent living, but they were unreliable in periods of economic crisis. Noblewomen always needed new dresses, regardless of the price of bread; their social inferiors were not so lucky and their orders dried up during harsh times. Aristocratic patronage had the added advantage of attracting new customers eager to bask in the reflected glory of a princess or a duchess.

The small number of mistresses who worked for court and Parisian noblewomen occupied the summit of their trade. These elite seamstresses were known either personally or by reputation to wealthy clients and to important cloth and fashion merchants. They belonged to the world of luxury and fashion, transmitting the latest styles to their clients and creating new nuances of cut and decoration. Mistress seamstresses at this level probably numbered a maximum of twenty women in the first half of the eighteenth century, rising to thirty or thirty-five by the end of the century. The *Livre commode des adresses de Paris* for the year 1692 recommended seven mistress seamstresses among the group working at this level. The author's criteria for selecting these women included both their reputation and their clientele. He specifically designated all of them as guild mistresses, which suggests that corporate membership was a prerequisite for achieving the highest position in the trade.[17]

To judge by this almanac, tailors continued to play a crucial role in clothing elite women in the 1690s: the author recommended eleven "ladies' tailors" in comparison to only seven seamstresses. The tailors' continuing monopoly over the formal two-piece dress probably helped them preserve their role in the high end of the trade through the 1690s. Their long corporate history, and the higher cultural value accorded to male skill, may have also enhanced their reputation. In a legal brief written during a legal conflict with the seamstresses in the 1720s, the tailors' officials emphasized their guild's long history of service to elite women, noting "the free and voluntary choice that these Ladies, women and girls, have made in all times for the unique ministry of Master Tailors in the articles of clothing which are for their use." Tailors did not dress merely ordinary women, the brief boasted, but illustrious ladies such as the queen of France, the duchess of Orléans, and numerous other court ladies.[18]

Eighty years after the *Livre commode,* the *Tablettes royales de renommée* signaled a rise in the number of seamstresses employed by court and Parisian aristocrats. The 1772 edition of the almanac listed twenty-six mistress seamstresses, selected once more on the basis of clientele and reputation. It named their clients among members of the royal court, such as Marie-Antoinette, the daughters of Louis XV, and the new duchess of Orléans. Another group of seamstresses were described simply as among "the most famous."[19] From a total of ninety-two tailors whom the author recommended, only seventeen specialized in female clothing. Seamstresses had apparently overtaken ladies' tailors at the summit of the industry over the course of the eighteenth century. Elegant ladies of the court and capital had switched allegiances, choosing more often to patronize female clothiers than male ones.

The seamstresses' victory, however, was limited, as the almanac revealed. With a total of ninety-two men versus twenty-six women, the upper ranks of male tailors far outnumbered the seamstresses. If we group the ladies' tailors with the seamstresses, we find a total of forty-three artisans working in the sector of women's clothing compared to seventy-five making men's clothing. This discrepancy derived from the high esteem accorded to Parisian tailoring in the late eighteenth century. Achieving the proper cut was essential to the fashionability of a man's suit. An elegant European gentleman would visit the city to have his suits sewn by a Parisian tailor. In women's clothing, by contrast, the quality and pattern of the cloth mattered much more than the cut and assembly. Paris was an important center for purchasing fabric and fashionable accessories, but the actual dresses could be made by a skilled seamstress anywhere. The almanac attested to this discrepancy, describing many of the tailors on its list as operating at a national and even international level, while the seamstresses were restricted to Parisian or court circles.

Probate inventories offer insight into the careers of the most prominent seamstresses. Françoise LeClerc became seamstress to the queen of France in 1725. At this date she purchased a house in Versailles, presumably for greater proximity to her royal patron. Apart from the queen, LeClerc enjoyed a large noble clientele, which she maintained even after her period of royal service had ended. Her probate inventory listed twenty-one regular clients, including the princesses of Montauban and Guimene, three countesses—one a lady-in-waiting to the queen—and five marquises.[20] A second member of this elite group was mistress Marie Anne Guichard. Guichard died in 1777 in her apartment on the rue Saint-Honoré, located at the center of the Parisian luxury trades. During her lifetime, Guichard worked extensively for Mesdames Adelaide and Sophie, two of Louis XV's daughters.[21]

Directly below this top niche of celebrity seamstresses lay a slightly larger group of highly successful mistresses, who attracted a stable clientele of noble and wealthy bourgeois women. Mistress Jeanne Dollé, who died in 1735, belonged to this group. According to her probate inventory, Dollé's clients included three duchesses, two countesses, a marquise, two maréchales, and several commoners. Another was mistress Françoise Môlé. When she died in 1714, Môlé's business records mentioned seventeen noble and nonnoble customers. A contemporary engraving of one of her clients, the marquise de Florensac, depicts her in a *manteau* dress perhaps made by Môlé herself.[22]

The 1755 probate inventory of mistress Marie Marguerite Oudry describes some of the services that seamstresses of this level provided for their clients. At the time of her death, she had started making a dress for an English woman, who lived in the Convent des Anglaises in the faubourg Saint-Antoine. Oudry had bought thirteen aunes of red- and white-satin and a hoopskirt to make the dress, at a cost of 130 livres. She had previously purchased fourteen aunes of taffeta for 84 livres, to make a dress for the countess of Roure. In addition to making new dresses, her bookkeeping indicates that she also mended the countess's clothes. Like Oudry, even high-level seamstresses offered mending and repairs for their clients.[23]

Beneath this upper rank stood a substantial middle body of seamstresses who acquired a mixed clientele of bourgeois women, and the wives of merchants, prosperous masters, and high-level servants. The lucky ones had one or more noblewomen as their privileged clients. Marie Louise Souters, who died in 1751, was a member of this group. Her clients included the wife of a Parlementary president, as well as the wives of the manservant of the duke of Burgundy, the concierge of the Hôtel de Soubise, and a bailiff of the jurisdiction of Servailles.[24] Another was Marie Germaine Pelée. At the time of her death in 1754, Pelée was engaged in repairing and altering two dresses with matching petticoats that belonged to the wife of a Parlementary president. Pelée had also begun repair work on a dress of gray damask with purple flowers for the countess of Gueslin, a red- and white-striped taffeta dress for the wife of the concierge of the château of Rosny, and a flowered satin dress that belonged to her brother-in-law's sister. She employed two permanent workers to help her make and mend her clients' dresses. Seamstresses at this level could live comfortably from their work, although they suffered during the off-season and periods of economic recession.[25]

An even larger, third category of seamstresses made their living from the "common" people described by the Caen seamstress, including masters' wives, shopgirls, servants, and other working women. They probably did more mending and alterations than new garments, and made more skirts and aprons than dresses. The articles of clothing they did produce were of lower-quality materials than those used for richer clients. Relying on a poorer clientele, these seamstresses were financially insecure. They and their customers appeared less frequently in probate inventories and have left fewer traces in the archives. The garments they made do not survive in museum collections, but were recycled through three or four generations and then used for rags or turned into paper.

Beneath these three levels of independent businesswomen lay a large underclass of mistresses who lived in extremely fragile economic conditions. Having failed to attract a base of regular clients, they constantly struggled to earn their living and were often forced to seek daily work with other mistresses. Arguing for a diminution of their *vingtième* tax in 1774, the seamstresses of Caen claimed that many mistresses in their guild were reduced to dependent labor: "There are in the guild a large number of mistresses who[,] having no work at home, have been obliged to go on daily work themselves to earn their living."[26] This decline often came with age and ill-health. In her old age, Edmée Boullet, a former guild official, eked a meager existence through day labor. She died alone in extreme poverty.

A similar trade hierarchy existed in provincial cities. In 1757, the officials of the Caen seamstresses' corporation divided its 109 members into four categories for a proportional assessment of the *capitation* tax. The top class included only 6 women, while the second consisted of 24 mistresses, the third of 34, and the fourth of 45 women. Six members of the last class were excused from paying the tax, being noted in the margins of the assessment simply as "poor."[27]

Guild Regulations for the Employment of Labor

Most guild statutes offered explicit rules for employing workers. These rules aimed to prevent successful masters from capturing a disproportionate share of the market and driving less fortunate colleagues out of business. The tailors' 1660 statutes contained a long series of such regulations. They stipulated, first of all, that masters could open only one shop, in which they could hire a maximum of six journeymen. They also forbade guild members from stealing their colleagues' workers, enjoining them to hire only those who had finished all tasks begun for a previous master.[28] Another set of articles prohibited the practice of putting-out by forbidding guild members from distributing work outside of their shops. They also banned masters from paying their journeymen by the piece, but only with "wages, bread, drink, bed and home." The statutes further dictated a wage scale based on skill and experience.[29]

To ensure minimum living standards among masters, the statutes encouraged those with surplus orders to hire their needy colleagues. One article called for the establishment of a site where poor masters could gather to be hired by successful ones "so that they can all be occupied by their trade and earn their living." Masters were also forbidden from hiring seamstresses or illegal workers (*chambrelans*) and from forming professional associations with anyone but another master tailor. The guild also restricted widows' rights in the labor market. Widows could continue their husbands' professions, but they could engage only one journeyman, who had to be approved by guild leaders each year.

The statutes exhorted journeymen and apprentices to work hard for their masters, except on Sundays and church holidays when they forbade them from working. Journeymen were to seek employment as soon as they arrived in Paris. If they did not succeed within a week, they were to address themselves to the clerk of the guild for placement or leave the city. Finally, the statutes forbade workers from taking jobs from illegal tailors or seamstresses. Violators of these rules risked fines and imprisonment.

These stipulations expressed basic principles underlying corporate organization. They spoke to concerns for fairness, an equitable distribution of work, the preservation of an equilibrium of wealth within the guild, and the fear of unrest by unemployed journeymen. They may also hint at the development of practices that rubbed against the grain of corporate ideology. By prohibiting masters from opening more than one shop, the statutes suggest that some may have already begun to undertake larger-scale production. Limits on employment raise the possibility that some masters increased their productive capacity by concentrating workers in their shops. Finally, the list of prohibited trade partners also suggests that ambitious masters may have formed associations with illegal workers, women, or used-clothes dealers. Whether or not these stipulations may be taken as evidence for the existence of such practices in 1660, they certainly flourished in the garment trades over the eighteenth century.

In stark contrast with the tailors, the seamstresses' 1675 statutes provided few directives regarding employment. Instead, they imposed only the most basic tenets of corporate labor practices. Mistresses were limited to engaging one apprentice at a time, but they could hire an indefinite number of female workers. Like master tailors, they could not employ workers who had not finished all chores begun for a previous mistress. Apart from these standard regulations, the seamstresses' statutes offered only one additional clause regarding the labor market. This was the establishment of a sexual division of labor between tailors and seamstresses. The statutes prohibited mistress seamstresses from hiring journeymen tailors and also forbade master tailors from employing seamstresses.[30]

Several reasons lie behind the reticence of the seamstresses' statutes regarding labor issues. The first was probably the fact that the guild had just been established. When they drafted their 1660 regulations, the tailors drew on several centuries of corporate existence. In 1675, seamstresses lacked sufficient experience with corporate practices and ideas to know what aspects of the labor market their guild could or should address. The female nature of the workforce only heightened their uncertainties about authority, social control, and wealth. Concerns for equality among mistresses may have also seemed less important given women's normative position of supplemental wage earner rather than head of household. Another explanation of the statutes' reticence resides in the different fears aroused by male and female workers. Journeymen were potent symbols of social revolt and defiance. To avoid social disorder they needed to be rigorously controlled and disciplined by their masters. The anxiety raised by young working women, by contrast, seems to have focused on the possibility of seduction or sexual abuse. The insistence on a sexual segregation of the trade thus addressed the most important fears regarding women workers, while neglecting those usually raised by men. Finally, the relative lack of mobility of the female workforce probably also lowered concerns about regulating the seamstress labor market. Whereas journeymen traveled around France as itinerant workers, and thereby generated instability in the supply of workers and additional anxieties associated with migrant laborers, seamstresses tended to stay in Paris.

The Structure of the Labor Market

By long-standing tradition, Parisian workers gathered each morning at specific sites in the city to seek work. Journeymen butchers assembled at the place de la Grève at five o'clock in the morning, along with masons, carpenters, painters, and other members of the construction trades. In the pastrymaking trade, this labor market took place on the rue de la Poterie, and for the joiners (*menuisiers*) on the rue des Ecouffes. By the turn of the eighteenth century, many guilds had begun to replace these traditional labor markets with formal employment offices. Like the tailors, they required masters and journeymen to address themselves to guild clerks who ran the offices. This requirement not only enabled the guild to prevent violations of corporate hiring regulations, it also allowed guild leaders to keep track of workers living in the city. In 1749, the royal government, responding to pressure from the guilds, imposed the *congé* system on journeymen. The *congé* was a document written by the worker's master, stating that he was satisfied with the man's labor and authorized him to leave the workshop. Henceforth, masters were forbidden from hiring journeymen who could not present a *congé* from their previous employer. The post-1776 guild reforms would reaffirm the *congé* system, despite the bitter opposition and hostility of journeymen.[31]

In contrast to these practices, no specific site existed for hiring workers in the seamstresses' trade and no evidence exists of guild-imposed hiring procedures. Guild assembly records offer no trace of an office established to supervise the hiring process, nor do they speak to the imposition of *congés* on workers. In fact, guild deliberations make no reference to employment practices whatsoever, focusing instead on the sporadic crises that threatened its institutional privileges. There is, moreover, no evidence that female workers organized to place newcomers and negotiate with employers over working conditions, as some male journeymen's associations did. The trade was too large, too decentralized, and too diverse to permit control by guild officials or insurgent workers.[32]

Instead of a unitary labor market, the seamstresses' trade harbored a myriad of informal ones dispersed across workshops, boutiques, markets, and other meeting places. The search for work must have focused on the Halles, the rue Saint-Honoré, and the left-bank parish of Saint-Sulpice, where seamstresses and other garment trades proliferated. Labor markets were intensely personalized, relying on personal contacts between mistresses and workers and informal networks of information and favor exchange. Contemporary documents offer numerous examples of sisters, mothers, and daughters working for the same mistress. Once one family member had found a job, she could hope to bring her female relatives into the workshop when the opportunity arose. Women in related trades, such as fashion merchants, linen-drapers, or laundresses, could also supply useful information and recommendations. Bonds of friendship and mutual assistance formed among women in cabarets, shops, and cheap boarding-houses allowed those in search of work to learn about new openings. The predominance of women in all trades involving clothing and decoration must have greatly enhanced the efficacy of these networks.

Yearly Workers, or ouvrières à l'année

Two extremes of labor existed in Old Regime France. On one end of the spectrum were highly skilled artisans belonging to rigidly controlled crafts, such as printing or cabinetmaking. On the other lay unskilled manual laborers working in loosely regulated industries, such as construction or portering. The seamstresses stood somewhere in the middle of this range. Their three-year apprenticeship offered a basic certificate of technical competency. It guaranteed to mistresses a minimum of skill and experience in prospective employees and provided workers with an advantageous position in the search for employment. The guild's supervision of vocational training thus constituted its chief contribution to regulating the labor market. Each apprenticeship contract was signed by guild officials, who scrutinized and formally approved the terms of the agreement. Guild leaders also appear to have established an upper limit on the number who began training each year. By restricting the size of the skilled labor force, they sought to control unemployment and maintain a higher premium on the skills apprentices acquired. Given the enormous size of the workforce, focusing their regulatory efforts on entry to the labor market was probably more effective than attempting to control hiring or employment practices.[33]

Apprenticeship was a crucial asset, but it did not guarantee permanent or well-paid employment. In *Les Contemporaines communes,* Nicolas-Edmé Restif de la Bretonne told the story of "The Pretty Seamstress," a girl he named Elisabeth Dardenne. Having completed three years of apprenticeship, "her work was well done, very solid; but in such little quantity that it did not meet the Mistress's expense." Limited to a daily contract, she struggled to improve her skills so as to obtain a permanent position. In addition to the basic credential of apprenticeship, mistresses judged workers on the range of techniques they mastered, on the quality and rapidity of their stitching, and on less technical considerations, such as manners, morals, and personal appearance. Literacy could also be a consideration, especially if the mistress planned to leave her employee in charge of the workshop during her absences.[34]

The most prestigious type of work in the trade consisted of a yearly contract with a guild mistress. Workers who obtained this form of employment were called *ouvrières à l'année.* They usually lodged with their mistresses, receiving food and housing in addition to an annual salary. Yearly workers represented an elite minority, enjoying the rare luxury of full employment throughout the year. Competition for these places was intense, with the most highly skilled, experienced, and best-connected workers possessing the greatest hope of success.

An annual worker's status in her employer's home depended on the mistress's commercial success and individual character. Some performed household chores such as cooking or cleaning, particularly if no servant were employed. One worker testified to police officials that she was sent to purchase wine for her mistress's household.[35] Annual workers' trade skills, however, usually placed them above menial chores. Because they received considerably higher wages than servants, using them for household labor was a wasteful expenditure of their time.

If they did not marry, yearly workers could remain with their mistresses over long periods. Marie Catherine Cardin lived with her mistress for sixteen years, until the latter's death in 1743. When Marie Germaine Pelée died in 1754, she employed two sisters as yearly workers, one of whom had been with her for approximately eleven years. In most cases, mistresses who hired yearly workers were unmarried or widowed and their workers were almost always single women as well. The limitations of space, combined with potential conflicts of authority and, perhaps, unspoken fears of sexual rivalry, prevented married mistresses from incorporating workers into their households. Mistress seamstresses enjoyed considerable economic autonomy, but it did not extend to turning the family home into workers' lodgings. For mistresses and workers who never married, long-term professional association could become an alternative to founding their own families.[36]

Daily Workers *or* ouvrières à la journée

For married mistresses and their many colleagues who did not have sufficient orders to maintain a permanent employee, daily workers were the preferred form of employment. Even mistresses who engaged yearly employees took on day workers as supplemental labor, especially during peak periods. Daily workers occupied a precarious position, which grew more fragile as immigration to Paris from the provinces saturated the market over the eighteenth century. The duration of their employment was highly variable, ranging from a few days to weeks or months, or even to the possibility of regular employment with the same mistress. Daily workers lodged in their own dwellings, but may have taken meals with their mistresses and received other nonmonetary forms of remuneration.[37]

A working day in mistress Fontaine's home reveals the different forms of employment that could coexist in one workshop. In January 1713, Fontaine sat down for breakfast with her three daily employees before they began their day's work. Marguerite de Couude was twenty-eight years old and married to a soldier in the French Guard. Her colleagues described her as a permanent member of the mistress's workshop, stating that she "work[ed] ordinarily for the said Fontaine." The other two women worked on a temporary basis. They were Marie Sorel, a sixty-year-old widow, and Marguerite Prevost, a twenty-year-old unmarried woman, both of whom declared that they worked only occasionally for Fontaine. Sorel may have been driven back onto the labor market by the death of her husband, while Prevost was probably hoping to accumulate a dowry from her daily wages. Sorel's age and Prevost's youthful inexperience may have disqualified them from more permanent employment.[38]

The highly cyclical nature of production in the garment trades increased workers' vulnerability. During the busy fall and spring months, mistresses took on temporary help to meet the rush of orders. They quickly shed these extra workers when the summer lull arrived.[39] One scholar has claimed that the highest number of arrests for prostitution occurred during the summer months, a phenomenon she attributed to unemployment among female workers in the garment trades.[40] The problem of unemployment was exacerbated by the restrictions imposed on the number of working days each year. Although not always scrupulously observed, the liturgical calendar officially prohibited labor every Sunday as well as on many feast days falling during the week. In six months, Jeanne Berset worked only 134 out of 184 days for her regular employer, mistress Marie Bailly. During the next full year she labored 268 out of 365 days.[41] Given the number of religious holidays and the low wages they received, it was crucial for workers to find employment on available workdays.

Like other artisans, seamstresses worked very long twelve- to fourteen-hour days. Their workday began at sunrise, around six-thirty or seven o'clock in the summer and at eight o'clock in the winter. The day's activities ended, in all seasons, around eight or nine o'clock at night. The young seamstress Cécile Godine reported to the police that she had returned from her day's work in January 1733 at nine o'clock in the evening. Another worker reported in November 1760 that she went home between eight and nine o'clock. During busy periods, work could continue until midnight or even through the night for particularly urgent orders.[42]

The average size of a seamstress's workshop is extremely difficult to determine, given the different forms of labor, seasonal fluctuations in employment, and a lack of precise evidence. Poor seamstresses would have worked alone or with one or two helpers at most, while the most prosperous kept one or two permanent employees and a handful of daily workers. Tailors probably hired more workers on average than their colleagues, because the production of men's suits involved a more structured division of labor than did women's dresses. The only quantitative data on workshop size comes from a survey of Parisian industry undertaken between 1791 and 1792 by the Revolutionary municipal government. Contained in the documents known as the *papiers Braesch,* the survey was intended to help the administration determine how much currency it needed to issue to allow employers to pay their workers. This survey—as reported by Daniel Roche—enumerated 96 tailors and only 9 seamstresses. The 9 seamstress entrepreneurs employed a total of 57 workers, giving an average of almost 6.5 workers per mistress. This figure was close to the average among tailors, where 96 men employed 781 workers, for an average of slightly over 8 in each workshop. Both averages were well below the overall mean of 16.5 workers per employer. This report is difficult to correlate to Old Regime circumstances, however, because the garment trades had entered serious crisis during these years. Moreover, the report favored large employers, for it only included those who reported a need for currency to pay their workers.[43]

Yearly Salary and Daily Wages

Like forms of employment, salaries and wages varied considerably, according to seniority, experience, age, and the prosperity of the mistress. In 1766, a sixteen-year-old worker reported the substantial salary of 24 écus, or 72 livres. In 1770, mistress Reine Briard des Coutures died in the crush of the panicked crowd at the fireworks display held to celebrate the dauphin's marriage. Her probate inventory revealed that she paid her yearly worker a salary of only 60 livres. In 1777, Marie Anne Guichard, seamstress to two of Louis XV's daughters, paid her first worker 200 livres a year and her second 100 livres. In all of these cases, provisions for food and lodging are unclear.[44]

The chief figure among employees was the "first worker." In Restif de la Bretonne's "The Pretty Seamstress," he described the unsympathetic Mademoiselle Margot as "dean of the annual girls" (*doyenne des filles-à-l'année*). Ordinarily the senior employee in the workshop, the first worker was responsible for the most important tasks, such as cutting cloth and supervising the atelier when the mistress was away. In accordance with this status, they received a higher salary than their colleagues. Before mistress Jeanne Dollé died in 1735, she employed her own daughter as "principal girl worker" at 100 livres per year, a "second girl worker" at 60 livres per year, and a servant-cook at only 36 livres.[45] Mistress Laurence Ducouroy employed three yearly workers at the time of her death in 1759. Demoiselle Henriette, who had entered the workshop two years before Ducouroy died, received 100 livres a year. Ducouroy had hired a second worker two months before her death, at an annual salary of 75 livres, and a third worker, only one month before she died, at 60 livres.[46]

These salaries demonstrate the variability of annual pay, as well as the considerable stagnation that existed over time. In 1770 a worker might receive the same salary as a colleague some thirty years earlier. Given the sharp inflationary trend across the eighteenth century, real earnings probably fell significantly among workers, although the provision of food and lodging might have cushioned the blow to a certain extent. If mistresses did not pay their workers more, it was in part because they could not charge their clients higher prices, as will be demonstrated in the next chapter. This stability in labor and product prices was characteristic of the Old Regime economy, in which the overall cost of living frequently bore little relation to the calculation of wages or the price of finished goods.[47]

Mistresses paid workers' salaries at the end of the year or at the termination of employment. They frequently gave cash advances for spending money, doctor's fees, medicine, or other expenses. Before she died, Laurence Ducouroy paid Henriette two sums of 94 livres and 68 livres, respectively, leaving little due on the woman's two years of salary. She also gave her second worker 6 livres during the first month of employment. When she died, Briard des Coutures owed a worker only 37 livres and 10 sous for the remainder of her salary of 60 livres.[48]

Wages paid to daily workers also varied widely. When one seamstress took pity on an impoverished girl without work, she hired her at a daily wage of only 6 sous a day, in addition to which she provided food, lodging, and some used clothing.[49] The example of Jeanne Berset and her mistress Bailly reveals the role of experience in determining wages. After completing three years of apprenticeship, Berset remained in her mistress's workshop for another year and a half. For the first six months, she received 8 sous a day, amounting to a total of 53 livres. After this period, Bailly raised Berset's wages to 10 sous a day, "given that she should know how to work better." In a year, Berset earned a total of 134 livres at this wage.[50] Wages for experienced, mature workers might be considerably higher. Police records offer an anecdotal example in a report on a young laundrywoman who drifted into prostitution. In a letter to police inspector Berryer, a brothel keeper referred to the young woman's mother as a "seamstress at twenty sous a day." Although the tone was contemptuous, this was not a minuscule wage even by the standards of skilled male trades.[51]

The low level of seamstresses' pay attracted the attention of at least one contemporary observer. In his introduction to "The Pretty Seamstress," Restif de la Bretonne denounced the "cruelty" of female clients whose thirst for luxury was only satisfied by driving down their seamstresses' prices. In turn, he claimed, mistresses could only pay their workers 10 or 12 sous a day, while the daily cost of living for a single woman was at least 20 sous. To make ends meet, workers were obliged to nourish themselves on fruit and low-grade meat, to "go naked" through want of clothes, and to engage in prostitution. The reliability of Restif's account is open to question, for the dramatic tension of his stories relies to a large extent on the danger and desperation surrounding the working girl, which stands in stark contrast to her innocence and beauty. His texts highlight the thin line separating legitimate from illegitimate labor, ill-paid work from the temptations of debauchery, and honorable marriage from illicit sex, suggesting that his interests lay more in exploring female sexual vulnerability than in the real problems of women workers.[52]

At 20 sous a day, a seamstress who found full employment on available working days could earn approximately 270 livres, enough to rent an apartment, feed herself, and purchase used clothing and other small necessities. At the low end of the scale, with approximately 100 livres a year a seamstress living independently would find life as difficult as Restif envisaged. Most of her wages would be spent on rent, with little left over for additional expenses. For these women, the provision of food during the workday constituted an essential supplement. Even short periods of unemployment or illness could spell disaster. Only those who could rely on parents for food and lodging could hope to save money for a dowry or the price of guild membership. Widows with children would find survival extremely difficult.

As was the case for yearly workers, mistresses paid daily wages at the termination of employment, with advances given along the way. Probate inventories reveal that many mistresses owed back wages to their daily workers. When mistress Marie Josephe Denizon died in 1781, she owed a worker 24 livres for daily work. Another mistress, Marie Anne Guelorget, owed 3 livres to a temporary worker whom she hired to supplement her two permanent employees. Françoise Ducasble owed 9 livres to her workers when she died in 1782.[53]

Salaries among seamstresses were similar to those in other skilled female trades. One fashion merchant paid his two workers 100 and 60 livres respectively. Another two fashion merchants who operated a joint enterprise declared that they had always kept three workers, whom they gave an annual salary of 150 livres each. Another girl declared that she had learned how to embroider from her aunt. She worked at this trade from the age of fifteen, estimating her annual earnings at 100 livres. Her parents appropriated all of this money as reimbursement for room and board. When her uncle died, he left the young woman an annuity that permitted her to put aside some savings from her pay.

Male artisans could earn significantly more than seamstresses. In 1751, a master blacksmith agreed to pay his new apprentice 20 sous a day during the training period. Ten years later, a master printer promised to pay an apprentice 15 sous every working day during the first year of training, and 18 sous during the last three years. In the same year, two apprentice plumbers entered contracts paying 20 sous a day during their first two years and 22 sous the last two. Judging from these figures, young men entering vocational training could earn twice as much as finished apprentice seamstresses.[54] In the roofing trade between 1755 and 1776 the guild's official wage rate for journeymen was 45 sous a day in winter and 50 sous in summer.[55]

The pay received by journeymen tailors in the eithteenth century remains obscure. The tailors' 1660 statutes set wages for the "best" workers at 4 livres a month, and for the less experienced at 2 or 3 livres. Daily workers were to receive 10 sous a day. Whether or not they were ever respected, these wages probably rose to a certain extent over the eighteenth century. In 1778, a journeymen tailor in Caen earned 7 livres a month, which produced an annual income of only 84 livres. His master probably supplemented this meager amount with food and perhaps wine, and his pay would have stretched much further in the provinces than in Paris. When this worker left his master after sixteen months of work, the man owed him 35 livres and 16 sous.[56]

Subcontracting and Putting-Out

The putting-out system occupies a central place in histories of the nineteenth-century garment trades. Historians have insisted that a crucial element in the modernization of the clothing trades, and in particular in the rise of the ready-to-wear industry in the 1830s and 1840s, was the systematic use of cheap male and female homeworkers. This reorganization of labor, they have argued, had more impact on the trade than the introduction of new technology such as the sewing machine, which merely reinforced tendencies already in existence.[57] This account implicitly contrasts the growth of putting-out in the first half of the nineteenth century with the Old Regime corporate system, in which highly trained journeymen worked together in the master's workshop, each being capable of executing an entire order. While putting-out clearly acquired an unprecedented scale and organization in the nineteenth century, it was by no means unknown to guild masters of the seventeenth and eighteenth centuries. Despite formal guild prohibitions, Old Regime master tailors frequently gave piece work to male and female homeworkers. The practice was so well known that in 1749 a Parisian master tailor would casually use the word "piece worker" (*apiésseur*), a common nineteenth-century epithet, to describe a journeyman home worker living in his building. Far from decrying the man or the practice, this master frequently gave sewing work to his neighbor.[58]

Many seamstresses also distributed work to outworkers. When she died in 1770, mistress Antoinette Talbot owed thirty-nine livres and fifteen sous for sewing work she had put out to her niece.[59] In addition to the salary of her yearly worker, mistress Briard des Coutures owed four livres and four sous to a seamstress for piecework.[60] Seamstresses also distributed work to specialized artisans who possessed the specific skills required for their clients' orders. These included embroiderers, needleworkers who performed fancy stitching and quilting work (*piqueurs*), and *découpeurs*, who specialized in decorative cutting and stamping. The *découpeur* used metal punches and rollers to make decorative perforations in cloth, and shears to make scalloped edges along the edge of trimming, sleeves, and collars. They also pressed decorative patterns into fabric by banging a hammer on heated metal stamps placed on the cloth. During the application of police seals on Marie Josephe Denizon's apartment, Jeanne Petit, "seamstress of hoop-skirts," appeared to request payment of a sum of thirty-four livres and eight sous for work she had performed for Denizon.[61] In another example, when she died in 1777 Marie Anne Guichard owed thirty-five livres to a female *découpeuse*.[62] Mistress Françoise Môlé owed sixteen livres to a linen-draper for decorations, five livres to a Mademoiselle Foyon "for sewing work," an undisclosed sum to a Monsieur Thierry, quilter of taffeta cloth (*piqueur de taffetas*), and eight livres to a tailor.[63] Techniques such as quilting and stamping were usually applied on cloth before a garment was cut and sewn; seamstresses who distributed such work thus took responsibility for organizing several steps of production. As these examples demonstrate, networks of subcontracted labor crossed trade and guild boundaries as well as the gender divisions imposed by the guild's statutes.

In some cases, seamstresses made their own decorations for clients' dresses, sewing ruffles and trimming from the same fabric as the dress. They also used ribbons, braid, lace, and tassels purchased from fashion merchants or mercers. In all likelihood, however, seamstresses did not make the elaborate and expensive decorations on lavish noblewomen's dresses. Instead, they sewed the dress and gave it to the client, who would then take it to her fashion merchant for trimming. It has been suggested that fashion merchants often organized the entire process of dressmaking: accepting dress orders, subcontracting the sewing work to seamstresses, and having decorations made by their own workers. The business records of elite merchants, such as Rose Bertin and Mademoiselle Eloffe, tend to undermine this hypothesis. They charged clients for furnishing and fabricating dress trimmings, but rarely for the dress itself.[64] If they did not fall into complete dependence on fashion merchants, seamstresses did accept occasional subcontracted work from them, as well as from merchant mercers, linen-drapers, tailors, and other artisans. Accused of illegally selling men's and children's clothing, a used-clothes dealer in Caen explained that she had had the clothing repaired by a mistress seamstress and a master tailor, and thus had not trespassed on guild prerogatives.[65]

The most ambitious seamstresses operated groups of homeworkers. In one of their periodic raids, officials of the tailors' guild found Denis Vau-hées, a journeyman tailor, working with a group of women in a room on the third floor of an apartment situated on the rue de Gesvres. Vauhées was making a pair of men's breeches, while the women were making articles of women's clothing. During the proceedings, mistress seamstress Michelle Trainquart arrived to claim ownership of all the articles of women's clothing in the room. She further stated that she had asked one of the women present, her former apprentice Marie Nicolle Gaillot, to work at home because she was in the process of moving her own household and could not take in workers. She did not explain Vauhées's presence in the room. Unconvinced by her story, the tailors' seized all of the articles of clothing present. Overall, seamstresses do not seem to have organized dispersed networks of homeworkers or used them to embark on large-scale production.[66]

Female Labor in the Tailoring Trade

As with the putting-out system, historians have viewed the widespread use of female labor as an essential aspect of the transformation of the garment trades in the nineteenth century. During the first decades of the century, struggling journeymen pointed to the growing reliance on female labor as proof of their trade's degradation and the loss of Old Regime corporate pride.[67] Tailors who protested this situation, however (as well as historians who have made similar observations), failed to acknowledge the long-standing importance of female labor in the Old Regime tailoring trade. Although the Parisian tailors' statutes explicitly prohibited masters from hiring women other than their female relatives, a good number regularly employed women workers with no family ties. Ladies' tailors relied particularly heavily on female employees. According to a contemporary technical work, women performed much of the sewing work involved in the fabrication of stays and corsets.[68] A female employee in a tailors' shop could also help the tailor attract and maintain a female clientele, reassuring both female clients and their husbands or fathers that no irregularities occurred during the fitting process (see figures 3.19 and 3.21).

Masters who made men's clothing also hired female workers, most often to sew breeches and waistcoats. Indeed, contemporary sources reveal the female tailors' worker (*ouvrière pour les tailleurs*) to have been a common category of labor, one that women frequently claimed in notarial and police documents. Such sources also reveal the existence of specialized female occupations in the tailoring trade, including breechesworkers (*ouvrières en culotte*), breechmakers (*culottières*), and waistcoatmakers (*gilettières*). While they could presumably sew women's garments if necessary, these workers possessed different skills and participated in distinct networks of employment and patronage. They maintained professional and personal ties to tailors and their male clients, not to mistress seamstresses.

Some female employees worked in their masters' homes. In 1759, police investigated the suicide of Catherine Germain, who had thrown herself from the fourth-floor apartment of master tailor Labbet. Labbet declared that Germain, a forty-nine-year-old native of Verdun, had worked for him for three years. During this time she had lived in his apartment, which doubled as his workshop.[69] It was more common, however, for tailors' female workers to work out of their own homes or that of a subcontractor. Marie Elizabeth Vieille, the twenty-nine-year-old wife of a wheelbarrow operator (*roulleur de brouettes*), described herself as a "worker working ordinarily for master tailors." Discovered by guild officials making velvet breeches in her apartment, she declared that she: "never works in the tailor's profession except when master tailors give her work and notably for Sieur Dupré who almost always keeps her busy." Dupré himself admitted that he "ordinarily [gave her] breeches to be sewn."[70] In January 1744, tailors' officials raided the fifth-floor apartment of Antoine Bernard, a finished apprentice tailor. They found him illegally working with several women at making velvet breeches.[71] In both cases, officials seized the goods they discovered, their owners' protests notwithstanding. The most daring women were not content to perform piecework for master tailors, but branched into cutting out and assembling male garments for their own clients. During one of their periodic raids, officials of the tailors' guild entered the home of Catherine Tangres, whom they found with another woman making a gray wool riding jacket, surrounded by patterns and other tools of the trade.[72]

Female labor was probably even more widespread among tailors outside of Paris, particularly in cities with weak guild institutions or a scarcity of skilled male workers. Among its other devastating effects, the 1720 plague in Aix-en-Provence created a shortage of male labor in the city's tailoring trade. This situation encouraged masters to rely on female homeworkers, who became accepted members of the trade in subsequent years. In 1727, as part of a new system of corporate taxation, guild officials required masters to provide a list of the men and women they employed in their own boutiques as well as any female employees who worked in their own homes. No one overtly criticized the use of women workers until 1750, when guild leaders called an assembly to discuss problems related to this practice:

> [It] was represented by one of the guild officials that girls working in the masters' workshops [who] have scarcely begun to know how to make breeches, retire to their homes to work with more freedom and being in consequence imperfect in their work they massacre and ruin what they make[,] the masters being unable to avoid giving them work because of the small number of workers that are in the town, and the smallest number being found in their boutiques, this gives clients occasion every day to come complain to the masters of badly made seams.[73]

The guild's officials called on masters to bring the women into their own workshops to labor "under their eyes," reminding them that their statutes explicitly prohibited homework. This prohibition apparently met with limited success. A number of masters after 1750 came forward to intervene in seizures performed on illegal workers, on the grounds that the women were their employees and that they owned the goods seized. In 1762, exasperated officials repeated the prohibition, with probably a similar lack of success. Female homeworkers were a well-established feature of the Aix tailors' trade in the first half of the eighteenth century, a labor force that appears to have persisted despite official condemnation.

Illegal Workers, or ouvrières sans qualité

Like tailors' guilds, the seamstresses' corporation struggled to eliminate or reduce illegal work practices. Given the low level of capital necessary to start in the trade and the fact that it was practiced within the home, it was relatively easy for a needleworker to set up shop without joining the guild.

In 1774, the seamstresses of Caen complained that their trade monopoly was "daily despoiled by more than two hundred illegal workers who go on day work to individuals who believe [they will] find a better deal by using these daily workers."[74] This was an enormous figure, considering that legitimate mistresses numbered only thirty-nine in 1769. The context of this complaint—a request for a reduction in their tax assessment—gave the seamstresses reasons to overestimate their rivals' numbers, but it was not unlikely that illegal workers equaled or outnumbered legal ones both in the provinces and in the capital.

As was the case for legitimate labor, different levels of illegal work existed. The lowliest women worked in their client's homes, mending and repairing garments or making simple items such as shirts and nightgowns. Anne Choimie, a thirty-two-year-old seamstress and wife of a journeymen plumber, testified that she had worked one day per week in the home of her clients, the Sieur and Dame Darsonville.[75] Marie Anne Boula, a twenty-one-year-old seamstress, accompanied her noble client to the island of Saint Dominique to act as her personal seamstress. The client promised to provide her with food, lodging, laundering, and any necessary medicine in addition to four hundred Saint-Dominique livres a year.[76] Employed to work in another person's home, women such as Choimie and Boula occupied a position closer to domestic servant than independent entrepreneur. They seem to have believed that simple mending and alterations for private clients did not infringe on the seamstresses' monopoly. One nonguild seamstress defended her nineteen years of illegal work by stating that she had only performed repair work, which she understood to be free to all women.[77]

More successful illegal seamstresses made garments in their own homes for their clients. A small number achieved success on a par with guild mistresses. They not only made new garments, they hired workers to aid them in their labors. In 1781, two officials of the seamstresses' guild organized a raid on the home of Dame Poiret. When they entered her apartment, they found her, along with two employees, working on articles of women's clothing. Poiret admitted that she had bought another seamstress's business for 350 livres, but insisted that she had been established in the trade for only nine or ten months and had every intention of joining the guild.[78] Illegal seamstresses who hired their own workers worsened their infraction in the eyes of the guild. With their bold defiance of corporate rules, they posed a greater threat to labor and product markets than solitary individuals. A sense of indignation at such affronts is palpable in guild reports.

In 1731, the female officials of the seamstress-tailors' guild in Caen found a woman named Barbot making a woman's dress. They noted that Barbot not only worked in her own home illegally "but furthermore [had] with her a girl unknown [to them] who aided the said Barbot in working at works of their profession, which does considerable wrong to the profession of seamstress."[79]

Despite guild rhetoric, illegal tailors and seamstresses were often not unknown or shadowy figures. Many held close personal and professional ties with established masters and mistresses, who were not only aware of and complicit in their illegal work, but willing to help them circumvent corporate sanctions. In 1747, Sieur Richard, a forty-five-year-old master tailor, heard that his guild was planning to receive fifteen master tailors *sans qualité;* that is, without the formal qualifications usually required of new members. He quickly informed a journeyman tailor of his acquaintance, so that "if he had the intention to be received as a master, he [could] profit from the circumstance." The journeyman responded that the opportunity "would please him, because he would no longer be exposed to seizures from the officers of the master tailors' guild, as they had done several days earlier." A few days later he and his wife approached Richard to ask him to mediate with the guild on their behalf.[80]

Ties between illegal workers and masters proved especially important in the late 1740s, when a crisis shook the tailors' guild. Alerted by numerous complaints, the Parisian police in 1749 undertook an investigation into the corporation's *bacheliers,* the sixteen officials elected to perform raids on illegal workers. Over a three- or four-year period, a group of these officials had established a system of extortion aimed against nonguild tailors. Instead of prosecuting illegal workers and turning seized goods over to the guild, they offered to return them to the offenders in exchange for an exorbitant payoff, often negotiated in a favorite tavern. Caught in their trap, a number of workers turned to master tailors for assistance. Gabriel Galloin, a fifty-one-year-old journeyman, was founded illicitly making a gray wool suit in his home on February 26, 1749. After seizing the garment, the officials arranged to meet Galloin in a cabaret near rue Saint-Honoré. They agreed to return his goods for a payment of eighty livres, a sum barely less than the value of the suit itself. In his own words: "Unable to resign himself to pay such a large sum for so few things, he went to the home of Sieur Lequay, master tailor, to beg him to intervene to arrange the matter, which was only finished by the means of eighteen livres which Sieur Lequay paid [for him]."[81]

Another witness, Armand Blot, a twenty-nine-year-old journeyman, declared that he had turned to illegal work to support his wife and children. Guild officials seized the pieces he had cut out of woolen cloth for a suit and breeches, as well as two old suits, five pairs of new breeches, and an old scarlet jacket. Determined to recover these effects, he met the officials in their cabaret, where they demanded a payment of three gold louis. Blot asked master Gardel to accompany him and his wife when they went to the cabaret to renegotiate the affair. "Out of consideration" for master Gardel, the *bacheliers* agreed to return the items for only thirty livres, still an enormous sum to a poor artisan like Blot.[82]

Nonguild workers were defined as illegals by corporate regulations. They were aware of their status and the dangers it entailed, and were eager to enter the corporate fold if possible. Master tailors knew them as outworkers, friends, and even as potential sons- or brothers-in-law. They saw no shame in hiring them or assisting them in confrontations with the guild. In a world of scarce resources, it came as no surprise that many could not become guild members and had to rely on illegal endeavors to survive. Masters and mistresses were conscious of occupying a privileged position in the world of work, which enabled them to offer precious information or influence. They drew on their corporate status to act as patrons to less fortunate workers, thereby accruing additional prestige and power within their communities.

Relations between Workers and Mistresses

Journeymen's associations, known as *compagnonnages,* are a legendary element of the eighteenth-century world of work. Nineteenth-century novelists, such as George Sand, wrote about them, as have guild historians from the late nineteenth century to the present.[83] Beyond their picturesque aspects of brawling and secret rituals, these organizations served highly practical purposes for itinerant workers on their travels around France. Journeymen arriving in a new town could find lodging and employment information at the inn patronized by members of their *compagnonnage* group. They could also hope for an advance loan on their wages and companionship with their fellow artisans.

Apart from formal organizations, extraordinary circumstances could provoke ephemeral associations among workers. Steven Kaplan has described the numerous *cabales* workers formed to protest masters' perceived treachery. Angry journeymen organized to blacklist masters' shops, to slow down the pace of production, or to demand higher wages.[84] In a 1726 guild assembly, the master tailors of Aix-en-Provence complained that the labor shortage in the city had emboldened the remaining workers. They were now demanding eighteen sous a day, the masters ruefully reported, whereas "they had been content with twelve sous" previously.[85]

In the seamstresses' case, there is no evidence of anything resembling the *compagnonnage* association, either in Paris or in the provinces. Nor are there traces of more informal, transitory organizations. If *compagnonnage* helped itinerant journeymen to find lodging and work in the cities they visited, the restricted mobility of female workers reduced the need for such associations. Once they arrived in Paris, young women workers stayed in the city or returned home; they did not embark on the *tour de France* that formed such an important part of young men's working experience. Expectations of female behavior also inhibited gatherings of young, single women in the public taverns where journeymen congregated to socialize and discuss grievances. Perhaps most importantly, the tremendous size of the labor force, and the constant fear of unemployment, must have hindered seamstresses from attempting action against their mistresses.[86]

If seamstresses did not form organized protest groups, police records offer numerous examples of individual grievances between mistresses and workers. Mistresses' complaints about their workers differed little from those of their male colleagues. Their employees did not labor as hard or as long as they should; those who lodged with their mistresses stayed out too late at night or did not return at all. In 1712, mistress Anne Labitte lodged a complaint with the local police *commissaire* about her former worker Fauchon, the sister of a tailor's wife. Labitte had been obliged to fire Fauchon, because "instead of working [she] ran from hither to fro and slept outside of her house." Following the girl's dismissal, Fauchon's sister came to Labitte's home to insult her, followed by Fauchon's brother-in-law, who physically assaulted her. This abuse led Labitte to lodge a formal complaint against the family.[87]

Workers also brought grievances to the police, most often because they did not receive their wages or personal possessions when they left their mistresses' homes. In 1723, Françoise Letourneur lodged a complaint against her former employer, mistress Nicolle de Burron. The king's procurator at the Châtelet, who heard the case, decided that de Burron could deduct fifty livres spent during Letourneur's illness, but he ordered her to pay forty-two livres in back wages and to return the woman's personal linen.[88] The conflict between the young Jeanne Berset and her mistress Bailly also involved the payment of back wages. Berset originally addressed herself to the consular jurisdiction, the tribunal that heard commercial disputes. For unknown reasons, this court sent the case back to the guild for judgment. The conflict was finally settled with an agreement drawn up by the guild's notary in the presence of both parties and the guild's officials. In general, law courts did not play a primary role in resolving conflicts between workers and mistresses. Mistresses and their workers took recourse to formal procedures only in extreme situations.[89]

Outside of work-related disputes, conflicts arose regarding frankly criminal behavior. Some workers stole from their mistresses, as those who lived in their employers' homes were well placed to do. For example, the charitable seamstress who hired a poor girl for six sous a day was paid back with the theft of her personal belongings. In bankruptcy cases, fashion merchants frequently credited portions of their loss to the thievery of their shopgirls. Such complaints were not particular to female trades but arose from all sectors of artisanal production. One major category of complaints, however, was gender specific. These consisted of conflicts revolving around the sexuality of young female workers. Some employees complained about being forced into prostitution by their mistresses. A month after her journeywoman's arrival in her home, mistress De Brossard presented the young woman with different men who "wanted to take liberties with her." When the worker resisted, De Brossard physically abused her and threatened to have her arrested if she left the workshop.[90] Like De Brossard, mistresses who lodged their employees wielded heavy economic and moral authority over them. Young women with families in Paris may have been able to resist such pressure, but recent immigrants were more vulnerable. Apart from outright coercion, mistresses could also tempt their workers with a share in earnings from prostitution, which could significantly outweigh the wages paid for sewing.

The female composition of the seamstresses' trade formed the worker's best guarantee against sexual abuse. In 1758, Agnes Romanet, a fifteen-year-old "worker in dresses" could find no work among mistress seamstresses. She was fortunate to be offered a place with a tapestrymaker, Sieur Maillard, where she could make good use of her sewing skills. The girl's parents permitted her to accept the job on the condition that Maillard's aunt be present in the workshop at all times. One day, however, the aunt did not come to work and Maillard took advantage of the situation to assault the girl.[91] The potential for sexual harassment of female workers by male employers or customers was a key to the guild's strong draw for women throughout the eighteenth century.

If some employers encouraged a worker's debauchery, a young woman's inclinations toward it usually shocked and outraged them. In 1766, sieur Jean Pierre Massol, a royally privileged surgeon, appeared before a police *commissaire* to file a complaint against his seamstress wife's apprentice Louise, aged sixteen. According to Massol, he and his wife had employed the girl out of pity. Her parents, a dishwasher and a coachman, could not pay for her subsistence, let alone any professional training. He was thus surprised when Louise began purchasing candy every day as well as numerous articles of clothing and gifts for a hired worker. Under interrogation, the girl admitted that she bought these items with money she received from men with whom she "amused herself" at night. Louise further declared that she left her mistress's home in the evenings under the pretext of personal affairs in order to perform paid sexual acts with men in alleys. Horrified by this behavior, Massol and his wife filed an official complaint with the police, probably to justify breaking the apprenticeship contract and expelling the girl.[92]

Immigration of Workers to Paris

Recent historical research has highlighted the geographical mobility of journeymen, including tailors, across the eighteenth century. For the city of Rouen, Michael Sonenscher has shown that only slightly over 5 percent of the journeymen tailors who registered with the guild's employment bureau between July 1778 and May 1780 were natives of the city.[93] He characterizes their employment patterns as involving very short periods of work and frequent itinerancy. This appears to have been true of southern France as well. A majority of newcomers to the Aix-en-Provence tailors' guild came from outside the city, most hailing from the region surrounding Aix, or other Provençal towns, although some had traveled from as far away as Italy, Flanders, and Germany.[94]

Although no statistical source exists for seamstresses, it is clear that a high proportion of nonmistresses working in Paris had immigrated to the capital. In a sample culled from police and notarial archives of some seventy garment-trade workers, only twenty-three were native Parisians. The rest were born outside the city, for the most part in areas that traditionally supplied immigrants to Paris. Several had come from the region around Paris, from towns such as Saint-Denis, Gonesse, and Bagneux. Others had arrived from the provinces of Picardy and Normandy to the north of Paris, or from Champagne, Franche Comté, and Lorraine to the southeast of the city. Only a handful of women had traveled farther. These included one from the town of Carpentras in the south of France, as well as a Flemish and a German worker. As this list reveals, women who worked in the Parisian garment trades came from small towns and cities, where they may have received rudimentary training. They did not come from rural agricultural villages as many domestic servants did. These women's geographic origins also stand in sharp contrast to those of mistresses and apprentices, who were almost all native Parisians.[95]

Between 1757 and 1777, police inspector Marais was responsible for overseeing the world of Parisian prostitution. His reports and those of his fellow inspectors furnish life stories of hundreds of prostitutes, providing insight into patterns of female migration and career possibilities for young migrant women. Although these cases represent girls who strayed from acceptable behavior, they help to indicate the array of strategies open to young women from the provinces and illuminate their lives before prostitution. Suzanne de Lille, a native of Metz, came to Paris at age eighteen, "with the intention of putting herself [into service] as a chamber-maid or rather in apprenticeship with some fashion merchant." Jeanne Beroud came to Paris at age twelve from a town near Metz. Having little money but "the intention to put herself to work there, she entered first into a linen seamstress's place and then a fashion merchant's."[96]

As these reports demonstrate, young women habitually migrated to Paris in their early to late teens. They left home for various reasons: lack of employment, the desire to seek specific types of vocational training, or an ambition to take advantage of the opportunities for economic or social success in the capital. The glamorous aura of the Parisian luxury trades exercised a particularly strong fascination over provincial girls. Economic crises in provincial towns could also push greater numbers of young women to seek work in the capital, as such a crisis did in the 1770s when a disruption of the textile industries of northern France resulted in increased migration to Paris. Because of this migration, the labor market in Paris became oversaturated, creating high unemployment and causing a rise in arrests for prostitution.[97]

In other cases, family crisis played a central role in the decision to leave home. The death of one or more parents, compounded by conflict with a new stepmother or stepfather, could prompt a flight to Paris. In inspector

Marais's reports, seduction also figures prominently as a motive for departure. Christine Defoix's widowed father sent her from their home in Sedan to live with an aunt in Reims. At the age of seventeen or eighteen, Defoix recounted, she was seduced by the comte de Ferary in Reims. Believing herself to be pregnant, she fled for the anonymity of the capital. Sexual abuse by family members, an affair that resulted in pregnancy, the pull of a lover's departure, all could lead a girl to leave home for the excitement and uncertainty of the capital.[98]

Many immigrants counted on assistance from hometown contacts, either from relatives who had moved to Paris or from compatriots who had established themselves in business there. When the adolescent Suzanne de Lille arrived in Paris, she sought out the "home of some people who had been indicated to her in her country [*pays*] as appropriate to help her."[99] On her arrival, Claudine Françoise Janeret met two girls from her native region who introduced her to a third compatriot, a journeyman wigmaker. Eight days later he procured her a job as a cook with a tax-office clerk (*commis aux fermes*) living on the same street as his own employer.[100] Despite such connections, the immigrant's situation in Paris was fragile. Hometown contacts could prove unwilling or unable to provide ongoing assistance. Lacking strong family ties in the city, these women more easily fell into unemployment and the perils it presented. Seamstresses' reputation for poverty and prostitution thus drew on the legions of provincial women who failed to build a stable career in the capital.

Unemployment and the Sex Trade: The Seamstress as Prostitute

Faced with a shortage of employment in her own trade, a seamstress's best alternative was to seek employment in a related needle trade, where she could make use of her specialized skills. It could be with a linen-draper, a fashion merchant, a tailor, or even a tapestrymaker, such as the abusive Sieur Maillard. If she could not find any skilled sewing work, a needleworker might turn to odd jobs while waiting for better employment. Isabelle Dubois, a twenty-three-year-old "girl seamstress" lived in a boardinghouse on the rue de la Tannerie, where she made beds every day in return for a small monthly wage.[101] Failure to find work could quickly result in homelessness, hunger, and a resort to begging or stealing one's bread. Declarations made by women arrested for mendicancy reveal the harsh consequences of even short periods of unemployment. In November 1778, police arrested Elisabeth Julie Lacroix, a forty-nine-year-old seamstress from Pontoise, who claimed that her husband had abandoned her some ten years earlier. She declared that she had been without work for four to five days and had not eaten since the previous day. In December, police arrested Marie Elizabeth Lambin, a twenty-seven-year-old Parisian seamstress who had been unemployed for three months. A number of women in related trades were arrested along with her, including a twenty-two-year-old laceworker from Gonesse, a forty-one-year-old Parisian used-clothes dealer, and a twenty-nine-year-old Parisian linenworker.[102]

Desperate women might enter the ranks of prostitution as a successor to begging or an alternative to it. The lowest-level prostitutes sought their clients in the streets, performing sexual acts in alleys, public parks, or in cheap rented rooms. Their activities were accompanied by the potential for arrest and imprisonment, as well as the dangers of venereal disease, pregnancy, and violence. These women sprang from—and continued to maintain contacts with—the Parisian working classes. Their clients also belonged to that world, including journeymen, laborers, and domestic servants.[103] A step above streetwalkers came women lodged in brothels, usually operated by an older woman. The privacy of the brothel offered some security from arrest and a guaranteed preselection of clients, thus shielding women from the worst problems of violence or abuse. Marais's reports reveal that the police often protected brothel keepers in return for information on noble and clerical customers. Many other prostitutes obtained clients from male or female pimps without living in a brothel.

The socioeconomic profiles of women taken into custody for prostitution closely resembled those of suspects arrested for begging, with a large proportion of garment and textile workers. Over seven weeks between December 17, 1771 and February 1, 1772, Parisian police *commissaires* sent at least eighty women to the prison of Saint-Martin on charges of prostitution and debauchery. The women ranged in age from sixteen years old to fifty-seven years old (mean = 27 years). The largest trade group among them was the linenworkers, who accounted for almost one-third of the women arrested. Seamstresses came second, with eleven individuals or almost 14 percent of the total. The next largest groups were the laundresses, domestic servants, and tailors' workers, with seven, six, and five women, respectively. The remaining inmates claimed a variety of occupations, including food vendors, physical laborers, workers for tapestry-makers, nurses, and one gold polisher.[104] Arrested prostitutes also declared a range of ages and geographic origins. In 1784, the police raided an apartment building on the rue des Paulies, where they detained a number of women on charges of prostitution: on the first floor, an eighteen-year-old dress worker from Dijon; on the second, a twenty-three-year-old Parisian dress seamstress and a thirty-year-old servant from Anger; on the third, a seamstress from Meaux and a thirty-five-year-old servant from Picardy; and on the fourth, a twenty-five-year-old Parisian who worked in the hatting trade and a twenty-year-old worker in decorations and trimming.[105]

Despite the desperate context of their declarations, these women's occupational claims merit credibility. As historian Erica-Marie Benabou points out, most parents needed to put their teenage daughters to work to help support the family, and very few would have deliberately assigned them to a career of prostitution. Most of these women would have therefore performed several years of legitimate work prior to their arrest. Their professional affiliation was a central element of their self-identity, which they clung to even as they engaged in prostitution. Paid sex was not a final career choice but a temporary response to unemployment. When work became available in their own trades, many prostitutes returned to legitimate labor.[106]

Women arrested for soliciting on the street or in cheap rented rooms represented the low end of the scale. At the other extreme of the spectrum, the reports of Marais and his successors documented an elite form of prostitution involving young women who entered paid affairs with socially superior men. In exchange for their sexual services, they were usually lodged in a furnished apartment and received monthly allowances and gifts of clothing and jewelry. Their clients included noblemen, professional men, merchants, clerics, and even successful servants and guild masters. A high proportion of these kept women had belonged to the garment trades, where their lovers "discovered" them working in a mistress's or master's boutique. Given their involvement in luxury trades, seamstresses, tailors, and fashion merchants became natural intermediaries between their employees and their clients.

To judge from police reports, fashion merchants and their employees greatly outnumbered seamstresses among kept women. The fashion-merchant's boutique certainly provided far greater opportunities for contact with rich men. They sold expensive wares to both male and female clients, and the large windows of their shops allowed shopgirls to see and be seen by people walking past. Seamstresses offered fewer chances for meetings, because they worked out of their own homes for an overwhelmingly female clientele. Young working women must have been sorely tempted to accept paid sex with rich men. Becoming a kept woman offered the possibility of escaping arduous labor in their mistresses' or masters' workshops. As Marais described one young woman's working conditions in a merchant mercer's shop, she was "malnourished, badly lodged and subject to a great deal of work."[107] Henriette Dubois L'Ecuyer, a seventeen-year-old Parisian, entered paid relations with a tobacco merchant. "Naturally lazy," according to Marais, she stopped going to her daily work as a seamstress. Instead, she supplemented the tobacco merchant's measly allowance by accepting clients from the tailor-pimp Brissault.[108]

Kept women also stood to earn substantial amounts of money. Instead of the paltry one or two hundred livres a year they might earn through long hours of tedious needlework, they could obtain more than one thousand livres a year as a rich man's mistress. One fashion merchant's shopgirl received ten louis a month from her lover, "which she used to dress herself and to regal her mistress."[109] Others are reported to have earned fantastic sums of up to two, three, or even four hundred livres a month.[110] Sexual patronage took young women out of their mistresses' homes, or their own cheap lodgings, into independent, furnished apartments with servants and fine clothing.

Most employers were appalled by their workers' ventures into prostitution. Other members of the garment trades were known to the police as active pimps. An actress named Demoiselle Dubois met her first sexual patron, an Italian count, through a master tailor. When she became dissatisfied with the count's allowance, Dubois took a new lover whom she obtained from another tailor, Brissault. Brissault, described in Marais's reports as a tailor to the "girls of the theater," was apparently a well-known pimp.[111] He also referred to a woman named Lacontat as a "seamstress and pimp [*maquerelle*]."[112] Like employers, parents' attitudes toward their daughters' involvement in prostitution varied. Most families opposed paid affairs with socially superior men, which almost never resulted in marriage. Some, however, were overcome by the financial benefits involved. As Marais reported of one young woman: "She has her mother with her who worked in sewing and who until this day passed for an honest woman, but misery and the Englishman's guineas seduced her, she delivered her daughter, who is not yet fifteen years old, to him for 400 livres a month."[113]

Despite the changes introduced in these women's lives, they did not leave the world of the trades entirely. In a number of cases, education and professional training were included in the benefits they received from their lovers. After Julie Brabant caught the eye of the Maréchal de Duras, he placed her in a convent to be educated for two years. Subsequently, he arranged her apprenticeship with a fashion merchant on rue Saint-Honoré.[114] A police inspector put another girl into training with a fashion merchant during the course of their affair.[115] Vocational instruction provided a respectable cover for the women's illicit activities; it also promised a means to retire respectably from *le grand monde,* as Marais called it. Once the first flush of youth and beauty had passed, new patrons would become increasingly difficult to procure. Faced with a descent through the lower ranks of prostitution, farsighted women planned a return to legitimate work.

Madelaine Queru thus requested that her noble lover finance her apprenticeship with a fashion merchant. Although she abandoned this position to engage in casual prostitution, she subsequently obtained a new patron who, according to Marais, agreed to rent a fashion merchant's privilege for her and to supply two thousand livres worth of merchandise. Another former lover promised to "do her a last favor to help her in this establishment." With this assistance, Queru was able to open a boutique on the rue Royale.[116] On another occasion, Marais announced that the Demoiselle Ménage, previously kept by a counselor of the Parisian Parlement, "is leaving the great world and is supposed to enter tomorrow, Monday, a fashion merchant's shop in the rue Montmartre in the quality of a shop girl." When her lover attempted to change her mind Ménage refused, "telling him that all of her views turned toward a more solid Establishment."[117] Despite the uncertainties and hard work of shopkeeping, it offered these women a more hopeful future than prostitution.

Conclusion

The most impressive element of the seamstresses' trade across the eighteenth century was its tremendous size. By the end of the century, over ten thousand women participated as apprentices, workers, or mistresses. Together, they composed one of the largest trade groups in the city. The size of the workforce contributed to its second outstanding characteristic, diversity, in forms of specialization, vertical hierarchies, labor contracts, and wages. At least four different specialities existed, dedicated to making different sorts of female outer- and underwear. Mistresses may be divided into four categories of success, ranging from celebrated prosperity to modest financial stability to bare survival to desperate poverty. Workers in the trade labored on annual or daily contracts. They might work for their mistresses for one or two days, several months, or decades. Both annual and daily laborers received highly variable salaries, supplemented by nonmonetary rewards. Wages alone did not keep up with the rising cost of living over the eighteenth century. Unemployment and underemployment were constant features of this trade, exacerbated by the immigration of workers to Paris. Arrests of seamstresses for begging and prostitution reveal the extent of these problems and the grave consequences they could entail.

Given its vast size and its dispersion across Paris, a third characteristic of the seamstresses' trade was its decentralized and informal labor market. Hiring took place through personal contacts between workers and mistresses and through networks of information exchange. It was impossible strictly to control, organize, or regulate work practices, and the seamstresses' guild seems to have wasted little effort in trying. Unlike most male guilds, the seamstresses' statutes provided few rules for employment, and guild leaders did not intervene frequently in hiring practices or disputes. Instead, they focused their efforts on limiting and supervising apprenticeship, thereby restricting the size of the skilled workforce. This relative laissez-faire freed mistresses to impose their own conditions on workers, who did not form labor associations to defend their interests. The highly dispersed and uneven nature of the labor market was not, however, a reflection of strength among mistresses. Instead, it accorded with the precariousness of employers' economic situations. As I will demonstrate in the next chapter, mistresses were subject to harsh cyclical patterns of demand and an inability to raise their prices with inflation. While some fared extremely well, the majority of mistresses lived in humble conditions.

Journeymen tailors and worker seamstresses shared technical skills and worked for a broad-based clientele in enormous trades with large guilds. They also suffered similar problems of under- and unemployment. In terms of mobility, sociability, and trade-based association, however, their experiences sharply diverged. Journeymen tailors were highly itinerant, traveling around the country in the traditional *tour de France*. They formed labor associations and put pressure on masters. By contrast, seamstresses were either Parisian or came to Paris from the surrounding region. In both cases, they remained within the capital, turning to alternate trades when jobs ran short rather than leaving the city in quest of work. Seamstresses also encountered different risks in the workshop; sexual harassment must have formed a much less common threat for journeymen, and prostitution did not function in the same way as an alternative source of employment.

Although it emphasizes forms of difference, this chapter has also revealed that elements of the garment trades ostensibly marked by formal and legal distinctions were in fact not that separate after all. Illegal workers were not necessarily pariahs, abhorrent on principle to guild members. Some guild masters took their side, interceding on their behalf with the corporation and testifying for them in police inquiries. The bullying and extortionate tactics of tailors' officials in the 1740s must have increased masters' sympathies for the outsiders. Among seamstresses, relations between mistresses and nonmistresses were undoubtedly ambiguous as well. In such large guild populations, individual master tailors or mistress seamstresses may well have felt a sense of detachment toward corporate leaders, allowing them to develop more sympathetic relations with legal and illegal workers.

Gender distinctions in the garment trades were also more complicated than legal documents suggest. The tailors' guild explicitly prohibited masters from hiring female employees, yet in Paris and the provinces they did so constantly. Female tailors' workers constituted a regular element of the trade, discernible in notarial and police archives and sometimes accepted by the corporation itself, as was the case in Aix-en-Provence until 1750. In their periodic raids, guild officials found illegal male and female needleworkers in the same ateliers, hard at work on both women's and men's garments. Clearly, the day-to-day exigencies of survival obliterated the segregation that guild statutes established between male and female workers, women's and men's clothing. Gender surely inflected these needleworkers' strategies and experiences of shared work, but in ways that fell beyond the binary divisions imposed by law. The next chapter takes this discussion one step further by showing how seamstresses and tailors wielded their needles to make and mend garments, the range of tools and techniques they used in their chosen trades, and the way they divided tasks in the workshop.

THREE

Tools, Techniques, and Commercial Practices

From the eighteenth century to the present, the seamstress has been a highly symbolic figure in France, frequently associated with sexual promiscuity and prostitution. In the 1780s, Restif de la Bretonne depicted the "Pretty Seamstress" and other working women as suspended between legitimate needlework and illicit sexual activity. The pretty seamstress was a plucky, hard-working girl, but terribly vulnerable to the forces conniving to corrupt her. The nineteenth century produced an increased social and cultural fascination with the seamstress, who became an archetype of the woman worker. In literature, Henri Murger's *Scènes de la vie de Bohème* (1851) recounted the affairs of Parisian "bohemian" artists and writers with sexually promiscuous working women. Murger depicted sewing, self-adornment, and seduction as related and quintessentially feminine skills, which women acquired through birth rather than formal training or experience. Nineteenth-century labor activists, politicians, and moralists used the figure of the needleworker to question the disarray to families and the body politic caused by the reorganization of French industry.

In recent years, historians of women and gender have paid close attention to these debates, highlighting the centrality of the needleworker in discussions of the social consequences of economic transformation. They have also examined the ways in which gender ideologies were both reinforced and significantly altered through debates about women's work and its place in French economic and social life. This literature has underlined the important place accorded to female garment workers in perceptions of the industrializing economy, a phenomenon obscured by modern assumptions about women's exclusion from the workplace in past generations. It has also revealed the extent to which ideas about women and their work helped shape political, intellectual, and economic debates, where women themselves had little voice.[1]

For all its merits, this historiography has paid little attention to the manner in which needleworkers actually performed their work and earned their meager salaries. It has examined discourses about women's work with fascinating results, but has not accompanied this analysis with an equivalent scrutiny of practices of female labor. We know very little, as a result, about how eighteenth- or nineteenth-century seamstresses made garments, the organization of production in their workshops, the range of techniques they employed, or their relations with clients and suppliers of raw materials and tools. By exploring these issues for the eighteenth century, in this chapter I seek to restore the seamstress to her craft.[2]

Technical Literature

The first known technical work in the sewing trades was a 1589 pattern book written by Juan de Alceya in Madrid, which demonstrated the most efficient way to cut the pieces for a garment from a piece of cloth.[3] Judged to be the most difficult element of the tailoring trade, cutting cloth occupied a central position in all subsequent technical works. Variations in the width of cloth produced in France and elsewhere, as well as the lack of uniform measurement standards, further complicated the issue. In 1671, Benoît Boullay, a tailor of the faubourg Saint-Germain in Paris, published the first French book on tailoring, *Le Parfait tailleur,* which offered guidelines for calculating the length of cloth needed for garments using fabric manufactured in different widths. Roslin's 1734 *Le Tarif des marchands fripiers, tailleurs, tapissiers, couturiers* [sic] *et autres personnes que veulent se faire des habits ou meubles* (The rate for merchants fripiers, tailors, upholsterers, seamstresses and other people who want to have clothes or furniture made) addressed a variation of the same theme. The work consisted of a series of mathematical tables indicating the length of cloth necessary to provide a given area of material for cloths of different widths. He intended this information to assist tailors and seamstresses who needed to calculate the length of cloth necessary to line a garment when the garment and lining used different sizes of cloth. Roslin also wished to help upholsterers estimate how much fabric they needed to cover pieces of furniture.[4]

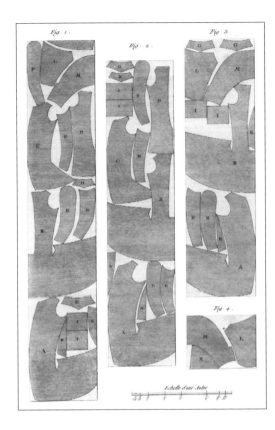

FIGURE 3.1 Pattern for a man's suit. From the *Encyclopédie,* courtesy of the Rare Books and Special Collections Library, University of Illinois at Urbana-Champaign.

Artisanal techniques of production attracted increased interest in the second half of the eighteenth century, as part of the larger Enlightenment project to celebrate craftsmanship and impose more rational and efficient methods on it.[5] The *Encyclopédie* volume containing an article on tailoring appeared in 1765. Although the text of the article was brief, it was accompanied by numerous illustrations. These illustrations depicted a tailor's workshop, a wide variety of tools and equipment, and several reduced-size patterns for garments, showing the manner in which the pieces could be cut with the least possible waste (see figure 3.1). In 1769, the Royal Academy of Science commissioned the most exhaustive Old Regime study of the garment trades, as part of its series of "Descriptions of Arts and Crafts." The book was titled *L'Art du tailleur, contenant le tailleur d'habits d'hommes, les culottes de peau; le tailleur de corps de femmes et enfants; la conturière; el la marchande de modes* (The art of the tailor, containing the tailor of men's suits; leather culottes; the tailors of women's and children's stays; the seamstress;

and the fashion merchant (hereafter *L'Art du tailleur*).[6] Its author, François-Antoine de Garsault, had written *L'Art du perruduier* (The art of the wig-maker) in 1767, and would publish *L'Art de la lingerie* (The art of linen-making) in 1771.

In *L'Art du tailleur*, Garsault recounted the history of apparel in France from the Middle Ages to the eighteenth century, and explained the different articles of clothing produced by tailors, seamstresses, and fashion merchants. He also included step-by-step instructions for making the most common articles of men's and women's clothing of the day. Garsault accorded particular attention to the stays and corset tailors, whom he considered the most technically skilled practitioners of the garment trades. A series of engravings accompanied the text, illustrating historical and contemporary garments, showing tools, and giving patterns for many of the articles of clothing he described. Garsault's work was recognized in his time as the authoritative account of the garment trades. The supplement of the *Encyclopédie* published in 1777 contained an expanded article on tailors and staymakers that followed Garsault very closely; the engravings as well as the text virtually replicated those in *L'Art du tailleur*.[7]

These technical studies devoted more attention to tailors than to seamstresses. The female trade occupied a small portion of Garsault's book and received only two pages of engravings, as compared to the many pages of text and illustration dedicated to tailors. This discrepancy may be explained in part by the technical realities of making men's and women's clothing. Both Garsault and the *Encyclopédie* emphasized the lack of special tools required to practice the seamstresses' trade. As the former stated: "The Seamstress has no particular instrument. A thimble, thread, silk, scissors and an iron, are sufficient for operating."[8] Seamstresses needed fewer tools because a woman's dress fit much less closely than a man's suit and thus used fewer pieces and called for less precision in cut and stitching (compare figures 3.1 and 3.2 for the man's suit with figure 3.2 for the woman's dress). Apart from strictly technical considerations, both women's dresses and women's work seem to have been intrinsically less interesting and important to the male authors who produced these technical works, and to the enlightened, male readership for whom they were intended. A close look at the dresses that survive in museum collections reveals that they required more skill than either Garsault or the *Encyclopédie* acknowledged. These texts therefore underline the low-prestige, low-skill image of the female trade as much as its inherent technical limitations.

The Workshop

The engravings included in technical literature offer a glimpse of the spatial organization of seamstresses' and tailors' workshops as well as the gestures and postures adopted by men and women at work. Of course, these studies presented a normative vision, which drew on moral judgments of labor and an idealized view of social relations and gender roles. The scarcity of information regarding the eighteenth-century workshop renders these images nonetheless precious to the historian. Where possible, I have supplemented published images with information drawn from archival sources such as probate inventories and police records.[9]

The *Encyclopédie* engraving depicts a tailor's shop occupied by an apprentice, several journeymen, and their master, all hard at work (figure 3.3). This image displays a clear hierarchical division of labor within the workshop. The apprentice does not cut or sew, but performs the menial task of heating an iron in the fire. The chief journeyman is shown cutting cloth at a separate table, while his colleagues sit on tabletops sewing in the cross-legged position still known in French as *à tailleur,* or tailor style. The master himself, distinguished by his fine dress, measures his client. He appears to be a successful artisan, employing a total of five journeymen and an ap-

FIGURE 3.3 Tailor's workshop. From the *Encyclopédie,* courtesy of the Rare Books and Special Collections Library, University of Illinois at Urbana-Champaign.

prentice. He has established no separation, however, between production and sales. Instead, he welcomes his client into the single room that serves as both workshop and boutique. To judge by the view outside the window, this room stood on the second or third floor, probably inside the master's own apartment. A second contemporary engraving focuses more closely on the encounter between master and client. This picture emphasizes the similarity between the tailor and his customer, showing both dressed in elegant suits and wigs. The journeyman in the background wears a simple cap and jacket, signaling his membership in a lower socioeconomic category (figure 3.4).

Given its apparent disinterest in the trade, the *Encyclopédie* did not provide an engraving of the seamstresses' workshop. For a contemporary equivalent, we must turn to the *Encyclopédie méthodique,* which depicted a seamstress's workshop composed of only two women, the mistress and her worker (figure 3.5). Seamstresses and tailors thus appear to differ, at least in the mind of outside observers, in the scale of their business operations. Despite its smaller size, the female workshop contains a similar division of tasks. Dressed in a fashionable *polonaise* gown, the mistress measures a client while her worker unfolds a piece of cloth at a workbench prior to cutting it. Again, no separation exists between the workshop and the commercial space. Dresses in progress hang from hooks on the walls and the table stands beside a window for natural light.

Other eighteenth-century engravings depict more populous seamstress workplaces. An almanac for the year 1765, published by the seamstresses' guild, shows an atelier containing six workers, the mistress, her female client, and a male onlooker, perhaps the client's husband (figure 3.6). In contrast to the sparse workshop of the *Encyclopédie méthodique,* the female guild emphasized in this image the vitality of the trade and the large number of workers it employed. A painting of a seamstress's workshop in southern France showed a similarly large workforce, depicting five employees sitting around a table listening attentively to their mistress's orders (figure 3.7).

Together these images suggest a common idea of the hierarchy of tasks in the garment trades, from the menial chores undertaken by apprentices to the stitching work of hired hands to the cutting of cloth performed by senior workers. These images also portray a difference in the posture of work between seamstresses and tailors. Tailors sat cross-legged on top of worktables; seamstresses performed sewing while seated on chairs, supporting their work on a table or in their laps. This distinction probably derived from considerations of female decorum and modesty rather than any difference in sewing technique. Resting the fabric on their laps, they sewed in the same basic fashion as did the tailors.

Evidence from probate inventories confirms this overall impression of the seamstresses' work spaces. These documents reveal, for example, that seamstresses rarely opened public boutiques. One rare exception was Marie Madeleine Bricon, a widow who died in 1770. Bricon kept a small, modestly furnished shop on the rue des Gravilliers to the north of the Halles district. It contained two counters, a stepladder, and several old planks that served as shelves, an old chest, two chairs, a display case, and a bench. Bricon had erected a partition against one wall of the boutique, presumably to provide privacy for customer's fittings. The value of these furnishings was estimated at only twenty livres. Bricon lived in the back room of the shop and the hallway that led to it. She had no recorded workers, but did employ a domestic servant who may have assisted in work-related tasks. This boutique was not a sign of prosperity, because Bricon's total assets amounted to a mere 388 livres.[10]

Unlike Bricon, the vast majority of seamstresses worked out of their own homes. Marie Josephe Denizon shared two rooms and a kitchen with her husband. The man was described as a a *bourgeois de Paris,* indicating

Le Maistre Tailleur

Ce Tailleur honneste homme en toute sa maniere
Excelle sur tous ceux de sa profession
Quand on le voit aller a la Procession
Il suit plutost la Croix quil ne fait la Banniere.

A Paris chez la veuve le Camu rue S.t Jacques a la teste d'Or

Avec privil. du Roy.

FIGURE 3.4 *Le Maistre tailleur* (The Master Tailor). Courtesy of the Cabinet des estampes, Bibliothèque nationale.

FIGURE 3.5 Seamstress's workshop 1. From the *Encyclopédie méthodique,* courtesy of the University of Illinois at Urbana-Champaign.

that he lived from investments rather than manual labor. The couple apparently had neither children nor live-in employees. The first of their two rooms was their bedroom, while the second served as Denizon's workshop. She had furnished it with a workbench, seven chairs, six armchairs, an ottoman, and two marble-topped chests of drawers. A fireplace provided warmth during cold months, supplementing the natural light from three windows overlooking the street. For additional illumination, Denizon had two torches and a pair of candleholders attached to the wall on either side of a large mirror. This mirror, along with a second one hung between two windows, would have increased the room's luminosity. Denizon had decorated her work space with plaster images of flowers and of Henry IV with his minister Sully. A green parrot with a white head, as well as a canary provided entertainment during long hours of work. This workroom contained enough space and seating for several workers, although Denizon's inventory recorded only one daily employee.[11]

Mistress Marie Germaine Pelée's large apartment included a kitchen, her bedroom, a second room, a small room (*cabinet*) on the floor above, and two small attic rooms. One live-in worker slept in the kitchen, while a second slept in Pelée's bedroom. To judge by its furnishings, the *cabinet*

FIGURE 3.6 Seamstress's workshop 2. The figure at the top of the page is Saint-Louis, the patron saint of the guild's confraternity. From *Almanach des Maî-tresses Couturières* (1765), courtesy of the Cabinet des estampes, Bibliothèque nationale.

FIGURE 3.7 *L'Atelier de couture à Arles* (Sewing Workshop in Arles), by Antoine Raspal, circa 1760, oil on canvas. Courtesy of the Musée Reattu, Arles.

on the upper floor was used as a workroom. It contained a small chest, five pairs of scissors for cutting cloth, some thread, a mirror, and a folding screen. The second room downstairs probably served professional purposes as well. Here we find three tables, a workbench, seven chairs, an armchair, and a casket, along with three clothes irons and two mirrors.[12]

Unlike Pelée and Denizon, many mistresses did not have enough space to separate work and daily life. In one- or two-room apartments, each room had to serve multiple functions for sleeping, living, eating, and working. Mistress Anne Malard lived in a one-room apartment furnished with six planks used as tabletops, a writing table, twelve chairs, an armchair, a commode, a large wardrobe, and a bed. She had decorated the room with three mirrors, over twenty religious pictures and portraits, and forty books. Bolts of fabric, dresses in progress, and supplies of needles and thread must have vied for space with Malard's own clothing, her furniture, food, and cooking utensils.[13]

The Division of Labor in the Workshop

As the *Encyclopédie* engraving suggests, apprentices occupied the bottom of the labor hierarchy. During their first year of training, apprentice seamstresses might not learn a great deal about the technical aspects of the trade. Instead, they performed mundane chores such as heating irons, sweeping up bits of thread and cloth from the floor, and handing cloth, thread, and needles to workers. Because production took place within the mistresses' home, apprentices also performed household chores. They prepared coffee and meals to sustain workers during long hours of sewing, or trudged across the city to make small purchases and deliver finished dresses. In the fictional workshop described by Nicolas-Edmé Restif de la Bretonne, apprentices "paid a small sum and they were of great use, rather for the time they saved the Workers, by running small errands, than by their work."[14]

After several months of menial chores and errands, apprentices could hope to begin training as professional seamstresses. Improving their sewing skills was a major aspect of this training. In most cases, they were not starting from scratch. Among popular classes that did not employ servants, mothers taught their daughters to help mend and darn the family's clothing. Preliminary instruction in needlework also took place outside the home. Historian Martine Sonnet has found that between 1760 and 1789 a place in school existed for one out of every three or four Parisian girls between the ages of seven and fourteen. Needlework was a fundamental element of the curriculum in all girls' schools.[15] Under the supervision of the mistress or a hired worker, the apprentice worked to expand her repertory of stitches and to sew more quickly and evenly (see figure 3.8 for the range of stitches used by eighteenth-century seamstresses and tailors). The relatively low cost of apprenticeship in the trade suggests that most girls acquired sufficient proficiency to be profitable members of the workshop before the end of their three-year training. Making dresses required many hours of relatively simple stitching that could be relegated to a capable apprentice.[16]

If the mistress fulfilled her half of the training contract, she would also teach her apprentice to take measurements, estimate the amount of cloth required for a client's order, cut pieces for a garment and, eventually, how to create a pattern on a live model. The long off-seasons of mid-summer and winter provided an opportunity for training, which was impossible during busy periods. Aside from these concrete skills, apprentices also acquired a general acculturation to the trade. A bright girl developed a sense

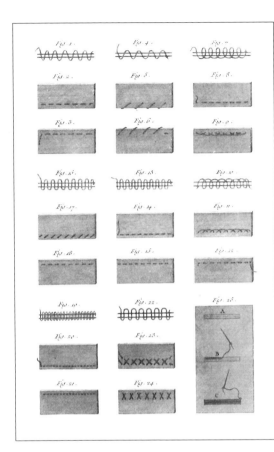

FIGURE 3.8 Stitches used by seamstresses and tailors. From the *Encyclopédie,* courtesy of the Rare Books and Special Collections Library, University of Illinois at Urbana-Champaign.

of the appropriate garments for different social events and categories, and acquainted herself with changing fashions. She learned how to choose suitable colors or patterns for different women and interact with socially superior clients. The apprentice's ability to acquire taste and a polished comportment would influence her prospects on the job market.

Once she finished apprenticeship, a young woman entered the paid labor force, where she spent most of her time stitching seams, ironing garments under construction, and doing finishing work such as hems and borders. The most-trusted workers cut cloth for their mistress, measured clients, and performed fittings. After two years of further work experience, a finished apprentice was eligible to perform her masterpiece and become a guild mistress. In the eyes of the guild, a total of five years of experience was therefore sufficient to qualify a woman as an independent seamstress. Unfortunately, no information has survived regarding the tests of skill imposed on prospective mistresses. In all likelihood, they required candidates to create patterns from a living model, to mark out the sections for several different garments on pieces of cloth, and to cut and sew them properly.

In August 1742, Honoré Martel undertook a test of competency that the tailors' guild of Aix-en-Provence imposed on journeymen working for masters' widows. Before a panel of twenty acting and former officers, master Montauban instructed Martel to make "a hood to cover a hat." Montauban asked the journeyman to specify how much cloth would be required for the hood and then allowed him to work on it. After an hour, the record reports, Martel abandoned the hood, "seeing that he would not be able to complete it." Montauban then told him to make a suit, consisting of a jacket, waistcoat, and breeches, to the measure of a master tailor present at the examination. After measuring his subject and estimating the amount of cloth required, Martel marked the pieces of the suit on a length of woolen cloth. On examining the work, Montauban declared the suit jacket to be extremely defective. He claimed that the back of the jacket was too short and tight because the side pleats were too narrow. When Martel requested permission to correct his errors, he was told that "once the work was cut one could no longer adjust it." The word "cut" was used here in a metaphorical sense, for Martel had only traced the pieces on the cloth with chalk. The journeyman failed this test, but succeeded in winning the guild's approval on his second try.[17]

Once they had attained guild membership, seamstresses and tailors were authorized to establish independent businesses. In a modest enterprise, with only one or two helpers, mistresses would spend most of their time performing sewing and cutting work for alterations or new garments. More prosperous mistresses employed workers to sew for them, devoting their time to client relations, selecting supplies, and keeping accounts. They received or visited first-time clients and measured them for their dresses. Accompanied by an apprentice, they took garments to their clients' homes for fittings and visited merchants' shops to purchase raw materials and discuss credit arrangements. They also maintained business records, keeping track of orders received, goods delivered, and payments pending. Because almost every client paid in installments, mistresses spent a good deal of time writing letters and making personal visits to collect their bills.

Cycles of Production

The garment trades lived by cyclical rhythms of production. Intensely active periods in the spring and fall were interrupted by long dry spells during the summer and winter months. These cycles were due in part to seasonal weather conditions, as women acquired lighter clothes in the springtime and switched to heavier and darker fabrics in the fall. The English novelist Tobias Smollet noted that a fashionable Parisian woman "must have her taffeties [*sic*] for the summer, her flowered silks for the spring and autumn, her sattins [*sic*] and damasks for winter." [18] Seasonal activity was also influenced by the social and religious calendars. The two principal celebrations of the year were Easter and Christmas. Even women who could not afford new garments would have their best clothes mended or redecorated for these occasions. Court aristocrats required new, formal dresses for a series of additional holidays, the most important being New Year's Day and Pentecost. Each major holiday called for a new dress with elaborate decorations, matching shoes, and accessories. [19] Seasonal and religious cycles overlapped at two crucial points: Christmas, heralding the arrival of the coldest weather; and Easter, marking the onset of spring. During the summer months, wealthy Parisians left the city for the country, creating a virtual halt in orders until the revival of social life in the fall.

A seamstress's journal from the early 1770s demonstrates these seasonal fluctuations. Across three years, seamstress Clément's monthly orders varied widely from month to month and for the same month in different years. In general, her busiest periods were the spring months from March to May and the months of October and December. The interim months of February and August were the lowest points (see figure 3.9). A second seamstress's journal echoes this pattern. From October 1768 to July 1770, Bridet-Clément recorded daily expenditures on thread, pins, and other supplies. Over this period her busiest months were November, December, and January, as well as March and April. The summer months of July, August, and September, and the month of February were periods of almost complete inactivity (see figure 3.10). [20]

Life cycles imposed another set of rhythms on production. A death within royal or princely families resulted in prolonged periods of mourning at court and among elite city dwellers. Less-exalted Parisians adopted mourning dress for their own family members: a widow mourned for eighteen months, a widower for only six. Mourning for a mother or father lasted six months, four and a half months for a grandfather, three weeks

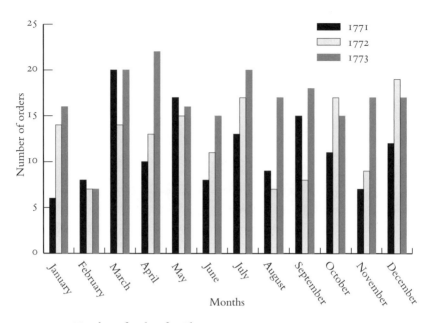

FIGURE 3.9 Number of orders for Clément, 1771–1773.

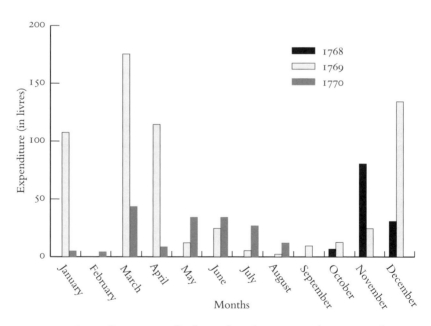

FIGURE 3.10 Expenditure on supplies by Bridet-Clément, October 1768 to July 1770.

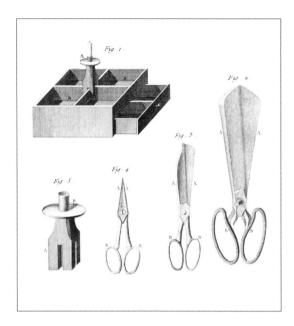

FIGURE 3.11
Tailors' thread box, candleholder, and scissors. From the *Encyclopédie,* courtesy of the Rare Books and Special Collections Library, University of Illinois at Urbana-Champaign.

for a sister or brother, and a week for a cousin. A death at court or in noble and rich bourgeois families resulted in many new orders for garment workers, because even mourning attire followed changing fashions. If clients could not afford new garments, they could ask seamstresses to mend or alter those worn during previous bereavements.[21]

Tools

Engravings in the *Encyclopédie* and *L'Art du tailleur* portray a wide array of tools. Although the texts attribute them to tailors, we may assume that most were used by seamstresses as well. The first tools depicted in the *Encyclopédie* engravings are two types of candleholders (figure 3.11). One was specially adapted for tailors, sitting on top of a box containing drawers for needles and thread. Whether or not they owned such a specialized item, seamstresses needed numerous candlesticks, torches, and lanterns for illumination, as well as boxes to organize their needles and thread. Good-quality scissors were another essential tool (see figure 3.11). Each mistress would own several different pairs of scissors, some for heavy cloth, others for delicate, precise cutting. In 1754, Marie Germaine Pelée owned five pairs of cloth-cutting scissors, valued together at approximately nine livres.[22] Seamstresses also needed a large number and variety of needles

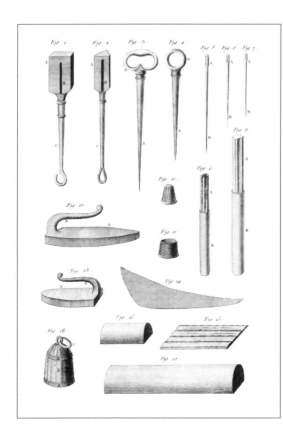

FIGURE 3.12
Tailors' tools, including
different types of irons
and ironing accessories,
thimbles, and needles,
from the *Encyclopédie,*
courtesy of the Rare
Books and Special
Collections Library,
University of Illinois
at Urbana-Champaign.

(see figure 3.12). Stronger and thicker needles were used for heavy fabrics
and attaching buttons or other decorations, thinner ones for light fabrics,
and long, straight ones for darning torn cloth. Eighteenth-century needles
were made from polished steel and therefore prone to rust. To prevent oxi-
dization, needle manufacturers packed them in paper pouches sealed in a
pig's bladder. According to Thérèse de Dillmont, author of the nineteenth-
century *Encyclopédie des ouvrages des dames,* storing needles in asbestos pow-
der helped protect them from rust. One can only wonder about the occupational diseases seamstresses acquired from this practice. Alternatively,
dipping one's fingers in an emery solution periodically while sewing also
helped to prevent rust.[23]

Along with needles and scissors, the thimble was an important tool for
seamstresses. One successful mistress offered herself the luxury of a silver
thimble and scissors.[24] As they do today, seamstresses and tailors used chalk
to trace patterns on cloth and mark alterations during fittings. They also
used pins in great quantities to hold pleats and hems in place for sewing.

The seamstress Bridet-Clément bought pins by the thousand, paying nine sous for a thousand small ones and fourteen sous for larger ones. Her clients used pins in their daily toilette as well, pinning stomachers, neckerchiefs, decorative collars, or cuffs onto their dresses instead of using buttons or other fasteners.

The iron was an omnipresent tool in tailors' and seamstresses' workshops. It was used for pressing cloth prior to cutting, forming pleats and hems, and providing a final finish to a garment. Like the *Encyclopédie*'s apprentice, seamstresses and tailors heated their irons in the embers of the fireplace. Without electric thermostats to guide them, they estimated the iron's heat by bringing it close to their cheeks or touching it with a wetted finger. Correct appraisal was crucial, because an overheated iron could burn valuable cloth. A careful seamstress or tailor performed a preliminary test on a scrap piece of cloth. The *Encyclopédie* cautioned needleworkers to examine their irons carefully after heating to ensure that no burning particles adhered to them. Irons came in different sizes and shapes and with a variety of accessories for holding and stretching cloth while ironing it (see figure 3.12).

In addition to the iron, seamstresses and tailors used lead weights to form and hold pleats. They also inserted small weights into women's dress sleeves to make them hang properly, a practice similar to the insertion of a metal chain in the hem of Chanel suit jackets. From August 1768 to April 1769, the seamstress Bridet-Clément spent a total of twenty-four livres on lead weights for dress sleeves. Finally, a number of seamstresses owned life-sized mannequins on which they could fit and assemble garments. Françoise Basson, widow of a *bourgeois de Paris,* possessed three mannequins, one of which had its own stand. These were particularly useful tools for sewing dress sleeves, which had to be attached from the outside.[25]

Supplies of Thread and Cloth

Apart from tools, seamstresses needed copious quantities of thread and cloth to make their clients' garments. This was a highly controversial aspect of their trade. The most frequent accusation leveled at needleworkers was that they deliberately overestimated the fabric needed for a client's order, with the intention of keeping the surplus for their own use. If not deliberately fraudulent, tailors and seamstresses were also suspected of incompetently wasting cloth, leaving their clients to shoulder the cost. Louis-Sébastien Mercier drew a vivid portrait of a stingy client's effort to save

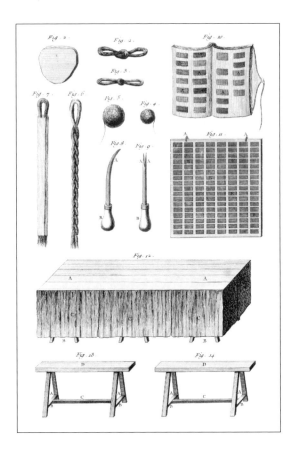

FIGURE 3.13 Types of thread, two pattern books, workbenches, and the *marquoir* (Fig. 8) and the *poussoir* (Fig. 9) used by stays tailors, from the *Encyclopédie*, courtesy of the Rare Books and Special Collections Library, University of Illinois at Urbana-Champaign.

money by purchasing his own cloth from a stand on the rue Tirechappe in Paris:

> The miser enters this narrow street, where hang thousands of fragments of cloth of all colors, all sizes and in all possible forms; and by force of going from one shop to another, he finds the cloth he is looking for. The thrifty scientist recognizes it at first sight. His glance is sure; he knows how many pieces he needs for the fabrication of his suit, and he has the cut all printed in his brain. He teaches a lesson to the surprised, and discontented, tailor, delivers the cloth and the lining to him: there is only what is required, nothing more. What accuracy! What precision! The tailor is silent, admires; and having recognized his master, he contents himself with the price of the confection.[26]

Not every client manifested such distrust in his tailor. Many successful Parisian tailors kept stocks of cloth to supply their customers, a practice that seems to have increased across the eighteenth century. The engravings of the *Encyclopédie* include two "sample books," complete with hooks to attach them to the wall of the workshop (see figure 3.13). By choosing cloth from the tailor's stock, a client could save himself the trouble of a separate visit to a cloth merchant's shop. Compared to women's fashions, the fabrics of men's suits changed somewhat more slowly, permitting successful tailors to risk purchasing expensive cloth in advance. Tailors who invested in a stock of fabric relied on credit from merchant mercers and drapers; if his orders dried up, if the off-season extended too long, or if he fell ill, a tailor could quickly find himself unable to keep up payments and, subsequently, be faced with bankruptcy. More cautious tailors did not purchase the cloth themselves, but used sample books provided by merchant mercers with whom they had provisioning agreements. This was a safer but less profitable practice.

In contrast to tailors, seamstresses almost never maintained stocks of cloth. In a sample of approximately fifty probate inventories, seamstresses possessed small pieces of cloth, most likely scraps left over from previous orders or from supplies used in repairing and altering garments. None of them, however, owned substantial amounts, indicating that they did not supply clients from their own stock and that they did not have a sideline in selling cloth or ready-to-wear garments. The price of fine textiles and the rapid changes in their design made accumulating stocks too hazardous and expensive for these modest artisans. The seamstresses' 1781 statutes spoke directly to this question: "Mistresses of the said Guild are also prohibited from keeping in their boutiques, workshops, or shops, any pieces of cloth, or from conducting a commerce in them, under punishment of confiscation of the goods, the appropriate damages, and a fine of 100 livres." In this case, it does not appear that the prohibition arose from the spread of the undesirable practice.[27]

While seamstresses did not keep stocks of cloth, they sometimes purchased cloth for their clients and included the cost in the final price of the dress. These orders allowed seamstresses some leverage in developing relations with merchants and a margin to increase their profits. Most clients, however, preferred to purchase fabric themselves, employing the seamstress only to cut and sew the garment. In December 1739, the marquise de Breuil sent a letter to mistress seamstress Françoise LeClerc, conveying a dress order and the fabric necessary for the dress. LeClerc was not a lowly practitioner of the trade but, as former seamstress to the queen of France, one of the most prominent. In her letter, the marquise explained that she had no money to send for the dress but would furnish a down payment when LeClerc delivered the finished garment.[28]

By purchasing their own fabric, rich and fashionable ladies could ensure that its color, design, and price suited them perfectly. They could also profit from the advice of well-known cloth merchants, whose commercial prestige and ties to cloth manufacturers enabled them to furnish authoritative counsel on changing styles. Today, famous *couturiers* order new fabric designs from manufacturers to suit their latest creations; in the eighteenth century fashion lay not in cut or design, but primarily in textile patterns and decorations, giving merchants mercers and fashion merchants the upper hand.

If they did not usually provide the fabric for clients' dresses, seamstresses did furnish the thread, hemming ribbon, and the other small items necessary for making and finishing them. At the time of her death, Marie Madeleine Bricon owned a special chest of drawers to hold her supplies. It contained three drawers of different types of ribbon, another drawer full of pins, a package of corset laces, hemming ribbon, over thirty rolls of thread, forty packages of needles, stationary, sealing wax, and lead weights. The notary evaluated these supplies at the considerable sum of one hundred livres.[29] Her colleague, mistress Marie Josephe Denizon, had a smaller inventory. At her death in 1781, the notary recorded six pieces of white ribbon, a piece of white linen cloth, and forty-eight pads covered with linen and filled with horsehair, all for use in making hip bolsters, which had replaced hoopskirts in fashion. The notary evaluated these supplies, along with two pairs of scissors, a thimble, and a case of needles, at sixteen livres.[30]

Among a wide range of suppliers, merchant mercers occupied the premier rank. The umbrella of the mercers' guild encompassed almost twenty specialties, many essential to the garment trades. Seamstresses acquired silk from specialist mercers, called *marchands d'étoffe de soye.* One of the most famous was Jean-François Barbier, who received supplies from over eighty different merchants in the Lyons silk industry. Barbier's shop in Paris was located on the rue des Bourdonnais, at the sign of the "Golden Beard." According to the *Tablettes royales de renommée,* it was "one of the most considerable boutiques for plain, brocaded and gold and silk-encrusted silk fabric, of fashionable accessories [*modes*] and of seasonal [fashions]."[31]

Court nobles, Parisian ladies, and visitors from the provinces flocked to famous boutiques like Barbier's to hear about, peruse, and purchase the latest styles. Many cloth shops were located near the Halles market, on and around the fashionable rue Saint-Honoré and the rue de Richelieu, or on the less-prestigious rue Saint-Denis. Seamstresses also bought thread, needles, pins, lace, and scissors from specialist mercers. In the second half of the eighteenth century, they purchased dress decorations, ribbons, and finery in the shops of female fashion merchants, who had begun to differentiate themselves from the mercers.

Apart from these established merchants, seamstresses could buy supplies from hawkers who set up stands or sold door to door. Ambulatory vendors selling pins, needles, thread, and ribbons were common in Paris, although their activities violated the trade monopoly of the mercers' guild. In 1758, on the rue de Cléry, officials of the guild arrested a man who had been selling cotton and thread with the cry: "Buy thread and cotton to make stockings, gloves, buy!" They also caught two women illegally selling small items of finery.[32] Such vendors offered cheap prices and convenient access, but their quality standards must have fallen well below those of merchants like Barbier. Still, the many seizures performed against them by the mercers' guild testify to their perceived interference in the trade.

A needleworker's typical day could involve a series of visits to clients and suppliers. Sieur Labbet, a master tailor living on the rue du Roule, left his house at nine o'clock on the morning of January 10, 1759. He left behind his journeyman, who spent the morning seated on a table sewing in the front room of the apartment, while a female worker sewed sleeves at a window in an adjoining room. Labbet first visited a buttonmaker on the rue des Fossés Saint-Germain-l'Auxerrois. He then walked the short distance to the home of Sieur Lavis, a master of the ballet, to drop off an order. From there, he went to Barbier's shop on the rue des Bourdonnais where he bought some gray velvet. His next stop was at another mercer's shop where he bought trimming material for a suit. On the way home, he encountered a former employee who now worked for the tailor of the Italian Comedy company. They shared half a bottle of wine at the Roi de France, a tavern on the rue de la Ferronerie, after which Labbet returned home.[33]

From October 1768 to July 1770, mistress seamstress Bridet-Clément kept a record of her daily purchases of thread, ribbons, lace, pins, lead weights, and small amounts of fabric. In this period, she paid an impressive total of 835 livres for these supplies. The number of purchases she made each month varied widely, from zero in February 1769 to a high of forty-one a month earlier in January 1769 (see figure 3.10). Her most frequent need was for thread, which she bought in many different colors and varieties, spending over 95 livres in a twenty-month period. She also acquired over eight thousand pins at a cost of between 9 and 14 sous per thousand. Less frequent expenses were for lace to decorate dress sleeves and collars, and for buttons, corset laces, a box to deliver a dress, and a hoopskirt. Bridet-Clément also regularly procured small pieces of cloth, making twenty-one different purchases of silk taffeta cloth, seventeen of linen, and two of woolen cloth in just under two years. The largest amount of fabric she bought was eighteen aunes of a black woolen fabric to make a widow's mourning dress, for 117 livres. The rest were much smaller pieces, ranging from one-quarter of an aune to three and a half or five aunes, enough for mending or to make a woman's skirt.

In the long run, Bridet-Clément's expenses far outweighed her income. When she filed for bankruptcy in 1781, she owed 4,565 livres to suppliers, including 500, 250, and 160 livres to three different merchant mercers, 120 livres to her lace merchant, 96 and 30 livres to two artisans who cleaned and dyed articles of clothing (*teinturiers*), 120 livres to a stockings dealer, and 60 livres to a "Jewish merchant." Her largest debt was of 1,800 livres to a Sieur Demontarcie for unspecified services. These high debts were countered by only 571 livres in uncollected bills from her clients. Although Bridet-Clément was undoubtedly exceptional in her level of activity and expenses, her example indicates the frequency of small supply purchases seamstresses made and the array of merchants on whom they relied for materials.[34]

Clients

Because they did not operate public shops, seamstresses relied largely on word-of-mouth to acquire clients. Those who worked for illustrious noblewomen attracted new clients through their patrons' celebrity. Like Molière's bourgeois gentleman, socially ambitious women pursued the cachet and the inside knowledge possessed by artisans who worked for "people of quality."[35] Less illustrious seamstresses relied on personal recommendations and neighborhood proximity to find clients. They also acquired customers from friends and relatives working in related trades, such as laundresses, linen-drapers, used-clothes dealers, and fashions merchants. The breakdown of one friendship offers insight into practices of information exchange. In a complaint to police, Demoiselle Domail, a twenty-year-old seamstress, recounted a tale of betrayed personal and professional confidence. According to Domail, some two weeks earlier the widow Pierrard, a silk-stockings launderer, visited her and declared that she wanted to patch up their quarrel. Pierrard supposedly told Domail: "we must forget the past, I no longer want to see the wife Lévêque, la Cécile, la Sophie, they are scoundrels' rogues [*gueuses des coquines*]."

To prove her sincerity, Pierrard told Domail that she was going to procure a good client for her, whom she had stolen from Cécile. A few days later, she came again, this time with a letter ostensibly written by the client, a lady from Madrid. Pierrard read the letter to Domail, whose apparent illiteracy aided the scheme against her. Domail recalled that the letter stated: "Madame I beg you to bring me a seamstress since I can no longer make use of the one you had given me due to the little difficulty that you have had together."[36] At five o'clock the next morning, the two women rented a carriage that took them as far as the bois de Boulogne. Pierrard suggested that they walk into the woods to meet the client's servant, who was coming to meet them. They had walked some way when the trap was sprung. On a signal from Pierrard, the three women named Lévêque, Sophie, and Cécile emerged from their hiding places. They attacked Domail, tearing her bonnet, mantle, and apron and breaking her fan. Two carters intervened to save Domail, later testifying to the violence of the assault.

Domail's attempt at revenge appeared in a subsequent police complaint. Following the attack, she apparently told a female acquaintance that the woman's husband habitually frequented a house of prostitution, naming her enemies as the prostitutes he visited there. Incensed by this accusation, the woman went to their house, where she verbally and physically assaulted Lévêque, Sophie, and Cécile. They responded with a complaint against Domail for slander.[37] As these events illustrate, professional concerns permeated social relationships among working women. Information and client exchange offered a way to initiate and cement friendship or exact revenge against enemies. In this female world of work, sexual slander was the weapon of choice in battles over commercial territory and personal enmity. When conflicts turned to violence, a woman's clothing and accessories were a privileged object of attack. Clothing, sexual honor, and work were closely related in these women's perception of themselves and their social world.[38]

Dissatisfied with word-of-mouth contacts, some garment workers adopted more sophisticated advertising techniques. In 1760, the tailors' guild assembly condemned several tailors who distributed printed tracts "which announce suits and all types of garments at very low prices . . . with the view of attracting a greater number of clients." Guild leaders declared that these commercial practices created unfair competition and hurt the trade's reputation "by the defective nature of low-priced merchandise[,] not apparent at first but by which the public will always end up being duped."[39] They ordered masters to follow accepted practices and limit themselves to cards simply stating their names and addresses with no mention of prices. Repeated prosecutions of master tailors through the 1760s and 1770s reveal that some members of the guild defied these orders. No evidence for this form of marketing has been found among seamstresses, but ambitious mistresses may well have adopted similar practices. These new and disputed commercial techniques foreshadowed advertising tools that became widespread in the nineteenth century.

The Imaginary World of Client-Seamstress Relations

Client relations were not only of interest to the artisans involved in them. In the late seventeenth century, relations between seamstresses and their clients also caught the attention of a handful of artists. The well-known engraver Arnoult produced an image entitled *The Good Seamstress,* which depicts a seamstress and her worker measuring a female client (figure 3.14). While the assistant carefully lays the client's mantua dress over a chair, "the good seamstress" measures the woman's upper arm. This engraving displays a common form of attire and a shared attention to appearances between client and seamstress. The two women are dressed in almost identical finery, wearing the same necklace, lace garnishes, and *fontanelle* headdress. Even the seamstress's assistant wears fine clothing, jewelry, and a fancy headdress.

Two additional late-seventeenth-century engravings portray the logical next encounter between client and seamstress, the fitting of the garment (figures 3.15 and 3.16). The luxury of the surroundings suggests that the interaction takes place in the client's home. In these images, the social distance between mistress and client appears to a certain extent in differences in apparel. In contrast to the rich fabric and decorations of the client's dress, the mistress in both images wears a mantua of plainer

La Bonne Couturierre

D'ouvriere en fut il jamais de plus habille ?   Paroissez a la Cour, ou Restez a la Ville,
Ie donne le bon air a mes habillemens .   Madame, et vous allez faire nombre d'Amans .
Se vend a Paris Chez N. Arnoult rue de la fromagerie aux halles au bon Raisin Avec Priuilege du Roy

FIGURE 3.14 *La Bonne couturière* (The Good Seamstress), by Nicolas Arnoult, shows a seamstress measuring her client's upper arm (late seventeenth century). Courtesy of the Cabinet des estampes, Bibliothèque nationale.

La Couturiere

A Paris Chez Chiquet   Rue S.t Jacq. a Pres les Mathurins   Avec privил. du Roy 1695.

FIGURE 3.15 *La Couturière* (The Seamstress) 1, by Nicolas de Larmessin, shows a seamstress arranging the skirts of her client's *manteau,* while her worker fits the sleeves (late seventeenth century). Scissors, thread, and pins and needles lie on the table on the left of the image. Courtesy of the Cabinet des estampes, Bibliothèque nationale.

La Couturiere

Je me plais d'habiller vne aussi belle fille
Qui vous; aymable Iris, dont lesprit est bien fait
Pour faire Vôtre Corps et vôtre habit parfait
Souffrez que l'on vous Erace vn ou deux points d'eguille.

A Paris Chez F. Guerard vis à vis la Fontaine St Severin à l'image nostre Dame.

FIGURE 3.16 *La Couturière* (The Seamstress) 2, by François Guérard, shows a seamstress fitting the top of her client's sleeve (late seventeenth century). Courtesy of the Cabinet des estampes, Bibliothèque nationale.

FIGURE 3.17 *La Couturière* (the seamstress) 3, shows a seamstress stitching a dress while her client watches (mid-eighteenth century). Courtesy of the Cabinet des estampes, Bibliothèque nationale.

cloth, covered by an apron. Despite these distinctions, the two mistresses are notably well dressed by the standards of 1695. Their sleeves are of a fashionable cut and their aprons are made of fine gauze or linen. They have decorated their cuffs, collar, and stays with lace and wear fancy headdresses.

These three engravings place client and seamstress in a shared female world of fashion and taste, which transcends their social and economic differences. The seamstresses appear to be engaged not so much in work as in a private form of feminine grooming. These images also underline the needleworker's role in creating a sexualized female appearance. The sexual theme, implicit in the images, is explicitly evoked in the legends that accompany them. The first (figure 3.15) reads: "There has never been a more competent worker/I give the right air to all my clothes /Appear at the Court or Stay in the City/Madame and you will get a number of Lovers."[40] The second (figure 3.16) describes the seamstresses' pleasure in showing off the young woman's body: "It pleases me to dress such a beautiful girl/As you lovable Iris, whose spirit is well made/To make your body and your dress perfect/Allow us to make one or two stitches."[41] An eighteenth-century engraving puts the demand for seductive clothing in the mouth of the client, who demands: "Lower the neckline of this dress my girl/You are hiding all my enticements/We are nice for such a short time/Hey, why not make the most of it?" (figure 3.17).[42]

In satiric fashion, these verses equate the seamstress's function with that of a virtual panderer. Her purpose is not simply to clothe the client, but to bestow a beautiful and seductive appearance on her. By highlighting a bustline or skillfully concealing less appealing features, the seamstress enabled her clients to procure male interest and attention. The point of this seductive capacity was not so much sexual gratification as it was the power it gave them over men and even other women, who could be awed or intimidated into submission. The artist's aim is to penetrate the secret world of feminine appearances, where high- and low-class women united to produce female beauty.[43]

This vision of the seamstresses' trade is key to understanding the sexualized aura surrounding garment workers from the Old Regime up to the twentieth century. The aura did not arise merely from their role in prostitution, although many did engage in paid sex to supplement their meager wages. Instead, as one of the culture's main creators of femininity and the female power of seduction, seamstresses were themselves seen as essentially sexualized beings possessed of a heightened femininity. These representations drew strength from the character of seamstresses' professional and private lives. In contrast to other women, garment workers lived in a distinctly female world. They ran independent businesses, took in female apprentices and journeywomen, and worked almost entirely for other women. As will be revealed in later chapters, a high proportion of seamstresses were single women. With the gender-specific nature of the trade, and its proximity to the body, came a slightly dubious respectability. Seamstresses knew perhaps too much about the female body, and its transition from gross nature to elegant culture, to be entirely honorable. Midwife or madame, they held the key to female secrets and the female sexual power that was such a strong feature of discourses about femininity in the Old Regime.[44]

Of course, seamstresses were not the only artisans charged with producing female beauty; linen-drapers and fashion merchants, along with male stays tailors, hairdressers, or shoemakers, were all well-known servants of the female appearance. By contrast with seamstresses, however, other female garment trades were depicted more often in relations with male clients than with female ones. Stories and images of linen-drapers and fashion merchants often depicted them in flirtatious exchanges with male clients who had entered their shops (figure 3.18). These images found an echo in the police reports of Marais and his colleagues, which described the seduction of shopgirls by socially superior clients and their entry to the world of high-class prostitution. For their part, male servants of female beauty were increasingly ridiculed in the late seventeenth and eighteenth centuries. In addition to his image of the seamstress, the engraver Arnoult also composed an image titled *Le Tailleur français* (The French Tailor), showing a tailor engaged in fitting a female client for a pair of stays. The legend printed below the image mocks the tailor's perceived role in helping female clients hide unwanted pregnancies: "He is honest, he is discreet/He adroitly hides a defect of Nature/and of an amorous adventure/he knows well how to keep the secret" (figure 3.19).[45] From this period forward, the propriety of male artisans in the world of female appearances was increasingly questioned, as social commentators, most notably Rousseau, castigated work in the needle trades as inherently feminine and feminizing. All forms of service to physical appearance could be ridiculed as servile and superficial; however, distinctions were drawn between "natural" female interest in appearances, either as consumers or producers, and unnatural, effeminate interest from men.

La Marchande lingere
Mon braue Caualier tout remply de franchise
Si vous voulez de moy quelque chose acheter
Voyez et si cela ne peut vous contenter
Je vous deployeray vne autre Marchandise

A Paris chez la veue le Camu rue St Jaqué a la toié d'Or   Auec priuil du Roy

FIGURE 3.18 *La Marchande lingère* (The Merchant Linen-Draper) (late seventeenth century). Courtesy of the Cabinet des estampes, Bibliothèque nationale.

Le Tailleur François

Il est honeste, Il est discret   _Et d'vne Amoureuse Aduenture_
Il cache adroitement vn defaut de Nature   _Il sçait bien garder le secret._
Se vend a Paris chez N. Arnoult rue de la Fromagerie aux halles où est Paris aux priuilege du Roy 1687

FIGURE 3.19 *Le Tailleur français* (The French Tailor) by Nicolas Arnoult, shows a tailor assisting a female client trying on a pair of stays (late seventeenth century). Courtesy of the Cabinet des estampes, Bibliothèque nationale.

Measurements

No standard measuring device existed for measuring bodies in the eighteenth century. Lacking a tape measure marked in inches or centimeters, the seamstress or tailor used a long strip of paper. They took each measurement from the top of the strip, marking it on the paper with a cut of the scissors. As the *Encyclopédie* observed, the difficulty of this method lay in remembering the significance of each mark. With practice, the author assured, the technique was easily mastered. Seamstresses and tailors kept these strips of paper for their regular clients so that they could accept new orders by mail or messenger.

Different measurements were necessary for different garments. In *L'Art du tailleur*, Garsault provided a detailed list of measurements required for making a woman's dress and skirt, a pair of stays, and other garments.[46] In 1796, the English *Taylor's Complete Guide* listed the following steps for measuring a woman for a fitted riding jacket:

> First measure under the arm straight down to the hollow by the hip, there mark your measure which will be the length of your body. Next down the back seam to the hip, then across half the back. Mark the measure and then proceed to the elbow and down to the hand. Next measure round the arm at the top and afterwards in as many places as you think proper. Be very correct in measuring round the wrist, as it must fit close and neat. Then measure round the body as for a coat. With respect to the breast be delicate and judicious and take half across with a proper consideration of ease for the rising prominence. Measure likewise from the top of the shoulder to the bottom of the stays before, or to what length the Lady may wish or as the ruling fashion may suggest. Then take the length of the petticoat from the hip to the ground and any other part you think proper. [47]

As the last sentence suggests, measurement was not an exact science. In assessing each client, tailors and seamstresses relied on experience to tell them which additional details they needed. The *Encyclopédie* urged tailors to remain alert for physical characteristics or deformities that could not be measured:

> In the time that he takes the measure, he should also observe that which he cannot mark on the paper, that is the body's structure, like the shoulders high or sunken, the roundness and turn of the stom-

ach, the chest flat or elevated, etc. so as to cut in consequence; if the subject has some defects of conformation, the art of the tailor is to alleviate them by more or less heavy garnishes, either of linen, wool, cotton, etc.[48]

The *Encyclopédie* thus emphasized the aesthetic as well as the artisanal dimension of the tailor's work. His responsibility lay not only in producing a well-fitted garment but also in disguising or repairing his customer's bodily flaws. As we have seen, this function took on tones of medical urgency in the case of whaleboned stays, which were believed to prevent deformities in children or cure existing ones. Despite these claims, the role of tailors in measuring women's bodies was more often seen as a salacious activity than the exercise of a therapeutic duty. As the engraving *The French Tailor* (figure 3.19) suggests, the practice of measuring raised particular interest and concern among observers when practiced by a male tailor on a female client. In 1675, Louis XIV stated in the seamstresses' letters patent that one of his motivations for creating the guild was to permit women to be clothed by female artisans if they so desired.[49] In the 1720s, in arguing for their right to make whaleboned stays, the Parisian seamstresses' guild highlighted the moral dangers in allowing tailors to measure scantily clad female clients. The salacious intent of tailors in approaching the female body, either to measure or fit garments, also attracted satirical treatment in literature and imagery (see figure 3.20, where a tailor focuses intently on the bosom of his female client as he measures her chest).

Amounts of Cloth

Having measured her client, the seamstress could form a reliable estimate of the amount of cloth she needed to make a dress. Based on figures from *L'Art du tailleur,* the standard dress of the 1760s, the *robe à la française,* required approximately five square aunes of cloth, if worn without a hoopskirt. Because manufacturers usually produced silk and cotton cloth in half-aune widths, the dress would have used nine and a half aunes of fabric (12.3 yards, or 11.1 meters).[50] The matching skirt called for approximately three and one third aunes of cloth at half an aune in width. An ensemble composed of dress and matching petticoat thus required almost thirteen aunes of material (15 yards, or 13.5 meters).

Dresses worn over hoopskirts required much more fabric. In the early years of the nineteenth century, Madame de Genlis recalled that her

FIGURE 3.20 A stays tailor measuring a client for a pair of stays (early eighteenth century). Courtesy of the Cabinet des estampes, Bibliothèque nationale.

trained court dresses, worn over a large hoopskirt, used between twenty and twenty-two aunes of cloth (26 to 28 yards).[51] An Englishwoman named Barbara Johnson, who left a journal recording her cloth purchases from 1746 to 1821, provides additional information. According to Johnson's notes, a "negligee"—the English word for the *robe à la française*—that she wore to the Stamford races in 1767 required twenty-two yards of material; in 1770 a second dress needed twenty-one yards. The largest amount Johnson purchased was twenty-five yards of white satin for a "negligee and puckered petticoat" in June 1763.[52]

The simpler dresses Johnson adopted in the 1770s and 1780s used less material. Her "nightgowns"—the English word for the fitted *robe à l'anglaise*—required only eleven and three quarter yards, twelve yards, or fourteen and a half yards. She purchased similar amounts of cloth to make the simple "gowns" that became popular in the late-eighteenth century. In 1781, Johnson had a "red double taffety [*sic*] gown and petticoat" made from nine yards of cloth, of three-quarters of a yard in width. She had a "brown taffety [*sic*] gown" made in 1785 with five and a half yards of fabric of one aune in width. In documenting the shrinking amounts of cloth required for the gowns of the 1770s and 1780s, Johnson's journal suggests that women's rising consumption of clothing in the latter decades of the eighteenth century was encouraged by the declining cost of dresses.

Making the robe à la française

Once they had obtained a client, cloth, and appropriate tools and supplies, seamstresses began the business of cutting and stitching garments. The next sections of this chapter will focus on the fabrication of three key garments in the female wardrobe: the dress, the skirt, and the stays. The final sections will examine the protracted and sometimes painful process of extracting payment for these wares. François de Garsault provided a step-by-step guide for making the *robe à la française* and matching petticoat, which I will follow here.

To make the *robe à la française,* the seamstress started by cutting the pieces of the garment, using a cloth or paper pattern and her client's measurements for guidance. Cutting was the most delicate and demanding aspect of the garment trades; stitches were easily removed and replaced, but a mistake in cutting would destroy valuable cloth. In 1660, the Parisian tailors' statutes obliged masters to reimburse their clients for any cloth ruined in this manner. Almost one hundred years later, in 1745, the tailors' corpo-

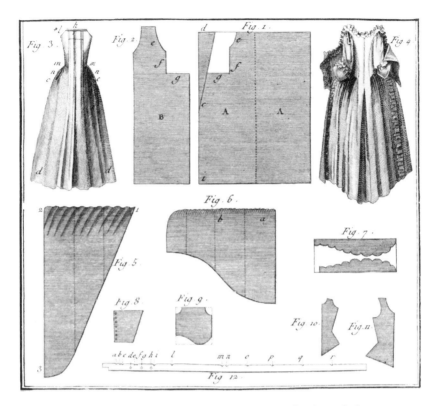

FIGURE 3.21 Pattern for the *robe à la française*. From *Encyclopédie méthodique*, courtesy of the University of Illinois at Urbana-Champaign.

ration of Aix-en-Provence required masters to perform all cutting themselves. Prior to the eighteenth century, most seamstresses and tailors made life-sized patterns for garments on their clients out of thin cloth, using the pattern as the lining of the finished garment. During the eighteenth century, the use of standardized paper patterns became widespread in the garment trades. Garsault recommended that needleworkers possess a set of patterns for each type of garment they produced, in a range of sizes, and he provided several reduced-size patterns to aid them. Figure 3.21 shows a pattern for the *robe à la française* and matching petticoat from the *Encyclopédie méthodique,* replicating the one Garsault included in *L'Art du tailleur.*

To cut the pieces of the garment, the seamstress first folded the cloth in half widthwise and then ironed and pinned the pieces of the pattern onto it. Next, she compared the client's measurements to the pattern, marking any discrepancies in tailor's chalk. Then she cut the pieces following the contours of the pattern or her chalk marks when they diverged from it.

Because each piece of the pattern usually had to be cut twice—once for each side of the body—folding the fabric in half allowed the needleworker to cut two identical pieces at once. According to Garsault, because of the popularity of patterned fabric, seamstresses encountered a particular difficulty in cutting out pieces for women's dresses: "The greatest difficulty which is met, when one has cloth with flowers or in compartments, is to fit them well and sort them regularly, economizing the cloth as much as possible; it is an affair of genius and talent."[53]

According to Garsault's pattern, the *robe à la française* consisted of four back pieces and two front pieces. The seamstress cut each of the four back pieces to the same length, straight across the width of the cloth. The two front pieces also used the entire width of cloth, but were cut slightly longer to provide extra material for the shoulder seams. Once the seamstress had cut them, she sewed the back pieces together lengthwise (figure 3.21; "Fig. 1" shows two joined back pieces). Then she folded the fabric in half widthwise and ironed it to create a horizontal line, marking the height to which the gores of the dress would reach. The seamstress then cut a diagonal line, running from a point one-eighth of an aune (5.8 inches) in from the top corner of the fabric to this halfway mark, (from d to c in figure 3.21, "Fig. 1"). The cut-out triangular pieces were retained to serve as gores in the dress skirts. In dresses worn over hoopskirts, the gores had to be much wider and were cut from separate pieces of fabric.

The needleworker then finished cutting the armholes and torso of the dress as far as the hips (e, f, and g in figure 3.21, "Fig. 1"). She left the remaining material to make the side pleats. Next she cut out the armholes and the torso for the two front pieces of the dress, again leaving extra material for the side pleats (figure 3.21; "Fig. 2" shows one front piece). If desired, the seamstress could make identical front and back pieces in a lighter cloth to line the dress. In most cases, however, she omitted this step. Surviving *robes à la française* often contain a bodice lining and are lined around the bottom hem to prevent fraying, but the dress skirts are usually unlined. Because women wore one or more petticoats under the dress, additional lining would have only increased the weight and bulk of their clothing.

Next came the more meticulous process of forming the many pleats of the dress (see figure 3.21, "Fig. 3"). The back pleats of the *robe à la française* consisted of two square box pleats, each composed of one wide pleat placed between two narrow ones. The seamstress carefully folded and ironed each into place. To make the hip pleats, she sewed the triangular gores to the edges of the back pieces and then formed three or four pleats out of this material ("Fig. 3," m, n, c), securing them with cross-stitches. Dresses worn over hoopskirts had no side pleats, but rather gores that came up as high as the hips. The last pleats went into the front pieces, and were also secured with cross-stitches.

Once she finished making the pleats, the seamstress made the collar of the dress, folding a length of fabric into a thin strip, pressing it flat, and attaching it at the top edge of the back piece. She then sewed a line of cross-stitches across the inside of the back of the dress, approximately ten centimeters below the collar, to hold the heavy back pleats in position. In some cases, she also sewed a rectangular piece of cloth, called the *quarrure,* on the inside of the back lining to help support the weight of the pleats. She might separate this cloth into two pieces, placed several inches apart. Ribbons or cords attached to either side of the split allowed the wearer to tighten the torso of the dress under the pleats. When these internal details were complete, the seamstress attached the top of the front pieces to the back, folding the extra length over to form the shoulder seams of the dress. She then stitched the two sides of the dress together, leaving an eight-inch gap at the sides for the pockets. The dress was left open in the front to display the stomacher and matching skirt. A folded and ironed strip of cloth sewn down each side of the front opening served as decoration and reinforcement for the dress.

The last steps involved mounting the sleeves and finishing the dress. First the seamstress cut out the pieces for the sleeves and their lining and sewed them together. She used a running stitch to form shoulder gathers along the top edge of the sleeve, then sewed each one shut lengthwise and mounted it into the armholes of the dress. The seamstress finished her job by trimming the bottom hem and the pocket openings with ribbon. Before sewing the final hem, she took the dress to the client for one or more fittings, noting any areas of the dress that did not fit properly and pinning the hem to the desired length. The result of this process was the *robe à la française* depicted in figure 1.1.

The matching skirt was a much simpler garment. It was made from five pieces, each cut straight across the width of cloth to the same length, and then sewed together lengthwise. The seamstress followed the same steps for the lining pieces, which she then sewed on to the skirt fabric. She formed pleats along the top edge of the fabric and secured them with a waistband. She sewed the skirt together from the top to the bottom, leaving two openings on the sides for the pockets. Finally, she trimmed with ribbon the openings, the top, and the bottom edges of the skirt.

Following Garsault's explanations, the techniques used to produce the dress and skirt ensemble appear simple and straightforward. An examination of surviving eighteenth-century dresses by contrast, suggests that the fabrication of dresses could be much more complicated. Reconstructed patterns based on dresses held in museum collections present a number of variations from the generic pattern Garsault provided. They show, for example, a variety of internal mechanisms used to support and tighten the torso of the dress or to take up and release the hip pleats. In many cases, seamstresses made the *robe à la française* in two steps, cutting and assembling the bodice lining first and then mounting the dress fabric over it. This lining could be a distinct garment within the dress, containing whalebone supports or reinforced eyelets to lace it shut.[54] Internal structures played a particularly important role in dresses worn over hoopskirts. An English *robe à la française* exhibited in the Victoria and Albert Museum could be worn either with or without a hoopskirt. Cords attached to the hip pleats inside the skirt allow them to be released or drawn in tightly to accommodate different-sized hoopskirts. Constructing these mechanisms, draping large amounts of cloth over them, and ensuring that the elegant exterior betrayed no hint of the complex contraptions hidden within required particular skill and expertise.[55]

Mounting the sleeves of the dress also posed problems, given the combined thickness of the gathered fabric and lining. The underside of the sleeve could be sewn into the dress from the inside, but the heavy gathers at the top had to be attached with invisible stitches, from the outside. Later in the century, the closely fitted back seams of the *robe à l'anglaise* constituted another test of skill, because they had to descend evenly and gracefully toward the tailbone. Making the fashionable dresses of the eighteenth century—which appeared light and elegant on the outside, but were filled on the inside with heavy pleats, cords, and ribbons—required a high degree of technical ability. Competence involved not only style or fashion sense but also talent, skill, and experience.[56]

The time required to make garments varied widely, depending on the complexity of construction and the decorative garnishes required. The skill and experience of the seamstress, the number of workers she employed, and the urgency of the client were also factors. In general, it probably took at least four working days to cut and stitch a *robe à la française*. Those with lavish decorations or complicated internal mechanisms took longer.

Given the high cost of fabric and an inherited respect for conservation, women of all social classes, including the queen of France, sent their dresses to be repaired, refinished, and altered. Dress decorations, as well as the length and width of sleeves and hems, were all adjusted to suit changing fashions. The arrival of the hoopskirt around 1718 called for more radical alterations. Fortunately for style-conscious French women, the *manteau's* trained skirts could be shortened and the excess used as gores to accommodate a hoopskirt. The scarcity of mantuas in modern museum collections thus derives not only from the passage of time, but from the fact that their owners altered them beyond recognition as they adopted new styles in the early eighteenth century.

Later in the century, women also had the *robe à la française* altered to meet the demands of fashion. Their seamstresses took in the voluminous back pleats of the dress, sewing them down to create the fitted back popular in the 1770s. They also cut frayed *robes à la française* at mid-thigh length to create the *casaquin* jacket. In fact, the *casaquin* style itself probably originated as a way to recycle frayed dresses. When high waistlines were in vogue in the 1790s, seamstresses used excess material in pleats sewn down in the *robe à l'anglaise* to bring the waist up for the new look. Most drastically, a needleworker could take a dress entirely apart and cut it into pieces for a new garment. A deconstructed *robe à la française* provided sufficient material to make a jacket and skirt ensemble. The large amounts of material used for dresses before the 1780s thus made it possible to re-create them as entirely different garments. Many surviving eighteenth-century dresses, jackets, and skirts bear the marks of one or several alterations.[57]

In addition to performing alterations, seamstresses mended garments. They carefully repaired torn linings, split seams, fallen hems, rips, burns, and other damage. Hems and tucks supplied material to patch holes in cloth, while special stitches disguised tears. If all else failed, seamstresses could camouflage irreparable damage by adding new decorations. A good seamstress knew the best ways to alter old garments to suit the current fashion, and performed almost invisible repair work. A needleworker's success—or failure—in these efforts must have strongly influenced her clients' loyalty. When Marie-Antoinette had garments altered, she sent them to one of her fashion merchants, Mademoiselle Eloffe, rather than giving them to a palace servant.[58] Mademoiselle Eloffe probably did not perform the work herself, but she hired workers capable of satisfying royal standards. The seamstresses' 1781 statutes underlined the importance of this work, confirming that mistresses "will also have, in competition with the Master Tailors-Fripiers, the right to mend, re-cut, and sew back together old dresses and other used women's, girls', and children's clothing, for people who order them, and without being able to conduct a commerce in them."[59]

The Fabrication of Whaleboned Stays

The production of whaleboned undergarments attracted close attention from technical writers. François de Garsault described tailors who engaged in this specialty as the most technically skilled members of their trade: "The Master Tailor, who has chosen this branch of his Art, is called a *Tailor of Dress Bodices and Corsets,* and although his science is less extensive in its work than that of the Man's Tailor, he has nonetheless more tools, and a more detailed and knowledgeable handling, given that this Art demands a great deal of precaution, address, and precision."[60]

L'Art du tailleur included a lengthy description of the procedures followed in making a pair of stays. Because these were essential items of the female wardrobe, and disputes between tailors and seamstresses often focused on this branch of production, it is worthwhile to review Garsault's explanation in some detail. According to Garsault, a pair of stays consisted of two back pieces, two front pieces, and two shoulder straps. The "whalebone" used to stiffen the stays was actually cartilage taken from the jaws of whales hunted in the Atlantic Ocean. In Paris, a small group of merchant mercers specialized in the sale of whalebone. One of them was Bénard the elder, mentioned in the 1772 *Tablettes royales de renommée.* Located on the rue de l'Arbre sec under the name of *La Pêche de baleine* (Whale Fishing), Bénard's store offered "whalebone of all sizes and quality, that he has cut to the greatest perfection."[61] In addition to the tailor's standard tools of scissors, needles, and thimble, the staysmaker used a special knife to cut and whittle the whalebone, a *marquoir* to trace lines for the seams in which it was inserted, a wooden ruler to guide it, a *poussoir* for pushing pieces of whalebone into the garment, and an awl to pierce eyelets for the laces (see figure 3.13).

Like his colleagues, the staysmaker began by taking his client's measurements (figure 3.22, no. 1, shows the different measurements necessary for the stays). He then selected appropriate patterns for the front, back,

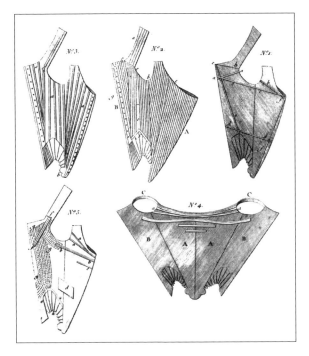

FIGURE 3.22
Sideview of a pair
of stays. "No. 1"
shows the measure-
ments necessary for
the stays. The other
images show the
placement of whale-
bone in the stays.
From François de
Garsault, *L'Art du
tailleur* (1769).

and shoulder pieces. The first layer of the stays was made from buckram, a coarse canvas often recycled from old sheets or sailcloth. The tailor wetted the buckram and then folded it in half. He ironed the pattern pieces onto the cloth, marking any differences with the client's measurements in tailors' chalk. Once he had cut out the front and back pieces in buckram, he ironed and basted them onto another piece of canvas or rough linen cloth. Cutting around the buckram, he created identical canvas pieces for the second layer of the stays.

Next, he used the *marquoir* and ruler to trace lines a quarter of an inch apart across the pieces. Once all of the lines had been marked, he gave the cloth to a needleworker who covered each line with a row of backstitches, effectively sewing the canvas and buckram together while creating a series of pockets to hold the whalebone strips. According to Garsault, this sewing work was usually performed by female employees, while the male tailor honed the whalebone, cut the cloth, and ensured the proper fit of the garment (see figure 3.23). The next procedure consisted of preparing the whalebone for the stays. The tailor cut a series of whalebone strips to the correct length and width for each pocket, and shaved them to an appropriate thickness. To make a comfortable and even fit, he ensured

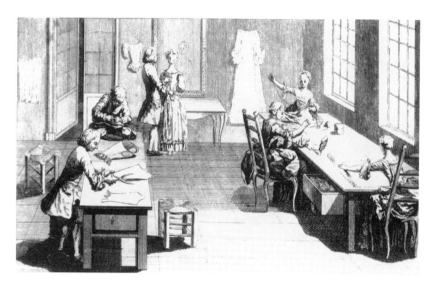

FIGURE 3.23 The workshop of the stays tailor. From François de Garsault, *L'Art du tailleur* (1769).

that the pieces destined for each side of the body were of similar size and strength. Once he had selected and prepared the whalebone pieces, the tailor inserted them in the stays, using the *poussoir* to push them all the way into the pockets. For proper fit and support, Garsault recommended that the pieces of whalebone over the kidneys and chest be stronger and harder than those inserted at the sides or the top and bottom of the garment.

After inserting all of the whalebone, the tailor sewed around the edges of the cloth with permanent stitches. If the client intended to lace the stays in the back, as was the most common style, he sewed the front pieces together and attached them at the sides to the two back pieces. Then he attached more whalebone on the inside of the stays, including one or more horizontal strips across the chest to prevent sagging, and two vertical strips beside the opening of the stays to reinforce the row of eyelets (see figure 3.22, no. 4). Once these steps were complete, the tailor ironed the stays inside and out to adhere the layers of cloth to each other and impart the proper rounded shape to the whalebone strips.

At this point, the stays were ready for a preliminary fitting. During the fitting process, Garsault indicated, a tailor should examine "with scrupulous attention" every inch of the client's torso in order to ascertain any faulty areas. He should ask the client if she (or he in the case of a child) felt uncomfortable or pinched anywhere, marking such places carefully with tailors' chalk. He should also note the proper placement of the shoulder-strap fastenings. Once the tailor performed necessary alterations, a female needleworker anchored the whalebone strips in place with strong rows of cross-stitches. Areas subject to greater wear and tear received additional rows of stitches. When warranted, Garsault remarked, the tailor could add more strips of whalebone across the chest to contain the bosom further. He then bordered the top and bottom of the stays with a band of fine buckram to prevent fraying and sagging. Another strip of whalebone was sewn over the area covering each shoulder blade to flatten it as much as possible (for these steps, see figure 3.22 no. 5).

To provide a smooth fit, the tailor filled empty spaces between the whalebone strips on the chest with paper or buckram. He followed the same procedure next to the eyelets, finally covering the entire area with a piece of buckram. After verifying the fit once more, the tailor wetted the cloth on the inside of the stays and ironed it carefully to mold all of the whalebone pieces into place. The final steps consisted of lining the stays on the inside and outside with fine silk or linen cloth, and sewing a strip of cloth down the front to form a pocket for the busk. With the addition of four hooks at the bottom for attaching a skirt, the garment was ready for delivery.[62]

Prices

Once they delivered a finished dress or a set of stays, seamstresses and tailors began the long process of securing payment for their work. The prices they charged varied according to a number of factors. Worried about the instability of prices in the garment trades in the years after the 1720 plague, the Parlement of Provence ordered the Aix tailors' guild in 1726 to publish an official price scale for different articles of clothing. In a guild assembly, one official protested that this was impossible, given "the variation that there always is in the fabrication of suits, the rise in food prices, the scarcity of journeymen, who [therefore] receive higher payment, and because sometimes it is necessary to make several suits in one night, so that the journeymen are paid more."[63] When the Parlement persisted in its demands, guild leaders enjoined the masters setting the rates to take into account the postplague rise in journeymen's wages, the complexity of current suit styles, the increase in rents for homes and boutiques, as well as the heavy dues imposed on masters to meet royal taxation.

A similar range of factors affected seamstresses' prices. As *The English*

Book of Trades stated in 1804: "The price charged for making dresses cannot be estimated: it varies with the article to be made; with the reputation of the maker; with her situation in life; and even with the season of the year."[64] Few concrete examples of prices exist. In the first years of the eighteenth century, an anonymous Parisian seamstress recorded in a daily journal her fees for making dresses, skirts, dressing gowns, and other items. She charged three or four livres for making a mantua-skirt ensemble, one to three livres for a skirt, and three livres for a lined corset. She usually did not furnish the cloth for her clients' dresses, but she did procure the small amounts of material used for the lining and decorations. On December 29, 1704, for example, she charged a client four livres for making a silk mantua and skirt as well as six and a half livres for the cloth she used to line them.[65]

In 1735, mistress seamstress Gaillard charged her noble client Madame Bercy de Conflans six livres for making a dress and between one and a half and three livres for the matching skirt. Twenty years later, she continued to charge de Conflans the same rates for making skirts and dresses. By 1764, Madame de Conflans had switched to a new seamstress, mistress Saulmont, who billed the noblewoman only six livres for a dress and skirt ensemble. These examples reveal an extreme stagnation of prices across the eighteenth century. Once a craftswoman and her customer agreed on a fee, it was apparently very difficult to raise it. Given the sharp increase in the cost of living over the eighteenth century, seamstresses would have experienced a real drop in earnings, which they seem to have passed on to their workers in stagnant wage rates.[66]

Another group of seamstresses provides additional information on labor prices. Between 1772 and 1775, the seamstress Tripier charged clients approximately eight livres for making a dress and between six and nine livres for a dressing gown. On another occasion, however, she charged ten livres merely for making the lining of a dress.[67] Mistress Marguerite Gaillard charged two livres and eight sous in 1763 for making two corsets.[68] A third colleague paid an outworker one livre and one sol for the painstaking labor involved in quilting a petticoat.

Tailors appear to have received higher remuneration for their services, although it is difficult to compare the time and effort involved in making a woman's dress and a man's suit. After waiting in vain for acquittal of his bill, master tailor Edouard Linch presented his client Patrick Farrely with a formal demand for payment. According to this document, Linch charged Farrely eighteen livres for making a full suit, including jacket, waistcoat, and breeches. If ordered separately, each element of the suit cost six livres. When he included braid decorations on the jacket, Linch raised a suit's price to twenty-four livres. The Aix guild set labor prices in 1726 at very similar rates. For a complete suit ensemble, they evaluated the tailor's work at twenty-seven livres. A twelve-year-old child's suit would cost five livres, a priest's long robe seven livres, and a parlementary magistrate's robe eight livres.[69]

Both tailors and seamstresses charged almost as much for alterations as they did for making a new garment. In September 1741, mistress Gaillard charged Madame de Conflans four livres for fixing the pleats and replacing the decorations on a dress, and for shortening the matching skirt. On the same day, she billed the noblewoman two livres for mending a blue-and-white damask dress and shortening its skirt, as well as three livres for repleating and redecorating another dress. The tailor Linch also performed mending and alterations, charging his client two livres and ten sous for repairing a suit, and six livres for altering and repairing a coat and breeches, which included the cost of the thread and silk he used. Clients had their garments altered or retrimmed to repair problems of wear-and-tear or fit and to keep them in line with evolving fashions in decorations or style. They saved a great deal on the price of fabric that they would have had to purchase for a new garment, but they spent almost the same amount on labor costs.

So far, I have examined prices charged for labor alone. Prices for dresses including both labor and fabric were many times higher. In the early 1770s, the seamstress Tripier usually charged her clients for the whole dress, including fabric and fabrication. Tripier charged the most for dresses of fine taffeta cloth, selling them for 144 to 155 livres each. Her clients must have found these prices prohibitively expensive, because only three out of fifty-two dresses she sold were made from this fabric. More frequently, she made dresses from *petit taftas,* a less expensive form of taffeta. Dresses in this cloth varied in price from 72 to 130 livres.[70] Given their expensive price, these dresses probably came as ensembles with matching skirts. Tripier also made many gowns out of linen and cotton, fabrics that became increasingly popular during the 1760s and 1770s. The most expensive were made of high-quality calico and sold for 90 to 100 livres, while those of lower-quality printed cotton fetched between 60 and 84 livres. Muslin dresses, probably resembling the simple chemise dress worn by Marie-Antoinette in Vigée Lebrun's portrait, cost between 61 and 66 livres.

Tripier's journal, like Barbara Johnson's, reveals the shrinking cost of the dress styles of the late eighteenth century. A cotton dress was half the price of a taffeta one, permitting women to buy more dresses or to begin buying custom-made garments for the first time. These gowns, however, were still extremely expensive in relation to female salaries and the cost of living. In probate inventories, seamstresses paid an average rent of 162 livres a year, barely more than the most expensive dresses Tripier sold. Even her cheapest cotton dress represented the better part of a year's wages to a working girl. Most Parisian women, including seamstresses themselves, could not afford the price of the fabric contained in new dresses.

Fashion Merchants

However extravagant for a shopgirl, the dress prices quoted in Tripier's journal bear no comparison to the amounts that noblewomen, particularly court aristocrats, paid for their elaborate dresses and for the ribbons, rhinestones, and tassels that decorated them. Mademoiselle Eloffe served as a fashion merchant to Marie-Antoinette and to many court noblewomen during the 1770s and 1780s. Her account book shows that the trimmings on a courtier's dress could cost ten times more than Tripier's most expensive dresses. The most elaborate decorations Eloffe provided were for dresses worn during a noblewoman's first presentation at court. The dress worn by madame du Boscage during this ceremony in 1787, for example, amply illustrates the tremendous luxury and expense involved. To decorate the dress, Eloffe provided three and a half aunes of crêpe cloth embroidered with gold and silver thread at one hundred livres an aune, three aunes of silver fringe, rhinestoned ribbons, and five and a half aunes of ribbon embroidered in blue spangle wreaths. All of these items were used in adorning the gown. Eloffe also supplied fine gold tassels and rhinestoned ribbons for the dress bodice and nine and a half aunes of lace for the bodice sleeves and collar, as well as bracelets and a stole. The dress skirt's trimmings consisted of embroidered ribbon, silver-hued fringe and tassels, and three aunes of crêpe with gold-colored dots. The total cost of these decorations exceeded 1,400 livres, including 96 livres for making the decorations and 15 livres for making the bodice's lace sleeves.[71]

The comtesse de Narbonne's presentation dress offers another example of extremely ostentatious display. In April 1787, Eloffe supplied the countess with two and a half aunes of crêpe embroidered with wreaths of silver spangles and bordered with silver sequins for decorating the petticoat, at a price of 300 livres. She also furnished two and a half aunes of crêpe embroidered with silver stripes to trim the dress skirt, six aunes of silver sequined ribbons embroidered with silver wreaths, rhinestones, silver tassels, a rhinestoned and tasseled belt, nine aunes of lace for the bodice sleeves, a lace collar, lace and gauze for several headdresses, flowers, two hundred pins, and a fan. The total bill came to 1,918 livres, including the 96 livre fee for making the decorations.[72]

These astronomical prices help explain why fashion merchants became such prosperous and influential figures within the Parisian luxury trades, while seamstresses occupied a much more modest place. Even apart from these once-in-a-lifetime dresses, noble and rich bourgeois women spent much more in the fashion merchant's boutique than they ever did for their seamstresses' services. Dress decorations, bonnets, shawls, and other items of finery were many times more expensive than the labor provided by a needleworker. The cachet of "fashion" allowed ambitious merchants to add a stiff mark-up to their products, further increasing their profits. These figures also offer insight into the temptation of high-level prostitution for fashion merchants' shopgirls. They spent their days and nights sewing extraordinarily lavish items of clothing, which they could never hope to wear.[73]

In addition to making and selling dress decorations, Eloffe also sold finished articles, such as neckerchiefs (*fichus*) and mantillas. On one occasion, she charged Marie-Antoinette sixteen livres and five sous for three and a quarter aunes of Italian gauze to make two large neckerchiefs and six sous each for making them. She also charged her six livres for the fabrication of a mantilla and three livres for making a petticoat.[74] Eloffe does not appear, however, to have branched into the production of women's dresses. Her journal does not record instances where she actually made dresses for Marie-Antoinette or other court women. Instead, she concentrated on the much more lucrative activity of making decorations for dresses and selling the ribbons, lace, gauze, rhinestones, and feathers used in their fabrication.

The account books of the most celebrated eighteenth-century fashion merchant tell a similar story. Rose Bertin's clientele was composed of many hundred men and women, including European royalty, distinguished French and foreign nobles, American elites, and, most notoriously, queen Marie-Antoinette. Bertin was known to contemporaries as the "minister of fashion" in reference to her easy access to, and perceived influence over, the queen. Her reportedly haughty and arrogant demeanor scandalized and amused elite observers, who had never seen a mere shopkeeper take on such airs.[75] The account records that Bertin left behind reveal that her work consisted of supplying the labor and materials involved in trimming dresses, and purveying hats, bonnets, ribbons, lace, neckerchiefs, shawls, and a myriad of other items worn on women's heads and shoulders. She occasionally furnished dresses to her clients, but these were usually for Marie-Antoinette herself or other royal clients.

Purveying finished dresses was therefore an exceptional aspect of Bertin's trade, undertaken for her most important clients. Indeed, most clients would have found it less expensive to have dresses made by their own seamstress, using Bertin's services merely for the final trimmings. Moreover, because clients would have the same dress refinished two, three, or even four times to prolong its fashionable life, it makes sense that Bertin would have decorated dresses much more often than she made them.[76]

Credit

Credit relations were universal in the garment trades. From the highest noblewoman to the lowliest shopgirl, seamstresses' clients almost never paid the full price of the garments they ordered. Instead, they made a small initial down payment and promised to pay the rest in installments. To keep track of these payments, needleworkers relied on a common set of simple bookkeeping techniques. Most kept bound journals in which they entered a daily record of sales and credit installments. Mistress Françoise Ducable, who died in 1782, kept "a little register covered in cardboard on which it appears the deceased marked credits for the works and merchandise of her estate of dress seamstress."[77] They also kept receipts and other records of payments made to suppliers, sometimes using a second journal for this purpose. For example, Marie Jacqueline Ouvrard kept a book covered in parchment in which she noted merchandise ordered from a fashion merchant.[78]

In their account books, seamstresses recorded the date, type of good or service rendered, price, and the client's name. When dealing with first-time clients, they often included the woman's address as well. For example, Tripier noted that a client named Mademoiselle Nicolet lived in a building on the rue Vieille du Temple, on the second floor at the back. Another customer, Madame Perpignan, lived on the rue Planche Mibray on the third floor of the building occupied by the baker Sieur Latour. Other first-time customers were noted as the sister, servant, or daughter of a regular client.[79] Beside each name, seamstresses recorded the details of the credit agreement, including the initial down payment and the schedule for installments. Many asked their clients to sign the page as a guarantee of good faith. Madame Perpignan wrote on July 22, 1774: "I acknowledge having received from Madame Tripier a finished dress and its skirt for the price of ninety livres at a rate of nine livres per week." [80] Like Tripier, conscientious seamstresses recorded each payment on the same page, directly beneath the record of the initial transaction. They often kept a separate page for each client to avoid confusion. When payments were complete, they drew a slash or cross across the entries. Finished account books were preserved as proof of outstanding accounts and as a record of business activities.

Most mistresses wrote in a crude script and they frequently made mathematical mistakes; however, they possessed the intellectual skills necessary to function as independent businesswomen in a trade that relied on credit. Their abilities distinguished them from dependent workers, many of whom were illiterate. At her death in 1754, Marie Germaine Pelée's two live-in workers stated that "they do not know precisely what could be due to the said succession by the people hitherto named or what could be due for works. [It] will result from the memoranda that the defunct took care to keep and that they presume should be found underneath the said seals." [81] Only one of the two could read and write. Literacy and numeracy might also set apprentices apart from workers. Many apprentices possessed basic reading and writing skills, which gave them precious advantages over older, more experienced, but illiterate workers. These girls might hope to be hired as permanent employees and eventually establish an independent business, unlikely aspirations for those who could not read or write.

Despite the care with which seamstresses recorded installment agreements, most of their clients failed to observe the fixed schedule. Seamstresses usually accepted this failure, as long as clients continued to make occasional payments. If a long period of time passed without any payment at all, they would take measures to ensure their account. As a first step they added up the total amount due and asked the client to sign a written statement of the account. They carefully conserved these documents, known as *arrêtés de compte,* as legal proof of the sums due them. If another long delay passed, a seamstress might write to her customer to request satisfaction of all or part of the bill, renewing this correspondence as often as necessary. On July 14, 1749, mistress Gaillard wrote to her noble client de Bercy: "The Need in which I find myself for money has made me take the Liberty of asking you for a 120-livre down payment. I count on your goodness and that you will not find it wrong [of me]." Gaillard was fortunate in receiving a favorable and relatively rapid response from her client.[82]

Many of her colleagues were less fortunate and found themselves obliged to take legal action against recalcitrant customers. When clients failed to pay over a period of years, mistresses could seek a sentence from the Châtelet of Paris ordering the defaulter to pay the sums due, plus interest and legal expenses. This was an extreme step. Seamstresses initiated legal proceedings only when convinced of the impossibility of collecting the bill by informal means. The maintenance of long-lasting client relations obliged them to accept extremely tardy bill collection, particularly from noble clients whose lavish spending often depended on extended credit.

Accounts recorded in seamstresses' probate inventories testify to their willingness to accord credit. Mistress Jeanne Dollé billed the duchesse de Retz 894 livres in 1723; in 1728 she received a sum of 89 livres as partial payment, followed by another 64 livres. When Dollé died in 1735, the duchess still owed her 741 livres. Prior to her death, Dollé had initiated legal proceedings against the duchess, who ultimately paid another sum of 170 livres to Dollé's estate.[83] Françoise LeClerc, seamstress to the queen of Louis XV, collected the most impressive record of credit.[84] The comtesse de Maurepas, for example, opened an account with LeClerc in 1728. By 1737, the countess's bill had reached 2,584 livres. She made three partial payments on the account, furnishing 467 livres in October 1737, 382 in August 1738, and 666 in March 1739. When LeClerc died in December 1739, the countess still owed her 1,981 livres. In another example, the princesse de Montauban's account with LeClerc amounted to some 518 livres in September 1735. LeClerc received two payments, one in July 1737 of 192 livres and another in August 1739 of 100 livres. The elevated sums involved suggest that LeClerc may have furnished raw materials as well as labor to her noble clients.[85]

Although she must have suffered from tardy payments, LeClerc frequently began new accounts for clients who were still in arrears on old ones. The marquise de Curze, for example, patronized LeClerc from 1723 until the seamstress's death in 1739. LeClerc added up her account with the noblewoman on at least three occasions: once in 1729 when the marquise owed 1,023 livres, again in 1737 when she owed 1,071, and finally in 1738 when she owed 254 livres. The marquise made twelve payments each of 24 livres on this account between October 1738 and November 1739. LeClerc began a fourth account with the marquise in January of 1739, which totaled

66 livres at the time of the seamstress's death. The hope of eventual payment, as well as the prestige of noble patronage, undoubtedly convinced LeClerc to renew credit relations with such clients. The woman's patience, however, was not infinite. In January 1733, she obtained a police sentence condemning the marquise de Farre to pay an account of 700 livres, covering the period 1715 to 1723.

Death severed the tightrope walk between the prestige of a noblewoman's custom and the fear of bankruptcy. When a seamstress died, her heirs were unlikely to continue her trade and had nothing to lose in adopting an aggressive attitude. Some seamstresses formed their own plans for such money after their deaths. At the time of her death, Louise Lange had begun making two dresses of white silk with stripes and flowers for the marquise de Torigny. Lange left written instructions for her executor regarding 300 livres that the marquise owed her, requesting that the money be used to pay for an annual mass for her soul. She donated the surplus to the poor of her parish.[86] A client's death also liberated seamstresses from constraint in demanding payment, if they did not work for other members of the family. In December 1733, mistress seamstress Catherine Marguerite Emery appeared at the application of police seals on the affairs of her deceased noble client, Marguerite Marincot. Emery demanded satisfaction of her bill of nine livres, which dated from two years earlier.[87]

When seamstresses insisted on payment, they sometimes encountered not only passive resistance, but outright intimidation and even physical violence. On July 4, 1760, Marie Anne Maurice, a seamstress living on rue Saint-Honoré, appeared before the police to make a complaint against Demoiselle Gallodier. Some days previously, Maurice had gone to Gallodier's home to ask her to pay a bill. In response, Gallodier and her chambermaid became verbally and then physically aggressive. Her lackey threw Maurice to the ground, kicking and punching her. Finally, he threw Maurice out the door and into the street. The *commissaire* noted that the bruises and cuts covering Maurice's face and body testified to the abuse she suffered.[88]

Prior to Maurice's visit, another tradeswoman met with the same treatment. On May 2, Françoise Ruch, a linen-draper, went to request settlement of her account with Gallodier. Her bill included 93 livres dating from January 1760, another 153 livres, as well as a loan of 50 livres in cash. Ruch had received only 12 livres since February and felt it was time for another installment. Gallodier responded by insulting and taunting the woman. When Ruch declared that she would not leave without being paid, Gallodier hit her with a fire shovel. This incident also ended with the ejection of the tradeswoman and a complaint to the police.[89]

Despite their numerous difficulties, lengthy credit relations had positive aspects. They created ties of patronage and moral obligation that could benefit seamstresses, allowing them to appeal to their well-connected clients in times of need. The marquise de Montbrun wrote to police officials several times on behalf of her former linen-draper, jailed for participating in the Jansenist convulsionary movement.[90] In 1776, Madame LeNoir, the wife of the lieutenant general of police, wrote to Guillaume-François Joly de Fleury, the procurator general of the Parisian Parlement to request that he accord an interview to her seamstress. Joly de Fleury agreed to meet with the seamstress, who came as a representative of her guild to protest its merger with another guild. The procurator general heard her out and promised to do what he could to help. Although he did not prevent the merger, the fact that such an elevated figure was willing to meet with the seamstress testifies to the efficacy of her patronage ties.[91]

Conclusion

A close examination of seamstresses' working techniques helps explain the trade's attraction for working women. The necessary tools of the trade were few and relatively inexpensive. Equipped with a needle, thread, scissors, an iron, and a thimble, a woman could set up shop as an independent seamstress. She did not require capital for stocks of cloth or to rent a boutique, and she could manage all of the steps of production on her own if necessary. Newcomers to the trade could acquire sufficient skill to be hired as workers during a three-year apprenticeship. After only two more years of work experience, they possessed the qualifications necessary to become mistresses and set up independent businesses. These characteristics of the trade encouraged thousands of women to undergo training and seek admission to the guild across the eighteenth century. They also rendered it easy prey for illegal workers, who infiltrated the trade in large numbers.

Despite the low-cost and low-skill aspects of this occupation, Enlightenment observers probably underestimated the degree of technical proficiency necessary to excel as a seamstress. Making elaborate formal gowns required a high level of skill and experience. Disguising bodily faults and accentuating good features also constituted a stringent test of capacity. Needleworkers were divided by their level of proficiency and experience, by their degree of literacy and numeracy, as well as by their ability to acquire and project a sense of taste and style. Those with rudimentary skills could find employment making simple garments and mending clothes for the poor families in their neighborhood. High-level seamstresses had to master more complicated techniques and demonstrate imaginative flair in suggesting dress styles and decorations or in performing alterations for their clients.

Seamstresses occupied an important place in the complex and interconnected networks of Parisian garment, cloth, and utensils trades. They were regular clients of merchant mercers, purchasing cloth, thread, needles, and other supplies on a continual basis. They ordered other raw and finished materials from linen-drapers and fashion merchants, and subcontracted work to specialized stitchers and cutters. Cycles of production in the seamstresses' trade must have produced wider ripple effects, strongly perceptible to the merchants who supplied them. Their capacity to form relations with suppliers, however, was limited by the fact that customers usually bought cloth directly from the merchant's boutique, thereby preventing seamstresses from putting a mark-up on cloth or developing beneficial commercial relationships with merchants. Because the value of cloth far outweighed the value of a woman's labor, seamstresses occupied an inferior position in the garment trades. When new techniques for advertising and distributing emerged, they could profit relatively little from them.

Despite these limitations, seamstresses' ties to elite clients could be long-lasting and advantageous. Aristocratic women followed the whims of fashion and adopted a succession of changing dress styles, but they could be very loyal to the women who made their clothes. The same needleworker might make dresses and mend garments for a noblewoman for twenty years or more. Elite customers always wielded the upper hand in these relations. They refused to allow seamstresses to raise their prices over decades of service and obliged them to accept very tardy—and partial—payment of their accounts. Nevertheless, credit relations were not all bad for seamstresses. They may have suffered anxiety and deprivation while awaiting payment—hardly daring to demand cash outright from their noble clients—yet seamstresses also benefited from the ongoing relations generated by the credit system. When faced with crises that surpassed their meager resources, they might turn to a long-time client for help. Noble women and their seamstresses exchanged more than fashion tips or idle chatter, they also formed gender-specific ties of patronage, which could mitigate the legal, social, and economic powerlessness of the working woman.

Based on the topography of the trade outlined in the previous three chapters, in part two I place the seamstresses' trade in the wider context of labor regulation, the guild system, and the state from 1675 to 1791. Seamstresses' incorporation in guilds was an essential aspect of the trade's success in the garment trades across the eighteenth century. Their interaction with guilds, moreover, adds a new dimension to our understanding of women's relationship to the state in early modern France. When given the opportunity, women proved eager to join guilds and were capable of administering their own corporate institutions.

PART TWO

Making the Guilds

FOUR

The Royal Government, Guilds, and the

Seamstresses of Paris, Normandy, and Provence

Scholars of women's work have tended to agree that female labor opportunities declined in Europe from the late Middle Ages through the end of the seventeenth century. According to this argument, as guilds grew in strength across the early modern period they gradually excluded women, with the active support of local and royal authorities. Those who retained guild privileges, notably masters' wives and widows, found their privileges drastically reduced over time. These limitations were but one aspect of an overall loss of independence for women, who became increasingly confined by law and male family authority. As Natalie Zemon Davis has written: "Women suffered for their powerlessness in both Catholic and Protestant lands in the late sixteenth to eighteenth centuries as changes in marriage laws restricted the freedom of wives even further, as female guilds dwindled, as the female role in middle-level commerce and farm direction contracted, and as the differential between male and female wages increased."[1]

The seamstresses pose a striking challenge to the thesis of a linear decline in women's economic and legal status during the early modern period. In 1675, when the triumph of absolutism, corporatism, and patriarchal marriage legislation might lead one to expect the nadir of women's experience, one discovers instead the creation of new independent seamstresses' guilds in Paris and Rouen. Moreover, after this date female needleworkers in many provincial cities and towns became members of tailors' guilds. By the 1750s, seamstresses held the title of guild mistress in at least fifteen cities and towns in the regions of Brittany, Normandy, Provence, Ile-de-France, Picardy, and Auvergne. In all of these cases, seamstresses were allowed to work for women and children only, and were explicitly prohibited from working for men. Using the cities of Paris, Caen, and Marseilles as case studies, in this chapter I seek to explain and account for the guild status achieved by French seamstresses and show its evolution over time.

A range of factors was responsible for the entry of seamstresses into the guild system. Among the most important was the royal government's efforts, under the ministry of Jean-Baptiste Colbert, to encourage and rationalize the French economy in the 1670s. The decision to award a guild to the Parisian seamstresses thus belonged to a wider effort to extend corporate association to hitherto unorganized sectors of the economy. The choice of the seamstresses, however, was not accidental. In defiance of the tailors' guild monopoly, seventeenth-century seamstresses had established themselves as the most important labor force in the production of made-to-measure women's and children's clothing. Legalizing their work promised to remove a source of dissension from the labor market and provide a new outlet for the domestic cloth industries that Colbert was eager to foster. This female trade was also large and coherent enough to support the burden of incorporation. Encouraged by the strong cultural association between sewing and femininity, women had streamed into the seamstresses trade during the first three quarters of the seventeenth century.

Gender was both crucial and tangential to the seamstresses' inclusion in guilds. By the mid-seventeenth century, a strong sexual division of labor already characterized the garment trades. Female needleworkers produced articles of clothing for women and children, while most tailors specialized in men's clothing. When it brought seamstresses into the corporate system, the royal government in some ways merely institutionalized the preexisting sexual division of labor. The king did not sanction the guild's creation because of new ideas about women and work; instead the royal government used ostensibly natural sexual divisions to divide a growing trade sector equitably. By granting legal and institutional status to this sexual division of labor, however, royal administrators inadvertently created a new and influential model of sexual difference. This model suggested that a woman's sex should determine all aspects of the work she performed, from the products she made to the people she worked with to the clients she served. Appropriate "women's work" was intrinsically and essentially tied to femininity. These were not new ideas, but rarely had they received the force of royal privilege and the full power of the law to enforce them.

The Parisian seamstresses' guild was thus born of the intersection of administrative, socioeconomic, and cultural factors. Once it was established in 1675, the guild became a model for reorganizing the garment trades in cities across France. For provincial seamstresses, the Parisian example was a source of inspiration, emboldening them to seek expanded corporate privileges. When they arbitrated conflicts between tailors and seamstresses, administrators also looked to the Parisian example, although they had to compromise between central initiatives and local guild traditions and practices.

Corporate Privilege, the Guilds, and the Royal Government

Guilds represented a small proportion of work in Old Regime France. In the rural villages where 85 percent of French people lived, peasants and craftsmen labored entirely outside of the guild system. Even within larger towns and cities, guilds encompassed a minority of the workforce. Most men and women worked in nonguild trades as domestic servants, unskilled manual laborers, or vendors of food and other small goods. In Paris in the 1720s, guild masters totaled some 32,000 in a population of approximately 500,000.[2]

Despite their numerical inferiority, trade associations wielded considerable economic, social and even political power in seventeenth- and eighteenth-century France. The guilds were *corps,* part of the constellation of corporate groups that included town councils, judicial officers, religious orders, and academic bodies. Like other corps, most guilds owed their existence to the royal title embodied in their "letters patent." These letters endowed a corporation with a collective legal personality, enabling it to own property, take loans, and initiate lawsuits. They also established a guild's monopoly over a particular sector of activity, along with the legal authority to enforce it.[3]

The logic behind corporate privilege was one of reciprocity between the king and his corps. Each group provided a crucial branch of public service; in return its members gained the right of quasiautonomous self-government, including the ability to meet in assemblies, elect leaders, and adopt regulations. In theory, the members of a corporate body were bound together by a collective spirit, which united their own particular interests to the wider public good. The guilds' domain of service was the world of work, the vast arena that constituted the meaning and the destiny of the Third Estate. Each guild received a detailed set of economic privileges. These included exclusive rights to produce and/or sell certain goods, ranging from buttons to pastries, from cabinets to custom-made articles of clothing. Guild masters enjoyed access to restricted markets in raw materials and labor, as well as the capacity to train apprentices, hire workers, and open a public shop. A master's corporate credentials served as a form of collateral for creditors and reassured potential customers. With its pooling of resources and administrative structure, the guild enforced joint regulations and prevented outside encroachment.

In exchange for these privileges, the king held guilds responsible for the smooth functioning of their sectors of economic activity. He expected them to supply the public with a sufficient quantity of high-quality goods at controlled prices. Guild leaders were required to enforce their regulations, and in particular to visit masters' workshops twice annually to ensure that they maintained adequate standards of production. The royal government also relied on guilds to organize and regulate the urban labor market. Masters transmitted trade skills to their apprentices and provided employment for the thousands of skilled workers who populated French cities.

In Paris and major provincial cities such as Rouen, Nantes, Bordeaux, and Toulouse, guild masters used these prerogatives to establish impressive manufacturing and commercial enterprises. They dominated rich merchant and luxury trades whose products circulated through local, regional, national, and international distribution networks. The six Parisian merchant guilds, collectively known as the Six Corps, conducted a lucrative and extensive trade in dry goods, furs, gold, and woolen cloth, among other items. The most prestigious artisanal corporations, which produced and sold their own specialty items, could rival the powerful Six Corps. By the time of Louis XIV, guild masters had helped make France the center of European luxury production, turning out the finest cloth, carriages, court dresses, and other goods for an international market.

Beyond their economic importance, the corporations also filled crucial social and political functions. Guild masters garnered a distinctive status and prestige in their communities from their corporate status. Along with other privileged subjects, they viewed society as a hierarchical collection of corporate bodies, which together guaranteed the harmony, stability, and cohesion of the social order. Enthroned at the summit of the Great Chain of Being, the king ruled over, recognized, and reconciled these collective entities, rather than individual subjects. As the attorney general of the Parisian Parlement Antoine-Louis Séguier proclaimed in what has become the most famous defense of corporate society:

All your subjects, Sire, are divided into as many different corps as there are different estates in the kingdom. The clergy, the nobility, the sovereign courts, the lower tribunals, the officers attached to these tribunals, the universities, the financial companies, all present, in all parts of the State, existing corps which can be seen as the links in a great chain, of which the first lies in Your Majesty's hand, as chief and sovereign administrator of everything that constitutes the corps of the nation.[4]

From the sixteenth century on, the royal government increasingly insisted on the crown as sole creator and supreme arbiter of the corporate system. A series of edicts denied the right of municipal or regional authorities to create new guilds or to confirm existing corporate privileges. The crown used its control of the guilds as a means to disseminate royal economic directives to craftsmen and merchants; guilds also served as an intermediary to transmit social and political ideologies to the world of work. These paradigms included both the internal solidarity that should prevail among corps members and the hierarchical relations of the workshop. Masters' strict supervision of their workers and apprentices served to repress the disorder and debauchery believed to be inherent in young men, thereby producing socially useful and disciplined workers. For the majority who labored outside the corporate system, the guilds were to stand as a paradigm of discipline, organization, and orderly labor relations.

Corporations were also charged with representing French society to the king who embodied it. By the end of the sixteenth century, the royal government had largely stripped the guilds of the role in municipal government they had possessed during the Middle Ages. Nevertheless, trade corporations continued to play important consultative and even participatory roles in municipal and royal administration. In some towns and cities, for example, guild leaders maintained ex officio participation in municipal councils, as was the case, most prominently, of the Six Corps in Paris.[5] In 1789, the guilds reenacted for the last time their centuries-old role as electoral bodies in elections of the Estates General. This was the case in provincial cities, but not in Paris.

Last, but certainly not least, the guilds constituted a crucial fiscal resource for the crown. Their officers often collected regular taxes from members on the king's behalf, such as the *capitation* and the *dixième de l'industrie*. As the source of all privilege, the king also expected a concrete return at exceptional moments of royal crisis or festivity. These sporadic payments culminated in the creation and forced sale of corporate offices in the late seventeenth and early eighteenth centuries. Introduced in order to finance Louis XIV's foreign wars, the purchase of these offices would leave French guilds deeply indebted by the end of his long reign. In the "symbiotic relationship" that bound the monarchy and the corps, each side gained concrete economic benefits from the other, as well as broader social and political legitimacy. Power was always tilted toward the crown, which extracted enormous amounts of money over time. Nevertheless, the state's broad-based reliance on the guilds gave the relationship a certain duality that has escaped many modern observers.[6]

Based on these common principles, the everyday world of the trades harbored a confounding degree of diversity, ambiguity, and differentiation. All guilds possessed of royal letters patent shared the same corporate status, but vast hierarchies of wealth and prestige divided them. From the mid-fifteenth century on, the merchant Six Corps enjoyed the official supremacy of the guild system. They marched at the head of all guild processions and represented the Parisian guilds in certain political contexts. The remaining 118 trade corporations spanned a wide range of economic sectors, sizes, and fortunes. In 1691, the royal government drew up a table dividing the Parisian guilds into four categories, ranging from the richest and most prestigious to the most humble and insignificant.[7]

The distinction between guild and nonguild trades, moreover, was much less clear than royal or corporate rhetoric might imply. Through much of the seventeenth century, distinct jurisdictions existed within the city of Paris that licensed nonguild artisans to work within their territorial limits. These were the *lieux prétendus privilégiés,* areas of the city that claimed exceptional judicial, administrative, and fiscal status, based on old seigneurial or ecclesiastical domains. In addition, several outlying suburbs issued their own masterships. The royal government abolished most of these exceptional jurisdictions in the 1670s, obliging suburban masters to join Parisian guilds. The largest area of artisanal liberty, however, remained untouched. This was the faubourg Saint-Antoine, located to the east of Paris, which remained free of guild control throughout the Old Regime. It offered a zone of competition and free-for-all economic possibilities a mere half-hour walk from the center of Paris. Despite strict regulations forbidding commerce with the faubourg, Parisian guild artisans developed complex professional connections with it.[8]

While some artisans resisted the guild system, many others in unincorporated sectors fell under its ideological sway. Mimicking the assemblies held by formal guilds, they met together to discuss common problems and drafted collective rules for practicing their trade. In times of crisis they sent representatives to municipal or royal officials, hoping to be recognized as legitimate spokesmen for their trade. Regional Parlements and police officials sometimes granted them quasiguild status, thereby creating a gray zone of nonroyal corporations in defiance of royal efforts at centralized control.[9] Practitioners of nonguild trades, such as innkeepers or food vendors, were also required to register with and report periodically to police officials. Most unincorporated trades therefore fell under some form of supervision and regulation. Local and regional administrators' urge to regulate, supervise, and control—to "police" in the full Old Regime sense—touched every level of the world of work.

As in so many other aspects of French life, Paris was the practical and ideological center of the guild world. Given its economic, political, and cultural importance, merchants and artisans from all regions looked to the Parisian example. Royal officials echoed this propensity, frequently requiring that provincial guilds utilize Parisian standards when they modified their statutes. Nevertheless, strong regional traditions and customs persisted. Historians have drawn the sharpest distinctions between the guild systems in northern and southern France. Guilds originated earlier and implanted themselves more firmly in the towns and cities of the north, while southern towns resisted the guild system through the medieval and early modern periods. Historian Maurice Agulhon has argued that the religious confraternity preexisted the guilds in Provence, and that, up to the eighteenth century, religious and sociable aspects of trade associations prevailed over economic ones.[10] Within these regional tendencies, guilds were also profoundly local institutions. Each municipality retained its particular traditions and institutions, inherited from centuries of economic life and negotiations with regional and royal authorities. These factors created a world of work crisscrossed by boundaries of law, economic specialization, individual self-interest, and local custom.

Women and Guilds in Seventeenth-Century France

Almost every woman engaged in economically productive work in Old Regime France. Like men, most women performed agricultural and domestic labor either on their own land, as sharecroppers, or as day laborers for richer peasants. Within the cities, domestic service employed the largest number of women, with servants of both sexes representing between 5 and 15 percent of the urban population.[11] Another large group of women worked as street or market traders, hawking vegetables, dairy products, fish, and other foodstuffs, or peddling trinkets, used bits of clothing, and other inexpensive articles. The least fortunate supplied their brute force in exchange for minimal wages, serving as porters or unskilled laborers on building sites.

With very few exceptions, French guilds restricted their membership to adult males of the Catholic religion. The vast majority of women were therefore excluded from the economic and social benefits of guild membership. This did not mean, however, that they had no place in the guild world. On the contrary, they were a constant presence in corporate workshops and boutiques, as mistresses in a handful of female guilds, as relatives of male guild members, or as hired workers. Women in the corporate sphere occupied the summit of female labor, possessing specialized skills that enhanced their family businesses or won them independent salaries.

Out of approximately sixty Parisian guilds prior to 1673, only two were composed exclusively of women.[12] These were the linen-drapers (*marchandes maîtresses toilières lingères canevassières*), who sold linen cloth and finished goods, and the hemp merchants (maîtresses linières filassières chanvrières), who sold flax, tow, and hemp. The linen-drapers' 1645 statutes gave them a quasimonopoly on the sale of all linen cloth and finished goods, which they traded in the Halle aux Toiles. Their statutes also authorized mistresses to travel or send representatives to all "cities or places where both new and used Linen Cloth, Sheets and Thread are made, fabricated, traded, and sold."[13] This was a striking affirmation in a society with strong legal and social restrictions on female autonomy.[14] With their control of the trade in linen cloth and goods, linen-drapers occupied a central position in the Parisian garment trades, employing hundreds of female workers to sew the finished articles they sold. The royal edict of 1691, which established a hierarchy of four "classes" of Parisian guilds, ranked them in the second level. A government study accompanying this edict estimated the guild to number four hundred mistresses, stating: "This community is very well-regulated and in good order; several mistresses conduct a quite considerable trade; those of the Palace and the Cemetery of Saints-Innocents are quite poor" (see figure 4.1).[15]

The *filassières* were merchants of flax, tow, and hemp, materials used in the manufacture of rope and coarse cloth. They served as intermediaries between provincial suppliers and weavers or ropemakers in the capital city. Like the linen-drapers, the *filassières* monopolized the import of

FIGURE 4.1 Linen-draper's shop. From the *Encyclopédie méthodique,* courtesy of the University of Illinois at Urbana-Champaign

these goods to Paris. The *filassières*' guild, however, was much smaller and played only a minor role in Parisian commerce. The report prepared for the 1691 edict described them as numbering only sixty mistresses, who practiced their trade conjointly with their husbands: "They are the ones who sell tow. And all of the mistresses of this trade . . . are wives of master rope-makers and these two trades are poor."[16] The edict of 1691 assigned them to the fourth class of Parisian guilds.

Apart from exclusively female guilds, a small number of Parisian corporations accepted both men and women. One was the guild of small grain and seed dealers (*maîtres-maîtresses grainiers-grainières*) created in 1595. The masters and mistresses of this corporation controlled the retail sale of seeds and legumes, as well as secondary cereals such as barley, millet, and buckwheat. Members of the Parisian bourgeoisie, traveling merchants, and master gardeners could conduct a wholesale trade in these items, but their goods were subject to inspection by corporate officials. In this guild, female mistresses shared the same status as male masters and its statutes reserved two of the four elected leadership positions for women. This was the only example of a truly mixed-sex guild in Paris.[17]

Women played a less prominent role in two unusual corporate bodies, the barbers-surgeons' community and the painters-sculptors' academy of Saint Luke. Female midwives composed a distinct and subordinate subdivision of the first group. They elected their own officials to oversee their affairs, but the surgeons controlled the corporation as a whole. Female membership candidates were examined "by the king's first surgeon or his lieutenant, by the four provosts of the College of Surgery, by the king's four surgeons at his Châtelet and by the four mid-wives' officials [*jurées*]."[18] The second organization, the painters-sculptors' academy of Saint Luke, also accepted female members. Its administrators appear to have been exclusively male, however, and women entered the community in relatively small numbers across the eighteenth century. In 1736, for example, only seven of sixty new members of the corporation were female. In 1762, nine out of fifty-seven were women.[19]

Outside Paris, the city of Rouen in Normandy possessed the only known additional women's guilds of seventeenth-century France. Rouen was a major industrial and commercial center, with perhaps the longest history of guild organization in France.[20] Drawing on this vigorous corporate tradition, women had obtained five independent guilds in this city, compared to only two in Paris. These included two linen-drapers' guilds—the new linen-drapers and the merchants of used linen—as well as the ribbon merchants (*marchandes rubannières*), the tow merchants, and the stocking- and feathersworkers (*maîtresses bonnetières-plumassières*).[21]

"Women's Work" in the Late Seventeenth Century: The Ambiguities of Law, Custom, and Practice

To judge from the short list of female guilds in Paris and Rouen, contemporary notions of appropriate "women's work" included needlework, textile preparation and sales, food vending, and assistance in childbirth. The feminine codification of such activities was not new, but an inheritance from classical and Christian traditions. In 1672, the playwright Molière used needlework to symbolize a traditional domestic and virtuous femininity, abandoned by outspoken *précieuses* of his day. In *Les Femmes savantes,* the "good bourgeois" Chrysale declares that in his father's time, women's "households were their learned speech, and their books a thimble, thread and needles." He thus contrasted the intellectual pretensions of contemporary women unfavorably with the modesty and homeliness of previous generations.[22]

If the gender codification of certain tasks was well known and deeply rooted, it was manifested in the late seventeenth century in a complicated mixture of law, custom, and practice. In some sectors, as we have seen, women drew on the acknowledged "femininity" of certain tasks to acquire independent guild privileges. This was a rare achievement. In most cities, professional needlework was off-limits to women, as were food-preparation trades and entire sectors of textile production. Male guilds enjoyed monopolies over these crafts, excluding women from activities nonetheless viewed as typically feminine. Every year, guild officials invested considerable time and money pursuing illegal female workers and the masters who hired them. In April 1692, for example, the Parisian embroiderers' guild successfully prosecuted a group of its own masters for having hired female workers (*fausse-ouvrières*). In the future, masters were enjoined to conform to guild rules and hire only qualified male workers. The fact that needlework and other skills were so strongly associated with femininity, therefore, did not entitle women to practice them for economic gain.[23]

As this example demonstrates, however, women could often be found as hired employees or illegal entrepreneurs in trades where they had no legal right to work. *Encyclopédie* engravings from the mid-eighteenth century depict women working alone or alongside male colleagues in a number of crafts ostensibly ruled by male guilds. These included the embroiderers, stockingmakers, manufacturers of buttons and decorative trim, fanmakers, enamelers, makers of artificial flowers, papermakers, wigmaker-barbers, saddlers, and makers of silk and golden thread. The editors of the *Encyclo-pédie* presented female labor in these trades as a simple fact, which apparently required no textual commentary.[24] Cultural notions of appropriate female tasks—sewing, making textiles and decorative objects, or decorating small objects—could thus overcome legal strictures, encouraging male employers to hire women in sectors where they were theoretically forbidden.

To make this picture even more complicated, one must also acknowledge the importance of female labor in myriad trades that had no association with typical "female" tasks. The wives and daughters of guild masters in many different trades participated in the family business on a daily basis, and their labor could be crucial to its survival. In many cases, the husband focused on productive labor with his journeymen, while his wife waited on customers and kept accounts. In other circumstances, wives and daughters played an integral role in the production of finished goods. Recognizing the importance of this contribution, some guilds authorized their members to hire their colleagues' female relatives. In 1692, the sentence pronounced against the embroiderers explicitly reaffirmed masters' capacity to hire other masters' daughters. Guilds also acknowledged women's stake in the family economy by allowing widows to continue their husbands' business in limited conditions and letting them transmit guild membership through marriage. Any task that women performed in the context of a family concern could therefore be considered an appropriate form of "women's work."

At least one late-seventeenth-century observer, conscious of the gaps among legal stricture, cultural codification, and practice, complained that male guilds should not be permitted to monopolize the few economic activities that were intrinsically appropriate for women:

> This liberty of certain works which do not depend on trade apprenticeship or the constraints of a guild [*jurande*] should be preserved even more for women and girls since we know the dangers to which necessity exposes the weakness of their sex[;] the greatest number know how to wash clothes, to do linen work, sewing[;] some make needlework tapestries, others mourning head-dresses, masks of hair[;] can we envy a widow, sometimes a lady, charged with several children, if she finds in one of these small works that with which to feed her family, and he who would wish to reduce them to begging for their bread in order to profit from the gift of such masterships would [he] not be entirely guilty?[25]

This passage underlines the ambiguity surrounding women's work in the late seventeenth century. The author did not problematize the question of how or why women performed certain tasks; he believed simply that women "knew" how to wash clothes or use a needle. His understanding of "women's work" drew on implicit assumptions about female skill, but he did not explicitly link them to women's essential or biological nature. Instead, he seemed to believe that these were skills women usually acquired in the course of everyday life. The moral focus of "women's work" therefore did not lie in a claim that women should perform certain types of activities, and refrain from others, at risk of violating their essential femininity. He argued merely that women who needed to earn a living should be permitted to exercise the few skills that they most likely already possessed. His goal was to provide succor to the poor and prevent the disorder and degradation inherent in idleness and poverty. These views reflected broader attitudes toward women's work in late-seventeenth-century France, in which the relationship between ideology, law, and practice remained largely unarticulated and unexamined. Notions of tradition and custom vied with explicit legal strictures, which in turn rubbed against everyday practices. Administrators and members of the world of work dealing with this complicated amalgam produced an array of local and strategic compromises without attempting to sort out the contradictions inherent in them.

Women both benefited and suffered from this situation. On the one hand, the gendered codification of trade skills enhanced women's economic position in the labor market, allowing them to acquire guild privileges or to work in certain trades regardless of legal restrictions. Women were likely to acquire the skills in sewing or textile production that enabled them to seek work in such trades, and male masters were likely to hire them, even though they could be prosecuted for doing so. On the other hand, the existence of recognized domains of "women's work" also discouraged women from entering other sectors. Their privileged relationship to certain trades thus stifled alternate possibilities of employment. Acquiring guild privileges in 1675, the seamstresses' trade perhaps best embodies the paradoxical strengths and weaknesses of "women's work." Once they acquired a guild their example did much to crystallize existing notions of "women's work," contributing to a new articulation and rigidification of the traditional sexual division of labor.

Seamstresses in Seventeenth-Century France

Prior to 1675, the Parisian garment trades furnished an excellent example of the clash between ideas about women's work and legal constraints obstructing it. Until this date, the tailors' guild held a monopoly over the production of made-to-measure clothing for men, women, and children. As their 1660 statutes stated, the guild held exclusive rights

> to make and sell all kinds of Suits and other ordinary articles of clothing, for the use of men, women and children, custom-made or ready-made, to display for sale, sell, [and] market them in all kinds of fabrics and leathers, and other materials if appropriate, and which may be appropriate in the future for the fabrication and perfection of the said garments.[26]

Despite this monopoly, seamstresses had established a strong presence in the trade by the mid-seventeenth century at least. The tailors' statutes indirectly acknowledged this situation by prohibiting masters from employing them: "No Master of the said trade may maintain two boutiques, nor receive any illegal worker [chambrelan], nor seamstress [couturière], nor associate himself with used-clothes dealers nor anyone but a master of the said craft and trade."[27] The statutes also forbade journeymen, at risk of imprisonment, from entering the employ of illegal tailors and seamstresses. A collection of several hundred seventeenth-century apprenticeship contracts held in Parisian notarial archives sheds further light on the seamstresses' trade before incorporation. The existence of this large group of contracts is in itself surprising, because seamstresses in this period constituted an illegal trade group. One might have expected formal, notarized contracts to be prohibitively public endeavors for artisans who risked prosecution for their work. Moreover, notaries should have refused to draw up the contracts, because their professional regulations forbade them from aiding illicit transactions. The large number of surviving contracts thus testifies to the vigor, size, and audacity of the seamstresses' trade prior to incorporation.[28]

To judge from these contracts, the pre-1675 seamstresses were already a strongly gender-specific trade group. The term *couturière* is found in apprenticeship contracts as an exclusively female trade appellation. No examples exist of male *couturiers,* although the tailors' guild had used the term up to the sixteenth century, and one scholar has found equal numbers of male *couturiers* and female *couturières* in sixteenth-century training contracts.[29] Moreover, the seamstresses accepted only girls and young women as their apprentices, never boys. The gender of the seamstresses' clients was not explicitly indicated in these apprenticeship contracts, but it is likely that most of them were women as well.

Pre-1675 apprenticeship contracts also reveal the emergence of distinct forms of specialization in the trade. Many women called themselves simply "seamstresses," while others specified that they were seamstresses in woolen cloth, in linens, in children's clothing, or in mourning garments. A small number of the women had family ties with tailors. Out of a sample of forty-five contracts, four seamstresses were married to Parisian master tailors, one to a tailor with no guild affiliation, and another woman's father was a master tailor. The rest were independent businesswomen who seem to have run their own enterprises.

Above all, the contracts underline the development of standardized training procedures in this trade. Seamstresses did not acquire skills at home from female relatives, but through several years of formal training outside the home. Relations between apprentice and mistress were governed by a notarized contract, which followed the standard guild model for apprenticeship agreements. Some seamstresses appeared several times, taking on a series of apprentices during careers of long duration.

Apprenticeship contracts thus reveal a well-established, large, and thriving female trade niche. At least two factors must explain the seamstresses' success in defying the tailors' monopoly. The first was the cultural association between women and needlework. Like embroidery, contemporaries may well have perceived seamstresses' work as a legitimate female activity and been willing to disregard legal strictures against it. The fact that seamstresses worked primarily for their own sex further situated their labor within the private, unregulated domain. The second factor aiding seamstresses was the sheer practical obstacles involved in expelling them from the trade. Because most worked in their own homes, guild officials would have faced severe difficulty in locating and prosecuting them. The lower wages that women received for their labor also made them more attractive than male tailors to their clients. Both ideological and practical considerations thus encouraged the success of seamstresses against the tailors.[30]

Colbert and the Edict of 1673

The catalyst for changes in the legal framework of the garment trades issued from events in the realm of high politics. In 1669, Controller General Jean-Baptiste Colbert issued a series of ordinances for the woolen cloth and textile dying industries. These ordinances contained detailed regulations for every step of production, which he intended to become a new national standard. He also took steps to encourage the domestic manufacture of high-quality silk cloth and lace, in order to eliminate expensive foreign importation and to provide new products for export. Turning from manufacture to commerce, Colbert promulgated a *Code du commerce* (commercial code) for trade and commerce across France in 1673, offering national rules for the conduct of merchants and traders. Throughout his tenure, the controller general took measures to encourage French economic development by establishing a handful of new commercial companies and granting exclusive monopolies on new techniques or products to royally sponsored manufacturers.[31]

In March 1673, Colbert trained his energies on the guild system, issuing a royal edict that ordered the incorporation of all unincorporated trades in cities and towns where guilds existed. The edict noted that artisans working outside the guild system suffered harassment and legal sanctions from local corporations. It also asserted that the lack of supervision over these trades posed a serious threat to public well-being. Without corporate officers to police production and commercial standards, consumers fell victim to shoddy merchandise and fraudulent trade practices. The extension of the guild system to all trades, the edict suggested, would resolve the problems of producer and consumer alike.[32]

This was not the first time that a French king had issued such an order; the edict's preamble recalled previous royal edicts of 1581 and 1597, which made similar demands. The edict of 1673, however, appeared at a time when the royal government held a particular interest in its success. Louis XIV had undertaken war with the Dutch in 1672 and he urgently required new sources of income to fight it. The edict stated explicitly that revenue generated by the new guilds would be directed "without any diversion towards the pressing expenses of the war."[33] Half of the fees paid by masters and mistresses in the new guilds would accrue to the royal treasury. As a supplementary measure, the 1673 edict ordered all existing guilds to update their statutes and pay to have them confirmed by the crown. A second edict assigned responsibility for these payments to municipal authorities. If the guilds could not furnish the necessary money, the municipalities would have to pay for them.

These stipulations underline the fiscal interests behind the 1673 edict. They have led some historians to dismiss it as a hasty and superficial grasp at an easily plundered source of revenue. It is clear, indeed, that monetary needs weighed heavily in the controller general's mind as he drafted the edict. Nevertheless, intense fiscal concerns do not preclude the existence of economic and administrative motives as well. Taxation and administrative reform had always been intertwined in the government's relationship with the guilds. With the 1673 edict, Colbert sought to generate new income as quickly as possible, but he also took the opportunity to increase efficiency and quality standards in production. This would not only help in the short-term war effort, it would further his twin goals of freeing France from foreign imports and expanding the country's export capacity. It would also help fulfil his desires to create new forms of employment for otherwise idle and impoverished French subjects, reduce social disarray and increase potential tax revenue. Ultimately, a strong French economy—favored by well-organized and regulated trades—would provide the foundation for a stronger monarchy. Seen in this perspective, the 1673 edict was wholly compatible with Colbert's other legislative projects, such as the *Code du commerce* or his series of regulations for the textile industry.[34]

The application of the edict offers perhaps the best clues to the intentions behind it. In its aftermath, members of the royal government drew up a report titled "Table of the Arts and Crafts to Establish as Guilds in the City and Suburbs of Paris Following the Edict of the Month of March 1673." This document targeted thirty-seven different Parisian trades for incorporation. It listed the population of each trade, the amount to be charged for mastership in each of the new guilds, and the sums that the royal government could expect from its half-share of new masters' fees. Among the thirty-seven trades, we find innkeepers, millers, and merchants of diverse goods such as firewood, wheat, coal, horses, wholesale leather, spirits, butter, and waxed cloth. Two occupations were indicated to be exclusively female, the seamstresses and the fresh-flower sellers.[35]

Judging from the information included in this list, the revenue that each trade could offer to the crown was an important criterion of selection, but it was not the only one. The seamstresses, it is true, would offer an impressive ninety thousand livres from their three-thousand-strong workforce. Each woman would pay sixty livres, half of which would go to the royal government. This was the largest sum calculated for any trade. Other professions, however, would provide much smaller amounts. The two hundred fresh-flower sellers, for example, would produce only an estimated six thousand livres. Aside from fiscal considerations, the predominance of merchants of important basic goods suggests a desire to regulate traffic in major items of public consumption. The millers' presence in the list supports this suggestion, given the tremendous sensitivity of subsistence issues in this period and the constant fear of dearth and the urban riots it could inspire. In the case of the innkeepers and boardinghouse keepers, a desire for greater surveillance of the Parisian itinerant population may have been at work. Overall, the crucial prerequisites for incorporation appear to have been a level of prosperity sufficient to support the financial burdens of guild status and a sufficiently stable and coherent workforce to make a success of corporate organization, with its elections, assembly meetings, and regulations. Desire from the trades' practitioners probably also played a significant role in their inclusion on this list.[36]

Unlike its predecessors, the legislation of 1673 produced remarkable results. According to Emile Levasseur, the Parisian guilds rose in number from 60 in 1672 to 83 several months after the edict, and finally to 129 in

1691. A similar response occurred in provincial towns and cities.[37] French artisans and merchants clearly perceived the 1673 edict as a legitimate invitation to enter the corporate world, and they responded with enthusiasm. Despite the new fees they would encounter, they judged the benefits of guild status to outstrip the drawbacks. The needs of the state therefore succeeded in fostering a substantial propagation of corporate organization among urban artisans in the 1670s, including some groups of female workers.

The Creation of the Parisian Seamstresses' Guild

In response to the possibilities offered by the 1673 edict, a group of seamstresses quickly organized to draft statutes for a new guild, and then submitted them to the king with a letter requesting incorporation. As the king stated in his letters patent:

> In execution of which Edict, several Women and Girls, having shown Us that in all times they have worked at sewing, to clothe young children and make Skirts, Dressing Gowns, Mantuas, Skirt Bodices and other clothes of convenience [*habits de commodité*] for persons of their sex and that this work was the only manner in which they could gain their living honestly: They entreated Us to establish them as a guild [*communauté*], and to accord them the Statutes that they had presented Us to exercise their Profession.[38]

This request adds weight to the impression given by the apprenticeship contracts, suggesting that by 1675 seamstresses had developed a strong professional identity, based on a set of precisely delimited products and the common gender of both workers and clients. Some form of association existed among them, which permitted a rapid response to the new legislation. The framing of their request also indicates some sophistication with the legal procedures and rhetoric of the guild world. Seamstresses were not only conscious of the gender composition of their trade; they were capable of manipulating it by emphasizing the precarious moral situation of working women. Their statement carried the tacit warning that if they could not work in this "honest" trade they might turn in desperation to less honorable forms of income.

The king transmitted these statutes to his procurator at the Châtelet of Paris and the lieutenant general of police, Nicolas de la Reynie, for their approval. In their report, these officials noted the tailors' utter failure to eliminate seamstresses from their trade, concluding that the establishment of a female guild could not cause any further harm. They thus informed the king that:

> The practice of using Seamstresses to make their Skirts, Dressing Gowns, Skirt Bodices and other clothes of convenience [*habits de commodité*] had introduced itself among Women and Girls of every condition to such an extent; that regardless of the seizures undertaken by the Tailors' Officials and the condemnations that had been pronounced against the Seamstresses, they continued working as previously. That this severity exposed them to suffer great vexations, but did not make them cease exercising their Commerce, and that their establishment as a Guild therefore did not greatly prejudice the Master Tailors' [guild], because up to the present they did not work less, even though they have no right to do so.[39]

Beyond practical considerations, the royal letters patent raised moral concerns, not for the female artisans in question, but for their elite female clients. The king's letters stated that he had consented to the new corporation: "Having moreover considered that it was quite within propriety and suitable for the decency and modesty of Women and girls to permit them to be clothed by persons of their sex, when they judge it appropriate."[40] Concerns for female modesty were thus an explicit motivation for the guild's creation.

In addition to these directly expressed explanations, we may identify a number of tacit considerations at work. Garment-making offered a source of employment to working women, who might otherwise be idle, indigent, and a source of social disorder. Disputes between tailors and seamstresses generated disarray in the labor market and legal expenses within the male guild. Properly organized and regulated, needleworkers would provide new outlets for French textile production, the most important industry in France and a particular object of Colbert's concern. It was no use pouring effort and subventions into silk, woolen, and lace manufacture if French women did not have sufficient access to finished goods made with these products. Incorporating the seamstresses also offered a new and highly lucrative source of revenue. Creating a seamstresses' guild thus promised to aid urban labor markets, stimulate the growth of domestic industry, and—not the least of considerations—provide ninety thousand livres to the crown.

The king granted the seamstresses' letters patent as a new guild on

March 30, 1675, and the Parisian Parlement registered the letters in September of the same year. This document granted the seamstresses the same legal status as other Parisian guilds. New mistresses were sworn in before the king's procurator at the Châtelet of Paris and thereby acquired the official title of *maîtresses couturières* (mistress seamstresses). As established by the new statutes, the guild's administrative structure and regulations were similar to those of other Parisian guilds. An electoral body composed of guild mistresses elected three of six administrative officers each year. With the authorization of the Archbishop of Paris, a guild confraternity was established in the parish church of Saint-Gervais under the patronage of Saint-Louis. The guild's basic regulations corresponded entirely with corporate norms. It was no more responsible to outside authority than any male corporation.

The seamstresses' trade privileges, however, did set them apart. The tailors' guild had possessed for centuries a monopoly on the fabrication of men's and women's clothing. The royal government could not simply dismantle these privileges, which had been repeatedly confirmed by the king's predecessors. As arbiter of the corporate sphere, the state therefore sought a compromise that would permit seamstresses to work in the trade with the least possible diminishment of the tailors' position. Royal officers found a solution by permitting seamstresses to work for women and children only. Tailors not only retained their rights to make women's and men's clothing, they also maintained a monopoly over the most expensive female attire of the period, the two-piece dress worn by court noblewomen.[41]

With this compromise, the royal government denied the seamstresses a monopoly on their sector of commerce, placing them in a situation of direct competition with the tailors. This was a highly unusual situation, because the guild system usually functioned to eliminate or at least minimize competition, not to foster it. Once again, we encounter the paradoxical effects of gender on female labor. The royal government could not have imposed such unequal trade rights on a male rival to the tailors' guild; however, it would have been impossible for a male trade to acquire even these limited privileges. The seamstresses' female gender both rendered possible and restricted their legal rights.

The sexual division imposed on the product market carried over to policies for hiring and guild administration. The 1675 statutes forbade mistress seamstresses from hiring journeymen tailors and barred master tailors from employing female workers. They also prohibited seamstresses' and tailors' elected officials from conducting inspection visits on the other guild's members. A gender barrier thus ran through all aspects of the new guild's constitution. Adopted in some ways as a simple institutionalization of preexisting practice, the new legal status accorded to sexual segregation in the garment trades would become a model for provincial towns and cities.

The Creation of Two Additional Female Guilds

The birth of the Parisian guild was quickly followed by the creation of a seamstresses' corporation in Rouen in December 1675. Rouen was the capital of upper Normandy, and one of the most important cities of eighteenth-century France. As discussed above, Rouen contained the largest number of women's guilds in the seventeenth century. It was thus not surprising that the city's seamstresses seized the opportunity to acquire guild status and that local officials agreed to the creation of a new female guild, despite the tailors' vociferous protests. Although no clear reference was made to the Parisian case, it must have played a crucial role in the timing of their demand. As in Paris, the Rouen seamstresses' guild obtained the right to work for women and children only, and not for men. By 1685, eighty women had paid sixty livres each to join the new guild.[42]

The Parisian fresh-flower sellers (*bouquetières*) were the third group to obtain corporate status as a result of Colbert's edict. In August 1677, the flower sellers received letters patent granting them a monopoly over the sale of "all sorts of Bouquets, Hats, Crowns [and] Floral Garlands."[43] In size and status, these tradeswomen most closely resembled the humble hemp merchants. Around 1691, the government study estimated the flower sellers' guild to number 120 mistresses, "almost all poor."[44] The edict of 1691 assigned them to the fourth class of Parisian guilds, along with the hemp merchants and other modest trades.

If their economic importance was minimal, the flower sellers were noteworthy for their statutes' emphasis on the exclusively female composition of their corporation: "The community will be composed only of women and girls, and no Boy will be permitted to achieve Mastership [*maî-trise*], nor intervene in the said trade, nor make or sell Bouquets. We prohibit all Mistresses from giving work to men." Moral concerns voiced in the seamstresses' letters patent also appeared more forcefully in the flower sellers' statutes: "if any Mistress, Apprentice or Journeywoman [*Compagne*] of the Trade was found guilty of having committed a fault of honor, she would lose her Privilege; and if she was a Mistress her shop would be closed; she would no longer be able to engage in the Trade."[45]

The enhanced articulation of moral anxiety caused by the flower sellers most likely arose from the fact that they sold their goods in public, rather than in their own homes. The possibility for confusion with women who sold illicit goods, and in particular with street walking prostitutes, thus became a major source of anxiety. The evidence suggests that flower sellers had good reason to fear for their reputation. In August 1698, the Parisian lieutenant general of police passed sentence against Marie Leroy, Marie Hébert, and a group of other women who had been arrested for illegal gathering and the disruption of public order. "Under the pretext of selling flowers and bouquets," the women had gathered around the bridges and quays of Paris, attracting groups of soldiers and vagabonds who "insult[ed] the passers-by, cause[d] quarrels," and "permit[ted] crooks and purse-snatchers to stop there and to commit several robberies." While the women escaped with a three-livre fine, future violators would pay fifty livres for the first offense and endure a whipping for the second one. This was merely one of a series of arrests performed against suspect flower sellers during the late seventeenth and eighteenth centuries.[46]

Royal Government and Women's Guilds after Colbert

Historians have posited a significant decline in the vigor and competency of royal administration from Colbert's death in 1683 through the end of Louis XIV's reign. They have characterized the royal government as composed of unimpressive ministers and weak policies, both unequal to the wars and economic crises that confronted the country.[47] With regard to guilds, they have argued that fiscal concerns increasingly overwhelmed regulatory ones. As proof, they point to the series of guild offices that the royal government created from the last decade of the seventeenth century to the end of Louis XIV's reign. The first of these offices arrived in 1691 in the form of a royal edict transforming the guilds' elected officials into venal offices. Additional offices quickly followed, including the "Auditors and Examiners of Guild Accounts" in 1694, the "Treasurer, Receiver and Payer of Guild Funds" in 1702, and the "Registrars of the Arts and Crafts" in 1704. Across France, guilds were obliged to purchase these offices to avoid losing their administrative independence to outsiders. The royal government not only permitted but expected the guilds to buy the offices, and it quickly authorized them to take new loans for this purpose. Given the crown's shaky record in repaying debts, corporations had stronger credit than the king and could thus serve as useful intermediaries for loans to the state.

These forced loans have been viewed as evidence of the predominantly fiscal interests of ministers after Colbert and their indifference to the actual functioning of the guild system. While understandable in view of the considerable sums involved, this conclusion again overstates the case. Ministers following Colbert certainly exploited the guild system, but they also continued to rely heavily on the guilds to regulate economic and social (re)production and to generate fiscal revenue. In this respect, the edict of 1691 deserves fresh appraisal. Often cited as a downward turning point in the government's treatment of the guilds, the edict of 1691 in fact addressed a series of administrative problems. Its preamble criticized numerous guild abuses, including the assignment of overly expensive and timeconsuming masterpieces (*chefs d'oeuvre*), excessive charges for mastership, sloppy recordkeeping, and poor supervision of apprenticeship. In order to redress these problems, it established a commission of royal councilors who would assign modest masterpieces for each guild and set a new tariff of moderate guild fees.

The threat to the guilds' independence was not merely intended as a lever to extort money; it was also meant as a wake-up call, to convince guild officials of the need to reassess and reform their management practices. In the seamstresses' case, at least, negotiations surrounding the purchase of these offices produced a set of new regulations that fundamentally affected the guild's administration over the eighteenth century. In all likelihood, this was not true for the seamstresses alone, but for other guilds as well. Royal administrators thus took advantage of the 1691 legislation to intervene significantly in the way guilds managed their internal administration and resources.[48]

This period of reform also witnessed the last major opportunity for the creation of new women's corporations. In the "Memorandum for the Establishment in Mastership of Arts and Crafts in the City and Suburbs of Paris," government officials targeted a new list of thirty-two nonguild trades. Several had previously appeared in the 1673 project, but had failed to attain guild status in the intervening years. This time, nine occupations were indicated as women's trades. These were the "fruit sellers and hucksteresses," (*fruitières regrattières*) the "hairdressers, hair merchants, [and] braiders," the "school mistresses," the "aides to postpartum women," (*gardes d'accouchées*), the "tripe cookers and sellers," the "old-stocking, linens, and suit menders," the "dairy, cream, and egg sellers," the "stitched-bonnet makers," and the herbalists. The launderers and the laundresses as well as the fish merchants were described as mixed-sex groups.[49]

This list testifies to the range of female trades practiced in late-seventeenth-century Paris and to the large numbers of women involved in them. The largest groups were the hairdressers and linenworkers, with an estimated 2,000 women each; the fruit sellers numbered some 1,000 and the herbalists at least 1,500. The remaining occupational groups were considerably smaller, with 100 schoolmistresses, 200 postpartum aides, 400 tripe vendors, 40 dairy vendors, and some 50 bonnet makers. The last group was the most economically successful. According to this report, they had started calling themselves "bonnet merchants," and they each employed as many as 40 or 50 workers. Altogether, this list represents some 7,300 women working in Paris in independent occupations.

As in 1673, female incorporation suggested a range of advantages to Parisian and royal administrators. The potential revenue was, again, an important motivation. As in the seamstresses' case, the price of membership would be minimal, but the women's numerical strength ensured a handsome profit to the crown. Each of the women would pay an entry fee, from which a "royal fee" would be deducted. With regard to the old-stockings menders, the report pointed out: "This community by its great number will produce more than the strongest of all the Parisian guilds by paying only six livres each for the royal fee at the time of their reception." Speaking of the female hairdressers, it stated that: "The community . . . will be all the better in that it will be very numerous and there will be among them some [who are] quite rich."[50] The incorporation of the seamstresses, which was proving to be a lucrative and successful venture, must have provided an encouraging precedent for administrators in search of new sources of fiscal revenue. Equally important for the author of the report, however, were the potential advantages female guilds offered to public utility. With regard to the old-stockings menders, he wrote: "The said [female] workers seem as useful as the cobblers and when they are in a guild, they will only make good merchandise and works." In at least one case, he also argued that corporate status would protect female workers from male harassment: "The constant persecutions exercised by the [male] merchant fruit-sellers on the [female] fruit-sellers in boutiques should excite the Public Minister to put them in a guild and regulate the quantity of butter, eggs and cheese which they should have." Finally, the author mentioned two cases—

the milkwomen, cream, and fresh egg merchants, and the fruit sellers and hucksteresses—where the women themselves had requested incorporation.[51]

Despite these arguments in its favor, the project was never implemented and the female trades in question never achieved guild status. Members of these mostly modest trades would have been hard-pressed to meet the financial demands of corporate membership, and they probably stood to benefit little in terms of credit and public reputation. Female market trades may have also seemed lacking in the requisite honor for guild status. The comments made in this report, nonetheless, demonstrate that female market women were recognized as fulfilling important public services in the same manner as male vendors or artisans. In the absence of explicit regulations and officials to enforce them, they posed similar dangers to the public. Government officials also acknowledged women's special vulnerability to competition from male workers. Guilds were ultimately rejected as a form of regulation, but the problem of supervising these small female street trades would trouble administrators throughout the eighteenth century.[52]

Seamstresses in the Provinces

While the end of the seventeenth century witnessed the last projects to create women's guilds in Paris, important innovations continued in provincial towns and cities. Like their Parisian colleagues, provincial seamstresses had established an economic niche in women's and children's clothing during the seventeenth century. In 1652, in the earliest example of seamstresses' encounter with the guild system, the tailors' corporation of Aix-en-Provence sought and received permission from the local Parlement to receive seamstresses as subordinate members for the production of women's and children's clothing. The growing problem for provincial administrators in the late seventeenth and eighteenth centuries was how to respond to this female workforce, particularly as the numbers of women engaged in illegal production grew and local tailors' guilds accrued significant debts through legal proceedings against them.

Three distinct solutions were available to provincial administrators, who chose among them based on royal council directives, local and regional practices, demands from trade members, and the market for women's clothing in their cities. The first possibility was to create a new, independent female guild, such as those in Paris and Rouen. After Colbert's death, and in the absence of strong central initiatives for the creation of new corporations, this path attracted few followers. The only other city for which we have records of an independent seamstresses' guild is Le Havre, the satellite port town of Rouen, which established a female corporation in 1722. Seamstresses who did not possess sufficient numerical strength, economic clout, or organization to obtain guild status in 1675 thus found that their window of opportunity had closed in subsequent years.[53]

An opposing alternative was to allow seamstresses to work in customer's homes or in their own dwellings, with no guild controls. This approach removed their work from the public arena, reducing them to a level akin to domestic service. The city of Nevers followed this practice and many other small towns probably did so as well, despite protests by local tailors' guilds.[54] Eschewing these two extremes, a number of cities and towns adopted the intermediate solution pioneered in the city of Aix-en-Provence, allowing seamstresses to work as subordinate members of the local tailors' guild. A striking anomaly in the guild world, this mixed-sex model emerged in cities such as Abbeville, Laon, Caen, Coutances, Angers, Le Mans, Saint-Malo, Rennes, Langres, Nantes, Saintes, Clermont-Ferrand, Marseilles, and Arles. These cities spanned five provinces and straddled the traditional cultural and institutional divide between northern and southern France. Examination of departmental and municipal archives would doubtless reveal additional cases (see figure 4.2 for a map of locations where seamstresses entered the guild system).

Although information is not available for all cities, it appears that this intermediate solution was frequently devised by tailors' guilds themselves. In Aix-en-Provence, the tailors requested formal permission from the Parlement of Provence to admit women to their guild in 1652. In 1728, the tailors' guild of Nantes reached the same decision, explaining that the demand for women's clothing in the city had grown beyond the masters' capacity to fill it.[55] They were also motivated by the eighteen thousand livres in debt they had accumulated through futile legal action against the seamstresses. In 1751, the tailors of Saintes told a similar story, stating that they had resolved to accept female members "considering the disadvantages that could result in that they are not a sufficient number of *couturiers* and tailors for women to serve the public; and that moreover there have been for all times different conflicts between the masters of their said community and the girls who work in the said trade of seamstress for women's and children's clothes."[56]

FIGURE 4.2 Map of cities and towns where seamstress entered guilds. Italics indicate those cities where seamstresses established independent guilds.

Acknowledging that they could not beat the seamstresses, provincial tailors forced the women to join them. This strategy allowed tailors formal control over the women's labor, because they generally excluded women from participation in guild administration. It also permitted tailors' guilds to profit from the membership fees and other dues paid by their erstwhile competitors. Instead of losing money in useless prosecution of seamstresses, the tailors obtained a new source of revenue. Finally, this approach provided a means to prevent what the tailors may have feared most, the creation of an independent female guild. They were all familiar with the Parisian situation; corporate pride and dignity, as well as economic self-interest, convinced them that a similar occurrence in their town would be disastrous.

Provincial tailors' guilds were vindicated in their calculations to a certain extent. They succeeded in preventing the creation of new seamstresses' guilds and they often retained control of guild administration. Their ability to dominate the new female subdivisions within their corporations, however, proved exasperatingly elusive. Shortly after their union with the tailors, for example, the seamstresses of Caen embarked on an aggressive and partially successful campaign to win administrative autonomy. Where tailors continued to monopolize corporate government, as in Aix-en-Provence, the numbers of women who joined the guild overwhelmed them. According to assembly minutes, the sheer mass of women proved impossible to dominate and, even more infuriating, the guild's male leaders were not above entering profitable collusion with them.[57]

In order to clarify seamstresses' status in provincial tailors' guilds, in the next sections I examine their experiences in the Norman city of Caen and the Provençal city of Marseilles. Although Normandy and Provence were among the richest of French provinces, they were marked by profound judicial, administrative, economic, and cultural differences. Provence entered France centuries later than Normandy, retaining proud memories of independence if little actual autonomy by the second half of the seventeenth century. Provence was a *pays d'état,* meaning that it possessed a provincial assembly, or estates, which theoretically safeguarded its administrative and political liberties. In reality, the estates of Provence did not meet after 1639 and the obedience of the general assembly that replaced them was ensured by the presence of the royal intendant at its meetings. Still, the lax guild tradition of the province and its distance from Paris, not to mention its economic and social specificity, made it a distinctive environment for the seamstresses' trade.

Normandy, by contrast, was a *pays d'élection,* subject to direct administrative control by the king's representatives. While one royal intendant supervised all of Provence, Normandy was divided into several *généralités,* each with its own intendant. Administrative and geographical proximity to Paris meant that the province felt the weight of royal control to a much greater extent than its southern counterpart. This was also a region with a very old and well-established guild system, whose members maintained close contacts with guilds in neighboring cities and Paris. Comparing Normandy and Provence reveals differences and similarities between provinces with extremely different administrative and corporate regimes.

Rouen was the capital of upper Normandy, and Caen was the capital of lower Normandy, the northern half of the province. In comparison to Rouen, Caen occupied a secondary position in French economic and cultural life, alongside other provincial capitals, such as Amiens, Metz, Nîmes, and Orleans. An important center of woolen cloth production through much of the eighteenth century, the city's industry encountered harsh competition from rural manufacture from the 1770s. The most important economic activity in Caen took place during its annual fair, one of the largest in Old Regime France. The city experienced little social or economic change prior to the 1750s, when growing immigration altered the traditional composition of the city. Its population grew from 26,500 at the end of the seventeenth century to a maximum of 40,000 around 1775, largely fueled by post-1750 immigration from the surrounding countryside.[58]

The Caen tailors' guild dated from 1576. Inspired perhaps by the examples of Rouen and Paris, the tailors began to admit seamstresses as subordinate members by the early 1690s at least.[59] They did not officially acknowledge the presence of women in their guild until 1712, when they revised their original 1576 statutes. Following what was becoming a standard pattern, the new regulations stated: "The Mistresses of the said trade will work only for women and children, and will not be permitted to work for men."[60] Aspiring mistresses were required to complete a formal, two-year apprenticeship with a mistress seamstress. Finished apprentices could enter the guild by performing a masterpiece and paying ten livres to the treasury as well as ten sous to each of four elected officials and to the masters present at the examination. These fees were significantly lower than those paid by apprentice tailors, who furnished fifteen livres to the guild and one livre to each official and examiner.

The 1712 statutes gave seamstresses no role in the guild's administration, assigning tailors' officials to judge mistresses' masterpieces and police their production standards. In cooperation with the all-male assembly, they were to set fees for male and female guild members. The statutes also established unequal rights for seamstresses' and tailors' family members. In the future, tailors' male and female children could enter the guild without completing an apprenticeship or performing the masterpiece. Mistresses' daughters enjoyed the same privilege, but their sons were obliged to undergo formal training like any outsider to the guild. Similarly, masters' widows could continue their husbands' trades as long as they did not marry a nontailor. Mistresses' husbands had to join the guild on their own account.

The seamstresses' frustration with these limitations led to a bid for independence several years later. In a formal request to the royal Council of Commerce, they asked "to be disunited from the Tailors' Community and to make a separate Corps and Community."[61] The tailors responded with a series of concessions, including the right for six female representatives to attend guild meetings and to participate in the evaluation of female masterpieces. Unsatisfied by this offer, the seamstresses continued their bid for independence. By 1719, legal conflicts between the two sides had generated considerable debt, and a new lawsuit was imminent. In order to resolve the conflict without further recourse to the courts, the controller general ordered the intendant in Caen to conduct hearings into the affair. Drawing on this official's recommendations, the royal council subsequently issued a judgment "bearing Settlement between the Mistress Seamstresses of the city of Caen and the Master Tailors."[62]

This judgment refused the women an independent guild, declaring: "His Majesty desir[es] that the Seamstresses, united with the said Tailors for a considerable time, remain in Community with them."[63] It also canceled all legal proceedings between the tailors and the seamstresses, appointing the intendant to oversee liquidation of the guild's debts. The seamstresses' initiative for independence had arrived some forty years too late. Their prior union with the tailors—and in particular the debt accumulated in the interim—convinced the royal government that the two trades should remain united. The 1719 judgment did, however, offer them considerable new advantages. They would henceforth elect four mistresses to oversee their affairs, hold their own assembly meetings, and bear independent responsibility for debts. The tailors would continue to conduct inspection visits on seamstresses and judge their masterpieces, but only with the cooperation of two female officers. This ruling also removed inequalities between masters' and mistresses' children by requiring daughters to complete one year of apprenticeship with a mistress prior to entering the guild. As a concession to the tailors, however, the royal government maintained their control of corporate finances. The tailors would continue to determine and collect the seamstresses' fees, but they would be accountable to the seamstresses for them.

In reaching this settlement, royal officials drew on preexisting corporate principles. Seamstresses performed an important public service, fulfilled rigorous guild requirements, and paid fees to the royal treasury. In return, the royal government recognized their right to self-governance. At the same time as they applied standard corporate principles to seamstresses, however, officials fell back on what had become an equally important principle, that of sexual segregation. They did not create a truly mixed-sex administration, such as the one used by the Parisian grain dealers' guild since 1519. Instead, they created two distinct administrative bodies, divided by sex. Male tailors met in one assembly, while female seamstresses gathered in a separate body. The two trade groups remained distinct and segregated subdivisions within the guild.

As in Paris, the sexual division of the garment trades both hindered and empowered women. The women's sex made it easy for officials to limit them to the field of female clothing, yet it also called for a separate administrative structure controlled by women. The logic of segregation, furthermore, permitted demands for formal equality between seamstresses and tailors; if one group's children were required to undergo apprenticeship, the other group should be subject to the same demands. Without gaining complete independence, the Caen seamstresses achieved a large degree of administrative autonomy in 1719. After this date, they were guild mistresses in a real sense, with recognized powers of self-government. They underwent formal apprenticeship, performed the masterpiece, and swore an oath before police. They elected officials and met in assemblies to discuss their affairs. As I will show in the next chapter, some sense of moral community existed among mistress seamstresses of Caen, which they developed and expressed through guild rituals, such as masses and burials.

The Seamstresses of Marseilles: Subordinate Female Guild Members

At the opposite extreme of the kingdom from the Norman city of Caen lay the Mediterranean port of Marseilles, one of France's most important commercial centers. In 1669, Colbert favored the city with the status of a *port-franc,* removing all tariffs on goods entering the port. This privilege greatly encouraged the city's commercial activity, particularly its trade with the Near East. Marseilles also enjoyed immunity from a series of regular royal taxes to the crown, a privilege it reimbursed through numerous "extraordinary" contributions over the eighteenth century.[64]

The founding date of the Marseilles tailors' guild remains unknown. In 1584 and 1610, guild leaders solicited and received new statutes. In 1675, the tailors decided to revise their statutes once more, declaring that they contained "several Articles conceived in ambiguous terms and other omissions," which had created expensive legal problems. They resolved that the new statutes would follow the model of the Parisian tailors' guild, to the extent that the "different situation" of the two cities permitted. In May 1675, they submitted their revisions to the local lieutenant general of police. Based on his positive judgment, the royal government approved the new statutes, which were registered by the Parlement of Provence in 1676.[65]

These statutes confirmed the close relationship between the trade guild and the religious confraternity, identified by Maurice Agulhon as a central characteristic of guilds in Provence.[66] The regulations called on the confraternity to sponsor a weekly mass for deceased guild members as well as a monthly mass for the king and his armies. They also devoted all confraternity dues to the decoration of its chapel and to "the assistance of poor Masters or their Families, such as poor girls to be married."[67] The most innovative feature of the new statutes was their accordance of formal trade rights to women for the first time. Masters' daughters were freely allowed to make articles of clothing for children up to the age of eight years old. Other women could acquire the same privileges by paying to join the religious confraternity. In future, master tailors would pay ten sous in annual confraternity dues, journeymen five sous, and male and female confraternity members three sous. The Marseilles tailors thus followed other cities in granting female trade rights, but they were unusual in placing seamstresses in the confraternity rather than the guild and in limiting them to the production of children's clothes.

As in Caen, the limited privileges furnished by the tailors' guild proved incommensurate with the women's ambition. Defying the restrictions imposed by the statutes, a number of seamstresses made a living by making and selling women's clothing. In 1694, the tailors formally requested that police officials enforce their statutes and prosecute seamstresses who worked for adult women. A judgment of the Marseilles police rejected this demand, authorizing seamstresses to produce female clothing in their own homes. To obtain this right, a needleworker would henceforth pay a membership fee of six livres to the guild's treasury, becoming a member of the corporation rather than the confraternity. The police ruling forbade women from operating public shops or employing any workers other than their own children. This ruling legalized seamstresses' work for their own sex, but only within the context of household and family production. The officials of Marseilles thus brought female trade rights in line with the rest of France, but compensated the tailors by limiting the location and scale of their production.

Despite this concession, some seamstresses were still determined not to play by the tailors' rules. In 1712, guild officials directed a new complaint to the lieutenant of the *sénéchaussée* of Marseilles, the city's higher court. This official reiterated the original police decision, prohibiting seamstresses from "having open boutiques, displaying their work in them, from working on men's clothing and having journeymen other than their own children." He did, however, permit seamstresses to hire as many female workers as they desired. The 1712 ruling gave the seamstresses of Marseilles the same basic trade privileges as Parisian seamstresses, except for the capacity to open a public boutique.[68]

Legal conflict continued through the 1730s regarding a new sector of production, whaleboned undergarments. In 1737, the intendant conducted a hearing into the complex set of circumstances surrounding the conflict. The results of this hearing reveal differing attitudes among royal and municipal authorities toward women's incorporation, as well as a new climate of doubt regarding the efficacy of the guild system itself. The municipal councilors, or *échevins,* did not believe that the two groups constituted a single guild, and suggested making the seamstresses "a separate corps, established as a mastership [*maîtrise*] and sworn trade [*jurande*]." The tailors rejected this idea. They pointed to the women's guild fees as proof that "the Seamstresses have always constituted a corps in community with the Tailors."[69] Moreover, they continued, granting independence to the seamstresses "would be even more unjust as the Tailors would remain solely responsible for the debts of the community which they assure to be very considerable."[70]

The royal intendant held the responsibility of judging between the claims of the different groups and recommending a plan of action to his superiors. His lack of enthusiasm for the guild system itself filtered clearly through his report. He commented in an aside that it seemed to him that anyone should be allowed to make the items under discussion. Apparently convinced by the tailors' financial arguments, he rejected the *échevins'* proposal for separating the trades. He also rejected the suggestion that seamstresses should be obliged to undergo formal apprenticeship and competency tests. As he explained:

It is to be feared with reason that the Tailors would quibble with them during their examination or about their masterpiece, and would refuse them under the pretext of incompetence[,] because of the interest they would have in excluding them to give themselves all the work in this art; it would be an even greater prejudice for the public if it were deprived of all of these [female] workers, whose great number necessarily excites either among themselves or among the Tailors a rivalry for the perfection of their work, to attract more clients; and [it] can advantageously replace the proofs of ability to which the seamstresses could be submitted to acquire mastership [*maîtrise*].[71]

The intendant did not believe, as his Parisian colleagues had in 1691, that strong guild regulations would help female artisans defend themselves against male abuse. Instead, he maintained that competition among seamstresses and tailors would provide a healthy stimulus to the trade, sufficient in itself to guarantee appropriate quality and quantity in production. He viewed apprenticeship and tests of competency, two cornerstones of the guild system, not only as irrelevant and unnecessary but as obstacles to the healthy functioning of the economy. On top of these protoliberal economic views, the intendant clearly distrusted guild officials, whom he suspected of venal self-interest.

To accompany his report, the intendant drafted a proposal for reforming the guild's regulations. The first article reasserted the corporate union between male and female sides of the trade, permitting both groups to work either in their homes or in a public boutique. These new rules explicitly guaranteed the seamstresses the same trade rights as their Parisian counterparts. The intendant accordingly raised the women's entry fees to the much higher sum of fifty livres, and obliged them to pay one livre in annual guild fees. In compliance with the Parisian statutes, he forbade seamstresses from hiring male workers.[72]

The seamstresses' experience in Marseilles reveals the important influence of the Parisian model. In moments of change and crisis, royal administrators—as well as guildsmen and women themselves—looked to Parisian regulations for guidance. Despite its tradition of proud independence, Provence was falling increasingly under the sway of the capital and royal efforts toward economic and administrative centralization. At the same time, however, the tailors' guilds of Provence continued to follow a distinctive path. Marseilles tailors dispensed with apprenticeship and the masterpiece for their female members, a negligence echoed in Aix-en-

Provence and quite at odds with the strict rules imposed on female guild members in Paris and Caen. The intendant's skepticism regarding corporate values may reflect his encounter with Provençal resistance to guild regulation as much as a philosophically grounded distrust of the principles of corporate regulation. It may also reveal something of the economic and political culture of the free port city, turned toward the outside world and away from the constrictions of municipal particularism.

Beginnings of a Turn Away from the Guilds

Whatever their provenance, the views of the intendant of Provence in 1737 foreshadowed a wider change in royal administrators' attitudes toward the guilds. Jean-Claude Perrot has claimed that the royal government accepted most requests for incorporation until the 1730s, after which it increasingly rejected them.[73] In the second half of the eighteenth century, the royal government's confidence in the guilds as a means to regulate economic and social production gradually eroded. Although they did not separate themselves decisively from the guild system, and they remained committed to corporate models of organization, royal ministers stopped creating new guilds and sought to respond to growing attacks on the guild system from physiocrats and other critics.

A piece of legislation from 1767 captures this ambivalent attitude. In August of that year, the crown issued an edict providing new "regulations for Professions of Arts and Crafts and others that interest commerce, and that are not in sworn mastership [*jurande*]."[74] The edict addressed an array of un-incorporated Parisian trades, among them a number of small vending and service occupations. Rather than obliging them to form new guilds, as the 1673 edict had done, it required their practitioners to register with the police on an individual basis. This move broke with previous strategies for supervising and regulating the economy. Abandoning efforts to expand corporate entities, the royal government created a direct relationship between individual tradesmen and Parisian authorities. The break with the past is even more striking given that a number of the trades listed in the edict had been mentioned in the projects of incorporation of 1673 and 1691, including such female artisans as hairdressers, bonnet makers, linenworkers, lace menders, and vendors of used clothes, tripe, and dairy products.

As this list suggests, women's work formed a key element of the legislation. The text clearly established women's right to work, at least in appropriate trades: "His Majesty intends that persons of the other sex, either married, widowed or single, be admitted to provide themselves with the said letters or patents for all the professions for which their sex may be susceptible, and that they shall be able to exercise them without difficulty after having been received in the form prescribed by the first article."[75] The author did not explain which professions were particularly apt for women, but the feminized nouns used to describe linenworkers and lace menders, among others, reveals a familiarity with the existing sexual division of labor. A subsequent ruling liberated several of the occupations—including all of the female ones—from the registration fees that had been imposed, stating: "It was of his [Majesty's] goodness not to demand finances from several trades for which the object is too unimportant and too mediocre."[76] These poor female artisans and merchants were still, however, obliged to register with the police.

From the late seventeenth century to the 1760s, royal and municipal administrators failed to devise a satisfactory method for regulating female market trades. Incorporation had offered one possibility, but attempts to create guilds in these trades failed and the program was abandoned. The government's new policy was not, however, one of complete liberty. The 1767 edict maintained a mitigated form of corporate discipline by requiring tradesmen to swear oaths of fidelity, in the same manner as new guild masters. It also explicitly invited them to meet in assemblies and elect officials to police their trades. In some ways, therefore, the corporate tradition survived in the 1767 edict.

The Shock of Abolition, 1776

If the 1767 edict betrayed an ambivalent attitude on the part of the royal government, the real blow arrived in 1776. In February of that year, Controller General Anne-Robert-Jacques Turgot promulgated six edicts liberalizing trade and commerce in the realm, including one abolishing the guild system throughout France. In his preamble to the edict, Turgot harshly criticized the trade corporations, developing a notion of social and economic organization at odds with the secular traditions of the French monarchy. In common with the physiocrats, Turgot believed that work was a basic human right, which could not be alienated by law: "God in giving man needs, in making the resource of work necessary for him, made the right to work the property of all men, and this property is the first, the most sacred and the most imprescriptible of all."[77] According to Turgot, the abolition of the guild system was essential to remove unnatural constraints on human labor and allow all French subjects to exercise their labor freely. Where Colbert had viewed corporate bodies as fundamental components of society, Turgot envisioned a nation composed of individuals with natural rights.

Turgot explicitly extended this project to women, whom he granted natural labor rights of their own. He castigated women's exclusion from the corporate system, arguing that the guilds had illegitimately appropriated female trades: "The spirit of monopoly, which presided at the making of these statutes, was pushed so far as to exclude women from the trades most appropriate for their sex, such as embroidery, that they cannot exercise on their own account." The controller general thus combined new philosophical beliefs with traditional views about women and the sexual division of labor to argue that women should be allowed to practice their "own" trades freely and independently. Women required the removal of artificial trade restrictions even more urgently than men, he suggested, because feminine weakness increased women's needs and limited their resources. By preventing female employment, he claimed, the guilds encouraged "seduction and debauchery."[78]

Unlike his predecessors, Turgot could not conceive of regulation or supervision as necessary to protect female artisans. Women had nothing to fear from male competition, he suggested, for in a free market men and women would follow their innate predilections for certain occupations and a natural sexual division of labor would emerge. Indeed, for Turgot, "women's work" was so rooted in the nature of femininity that it offered the outstanding example of innate labor rights. He thus made use of "women's work" to situate human labor in a natural world that anteceded legal stricture. This observation suggests that his defense of female labor drew as much from its utility as an ideological tool to support his larger arguments, as it did from a concern with poor women workers.

In response to Turgot, the Parlement of Paris emerged as the principal spokesmen for the guilds. Parlementary magistrates eagerly took up this opportunity to defend corporate society against what they perceived as ministerial despotism. During the royal *lit de justice* held to force registration of the edict, parlementary Attorney General Séguier offered a strong defense of the corporate system in which he described the corps as constituting a Great Chain of Being, emanating from the sovereign himself. Destroying the guilds would shake the foundations of society and, he hinted, ultimately undermine royal authority. Séguier rejected Turgot's ideal of "indefinite liberty," as he called it, arguing that true liberty could only exist within tradition and a system of law.

In defending the trade corporations, Séguier did not deny the validity of certain criticisms; in fact, he conceded that the guilds should be significantly reformed. For example, he suggested that the most poor and unskilled trades be freed from guild control. He also recognized the guilds' treatment of women as one of their principal faults, and proposed two complementary solutions. On the one hand, he called for liberating the sale of fresh flowers and fruit, two primarily female trades, claiming that these activities were "the very essence of liberty." On the other hand, Séguier also insisted that a certain number of male corporations should be obliged to accept women: "There are some [guilds] finally where one should admit women to mastership, such as the embroiders, the fashion merchants, the hairdressers; it would be to prepare an asylum for virtue, which need often leads to disorder and to libertinism."[79]

Despite their strong differences on the guild system, Séguier and Turgot thus agreed on the need to allow women to practice a certain number of intrinsically female trades. They did not ponder or debate what trades these might be, because the list of appropriate female trades seemed obvious to both of these fierce political opponents. As their references to virtue and debauchery suggest, their shared concern with female labor was probably influenced by the rise of prostitution in the 1770s. Overall, their comments suggest that a significant transition had taken place in ideas about women's work across the eighteenth century. The late-seventeenth-century author was concerned with female poverty and begging; in 1776, both advocates and critics of the guild system believed that female unemployment would lead to prostitution. Both sides now viewed women's work as inextricably connected to female sexual morality. These concerns had certainly existed previously, but they did not dominate discussions of women's work to the same extent.

Reestablishment and Reform of the Guilds

Turgot's abolition of the guilds lasted only six months. Faced with strident protest from the guilds and the Parlements, the monarchy quickly reversed the edict. In August 1776, Turgot left his ministry in disgrace and the king issued a second edict restoring the Parisian guilds. This legislation introduced a number of significant reforms to the system. The corporations declined in number from over 120 to 50 through mergers of related trades. The edict set membership fees in all of the new corporations at much lower levels than previously and eliminated the requirement for apprenticeship. It also established limited economic competition among the new guilds and permitted masters to be members of several guilds at once. Finally, the edict liberated the humblest trades from corporate control so that they might serve as an "open resource to the most indigent part of our subjects."[80] Included in this number were the female flower sellers and hemp merchants, along with the male brush makers, gardeners, weavers, and rope makers.[81]

One of the edict's most radical measures consisted of opening all guilds to women. In the future, a woman could join any guild simply by paying the set membership fee.[82] Widows would no longer automatically inherit their husbands' privileges but would be obliged to become mistresses on their own account after a one-year grace period. The same rules applied to men in women's guilds. This reform represented a fundamental change in women's relationship to the corporate world. Whereas they had previously acquired guild status as an exceptional, usually unequal, form of privilege, henceforth all women could enter guilds on the same basis as men. The reformed guild system was not, however, completely gender-blind. The edict explicitly disqualified women from administrative functions in predominately male guilds, as it did to men in female guilds.

An examination of reception records for 1778 suggests that women did not immediately rush into formerly male guilds. In that year, a total of 1,896 new masters and mistresses entered the reformed Parisian guilds. Among them 100, or some 5 percent, were women joining male corporations. As Séguier and Turgot predicted, the largest numbers were found in the textile and needle trades, including 18 in the new draper-mercers' corporation, 17 in the glovemakers', 12 in the embroiderers and button-makers', and 10 in the tailors', used-clothes, and furniture-dealers' guild. If we add the 110 new mistress seamstresses, the 15 female linen-drapers, 28 fashion merchants, and 1 female painter, we arrive at a total of 254 women, or almost 13.5 percent of the total. Women were a small minority among new guild members, but men who joined female guilds formed an even smaller group. In that year, only three men joined a women's corporation, including one linen-draper, a fashion merchant, and a new member of the seamstresses-*découpeurs'* guild.[83]

In the clothing trades, women's guilds gained substantial new territory from the reforms of 1776. For the first time since 1675, the royal government accorded corporate status to a female trade: the fashion and feather merchants (*marchandes de modes-plumassières*). Its members would include celebrated fashion merchants such as Mademoiselle Eloffe and Rose Bertin. The seamstresses' initial experience of 1776 was one of anxiety and disappointment, for the August edict formally united them with another trade group, the *découpeurs,* who cut and stamped decorative patterns in cloth. In a formal memoir to the crown, the seamstresses declared themselves mystified by this union, claiming that their future partner was a male trade and therefore a wholly inappropriate choice.[84] The guild's new statutes of 1781, nonetheless, testified to the seamstresses' substantial achievements in the expanding Parisian economy. The corporation gained important new privileges, including a total monopoly on the fabrication of women's clothes and the right to make some articles of clothing for men in competition with the tailors.[85]

Reestablishment in the Provinces

The royal government reestablished provincial guilds more slowly. Edicts reinstituting the corporate system appeared for Lyons in January 1777, for the jurisdiction of the Parlement of Paris in April 1777, for Normandy in February 1778 and April 1779, and for Roussillon and Lorraine in May 1779.[86] In these provinces, seamstresses were among the humble trades removed from guild control. Henceforth, women who wished to work as seamstresses could do so simply by registering with the municipal police. More than one hundred years of corporate status among provincial seamstresses thus came to an end with the post-Turgot reforms. The seamstresses' status remained ambiguous, however, for these edicts also reestablished tailors' guilds in these provinces, along with their monopolies on made-to-measure clothing. Provincial seamstresses thus found themselves in the paradoxical position of being explicitly freed from guild control, while the garments they made fell back into the tailors' exclusive domain. Because women could now join male corporations, there was room to argue that they should be obliged to do so if they wanted to make and sell women's garments.

After 1776, tailors in some provincial towns complained bitterly to royal authorities about women's infringement of their monopolies. The tailors of Clermont-Ferrand wrote to the procurator general of the Parisian Parlement to demand that female tailors (*tailleuses*) be obliged to join their guild. A plaintive letter from the tailors explained:

As formerly the master Tailors and [female] Tailors have always been in a corps in the city of Clermont, article 3 seems to authorize women and girl tailors to exercise the professions of Seamstress, Embroideress and Linen-Worker with the obligation of making the declaration presented by article 2 and without paying any fee. Article 5, on the contrary, gives them the faculty to be admitted and received in guilds by paying the fixed fees.[87]

The tailors complained that a "multitude of women and girls have established themselves in the city of Clermont in Auvergne, working and making Dresses and Stays for women." The tailors had tried to impose guild membership on them, in accordance with article 5 of the 1777 edict, but the women had refused, stating that "they had the Liberty to freely exercise their profession without paying any fee." The guild requested clarification of these apparently contradictory articles, inquiring whether the *couturières* named in the edict corresponded to the women they called *tailleuses*. The king's procurator, Joly de Fleury, responded to the tailors' complaints in a letter affirming the women's right to practice their trade freely. According to Joly de Fleury, the *tailleuses* of Clermont-Ferrand were indeed the *couturières* of the 1777 edict: "One can and one should understand [that the trade of] tailors for women, like the estate of seamstresses, is to make Dresses and Stays for women; one cannot assimilate them to the tailors for men and, by making the declaration prescribed by article two of the edict, they thus have the faculty to exercise their professions freely."[88] Seamstresses in this town successfully resisted the reimposition of corporate ties, preferring to work in anonymous liberty.

For all the confusion and controversy it generated, the reformed guild system inaugurated in 1776 lasted only fifteen years. In 1791, the National Assembly abolished the guild system across France, an act that was never reversed. As Turgot and the Marseilles intendant had desired, seamstresses would henceforth compete with tailors in a putatively free market.

Conclusion

Before 1675, the Parisian tailors' guild held a monopoly over the production of made-to-measure clothing. In defiance of this prerogative, seventeenth-century seamstresses established a growing trade niche. A long tradition of formal apprenticeship existed among them, which transmitted different forms of specialization. The seamstresses' trade resembled other forms of "women's work" in seventeenth-century France in making use of skills culturally coded as "feminine" that were nonetheless legally restricted to male guild members. The strong cultural association between needlework and femininity helped seamstresses to challenge the tailors' monopoly, creating a situation in which women routinely violated the law to practice a stereotypically "female" trade.

On its own, the combination of cultural codification and everyday practice did not suffice to change the law. This opportunity resulted from Colbert's 1673 edict calling for the creation of new guilds in all unincorporated trades. If not for the fiscal and managerial needs of the centralizing state, the seamstresses would probably have remained an illegal labor force. In 1675, the seamstresses obtained the same legal rights as male guilds, but sexual difference nonetheless lay at the heart of the new guild's constitution. Seamstresses were allowed to make clothing only for other women and children and could hire only female workers. These stipulations stemmed in part from concerns about the purity of elite female clients, but they were not part of an attempt on the government's part to reshape gender ideologies. Instead, sexual segregation offered the easiest way to compromise between the centuries-old privileges of the tailors and the new claims of the seamstresses. It offered seamstresses' legal status for their labor, while restricting them to an easily delimited sector of the garment trades. Royal officials probably saw this as a fair and reasonable compromise, because seamstresses already worked predominantly for women. This settlement had the additional advantage of preventing seamstresses' husbands or fathers from encroaching on the tailors' trade through their wives' or daughters' privileges. As seniors in the corporate world, tailors retained their full gamut of privileges.

After 1675, the Parisian seamstresses' guild served as both a positive and a negative model for provincial towns and cities. As the demand for women's clothing rose beyond tailors' ability to satisfy it, their guilds began to accept seamstresses as subordinate members. The Parisian example warned of the possibility of an independent female guild, encouraging tailor's guilds to accept women before they acquired sufficient clout to obtain guild status on their own. When seamstresses entered tailors' guilds they acquired the same privileges as their Parisian colleagues, with the right to work for women and children only and to hire female workers.

Over time, seamstresses in Paris and the provinces successfully augmented their privileges. Once they had entered the guild system and acquired the right to press lawsuits and represent themselves to authorities, the logic of seamstresses' corporate status allowed them to push for equal rights with male guilds. They did not claim to make clothes for men, but they successfully expanded their rights over women's apparel. Turning from administrators' attitudes toward women's work to the practitioners themselves, in the next chapter I will examine how tailors and seamstresses reacted to the new legal configuration of the garment trades after 1675 and the forms of identity they derived from their corporate status.

Before turning to these questions, several points raised by the seamstresses' encounter with the guild system from 1675 to 1791 should be underlined. First, this case study demonstrates the lack of official prejudice against female labor. Far from restricting or discouraging women's work, royal and municipal administrators felt that it needed to be encouraged and protected to prevent widespread female destitution and the social disorder it generated. They also valued female trades as a means to satisfy the needs of the urban populace and to stimulate domestic production and consumption. Administrators were less sure of the proper way to regulate women's work. In many cases, female trades seemed too humble or disorganized to form guilds; they also faced the obstacle of resistance from established male guilds. During certain periods of economic and political reform, however, royal ministers agreed to grant women new guilds, with all of the privileges and obligations that accompanied corporate status. The regularizing and centralizing tendencies of the state in the late seventeenth century could thus serve to create greater equality for women rather than reducing it.

The seamstresses' varied experience in French cities and towns highlights important regional variation in the guild system itself. This diversity suggests that provincial guilds continued to function within a regional and municipal dynamic, despite efforts at centralized royal control. The contrast between Normandy and Provence, moreover, indicates that existing corporate traditions—including the prior existence of female guilds—had a powerful influence on women's capacity to acquire guild status. Where the corporate tradition was strong, seamstresses could attain formal mistress status, with the privileges and constraints inherent in it. Where guilds were weaker, and women had no previous corporate role, they remained auxiliary and largely voiceless members of tailors' guilds. Ironically, therefore, the incorporation of women was not a symptom of the weakness or decline of the guild system, but a sign of its strength. It was the vitality of the guild tradition within northern cities that furnished women with the conceptual and legal tools to argue for their autonomous corporate rights.

For advocates of the guild system, the seamstresses offered proof that women were not incompatible with guilds and that, on the contrary, they might thrive within them. The seamstresses' success provided evidence that women's work belonged in the same regulatory framework as men's, and that women were apt candidates for membership in the corporate world. This lesson may account for efforts to bring market women into the guild system and help explain the short-lived August 1776 reforms, which opened all formerly male guilds to women. Despite the radical nature of the reform, royal administrators probably expected women to join guilds appropriate to their sex. The record shows that most of them did, entering trades with a long history of female employment.

Proving women's aptitude for corporate organization was not the seamstresses' most widespread legacy. More important was their contribution to a new articulation of the sexual division of labor. The traditional haziness of women's work disappeared in a trade explicitly defined by the gender of its practitioners, products, and clients. The task of the law was no longer to impose a vision of social, economic, and moral exigency on the world of work, but to allow a natural division of labor based on sex to emerge. The seamstresses' example therefore helped to naturalize and essentialize women's association with needlework. From being a traditional connection, subject to condemnation by guild rules, it became an innate aspect of femininity. For Turgot, no external institutional structures were necessary to protect female labor, because it was already inscribed in their female nature. In a free market, men's and women's inherent tendencies toward certain trades would emerge. The perverse and artificial labor market imposed by the guild system would wither away, and a natural sexual division of labor would take its place.

This new way of looking at women's work must be understood in the broader context of changing ideas about nature, the human body, the individual, and of labor itself. These ideas came from the general conceptual shift of the Enlightenment, from the corporation to the individual, and from laws and customs governing social conduct to "natural" ways of life and behavior. Shifting women's work from an ambiguous mixture of custom, law, and practice to an essentialized notion of innate female skill was one part of much larger cultural and political changes, which surfaced in the realm of fashion as well.

FIVE

The Tailors and the Seamstresses:

Corporate Privilege, Gender, and the Law

On August 16, 1741, four mistress seamstresses appeared before the substitute lieutenant general of police in Caen to lodge a complaint against two officials of their guild, Sieur Morin and Sieur Duchêne. The women explained that the regulations of the joint seamstress-tailors' guild required tailors' participation in the burials of masters' wives and married mistress seamstresses. In both cases, master tailors were to carry the woman's coffin in the funeral procession, while two acting and two former officials carried the corners of a pall draped over it. When an unmarried mistress died, however, the tailors were supposed to cede their role in the funeral ceremony to four unmarried mistresses. In two recent cases, the plaintiffs reported, the tailors' officials had egregiously violated these regulations.

When married mistress Carnel went to her grave some two weeks earlier, the officials failed to attend the burial. To this neglect they added their outrageous behavior an hour later at the funeral of an unmarried mistress, Demoiselle Le Bouteiller. According to the four plaintiffs, Le Bouteiller's parents had asked them as unmarried women to hold the corners of the pall in the established manner during their daughter's burial. As they approached the coffin, however, Morin, Duchêne, and their confederates appeared to prevent them from participating in the ceremony. The tailors warned the seamstresses away from the sheet, jeering that they would not permit them even to furnish a body for the coffin. They continued, in "harsh and ironic terms . . . go on, go on, my ladies, undress yourselves, you have lost your display [*étalage*]," referring presumably to the fine garments and airs the seamstresses had donned for the ceremony, which wilted rapidly under the attack. The tailors advised them to give their clothes to the female bystanders observing the scene, whom they would rather see carry the pall. "For you, nothing," they concluded. At the end of these remarks, the men broke into fits of laughter, which persuaded the onlookers that there had indeed been "ill-conduct" on the women's part. The seamstresses were obliged to withdraw and watch as the burial continued without them. At the cemetery, they renewed their efforts to honor their departed colleague, with the same humiliating results. When they approached to sprinkle holy water on the grave, the tailors continued their loud laughter and mockery.[1]

It is a well-known anthropological dictum that jokes offer a fruitful avenue for understanding any culture or society. In this chapter I seek to explain why the Caen tailors thought it was so funny to humiliate the seamstresses at a burial and why the seamstresses sought vengeance in the courts, rather than responding with insults and laughter of their own. The answer lies in the complicated relationship among gender, guild status, and the law that emerged in the garment trades during the late seventeenth and early eighteenth centuries. Until seamstresses obtained guild privileges, tailors held exclusive rights to produce men's and women's clothing. They enjoyed the economic advantages of guild status, as well as its honor and prestige. The seamstresses' entry to the guild system and their acquisition of administrative powers signaled the end of these exclusive privileges. Henceforth tailors had to share a major sector of their trade and their corporate status with women who reeked of subterranean, and thus dishonorable, labor. The Caen tailors brought seamstresses into the guild on their own initiative in 1712, but they did not anticipate the women's independent spirit or the respect they would receive from royal, parlementary, and police officials. Above all, the tailors did not understand that endowing corporate status on the seamstresses would transform their legal identity. As women, seamstresses had limited legal rights. As members of a guild, they possessed a collective legal personality equal to that of male masters, which allowed them to initiate lawsuits and demand equal treatment within the law.[2]

In the chapter that follows I examine a series of conflicts between seamstresses and tailors in Paris, Caen, and Marseilles that demonstrates how women's new corporate rights challenged and ultimately transformed privilege in the garment trades. These legal battles reveal the ways the two groups understood their corporate status and the relationship to the law it conveyed on them. The confrontation between seamstresses and tailors also raises wider questions about the place of women in the guild system.

What were the parameters for women in the traditional guild system, as represented by tailors' guilds? Could the guild system easily accommodate new groups of women, given its ostensibly gender-neutral legal framework, or did the inclusion of women necessitate a fundamental transformation of corporate structures? To what extent did women's legal and social identity change as guild members, and how did men react to their new privileges? Finally, what factors other than gender affected struggles between seamstresses and tailors?

The answers to these questions offer new insight into the significance of guild membership for male and female artisans in Old Regime France. As I will show, the seamstresses and tailors differed in their conceptions of corporate status, particularly as the corporation related to the family and gender. When challenged by seamstresses, tailors declared the family to be central to the life of their guild. Masters were not individuals, but male family heads, with crucial responsibilities to their wives and children. The threat posed by seamstresses surpassed their economic privileges to endanger their male role as family leaders. For the female artisans, by contrast, gender was the primary focus of their corporate identity. A seamstress was above all a female artisan who worked for and with other women. She belonged to a guild as an individual, not as the representative of a family unit. Seamstresses believed that all female needleworkers, including tailors' kin, should fall under their jurisdiction. They looked with scorn at the privileges and skill women acquired in the patriarchal workshop, and expressed pride in their own legal and professional autonomy.

Corporate Privilege and the Law in Old Regime France

The importance of corporate privilege derived from the fact that Old Regime France possessed no written constitution outlining a set of fundamental laws. The king held absolute power to create new laws and confirm or revoke existing ones. French subjects held no basic civil rights other than the particular and exceptional privileges granted by the king and his ancestors. Privilege existed in myriad varieties. The First and Second Estates enjoyed the well-known prerogative of exemption from direct taxation, while different provinces negotiated their own liberties when they entered the French kingdom. The king also granted rights to corporate groups such as guilds, academic bodies, and royal officers. Even individuals could obtain royal privileges, usually in the form of a monopoly over a particular branch of manufacture or commerce.

Privilege bestowed a distinctive legal position on its proprietors. In contrast to other French subjects, owners of privilege possessed well-defined legal rights that the royal government could not ignore or arbitrarily dismiss. Of course, royal ministers exploited the system of privilege to meet the needs of state. When the royal treasury fell short, ministers demanded new fees for the "confirmation" of existing prerogatives or obliged officeholders to finance "raises" in their annual stipends. To the end of its existence, however, the royal government remained beholden to the concessions it granted. Its dependence on the income from the sale and confirmation of different types of privilege—to royal officeholders, guild members, and individual manufacturers—led it continuously to enlarge and protect the system of privilege throughout the Old Regime.[3]

In the guild world, royal letters patent bestowed a collective legal personality on each corporation, meticulously outlining its economic rights. Their owners guarded these documents zealously, because they constituted essential proof of their prerogatives. In May 1756, the Parisian tailors' guild was obliged to produce documentation of its trade privileges to serve as evidence in a court case. A search through the guild's archives revealed the alarming fact that most of these documents had disappeared, leading its officers to note "that it is nonetheless in the interest of the guild and its members to recover and conserve the titles and documents which belong to it with the greatest care because it is upon the possession and enjoyment of these titles that the existence of the guild and the preservation of all its members depends."[4] Like the tailors' guild, corporations undertook frequent legal action to defend their privileges against encroachment from other corporate bodies or individuals. Their elected officers acted on behalf of the entire membership, hiring lawyers, initiating lawsuits, financing different types of legal action, and conducting raids on suspected illegal workers.

The litigious nature of the corporate system was legendary in its own time and remains one of its most notorious features. From the buttonmakers' enduring dispute with the tailors over cloth-covered buttons to the fight between caterers and roast-meat sellers over the sale of prepared meats, corporate battles have served critics from the Old Regime to the present as evidence of the pernicious and absurd nature of the system. The stakes in these apparently trivial disputes should not, however, be underestimated. To take the first example, tailors would lose important clients if hampered by overly slow or expensive buttonmakers; however, buttonmakers stood to lose the greater portion of their business if they allowed tailors to produce and sell buttons.[5] The corporate ideal of a fair allocation of resources could not prevail without lengthy, often acrimonious negotiation among guilds, each possessing claims to new or emerging sectors of production. Because guild statutes accorded ownership of detailed trade rights, it was inevitable that the legal system would become a central arena for settling disputes. The stakes involved were as much cultural and social as economic. Guild masters' honor demanded a firm response to aggression from other guilds, which they sought from the justice system. Failure to do so led to a sapping of corporate morale and a loss of reputation in the eyes of the outside world, which only encouraged further violations. Like their fellow subjects, guild masters relied on the law as a "principal form of regulation and enforcement."[6]

The Legal System and the Guilds

As sole creator of the guilds, the king was in principle the unique arbitrator of the corporate sphere. In practice, he delegated this authority to numerous levels of jurisdiction. The royal council habitually acted as the highest court for corporate affairs, as for all other matters in the realm. After 1661, the council held the power to overturn judgments from the nation's sovereign law courts, the Parlements.[7] The royal controller general took a personal interest in some guild disputes, seeking information from the intendants and presenting cases to his fellow counselors. Beneath the royal council, the Parlements played a crucial role in corporate affairs. France contained a total of twelve of these courts at the beginning of the eighteenth century, which grew to sixteen by 1789.[8] Parlements exercised wide powers over the guilds, judging cases on appeal from lower jurisdictions, registering acts of royal legislation affecting them, and assessing all new or revised guild statutes. In their legal battles, guilds looked to these senior members of the corporate world for patronage and protection. The close ties between the guilds and the Parlements surfaced most vividly in 1776, when the latter emerged as the foremost spokesmen against Controller General Turgot's abolition of the guilds.[9]

In Paris, day-to-day supervision of the guilds lay within the purview of the royal procurator at the Châtelet of Paris. In 1658, the king assigned this officer legal responsibility for trade corporations, with the title of "first judge and preserver of the privileges of the corps of merchants, arts and crafts, masterships and sworn trades [guilds]" in the city and suburbs of Paris. Every Tuesday and Thursday, the royal procurator judged cases presented by guild officials, masters, journeymen, or apprentices. He was also responsible for swearing in new masters and mistresses, overseeing the election of guild officials, and approving assembly deliberations.[10] The royal procurator did not issue binding rulings, but only *avis,* or advisory statements. To acquire legal status, his *avis* required approval from the lieutenant general of police, a post created by Controller General Colbert in 1667. These two officers also reviewed any new or revised guild statutes and reported their opinions to the crown.[11] Finally, an additional judicial chamber existed solely for commercial disputes. This was the "consular court," which Colbert established in Paris and numerous provincial cities as part of his efforts to regulate and reanimate trade. Consular courts settled conflicts between merchants, investors, and tradesmen regarding fraud, bankruptcy, and other commercial affairs.

On an individual level, guild masters and their workers encountered the law most frequently in the person of the forty-eight neighborhood police *commissaires.* These officials, subordinate to the three lieutenants of the Châtelet, played the combined roles of police officer, ombudsman, and magistrate. They resolved a vast array of community disputes, including many work-related problems. A master accused of fraud, a merchant whose clerk stole the merchandise, a shopgirl sexually assaulted by her customer would all make their way to the local commissaire to seek punishment against wrongdoers, publicly reclaim their honor, and obtain financial compensation. A strong adherence to this form of local police justice saturated the neighborhoods and ateliers of the working people.[12]

In provincial cities, the judicial process functioned in much the same manner through a hierarchy of jurisdictions extending from local police officials through city courts to regional Parlements. The royally appointed intendant was another extremely important actor in provincial guild litigation. In direct and constant contact with the controller general and other royal ministers, this official brought the arm of central control into the affairs of provincial guilds. When legal conflicts between guilds dragged on for many years, or involved especially heavy stakes, the intendant might intervene personally. Their reports played a crucial role in decisions taken by the royal council. In many cases, the king increased the intendants' administrative and judicial powers by appointing them as first president of the provincial Parlement, allowing them to combine their extensive prerogatives with a heavy influence over the Parlementary magistrates.[13]

Corporate bodies in Paris and the provinces skillfully manipulated these multiple jurisdictions. If a judgment went the wrong way, officials immediately set about mustering the money and legal justification to sponsor an appeal. Guild lawyers wrote, and sometimes published, legal memoranda (*mémoires*) for their clients, putting forward the strongest case for their clients and attempting to attract public sympathy. In their struggles for individual and collective access to resources—be they economic, social, or cultural—guild members drew on legal rights painstakingly outlined in their statutes and on a long tradition of seeking justice from local police officials, the Parlements, and even the king in council.

Women, Law, and Guilds

How did women fit into this complex legal system with its multiple level of jurisdiction? This question is complicated by the fact that France did not possess a unitary civil law code, but rather hundreds of distinct systems of customary and written law.[14] Women's legal status varied significantly across the country, depending on the law codes of the provinces or cities where they lived. The customary law of northwestern France, and particularly the custom of Normandy (*coûtume de Normandie*), applied the greatest restrictions on women. In Normandy, married women could not write wills independently of their husbands, nor could widows act as tutors to their children. Together, daughters could inherit a maximum one-third portion of their father's estates, if he chose to leave them anything at all. The only inheritance portion to which women were legally entitled was a dowry for marriage. An adult woman who was unmarried at her father's death fell under the tutelage of a brother or another male relative. By contrast, the written law of the South of France granted women a more equitable status. Southern women usually exercised independent control over the revenue they acquired after marriage. Fathers were free to leave daughters as much as they desired and, outside the nobility, daughters and sons usually inherited equally. The customary law of Paris fell somewhere between these two extremes. Husbands assumed sole authority over the couple's joint financial community, but sons and daughters inherited equally from their parents. Married women could write wills and act as guardians to their children.[15]

Above and beyond these regional differences, certain features of women's legal status remained constant across France. One such characteristic was their exclusion from all public positions and venal offices. As the *Encyclopédie* article on "woman" explained: "According to Roman law, which is in this point followed throughout the kingdom, women are not admitted to public charges, thus they cannot occupy the office of judge nor exercise any magistracy, nor perform the function of barrister or attorney."[16] Another common feature of women's legal status was the different rights possessed by married and unmarried women. With the exception of Normandy and a few other provinces, widows and single women over the age of twenty-five enjoyed complete control over their property and could enter contractual agreements without male approval.[17] Married women uniformly suffered the lowest level of legal responsibility, being barred from signing contracts or initiating lawsuits without their husbands' authorization. Wives could be witnesses for civil and criminal affairs but not for wills or many other notarized acts.[18]

If single women enjoyed enhanced legal status, the greatest freedoms the law accorded to women were for those who engaged in trade and commerce. Under the title of *marchande publique,* married and single women could assume independent responsibility for any commercial contract or debt. This category had existed since the Middle Ages, allowing women the legal authority necessary to conduct autonomous businesses. As the jurist Pothier explained in his *Traité de la puissance maritale:* "The utility of commerce and necessity resulted in women's dispensation from marital authorization."[19] The long existence of this legal category emphasizes the important role that the French crown accorded to women in production and commerce and the autonomy women traditionally acquired through their labor.

Guild mistresses occupied another distinct category, acquiring all of the rights of the *marchande publique,* as well as the benefits of the guild's collective legal personality. Their officers could initiate lawsuits on behalf of the entire corporation, negotiate with judicial and administrative authorities, and offer their own interpretations of the legal documents enshrining their collective existence. Instead of being represented by husbands or fathers, mistresses were represented by elected officers in guild-related lawsuits. Any judicial ruling that affected the guild's privileges required mistresses' approval or at least their participation in discussions leading up to it. Guild membership endowed women with the same legal status as men for work-related issues. As one historian has remarked: "Where [women] were entitled to a corporate identity of their own—as was the case in Paris and Rouen in particular—their corporations enjoyed privileges that were entirely comparable to those possessed by the masters of other corporations."[20]

Integrating women into the guild system was not, however, a straightforward or easy process. When seamstresses acquired guild status, their new prerogatives did not enter a vacuum, but clashed with preexisting forms of male and female privilege. Tailors' guilds had enjoyed for centuries a monopoly over the production of made-to-measure clothing, and they had extended these rights to their wives and daughters under limited conditions. When seamstresses obtained a guild based on their female gender, they set out to eliminate women's familial rights and bring all female labor under their control. The tailors responded with a campaign to retain the broad definition of their mastership. The introduction of women into the guild system thus created as many legal problems as it resolved.

The Seamstresses after 1675: Staking Out a New Legal and Economic Terrain

In Paris, a series of conflicts in the 1670s revealed the new divisions caused by the seamstresses' guild and the rapidity with which the needleworkers assimilated their new corporate identity. The royal council granted the corporation's existence in January 1675, whereupon it ordered that copies of its decision be distributed to interested parties. By February 1675, a group of seamstresses had already joined the guild, although its letters patent were not issued until March and did not come into force until the Parisian Parlement registered them in September of that year.[21] The women's eagerness is understandable, because guild membership offered significant advantages. It permitted seamstresses to work for customers, hire workers, and accept apprentices, all openly and under the protection of law. Guild regulations offered a public validation of their trade practices, competence, and probity. The prestige of becoming a mistress in a royally incorporated body provided an additional enticement. Mistress seamstresses joined a small elite of female guild members in Paris with special legal privileges and a distinctive corporate status.

These advantages quickly brought the corporation its first members, but they did not suffice to win over the majority of seamstresses. The royal government had estimated the trade to number three thousand in 1673. Twenty years later, a new government study reported the guild's population at only one thousand women.[22] If these figures are reliable, only one-third of seamstresses joined the guild. There were a number of reasons for this limited drawing power. The first was the entry fee of eighty-eight livres. Relatively small by corporate standards, this represented an enormous sum for a poor worker, equal to perhaps one year's salary. Many seamstresses simply could not afford to make the leap from illegality to corporate citizenship. The benefits of guild membership also probably failed to impress many of the trade's practitioners. With its regulations, quality controls, and taxation, corporate status did not always appeal to craftswomen who were well accustomed to violating legal barriers. If some embraced the opportunity to enter the corporate world, others preferred obscurity and marginality, with the freedoms thereof. Women who made goods prohibited by the 1675 statutes, those who had strong ties to master tailors, and those who simply had no desire to endure official interference and expense all declined to enter the new guild.

The creation of the Parisian seamstresses' corporation thus forged in the trade a new division between corporate insiders and outsiders. Although the consequences of refusing corporate membership may not have been apparent immediately, the legal rights bestowed by incorporation fostered a sharp imbalance of power between the two groups. Mistress seamstresses possessed an array of legal resources to enforce their trade monopoly. They were empowered to raid illegal workshops, seize materials and tools, and bring offenders before the royal procurator at the Châtelet of Paris for sentencing. Aside from these coercive powers, their legal prerogatives had significant ramifications for their economic and social clout within the trade.

Recalcitrant seamstresses were not the only opponents of the new guild. The tailors' guild did what it could to prevent the birth of the female corporation. In February 1675, guild officials seized goods in the home of a freshly minted mistress seamstress, claiming that their statutes granted them a monopoly over the production of women's clothing. They did so despite the fact that the woman could produce both her receipt of entry to the seamstresses' guild and a copy of the royal council decree bringing it into existence. This show of force apparently succeeded in intimidating many seamstresses. A royal edict issued in response to the seizure declared that no new candidates had presented themselves for admission in its aftermath.

The royal council quickly stepped in to protect the fledgling corporation. It dismissed the tailors' legal actions, reminding them that the women's statutes prohibited them from inspecting seamstresses' workshops. The royal council also condemned nonmistresses' attempts to evade guild control in privileged jurisdictions, forbidding them from practicing the trade in "the city and suburbs of Paris, [or] the Houses of the Temple, Saint Jean de Latran, Saint Martin, Colleges, Hostels, and other places, under any pretext whatsoever." These sites belonged to a small list of areas within Paris that remained free from corporate control, in which seamstresses apparently sought shelter from both the male and female guilds. This condemnation was part of the crown's broader rejection of the exemptions claimed by such areas. By the end of the 1670s, the royal government had eliminated most of these separate jurisdictions.[23]

Resistance within the trade continued despite this official show of support. In May 1675, the royal council issued a second decree indicating that, despite a revival in admissions, many seamstresses continued to evade the guild. The king's procurator at the Châtelet had sworn in six new officials (jurées), but they had no authority over illegal workers until the Parlement of Paris registered the corporation's letters patent. The royal council now established a two-week deadline for payment of the entry fee of eighty-eight livres, half of which went to the crown, while the other half accrued to the guild's treasury. Subsequent candidates would have to pay additional fees to the jurées, and a stiff fine of one hundred livres for illegal work. The edict revealed a combination of fiscal and administrative interests behind this move, denouncing the harm done by recalcitrant seamstresses both to the integrity of the new seamstresses' guild and to the king's coffers.[24]

Like its predecessors, this edict failed to persuade all seamstresses to enter the corporate fold. A year later, the royal council issued a third injunction on all trade members to join the guild. This time, the council's decree targeted a new group of troublemakers, women who refused to seek guild membership because "they are daughters of Master Tailors, and they claim that the Art of the statutes of the Master Tailors gives them the right to work in this quality." Rejecting this claim, the council ruled that "even Master Tailors' daughters will be obliged to pay the sum of eighty-eight livres." [25] With this ruling, the royal council aimed a broadside at a set of preexisting female corporate privileges. It was no longer attacking hidden, illicit seamstresses, but members of guild masters' families, who enjoyed a set of legally guaranteed trade rights.

In 1660, the tailors' statutes had explicitly allowed masters' daughters to make children's clothing for their own account, as long as they did not marry outside the trade. They forbade all women from practicing the trade, except for: "daughters of Masters of the said estate, who remain to be provided for [demeurent à pourvoir] and need to earn their living, to whom it will be permitted to clothe small children up to the age of eight years only and with the permission of our Procurator at the Châtelet and the consent of the said Officers of the said trade." [26] These trade rights were part of a range of prerogatives women held through kinship ties to male guild members. Few corporations went so far as to allow masters' daughters to work on their own account, but virtually all permitted widows to continue their husbands' trades under restricted conditions. As a rule, widows played no role in the guild's administration, and they lost their trade privileges on remarriage to a member of another trade. Widows could, however, transmit their privileges through marriage, a prerogative sometimes extended to daughters as well.[27]

When it ruled against tailors' daughters, the royal council rejected the traditional privileges of the guild family in favor of the new female corporation. Its actions did not represent a crusade on behalf of independent women's rights, but an effort to protect a corporate institution created by royal fiat. Having required artisans to form guilds in 1673, the crown was determined to ensure the legitimacy and vitality of these organizations. Failure to do so would discourage other artisans from forming or joining the new corporations it hoped to create. This move had financial as well as administrative ramifications, for royal officers were also seeking to protect the revenue they expected from the guild.

This decision did not end the dispute. In July 1677, seamstress officials complained to the lieutenant general of police that a number of tailors continued to employ women in their workshops. In response, he issued an ordinance permitting the women to inspect tailors' workshops in the company of a police *commissaire*.[28] This ordinance significantly altered the 1675 statutes, which had prohibited the two guilds from inspecting each other's members. Carrying the logic of the statutes one step further, the Parisian police official now empowered seamstresses to supervise all female labor in the garment trades.

The tailors did not overlook the new sexual divisions emerging in their trade. Prompted by the police ruling, three master tailors, apparently serving as proxies for their guild, lodged a formal opposition to the seamstresses' statutes. They demanded the right to employ women, specifically their own daughters, as well as servants, orphaned masters' daughters, and masters' nieces. Demonstrating their adroitness with gendered arguments, they pointed out the scarcity of alternative economic opportunities for their female relatives given that women could not join male guilds. The tailors lost the first round of this battle when the seamstresses obtained a favorable ruling from the Parlement of Paris in February 1678, a decision the tailors promptly appealed. On April 22, 1678, the Parlement of

Paris issued a final ruling against the male guild, authorizing masters to employ only their own daughters and one female servant. As an exception, it permitted tailors who specialized in women's clothing to employ all masters' daughters. Finally, the Parlement's ruling validated the police ordinance that allowed officials from each guild to inspect members of the other guild.[29]

In making this decision, the Parlement sought a compromise between the principle of sexual segregation underlying the seamstresses' guild privileges and the traditional family prerogatives of the tailors' guild. It did not eliminate the rights of tailors' daughters but restricted them to working for their fathers or for ladies' tailors. In doing so, the Parlement echoed the royal council's and police officials' support of seamstresses' claims to represent all female labor in the garment trades and confirmed sexual segregation as a new status quo. The positions of the three parties were substantially altered by these conflicts. Seamstresses' trade identity had clearly undergone a significant transformation by the end of the 1670s. With an immediate grasp of the stakes of guild membership and the legal resources available to corporate groups, guildswomen took strong action to defend their privileges and to conquer new territory. Their perception of the trade rights of tailors' daughters as an injustice reveals their view of themselves as a legally constituted group with guaranteed prerogatives. The guild's action against illegitimate female needleworkers also underlines the particular nature of their privileges. Seamstresses brandished their female sex to obtain incorporation, but their guild strategies revealed little interest in defending women's labor rights as a whole. They did not defend women's economic opportunities per se, but their own exclusive privileges as guild members.

On the opposing side, the tailors' battle drew on mixed motives. First of all, the tailors struggled to maintain a source of cheap labor. Deprived of inexpensive female workers, they faced higher expenses for employing skilled male journeymen. The tailors were also inspired by their responsibilities as family heads. In French, one sense of the word *pourvoir,* used by the tailors in the passage above, is to settle girls with husbands. By safeguarding their daughters' privileges, master tailors tried to maintain the young women's ability to acquire a dowry for marriage or to support themselves outside the family if necessary. Their masculine pride and honor also motivated them to retain their full range of privileges as master tailors and family heads. For them, a master tailor was not merely an individual entitled to practice a trade, but a husband and father who provided economic opportunities for his family. The seamstresses' victory thus represented a loss of economic, social, and cultural position for the tailors.

The biggest losers in this decision were the tailors' daughters. Whereas they had previously possessed the right to make children's clothing on their own account, henceforth they were obliged to choose between joining the seamstresses' guild, working in their fathers' workshops, or seeking employment from ladies' tailors. Their status as masters' daughters diminished as a direct result of the creation of the seamstresses' guild. While mistress seamstresses now exercised their trade as legally responsible and independent businesswomen, tailors' daughters fell back into dependence on the male heads of their families.

A Mixed Guild: Seamstresses against Tailors' Widows in Caen

In the provinces, seamstresses and tailors also struggled over the interplay of gender, privilege, and family. In fact, their legal battles were more complex, because both trades belonged to a single guild in many towns and cities. Given the exceptional nature of provincial seamstresses' corporate status, neither guild members nor royal or municipal officials could be certain of the exact rights they possessed. Royal officers were long familiar with the inequality and hierarchy inherent in the guild system and in other corporate institutions, but the new factor of gender introduced unprecedented and vexing problems.

Unlike the Parisian case, royal regulations had resolved from the outset the problem of tailors' daughters in Caen. A 1719 ruling required both tailors' daughters and seamstresses' sons to undergo apprenticeship prior to entering the guild. Moreover, daughters were not allowed to practice the trade without obtaining guild membership. The status of tailors' widows, however, was more ambiguous. The guild's 1712 statutes and the ruling of 1719 both maintained traditional corporate rights and restrictions on masters' widows. As in other guilds, they could continue working in the trade unless they married a nontailor. Because tailors could work for men and women, their widows were tacitly empowered to make and sell women's clothing, even if their husbands had specialized in men's clothing. These rights formed the basis of repeated legal conflict between seamstresses and tailors from the 1720s to the 1740s.[30]

As was the case in Paris, the seamstresses of Caen initiated the crisis by undertaking legal action against tailors' female family members. In 1722,

1723, and 1740, their officials obtained a series of police sentences ordering tailors' widows and daughters either to be received as mistress seamstresses or cease making women's clothing. Matters came to a head in November 1742, when the lieutenant general of police authorized a raid on the workshop of Anne Vauquelin, who was accused of working in the trade illegally. Having obtained the tailors' participation on the basis of this claim, guild officials raided the woman's home and seized her merchandise. On learning that the woman was a master tailor's widow, however, the tailors' officials angrily requested the annulment of the seizure. In July 1743, the lieutenant general of police rejected this demand, ruling that tailors' widows did not inherit the right to work in their husbands' occupation, specifically not in the production of women's and children's clothing. In the future, they would have to become mistress seamstresses if they wished to work in the trade.[31]

Both parties reacted quickly to the new ruling. Bypassing the Parlement of Normandy, the tailors appealed the case directly to the royal council. This led seamstresses to address their own request to the council for confirmation of the police sentence. After consulting with members of the Bureau de commerce—the royal advisory body for commercial affairs—the council passed judgment in the tailors' favor. On July 24, 1744, it decreed that widows of masters who did not remarry could continue to work for women and children. The seamstresses appealed this decision in turn, claiming that they had received inadequate opportunity to respond to the tailors' case. To settle the dispute, the intendant of Caen, Louis Arnaud de la Briffe, possibly acting on orders from the controller general, ordered his deputy in Caen to investigate the matter. Between July and November 1745, the subdelegate received representatives from the guild on at least two occasions. Accompanied by their lawyers, tailors' and seamstresses' elected officials appeared separately to present their statements.[32]

The tailors appeared first, offering a defense based primarily on the legal precedent for their widows' rights to produce women's clothing. They recalled that the 1712 statutes as well as the 1719 settlement guaranteed this prerogative, which was completely in accordance with the situation in Paris and Rouen. To prove this point, they produced a letter dated August 16, 1743, written by a Parisian master tailor's widow "who works for women without being a seamstress, because she enjoys the privilege of her late husband." For additional legal justification, the tailors turned to the tenets of civil law, citing the well-known jurist Domat's comments on the privileges of venal officeholders' widows: "It is a right of office that the quality, rank and the privileges of officeholders [*officiers*] pass to their wives and remain with them when they are widows, because the man and the woman together are one in flesh, so that the wife holds from the husband everything that can pass to her sex."[33]

This statement aptly summarized the nature of privilege that tailors defended in both Paris and Caen. Mastership belonged to the family unit, represented by its male head. Sons inherited direct claims to mastership from their fathers, which they used to build families of their own. Women could not hold guild privileges independently, but they could exercise them provisionally until they entered unions with other men. When they married, they transmitted the patriarch's prerogatives to their new husbands. The family thus constituted a discrete corporate group within the guild, with the master acting as a caretaker of family privilege.

The tailors further supported their position with economic arguments, claiming that women's clothing offered the only viable trade option for their widows. According to the officials, the seamstresses' demands would "cut off the principal and almost unique resource which remains to widows after their husbands' death, that is the just faculty which belongs to them to work for women and children as well, without which they would be deprived of the means of subsistence, because it happens very rarely that the public addresses itself to a woman for men's garments." The tailors might have added that legal restrictions on women's inheritance rights in the customary law of Normandy would render their widows' economic position particularly difficult.[34]

The seamstresses countered this paternalistic view of corporate privilege with an appeal for equal treatment and fairness. Armed with a certificate signed by twenty-six colleagues, guild officials Jeanne Bienaimé, wife of Dupont, and Marie Ferey presented the seamstresses' response. Their statements pointed out the logical inconsistencies in existing regulations for male and female guild members. They argued, for example, that if tailors' daughters had to complete a two-year apprenticeship and be accepted as mistress seamstresses in order to make women's clothing, it was only logical that their wives and widows fulfill the same requirements. They also claimed that if the 1712 and 1719 regulations endowed masters' widows with the de jure status of mistress seamstress, the rules should have permitted widows to accept female apprentices. Instead, the 1712 statutes explicitly prohibited widows from taking apprentices, while authorizing mistress seamstresses to have one apprentice at a time. Hence, the guild's own statutes implicitly denied tailors' widows the prerogatives of a mistress seamstress. Rejecting the tailors' comparative arguments, the seamstresses insisted on the particular situation of Caen. Paris and Rouen should not serve as models for their guild rights "because each city has its customs and particular regulations with respect to the different professions that are practiced there."[35] They also deemed seventeenth-century law texts irrelevant to their situation, because these authors had written about officeholders, not tailors and seamstresses.

The issue of female guild status assumed central importance for both sides in the debate. Seamstress officials claimed that women belonged to a distinct and separate corporation within the tailors' guild. In their eyes, their elected representatives and separate assembly meetings proved the existence of two corporations, each with "different attributes and faculties." The only factor uniting seamstresses and tailors, they claimed, was their common sewing skills. Tailors' spokesmen indignantly rejected these claims of independence, which they characterized as a revolt against royal authority: "Everything announces here the spirit of revolt, the lack of respect on the part of the Mistress Seamstresses for the decisions [that have] Emanated from the very authority of his Majesty."[36] They drew an implicit parallel between the king's authority over his realm and the master's authority over his household: the illegitimate meddling of the seamstresses undermined both. They complained of the "perpetual chicanery" that seamstresses "have exercised against Masters' wives to make them fall into the trap that they have set for them." Tailors' wives and widows, they declared, "cannot be submitted to the yoke that the mistress seamstresses would like to impose on them, not only without any law, but even against the authority of the sovereign."[37] Order could only be restored, they implied, by reaffirming appropriate male control of the guild.

The seamstresses' officers responded to this attack by claiming the moral high ground. Their statement complained about the difficulty of gathering seamstresses to defend their rights "because of the attachment they have to their work, and to retreat and prayers during their free moments." They also claimed that master tailors hired journeymen to do all their work, allowing them to devote their time to "finding ways[,] while emptying a bottle, to harass and file suit against the defendants."[38] Although one should not underestimate the rhetorical nature of these complaints, they may hint at important differences between seamstresses' and tailors' work identities. It would not be surprising if, like other male artisans, many tailors experienced trade sociability in taverns and drinking parties. The seamstresses, by contrast, may have spent more of their spare time engaged in religious devotion. As chapter 8 will discuss, seamstresses possessed a high number of books, which were usually devotional in nature, in comparison to other artisans. Seamstresses therefore may have combined work with prayer and religious reading, deriving a self-consciously virtuous and honorable trade identity from this mixture.

Apart from castigating the tailors' debauchery, seamstresses also denigrated the trade skills women acquired in the patriarchal family workshop. As they demanded, "how in fact would the wife of a tailor or his widow, who had never had other exercise but to sew men's suits under the obedience of her husband, want to meddle in cutting, cutting out and making up women's and children's clothes?"[39] They suggested that a tailor's wife would possess only simple sewing skills, while the mistress seamstress must know how to make patterns, cut cloth, and sew women's dresses. The tacit issue here was not only skill, but independence. The seamstresses implicitly contrasted their independent economic status with a wife's subordinate role in her husband's workshop. A subsequent statement addressed this question from another angle, claiming that the tailors' wives had "no quality" to initiate legal proceedings without being authorized by their husbands. These claims surely reflected seamstresses' pride in the legal autonomy that allowed them to pursue independent lawsuits.

Like Parisian masters' daughters, tailors' wives or widows in Caen never spoke officially during this affair. Because they possessed a legal identity only as an extension of their husbands, they did not participate in the negotiations between corporate bodies regarding their fate. According to the tailors, the women themselves had protested seamstresses' attempts to control their labor, stating that they "strongly opposed their claim and reproached them that they had no capacity [titre] to oblige them to be received as Mistress Seamstresses." Their own words, however, never formed part of the official record.

Despite their heated rhetoric about tailors' wives, the major ambition at stake for seamstresses in this conflict was ultimately not the wives and widows at all, but the trade rights of tailors themselves. In their statements before the subdelegate, the seamstresses issued the startling claim that they alone should be allowed to make women's clothing. They further declared that, during the negotiations surrounding the 1719 agreement, the tailors had agreed to make only male clothing in the future if seamstresses would work only for women. To support these assertions, the seamstresses argued that the wording of the legal documents themselves reflected the tailors' renunciation. They claimed that the articles of the 1712 and 1719 regulations that limited the seamstresses to women's clothing had actually signified an exclusive monopoly on the production of women's clothing. After 1719, they claimed, the trade had been segregated along gender lines with female seamstresses making clothes for women and male tailors making clothes for men.

This was an extraordinary claim. In every French city where seamstresses acquired guild status, they did so with the explicit condition that tailors' preexisting privileges remain unchanged. The advantages of seniority, plus the unspoken weight of male social and economic predominance, meant that seamstresses gained only a portion of the garment trades in competition with the tailors. Now, the Caen seamstresses attempted to reverse the situation, using the restrictions imposed on them as an advantage in their favor. Arguing from an assumption of legal and logical equality, they declared that if female seamstresses made clothing for women only, male tailors should be restricted to male clothing. With these assertions, the battle took on new stakes; seamstresses were not only at tacking widows' capacity to make women's clothing but tailors' access to this market as well.

In a second statement, the seamstresses increased their bravado, asserting that Parisian tailors themselves held the right to work for men only. According to this statement, the Parisian seamstresses' 1675 statutes had granted the female guild a monopoly on the production of women's clothing, wholly excluding the tailors from this branch. To prove this claim, they cited article 2 of the seamstresses' statutes which prohibited cross-gender hiring among tailors and seamstresses, as well as the total administrative segregation of the two guilds. These claims underline the extent to which the seamstresses were attempting to manipulate the legal documents, because the first article of the 1675 statutes clearly maintained the Parisian tailors' right to make clothes for women. The seamstresses and their lawyers apparently hoped that neither the tailors nor the royal council would bother to verify the contents of the Parisian statutes.

In the context of these legal disputes, the tailors' scandalous behavior at the burial of the mistress seamstress four years earlier in summer 1741 becomes more comprehensible. Corporate privilege held conflicting meanings for male tailors and female seamstresses. Tailors' identity as guild masters contained a strong familial element and was closely associated with their ability to transmit privileges to family members. They conceived of a guild world composed of male-dominated families in which women had an important role to play as wives and daughters, but not as independent actors. Their attack on the seamstress's burial thus arose from a sense of injury over female interference in male control of guild rituals. The specific insults they used also emphasized the sexualized component of female honor; they told unmarried seamstresses that they might as well undress because they had already lost their "display" before the gathered crowd. Their actions and words rejected the women's attempts to display a public and guild-based form of honor, suggesting that the only honor women could possess was private, domestic, and sexually modest.

Seamstresses clearly formed another view of the possibility for a female honor derived from their guild membership. They were proud of their guild status, of their role in public corporate ceremonies, and of the legal independence that allowed them to defend this role. They were equally gratified by their ability to represent themselves and other women in public places: in church and before the intendant and police officials. Their guild honor was not, nevertheless, gender neutral. For the seamstresses, as for the tailors, sexual purity and modesty formed crucial elements of a distinctly female honor. This emphasis may explain the exclusion of men from unmarried mistresses' burials, as a celebration of their chaste virtue. Even in death, the putatively virgin female body should not be touched by men, because male hands would pollute her purity as she entered the grave. It also explains their hostility to the tailors' alleged excessive drinking and tavern haunting. In contrast to the tailors, however, seamstresses believed that their corporation was a source of female honor, not a pretext for abandoning it. Guild status permitted women to make an honest living working for female clients in exclusively female workshops and to protect this honor in the courts.

The reaction of the wider public to the burial scene suggests a mixed response to these claims. The police official supported the seamstresses, condemning the tailors for their infraction and imposing a symbolic, if not very expensive, fine. The bystanders, however, seemed less sure of the seamstresses' position. According to the women's report, it was the observers' acceptance of accusations of "misconduct" that made them withdraw from the burial ceremony. A degree of uncertainty seems to have prevailed among male and female residents of Caen regarding the honor and prestige of guildswomen's public functions. Guild status endowed seamstresses with the capacity to defend their activities in court, but not with a convincing public persona vis-à-vis the other inhabitants of the city.

In the larger legal conflict regarding tailors' rights to make women's clothing, the royal council delivered a ruling that severely checked the seamstresses' pretensions. The council's edict permitted widows to work in their husbands' trade for men or women until remarriage, with a potential fine of two hundred livres on the seamstresses if they interfered with this right. Tailors and their widows retained the capacity to work either for men or for women, as they saw fit. After this date, the seamstresses continued to exist as an almost discrete unit within the tailors' guild. Seamstresses and tailors were bound by formal corporate ties, but they were also divided by conflicting, often bitterly opposed, visions of male and female roles in the guild. Tailors experienced the seamstresses' incorporation as a corrosive assault on their economic, familial, and corporate authority. Seamstresses, by contrast, saw their attachment to the tailors' guild as a constant constraint to their freedom. Their vision of corporate independence, based on the examples of their colleagues in Paris and Rouen, remained frustratingly beyond their grasp.[40]

Tailors' Wives, Whalebone, and Guild Status in Marseilles

In Paris, two independent guilds disputed issues of gender, corporate status, and privilege; in Caen these problems opposed a distinct guild within a guild. The tailors and seamstresses of Marseilles belonged to a third category. Unlike the previous cases, the Marseilles seamstresses possessed no administrative body to represent them or make decisions on their behalf. Their membership in the guild endowed them with a tacit capacity to participate in corporate decision making, yet no mechanism existed to name representatives for this purpose. A series of legal conflicts in the 1720s and 1730s generated ad hoc representatives of the trade, who became victim to accusations of manipulation and self-interest.

Precisely because of the instability of representation among seamstresses, the Marseilles dispute allows a greater diversity of voices to emerge than did the previous cases. Whereas elected officials presented seamstresses as a bloc in Paris and Caen, different groups competed to speak as their legitimate voice in the southern city. In particular, the Marseilles case highlights the importance of economic issues, behind legal conflict in the garment trades. It also reveals the blurring of lines between the two groups of women—seamstresses and tailors' female relatives—opposed to each other in the previous cases. Women calling themselves "seamstresses" in Marseilles were as likely to be tailors' wives or daughters as independent artisans. The law did not merely reflect existing social or economic categories, but rather was a tool that could be manipulated by particular interests.

In February 1675, at the moment when Parisian seamstresses were embarking on their new corporate existence, the tailors of Marseilles revised their sixty-year-old guild statutes. Their new regulations endowed masters' daughters with the same trade rights as Parisian tailors' daughters. Adopting the precise wording of the Parisian guild's 1660 statutes, they prohibited all nonguild members from working in the trade, except for "Masters' Daughters of the said Status, who remain to be provided for and who need to earn their living, to whom it will be permitted to clothe small Children up to the age of eight years-old only." On marriage to a nontailor, they would lose this privilege. The Marseilles statutes permitted women who were not related to a master tailor to acquire the same trade rights, by paying a fee to join the guild's confraternity.[41] By 1712, seamstresses had become subordinate guild members, with the right to work for adult women and employ female workers, but not to open public shops.[42]

These female trade rights remained unchanged until the late 1720s, when a series of legal conflicts erupted between the tailors and the seamstresses. As was the case in Caen, the disputes culminated in a formal hearing between tailors and seamstresses before the intendant. This time, however, trouble did not arise directly from contention over tailors' female relatives. Instead, the conflict focused on the use of whalebone in women's undergarments. As we have seen, this was an issue that generated legal disputes between Parisian tailors and seamstresses in the same decade. Problems began in Marseilles in 1728, when tailors' officials appeared before the municipal officers claiming that seamstresses were using whalebone in violation of their trade restrictions. The tailors succeeded in obtaining a sentence prohibiting seamstresses from making whaleboned stays. The officers' sentence also forbade women from clothing boys above the age of eight and from hiring male workers. It did not affect seamstresses' capacity to hire as many female workers as they desired and to make other articles of women's and children's clothing.

Four years later, the case was reopened. In December 1732, three women calling themselves "seamstresses" lodged an appeal to the 1728 ruling before the Parlement of Provence. The Parlement again ruled in the tailors' favor, reaffirming the municipal officers' decision to deprive seamstresses of the right to produce garments with whalebone. Henceforth, tailors' daughters would be the only women allowed to use whalebone in making women's and children's clothing. The sentence imposed a stiff fine of three hundred livres for violators, six times the fee required for joining the guild. On the strength of this ruling, tailors' officials began to prosecute seamstresses whom they caught making whaleboned garments.

At this point, however, the story becomes more complicated. According to the intendant's subsequent report, the municipal officers of Marseilles claimed that the 1728 judgment was the fruit of conspiracy between the tailors and six so-called seamstresses, who were in reality members of tailors' families. The officials told the intendant that six women had appeared before them to accept the sentence on behalf of all seamstresses. Each of these women, they declared, was actually the wife or daughter of a master tailor. They made similar accusations with regard to the 1732 appeal. This appeal, they stated, was lodged by three tailors' relatives masquerading as independent seamstresses, with the purpose of obtaining an authoritative ruling on whalebone in favor of tailors and their daughters. Far from opposing the Parlementary ruling, the women had formally approved it. To cover up this detail, the tailors had printed an abridged version of the ruling, which purposefully failed to mention that the judgment was delivered with the consent of both parties.[43] The intendant lent credence to the municipal officers' accusations, pointing out that the three "seamstresses" involved did not appear on a list of 250 female guild members submitted by the tailors. The fact that tailors' daughters were the only women authorized to use whalebone by the 1732 Parlementary sentence certainly adds weight to suspicions of family interest.[44]

Shrouded in suspicion, this ruling prompted a series of appeals and counterappeals, producing a new group of spokeswomen for the female needleworkers. In 1734, five "seamstresses" submitted a request to the Parlement at Aix to be received as a third party to the ruling. Contesting the representative capacity of the original trio, they argued that the ruling was invalid because other seamstresses affected by it had not been consulted. The Parlementary magistrates apparently found these women's arguments persuasive, for they ultimately supported seamstresses' right to work with whalebone. Their sentence of June 28, 1735, reverted to the regulations of 1694, permitting seamstresses to use whalebone and prohibiting tailors from interfering with their commerce in such items. The tailors' subsequent attempt to overturn this decree failed. The magistrates rejected their appeal and expressed their exasperation by condemning the guild to pay the trial fees and by imposing an enormous—and in all likelihood unenforceable—future fine of one thousand livres for attempts to prevent seamstresses from using whalebone.

Although they ruled against the tailors, Parlementary magistrates offered them some compensation for the loss of exclusive rights to whalebone. This took the form of a new prohibition on public boutiques among seamstresses. This was a largely symbolic gesture, for few seamstresses operated public shops even in cities where they were permitted to do so. Because seamstresses fabricated custom-made clothing for individual clients, they had few wares to display in a boutique, and most were too poor to invest surplus capital in renting a public display area. While it is possible that Marseilles seamstresses concentrated more heavily on ready-to-wear garments than did their colleagues, it is doubtful that they could muster the resources to venture into this sector any more than could their Parisian colleagues. The high price of cloth rendered investments in stocks of material or ready-to-wear clothing too expensive and too risky for the vast majority of seamstresses. It is thus more likely that the public shop served as a symbol of high-status commercial work as opposed to the lowlier status of homeworkers.

Whatever the Parlement's intentions, this compensation proved insufficient for the tailors. Refusing to abandon the struggle, they protested the decision in writing to Controller General Orry. The minister responded by instructing the intendant of Provence to conduct a formal hearing into the matter and then draft recommendations to resolve the conflict. Like his colleague in Caen, the intendant received both tailors' officials and city officers, who presented their version of events in a series of statements. Seamstresses, however, had no elected officials to intervene in the affair, and hence were represented by the five women who had successfully appealed the 1732 ruling to the Parlement in Aix. After allowing each party to respond to the statements of the other, the intendant submitted a report and suggestions for revising the guild's statutes.

As might be expected, these hearings elicited different readings of the social identity of seamstresses and tailors, the nature of their work, and the most advantageous economic possibilities available to them. The tailors informed the royal official that many masters concentrated exclusively on the fabrication of stays and other whaleboned items. Seamstresses' invasion of this sector, they insisted, would lead to their bankruptcy and a loss of public confidence in the guild, because the women sold low-quality goods under the "set price." As the tailors claimed: "Working whalebone requires strength and capacity, and since the one and the other are lacking to women, who have also undergone no examination at all in stays, they can only make defective works to the public prejudice." They insisted that the seamstresses of Marseilles had sent their stays to the French West Indies, where their poor quality prevented them from being sold. Seamstresses had supposedly also given these articles to used-clothes dealers in Marseilles, who experienced similar difficulties selling them.[45]

Like their colleagues in Caen, the five seamstresses responded with a mixture of legal and moral arguments. They pointed out that the tailors' 1675 statutes did not prohibit seamstresses from using whalebone. Moreover, in the neighboring city of Aix-en-Provence, they noted, seamstresses were permitted to make all types of whaleboned garments in competition with the tailors. In addition to these practical arguments, they invoked moral considerations by stating that "it would be indecent if women were obliged to employ men for these sorts of garments that approach them so closely." The seamstresses did not argue that tailors should be excluded from making stays, but that the royal government should maintain women's ability to decide whether they wished to hire male or female artisans. This argument had echoes reaching back to Louis XIV's explanation for his creation of the Parisian guild in their 1675 letters patent.[46]

Throughout the negotiations, both sides attempted to profit from the lack of fixed representation among seamstresses. The tailors maintained that the five seamstresses' claim to be a "third party" to the Parlementary ruling was unfounded, because all seamstresses in the guild had signed a written acceptance of the decree of 1728. Furthermore, they suggested that the five women had no authority to undertake legal action on behalf of their female colleagues. Any rights won by the five seamstresses on appeal should apply to those women alone, not the trade as a whole. In addition to denying their opponents' representative quality, the tailors also fashioned their own version of collective "consent" from the seamstresses. In their negotiations with the intendant in 1737, they proudly produced a declaration signed by thirty-four seamstresses, by which the signatories renounced the right to work with whalebone and accepted the 1732 Parlementary ruling. According to the tailors, these thirty-four women were the most experienced of the two hundred and fifty seamstresses in the guild. Surely, they argued, these senior seamstresses understood the interests of the trade better than the five appellant mistresses, none of whom had belonged to the guild for more than seven years.

In fact, the tailors claimed, the five women who opposed them were the only members of the guild who engaged in staymaking, an assertion that sits oddly with their claims for the damage perpetrated by seamstresses in this sector. These women's self-interested position thus did not represent the interests of seamstresses as a whole. Instead, the tailors insisted, "the liberty which the decree of 1732 accords the seamstresses to work in an open boutique and to procure themselves customers through the display of their work to the public is much more advantageous to them than the faculty to make whaleboned works in the obscurity of a room with no sign."[47]

When it was their turn to speak, the five seamstresses rejected the tailors' attempts to fashion a form of ad hoc representation among the female half of the guild. They firmly supported the municipal officers' claims of conspiracy between tailors and their relatives in obtaining favorable judgments. The thirty-four women who had signed the 1732 document, they claimed, were "for the most part the wives, daughters and relatives of tailors, who furthermore not knowing how to make works with whalebone and only making women's dresses [*habits*] have more interest in working in an open boutique than in a [private] room, in order to procure clients."[48] Contrary to the tailors' pretensions, they declared, a larger group of women had refused to sign the declaration. Their wish to use whalebone was so strong, the seamstresses reported, that they had contributed to the legal expenses of the 1734 appeal.

As these back-and-forth arguments reveal, the collective legal identity of seamstresses as guild members had little efficacy in the absence of formal procedures for naming representatives. Their corporate status entitled them to participate in decision making, but the absence of accredited officials made it extremely difficult to produce binding decisions. Perhaps the most telling factor of these disputes is that while both sides claimed to be defending collective interests, the vast majority of seamstresses took no active part in the proceedings. Throughout the legal episodes, no more than fifty out of two hundred and fifty seamstresses participated in organized discussions of their trade privileges. The others remained silent, perhaps too ill informed, indifferent, or preoccupied by their daily tasks to intervene. This may have been the case in Caen and in Paris as well, where the official voice of the guild masked the limited nature of participation.

Although it is impossible to know how "ordinary" seamstresses reacted to these events, the statements recorded by the intendant suggest that the conflict of identity among seamstresses arose from deeper fractures within the trade. Far from being a united group, seamstresses in Marseilles fell into at least three or four different trade specialties, including ladies' dresses, children's clothing, hoopskirts, and whaleboned stays. The recent origins of the last group were confirmed by the municipal officers who stated that "in all time the seamstresses have had the faculty of working on garments for people of their sex, but they have never possessed [the right] to make whaleboned dress bodices [*corps de robe*], except for small children under age eight."[49] The women were also split into different social groups, which did not correspond neatly with these forms of specialization. Some had joined the guild as newcomers to the trade, others were relatives of mistress seamstresses, while yet others were the daughters, wives, or sisters of master tailors.

The persistent confusion between seamstresses and tailors' relatives emerges in the frequent use of the term *tailleuse-couturière* (female tailor-seamstress), to describe female needleworkers. Seamstresses themselves may have had little sense of belonging to a gender-specific, coherent female trade, sharply separate from the tailors. In revealing the ambiguities behind the trade appellations, this case may offer a truer sense of the ambiguous sentiments of needleworkers across France. Lawsuits and legal briefs prepared by guild officials portray a cohesive corporate vision, but it may have been one that was shared by a small number of highly active members. In practice, seamstresses may have had closer ties to male artisans and tradesmen than their statutes or official declarations suggested.

In all likelihood, however, women's exclusion from guild administration in Marseilles did more than merely reflect underlying disunity in the guild. It probably also acted to discourage the creation of a distinctive female corporate identity. Compared to their Parisian and Norman colleagues, the southern seamstresses were relatively passive members of the corporate sphere. They did not attempt to oust the tailors' female relatives from the guild or assert their control over all female labor within the garment trades. Nor did they agitate for administrative participation in the guild. In Caen and Paris, a clear distinction existed between guild mistresses, who participated in decision making, and tailors' wives or daughters, who did not. This differentiation was lacking in Marseilles, where all women were excluded from guild administration.

If seamstresses were not always clear on their affiliations, observers were even less certain. The Parlement's fluctuating judgments in Marseilles hint at the magistrates' inability to sort out the divisions of the trade. Like its counterpart in Normandy, the Parlement in Aix took seriously its role as arbiter of corporate privilege. Asked to pass judgment among tailors, their female relatives, and seamstresses, its magistrates acknowledged that each party possessed legitimate claims on the trade. To reach a compromise, they tried to isolate different areas of privilege, and divide them fairly among the claimants. An equitable division of labor was impossible, however, when the identity of the female groups was constantly thrown into question. The alternating decisions taken by the Parlement reveal the considerable potential for manipulating magistrates, especially since they did not live in Marseilles and may have had little familiarity with the particularities of the garment trades in that city.

After hearing representatives of both sides, the intendant of Provence drew up a new set of regulations based largely on the Parisian model. As discussed in the previous chapters, the new rules allowed seamstresses to open public boutiques and hire as many female workers as they desired, but not to employ male workers. They could produce simple whaleboned garments, such as hoopskirts, corsets, and bodices, but not the complicated and expensive whaleboned stays. The intendant's reliance on the Parisian model did not extend to separating the two trades. Instead, he recommended that seamstresses and tailors remain in a joint guild. He offered the seamstresses no new administrative powers or access to decision making in the guild. This solution apparently settled or covered over the worst tensions in the guild, because no traces exist of subsequent litigation between tailors and seamstresses to the end of the Old Regime.

Corporate Self-Defense: The Parisian Tailors' and Seamstresses'
Response to the Turgot Reforms

A final context in which to assess tailors' and seamstresses' ideas about corporate status, gender, and family lies in the appeals they wrote to oppose Turgot's abolition of the guild system in 1776. Before the abolition edict appeared in February of that year, rumors of its impending arrival led some guilds to attempt to prevent this ruinous event by commissioning *mémoires* defending their privileges. Once the edict took force, a new shower of appeals appeared, some in printed form, others as letters addressed to individual authorities. Written in a moment of severe crisis, these documents reflect the circumstances of their creation, containing arguments and language adapted to the particular economic, political, and ideological context that produced them. Even more than previous legal briefs, they must be read as rhetorical and strategic statements, for the stakes at risk were of unprecedented magnitude and the struggle mobilized legal actors who usually had little time for artisans and their affairs.

In the desperate struggle to preserve their existence, seamstresses and tailors did not abandon the representations they had developed in previous legal cases. They did, however, cast them in new ways designed to elicit maximum sympathy from their readers. The tailors' and seamstresses' 1776 appeals provide a reappropriation of the outstanding aspects of their guilds, in which we find existing models of guild identity expressed with new valences. The Parisian tailors brought the guild family to the forefront of their appeal, emphasizing the intimate connection between the corporation and the family. Parisian seamstresses, by contrast, insisted on the exclusively female composition of their guild and the need to protect vulnerable female workers from male competition. At the moment of extreme crisis in 1776, guild leaders isolated and crystallized what they felt to be the very essence of their corporation and asked their lawyers to cast it in the most effective manner possible.[50]

The seamstresses' guild produced at least three appeals against abolition. The first appeared in February 1776, shortly before Turgot's edict. Titled "Supplement to the *Mémoire* to Be Consulted of the Six Corps, for the Seamstresses' Guild," it was the only one to appear in published form. The title referred to a legal brief published by the powerful Six Corps some days earlier on February 1, 1776. Both documents were written by Jacques-Vincent Delacroix, a lawyer attached to the Parisian Parlement.[51] His prominence, and his well-publicized association with the Six Corps, undoubtedly led the seamstresses to seek him out as an able and influential advocate for their cause.[52] Following this published text, they addressed two additional appeals to individuals, the first to Marie-Antoinette and the second to the procurator general of the Parlement of Paris, Joly de Fleury.

Delacroix's *mémoire* on behalf of the seamstresses served as a model for the two later documents. His text began by accusing men of appropriating inherently female skills. Women possessed a natural and moral claim to certain activities, which men had unfairly taken from them: "There are in society charges that demand only softness, intelligence and justice; honors that can reward peaceful heroism and beneficence; works that require only a vivid and brilliant imagination, only grace and finesse in execution. Without doubt, women had the right to claim them, man has robbed them because he is stronger."[53]

Delacroix went on to list a series of female virtues that surpassed traditional notions of femininity, including grace and elegance as well as intelligence, eloquence, and scientific ability. He suggested that women should develop their talents to their full potential and exercise professions like the law, medicine, and literature. His Rousseauian inclinations, however, also emerged in this text. Instead of embellishing themselves and "speaking in a circle," he argued, rich women ought to devote themselves to useful activities and lead simpler, more virtuous lives.

Turning to the artisanal trades, Delacroix declared that guilds were created to give order to the world of work, to provide surveillance against fraud, and to enlighten ignorance. Here again, however, men had excluded women as "if they were incompetent, incapable of works that demand only taste and elegance." In making this argument, Delacroix implicitly echoed Turgot's criticism of the guilds' nonadmission of women. He differed from Turgot, however, in using this male bias as a crucial argument for preserving the seamstresses' guild. This corporation, he claimed, was the unique female guild in France and the sole haven for women's work. It was the best-regulated of all guilds, characterized by order, justice, economy, and a wise beneficence toward its members. Delacroix similarly idealized the guild officers: they distributed charity among poor mistresses, conducted orderly inspection visits, avoided extraneous expenses, made all decisions with laudable impartiality, and had demonstrated zealous service to the state on numerous occasions. Even if all other guilds were abolished, this rare haven of female labor should be preserved.

In this text, women's work consisted of taste, not skill, and the guild's functions were viewed as moral rather than economic. Apprentices' principal task, Delacroix declared, was to learn moral standards, not professional skills. Echoing Rousseau's *Emile,* he stated that the most important lesson for a young girl was "that of making herself respected by her modesty and the purity of her actions." Earning a living was apparently a negligible consideration. The officers accordingly looked for moral fiber, not proficiency, in potential mistresses: "the guild officials worry less about the competence of the mistress than the wisdom of her conduct and the excellence of her principles." Guild officials' chief role was to uphold the moral purity of their mistresses: "What makes them infinitely precious is the severity with which they denounce the mistresses who would expose their students to seduction and would not guarantee them from dishonor."[54]

Implicitly countering Turgot's faith in the free market, Delacroix declared that female workers could never equal the strength and cunning of men, and therefore could not successfully compete with them. He referred to men as "tyrants" and "pirates," recounting a series of battles that female trades had lost to men. Without guild protection, seamstresses would soon join this number and inevitably turn to prostitution to support themselves. Female customers would then be left to the mercy of male tailors. Delacroix referred to the tailors' "vulgar hands" that touched women's bodies during the fitting process and "the curious eye which prolonged its observations, under the pretext of a more scrupulous exactitude."

A second group waiting to exploit weak, young female workers was sexually corrupt mistresses, whom he vilified as worn-out prostitutes: "These odious and decrepit creatures who, no longer being able to traffic in their outmoded persons, put a price on indigent beauty, would bless the day when their empire would be suddenly enlarged, where their resources would be multiplied."[55] Without the guild's supervision, these women would prey on innocent girls, forcing them into prostitution for their own profit. The story recounted in the *mémoire* involved oppressive men, wise guild officers, pimping mistresses, and tender apprentices. All relations implied domination or subordination, with the virginal female body at stake in the struggle.

These themes reappeared in the appeals sent to Marie-Antoinette and Joly de Fleury. Both relied heavily on the published *mémoire*, copying large sections verbatim. The seamstresses addressed the first to Marie-Antoinette, hailing her as "the most amiable Queen who has embellished the throne of France." Reiterating Delacroix's claim that Louis XIV's queen, Marie-Thérèse, had patronized the guild's creation, it called on Marie-Antoinette to renew her predecessor's support for working women. With this petition, a female guild thus appealed to the highest female authority in the kingdom for help in conserving the sexual purity of French women and an important source of charity for poor women. It is unknown whether Marie-Antoinette ever received the document and, if so, how she responded.

The guild sent the second appeal to Joly de Fleury, procurator general at the Parlement of Paris. While Delacroix's brief and the letter to Marie-Antoinette appear to have been written before Turgot's edict, this text was written afterward, as a plea for the guild's reestablishment. Echoing the published document, the author emphasized the charity distributed to poor mistresses through the guild. The letter also insisted that even if the guild system was abolished, the "weakness of the [female] sex" necessitated maintaining the seamstresses' corporation. The seamstresses asserted their willingness to correct any abuses within their guild and to accept union with another trade. As Delacroix had done, however, they insisted that such a union should only take place with another women's guild: "It [the guild] would not believe it to be appropriate to unite them with professions or guilds regulated or governed by men." Finally, the letter pointed once more to the guild's charity to poor mistresses as a compelling reason to resurrect it.[56]

The relationship between these texts and the guild leaders who commissioned them is difficult to assess. In some ways, the texts clearly corresponded to officials' perceptions of the guild and its corporate identity. For example, passages in Delacroix's brief that refer to the guild's ideal administration echo statements pronounced during guild assembly meetings. As I will discuss in the next chapter, the officials' sound financial and administrative management was a frequent theme of assembly minutes. Over the eighteenth century, the guild's leaders fashioned a corporate self-image based on their exemplary administration, and it was natural for guild officials to wish to see themselves portrayed in a flattering light. It is also clear that the gender-specific nature of the trade, and the desire to avoid mixing with male artisans, reflected strong and long-cherished feelings within the guild. From the first decades of its existence, the corporation's distinctive gender composition had constituted its central feature and main claim to existence. In Paris and Caen, a distinct form of female corporate honor emerged based on the trade's exclusively female composition and clientele. From 1675 to 1776, seamstresses were vehement in defending their autonomy from male control. Moreover, female corporate leaders might well have feared losing their unusual degree of authority and freedom of speech and action in a mixed-sex guild.

The prurient sexualized imagery in these documents, however, is more difficult to attribute to guild officials. To be sure, seamstresses frequently invoked moral issues in legal conflicts before 1776. In 1675, they claimed that the trade was their only means to earn an "honest living." In the 1720s, Parisian seamstresses evoked undesirable physical contact between tailors and their customers to support their right to make corsets and stays. In Caen in the 1740s, seamstresses accused male tailors of excessive drinking, in contrast to their own devotion to prayer and work. Nevertheless, the hyperbolic language used to depict guild mistresses as pimps and prostitutes in 1776 was a new turn in guild rhetoric. Surely, guild leaders did not believe that their mistresses were all decrepit prostitutes, eager to lure innocent young apprentices into the world of prostitution. In their day-to-day guild administration, they concerned themselves with economic and institutional issues, rather than questions of sexual morality. They judged mistresses' masterpieces, supervised apprenticeship contracts, raided illegal workers' apartments, and initiated lawsuits to defend their privileges. Assembly minutes never refer to a moral police of the trade or its practitioners. Reducing female honor to individual chastity, this document disavowed seamstresses' efforts in Paris and Caen to project a trade-based, public, and corporate brand of female honor.

How, then, may we explain the choice of language and imagery in this text? The first place to look for answers is Turgot's edict abolishing the guilds. Even before the edict was issued, copies must have circulated in Paris, and it is highly likely that Delacroix had read Turgot's preamble. In this document, the controller general explicitly raised concerns about women's exclusion from incorporated trades, and he castigated guilds for contributing to female unemployment and prostitution. The sensitivity of this issue may be judged by the fact that Attorney General Séguier also took up the problem of prostitution in his defense of the guilds. It was therefore natural for Delacroix to respond to these concerns and argue that far from increasing prostitution, the seamstresses' guild was the best defense against it. As a savvy lawyer, he focused on the area of greatest anxiety surrounding women's work, fashioning a case designed to have a maximum effect on its readers.

Beyond the immediate demands of the situation, Delacroix's *mémoire* also played on a set of themes and tropes that concerned him as an individual. Delacroix had come to national prominence through his defense of the modest Veron family against the aristocratic Morangies family in the early 1770s. According to historian Sarah Maza, Delacroix frequently positioned himself in legal cases as the defender of the weak against "violent and arbitrary authority." His favorite rhetorical strategy was the opposition of idealized representatives of good and evil, making him one of "the ablest practitioners of the new melodramatic style of forensic argument." Specifically, Delacroix was a practiced expert in wielding highly melodramatic, sexualized imagery. Several of his earlier cases involved issues of gender and sexuality, in which he explicitly connected female sexual virtue to the moral health of the nation. In 1776, Delacroix published a work titled "How Much the Respect for Morals Contributes to the Happiness of States." In this pamphlet, he argued that women's morals consisted primarily of maintaining sexual purity and that female morality was of prime importance to the overall well-being of the state.[57]

By taking on the seamstresses' case, we may hypothesize, Delacroix could bring together his resistance to the ministerial "despotism" that capriciously threatened the trade corporations and his concerns for moral virtue and purity. Destroying the guilds threatened not only economic production or social order, it endangered the moral health of the French nation. With this intervention, he drew the seamstresses' guild into the wider political and cultural developments of the late Old Regime, in which highly gendered and sexualized language served to make arguments in the public sphere. The seamstresses' reactions must have been mixed. Having hired a well-known and presumably expensive legal counsel, they adopted his strong rhetoric in the appeals they sent to the queen and to the royal procurator. They probably had private questions about his depiction of their mistresses as pimps and aging prostitutes, but they could certainly agree that a female guild offered essential protection to economically and sexually vulnerable women.

The sexual and moral concerns evoked by the seamstresses' appeals offer a striking contrast to the arguments put forward in a *mémoire* published by the tailors' guild on February 17, 1776. Whereas the seamstresses' texts largely elided economic concerns, the tailors' *mémoire* strongly emphasized them. It argued that consumers benefited from guild masters' desire to preserve their public standing: "The desire not to compromise his reputation at all, makes him use better materials; his interest is not only not to deceive, but to avoid being the involuntary instrument of fraud."[58] Masters' public status, the tailors further argued, supplied the confidence essential for credit relations. Without the guarantees offered by guild supervision, no artisan would be able to acquire credit or dare to undertake business, and "the Arts will die from this liberty." Their corporation was thus a social and economic bulwark, which served to maintain fragile ties of trust, loyalty, and cooperation.

The tailors' appeal thus depicted the corporation as fulfilling crucial economic and social functions, rather than sexual ones. Master tailors were represented as honorable, trustworthy merchants rather than at best vulnerable, and at worst venereal, individuals. Guild officials also fulfilled significantly different functions. They were prosperous senior craftsmen not moral or sexual watchdogs:

> They only achieve the rank of Guild Officer, after a long and honest exercise of their estate; when after having overcome all the dangers, they begin to collect the fruits of their labor, and joining a type of ease with a firmly established reputation, they cede to the desire to be doubly useful, to merit the benevolence of the Magistrates, after having justified the Public's confidence.[59]

Despite its emphasis on economic concerns, the tailors' appeal was not devoid of morally freighted arguments. The last section of the document dealt with the disastrous effects guild abolition would have on masters' families, specifically their widows and daughters. In the past, it stated, the family always seemed a "precious object" in politics: "A father [who is a] good worker is an estimable Citizen; his example, his talent, his name, become for his children the most profitable part of his succession." The tailors also stressed the importance of privileges accorded to masters' widows. When masters died "an enlightened indulgence leaves the widow in possession of the privilege which was in some ways the title for which she consented to submit to the charges, the burdens, the fatigues, the perils of maternity." Without guild protection, journeymen would abuse defenseless widows and orphans.[60]

According to the tailors, legitimate marriage would decline as well. At present, they argued, all "honest" workers aimed to marry once they had achieved an estate. In order to protect his public reputation, a master avoided scandalous relations, seeking "in the breast of hymen a caution that nourishes him." In his wife, a master found "an assiduous companion to his labors, an affectionate consoler in his pains, which she shares and softens." In his children, he foresaw the aid that would one day lessen his fatigue and increase his profits. If a worker could not aspire to mastership, he would have no reason to be scrupulous in his conduct, and would prefer "a sterile libertinage to a fecund chastity, a shameful and murderous debauchery will become his unique occupation." Girls would avoid marriages with workers: "Who is the girl who will dare to contract the terrible tie of marriage with a being with no quality, of whom nothing assures the fate and whom the first accident may reduce to the last indigence?"[61] The inevitable decline of legitimate marriage would weaken public morality and reduce reproduction.

The tailors' legal history suggests that these references to widows and daughters were not mere rhetorical flourishes. Their battles with seamstresses in Paris and the provinces demonstrated a stubborn determination to defend their wives' and daughters' trade privileges. Throughout the Old Regime, the family lay at the center of the tailors' perception of their guild status. They conceived of the master as a head of household, who provided economic security to his wife and children. Like the seamstresses, however, the tailors' corporate identity took on new overtones in the struggle of 1776. Sarah Maza has described the increasing use of "private affairs," and in particular the family, to debate "public affairs" in this period. By arguing for their existence on the basis of "family values," the tailors gave new political and cultural valence to their long-standing reliance on the family. As their female colleagues had done, they fashioned a self-defense that framed their perceived raison d'être in the ideological terms of the day.

Seamstresses and tailors fought for their corporate existence in 1776. As they did so, they drew on the aspects of their guilds that they believed to be crucial, family in the tailors' case and female gender in the seamstresses'. These were notions that emerged from their everyday practices of work and the ways they acquired guild status. They were also honed and articulated in decades of struggle between the two groups. The expression of these ideas in 1776 represented a new level of politicization of guild identity. In the struggle to maintain their existence, guild leaders worked with their lawyers to devise the most convincing and urgent justifications for their survival. It was not surprising that they drew on earlier notions and cast them in a manner appropriate to the political and cultural tropes of their day. The overlap between guild affairs and wider political or cultural developments demonstrates the adroitness of corporate lawyers in picking up on current themes. It also suggests a loss of legitimacy for the corporate system itself. In the context of 1776, guild lawyers could no longer confine themselves to arguments based on legal precedent, statutes, or privilege. They were forced to define the corporations in terms that critics could understand and appreciate. In doing so, they crystallized long-standing notions of corporate identity, but they also added new and sometimes disturbing elements to corporate self-representation.

Conclusion

Seamstresses and tailors engaged in legal disputes over the relations among gender, guild status, and family from the moment women acquired independent guild privileges. In Paris in the 1670s, they fought over the status of tailors' daughters. Seamstresses won this battle when they acquired jurisdiction over all female labor in the garment trades. In Caen in the 1720s, seamstresses and tailors struggled over the rights of tailors and their widows to make women's clothing. This time the seamstresses were unsuccessful, although they did achieve greater autonomy within the guild than the tailors had anticipated. In Marseilles in the 1730s and 1740s, the two groups disputed seamstresses' right to use whalebone to make hoopskirts and stays. This case revealed the lack of clear differentiation between tailors' female kin and independent seamstresses, a characteristic encouraged by the women's exclusion from guild administration. Finally, in 1776, the Parisian tailors' and seamstresses' corporations sponsored legal *mémoires* to protest the abolition of the guild system. These documents reveal the new political spin placed on old arguments, as the two groups struggled to redefine themselves as essential features of French social and economic life.

In tailors' guilds, the family remained a largely tacit feature of guild life, until it was placed in peril. The seamstresses' new corporate privileges raised the question of the guild family in a new and revelatory manner. When threatened with the erosion of their family privileges, master tailors in Paris and Caen asserted their capacity to employ female dependents as a crucial part of their mastership and their prerogatives as patriarchal family heads. They perceived the loss of these rights as an assault on their status as both guild masters and men. The Parisian statutes' injunction on guild officials to rule as "good fathers" thus represented much more than empty guild rhetoric. Whether or not they had articulated these notions before 1675, the creation of the seamstresses' guild forced them to acknowledge the importance of family to their guild.

For the seamstresses, corporate status held a quite different meaning. Guild membership provided a means for women to escape the patriarchal family and its constraints. Mistress seamstresses assumed autonomous legal responsibility for their business affairs. They initiated lawsuits, presented complaints to royal officials, and appeared in public as representatives of their guild. It was the independence offered by corporate status that they found exhilarating, as well as the unusual legal autonomy the guild accorded them. In Paris and Caen, therefore, women's inclusion in guilds had significant social and cultural as well as economic ramifications. Corporate statutes constituted formal recognition of the seamstresses as a collective, legal group, endowing them with a fixed identity backed by the power of the state. The law did not bring seamstresses into being, but it did constitute them as a group with shared privileges and interests, which distinguished them from other women. Through incorporation, seamstresses acquired the capacity to designate other groups of women as illegitimate and to receive state support in their efforts to eliminate them from the labor market.

Seamstresses' aggressive use of their legal rights reveals how quickly these women assimilated the ramifications of corporate status. Little delay occurred between their acquisition of rights and their attempts to reinforce or increase them. These case studies also demonstrate the surprising accessibility of corporate identity to women. Despite the rare and unusual status of female guilds, seamstresses rapidly fashioned a self-confident, gender-specific corporate identity. They not only strove to defend their position but to improve it, attacking the trade rights of tailors' wives and daughters, and even questioning tailors' prerogative to make female clothing. In these battles, the law was often on their side. Once they acquired rights over the "female" side of the trade, a strong basis existed for them to demand rights over all female articles of clothing or all women workers. It does not seem to have occurred to them, however, to formulate requests to make male clothing. They stretched their arguments very far, but only within the sphere of female garments and female workers. This self-imposed limitation indicates the extent to which this was a "gendered" trade.

The case of Marseilles, however, shows the dangers of simply equating guild identity with lived identity and reducing seamstresses to their gender affiliation. Some seamstresses had closer ties to tailors than to their female colleagues. Gender might function as a less salient factor for women than kinship or trade specialization. The lack of corporate representation among Marseilles seamstresses, however, seems to set this case apart. Unlike their colleagues in Paris and Caen, the southern women did not take leading roles in guild ceremonies or assemblies. They did not listen to female officials draw sharp distinctions between independent seamstresses and tailors' wives. As a result, they had few opportunities to nourish their identity as a group of independent, incorporated, female artisans, or to brandish this identity in opposition to tailors' female relatives. In Paris and Caen, seamstresses possessed a stronger sense of guild identity, fostered by the existence of female administrative institutions. In the next chapter I will investigate women's exercise of their corporate administrative powers by examining the management of the Parisian seamstresses' guild during the eighteenth century. As I will show, officials often lived up to their claims of exemplary conduct, but they also gained substantial concrete benefits from their role in corporate leadership.[62]

More generally, legal conflict between tailors and seamstresses reveals the results of the spread of sexual segregation as a tool for organizing society and the economy. After the Parisian seamstresses received a guild defined by its sexual division of labor, subsequent legal decisions followed the logic of segregation that their statutes established. Across France, authorities based legal decisions within the garment trades on this principle. Those affected by these judgments received them as a new and often shocking innovation. For some women, like the seamstresses, the use of sexual difference as a criterion of decision making offered important advantages. They were quick to seize and manipulate it as far as they could. Other women derived forms of corporate privileges from other institutions, such as the patriarchal family. Finding themselves disadvantaged by the new distinctions based on sex, they clung to their existing privileges as long as they could. For them and their male relatives, the extension of gendered distinctions into their families and corporate associations was deeply upsetting. Even in the seamstresses' case, adherence to the interests of their own sex was often instrumental, because they used their privileges largely against other women and in favor of their own particular trade rights.

SIX

Women's Corporate Self-Government:

The Administration of the Parisian

Seamstresses' Guild

Historians have characterized Old Regime France as a corporate society, but they have uncovered little about the institutional lives of its corps. As a result, well-known stereotypes of closed, exclusive, and archaic guilds retain currency within historical scholarship. According to this view, guild leaders formed a closed and selfish oligarchy that funneled funds to their own pockets and cared little about the needs of ordinary masters. Guilty of poor administration, petty litigiousness, and jealously stifling technology, they stood little chance against ministers determined to plunder their resources to meet government debts. Corporate leaders responded to external pressure by closing their ranks to outsiders, creating a quasi-hereditary system. This view of the guilds may be traced in a direct line from eighteenth-century physiocrats to twentieth-century historians.[1]

Until recently, the lack of studies of individual guilds prevented serious questioning of these stereotypes. In the last ten to fifteen years, however, a number of revisionist studies has offered a more nuanced interpretation of corporate administration. As Steven Kaplan concludes in his study of Parisian bakers: "The guild was rotten in many places, but it showed more resourcefulness and resilience than anyone could have plausibly expected."[2] With regard to guild recruitment, Kaplan found that, rather than becoming more exclusive, the bakers' corporation remained open to newcomers throughout the eighteenth century.

These questions are important not merely to salvage the reputation of eighteenth-century guild officials, but because they address crucial elements of Old Regime politics, economy, and society. Guilds were the most common corporate bodies of Old Regime France and among the few widely available to members of the Third Estate. As semipublic institutions, trade corporations formed a central element of urban police and administration, acting to regulate economic production, labor markets, sales practices, and trade training. For their own members, guilds provided not only economic privileges and social status, but forms of self-governance and ongoing relationships with municipal and royal officials. Whatever their flaws, they offered some of the most salient institutional structures and organizing principles of urban life. A study of guild administration thus promises new insight into Old Regime society and relations between subject and government under an ostensibly "absolutist" monarchy.

Seamstresses were at once exemplary and exceptional members of the guild system. They confronted many of the same problems as their male counterparts: holding guild elections, policing members, collecting taxes, negotiating with royal and municipal officials, and resisting encroachment from illegal workers. As one of the largest guilds in the capital and one of a handful composed exclusively of women, however, the seamstresses encountered distinctive exigencies of their own. In this they allow us to examine the particular question of female corporate self-government, as well as broader issues of corporate administration and interaction between guild and state.

From its formation in 1675, the royal government appears to have fashioned a special mission for this female corporation, intending it to be a widely accessible haven for modest working women. During the 116 years of its existence, the seamstresses' guild largely fulfilled this role. Like Steven Kaplan's bakers, the 350 women who served as guild officials between 1675 and 1791 acted as mostly dedicated and responsible, if self-interested and undemocratic, wardens. They created and oversaw one of the largest systems of trade training in Paris and sheltered mistresses from the burdens of royal taxation. They successfully steered the guild through a series of financial crises, emerging with a rare record of financial surplus and with little trace of the internal conflicts that marked so many other guilds.

Administrative Structures of the Guild

Three tiers of authority administered the seamstresses' corporation. Its six elected officials, or *jurées,* constituted the first level. The 1675 statutes stipulated the annual election of three officials, each serving a two-year term to ensure continuity in administration. Elections took place on the Friday before the feast day of the Trinity, which arrived in late May or early June. The officials were responsible for enforcing the corporation's statutes and protecting its best interests. They assigned the masterpiece to aspiring mistresses and presided over its fabrication, assisted by a senior mistress who accompanied the candidate through the process. The statutes called on *jurées* to perform at least two annual inspection visits on each mistress and as many additional visits as they wished. They were also empowered to raid the homes of needleworkers suspected of violating guild privileges.

The guild's assembly constituted the second tier of administration. It was composed of the six acting and all former officials. Throughout the eighteenth century, the assembly held the highest level of authority within the corporation, examining and endorsing new policies on behalf of the membership as a whole. Once elected to the guild's leadership a woman maintained life-long participation in the assembly as well as permanent voting rights in annual elections.

The final level of authority for the seamstresses' guild resided in the royal government officials who held jurisdiction over the Parisian corporations. The royal procurator at the Châtelet served as magistrate for guild-related affairs; he also involved himself in day-to-day aspects of corporate life, swearing in new guild members, supervising elections, and authorizing decisions taken at assembly meetings. His actions were overseen by the lieutenant general of police, who held final authority over the Parisian guilds. New or amended guild statutes required the approval of both officials and the Parlement of Paris.

Guild Elections

The right to autonomous self-government constituted one of the central principles of the corporate system. Contrary to what one might expect in the "absolutist" Old Regime, guild leaders were elected by masters and mistresses, not appointed by police officials. The royal procurator of the Châtelet attended and supervised elections, but he did not interfere in the voting process. The procedures followed for these elections, however, were far from democratic. As historian Gail Bossenga suggests, guild government corresponded to a "corporate notion of representation" rather than a democratic one.[3] Most guilds ranked their members hierarchically according to seniority. In common guild parlance, former officials were *anciens; modernes* had belonged to the guild for more than ten years; and *jeunes* had less than ten years' seniority. *Anciens* could usually vote in all guild elections, while only a small number of *modernes* and *jeunes* participated. The 1710 statutes of the Parisian bakers' guild, for example, directed that three new officials be elected every year by an electorate composed of all *anciens,* twenty *modernes,* and twenty *jeunes.* The much larger tailors' guild enfranchised forty acting and former officials, forty *modernes,* and forty *jeunes.*[4]

The seamstresses' 1675 statutes offered somewhat perplexing hierarchical categories, deriving perhaps from their inexperience with corporate terminology. According to these statutes, the new guild's electorate included "the officers in Charge, all of the mistresses who will have served in charge, forty *anciennes,* twenty *modernes,* and twenty *jeunes* who will be called to the Election in turn."[5] The statutes did not indicate how electors were chosen "in turn" nor did they explain the categories, which drew a highly unusual distinction between *ancienne* mistresses and those who had served as guild officials. The seamstresses themselves did not persist in this usage, for subsequent documents used the term *ancienne* in the same manner as other guilds, to refer to former officials. Given this uncertainty, we may only conclude that the 1675 statutes offered limited representation to junior guild members, with a clear bias in favor of former officers.

According to the royal procurator's election records, the seamstresses' electorate totaled approximately 80 in the first decade of the guild's existence. By the 1730s, this group had grown to around 110 women, drawing new participants from the growing pool of former officials. The size of the electorate averaged between 95 and 110 through the 1770s, attaining a high of 140 in 1742.[6] This increase in the electoral pool did not pass unnoticed. In a revised set of statutes written in the 1770s, an unknown commentator—in all likelihood the royal procurator at the Châtelet or the lieutenant general of police—referred to ongoing problems in guild elections. He explained that extending suffrage to a large number of ordinary mistresses had been necessary in the early years "because there were too few former officers to compose an election."[7] In the 1770s, however, the size of the voting body undermined its good order, leading to "chaos" during the voting process. Accordingly, he proposed limiting the number of non-*jurées* who participated in elections. This project was probably not put into effect, for the seamstresses' did not receive new statutes until 1781 and they contain no reference to this plan.

Instead, the 1781 statutes declared that the new guild's *syndics* and *adjoints,* as the senior and junior officials were henceforth called, would be elected following procedures outlined in the royal edict of August 1776 that reestablished the Parisian guilds. According to this edict, guild leaders were henceforth supposed to be named by a group of thirty-six "deputies," who composed a new guild assembly. These deputies, in turn, were to be chosen by an assembly of four hundred mistresses. To maintain order, the deputies would meet in separate groups of one hundred based on the neighborhoods in which they lived. Syndics, deputies, and assembly members were all to be chosen among mistresses who had paid full fees to enter the reformed guild. These rules were not specific to the seamstresses but intended for all of the new corporations.

Considered overly large by some observers, the guild's electoral pool contained no more than 5 percent of the total population up to 1776 and hence was scarcely representative. The extent to which it was a true vote is also open to question, for voting patterns reveal a strikingly high degree of consensus. In the 1730s, four or five candidates might stand for the three available positions, but three candidates received almost all the votes. After 1745, such multi-candidate elections became less common. On rare occasions, the vote might split among credible candidates, as in 1752 when voters divided over the choice between Marie Anne Jacquet and Marguerite Louise Briant for the third position, or in 1767 when five candidates fought a tight race. In most cases, however, the three winning candidates received close scores, with an occasional outsider achieving a distant fourth place. Between 1769 and 1774, four elections were noted simply as "unanimous." After 1750, the guild's elite appears to have tightened its grip over the elections, using them as a means to sanctify chosen candidates rather than as a true process of selection. Those who opposed their choices rarely registered their disapproval by running for office themselves.

There is also evidence that successful candidates paid a high price for their office. In July 1771, Catherine Marthe Blesson, an acting official of the guild, filed a complaint with the royal procurator at the Châtelet of Paris. She alleged that in May she had given Marie Jeanne Sibille, then acting official and guild accountant, the sum of 1,200 livres to cover the "fees and dues" of her election. She now demanded that Sibille account for the money and return any surplus to her. The corporation's rules and regulations included no mention of an election fees, but this example suggests that substantial confirmation fees were a regular part of the electoral process. The royal procurator rejected her demand and required no account of the money from Sibille.[8]

Between the guild's birth in 1675 and its death in 1791, some 350 women
served as *jurées*. Most were mature women with substantial professional
experience, who worked as seamstresses before, after, and during their
period in office. At least 50 are known to have taken one or more apprentices during their careers.[9] In 44 cases where information is available, the
average time span between entry to the guild and election as a *jurée* was
almost twenty-one years (median = 21). Marie Marthe Lachaise attained
this position most quickly, winning election in 1756 only seven years after
she entered the guild as a mistress's daughter. Two other women, one a
mistress's daughter and the other a finished apprentice, shared the prize
for the longest wait, at thirty-four years each.[10] The guild's new statutes of
1781 confirmed existing practices by prohibiting the election of mistresses
with less than ten years of seniority.[11]

Although the circle of guild leaders was self-selecting, newcomers continually replenished it. Before 1776, there is no evidence of a mistress being
elected to office more than once. In the absence of corporate archives or
the officials' private papers, the path toward election remains obscure. Professional reputation and financial success were apparently not the most important factors. In 1773, for example, a printed guide to the Parisian commercial and retail trades offered a list of twenty-eight of the most famous
seamstresses within the capital.[12] Among them only two women served
as *jurées*. Patronage and mentoring bonds were probably more important
than professional success in admitting mistresses to the restricted circle of
guild administration.

Family ties played a significant but not a predominant role. In only
twenty-one identifiable cases did daughters of former officers become officers in their turn. Among them, we find four pairs of sisters. Geneviève
Françoise Para, wife of Briant, served as *jurée* from 1721 to 1722. Her two
daughters, Marie Charlotte Briant and Marguerite Louise Briant, were
also elected to this post, the former in 1748 and the latter in 1753, after an
unsuccessful bid the previous year. In another example, Louise Bellemer,
wife of Deveaux, became *jurée* in 1736. Her daughters Marie Anne Deveaux
and Ursulle Louise Deveaux both became mistresses during their mother's
two-year term in office, benefiting from the reduced entry fee required of
jurées' daughters. Marie Anne was elected to office in 1752, a post to which
her sister acceded in 1760. In some cases, service to the guild continued

across three generations. Marguerite Benoist, wife of Billard, acted as *jurée* sometime before 1718. Her daughter, Louise Henriette Billard, wife of Josset, won election in turn in 1733. Billard's two daughters, Marie Henriette Josset and Marie Louise Josset, followed their mother and grandmother into this position some twenty years later, the former elected in 1754 and the latter in 1767.[13]

These examples notwithstanding, most jurées found their way to corporate leadership without inherited access. Moreover, most were newcomers to the seamstresses' trade. Out of forty-four cases where information is available, thirty officials were newcomers to the trade who entered the guild through apprenticeship. Only ten were mistresses' daughters, while the remaining four became mistresses through outright purchase. If these examples are representative, less than one-quarter of *jurées* had mothers who had belonged to the guild. The relative weakness of familial transmission remained stable over the eighteenth century, guaranteeing newcomers the same ability to join the guild elite. As the next chapter will reveal, this finding corresponds to the overall weakness of mother-daughter transmission in the guild. Although there is no means to gauge the possibility, non-maternal kinship ties may have substituted for maternal ones. The high proportion of unmarried women elected as *jurées* — 39 percent of a sample of 191 *jurées* — highlights the potential importance of non-maternal kinship bonds, such as between aunts and nieces.

Overall, mentoring and patronage were probably more important than familial relations. The life stories of two *jurées* reveal the formation of patronage ties among unrelated mistresses. In 1734, mistress Renée Chollet accepted two orphaned sisters, Barbe and Marie Louise Chartrain, as apprentices for a four-year training period. The girls probably had some previous knowledge of the trade, for their deceased mother was also a guild mistress, perhaps a friend or acquaintance of Chollet. In the apprenticeship contracts, Chollet agreed to give the girls lodging and food in addition to vocational instruction.[14] Four years later, Barbe Chartrain and her sister emerged from this tutelage to become mistresses in their own right, using their mother's status to abbreviate the normal period of work experience required after training. In 1753, Renée Chollet won election to the post of *jurée*. Ten years later her protégé Barbe Chartrain was elected to this position.

Throughout their lives, both Chollet and Chartrain remained unmarried. When Chollet died in 1768, she and Chartrain were neighbors on rue Mauconseil, located near the central market district of the Halles. Although she was quite poor at the time of her death—receiving fewer than one hundred livres in annual revenue from annuities—Chollet instituted a priest of her parish as the executor of her estate.[15] Her will bequeathed fifty livres to the poor mistresses of her guild, as well as a dress and other personal effects to Barbe Chartrain. As this case suggests, personal bonds among *anciennes,* whether based on family, apprenticeship, or friendship, served as a means of recruiting and reinforcing the guild's leadership. Among the two thousand guild members, a core group of elders maintained close personal and professional relations. With ties dating back to adolescence, these women met frequently in guild assemblies and enjoyed social relations beyond the corporate offices, exchanging visits, gifts, and perhaps clients or trade secrets.

The Guild Assembly and the jurées

The guild assembly served as a forum for a wide range of issues. The most serious of these issues involved threats to the guild's privileges or to its institutional autonomy. A lawsuit initiated by another guild, a raid performed on a mistress by corporate rivals, or the imposition of new taxes all called for the immediate convocation of an assembly. This institution also addressed more mundane questions, such as granting monthly stipends to impoverished *anciennes* or undertaking new construction on the guild's offices. In general, all decisions involving new or extraordinary expenses required formal ratification by the assembly. It acted as the voice of the guild, serving to validate the *jurées'* actions on behalf of the entire membership.[16]

The seamstresses' 1675 statutes made no reference to an assembly, but it must have existed from the first years of the guild's creation. Such meetings probably played a vital role in formulating strategy during the difficult period of the 1690s and 1700s, when the royal government imposed a series of venal offices on the guilds. Formal procedures for assemblies, however, did not emerge until 1718. In a meeting of July 1718, the record noted that "in the past several years a number of extraordinary assemblies have been held for the affairs of the said community." Guild leaders regretfully noted that many *anciennes* did not attend because of the "loss of time that the said assemblies caused them[,] taking them away from their own individual and daily affairs." Heavy absenteeism rendered the meetings virtually useless.[17]

The June 1718 meeting thus took measures to raise assembly attendance, resolving to distribute two tokens, worth twenty-five sous each, to every woman present at an assembly. This was a large sum, amounting to significantly more than a worker's daily wage. To prevent abuses, the number of such meetings was restricted to four each year. Assembly members also agreed that future meetings would occur between two o'clock and five o'clock in the afternoon in the guild's offices. By the 1740s, the number of annual meetings had risen from four to twelve, a pace that persisted until the guild's demise. Reimbursement for assembly attendance weighed heavily on corporate finances. During the 1750s, the treasury spent over one thousand livres each year on assembly tokens. The corporation spent another thousand livres a year on the twelve pounds of sugar distributed to each *ancienne* as a New Year's present.[18]

The financial rewards adopted in 1718 succeeded in restoring high attendance rates. In 1718, the first year for which we have records, up to seventy-seven *anciennes* attended assembly meetings. From the 1720s to the 1740s, these gatherings regularly attracted fifty members or more. During the mid-1750s attendance appears to have fallen off, but the disappearance of records after the early 1760s makes it impossible to confirm this suggestion. Some *anciennes* accumulated impressive attendance records. In the first half of the century Marie Gilles, wife of Bricogne, participated in assemblies from at least 1718 to 1753, a record nearly equaled by her widowed colleague Marie Ménard, who attended from at least 1718 to 1745. Another four women appeared at meetings from at least 1725 to 1745. Over the years, these women accumulated substantial experience in guild affairs, becoming living storehouses of corporate memory and tradition.

A subtle balance of power existed between the acting officials and the *anciennes.* For day-to-day affairs the acting *jurées* took charge. They performed the routine duties of signing apprenticeship contracts, admitting new mistresses, and supervising trade practices. Selected among the three second-term officers, the *comptable,* or guild accountant, played the most important role among acting officials. She recorded all incoming revenue and outgoing expenses, and at the end of her term she prepared an account of the guild's financial activities for that year. Given these responsibilities, the accountant acted as the leader among the six *jurées* and usually chaired assembly meetings.[19] Her capacity to conduct financial affairs, however, often depended on explicit consent from the assembly. From at least 1745 on, the assembly signed an annual mandate, or *procuration,* formally authorizing that year's accountant to collect payments due to the guild and to issue receipts in its name. This act also required the presence of the five remaining *jurées* and two *anciennes* for the collection of all incoming payments, and called on the accountant to summon a guild assembly in the event of crisis.

During assembly meetings, acting officials usually took the chair, often seeking approval for their own proposals rather than advice from the *anciennes*. Assembly members frequently complied, authorizing the officers to proceed in whatever manner they deemed most appropriate. For particularly sensitive matters, however, the assembly sometimes insisted on the formation of a committee composed of several of their number and the elected officials. With their long participation in guild affairs, the *anciennes* doubtless wielded strong influence over the officers, who had only one year of previous leadership experience and probably had been handpicked by the *anciennes*. Strong explicit and implicit limitations thus existed on the acting officials' authority and freedom of action.[20]

This balance of power appears to have functioned successfully on the whole. To all appearances, relations between *anciennes* and acting officials did not explode into the conflict and bitter acrimony found in other guilds. Existing assembly records contain no references to scandal, dissension, or discord within the guild elite or between it and the rank and file. Indeed, the guild's notary recorded almost every decision made in the guild assembly as unanimous. Disagreements surely occurred, which the notary must have excluded from the official minutes on his own initiative or at the request of guild leaders. This peaceful image nonetheless concurs with the unanimous or near-unanimous results of many elections, as well as with the mute testimony of police and court documents. Records from the royal procurator's tribunal contain numerous cases where acting officers prosecuted errant mistresses, but only two known instances involving litigation among guild leaders. The impression of consensus among the guild elite offers a striking contrast to other guilds, in particular the master tailors. Whether involving extortion by subofficials, financial corruption, or rigged elections, documents from police, judicial, and guild archives testify to the corrosive conflicts that erupted within tailors' corporations in Paris and elsewhere.[21]

The *anciennes* of the seamstresses' guild were extremely proud of their administrative record. In 1719, they congratulated themselves in an assembly meeting on their "vigilance, good conduct, and economy in the government of their community's affairs." In 1736, they reiterated the importance of the assembly in the "regulation of the affairs and police of their community," which "they dared advance [was] one of the best regulated" among the Parisian guilds. Although they did not explicitly refer to their gender or the exclusively female membership of the guild, their insistence on the peacefulness, frugality, and good conduct of their administration may have underlined a set of virtues they believed to be particularly appropriate for a female corporation. The guild's financial record, indeed, suggests that they had reason to be proud of their success among Parisian corporations.[22]

The Guild Office

The guild's life daily centered on its corporate offices. Before 1719, the corporation rented headquarters on rue Sainte-Croix-de-la-Bretonnerie in the Marais district on the right bank of the Seine. In March 1719, the assembly met to consider purchasing a building in order "to avoid the changes to which the guild's office is subject by the changes of owners and principal tenants." The *jurées* had already identified a property, which a master locksmith had placed on the market for 28,000 livres. The building was located in the Marais district on the south side of rue de la Verrerie, between rue des Mauvais Garçons and rue des Deux Portes (since transformed into rue des Archives).[23]

The acting officials reminded assembly members that the guild possessed a 650 livre annuity on the clergy, informing them that the payers of the annuity had expressed a desire to refund its principal of 13,000 livres. The guild's treasury held another 16,566 livres in cash. With the consent of the king's procurator at the Châtelet, who was present at the meeting, the assembly approved the use of these sums to buy the building. The guild's capital of almost 30,000 livres in cash and investments offers impressive testimony to its financial success in the forty-five years since its creation. Assembly records make no mention of the origins of this money, but it must have come from membership and apprenticeship fees, perhaps augmented by successful speculation during the John Law banking experiment.[24]

It is not clear why the *jurées* chose this particular building. The only recorded explanation was that it was "very convenient by its location."[25] This may have been a reference to the close proximity of the confraternity church of Saint-Gervais and the guild notary's office, which was located beside the cemetery of Saint-Jean. Both were within a five-minute walk of the building. The convenience of their mistresses was apparently not a paramount concern. Seamstresses lived in virtually every neighborhood of Paris, including the street on which the building was located, but the Marais district was by no means the most important area of concentration.

After successfully negotiating the purchase, the guild retained owner-ship of the property until the late 1770s. The building contained a ground floor, a mezzanine, three upper stories, an attic, cellars, and a courtyard with a water pump. The corporation occupied the first-floor mezzanine and the entire second floor, using the former as living quarters for its guild clerk and the latter for its offices. According to a description from the late 1770s, the mezzanine contained an antichamber, two bedrooms, and an all-purpose living room. On the floor above, the guild's offices consisted of a large main room, a smaller back room, perhaps used as a kitchen, and a balcony overlooking the courtyard. In 1778, an architect estimated the rental value of the guild's offices and mezzanine at 680 livres a year.[26]

The main room of the guild offices must have been quite large, for it was home to assembly meetings that might gather seventy-five mistresses at once. For sixty years, this room was the heart of the guild's life, a scene of bustling activity almost every day of the year. Here up to four hun-dred apprentices and their families met each year with guild mistresses, to sign apprenticeship contracts in the presence of the acting officials and the guild notary. On busy days, more than ten families appeared for this pur-pose. The main room was also the chamber where aspiring mistresses came to perform their masterpieces. Between 1735 and 1776, over four thousand anxious candidates passed through the carriage doors into the courtyard, taking the stairs up to the office where the *jurées* awaited them.

The remainder of the building consisted of two ground-floor shops and private apartments on the third and fourth floors. The guild rented them to paying tenants, thereby obtaining a continuous source of rental income. In July 1733, it renewed the lease of a small ground-floor boutique and cel-lars to a servant (*officier de maison*) and his wife, for an annual rent of 60 livres. Given the man's occupation, his wife probably ran her own small business in the boutique, perhaps as a mistress seamstress. On the same day, the guild also renewed the lease of Pierre Grosset, a master lutemaker, and his wife. They occupied the second, larger boutique, its back room, a room on an upper floor, and attic and cellar space for 350 livres in an-nual rent. In 1740, the guild renewed the couple's lease once more. The husband's business had apparently prospered in the interim, for they took both ground-floor shops—which the guild promised to have opened into one—the back room, an upper-story room, a kitchen, a small room above the kitchen, and a mansard room in the attic. Their rent rose to 430 livres a year. In 1760, the guild renewed a lease for nine years to Louis François Rogier, a merchant mercer, and his wife. This couple occupied the single enlarged shop, its back room, one room on the mezzanine, and cellar space at an annual rent of 400 livres.[27]

In 1778, royal officials charged with auctioning the building noted the presence of five tenants, all women, who paid a total of 1,600 livres in annual rent. Dame Roger paid an expensive rent of 500 livres, probably for the ground-floor commercial space and living quarters upstairs. Two of the women bore the last names of former guild officials, suggesting that the guild might have offered first choice on the apartments to its own leaders.[28] In 1735, Edmée Boullet, an elderly, impoverished *ancienne,* died in the small two-room apartment she occupied in the attic of the house.[29]

Assembly records reveal an ongoing process by which guild leaders safeguarded the corporation's institutional existence within its offices. On September 27, 1736, the assembly agreed to commission a master cabinet-maker to construct cupboards for the offices to store the guild's papers, strongbox, and silver. The artisan's wages were to be determined by an expert appointed by the king's procurator at the Châtelet.[30] In 1740, the assembly further ensured the security of the guild's offices by commissioning shutters for the windows. At the same meeting, it authorized the acting *jurées* to purchase tables, chairs, and other furniture to furnish the main room, as well as cloth to cover the mattresses and sheets for "the small bed."[31] The record does not specify if the bed served for exceptional use by acting officials or if it was in the guild clerk's apartment.

Along with the stability of a permanent office and revenue from rental income, ownership of the building entailed the expense and trouble of continual repairs. In November 1738, the guild assembly learned that the building's cesspool was full. Its members agreed to hire a worker to drain the pit for a fee of 78 livres.[32] At the same time, they authorized the employment of a master mason to perform repairs to the building. In July 1753, guild leaders sought formal permission to repair an adjoining wall from Abraham François Macé du Montour, a former infantry captain who owned the building next door.[33] A year later, the need for serious, and extremely expensive, renovations obliged the guild to move to temporary quarters.[34] A royal council decree of May 1755, apparently judging the cost to be excessive, ordered the cessation of work and the immediate sale of the building. The *jurées* convoked an assembly meeting to deliberate strategies for retaining the property. The *anciennes* decided to put their own resources at the disposal of the guild. They collectively furnished 12,000 livres to supplement some 9,000 livres in the guild's treasury that they were authorized to spend on repairs. If this sum proved insufficient, the *anciennes* pledged to contribute more of their own money.[35]

The extent of damage to the house, and the leaders' willingness to furnish their own money to repair it, were both quite remarkable. The house had cost only 28,000 livres in 1719; now the guild proposed to pay over 21,000 livres for renovations. To amass 12,000 livres, the *anciennes* would have had to furnish at least 200 livres each, a substantial sum considering that some seamstresses earned not much more for a year's work. The only plausible explanation for this generosity is that the *anciennes'* contributions took the form of loans, which the guild treasury would reimburse over time. The alternate possibility — that their devotion to the guild persuaded them to pay out of their own pocket — seems impossible, despite the exaggerated claims of guild rhetoric. This was not the first or the last time the *anciennes* would use personal contributions as means to exert moral pressure on the royal government.

In 1755, the seamstresses succeeded in retaining their house and completing extensive repairs to it. By 1778, however, repercussions from the political sphere moved beyond their control. In August 1776, the royal government reestablished the Parisian guilds, reversing their six-month abolition under Controller General Turgot. Among the reforms introduced by this edict was the government's decision to assume responsibility for repaying all guild debt. To finance this measure, the edict announced the seizure of corporate real estate properties. Starting at the end of 1777, the royal government began auctioning off these properties and recouping the profits for the royal treasury. Income from these sales outstripped expectations, reflecting the booming property market of late-eighteenth-century Paris. In December 1778, for example, a building owned by the stockingmakers' guild, evaluated at 34,500 livres, sold in auction for 51,500 livres. The tailors' building was estimated at 38,600 livres, but sold for 52,050 livres on June 12, 1778. The seamstresses were the next victims. On August 21, 1778, their house on the rue de la Verrerie, evaluated at 29,000 livres, sold for 36,150 livres.[36] The guild could remain in its offices but would henceforth pay rent to the building's new owner. After sixty years of proud property ownership, the guild was reduced to tenant status once more.

Throughout the eighteenth century, acting *jurées* met regularly at the guild offices to conduct routine business and discuss new or ongoing crises. In 1781, the guild's revised statutes required the six officials to meet every Tuesday "to expedite current affairs."[37] The huge size of the guild made routine administrative chores an enormous task. Every year, up to 400 new apprentices undertook trade training with a guild mistress. In a sample of approximately 800 contracts, almost 90 percent were drawn up in the guild's offices in the presence of the *jurées*. The reception of almost 140 new mistresses each year was even more time-consuming. Most candidates were finished apprentices who were required to complete a competency test prior to joining the guild. The *jurées* devised, supervised, and inspected their masterpieces. They also physically presented candidates before the royal procurator at the Châtelet of Paris to be sworn in as mistresses. Other major tasks included inspecting guild members' workshops, drawing up annual tax assessments, appearing in court to prosecute delinquent seamstresses, and presiding over at least twelve assembly meetings each year. Given these responsibilities, the *jurées* could not hope to police production practices adequately. In order to fulfill the minimum requirement of two annual inspection visits on each mistress, they would have to make between 3,500 and 6,000 visits a year. Discovering and pursuing illegal workers outside of the guild was an almost impossible task.

The only full-time aid for the officials came from the guild clerk, who lived in the mezzanine apartment. In addition to accompanying the *jurées* on their visits, the clerk performed routine office chores, such as maintaining records, writing letters, taking notes at meetings, and processing seized goods. He and his wife would have also assisted in meal preparation, fire keeping, and cleaning. In the 1750s, the guild spent approximately six hundred livres annually on office supplies, such as ink, paper, candles, food, and firewood.[38] Guild officials also received expert assistance from two key figures, a lawyer and a notary. The corporation demonstrated great loyalty to its notary, employing the same office over at least sixty years. Pierre François Masson served the seamstresses from 1705 to 1740, and his successor, Guillaume Delaleu, served from 1740 to 1774. Their office was located in the Marais district, a short walk from the guild building. They made extremely frequent trips to the rue de la Verrerie, most often to write apprenticeship contracts, but also to take minutes of guild assemblies and to draft leases or other financial transactions. In 1716, for example, Pierre

François Masson and his junior colleague appeared in the guild offices on at least ninety-four days to write a total of 403 apprenticeship contracts. To lighten his workload, Masson had copies of the guild's standard apprenticeship contract printed in bulk so that he could merely fill in the details specific to each case. During their decades of service, Masson and Delaleu acquired an intimate knowledge of corporate affairs, as well as close personal contacts with the *anciennes.* They furnished crucial advice and guidance during crises. They also helped officials draw up the annual financial accounts and probably found sources of credit for the occasional loans the guild required.

Given the rockier course of judicial affairs, the corporation did not demonstrate the same faith in its lawyers. In 1744, the guild intervened in a case between a mistress and her client. Apparently unsatisfied with the performance of their lawyer, the assembly authorized the acting *jurées* to replace him with another one. With the grave stakes at risk in legal conflicts, it was essential for the seamstresses to feel confident in the skills and dedication of their lawyer. In 1776, as we have seen, the guild hired the well-known attorney Jacques-Vincent Delacroix to draft their official protest against abolition of the corporate system.[39]

Policing the Trade against Mistresses and Outsiders

In their efforts to police production standards and protect their monopoly, guild officials relied on the judicial authority of the king's procurator at the Châtelet. They brought offenders before his court prior to obtaining a final judgment from the lieutenant general of police. Records of proceedings involving the seamstresses' guild, available in the archives of the king's procurator from the 1680s to the 1780s, demonstrate the strong support this official accorded to the corporation. Most frequently, perhaps, *jurées* used the procurator's court to prosecute seamstresses who violated delayed payment agreements for their membership fees. In return for an initial installment, guild officials often permitted women to work in the trade until they accumulated sufficient funds to complete the fee. If the allotted time—usually six months—passed without additional payments, the officers asked the procurator to force the offender to pay in full or abandon the trade. On May 20, 1740, for example, acting officials appeared before the king's procurator to demand the execution of a writ they had obtained from a bailiff of the Châtelet ten days earlier. This document required Marie Anne Laurent to complete membership payments within three days. After this deadline, the guild would confiscate her fifty-livre deposit and she would lose her right to work as a seamstress. In Laurent's absence, the king's procurator complied with the *jurées'* demand. In cases where the accused did appear in court, the procurator generally awarded an extension of the deadline.[40]

Jurées also appeared in this tribunal to protest their own mistresses' failure to pay fees for annual inspection visits. Guild regulations set a fee of ten sous for each of the two yearly inspections. Corporate officers generally tolerated a failure to pay over one or two years; when the delay grew longer, however, they took the cases to court. The royal procurator usually ordered defaulting mistresses to reimburse their back fees as well as the expenses of the legal proceedings. Less commonly, guild officials took action against mistresses whom they judged to have produced inferior or illegal articles of clothing. In January 1682, they confiscated trade goods in the home of a mistress seamstress, accusing her of unspecified improper work practices. Several days later, the royal procurator fined the mistress thirty sous and ordered her to work in the future in accordance with the guild's statutes. The sentence was passed in absentia, because the woman did not appear in court.[41] The rarity of such cases points to the practical difficulties involved in quality control. Given the burdens of their administrative duties, acting officials were hard-pressed to fulfill the investigative aspects of their functions. They may have devoted as much energy to collecting the annual visit fee as to actually conducting the visit itself.

In addition to visiting their own mistresses, officials sometimes performed raids on illegal seamstresses. Like other guilds, they were first required to obtain an ordinance from the lieutenant general of police, authorizing the search and confiscation of trade tools and illegally manufactured goods. Once they had obtained this authorization, they had to obtain the participation of a police *commissaire* in the raiding party, along with a bailiff from the Châtelet and the guild clerk. On January 26, 1781, two *jurées* appeared before a Parisian police *commissaire* to require his presence at a raid on Dame Poiret, whom they described as a *couturière sans qualité*. The guild officials presented the police officer with an ordinance from the lieutenant general of police, dating from July 1780, authorizing them to perform the search and seizure. The six-month delay in their appearance suggests a considerable backlog in the guild's inspection schedule.[42]

Once a raid had been performed, the royal procurator at the Châtelet passed judgment on its validity and the penalty to be applied. In many cases, the defendant did not appear in court, preferring to abandon her merchandise rather than risk a fine. By that date, she was also likely to have left the premises where the raid had taken place. The king's procurator usually supported the guild's actions, judging the seizures valid and granting the guild possession of the seized goods. While he did not apply heavy fines to offending seamstresses, he usually sentenced them to pay the legal expenses of their prosecution.

To judge from police records, seamstresses' raiding parties were relatively rare. The tailors' guild pursued illegal workers more aggressively, organizing frequent, large-scale forays into neighborhoods suspected of harboring illegal workers. On March 19, 1768, the tailors seized the goods of eight *ouvriers sans qualité* whom they found working in private rooms in the vicinity of the Saint-Germain-l'Auxerrois parish church.[43] On May 10 and 11, 1769, tailor officials raided fifteen illegal workers in and around the faubourg Saint-Germain.[44] Like other guild officials, they often relied on tips from informants with their own scores to settle. The new luxury boutiques along rue Saint-Honoré selling different articles of clothing and accessories also attracted their scrutiny.

The tailors' repressive efficiency stemmed from the administrative structure they had developed for this purpose. Their 1660 statutes called for the election of sixteen junior officers (*jeunes bacheliers*) each year to perform weekly visits on illegal workers. These officials paid the legal fees to prosecute illegal workers; in return they received all profits from the seizures. Spurred by these rewards, they tirelessly pursued illegal workers, conducting raids from early morning to late evening.[45] The seamstresses did not imitate this administrative technique and never approached the tailors' level of intervention within the trade. Indeed, the women's less aggressive attitude to pursuing illegal workers may have derived from the fact that they could rely on the tailors to do their work for them. A 1693 royal council declaration allowed tailors to conduct visits on seamstresses, and allowed female officials to do the same on male workers. While officers of the seamstresses' guild rarely exercised this prerogative, tailor officials frequently targeted women for their inspection visits, and often discovered them making male or female clothing. Because the tailors and the seamstresses shared the right to make women's clothing, nonguild seamstresses violated both guilds' monopolies and were vulnerable to prosecution by either one. There is no evidence of cooperation between tailors and seamstresses on these raids, but the female guild certainly benefited from the tailors' zeal.

As much as they profited from tailors' repressive efficacy, individual mistresses could also be victims of it. On February 10, 1747, tailors' officials raided three boutiques on rue Saint-Honoré, accusing their proprietors — a master hatter, a master trunkmaker, and a master buttonmaker — of illegally selling and renting masked ball costumes (*dominos*). The buttonmaker and the trunkmaker each declared that they had merely rented space in their shops to mistress seamstresses who actually owned the garments. Master buttonmaker Sieur Tempe told the officials that "the ball gowns belong to the Dame Françoise Perrin, mistress Seamstress living on the rue de la Coutellerie whom he allows to use a portion of his boutique for the sale and rental of these ball gowns." Sieur Blaye, the hatter, first declared that the ball gowns belonged to the widow of a merchant mercer, and then added that his wife was an apprentice seamstress whom he was about to have received as a mistress. The tailors rejected these explanations, maintaining that the ball gowns fell within their exclusive trade monopoly.[46]

Twelve years later, the tailors' guild continued to pursue illegal ball gown sales on this street. In February 1760, officials prosecuted Marie Marguerite Chausse, a mistress seamstress. She stated that as a mistress she had the right to sell masked-ball costumes and the other articles of women's clothing found in her possession. The tailors declared once more that their 1660 statutes excluded outsiders from making or selling these items. They further charged that she was not even selling on her own behalf, but was acting as a front for Sieur Jacquard, a wigmaker, who owned the boutique she rented. The police *commissaire* present at the raid allowed the tailors to seize Chausse's goods in anticipation of the royal procurator's ruling.[47] The seamstresses did not acquire the formal right to make and sell these articles until 1781, when their new statutes enshrined this capacity.[48]

In the case of ball gowns, the tailors' prerogatives were more or less clear, and the seamstresses' guild had to accept their intervention. In other cases, however, the female corporation took action to defend a mistress, and by extension the collective privileges of all members. On August 1, 1748, an assembly meeting learned that the used-clothes and furniture dealers' guild had confiscated items of second-hand clothing and mended clothing sold by mistresses, on the pretext that seamstresses could only sell custom-made garments. Declaring that mending and second-hand clothes constituted an essential element of the guild's trade privileges, the assembly instructed the acting *jurées* to intervene in the legal proceedings. It authorized the guild's officials to take any measures necessary to win the trial, but in case of failure required them to convoke an assembly before filing an appeal.[49]

The Confraternity

Investigation and surveillance constituted one aspect of the guild's stewardship of the trade. Another element of corporate life was its social and spiritual activities. At the same time that seamstresses received their letters patent in 1675, they also obtained a religious confraternity dedicated to Saint-Louis, established in the parish church of Saint-Gervais. According to the first article of the confraternity statutes, the archbishop of Paris held final authority and jurisdiction over the association and any future conflicts involving it. The curé of Saint-Gervais was responsible for its daily functions, and he assigned a chaplain to conduct religious services for the group. The statutes also provided for the annual election of two administrators by an electoral body composed of all previous administrators and the parish priest. Acting officials were to keep membership lists, take minutes during assembly meetings, and prepare annual financial accounts.

As outlined in the statutes, the confraternity was an association of sisters united in charity, solidarity, and spiritual devotion. One article called on new members to go to church for confession and communion the day they joined. Another required sisters to "pray to God once a day for each other's needs so as to be more perfectly united by these bonds of charity." If a sister fell ill, her colleagues were enjoined to pray for her quick recovery. If prayer failed, sisters should attend the administration of the last sacrament. When death arrived, the confraternity paid for memorial services performed for the dead woman's soul. All sisters were obliged to attend the funeral and to take communion as a sign of respect for the departed. The last article of the statutes called for charity to impoverished members: "If it occurs that one of the Sisters becomes poor and denuded of goods, she will be aided, if possible, by the Confraternity . . . and the Sisters are exhorted to help them individually." No further information was offered regarding the amounts to be given or the means of distributing such charity.[50]

Neither guild nor confraternity statutes addressed the relationship between the two associations, leaving it unclear if they were overlapping bodies, if workers or apprentices with no guild affiliation could join, or if membership was compulsory for all mistresses. The guild's statutes further confused the matter, assigning responsibility for the religious association to two acting guild officials, rather than confirming the autonomous elections stipulated in the confraternity regulations. To judge from the scarce documentation available, the confraternity did not in fact possess its own administrative structure. Instead, each year one of the three senior guild officers acted as the *clergesse*, or chief administrator of the religious group.

The *clergesse* was responsible for collecting confraternity dues and, presumably, for organizing the celebration of masses, funerals, and other religious events in collaboration with the priests at Saint-Gervais. This role apparently demanded a great deal of time and energy; in 1750, this officer received a raise in her annual stipend of 50 livres "because of the errands of [the] confraternity." In the same year, the king's procurator at the Châtelet convoked a guild assembly to address the grievances of the acting *clergesse*, who complained that her predecessor had not surrendered 124 livres left over from the previous year. She demanded that her predecessor surrender the money, which the latter did some weeks later. In this rare case, a member of the guild's leadership turned to outside authority against a fellow member. This was a grave decision, for it involved surrendering guild autonomy to outside authority and implicitly admitting that its leaders could not manage their own affairs.[51]

In practice, it also appears that admission to the corporation entailed de facto membership in the confraternity. According to a 1693 royal declaration, five livres of the entry fees paid by new mistresses accrued directly to the confraternity treasury and one livre to the *clergesse*. Every mistress was obliged to pay an annual fee of ten sous toward the confraternity.[52] The records unfortunately offer no indication of mistresses' participation in this association or the nature of the religious ceremonies performed. We have no way to measure the extent to which it offered financial or spiritual aid for mistresses or a forum for trade-based religious sociability. It is probably significant, however, that the few surviving wills of mistress seamstresses make no mention of the guild confraternity. Instead, mistresses looked to their own friends and family to organize their funeral services, commemorative masses, and other religious rituals for the well-being of their souls.

The guild itself took charge of religious rituals conducted for public display. After the birth of each of Louis XV's three grandsons in 1753, 1754, and 1755, the corporation paid for the celebration of a Te Deum and a public mass, distributing flyers to advertise the event. The expenses involved in these celebrations were considerable; for one event the guild spent 862 livres and 7 sous.[53] In each case, the assembly approved these expensive celebrations as an expression of the "universal joy" felt at the birth of the dauphin's sons. In fact, these were acts of symbolic homage, a prudent strategy in the continual process of negotiation between guild and royal government. They also served to assert the seamstresses' honor within the Parisian corporate sphere and in the public eye. The guild thus demonstrated its wealth and its role in the city's public life by sponsoring collective ceremonies of religious devotion and fidelity to the royal family.

Charity

Although no concrete evidence survives regarding charitable activity in the confraternity, the guild itself distributed monthly stipends to some poor mistresses. To receive this aid, it was not sufficient to be poor, sick, or elderly; one had to be a former guild officer. Guild records reveal that all recipients of regular charity were in fact *anciennes*. On August 10, 1733, three widowed *anciennes*—Françoise Faget, Marie Dormont, and Catherine Toussaint—appeared before the guild assembly to request aid, declaring that "the various accidents which happened to them having reduced them to extreme indigence, and their infirmity and great age making it impossible for them to work and earn enough to provide for their necessities, they are on the brink of perishing from misery if the community does not accord them help proportional to their needs."[54]

The women added that two of them were almost completely blind, probably the outcome of long years of sewing in ill-lit rooms. The assembly agreed to grant Faget six livres every month for the rest of her life, and four livres a month to each of the other two women. In 1740, Jacqueline LeRoy appeared before the assembly, declaring that she was seventy-six years old and had served as a *jurée* twenty-five years previously. She was virtually bedridden and unable to work. The assembly decided to pay her six livres a month for life. These were modest sums, representing between one and two weeks' wages, but they made the difference between meager survival and starvation or homelessness.

In 1776, the seamstresses addressed a *mémoire* to the king, in which they stated that ten *anciennes* currently received pensions from the guild. Six were in the amount of 36 livres per year, two of 50 livres, one of 72, and the highest was of 120 livres. The guild claimed that recipients of this aid were aged seventy-five, eighty-four, and eighty-seven years old. Their modest pensions were supplemented by the women's share in the admissions fees paid by new mistresses and the tokens they received for attendance at assemblies. Together, the document estimated, these two sources amounted to approximately 150 livres a year; combined with pensions of 36 or 50 livres, this was enough to support an elderly woman. The pious tone with which the text refers to the guild's charity to poor and elderly mistresses was at odds with its admission that only former officers received regular pensions. The authors did claim that many other mistresses received occasional charity payments, but they did not specify whether these women were *anciennes* or ordinary mistresses.[55]

Funding for the guild's charity stemmed from two sources. In a declaration of 1693, Louis XIV permitted the corporation to accept twenty unqualified mistresses (*maîtresses sans qualité*) annually as a means of paying off debts incurred in purchasing the guild offices of 1691. This declaration further stipulated that thirty livres from each woman's entry fee would henceforth be dedicated to charitable aid among mistresses, amounting to a total of six hundred livres annually. The seamstresses' 1776 *mémoire* revealed that rent paid by tenants in the guild's building also went to support charity payments for former officers. This innovation was apparently introduced after the building's renovation in 1755 to reward *anciennes,* who had furnished more than thirty thousand livres to fund repair work. Charity in the corporation thus circulated almost exclusively among former guild officials, who justified their privileges based on personal sacrifices and service.

Regular Taxation

Apart from overseeing internal administration, corporate officers served as intermediaries between the royal government and guild members for the payment of taxes. The Parisian corporations collected two more-or-less regular taxes from their members on behalf of the king: the *capitation* after 1695, and the *dixième de l'industrie,* replaced by the *vingtième,* after 1749.[56] Each year, the lieutenant general of police determined the amount each corps owed and communicated the sum to its officials. For the *dixième* tax, this officer also appears to have assessed the guilds' membership himself. In 1742, for example, Lieutenant General de Marville informed the seamstresses that they owed 3,987 livres for that year's *dixième* tax. At an assembly meeting the guild decided to pay part of that sum with 1,000 livres remaining from the previous year's accounts. The mistresses would

Class	Number of mistresses	Percentage of total population	Amount paid (in sous)	Percentage of total tax burden
1	6	5.5	20	10
2	24	22.0	15	30
3	34	31.0	12	34
4 (taxable)	39	36.0	8	26
4 (excused)	6	5.5	0	0

furnish the rest, according to an assessment drawn up by Marville. In this case, the lieutenant general of police permitted the use of corporate funds to reduce ordinary mistresses' tax burden.

For the *capitation,* by contrast, the guilds seem to have appraised their members themselves. Although almost no information is available regarding the Parisian seamstresses' payment of this tax, the example of Caen sheds some light on how this process worked. On one occasion, in 1757, the guilds of Caen were assigned the responsibility of collecting the *capitation* tax from their members. This experiment was apparently never repeated, but the detailed records kept by the city's seamstress-tailors' guild offer insight into the procedures they followed for self-assessment.

The intendant of Caen assigned the seamstresses a collective *capitation* tax of fifty livres. Together with a supplement of four sous per livre, the guild owed a total of sixty livres.[57] In assessing their members for this tax, the female officers divided their 109 mistresses into four classes based on financial prosperity. The mistresses in the first class, numbering only 6 women, paid twenty sous each. The 24 women in the second class furnished fifteen sous each. The 34 members of the third class paid twelve sous each, and the 45 in the fourth class paid only eight sous. Six "poor" mistresses were excused from payment. Together, the payments equaled exactly sixty livres. In addition to the considerable mathematical prowess necessary to arrive at this assessment, officials possessed substantial information regarding their mistresses, including address, marital status, fortune, and employment of workers, servants, or apprentices (table 6.1 shows the distribution of this tax).[58] The preparation of a similar assessment for approximately 2,000 Parisian mistresses would have been a formidable undertaking. Between 1750 and 1760, the guild's leaders claimed to have spent some four hundred livres annually to prepare this assessment.

The Parisian guild also made annual payments to support the city's militia. Corporate participation in urban militias dated to the late Middle Ages, when guilds dominated municipal government in many cities. While masters originally served as militia members themselves, by the eighteenth century this duty had long been replaced with monetary payments. The seamstresses' financial records report highly varied costs for different aspects of the municipal militia. In 1744, their accounts noted an expense of some 220 livres toward the civic militia. In the mid-1750s, the guild reported paying some 65 livres annually for the upkeep of a battalion of the Parisian militia. In 1791, the guild claimed to have spent 1,000 livres each year to support a member of the militia.[59]

Venal Guild Offices and Financial Administration

Like other corporations, the guild's financial administration was inextricably linked to the royal government, and in particular to the exceptional taxation it imposed through a series of venal offices starting in the reign of Louis XIV. Established in 1675, the seamstresses' guild was confronted only sixteen years later with the edict of 1691, which transformed elected guild officials into venal officeholders. Despite harsh criticism of guild abuses in the text of the edict, the royal government permitted the corporations to purchase the offices and thereby remove them from the open market. Indeed, the hidden purpose of the exercise was to induce them to do just that, because the expenses of Louis XIV's foreign wars required revenue from all possible sources. The guilds felt obliged to buy the offices; the alternative, as the seamstresses stated in 1745, was to allow them to be "raised by one of their individual mistresses or any other stranger, which would cause certain disorder in the said guild's affairs."[60]

The prices set for the offices varied from several thousand livres to several hundred thousand. The mercers' guild paid the highest sum of 300,000 livres. The remaining members of the elite merchant Six Corps paid between 40,000 and 120,000 livres each. More modest corporations, such as the candlemakers and roast-meat sellers, gave 30,000 livres each. The harnessmakers and the secondary-seed merchants paid the relatively small sums of 10,000 and 8,000 livres respectively.[61] The seamstresses' guild was charged a respectable 33,000 livres. Its mistresses were mostly humble artisans, but their numerical strength argued for this fairly substantial fee. The government's estimate of the guild's financial capacity proved reliable, because its officers managed to remit the sum on June 27, 1691, only three months after the edict's proclamation. The largest portion of the money, 27,500 livres, came from the sale of three annuities the corporation owned on the Hôtel de Ville of Paris.[62] The crown's initial wager—that high profits could be generated by imposing low fees on a huge female labor force—proved to be sound.

The 1691 offices were formally "reunited" with the seamstresses' guild two years later by a royal declaration of April 28, 1693.[63] This declaration established a series of new regulations for the corporation that superseded stipulations of the 1675 statutes. The declaration significantly raised admission fees and established a new royal tax (*droit royal*) on incoming guild members. Future mistresses who joined the guild through apprenticeship paid 150 livres, from which 20 accrued to the royal coffers. Mistresses' daughters paid only 40 livres and were not subject to the royal tax. The 1693 declaration also took the unprecedented step of creating an entirely new means of entry to the guild. Henceforth, the royal government allowed the yearly admission of twenty mistresses *sans qualité*, that is, without the regular qualifications of apprenticeship or family inheritance. These mistresses paid 200 livres each for entry to the guild, out of which 125 livres entered the guild's treasury. The *anciennes* and the *jurées* received a portion of the fees of finished apprentices' and mistresses' daughters, but nothing from the unqualified mistresses.

A mixture of benevolent and fiscal motivations lay behind these stipulations. By creating a third path of membership, the royal government presumably intended to ensure the guild's accessibility to outsiders. Women who had not undergone apprenticeship could still hope to join the guild, paying only fifty livres extra for this opportunity. The royal government also aimed to safeguard the guild's financial stability. The original statutes had attributed only ten livres to the treasury from new mistresses by apprenticeship and five livres from mistresses' daughters. Henceforth, thirty livres and ten livres respectively would accrue to the guild. This new system of allocation was meant to assist the guild to recoup the 33,000 livres disbursed in 1693. By ensuring the guild's financial health, the royal government not only offered security to its members, it also ensured the corporation could meet future fiscal needs. Because the royal government relied on the guilds for income, it was in its own interest to help them restore liquidity as quickly as possible.

Finally, the 1693 declaration also included measures to reward guild leaders for their rapid purchase of the offices. The 1675 statutes had granted *jurées* two livres each from the admission of a new mistress by apprenticeship; henceforth they would receive four livres, a significant increase considering that one hundred women might enter the guild by this path each year. The *anciennes'* portion also rose significantly. Whereas the statutes had awarded an unspecified number of *jeunes, modernes,* and *anciennes* one livre from each new mistress's fee, the 1693 declaration allotted three livres to each of twelve *anciennes* selected on a rotating basis. Royal favor obtained through the purchase of offices thus accrued not only to the guild as an institution, but to the guild elite who brokered the payments.

The 1691 offices were the first in a long series. The crown created a second set of offices in 1694, the "auditors and examiners of guild accounts." This time the seamstresses were required to furnish 27,500 livres to purchase the offices.[64] Having emptied their treasury in 1691, the guild could not meet the cost from existing funds. The *anciennes* therefore resolved to finance the purchase in part through their own money, presumably in order to minimize the need for outside loans.[65] It is unfortunately not known how much they furnished or what means individual women adopted to muster the money. Although assembly minutes do not acknowledge the fact, their contributions must have taken the form of loans to be reimbursed at a later date. To supplement this private money, the guild obtained another 3,500 livres by selling an annuity of 250 livres to Jean Trochet, a merchant *bourgeois de Paris.*

The guild's quick payment of these offices called forth a new series of financial concessions from the government. To allow the corporation to recover the expense, the king agreed to forgo the twenty-livre royal tax imposed on admission fees by the 1691 edict. Proceeds from the tax would serve instead to repay guild debt. The 1696 decree also permitted the guild to use for this purpose all sums normally allocated to its treasury from admission and apprenticeship fees. Guild officers probably used this money to reimburse the *anciennes* who had contributed to the payment.[66] At this difficult moment, however, the guild elite also proved its capacity for altruism. Perhaps in exchange for the state's decision to renounce the royal tax, the *anciennes* agreed in 1696 to forgo temporarily their share of guild fees as another means of replenishing guild coffers.[67] This sacrifice reveals that, although *anciennes* benefited personally from dealings with the royal government, they were also willing to forgo personal income for the greater good of the corporation.

Ten years later, in August 1704, royal ministers created a third set of guild offices, the "hereditary guild clerks." Once more, the *anciennes* assumed a personal role in purchasing the offices, which were priced this time at 15,000 livres. The controller general's receipt for the guild's payment indicates that a total of fourteen *anciennes* pooled their funds to help meet the price. We can only speculate about the influence these women acquired in the corporation by shouldering this burden. They may have been able to promote their own protégés in guild elections or acquire a stronger voice in decision making.[68]

Far from being destroyed by these extractions, the seamstresses' guild rapidly recovered its financial health. An assembly meeting of 1718 noted that the guild had not only reimbursed all of its debts, but also purchased new annuities on the Hôtel de Ville, the postal service, and the clergy. Its finances benefited not only from the stipulations of the declaration of 1693, but from the annual stipends attached to the offices the guild had purchased, and perhaps from the strong advantages that the John Law period offered for shedding debt. Assembly minutes emphasized the remarkable vigor of the seamstresses' finances in comparison to the bankrupt state of many other Parisian guilds. As the officers declared, the guild's good fortune was "a certain proof of their vigilance, good conduct, and economy in the government of the affairs of their community."[69] Given this bright financial scenario, the record continued, the *anciennes* were justified in demanding the reinstatement of their share in guild fees, suspended since 1696. Assembly members decided not only to reinstate their allocations, but to increase them significantly. The 1693 edict had required that thirty livres enter the guild treasury for mistresses who entered the guild by apprenticeship and ten from mistresses' daughters. The 1718 assembly now reduced these sums to ten and five livres, respectively, dividing the difference each month among the *anciennes,* as foreseen by the 1675 statutes. After a twenty-five year hiatus, the *anciennes* would enjoy the material benefits of their status once more.

On March 29, 1745, under financial pressure from the War of the Austrian Succession, the government of Louis XV created a final set of guild offices, the "inspectors and controllers of the officers of the guilds of the kingdom" (*inspecteurs et controlleurs des jurés dans les communautés d'arts et métiers du Royaume*). The price of the seamstresses' offices was set at forty thousand livres. This time procuring the necessary funds posed a greater challenge than in the past. The guild treasury held nowhere near this amount, and the *anciennes* were apparently no longer able to invest their own money or take private loans for this purpose. In an assembly meeting convoked to discuss the problem, guild leaders rejected the possibility of making ordinary mistresses shoulder the expense, given "the indigent state of all the mistresses who compose the guild . . . and the impossibility in which they would be at present to acquit and furnish [the cost]."[70] The assembly thus formed a committee composed of the six acting officials and four *anciennes* to investigate alternate funding possibilities.

On April 15, 1745, the group reported that a source of funding could be obtained through the resolution of a long-standing legal dispute. In 1710, a royal edict had created a set of offices titled the "treasurers, payers and receivers of guild fees." Unlike other offices, these posts had fallen into the hands of private proprietors. Relations between the guild and its venal treasurer, Sieur Hamel, were particularly acrimonious. By 1738, Hamel had obtained the suspension of all payments owed to the guild since 1732, based on his claims that the guild owed him dues from its reception of new *jurées*, mistresses, and apprentices.[71] In 1745, litigation between the two sides continued under the jurisdiction of the royal commission established to audit guild debts.

Reporting back to the assembly, the finance committee recommended settling with the estate of Sieur Hamel, who had since died. Releasing the blocked payments promised a significant windfall, because they included all stipends owed for guild offices since 1732, or at least 800 livres for each year.[72] On April 25, 1745, guild representatives signed an agreement with Sieur Hamel's heirs, by which the latter accepted payment of 3,000 livres in lieu of the dues he had claimed. To supplement the money acquired through this agreement, the assembly authorized the *jurées* to accept a loan from André Guenisey, a *bourgeois de Paris*. In October 1745, the guild constituted a 750 livre annuity in his favor, in exchange for 15,000 livres in cash.[73]

As in the past, the royal government took measures to ease the financial pain of these payments. To assist the guilds in recuperating their expenditures, a royal edict accompanying the 1745 offices provided for an increase in guild fees. Henceforth, the government authorized all Parisian guilds to charge masters twenty sous, instead of ten, for each of the two required annual inspection visits. The additional revenue generated would go directly to reimburse guild debts. Many guilds were satisfied with this offer, but the leaders of the seamstresses' guild feared it would only worsen their financial problems "seeing how difficult the collection of this increase in the visit fee would be for a number of mistresses in the guild who[,] being for the most part reduced to the utmost misery[,] could not even pay the old fees and other guild charges."[74]

To spare their mistresses, the guild's representatives requested that the visit fee be transformed into an increase in the fee for the guild apprenticeship contract (*brevet d'apprentissage*). That way, the financial burden would fall on apprentices and their families, rather than indigent guild members. The royal decree of September 21, 1745, which formally sold the offices to the guild, granted this request, creating an increase of three livres, sixteen sous, and six deniers in the price of the apprenticeship contract. The total price of the document rose to twenty livres from its previous level of sixteen livres, three sous, and six deniers.

After 1745, the crown ceased creating guild offices. This did not mean, however, that the corporations suffered no further extraordinary taxation. The seamstresses' guild furnished at least two subsequent payments to the king. In August 1758, under the pressures of the Seven Years' War, the royal government announced a "raise" in the stipends attached to offices purchased by the guilds. Far from demonstrating royal benevolence, this announcement instituted a new round of forced loans, because the raise was financed by the guilds themselves as owners of the offices. The seamstresses found themselves obliged to pay 25,000 livres in exchange for an annual raise of 1,250 livres.[75] Demonstrating its recovered financial vitality, the guild supplied this sum from its own treasury.[76] Finally, in 1771, the seamstresses paid 20,000 livres to the royal government as an ostensibly "voluntary" donation (*don gratuit*), in celebration of the dauphin's marriage to Marie-Antoinette the previous year.

From 1691 on, the *jurées'* repeated refusal to pass on royal extractions to ordinary mistresses set them apart from other corporations. In Paris and the provinces, guild officials most often transmitted the cost of debt repayment to ordinary masters in the form of weekly or monthly dues or increases in membership fees. In 1694, for example, the Aix-en-Provence tailors' guild decided to reimburse loans taken for the 1691 offices by raising masters' annual dues. When this measure failed, the guild raised both admissions fees and the weekly tax imposed on masters for their workers. Their colleagues in Marseilles similarly raised guild entry fees and annual dues to meet debt payments in 1732.[77]

The female officials offered a simple explanation for their refusal to adopt such methods: the majority of their mistresses were simply too poor to meet additional financial demands. At a time when most mistresses could not pay existing guild fees their leaders declined to add new ones. This philanthropic explanation is supported by the officials' efforts to shelter mistresses from other fiscal pressures, such as the 1742 *dixième de l'industrie* tax. They also used guild funds to pay 220 livres to support the Parisian militia in 1744. A subsequent royal audit would condemn this generosity, ruling that the mistresses should have paid the tax themselves. Members of the guild's elite thus recognized the widespread poverty among their mistresses and avoided exacerbating it. Altruistic considerations aside, they realized that creating one more fee that their members could not pay would only increase their bureaucratic problems.[78]

Like other French corporations, the seamstresses' guild contributed substantial sums to the royal government from the late seventeenth century to the last decades of the Old Regime. The guild was clearly helpless to resist this fiscal pressure, but there is no evidence that its leaders ever seriously tried to avoid paying. Their compliance stemmed from a belief that the consequences of refusal would be much higher than the cost of the offices; the loss of administrative autonomy would intolerably diminish their corporate existence. Moreover, their acquiescence also derived from an understanding that such impositions constituted a normal, if disruptive and difficult, element of the corporate system. In moments of crisis, it was to be expected that the king turned to the corporations he created and whose privileges he upheld. Guild leaders had a shrewd sense of the advantages to be gained by rapid and graceful submission. Seamstress officials' success in obtaining new concessions, both for themselves and for the guild as a whole, demonstrates the possibilities that opened up in the negotiations regarding these offices.

The royal government's financial need led it to intrude in guild affairs beyond simple demands for money. In their attempts to secure the guilds' financial solvency and obtain the good will of corporate leaders for future payments, royal officials tinkered significantly with existing regulations. Specifically, they revised existing admissions standards and the allocation of resources within corporations. Such measures had significant consequences for the artisans who belonged to guilds or who aspired to join them. The seamstresses, for example, gained a whole new path of entry, which allowed women without apprenticeship or birth qualifications to obtain membership. From 1735 to 1776, some nine hundred seamstresses benefited from this possibility. Without regularizing the process, the royal government authorized many other Parisian guilds to admit "unqualified" masters to meet the expense of royal offices. State intervention thereby altered the composition and reproduction of the guilds, opening them to outsiders and conferring financial benefits on their leaders. In the process, the state reshaped the corporate community, and it may have helped to heighten the distance between guild officials and their rank and file.

Royal Control of Guild Finances: The Royal Commission to Audit Guild Debts

If fees and other financial benefits acted as a carrot for guild leaders, the royal auditing commission created in 1716 was a heavy stick. Alarmed by the magnitude of corporate debt in the second decade of the eighteenth century, Louis XV's Regency government established a commission in 1716 "to proceed to the liquidation of the debts, and the examination and revision of the accounts of the corps of merchants and craft guilds of the city and suburbs of Paris." This commission carried out its work on a sporadic basis from 1716 to 1788. Its activities enabled the royal government to control not only guild finances, but detailed aspects of their internal administration as well.[79]

Between 1716 and 1739, the commission examined the accounts of Parisian guilds for the period from 1689 to approximately 1720. The seamstresses' turn did not arrive until 1731, a result, perhaps, of the guild's relative financial stability to that date. Far graver cases demanded the commissioners' attention. Its financial success may also explain the seamstresses' refusal to cooperate fully with the audits. In 1731, the commission examined their account records from 1689 to 1694. On July 4, 1736, the procurator of the commission appeared before his colleagues to complain about the guild's failure to furnish its more recent accounts. He had instructed the seamstresses to produce all records since 1729, "which they absolutely neglect to do[;] what marks their disobedience even more and seems very extraordinary to us, is that they join to this first refusal that of refusing to produce the statutes of their guild." The commission ordered acting officials to produce the necessary documents within one week, or each woman would face a fine of three hundred livres.[80]

Despite its severity, this order failed to compel the guild's compliance. Instead, the acting officials convoked an assembly at which they informed their colleagues of the commission's ruling and obtained their authorization to undertake necessary measures to oppose it. They did not explain the motivation for this resistance, but it may have arisen from resentment at outside interference in their finances, given the guild's largely positive record. On July 18, the procurator noted their continuing disobedience, telling the commission that "the refusal is too marked not to oblige him . . .

to follow the execution of our . . . judgment."[81] The seamstresses may have nonetheless evaded this judgment, for no record exists of additional audits until the year 1756, when the commission audited the financial year 1744–1745. Following this date, the guild's finances were regularly reviewed.

The commission's audits reveal considerable variation in the corporation's financial activities from year to year. The period 1691 to 1693 contained remarkable differences, with revenue in the fiscal year 1691–1692 of almost 39,899 livres for expenses of 39,499 livres, and revenue the following year of only 801 livres for expenses of 1,232 livres.[82] The exceptional activity of 1691–1692 is explained by the purchase of guild offices in that year, but it is unclear why guild finances shrank so dramatically in 1693. In normal times, the guild's annual revenue varied between 12,000 and 25,000 livres, with expenses between 7,000 and 22,000 livres. As the guild's financial success implied, incoming revenue almost always exceeded expenses, sometimes by as much as 10,000 livres.

In its review of guild accounts, the commission subjected every expenditure or receipt to close scrutiny. Its auditors rejected any payment judged to be excessive or to have been made without proper approval. Even fees paid to royal officials did not escape this assessment. For example, the commission regularly reduced payments made to the royal procurator at the Châtelet of Paris. An audit conducted on February 1, 1770, for the fiscal year 1760–1761, declared that "seventy livres paid to Monsieur the king's procurator will be passed for thirty-six livres, the twenty-four extra livres will be barred." In an audit of the year 1761–1762, performed on the same day, the commissioners reduced another payment to the royal procurator from seventy livres to thirty-six livres. These expenditures probably represented reimbursement for the procurator's presence at guild assemblies or elections, or for cases presented in his tribunal. By adding a little extra to his fees, the officials may have hoped to obtain a more favorable hearing, a practice rejected by the commission.[83]

Even more frequently, the commissioners contested fees paid to the guild's notary. For example, they systematically rejected the twelve livres paid each year to the notary for his assistance in drawing up the financial statement.[84] On February 1, 1770, in its audit for the years 1760–1761, the commission reduced a fee for unspecified services from eighty-two livres and twelve sous to forty livres and twelve sous. The commission also punished the guild's failure to collect sums due to it. For example, the audit of the financial year 1761–1762 augmented that year's income by twelve hundred livres for uncollected rent on the guild's house.[85]

With these modifications, the commission's audits inevitably resulted in a financial statement that differed from the guild's original accounts. Although the commissioners performed their audits well after the fiscal year in question, they held the acting *jurées* of that year personally responsible for any discrepancies. In some cases, they permitted recourse against guild mistresses, but ex-officials had little hope of collecting for ten- or twenty-year old expenses. Despite the pains taken to obtain it, the assembly's ratification therefore did not liberate *jurées* from responsibility for guild finances. In the eyes of the crown elected officers remained the unique financial actors of their communities and held sole liability for their mistakes. Guild officials possessed the right to appeal the commission's rulings, and those judged to be in deficit invariably did so. Appeals served at the least to delay payment and, at best, to reduce or overturn the judgments definitively.

Over the years, the most serious problems the guild encountered with the commission involved its officers' repeated failure to collect full fees for apprenticeship contracts. The decree that regulated the seamstresses' purchase of royal offices in 1745 raised the fee for the *brevet d'apprentissage* by 3 livres, 16 sous, and 6 deniers. After 1745, guild officials should have credited 9 livres, 16 sous, and 6 deniers to the treasury from each contract, instead of the 6 livres they previously allotted to it. Successive administrations failed to do so, placing only 9 livres in the treasury for every apprenticeship contract. The commission spotted this error as early as 1756 when it examined accounts from the fiscal year 1750–1751. In their audit, the commissioners noted that 3,780 livres in revenue from 420 apprenticeship contracts was short by some 346 livres and 10 sous, owing to the money missing for each contract.[86]

For unknown reasons, guild leaders did not address this matter until December 1761, when they issued a formal request to the royal council for the retroactive suppression of the additional sixteen sous and six deniers. They explained that the *jurées* had collected the correct sum of twenty livres for each contract, but mistakenly included the sixteen sous and six deniers in the guild notary's fee for drawing up the contract.[87] Because they did not profit personally from this mistake, guild officials argued that they should not be obliged to rectify the shortfall. These were considerable sums, they pointed out, given the large number of new apprentices each year. In its final arguments, the guild attempted to apply moral leverage to the crown, recalling its past services and present virtues: "The guild should have hoped even more for this grace from the goodness of his Majesty's justice since it was free from all engagements, it owed nothing and it had furnished the sum demanded of it by virtue of the edict of the month of August 1758 from its coffers without having recourse to any loans."[88]

The king, represented by Controller General Bertin, was unsympathetic to these arguments. For future contracts, the royal council abolished the entire 1745 increase of three livres, sixteen sous, and six deniers. With regard to past errors, the council ordered the seamstresses to renew their appeal before the royal commission for guild finances. The acting officials returned to the commission in March 1762, repeating that a simple mistake had occurred and defending themselves against any suspicion of fraud. The new arguments they put forward reveal their increasing apprehension of a negative judgment. They claimed that previous guild leaders were not only morally innocent, but also practically incapable of paying the charges: "The major part of these *jurées* who were not very opulent in the past find themselves today insolvent." Guild officials also insisted on the futility of any recourse the commission might award them against the mistresses or apprentices involved in the contracts: "The major part of those upon whom one would wish to exercise [the payment are] insolvent and not in a situation to satisfy the other charges of the guild."[89]

The commission transmitted their request to the Parisian lieutenant general of police, de Sartine, for his opinion. De Sartine responded favorably, recommending that guild officials be discharged from financial responsibility. Disregarding this advice, the commissioners decided to reject the seamstresses' request, granting them only a dubious recourse to the apprentices for the missing money. Although they made no explicit accusation of fraud, the commissioners' severity indicates an unwillingness to accept the seamstresses' version of events.[90] Based on this ruling, the commission pressed the former *jurées* for payment. In April 1768, it passed judgment on an appeal submitted by officials from the fiscal year 1750–1751. Reaffirming its original decision, the board condemned the women to supply 346 livres and 10 sous in missing income from apprenticeship contracts. On the same day, they also reaffirmed a sum of 303 livres and 8 sous judged against the 1754–1755 officers.[91] On February 1, 1770, the commission raised from 2,448 livres to 2,672 livres and 8 sous the receipt for 272 apprenticeship contracts in the year 1761–1762.[92]

Four years later, however, the commission had apparently lost heart for the battle. It abandoned its claim to the extra fees for the year 1761–1762 and agreed to accept the original sum collected by the guild.[93] From this date forward, the commissioners proved increasingly lenient both in their initial audits and in their judgment of appeals. A significant evolution in attitudes seems to have occurred over time. During the 1750s and 1760s, the commission applied its findings relentlessly and previous officials were forced to furnish the sums judged due. During the 1770s and 1780s, the commission became markedly clement, often accepting the guild's original accounts and granting favorable judgments on appeals from previous audits.

Across the eighteenth century, the royal government used the auditing commission as a tool of intervention in the financial affairs of Parisian guilds. The crown held corporate leaders responsible for their activities, reaching several decades into the past to call former officers to account. Financial control allowed royal officials to encroach on myriad aspects of guild life. They supervised guilds' relations with lawyers and notaries as well as the details of the daily administration conducted in guild offices. The very knowledge that the commission would one day audit their accounts must have exercised a strong influence over guild leaders. They had to assume that the commission would eventually discover and punish any irregularities. The existence of the commission offers one explanation for the increasing role played by the *anciennes'* assembly over the eighteenth century. Fearful of the auditors' judgments, acting officials sought to divest themselves of personal responsibility for financial decision making. The officials would discover, however, that the assembly held little authority in the eyes of the royal commissioners, who held only acting officers accountable.

Conclusion

The seamstresses' guild confirms one long-held historiographical belief about the eighteenth-century guild system: its leadership consisted of a small elite that monopolized authority within the corporation. Former officials maintained power and influence through permanent seats in the guild assembly and used their control of elections to bring friends and relatives into their circle. The small group of assembly members enjoyed not only influence and power but also concrete material benefits, including a share of membership and apprenticeship fees, tokens for attendance at assemblies and other events, and an annual present of sugar. Their daughters enjoyed reduced membership fees, and they could hope for charitable support in their old age.

On the whole, guild leaders appear to have supplied good management in exchange for their power and privilege. As they continually pointed out, the corporation maintained impressive financial stability throughout the eighteenth century, demonstrated by its numerous capital investments. While most Parisian guilds encountered crippling debt, the seamstresses emerged from the period of royal-office creation in a positive financial situation. This success permitted guild officers to shelter mistresses from the effects of royal taxation. Unlike other corporations, they did not pass on the price of royal offices to their members in the form of dues or increased fees.

Despite its benevolent attitude, the guild's elite was quite isolated from the general population. Eighty ordinary mistresses participated in elections, but none of them appeared at assembly meetings. The rank and file probably encountered the guild on rare occasions: signing apprenticeship contracts, performing the masterpiece, or during annual inspection visits. Assembly meetings rarely discussed issues pertinent to mistresses' daily lives, and the guild played little role in the manufacturing or commercial side of the trade. When guild leaders referred to mistresses, it was usually to emphasize their poverty. The juxtaposition of the mistresses' anonymous poverty with the guild's financial prosperity reveals a striking contradiction at the heart of the seamstresses' corporation. Usually humble and modest artisans, seamstresses collectively formed a highly successful guild. Their leaders were capable of shrewd and competent navigation of the difficult political, financial, and economic waters of eighteenth-century Paris. They were far from the semiskilled quasi-prostitutes described by Mercier or Restif de la Bretonne.

Another noteworthy feature of the seamstresses' corporation was its constant interaction with the royal government. As their example demonstrates, royal government and guilds were engaged in a mutually binding relationship throughout the late seventeenth and eighteenth centuries. Whether through the royal procurator at the Châtelet, the commission to audit guild finances, or the imposition of royal offices, the crown exercised strong controls over the corporations and heavily drained their resources. Fiscal needs combined with administrative concerns led the royal government to intervene continually in corporate administration and recruitment across this period. The result of this intervention, however, was not merely to subdue the corporate system to monarchical control. The royal government could not intercede so forcefully in guild affairs—and rely so heavily on financial extractions from the corporate system—without becoming enmeshed in complex economic, political, and moral obligations. It had to help the guilds meet their debts, even when doing so meant a momentary reduction in revenue. Royal officials were also compelled to attend to the guilds' particular needs and even to award their leaders new monetary gains to ensure rapid compliance with the state's fiscal demands. The relationship between royal government and guilds was a constant process of negotiation, which combined coercive power with bribes and compromises.

In most cases, the royal government treated the seamstresses like any other Parisian guild. It did not impose special checks or controls on this rare female corporation, nor did the royal financial commission supervise the guild's finances more closely than those of male guilds.[94] The seamstresses were even capable of resisting the commission's investigation of its affairs. The creation of a third path of guild membership in 1693 does appear to have been unique among Parisian guilds, and the act was probably related to a desire to provide increased access to guild structures for women who had few alternative economic choices. Nevertheless, male guilds, such as the tailors', adopted similar measures on a sporadic basis, accepting unqualified masters for high fees in order to reimburse their debts.

The next section, part 3, will clarify the contradictions within the seamstresses' guild by examining the lives, career patterns, and fortunes of the mistresses and workers who practiced the trade. There I will address the system of apprenticeship that brought young women into the trade, and trace the paths that seamstresses followed to guild membership. I will also investigate the relationship among marriage, work, and family within this trade, showing that trade considerations played a strong role in the decisions women made about the families and households they formed. In the final chapter, I continue the seamstresses' story to the turn of the twentieth century, to reflect on continuities and discontinuities in the trade.

PART THREE

Making the Mistresses

SEVEN

Career Paths in the Seamstresses' Trade:

From Apprenticeship to Mistress-ship

Historians have begun to elucidate the male career path from apprentice to master, both in its idealized form and in its practical difficulties. Much less is known about women's career patterns.[1] Most studies of work in early modern Europe have emphasized the lack of defining occupational transitions in women's lives. They have characterized female labor as an integral part of a wider family economy, in which girls learned skills at home from their mothers and female careers were subordinate to male familial and occupational strategies. Apprenticeship or guild membership among women has been dismissed or treated as a rare exception. Given their domestic responsibilities and economic disadvantages, it is argued, women could not follow a linear path of career development. Instead, they worked sporadically, adapting their economic activities to their place in the life cycle and to the needs of their families.[2]

Seamstresses offer a sharp contrast to these conclusions, revealing a strong demand for vocational training and corporate institutions among Parisian women. Over the eighteenth century, between 300 and 400 young women began apprenticeships with a mistress seamstress each year. Seamstresses also consistently formed the largest group of new guild members each year. With an average of 138 mistresses, they composed approximately 10 percent of all guild entries. When given the opportunity, the seamstresses reveal, women surged into organized forms of trade training and work.

Two crucial moments marked a seamstress's career: apprenticeship and reception as a guild mistress. These benchmarks defined the privileged women who attained them as much as the many who did not. During three years of apprenticeship, adolescent girls acquired skills to work as professional needleworkers. Those who successfully completed training occupied the best position in the labor market, with a better chance of obtaining the coveted annual positions than their less qualified colleagues. The apprenticeship contract also brought young women into contact with the guild for the first time. Most apprentices signed their contracts at the guild's offices before its elected officials. Apprenticeship thus served several functions. It was a means to transmit professional skills to a new generation, to inculcate the social relations of labor within the workshop, and to introduce young women to the formal structure of the guild.

After two years of work experience, a finished apprentice was qualified to join the guild in her own right. Most, however, failed to achieve this status. They disappeared from the trade at marriage or continued working as dependent workers, and sometimes as illegal entrepreneurs. Those who did become mistresses usually worked for eight or ten years before acquiring this status. Entry to the guild thus represented a combination of many years of training and hard work, along with talent and good fortune. A mistress seamstress was entitled to establish her own workshop, take on apprentices, and hire workers. She enjoyed a status few women could claim, that of a full-fledged corporate citizen with established rights and obligations toward the guild. Of course, she would be required to pay new taxes and submit to the scrutiny of guild officials, but she could work openly under the protective mantle of her corporation. Over time, she might aspire to become a guild officer and thereby obtain a permanent role in the guild's administration.

Demand for Apprenticeship

Apprenticeship in the seamstresses' trade did not begin with the establishment of the guild in 1675. Notarized contracts testify to a tradition of vocational training among seamstresses from the mid-sixteenth century at least. The guild's creation did, however, bestow new forms of supervision and a new significance on professional training. Previously, apprenticeship was essentially a private arrangement between the girl's family and her instructor, with the sole purpose of transmitting trade skills. After 1675, apprenticeship became a formal prerequisite for entry to the guild, and a series of regulations governed its practice. The seamstresses' statutes required a minimum of three years of instruction with a guild mistress and two years of additional work experience. The statutes limited each mistress to training only one girl at a time, a measure intended to ensure the quality of instruction. A royal declaration of 1693 further stipulated that every apprenticeship be formalized with a notarized contract signed by at least two acting guild officials.[3] When they signed the apprenticeship contract, guild officials certified its compatibility with corporate regulations. They also collected a fee for their services and alms for the poor.

From the first decades of its existence, the guild-sponsored system of apprenticeship proved enormously popular. In 1716, the first date for which figures are available, at least 403 girls entered a notarized training contract with a guild mistress.[4] Between 1746 and 1759, the guild recorded a yearly average of 419 new apprentices. Because most contracts ran for three years, at any given time there were approximately 1,200 apprentices engaged in learning their trade.[5] With a guild population of over 2,000 mistresses, half the mistresses must have had an apprentice in their workshop. Seamstresses probably constituted the largest group of apprentices, male or female, in eighteenth-century Paris.[6]

Several factors account for the popularity of apprenticeship. One was the nature of the trade itself. Needlework was relatively easy to learn and had low start-up costs. Seamstresses did not need to buy stocks in cloth or rent and furnish a public boutique, but could establish themselves in their own homes with only their skills and some simple tools. Even those who did not become mistresses could use their skills to earn a living as dependent workers. The abundance of mistresses also made it easier for parents to find a mistress. In smaller trades, they may have had difficulty locating a skilled practitioner willing to train their daughters. The fact that seamstresses worked almost exclusively for female clients was also attractive. By placing their daughters in a female trade, parents could reduce the risks of sexual abuse or seduction that were posed by employment with an older man or interaction with male customers.

The guild's institutional structure constituted another advantage of the seamstresses' trade. Corporate supervision of mistresses offered parents hope of locating a trustworthy, competent, and morally sound mistress. If the woman failed in her duties, the girl's guardians could count on the support of officials for redress. The guild also established a relatively simple and inexpensive procedure for procuring the apprenticeship agreement. Some 80 or 90 percent of seamstress apprenticeship contracts were drawn up by the guild notary and signed in the guild offices. One day a week the guild held an open house at which apprentices and mistresses could come to have their contracts drawn up by the guild notary. Those who could not attend this weekly appointment could arrange to be received in the guild office on another day.

These benefits of the seamstresses' trade stood out even more strongly given the lack of alternatives. The more prestigious linen-drapers' guild was too expensive for many families, both in terms of the prices demanded for apprenticeship and the capital required to set up in the trade. The fresh-flower sellers and the hemp merchants, the two remaining female guilds, were cheap but relatively small and poor trades. Outside of the guild system, other female trades were also largely poor and unskilled, as was the case of the market trades discussed as possible targets for incorporation in the 1690s. The seamstresses thus offered the best hope for a young woman of achieving independent trade status and acquiring corporate membership.

To stem the flow of new trade members, guild leaders appear to have imposed a quota on the pool of incoming apprentices each year. This possibility is suggested by the stability in the number of new apprentices. Between 1746 and 1759, the standard deviation from the average of 419 girls was only 28. If no limitations were issued from above, it is probable that demand would have fluctuated more from year to year. This finding suggests that officers of the seamstresses' guild attempted to limit the size of the workforce by restricting access to vocational training. Because in this huge trade they could do little to control actual practices of hiring and production, they intervened instead at the moment of skill acquisition. Demand for apprenticeship, however, was not immune to conjunctural difficulties. Between May 1760 and the following May of 1761, a year of economic hardship in Paris, only 272 young women undertook trade training, a number much lower than the average of 419 found between 1746 and 1759. In hard times, parents had no money to spare for apprenticeship, while mistresses with few orders had little need for an apprentice's work. The drawing power of the seamstresses' trade also appears to have diminished somewhat over the eighteenth century, as the expanding and diversifying Parisian economy created new opportunities for female labor.

The parish of Saint-Jean-en-Grève, which actively sponsored vocational training for orphaned children, supplies the best testimony to this effect. Two sets of registers that record children placed in apprenticeship by its officers survive from the charitable foundation of the parish. The registers cover two periods, one at the beginning of the century and the other at the end. The first set of registers records the years 1710, 1713, and 1715 to 1717. They list fifty youths, divided evenly by sex, whom the parish foundation put into apprenticeship during the period recorded. Twenty-four of the twenty-five girls received training from a mistress seamstress, the twenty-fifth from a linenworker. By contrast, the twenty-five boys entered a total of fourteen different trades, ranging from humble cobblers to high-status textile merchant-manufacturers. Six boys undertook training with master cobblers (*savetiers*) and five with master shoemakers (*cordonniers*), the largest trade groups represented. Richer trades, including gilding and clothmaking, received only one or two boys each.[7]

The second set of registers lists one hundred and twenty-six apprentices for the years 1774, 1775, 1777 to 1782, and 1785 to 1787. In these years, girls outnumbered boys seventy-five to fifty-one. While the seamstresses remained the most attractive trade for girls, with forty-three of the seventy-five, the parish also turned to a host of new crafts. It placed six girls with fashion workers and two with more prestigious fashion merchants. Seven began apprenticeship with linenworkers and one with a linen-draper who reported no guild affiliation. Five additional girls studied with lace workers, three with embroiderers, two with female gilder-polishers (*doreuses-polisseuses*), two others with male painter-gilders (*peintres-doreurs*), one with a stockings worker (*ouvrière en bas*), and finally, one with a lace bleacher. Artisans involved in the contracts included men and women, and members of incorporated and unincorporated trades. The example of this parish suggests that a range of new occupations opened up for women across the eighteenth century, primarily in the garment and fashion trades. Whereas seamstresses had been pioneers in driving new forms of consumption at the beginning of the eighteenth century, by its last decades they had been joined and partially displaced by practitioners of new commercial and productive specialties aimed at a wider and more acquisitive market. These records also show strong support for female apprenticeship from charitable institutions.[8]

The Apprenticeship Contract

The eighteenth-century apprenticeship contract was a highly formalized document. In his *La Science parfaite des notaires*, Claude-Joseph Ferrière outlined the general terms used for contracts in Paris. He provided thirteen different types of contracts relating to trade training, including one used to transfer apprentices to a new master and another for annulling the agreement altogether. The level of standardization in terminology during the eighteenth century was so high that notaries often ordered preprinted contracts, leaving blanks for the specific details belonging to each case. The seamstresses' notary went one step further, procuring customized contracts for the guild that included the name of the corporation as well as the appropriate female form of words such as "apprentice" and "mistress." For the four hundred contracts he wrote each year, these custom-made forms were a tremendous time saver.[9]

This study is based on a total of 846 seamstress apprenticeship contracts, which included 743 individual apprentices. The notarial office that served the guild through most of the century offers the most extensive collection of these documents. Of the 720 contracts consulted from this office, 403 come from the single year 1716; the rest were scattered across the 1730s, 1740s, and the early 1750s. The sample also includes a number of contracts from the years 1751 and 1761, drawn up by many different notaries. These contracts were located using comprehensive archival indexes prepared for these two years. Unfortunately, the largest group of contracts, those drawn up by the guild notary, appears to have disappeared for 1751 and 1761, leaving a highly reduced sample. The period after 1761 is represented by a handful of additional contracts acquired by chance.[10]

Five parties were habitually featured in apprenticeship contracts: the apprentice, her legal guardian (if she were a minor), the mistress, the acting guild officials, and the notary. The first party to appear was the person or people who presented the child in apprenticeship. This could be the child's parents, her legally appointed tutors, or even an unrelated individual who agreed to pay for the training and accepted moral and legal responsibility for her conduct during service. If she were over twenty-five and unmarried, a woman could engage in a training contract under her own authority. The second figure to appear was the mistress. According to the printed contract used by the seamstresses' notary, the mistress formally accepted the girl as her apprentice and promised to "to show and teach her said trade of seamstress and everything that depends on it, to treat her gently and humanely, as is appropriate." This pledge addressed the two principal sources of anxiety for apprentices' parents, that the mistress might conceal trade secrets or treat the girl brutally. Such stipulations were not specific to seamstresses but figured in some form in almost all apprenticeship contracts. Apart from these initial promises, each contract individually specified conditions for the provision of food, lodging, and other amenities. Mistress seamstresses always appeared alone for these contracts, whether they were married, widowed, or single. Guild status allowed married women to engage in business-related contracts without their husbands' authorization.

After the mistress, the apprentice was the third person to appear in the contract. She formally agreed to enter her mistress's service and offered a series of pledges regarding her behavior during the training period. She promised "to learn within her power that which she will be shown and taught by her Mistress, to serve her loyally without being absent."[11] She also agreed, in the event that she fled prematurely, to be "sought in the city and suburbs of Paris to be brought back to her said mistress to complete the time of the present [contract]." This was a critical stipulation for all training agreements. Masters and mistresses counted on retaining their apprentices until the end of their period of service, for the young people's work only offered a profit in the final stages of training.

Following these mutual obligations, the next issue addressed by the contract was the mistress's fee. Because the price varied in each case, the notary's printed form left a large blank for this sum and any details regarding modalities of payment. The final participants in each contract were the guild's officials. In the guild's printed forms, these officials approved the documents as being in conformity with corporate regulations. They also acknowledged receipt of the necessary fees, including "twenty sous for the poor" of the Hôpital général of Paris. The standard notarial conclusion followed, by which the parties gave their addresses at their homes or offices, promised to honor the contract, and signed their names.

This was the standardized contract used by the guild's notary for 80 to 90 percent of seamstress apprentices. The remaining 10 or 20 percent of contracts were drawn up by notaries other than the guild notary. It is unclear why these apprentices and their mistresses decided to forgo the established procedure. Familiarity with an individual notary was probably an important consideration, particularly for families who engaged in many financial or commercial transactions. This was a more expensive choice, because nonguild notaries not only charged more per contract, they also took responsibility for obtaining the acting officials' signatures. This service must have significantly raised the cost of the contract.

Nonguild notaries used their own formulas, slightly different in wording from that of the guild's notary. In these documents, the mistress's promise to teach the trade often took on a more elaborate form: "She promises during the said period to show and teach her said trade of seamstress and everything in which she involves herself and intervenes without hiding anything."[12] In addition, nonguild notaries often established the apprentice's right to refuse illegitimate requests on the part of her mistress. The apprentice was required to obey her mistress only "in all that she will order that is licit and honest." One contract made the girl promise not only to learn the trade to the best of her ability but also to "comply with her mother's and father's good intentions [and] to follow in all things the beneficial recommendations of her mistress."[13] The majority of the nonguild notaries also explicitly assigned responsibility for retrieving a fugitive apprentice to the girl's major guarantor: "In the case of absence the [guarantor] obliges himself [or herself] to have her sought in the city and suburbs of Paris, for, if she is found, to be brought back to her mistress to complete the time remaining until the expiration of the present [contract]."[14]

The significance of these differences should not be overemphasized. All apprentices held a de jure right to refuse mistresses' illicit demands. A mistress faced with a delinquent apprentice would address herself immediately to the girl's guardians, even if the contract did not explicitly assign them responsibility. The differences among these contracts lie more in notarial idiosyncrasy than in qualitative issues perceptible to the parties involved. More important contractual distinctions existed between the seamstresses and the linen-drapers, the other major female guild in eighteenth-century Paris. The officials of this guild bore the title of "respectable people," or *honnêtes personnes*. Its regulations required that an apprentice's guardian and mistress both certify she was "of good life and morals, of the Catholic, Roman, and apostolic religion," the latter a detail occurring very rarely in seamstresses' contracts. Should she prove otherwise, guild officials would cancel her apprenticeship and bar her from entering the guild. The contract also specifically prohibited linen-drapers from sending their apprentices to inns or hospitals on work-related errands. On completion of the training, the mistress had to present the contract to the guild's officials. If she lost or expelled her apprentice, she was to inform the guild within one week. Failure to do so nullified the contract and brought a potential fine of one hundred livres. The contract also forbade mistresses from granting reductions in the length of training.[15]

These stipulations suggest a desire on the part of the linen-drapers' guild to control apprenticeship practices closely. Given its relatively small membership, the linen-drapers' guild could intervene in the training process to a much greater extent than the seamstresses' guild. If, as has been suggested, apprenticeship among the prestigious linen-drapers served as a form of finishing school for girls of the upper bourgeoisie, the contracts' severity may reflect elite parents' concerns for their daughters' moral and physical well-being.[16] Records from the law court of the king's procurator at the Châtelet indicate that the linen-drapers' guild interceded frequently in disputes between apprentices and mistresses, while the seamstresses' guild did not. The seamstresses controlled the reproduction of the trade by monitoring the number of incoming apprentices and supervising the framing of the contract. Their ability to supervise actual practices of apprenticeship was much more limited.

Apprentices and their Guardians

Among seamstresses, a major guardian or sponsor usually placed the girl in apprenticeship. In almost three-quarters of the cases (468 out of 646, or 72 percent), this was one or both of the parents or a parent's representative. Of the total group 13 percent came with both parents (81, or 13 percent), including thirteen cases involving a mother and a stepfather. A larger group of slightly over 40 percent (272, or 42 percent) was accompanied by a father acting alone, including four stepfathers and eight cases of representatives of a father who lived outside of Paris. Most of these contracts did not indicate whether the mother was dead or simply absent, because her legal consent was not required for the procedure. Between 15 and 20 percent of the apprentices (112, or 17 percent) appeared with their mothers alone. Most were widowed, but twenty-one were wives whose husbands' absence or illness had left them with de facto responsibility for their children. As these figures suggest, parents usually chose apprenticeship for their daughters and undertook the actions and expenses necessary to obtain it. Fathers were the most important figures in this process, but mothers played a significant role as well.

A substantial minority of girls (88, or 14 percent) appeared with a nonparental family member. Uncles and aunts most frequently placed girls in apprenticeship, with twenty-four and twenty-five cases respectively, and two cases of a pair of aunts and uncles appearing together. The next most common relatives were siblings, including six brothers, six sisters, and three brothers-in-law. Grandparents came a close third, with five grandmothers, five grandfathers, and two cases of a set of grandparents sponsoring a young woman for apprenticeship. Cousins appeared least frequently; the sample includes only four female cousins, four male cousins, and two second cousins. Among relatives, the mother's family seems to have played a more important role in sponsoring girls' professional education than the father's family: thirty-eight maternal uncles and aunts appeared compared to only seven paternal ones. The same was true among grandparents, with seven on the mother's side and three on the father's. A father, while he was alive, almost always took legal and financial responsibility for his daughter's future. When he died, the mother's family stepped into the breach to provide daily care and vocational training. Whether this pattern was also true for boys remains to be explored.

Beyond kinship ties, sentimental or religious bonds could also lead adults to take responsibility for a girl's vocational training. Eleven girls were placed into apprenticeship by a nonrelated legal guardian, another four by a godfather, and three by a godmother. Two additional apprentices were presented by their own mistresses, while fourteen appeared with representatives of charitable institutions or other patrons.

A final group of apprentices consisted of those who entered trade instruction under their own authority. In the total sample, approximately one in ten apprentices (n = 59 or 9 percent) placed themselves in apprenticeship. The largest group of independent apprentices (n = 25) declared themselves to be unmarried majors. Another seventeen were orphaned minors or women who simply described themselves as unmarried girls (filles) without specifying their age. Finally, sixteen autonomous apprentices were married women, including two widows, and one woman who was placed in apprenticeship by her own husband (see table 7.1 for a breakdown of sponsors).

Apprentices' Geographic and Social Origins

The women and girls who entered trade training were overwhelmingly Parisian in origin. Out of 519 cases where information is available, over 90 percent of apprentices' parents declared a residence in the capital (460 of 514 cases, or 91 percent). Those from outside Paris rarely came from very far away. In most cases, they arrived from towns that now are engulfed by the twentieth-century capital, such as Gennevilliers, Vaugirard, St. Denis, Montreuil, and Chevreuse. Some came from larger towns in the surrounding region, including Senlis, Saint-Germain-en-Laye, Chartres, and Beauvais. Six apprentices with parents in Versailles underline the importance of the court in attracting women to the garment trades. Apprentices from the most distant areas came from Lille and Tonnerre. Demand for entry to the seamstresses' trade was thus an urban and predominantly

TABLE 7.1 Relation of guarantor to apprentice, in order of occurrence

Relationship	Number of cases	Percentage of total
Father	272	42
Mother	112	17
Other family	88	14
Both parents	81	13
Herself	59	9
Nonfamily sponsor	16	2
Legal guardian	11	2
Godparent	7	1

Parisian phenomenon; peasants' daughters did not come to Paris to become needleworkers as they did, for example, to enter domestic service. Because three-quarters of mistresses were finished apprentices, the guild itself was composed largely of women raised in the capital.[17]

The professions of apprentices' fathers support the impression of a trade population well-implanted in Paris and emphasize the broad social scale from which apprentices were drawn.[18] Of 339 living fathers who declared a profession, the largest group belonged to the world of artisanal crafts and commerce: seventy-three were Parisian guild masters and another three enjoyed trade privileges from nonguild institutions. Forty-two were artisans with no guild title, and fourteen explicitly declared themselves to be journeymen (*compagnon* or *garçon*).[19] In addition to these craftsmen, thirty-seven of the girls' fathers were merchants, with twenty belonging to the prestigious merchant guilds known as the Six Corps. A smaller group of twenty-nine fathers worked as unskilled laborers, porters, or in small unincorporated trades. These fathers included twenty-one wage earners (*gagne-deniers*) and three coachmen.

The second largest group of fathers belonged to the world of service. Among these fifty-nine men, twelve were simple servants (*domestiques*) and six were manservants (*valets*). The remaining fathers bore a range of appellations, including doorman (*portier*), chef, coachman, butler *(maitre d'hotel)*, and household officer.[20] As these titles indicate, the category of domestic service encompassed a wide variety and hierarchy of positions. A *domestique* could be one of very few servants in a bourgeois household. A coachman or butler belonged in a grander noble residence with a large staff of attendants. These servants were not always the humble creatures of historical convention; a butler, for example, would occupy a respected and well-remunerated position in a noble household. Another five fathers were self-employed in the service industry, one as a "master hotelkeeper," another as an innkeeper; two as boardinghouse keepers (*maîtres de pension*), and one as a renter of furnished rooms.

Following the service occupations, another thirty-six fathers described themselves as *bourgeois de Paris,* in theory men whose income derived from property rather than salaried labor. The economic and social reality behind this self-description, however, is far from self-evident. Merchants, craftsmen, or domestic servants who earned enough to make significant investments could disguise their origins, and their continuing participation in paid labor, by this title. Historians have found even humble laborers claiming the status of *bourgeois.* The *bourgeois* fathers in this sample could thus have been born into this status group, they could have achieved it through many different kinds of work, or they might have been merely self-aggrandizing working men.[21]

The remaining fathers belonged to royal or municipal government institutions or worked as independent professionals. Fifteen were employees of judicial, administrative, or fiscal institutions, while another five fathers worked in some form of royal service, for example as a royally privileged writer, a royal pastry chef, or simply as "employees in the king's service." Ten fathers engaged in military or police service, one as a corporal of the watch, another as a night watchman, and six more as Swiss guards. Finally, a handful of fathers represented the social summit among apprentices. They included a royal councilor, a contractor for the royal navy, a provincial nobleman (*écuyer seigneur*), and the director of a provincial tax court (*directeur des aides*).

This list of occupations demonstrates the wide array of social groups that constituted the seamstresses' trade. Apprentices' fathers ranged from unskilled manual laborers to noblemen and holders of royal office. Training in this trade satisfied different social and economic strategies. For families of the highest level, apprenticeship was probably not intended as real vocational training, but as a form of feminine socialization akin to that offered by the linen-drapers' guild. These families sought mistresses of high repute with noble clients and a large staff of workers to spare their daughters physical drudgery. During apprenticeship, the girls acquired a taste for fashionable clothing and accessories as well as appropriate womanly skills in needlework. When sufficient funds for a dowry could not be spared, elite girls may have been steered toward trade instead of marriage. A younger daughter, or a child whose family fortunes had declined, could thus find herself destined for a career as a mistress seamstress.

At the middle level of master artisans, merchants, and prosperous servants, apprenticeship offered useful skills and a means to accumulate a dowry, even if the girl ultimately abandoned the trade after marriage. Artisanal families were particularly likely to put their daughters into apprenticeship when they had no use for them at home. This explains why few of the apprentices had fathers who participated in clothing production or other trades that seem to have relied heavily on female labor. Only two were master tailors, one a used-clothes dealer, and two others were merchant mercers. By contrast, we find seven lockmakers, four shoemakers, nine wine merchants, and seven cabinetmakers, trades that probably offered limited employment to girls either in the workshop or in sales. Like these men, the large group of domestic servants and employees who placed their daughters in training had no work to offer them at home. The seamstresses' trade provided a way of profitably occupying a young woman who was unnecessary for the family business.[22]

For the most humble families, apprenticeship in the seamstresses' trade offered a step up the social scale. Unskilled laborers sought to ensure their daughters' ability to support themselves and contribute to family income. Formal apprenticeship promised a more stable and secure position in the labor market than the girls' mothers or fathers enjoyed. Journeymen whose access to guild membership was permanently blocked could hope to see their daughters earn a corporate status forever beyond them. The importance of charity in sponsoring apprentice seamstresses highlights the role of the trade as a form of upward mobility for poor families.

Length of Apprenticeship and Age of Apprentices

Most seamstresses observed the three-year training period required by the guild. In a sample of 735 apprenticeship contracts, more than three-quarters (565, or 77 percent) lasted exactly three years. Another 122 (17 percent) extended to four years, 30 for five years (4 percent) and eleven for six years (1.5 percent). One apprentice each entered service for seven and eight years. Overall, the average duration of apprenticeship was three years and four months (median = 3 years) (see table 7.2). In other Parisian trades, apprenticeship could last considerably longer. Steven Kaplan sampled 293 contracts from a broad selection of corporations, finding an average length of four years and ten months.[23] The seamstresses' vocational training was

TABLE 7.2 Length of apprenticeship

Length (in years)	Number of apprentices
3	565
4	122
5	30
6	11
7	1
8	1

also shorter than the four-year minimum imposed by the linen-drapers' guild. The required period for seamstresses did, however, match that of the tailors, their closest counterparts in trade privileges and technical concerns. Seamstresses also entered apprenticeship at a younger age than their male counterparts. Kaplan found an average age of 15.91 years at apprenticeship, while a sample of 565 seamstresses' contracts showed an average age of 14.4 years (median = 14 years).[24]

Apprenticeship for many seamstresses coincided with the onset of puberty, with its physiological changes and new emotional challenges. The most explicit lessons these adolescents received about menstruation and sexuality may have come from their mistresses or older workers, rather than their own mothers or sisters. In the workshop, they learned to be sexually mature women at the same time as they acquired trade skills. The two forms of knowledge must have merged unconsciously, each inflecting and shaping the other. As they emerged from apprenticeship, seamstresses' adult femininity would have been strongly marked by the feminized culture of clothing and fashion and the female labor relations they encountered in the seamstresses' workshop. Henceforth, being a woman meant knowing how to make and wear clothing, and sharing or competing in these practices with other women. Male apprentices must have similarly imbibed their trades along with their emerging adult sexuality and emotions. The fact that male puberty arrived later may help explain the older age of male apprentices.

It is important to note, however, that average-age statistics mask a wide spectrum. The youngest apprentice seamstress was six and a half years old, and the oldest whose age is known was twenty-eight years old. Both ends of this scale were exceptional. The thirty-three girls below twelve years old were younger than any of the boys Kaplan documented. Indeed, Kaplan claims that boys under twelve were believed too young for apprenticeship, being "barely capable of enduring a too serious occupation, of waiting attentively or of taking on grueling work."[25] Guild regulations in effect in the 1750s confirmed the practice of early apprenticeship, establishing a minimum age of ten years old for new apprentice seamstresses. Given the strong feminine associations of needlework and the fact that many girls began to sew before they started formal training, seamstresses' families may have perceived this trade as more "natural" for the young girl. Embarking on apprenticeship may have seemed like an extension of an innately female activity, rather than an abrupt entry into the discipline of a new craft.

At the other end of the spectrum, married and widowed apprentices violated one of the basic norms of apprenticeship. Most male guilds excluded married men from apprenticeship and prohibited apprentices from marrying during their period in service. The patriarchal model so central to corporate ideology could not tolerate the phenomenon of the apprentice who had established his own family, for a master could hardly expect to exercise paternal authority over a young man who held similar powers over his own wife and children. The practice of accepting married apprentices among seamstresses suggests that a mistress's authority was not conceived along the same hierarchical model as a master's. While the master's paternalistic authority drew legitimacy from its familial, regal, and even theological parallels, there were few models for female authority in this society. As a result, the mistress's role and her relationship with her apprentice could be conceived of less formally and less rigidly. It was not incompatible for a mature wife or widow to place herself in apprenticeship with a mistress who might be herself unmarried or only slightly older.

The wide disparity in ages emphasizes once more the multiple life strategies to which apprenticeship corresponded. For young girls, apprenticeship offered not only trade skills but a form of foster care in families broken by death, dislocation, or poverty. In one case, a priest sponsored the apprenticeship of a six-year-old girl whose mother had died. The girl would lodge with her mistress throughout the six years of the contract. Her father, who was still alive, did not appear to sign the contract. At least two of the four nine-year-olds had also lost their mothers prior to being placed in apprenticeship. Five of the eight ten-year-olds were presented by their mothers or unrelated guardians.[26] Young apprentices required a strong emotional and professional commitment from their mistresses. In comparison to a thirteen- or fourteen-year-old, they possessed fewer useful skills and shorter attention spans, and they provided little profitable labor to their mistresses during their training periods. Even after three years of instruction, they would require several more years of experience before entering the labor market. They would, however, be relatively docile and submissive charges, less difficult than a willful sixteen- or seventeen-year-old.

Apprentices of advanced age offered considerable advantages to prospective mistresses. They came to training emotionally mature, possibly with a high level of existing skill and the capacity to learn quickly. Mature apprentices, however, also presented important drawbacks. Those with their own households, particularly married women with children, could less easily be pressed into long hours of service. Older apprentices might also be more reluctant to perform household chores or behave respectfully toward their mistresses. At worst, they had an independent spirit, set habits, and if raised in humble circumstances, could not acquire the polish necessary to serve socially elite clients.

The strongly inverse relationship between length of apprenticeship and age demonstrates the slower learning curve of young apprentices. Under twelve years of age, the average duration of instruction was 4.4 years. At age twelve, this average dropped to 3.7 years; for thirteen-year-olds it fell again to 3.4 and for fourteen-year-olds to 3.3 years. By age fifteen, almost all apprentices entered three-year contracts, suggesting that their mistresses viewed the three-year period as sufficient time in which to instruct their charges and extract a return on their investment in the apprentice. These figures may also reflect a more businesslike attitude among older apprentices eager to complete their training as quickly as possible to enter the labor market.

The Price of Apprenticeship

In our sample, no apprentice received a salary from her mistress. On the contrary, most paid for their training. From a total of 696 apprentices, 154 paid nothing for apprenticeship (22 percent), while the remaining 542 paid fees (78 percent). Overall, the average price charged by mistresses was 94 livres (median = 30 livres), with a range from 8 to 900 livres. This average rises to 121 livres if we exclude those who paid nothing (median = 100 livres). Compared to the prices demanded by the guilds in Steven Kaplan's study, these figures appear somewhat low. Nevertheless, Kaplan

TABLE 7.3 Evolution of the price of apprenticeship over time

Years	Average price for all apprentices (in livres)	Average among only those who paid (in livres)	Percentage of paying contracts
1716	72 (n = 406)	90 (n = 325)	80
1730s	103 (n = 61)	153 (n = 52)	85
1740s	117 (n = 106)	120 (n = 81)	76
1750s	155 (n = 77)	206 (n = 58)	75
1760s	119 (n = 48)	212 (n = 27)	56

found similar fees among the "solid" trades of lockmakers, joiners, sculptors, and pastrymakers.[27]

The price of apprenticeship in the seamstresses' trade appears to have risen significantly over the eighteenth century. The 406 contracts from 1716 cost on average 72 livres, or 90 livres among the 325 girls who paid for apprenticeship. In the 1730s, the average for 61 contracts rose to 103 livres, or 153 livres among the 52 girls who paid fees. In the 1740s, 106 contracts show an average price of 117 livres, or 120 livres for the 81 paying contracts. During the 1750s, a total of 77 contracts offered an average price of 155 livres, which rose to 206 livres among the 58 girls who paid for apprenticeship. Finally, in the year 1761, the average price for 48 contracts was 119 livres, or 212 livres for 27 paying contracts.

The cost of apprenticeship thus followed the inflationary trend of the eighteenth century (see table 7.3). As prices rose, however, the number of seamstresses who paid for apprenticeship declined. This finding suggests a growing gap between those who could pay—and who furnished substantial fees—and those who could not afford apprenticeship fees. The latter presumably received few amenities and perhaps lower-quality instruction. The discrepancy in size and origin of the sources, however, prohibits firm conclusions; it should be borne in mind that the samples from 1751 and 1761 represent only apprentices who did not go to the guild notary's for their contract. Families who paid more to use their own notary may have also been willing to pay more for training.

A number of considerations determined the price each mistress charged for her services. The most obvious were the material services she agreed to furnish, because apprentices who ate and lodged with the mistress imposed considerable expense on their new households. The impact of these services on prices becomes apparent when we divide contracts into those offering instruction only and those including additional services. In a total of 655 cases, 375 mistresses contracted to provide only vocational training, while apprentices' guardians accepted responsibility for furnishing food, lodging, and laundry. Among these 375 cases, 102 apprentices (25 percent) paid nothing for their training. Together, they accounted for more than two-thirds (70 percent) of all the apprentices who did not pay. The average price for those who did pay for these instruction-only contracts was 21 livres, against an average among all paying contracts of 121 livres.[28]

By contrast, apprentices who received material benefits such as food, lodging, and laundering paid much higher fees. A group of 217 such apprentices furnished an average of 199 livres for their apprenticeship, as their mistresses adjusted their fees to account for the additional expense. Among the different services, provision of food, and in particular bread, had the strongest influence on price. In an additional seventeen cases, for example, the mistress agreed only to lodge her charge, providing no food for the entire contract or a significant portion of it. The prices paid in these cases were low (average = 21.4 livres), indicating the dominance of food over lodging in the calculation of price.

In other cases, the mistress agreed to give her apprentice soup and meat but demanded that the guardians supply bread during the whole of the contract or at least the first half. At an average price of sixty-three livres, these contracts cost more than those with no food at all, but less than those that included bread. One contract explicitly linked the parent's monetary contribution to the price of bread. It stipulated that if the price of bread rose above four sous per pound, the father would be obliged to provide four pounds of bread each week. In keeping with its central place in the Parisian diet, bread seems to have been the largest expense in an apprentice's nourishment.

The service of laundering clothing had less effect on price. Another group of fifty-two apprentices received lodging and food, while their own families paid to launder their clothes. The average price of these contracts was 185 livres, compared to 199 livres for contracts that included food, lodging, and laundering. We may surmise that mistresses estimated the cost of laundering at around 15 livres. With only one exception, the apprentice's guardians always accepted the responsibility of supplying clothing for the duration of the contract.

Apart from these concrete services, prices were subject to nonmaterial considerations that cannot be measured statistically. Mistresses with successful businesses and high reputations could place a premium on their services. Their position enabled them to handpick apprentices, selecting those who could pay the largest fees or those with the best skills. Less fortunate mistresses had to be moderate in their demands. Prior contact between the mistress and the apprentice's family — whether as friends, neighbors, clients, or relatives — could also induce a mistress to lower her price or dispense with it altogether. A woman interested in forging links with a particular family might charge significantly less for training. Such calculations, for example, must explain mistress Marie Françoise Bourlot's decision to accept nine-year-old Marie Louise Comte for only ten livres for a three-year contract providing food, lodging, and laundry. Comte was presented in apprenticeship by the powerful duc de Noailles, her father's former employer. The duke's patronage could have considerably enhanced Bourlot's trade.[29]

The distinct cultural or nutritional concerns that some parents brought to their daughters' education are revealed in a small number of contracts. Four stipulated that the mistress would fed the apprentice "good flesh only." Five apprentices received explicit permission to spend Sundays and holidays with their parents or other relatives. Provisions for nonvocational learning were rare. One apprentice would attend catechism during Lent and a second would be allowed to prepare for her first communion at church. A third apprentice would study with a master of reading and writing during the first year of her contract. The vast majority of parents were more concerned with their daughters' trade training and daily care than with additional forms of learning.

Apart from the mistress's fee, parents were also obliged to satisfy the charges of the guild and the notary who drew up the contract. Guild supervision of apprenticeship did not come free. The royal declaration of 1693 set the guild's fee at twelve livres, dedicating half to the guild treasury and one livre to each of the six elected officials.[30] Apprentices paid an additional tax of one livre for the poor of the Hôpital général. In 1745, guild leaders received permission to raise apprenticeship fees by an additional three livres, sixteen sous, and six deniers. After this date, the total price of the guild-supervised contract, including the notarial fee, was twenty livres.[31] Apprenticeship fees were a lucrative source of income to the guild, generating an average of 3,676 livres between 1745 and 1759, or 21 percent of annual corporate revenue.

Given the bulk of business provided by the corporation, the guild's notary accepted a low price for his services, charging three livres, three sous, and six deniers prior to 1745, and four livres subsequently. According to guild officials' statements from 1762, other notaries charged at least five or six livres to draw up an apprenticeship contract. Still, with roughly four hundred contracts a year, the guild notary could earn more than one thousand livres annually from this business.[32]

Choice of Mistress

Unfortunately, notarial contracts offer no explicit explanation for families' choice of mistresses. Explicitly mentioned kinship ties are very rare, and a comparison between apprentices' and mistresses' names does not yield more than a handful of cases suggesting a family relation. In 1716, in the only example of sister-to-sister training, Nicolas Robert, the coachman of the cardinal of Rouen, placed his seventeen-year-old daughter Marguerite Robert into apprenticeship for three years with her sister, Mistress Elizabeth Catherine Robert. The father did not pay for the training, but agreed to continue lodging the younger daughter in his quarters in the cardinal's house on the rue Vieille du Temple, a short walk from her sister's apartment on the rue de Bretagne.[33] Some seamstresses must have trained their sisters without entering a formal contract; however, such informal training offered no qualifications for guild membership.

Neighborhood proximity appears to have played an important role in orienting choice. Out of 644 cases, roughly 40 percent (n = 256) of mistresses lived in the same parish as their charges, including almost 10 percent (n = 59) who lived on the same street. Another quarter of the mistresses (n = 167) lived in a parish adjoining the one where their apprentice's family resided. In some cases, a mistress's reputation alone may have been enough to attract apprentices. Of 824 mistresses, 46 were former guild officials. These women were experienced craftswomen and well-versed in guild politics, making them ideal mentors for apprentices anxious to advance their careers. Other seamstresses acquired a high reputation through commercial success. Parents interested in procuring a good mistress learned about these women through inquiries among merchants, other parents, or perhaps at the guild offices. The fact that one-third of mistresses (223 out of 644) lived in a nonadjoining parish testifies to the capacity of such information networks to bring Parisians together from all parts of the city.

Apart from informal information exchange, a type of brokering system appears to have existed to help anxious parents locate a mistress. Evidence to this effect is provided by a group of thirty-seven apprentices who undertook two contracts on the same day or within the space of several days. The first document looks like a normal apprenticeship contract signed by acting guild officials along with the other parties involved. The second contract, however, stated that the first mistress took on the apprentice only to please another colleague. The purpose of the second contract was thus to transfer the girl to another mistress, for whom she was apparently destined all along.

This set of contracts poses a problem for interpretation. The most obvious explanation is that of fraud. Because guild regulations limited mistresses to one apprentice at a time, those who wished to take two or more apprentices might well ask another mistress to appear before the guild officials for a first contract with the intention of transferring the validated apprenticeship to herself in a second contract. Accumulating apprentices in this way would provide mistresses with a source of cheap labor as well as hard cash in the form of parental fees. Some mistresses clearly did cheat the system. When spinster Marguerite Gabrielle Gaillard died in 1763, three apprentices lived in her home. Each had signed an apprenticeship contract with Gaillard before the guild's notary. The girls' families paid between 150 and 200 livres each for the training, sums that were partially refunded after her death.[34] In 1788, mistress Marie Marthe Gilles, widow of a master tailor, also had three apprentices, alongside a yearly worker.[35]

The plausibility of fraud, however, falters before the fact that the guild notary oversaw the second set of contracts, for which he had a special set of forms printed. Although he might have forgotten a mistresses' name or face after a period of months, the two documents in these cases were signed on the same day or within a month at the longest. His close ties with the guild surely would have prevented him from normalizing a blatantly fraudulent procedure. A second explanation for these dual contracts lies in the existence of some form of brokering system. When they failed to find a suitable mistress on their own, families could seek a mistress to act as an intermediary. The mistress agreed to take the child on provisionally while she located another seamstress willing to undertake the apprenticeship for the full three-year period. The guild offices on the rue de la Verrerie may have served as the focal point for this system, with families addressing themselves to the offices to be directed to an intermediary.

The fees charged for this brokerage service emerge from the contracts themselves; the first one often stipulated a price of 8 to 10 livres for instruction only, which the mistress did not refund when she transferred the girl to her new mistress. These were substantial finders' fees, but not unreasonable in light of the 150 to 300 livres families paid the second mistress for instruction, food, and lodging. In one case in April 1716, Jean Noel, a shoemaker (*cordonnier*) of the faubourg Saint-Antoine, placed a girl named Jeanne Charlotte François in apprenticeship with unmarried mistress Marie Anne Lejeune. François' father was the caretaker (*concierge*) of a château outside of Paris, who had authorized Noel to act for him in the matter. Lejeune agreed to provide trade instruction only over three years for a 10-livre fee. The woman reappeared on the same day, however, to transfer the contract to a colleague, mistress Anne Debachelier. This time Debachelier promised to provide food, lodging, and laundering to the apprentice over three years for a fee of 150 livres.[36]

Some twenty years later on June 16, 1739, widow Elizabeth Longue placed her eleven-year-old daughter Marie Elizabeth Piercain in service with mistress Louise Héleine Poulard, who again promised to provide trade training only for five years in exchange for a 10-livre fee. The same day, Poulard transferred the contract to another mistress, Marie Marguerite Couturier. This time, the mistress agreed to feed and lodge the girl over the same period for a hefty fee of 300 livres.[37] The need for such a brokering system makes sense given the evidence for a quota on the number of apprentices each year. If demand for positions exceeded supply, mistresses would have held most of the cards in apprenticeship negotiations. Those in a position to procure mistresses for interested families could demand a substantial fee. This brokering system would have been particularly attractive to families anxious to secure a high-quality mistress for their daughters.

A much smaller sample of linen-draper apprenticeship contracts offers revealing contrasts with the seamstresses. In a sample of twenty-six linen-draper contracts, every apprentice lodged with her mistress. Out of twenty-two contracts with full information, six girls paid nothing for their apprenticeship. The other sixteen girls paid an average of 462 livres, much higher than the average among apprentice seamstresses. These girls came from families even more firmly entrenched in the Parisian bourgeoisie or successful guild world. Four fathers were *bourgeois de Paris,* including two merchant *bourgeois de Paris,* while another three were guild masters. Three fathers worked for Parisian administrative or judicial institutions: one was a secretary of a counselor at the Parlement of Paris, another an inspector at the salt warehouse, and the third a bailiff at the Châtelet of Paris. One father represented both the only unskilled worker and the sole non-Parisian in the sample. Compared to the seamstresses, linen-drapers formed a smaller elite of female merchants, drawn from the well-to-do commercial and professional classes of the city.

Charitable Apprenticeship

In the 1760s, officials of the seamstresses' guild claimed that at least half of their apprentices were sponsored by some form of charity. This was an exaggerated estimate. Among 743 apprentices, slightly more than 10 percent (n = 85, or 11.4 percent) received support from charitable sources. Charity played a significant role in apprenticeship, but a considerably less dramatic one than the guild claimed.[38] The most important organizations in sponsoring apprenticeship in Paris were the charitable foundations attached to the city's parishes. Among them, the parish of Saint-Jean-en-Grève was one of the most active. The numerous bequests received by its charitable foundation for this purpose suggest that it had established a reputation by the beginning of the eighteenth century as a strong supporter of apprenticeship. On December 7, 1711, for example, it received a 600-livre annuity, bequeathed by an anonymous donor to place orphaned children in apprenticeship.[39] Some bequests identified even more specific candidates for such assistance. In 1715, a parishioner gave 18,750 livres, in the form of a 750-livre annuity, for the annual placement of "five poor girls, orphaned of father and mother, native of Paris" in vocational training.[40] Another gift for apprenticeship was made along with a bequest of 2,000 livres for twelve annual masses of the Holy Spirit. As the last example suggests, donations for vocational training were often made in the spirit of religious devotion.[41]

These funds permitted the parish of Saint-Jean-en-Grève to place a large number of children in apprenticeship, at least 50 in four years between 1710 and 1717, and 126 in eleven years between 1774 and 1787. Within our sample of apprenticeship contracts, 32 seamstress apprentices received funding from Saint-Jean-en-Grève, by far the largest single charitable sponsor in the group. In the years 1751 and 1761 alone, the parish funded at least 7 and 8 girls respectively. In each case, the foundation furnished a standard payment, which grew from 75 livres in 1716 to 150 livres by the 1740s. These sums enabled apprentices to contract for three years of instruction, plus food, lodging, and laundering.[42]

Beyond merely paying for the contract, the administrators of the foundation helped supervise the training process. Each year, they selected candidates among the "worthy" poor children of the parish. To benefit from this aid, a child had to be born and baptized in the parish and be orphaned of at least one parent. The apprentices they chose did not belong to the poorest, transient classes but were established residents of the area, known and approved by the parish priest and churchwardens. Foundation administrators accompanied the selected children to the notary's office to draw up the contract. In the seamstresses' case, they came to the guild offices, located in the same parish, to pay the necessary sums and to sign the notarial contract. Foundation administrators also inspected each workshop halfway through the training period to ensure that instruction was occurring in a satisfactory manner. When necessary, they authorized the transfer of an apprentice to a new master or mistress. Ultimate responsibility for the children, however, resided in the parents or other major guarantors, who featured in the notarial contract in the regular fashion.

Other parishes mustered fewer funds for sponsoring apprenticeship. In our sample, twelve additional parishes funded a total of twenty-three seamstresses. Foremost among them were Saint-André-des-Arts with six girls in 1716, Saint-Paul with five apprentices over three years, and Saint-Jacques-de-la-Boucherie with three in two years. Each parish furnished a different sum for the training, varying from a low of 75 livres, paid by the foundation of Saint-Charles in 1744, to a high of 325 livres, supplied by Saint-Eustache parish in 1743. Some provided bread rather than cash, an expedient to which the foundation of Saint-Paul turned, perhaps as its income from annuities was consumed by inflation or devaluation.[43]

Charitable foundations enabled the wealthy merchants, functionaries, and bourgeois men who ran them to develop influence and patronage in their neighborhoods. In one case, a notary appeared in a contract as both the drafter of the document and as an administrator of the parish foundation sponsoring the apprentice. Dominating labor markets, notarial transactions, petty justice, and charitable institutions, these men supervised and intervened in the lives of the poor men and women around them, forging ties of dependence and mutual obligation. A man who obtained free training for a poor family's son or daughter could expect to receive gratitude and local support in exchange. He could also hold needy families to certain standards of comportment in religious, social, business, and familial affairs. Apprenticeship thus played an important role in local systems of mentoring and social control.

Outside of the formal charity system, some apprentices received private subsidies. Nobles or wealthy commoners left annuities for this purpose, entrusting the distribution of funds to their own testamentary executors rather than a parish foundation. Well-placed benefactors sometimes singled out a child of their own acquaintance, such as the daughter of a favorite servant or employee. Among our sample, a countess, a duchess, and the widows of an honorary secretary of the king and of the second president of the Parlement of Paris each sponsored one girl for apprenticeship. The duc de of Noailles paid for the apprenticeship of his former Swiss Guard's daughter, while the seigneur de Villeron, president of the royal Grand Conseil, did the same for the daughter of his hunting steward. Finally, pious charitable impulses moved five priests to supply funds to sponsor girls for trade training.

Charitable funding for apprenticeship provided a minor but important means of access to the trade, which could take on several forms. Charitable sponsorship might be one link in a chain of municipal patronage, a reward for a parent's years of faithful service or simply the pious gesture of a rich man or woman facing death. Donors and administrators of this aid acted from feelings of piety and altruism, as well as concerns about social order and self-sufficiency for the poor. Far from being excluded from such aid, girls attracted special attention from donors who were aware of the limited range of trades available to women and fearful for poor girls' physical and moral well-being. Female apprenticeship was normal not only for the artisans involved, but also for the social and religious elite who sponsored it.

Allouage

Apart from apprenticeship, alternative forms of trade training existed in Paris in the eighteenth century. Like apprenticeship, *allouage* training was also ruled by notarized contracts.[44] Both contracts established a set of mutual obligations to be followed during a strictly defined period of vocational training. The language of the *allouage* contract closely followed the corporate model, mimicking many of the standard terms of the apprenticeship document. The fundamental distinction between *allouage* and apprenticeship was that the former offered no qualifications for entry to a guild. Finished apprentices gained a certain status vis-à-vis the corporate organization that regulated their trade, most importantly the right to stand for membership after several years of supplementary work experience. An *alloué* who fulfilled all the terms of his or her contract had no hope — at least in theory—of ever joining a guild. For guild masters, *allouage* was advantageous in that the guild system imposed no limit on the number that each master could accept. For nonmasters, it was the only kind of instruction they could offer, because they had no ties to a guild.

On the surface, little distinguishes the small group of seventeen seamstress *allouées* from apprentices. Like apprentices, these pupils ranged in age from seven to over twenty-five years old. Their origins were also similar; the young women's fathers were guild masters, journeymen, and *bourgeois de Paris*. Almost all had Parisian origins, the two outsiders coming from nearby Varennes and Melun. Only one planned to live at home during the training period, while the rest would lodge and take meals with their mistresses. The *allouées* also paid fees similar to the apprentices. Apart from three who paid nothing, the rest paid an average of 182 livres, a figure comparable to the average paid by apprentices who lodged with their mistresses.

Given their Parisian origins, their apparent economic stability, and their familiarity with the guild world, their families' motivations for choosing *allouage* over apprenticeship call for some explanation. In some cases, the reason may be deduced from information given in the contract. Two girls, aged seven and nine years old, did not meet the guild's minimum-age requirement for apprenticeship. One of these contracts explicitly stated that the girl would enter formal apprenticeship when she reached the minimum age of ten years.[45] Three other *allouées* were daughters of deceased mistress seamstresses and could thus enter the guild without undergoing formal apprenticeship. For the older women, a different process of decision making was at work. Several indicated in their contracts that they had already begun to work in the trade. They therefore sought additional instruction, as one woman put it, "to perfect herself in her trade."[46] Another woman declared that she had previously learned how to make children's stays; she now wished to enter *allouage* to be trained in making women's clothes. Having resigned themselves to the status of permanent worker, these women sought new skills to improve their position in the labor market or perhaps to work illegally as independent seamstresses.

The other cases suggest different hypotheses. The non-Parisian families may not have understood the stakes at risk in the *allouage* contract. Alternately, they may have planned to bring the girls back home to work once they acquired skills. Another father, who was a Parisian merchant mercer, may have intended to use the girl in his own business. As was the case with the apprentice seamstresses, therefore, *allouage* appears to have fulfilled varying needs. Although tainted with a low-status image, *allouage* was a sensible decision for most of these young women. Like other eighteenth-century artisans, however, seamstresses engaged infrequently in this form of training.

A second alternative to apprenticeship was offered by free charity schools established by a handful of Parisian parishes. In 1678, only three years after the creation of the seamstresses' guild, the parish of Saint-Eustache established the lay community of Sainte-Agnès, with a mission to teach poor girls vocational skills. In its first year, it employed three mistresses, a seamstress, a linen-draper, and an embroiderer, who were responsible for training 40 girls. Two years later, their numbers had grown to fifteen mistresses and over 200 girls.[47] By the end of the century, there were some 450 students. This was a huge number, considering that mistress seamstresses accepted no more than 400 new apprentices each year. Several similar institutions existed in Paris by the end of the seventeenth century, including the community of Sainte Anne, the Filles de Saint-Joseph, the Filles de Saint-Maur, and the Instruction chrétienne. Like *allouage,* this training system offered no hope of guild membership, but it did furnish girls with the skills necessary to work in a variety of needle trades. The seamstresses' trade, however, seems to have been excluded from the curriculum. In the first years of the community's existence, the superior of the community of Sainte-Agnès declared the seamstresses' trade off-limits to the sisters and their pupils due to the excessive immodesty of female fashion. Instead of women's clothing, these charity schools focused on embroidery, linen work, tapestry making, and lace making. Further investigation of alternate systems of apprenticeship will be necessary to measure their contribution to the Parisian economy and the degree of competition they offered to guild-based training. The timing of the creation of these schools—which coincided with that of the seamstresses' guild—suggests that the last three decades of the seventeenth century witnessed a sharp rise in concerns over female training and employment.[48]

Mobility among Apprentices

The formality of the notarized contract lends an aura of permanence and stability to the practice of apprenticeship. Hidden behind these appearances lay a high level of mobility and failure among apprentice seamstresses. The guild notary's archives testify to this reality through the amendments and supplements he attached to a number of the original contracts. Among our sample of 743 girls, at least 84 did not complete apprenticeship with their original mistress, a figure that would certainly be higher if complete information were available. In seven cases, the apprentice's motivation for seeking a new mistress was clear: the death of the original mistress had effectively severed their contracts. The remaining cases offered no explanation for the break, but we may imagine a variety of possible reasons. A family's inability to continue payments, irreconcilable conflict between mistress and apprentice, a relocation of one of the parties, or the eruption of family crisis were all factors that could lead to termination of the contract.

The waiting period between leaving one mistress and obtaining another one varied considerably. Nine girls found a new tutor within two weeks, but others had to wait much longer. The longest period between the cessation of a first contract and the beginning of a new one was three years, a longer interruption than most guilds permitted. The majority of cases fell between these extremes, with the average apprentice finding a new mistress within six months. This interval represented the delay needed to recover from illness, to resolve family problems, or to become frustrated in the pursuit of other opportunities. The contracts usually lasted for the time left in the original contract; very few stayed longer than the time it had stipulated. Some girls merely changed mistresses, others dropped out altogether. Of the total sample, at least thirty-seven apprentices terminated their apprenticeship with no record of a subsequent transfer to a new mistress. In two cases, the apprentice was obliged to cease trade training due to physical weakness. One was stated simply to be ill, and the other suffered from poor eyesight, a disability that rendered her unfit to practice the trade. It is highly likely that this group does not include all the girls who abandoned apprenticeship in our sample.

The notarial contract offered a cordial way to resolve differences. Records from the law court of the royal procurator at the Châtelet document more bitter conflicts. Disputes between mistresses and apprentices' guardians constituted the most common reason for seamstresses to appear in this tribunal. Mistresses whose apprentices had fled or defaulted on their fees brought the majority of complaints. Apprentices' families initiated legal proceedings less often. They did so to demand that mistresses who rejected their apprentices refund sums they had paid in advance. We do not see complaints about excessive work or violence, although such problems must have occurred. Parties to these disputes almost always brought along an attorney, underlining the legal sophistication of the Parisian world of work. Unfortunately, the court records provide almost no information regarding the precise nature of their respective complaints. Unlike the linendrapers, the seamstresses' guild itself almost never intervened in these conflicts. Its active supervision of apprenticeship appears to have ended with the signing of the contract.[49]

Life after Apprenticeship

Apprentices who completed trade training enjoyed the strongest position in the labor market. They had the best chances of finding continual employment and were most likely to obtain the annual appointments that constituted the best jobs in the trade. Women who did not complete apprenticeship might still find work, but they occupied a lower status in the hierarchy of labor. Possessed of the highest skills, best connections with mistresses seamstresses, and a formal qualification, finished apprentices also had the strongest chances of becoming mistresses.

For all their privileges, however, many did not achieve mistress status. At a cost of 150 livres, plus the sums required for the masterpiece, guild membership was an expensive goal. With annual salaries of some 100 to 150 livres, a lifetime of work might not permit a seamstress to accumulate sufficient funds. For an average of 419 new apprentices a year from 1745 to 1759, we find an average of some 100 mistresses entering the guild by the path of apprenticeship during those years. If these figures are representative, only one-fourth of young women who undertook apprenticeship became mistresses. A similar pattern occurred in the provincial city of Caen, where the average of 14 new apprentices annually in selected years between 1722 and 1779 contrasted with an average of 4 new mistresses per year.

The Parisian seamstresses' guild itself offered a pessimistic vision of career paths in the trade, declaring in 1762 that

> most of these apprentices did not continue their apprenticeship, others have died, others in truth have established themselves [as mistresses] with the help they received from charitable people; but these people with their deaths have not been able to procure them what they expected, in such a manner that they now find themselves reduced to lacking the necessities and consequently unable to pay the ordinary charges of their Community, even less the Extraordinary ones.[50]

A large range of possibilities existed for women who did not become mistresses, not all of which were negative. Most would work in the trade during their late teens and early twenties. For many of these young women, it made more sense to save money for a dowry than for the guild membership fee. Upon marriage, these women would most likely transfer their activities to their husbands' trade, helping out in the workshop or taking charge of the commercial side of the business. If necessary, when widowhood or hard times arrived, they could return to work as seamstresses. Other women continued as dependent employees throughout their lives. This would be particularly true of those who did not marry or whose husbands did not need their labor, such as domestic servants or journeymen. Finally, a skilled needleworker could also find numerous sources of employment in the capital's bustling garment and accessories trades or, if she dared, she could establish herself as an independent seamstress without mistress status.

It was the culmination of many years of hard work and saving for the one hundred finished apprentices who succeeded in joining the guild each year, assisted perhaps by a bequest or an advance on their future inheritance from parents. The timespan between finishing apprenticeship and entering the guild may be calculated by comparing apprentices' names with the lists of new mistresses kept by the royal procurator at the Châtelet of Paris. As these comparisons reveal, the time period required to become a mistress varied a great deal. The youngest women were in their late teens, while the oldest was 54 years old. The median age of new mistresses was 26 years, and the mean just slightly higher at 26.9 years. Because most would have finished apprenticeship around age 17, it appears that almost ten years of work in the trade usually preceded a woman's entry to the guild.

Reception of Mistress Seamstresses

Guild reception records kept by the royal procurator at the Châtelet of Paris survive for the period 1735 to 1789.[51] According to these records, a total of 7,425 mistresses entered the seamstresses' guild from September 1735 to the end of 1789, the last year for which records exist. An additional 12 mistresses purchased *lettres de maîtrise* in the guild in 1767 without appearing in the Châtelet registers. Based on these figures, an average of 138 mistresses entered the guild each year between 1736 and 1789 (see figure 7.1 for a graph of entries over this period).

While much smaller than the number of new apprentices, this figure was consistently the highest among all Parisian guilds. In 1736, the pro-

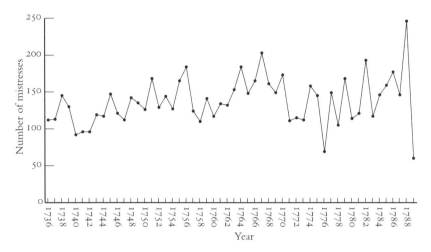

FIGURE 7.1 Admission of mistresses to Parisian seamstresses' guild, 1736–1789.

curator swore in a total of 1,012 men and women as members of the 124 Parisian guilds. Among them, seamstresses composed the largest group with 111 mistresses, or almost 11 percent of the total. The next largest group was the 83 merchant mercers (8 percent), who entered a highly segmented guild encompassing numerous forms of specialization. Some thirty years later in 1762, a total of 1,035 new masters and mistresses entered the guilds. The seamstresses' proportion had grown to 13 percent (n = 135). The shoemakers now occupied second place with 8 percent, and the merchant mercers had fallen to third position with slightly over 7 percent.[52]

Across the eighteenth century, the level of entries to the seamstresses' guild did not vary drastically (standard deviation = 26). Dividing entries by decades shows that they rose from the 1740s through the 1760s, with a slight drop during the 1770s, and a revival in the 1780s (see table 7.4). Within this overall pattern of stability, considerable annual variation existed. Four periods in particular witnessed a significant decline in admissions. These were the early 1740s, the late 1750s to early 1760s, the early 1770s, and the year 1776. These slowdowns corresponded to wider economic and political crises, underlining the guild's vulnerability to conjunctural difficulties. For example, serious grain shortages struck Paris during both the early 1740s and 1770s, resulting in grave economic dislocation, proliferating unemployment, and increased levels of mortality. Like other Parisians, seamstresses' resources were consumed by the necessities

TABLE 7.4 Total number of new mistress seamstresses by decade

Years	Total
1740–1749	1,177
1750–1759	1,418
1760–1769	1,558
1770–1779	1,305
1780–1789	1,469

of life during these years, exhausting any savings they had accumulated toward guild membership. Between 1758 and 1762, France's engagement in the Seven Years' War appears to have created a noticeable but less serious disruption (see figure 7.1).[53]

The temporary abolition of the guild system between February 1776 and August 1776 caused an abrupt and total cessation of admissions. In obedience to royal orders, the king's procurator at the Châtelet did not accept any new members in the now defunct guilds. The continuing disorder sown by these events is revealed by the fact that admissions did not recommence until October 1776, some three months after the guilds' official reestablishment. The procurator's records show that entries to the new *couturières-découpeuses'* guild rapidly recaptured and even surpassed its old levels. These newcomers would have been joined by an unknown number of pre-1776 mistresses returning to the guild who were not recorded in the procurator's registers. The August edict gave former guild members a choice between rejoining their reformed corporations as full members or as adjuncts. The latter played no role in guild administration and could not accept apprentices. For the moment, the number of pre-1776 mistresses who returned to the guild remains unknown. Continuity between the pre- and post-1776 periods is suggested, however, by the fact that many acting guild officials in the post-1776 period had served before 1776.

The Recruitment of Guild Mistresses

Three paths to membership existed in the seamstresses' guild prior to 1776. The 1675 statutes envisioned two routes, entirely in accordance with standard corporate practice. First, mistresses' daughters could enter the guild simply by paying a set fee to the guild treasury and acting officials. The second path was that of apprenticeship, plus work experience and the masterpiece. Originally set at 88 livres, the royal declaration of 1693 augmented the fee for finished apprentices to 150 livres. By 1776, the price had risen to 175 livres. The royal edict of August 1776, which reestablished the guild system in Paris, lowered this price to 100 livres.[54] In addition to these two normative paths, a royal declaration of 1693 took the highly unusual measure of creating a new form of access to the guild. In order to encourage the guild's accessibility and provide funding for charity, it permitted the annual acceptance of twenty women with no formal qualifications either of birth or experience. Instead, they purchased guild membership outright for a fee of 200 livres, a price that must have risen over time. This path of entry constituted a distinctive aspect of the seamstresses' guild, for no other Parisian guild accepted unqualified members on a routine basis.[55]

Of these three possibilities, apprenticeship was by far the most common. Together, seamstresses entering this path accounted for 4,131 of the 5,509 mistresses accepted between September 1735 and February 1776 (75 percent).[56] Women who entered under the terms of the 1693 declaration composed the second largest group, with 905 mistresses (16.4 percent). Mistresses' daughters numbered only 458 (8.3 percent). Across the eighteenth century, only fifteen mistresses are recorded to have made use of other forms of access (0.3 percent). Three women entered through the privileges of the Hôpital de la Trinité and twelve purchased *lettres de maîtrise* in 1767.

A graph of new entries, broken down by path of admission, shows that the relative importance of the three major paths did not alter significantly from September 1735 to February 1776 (see figure 7.2). The consistently high number of apprentices and *sans qualité* mistresses indicates that the guild remained accessible to outsiders throughout the eighteenth century. The seamstresses' guild was composed almost entirely of first-generation corporate citizens. In defiance of corporate values—and the most common critiques of the guild system—fewer mistresses' daughters entered than women with no qualifications at all.[57]

These figures reveal a paradoxical situation: demand for access to the seamstresses' guild was extremely high, yet few women transmitted their guild status to their daughters. One obvious reason for this discrepancy was the fact that a high proportion of seamstresses did not marry, as will be seen in the next chapter. This demographic fact alone meant that relatively few daughters existed to become mistresses. More significantly, it may also be the case that low generational continuity resulted from distinctive strategies of female guild membership. Women did not use their

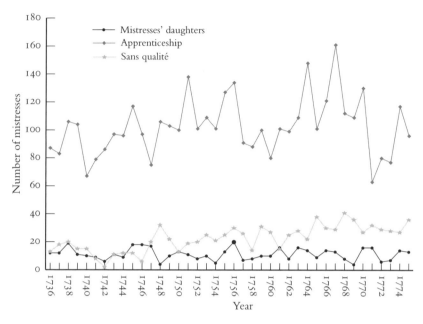

FIGURE 7.2 Breakdown of admissions to Parisian seamstresses' guild by path of entry, 1736–1775.

guild status to create dynasties of needleworkers, we may hypothesize, but to attract good mates for their children. In the same manner that an individual seamstress used income from the trade to improve her marriage prospects, she and her husband may have employed their combined wealth and status to attract a high-quality mate for their daughter. The mark of success for a mistress seamstress might thus have consisted of marrying her daughter to a man capable of freeing her from manual labor, rather than having her join the seamstresses' guild. Despite their independent corporate status, mistress seamstresses thus appear to have accepted the wider cultural preference for the family economy over female economic independence.

Statistical analysis shows a significant correlation between the number of apprentices and daughters accepted each year, a weaker connection between apprentices and unqualified mistresses, and no correlation at all between daughters and unqualified mistresses.[58] These results suggest that guild leaders did not systematically adjust the number of *sans qualité* mistresses they accepted depending on the number of apprentices or mistresses' daughters who presented themselves each year. The lack of absolute correlation among the different paths of entry is understandable in light of the different conditions and strategies that led each type of mistress to seek guild entry in a given year. Mistresses' daughters, for example, might have worked with their mothers, seeking independent membership only when the older woman died. Other daughters would have waited for the year in which their mothers won election as corporate officials, because *jurées'* daughters paid even lower entry fees than did mistresses' daughters. By contrast, the number of finished apprentices who presented themselves was more sensitive to conjunctural conditions. In periods of economic crisis, workers lost their meager savings and were forced to delay guild entry. In times of low interest, they would be tempted to borrow the money they needed to pay the fees. Finally, the quota imposed on unqualified mistresses meant that demand almost always exceeded supply. Given the constant push from below, the number of these mistresses accepted in a given year depended on the leniency of individual officials, who were more or less willing to violate the quota limit.

Reception to the Tailors' Guild

The tailors' guild provides a significant point of comparison with the seamstresses, because both corporations produced made-to-measure clothing and they shared the right to make women's and children's clothes. Overall, the royal procurator's records reveal significantly lower entry levels among tailors than their female counterparts. Between 1735 and 1789, 4,439 masters entered the guild.[59] The annual average was 82 new masters, compared to an average of 138 for the seamstresses. This discrepancy results in part from the fact that boys of the artisanal classes had more opportunities available to them than girls. A young man could choose from a handful of trades, while a young girl had relatively few options, particularly if she were interested in becoming a guild mistress. Moreover, the tailors' higher entry fees made joining their guild more difficult.

The disparity between the numbers of new entrants to the seamstresses' and to the tailors' guild during this period would suggest, by extrapolation, that the seamstresses' guild population greatly outnumbered that of the tailors. However, contemporary estimations of guild size counter this hypothesis. Savary des Bruslons ranked the tailors second among Parisian guilds in the 1720s with 1,882 masters; the seamstresses came fourth with 1,700 mistresses. If Savary des Bruslons' figures were accurate, the explanation for this discrepancy must lie in differing career expectancies. In order for the tailors' guild to accept fewer masters but have a greater over-

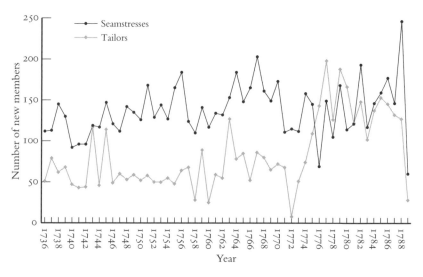

FIGURE 7.3 Admission to Parisian seamstresses' and tailors' guilds, 1736–1789.

all population, master tailors must have had longer careers than mistress seamstresses. The total guild populations, taken together with the membership figures discussed above, permit us to calculate a career expectancy among master tailors of approximately twenty-five years, while the seamstresses' would have been approximately twelve years. These figures, while remaining tentative, reinforce the impression created by the low levels of generational continuity in the seamstresses' guild. The trade was not only noncontinuous over generations, but within a large proportion of individual women's lifetimes as well.

A graph comparing entries to the tailors' and seamstresses' guilds demonstrates that women consistently outnumbered men from 1736 to 1776 (figure 7.3). It also shows that the tailors' guild was affected by the same conjunctural setbacks as the seamstresses. Like those for seamstresses, tailors' admissions dropped in the early 1740s, again during the period 1758 to 1761, and once more in the early 1770s. After the shock of 1776, the tailors' guild recovered rapidly and, with their union with the used-clothes dealers, surpassed the seamstresses' rate of admissions for the first time. Beyond these generalized moments of crisis, however, there was little overall correlation between tailors' and seamstresses' annual entry patterns. The two guilds followed distinctly different rhythms of admissions.[60]

The lack of correlation between seamstresses' and tailors' admissions levels did not result from economic factors specific to men's and women's clothing. Instead, they derived from the different paths of entry available to candidates for membership in each guild. Whereas seamstresses chose from three main options, tailors had at least six alternatives. Like seamstresses' daughters, masters' sons could enter the guild after performing a test of competency and paying a nominal fee. They could also enter as finished apprentices by completing three years of work experience, performing a masterpiece, and paying a fee of around four hundred livres.[61] The tailors' corporation, however, treated finished apprentices in a very different manner than did the seamstresses. In a striking contrast to the female corporation, the tailors deliberately restricted the number of outsiders who could achieve mastership by this path. According to their 1660 statutes, a maximum of ten finished apprentices could enter each year. Although they did not always respect this precise limit, the number of apprentices remained consistently low.

A much larger group of master tailors entered through two categories for which the seamstresses had no equivalent. In common with a number of male guilds, the tailors permitted men who married a master's widow or daughter to join the guild under the same conditions as finished Parisian apprentices. They were required to pay heavy fees and complete a masterpiece, but the statutes imposed no limitations on the number who made use of this path. Masters also entered the guild by making use of privileges offered by exterior sources, including royal *lettres de maîtrise*, and work at the Hôpital de la Trinité.

The royal procurator's records reveal the proportional weight of each of these paths from September 1735 to March 1776. Of the 2,681 men who became masters during this period, 591 were sons of masters (22 percent), 361 were finished apprentices (14 percent), 839 had married a master's daughter (31 percent), 227 had married a master's widow (9 percent), 72 had served at the Hôpital de la Trinité (3 percent), and 591 were *sans qualité* or had purchased a *lettre de maîtrise* (22 percent). An additional 60 tailors entered by nonspecified paths.[62] Marriage thus played the most important role in the reproduction of the tailors' guild, representing 40 percent of the total. Masters' sons accounted for half as many new guild members, or around one-fifth. An equal number of masters entered the guild by purchasing mastership outright in the form of a *lettre de maîtrise*. Apprenticeship represented a minor means of access, less important than marriage or mastership letters.[63]

This situation constituted a complete subversion of corporate ideology, which recognized only two normative forms of trade transmission, heredity or apprenticeship. Either one inherited one's trade skills and guild status by blood, or one acquired them through the hard schooling of apprenticeship and work experience. The ascension from callow apprentice through skilled journeyman to confirmed master was one of the hallmarks of the guild system, celebrated in theory if shakier in actual practice. In many ways, the corporate system based its claim of fostering healthy social relations and the smooth functioning of economic production and distribution on the values and practices inculcated during apprenticeship. The tailors' guild defied this ideology by blocking the path of finished apprentices in favor of those who bought or married their way into the guild. The average journeyman had little hope of joining, unless he could find a bride in a master's family or muster the heavy costs of a *lettre de maîtrise*.

Reliance on marriage as a form of guild reproduction helps explain the crucial role of family in tailors' guild ideology. The tailors' legal fight to protect their daughters' and widows' privileges, discussed in chapter 5, also acquires new significance in the context of these statistics. If 40 percent of masters acquired their guild status through marriage, they would be likely to defend female privileges ardently. Moreover, their wives would be attuned to any attempt to diminish their prerogatives and would encourage their husbands to take action. These figures also point to the existence of gendered strategies of upward mobility among tailors. Many masters choose not to have their sons continue in their trade, presumably encouraging them to attain family ambitions by entering more prestigious trades, perhaps as merchant mercers or drapers. Meanwhile, their sisters sustained the status quo by marrying journeymen tailors. This strategy condemned women to remain within a male-dominated family economy and denied them the socioeconomic ascension promised to their brothers.[64]

Nevertheless, this situation must have also allowed women considerable prestige in marriage. When she married a tailor, a master's daughter or widow gave him a corporate status he may otherwise never have possessed. Raised in the trade, she had considerable technical skills and a strong grasp of the capital's commercial practices. If her husband was a provincial journeyman, unfamiliar with Parisian customs and perhaps even with the dialect of the capital, she could offer crucial advice and guidance. These wives also possessed superior knowledge of guild politics, and perhaps involved themselves in behind-the-scenes corporate strategizing. A daughters' husband might well work in association with his father-in-law, perhaps buying him out when the latter chose to retire. Strong economic

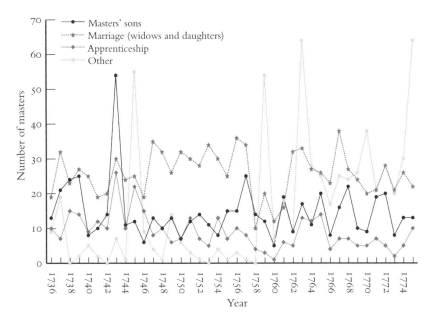

FIGURE 7.4 Breakdown of admissions to Parisian tailors' guild by path of entry, 1736–1775.

and social ties with their families of origin would have further fortified these women's status in marriage. The tailors' example suggests the need for further investigation of Parisian women's role in integrating provincial men into the capital's economic and social structures. These figures also suggest that women in eighteenth-century Paris were more likely to practice their fathers' trades than their mothers'. While 839 masters' daughters effectively continued their fathers' trade by marrying tailors, only 458 seamstresses' daughters took up their mother's trade by joining her guild. Fathers' trade practices played a central role in shaping their daughters' careers and their marriage prospects, reflecting the patriarchal nature of the tailoring family.

A graph of the tailors' paths of entry from 1736 to 1776 shows that their proportional weight remained more or less constant throughout the period (see figure 7.4). The obvious exception to this rule is the group of *sans qualité* masters who entered in large groups, but only in certain years. The explanation for these sporadic admissions lies in the guild's encounters with royal taxation. The years when it admitted a large group of *sans qualité* masters were those when it disbursed a substantial sum to purchase royal guild offices. After its purchase of the first guild offices in 1691, for example, the guild sought and received authorization to admit four un-qualified masters. In 1738, corporate leaders took their own initiative in accepting forty-three royally privileged tailors as regular masters, obtain-ing a total revenue of 25,800 livres, which they intended to use for debt re-payment. The government accepted this maneuver as an exceptional mea-sure, but forbade the guild from repeating it without advance approval. Royal officials granted this permission on at least two subsequent occa-sions, allowing the guild to receive forty masters in 1745 and another sixty in 1759.[65]

Without going so far as to regularize the admittance of unqualified masters—as it did in the seamstresses' case—the royal government thus permitted a large male guild to accept substantial groups of unqualified candidates on isolated occasions. By so doing, royal officials both ensured the continuing solvency of the guild and provided new access to corporate institutions for provincial and Parisian journeymen. This policy, however, could only work in a very large guild. Although a small guild would have been engulfed by these mass admissions, the group of two thousand mas-ter tailors could absorb the shock of forty or fifty new masters without excessive dislocation of product and labor markets. Even so, it was a policy that must have aroused considerable resentment and hostility among the rank and file.

The small number of master tailors accepted through the Hôpital de la Trinité offers a final contrast to the seamstresses' guild. This hospital offered artisans free access to mastership in exchange for six years of trade instruction to the orphaned children residing there. In theory, seamstresses could also gain access to the guild through work at the Hôpital de la Trinité, but from 1735 to 1789 only three women are recorded to have made use of this possibility. Hospital records indicate that the six theoretically available positions for seamstresses remained consistently vacant. This was not true of the tailors or the linen-drapers. The seamstresses' absence sug-gests that access to the guild by regular means was considered to be no more difficult than the six years of teaching required by the hospital.[66]

Apprenticeship and Guild Membership Outside of Paris

Recruitment among provincial tailors and seamstresses reveals significant contrasts with the Parisian case. In the city of Caen, the lieutenant gen-eral of police presided over the admission of new guild masters and ap-prentices.[67] In the nineteen years sampled between 1724 and 1775, a total of sixty-two new masters joined the Caen tailors' guild, or an average of 3.3 a year. Unfortunately, the record specified their paths of entry in only forty-four cases. Within this group, men with inherited ties to the guild accounted for almost half of the new masters. Nineteen were masters' sons and two were sons of mistress seamstresses. The remaining twenty-three masters had origins outside the guild, including fifteen apprentices, seven owners of *lettres de maîtrise,* and one master who entered by direct order of the intendant. No individual entered through marriage to a master's daughter. In contrast to the Parisian situation, therefore, the Caen tailors closely adhered to normative ideals of corporate reproduction, relying primarily on apprenticeship and inheritance for new recruits.

These patterns of recruitment were fundamentally shaken by the reforms of 1776. Although Parisian guilds were reestablished by royal edict in August 1776, provincial guilds had to wait two or three years for edicts ordering their reestablishment. Legislation for the city of Caen did not arrive until April 1779, leaving its corporations in a state of limbo until that date. The tailors' ambiguous status did not prevent them from receiving 18 new masters between September 1776 and March 1779. When the edict arrived, demand shot up immediately for the now combined tailors–used-clothes' dealers corporation. From April to December 1779, a record of 36 new masters joined the guild. In 1780, the guild numbered 130 members.[68] Most incoming masters, however, were not the outsiders that reform legislation had aimed to integrate. Instead, most were masters' sons. Fearful of drastic reform or abolition of the guild system, these individuals sought to exploit their inheritance—and reaffirm their corporate status—before it was too late. Journeymen, on the other hand, were perhaps too pessimistic about the guild's future to invest their hard-earned savings in mastership. After 1780, interest in the guild appears to have dwindled. Existing records suggest that far fewer tailors were admitted after this date; unreliable documentation for these years, however, precludes firm conclusions about admissions patterns in the 1780s.

If the tailors presented significant differences from their Parisian colleagues, the recruitment patterns of seamstresses in Caen closely resembled the Parisian case. As in the capital, the number of incoming seamstresses in Caen consistently surpassed the tailors up to 1776. In the nineteen years sampled from 1724 until 1775, new seamstresses outnumbered tailors by 72 to 62. Seamstresses also outnumbered tailors in the overall guild population; the guild's 1757 *capitation* tax assessments listed 99 master tailors for 109 mistress seamstresses.[69]

The origins of mistresses in Caen also resembled the Parisian model. Of seventy-two mistresses accepted, nine entered by unspecified paths. The remaining sixty-three were largely outsiders: forty-eight were apprentices and one had purchased a *lettre de maîtrise*. Only fifteen women (24 percent) entered through their parents' privileges: eight as mistresses' daughters and seven as tailors' daughters. As in Paris, few daughters followed in their mothers' footsteps. The presence of master tailors' daughters obviously sets Caen apart, for these women had no claim to membership in the Parisian seamstresses' guild. Nevertheless, they recall the important role of masters' daughters in the recruitment of the tailor's guild in Paris. Once again, girls were just as likely, if not more likely, to take up their father's profession as their mother's.

After 1776, the seamstresses' fate diverged from that of their Parisian colleagues. The royal edict of April 1779 reestablishing guilds in Caen explicitly liberated the seamstresses' trade from guild control. Henceforth, any woman could practice the trade freely. The Caen seamstresses, however, refused to abandon their corporate organization until this edict arrived. During the ambiguous years of 1777 and 1778, they received eleven new mistresses. While the record shows no entries after that date, the guild did elect new officials in 1779, the last sign of life from the female side of the guild. These actions suggest the tenacity with which seamstresses held on to their corporate existence in Caen.

The tailors' guild in Aix-en-Provence offers a third example, substantially different both from its Parisian and Norman counterparts. With sixty-seven members in 1733, it was smaller than the Caen tailors' guild, but it was still among the largest trade corporations in the city.[70] Between 1745 and 1775, a total of seventy-two new masters entered the guild. In contrast to the previous cases, over half of these men (n = 38 or 52 percent) were masters' sons. The second largest group (n = 16) entered the guild by marrying a master's daughter. In Aix, masters' sons-in-law were treated even more benevolently than in Paris, enjoying the status of a master's son rather than that of a finished apprentice. Guild records show that most of these bridegrooms came from outside the city of Aix. Because they had not completed apprenticeship in the city, they did not qualify for membership by that route and therefore had strong motivations for seeking a bride among local masters' daughters. The remaining thirty-four masters entered the guild through alternate paths. Ten owned *lettres de maîtrise* and two achieved mastership through work at the city's Hôpital de la charité, which held privileges similar to the Hôpital de la Trinité of Paris.

As was the case in Paris, the guild appears to have severely limited the numbers accepted by apprenticeship. Between 1745 and 1775, the guild records show only six masters admitted through the path of apprenticeship. Given the strength of generational continuity, assembly minutes frequently revealed fourth- and fifth-generation master tailors. The guild was a collection of extended kin groups, consisting of fathers, sons, brothers, uncles, and cousins.

These relatively stable patterns of recruitment were violently shaken by the 1776 edict. Its immediate effects were revealed by the group of sixteen masters' sons who entered the guild that year. Like their Norman colleagues, these sons sought to secure their corporate inheritance before it was too late. In Aix-en-Provence, however, the long-term effect of 1776 was to open the guild to outsiders. Between 1776 and 1790, the guild accepted forty new masters by apprenticeship, thirty-four more than it had admitted during the previous thirty years.[71]

Unfortunately, no record exists for the admission of seamstresses. Disputes reported in the guild's assembly minutes suggest that the frequency of fraud among guild officials would have undermined the validity of such records in any case. Nevertheless, we do possess a number of membership lists established for the payment of annual guild dues. In 1733, the latest existing record lists 67 master tailors for 111 seamstresses. During the first decades of the century, seamstresses strongly outnumbered tailors in Aix as they did in Caen.

The results of this regional comparison suggest that while gender strongly affected women's corporate experience, it was less important for men. Seamstresses manifested a high demand for guild entry in the very different municipal and economic contexts of Paris, Caen, and Aix-en-Provence. Before 1776, their entry levels consistently outnumbered those of master tailors. Moreover, access to the female trade remained open to newcomers in Paris and Caen throughout the eighteenth century. Seamstresses' guilds did not close themselves to outsiders. After 1776, however, their corporate fortunes diverged, as seamstresses in Paris continued as a guild and their provincial colleagues returned to a world of free labor.

The tailors presented much more varied patterns. Levels of generational continuity differed significantly between the southern city of Aix and the two northern cities. The Aix guild included a very high proportion of masters' sons, while their numbers were lower in Caen and even lower in Paris. Marriage to a master's daughter or widow was a crucial source of recruitment in Paris, but was much less important in Aix and apparently nonexistent in Caen. The Paris guild was also unique in selling off large numbers of masterships during the eighteenth century. Throughout the century, the capital city thus offered the greatest opportunities to outsiders. To gain access, however, newcomers were obliged to join guild families or produce hefty sums of money. Apprenticeship alone was often not sufficient for acquiring guild status.

Tailors' experiences diverged again after 1776, with the dominance of masters' sons in Caen contrasting with the influx of outsiders in Aix. These results demonstrate that men's experience in corporations was much more varied than women's; their gender did not play the predominate role in shaping their relationship to the guild system that it did for women. Instead, recruitment patterns were shaped by the differing requirements of guild regulations, marriage, and the specific contexts in which they lived. In turn, different patterns of guild recruitment produced distinctive social and cultural worlds, and, we may assume, different corporate and work identities.

Conclusion

Apprenticeship and recruitment patterns reveal high demand for the seamstresses' trade. Every year, several hundred Parisian girls began formal apprenticeship with a guild mistress, joining what must have been the largest pool of apprentices in the city. With some 130 new mistresses every year, the guild also possessed the highest entry levels of all Parisian guilds. These figures result from the easy access to the guild as well as from restrictions imposed on female labor. They demonstrate the capacity, or perceived capacity, of the trade to absorb a large workforce. The numbers also indicate the attractiveness of the guild that regulated the trade. When the opportunity presented itself, women in Paris and the provinces streamed into institutionalized forms of trade training and work. Young women did not perceive their lifestyles or their family lives to be incompatible with formal vocational training or guild status nor did their parents, who chose this path and furnished money for it. Moreover, the charitable bequests donated to sponsor poor girls' training, and the involvement of parish foundations in distributing it, testify to wider social and cultural support for female apprenticeship.

By joining the guild, seamstresses demonstrated a strong commitment to their careers. They surely would not have invested money in guild status if they believed that a husband or father might require them to put aside their trade at any moment. Having achieved this status, however, mistress seamstresses steered their daughters in another direction. Becoming a mistress seamstress responded to the needs of a single generation, it was not used to establish a dynasty of female guild members.

Together, the large numbers of apprentice and mistress seamstresses demonstrate the thought, time, and investment that went into preparing and establishing female careers in the cities of eighteenth-century France. Many parents did not teach girls skills at home, nor did they wait for a husband to come along to train them. Instead, they actively sought forms of vocational training for their teenaged daughters so that the girls could begin to contribute to the family income or put aside money for a dowry. This finding seems to suggest a level of commitment to the individual life-span and to female life possibilities that existing historiography does not predict. Drawing on this insight, in the next chapter I will sketch the social portrait of the trade, examining the families and households that mistress seamstresses composed and the ways in which they used their mistress status to negotiate the marriage market. I will also illustrate varied levels of fortune among seamstresses and the material worlds in which they lived.

Before leaving the topic of apprenticeship, however, it is worth underlining the suggestions this study offers regarding the role of gender in the acquisition of trade skills and guild status. On one level, apprenticeship appears to have been an essentially gender-neutral process that allowed both girls and boys to acquire trade skills that might one day lead to membership in a guild. Seamstresses' apprenticeship contracts were essentially the same as those in male trades in terms of their basic terminology, their price structures, and the role of the guild in supervising training. On further reflection, however, it becomes clear that apprenticeship was a fundamentally gendered process, and that one of its main functions was to impart and reproduce gender among the working people of the Old Regime. Boys did not enter an artisan's workshop simply to learn techniques of production; they went to learn their trade, invariably, from another man. When women received their own guild, one of its primary effects was to normalize and enforce an exclusively female form of training.

The process of learning to be an adult man or woman was thus an implicit element of apprenticeship. Artisans' perception and practice of their trades must have been tied up with their gender identity, because they learned to be adults at the same time that they learned to practice their trades in the company of other men or women. It is hardly surprising that folk tales, anthropologists, and labor historians note a great deal of sexual imagery and symbolism around the tools and techniques of production, because men and women attained sexual maturity at the same time that they acquired technical proficiency. Male hostility to women's work in their trades stemmed not only from economic concerns, but from a profound sense of attack on their masculine identities.

With this in mind, the fact that boys in different trades entered apprenticeship later than the seamstresses might well stem from the later age of male puberty. The beginning of apprenticeship was thus adjusted—consciously or unconsciously—to ensure that puberty would occur during the boys' years of training. The acquisition of skills had to accompany the acquisition of an adult mind and body; if too young, the boy would not absorb the training, too old and he might be intractable and uncontrollable. Among women, the fact that training could begin at a very young or an advanced age suggests that the model of femininity and the acquisition of adult womanhood were not perceived to be a problem in the same way as these issues were for men. Women might be expected to grow into femininity more or less naturally, while boys needed to be broken into the discipline and self-control of manhood.

EIGHT

Marriage, Fortune, and Family:

The World of the Mistress Seamstress

On June 7, 1749, a mistress seamstress presented herself before the Parisian police to lodge a complaint against her husband, a domestic servant. While she worked hard, her husband dissipated himself in drunken debauchery, leading his wife to complain: "She would have believed that, on his side, her husband would have done what he could to procure himself a little establishment, the plaintiff's aim being to take him out of servitude by means of the profession she practices, in which she earns her living very respectably [*fort honnêtement*]." [1] By emphasizing the wife's economic autonomy and the possibility of upward social mobility through a female trade, this statement offers an unexpected account of women's work and the family in early modern France.

Twenty years have passed since the appearance of pioneering studies of European women's work. These studies argued that the family was the basic economic unit of eighteenth-century France, the remunerated labor of both husband and wife being crucial to the family's survival. This notion of the "family economy" emphasized both the limitations imposed on women's work and the essential economic contribution women provided to their kin. Men dominated the household economy, using female labor to meet their own productive or commercial needs. The combination of women's low wages and their minimal inheritance rights rendered female survival outside of marriage extremely difficult. Despite these limitations, the family's need for women's labor meant that they permeated the workshops and markets of France. Their vital role in economic production granted women substantial informal power in the family. [2]

The seamstresses' trade offers a sharp challenge to this historiographical consensus. Whereas previous studies assumed the preeminence of male concerns in marriage choices, seamstresses used their professional skills and guild status as a negotiating tool in the marriage market. After they married, mistress seamstresses often worked independently of their husbands. The large number of unmarried seamstresses, moreover, suggests that participation in the trade allowed some women to choose spinsterhood over family life. Unmarried and widowed seamstresses established households composed of female workers, apprentices, and sometimes their adult daughters or nieces. In these homes, economic, social, and emotional ties overlapped, creating a distinctive female living environment. In contrast to assumptions about the dire poverty of both single women and seamstresses, these women could be financially successful; records show their purchases of expensive silverware and their investments in annuities, among other forms of wealth.

Seamstresses participated in the new modes of living of the eighteenth century, which involved greater consumption of clothing and other goods, enhanced comfort in everyday life, increased literacy, and new notions of individual and familial intimacy. Given their contact with socially elite clients, seamstresses were well placed to learn these new styles of living, and they had good reason to display them in homes that also served as professional headquarters. Their large numbers served to propagate such practices to a wider Parisian audience, assuring that the new forms of consumption were, and were seen to be, a particularly feminine phenomenon.

The Marriage Contract as a Historical Source

Notarial marriage contracts contain precious information for a study of alliance patterns, including names, addresses, and professions of the parties involved, as well as the value and composition of dowries and the financial provisions grooms made for their future brides. The proportion of seamstresses who participated in formal marriage contracts cannot be determined with certainty. Examination of notarial archives reveals surprisingly few seamstress brides, in light of their numerical strength in the Parisian population. A sample of all 1761 notarial marriage contracts, for example, contained only twenty-three seamstresses. At least two factors must account for this small number. The first is the absence of the poorest women from notarial documents. Poor couples had little to gain from a contract intended to protect family patrimony, and they may have been reluctant to pay the fees required to obtain it. Unfettered by annuities, real estate, or other property, they might indeed avoid contact with the notarial office throughout their lives. The modest dowries of many seamstress brides suggest, however, that the price of the contract did not discourage all poor couples.[3]

A more important explanation for seamstresses' absence from marriage contracts is probably notarial omission of the bride's profession. Notaries almost always indicated the occupation of the groom, but they often neglected do so for the female partner, even in cases where the woman clearly engaged in remunerated labor. For example, it is routine to find that the notary designated no occupation even though a bride declared she had acquired her dowry from "her own earnings and savings." In general, women's work must have featured more heavily in calculations and negotiations surrounding marriage than notarial documents suggest.

With few exceptions, therefore, our sample is composed of women who explicitly mentioned a profession, and it disproportionately represents the most successful seamstresses. These seamstress brides belonged to the population of fortunate skilled workers and established mistresses, women with a strong and self-conscious trade identity. With these caveats, the sample includes seventy marriage contracts, ranging from 1699 to 1761. Forty-seven of the brides claimed to be mistress seamstresses. Another twenty-three were nonmistresses, although some acquired guild membership after marriage.[4]

Grooms' Social and Economic Origins

Seamstresses belonged to the low to middling milieus of the artisanal trades, domestic service, and modest functionaries. Apprentice seamstresses were born into these circles, and they remained within them when they married. They most frequently formed unions with craftsmen and merchants. In a sample of 159 marriage and apprenticeship contracts, half of the seamstresses' spouses belonged to the world of work (n = 83 or 52 percent).[5] Thirty-four husbands were masters in craft or merchant guilds, twelve were journeymen, thirty-four were artisans who declared no guild affiliations, and one spouse held a royal privilege for his trade. At the lowest level, two husbands were unskilled laborers. The second largest group of husbands consisted of domestic servants (n = 37 or 23 percent). As with the apprentices' fathers, these men performed a wide range of tasks for their employers, twelve as simple *domestiques,* four as coachmen, five as cooks, two as valets, and two as cleaners (*frotteurs*). With three butlers and nine household officers, twelve husbands occupied high levels of service, including one employed by the king.

Seamstresses' husbands also included a substantial number of *bourgeois de Paris* (n = 23 or 14 percent). In many cases, however, rather than indicating elevated social origins this title represented the achievements of middle age. Only 5 percent of grooms in marriage contracts claimed this status, while 20 percent of married mistresses in apprenticeship contracts had bourgeois husbands. These men may have followed a path similar to that of mistress Françoise Môlé's husband, who appeared in their 1685 marriage contract as the butler of the comte d'Aujan and was described as a *bourgeois de Paris* in his wife's 1714 probate inventory.[6] The remaining husbands worked primarily as salaried employees at municipal or royal institutions. This group consisted of four clerks, four employees, two bailiffs, a building inspector, a guard at the Hôtel de Ville, and a rider of the watch. A building contractor, an architect, and a barrister at the Parlement of Paris represented the highest social levels.

If seamstresses remained close to their socioeconomic roots when they married, they chose men with markedly different geographic origins from their own. Three-quarters of the seamstresses in our sample of marriage contracts were Parisian, compared to only one-fifth of the grooms.[7] In general, mistresses were most likely to be Parisian: 80 percent of their parents listed a Parisian address. They were also more likely to marry fellow Parisians. Almost one-third of their grooms had parents who lived in the capital. By contrast, half of the nonmistresses were provincials, and almost all their grooms had non-Parisian origins.

Most mistress seamstresses were at home in the capital, or at least in their own neighborhood of it. They found their way easily about the city's crowded streets and alleys and benefited from a network of relatives and friends ready to provide assistance, listen to complaints, and offer advice. Mistresses' husbands, by contrast, were closer to provincial ways of life and perhaps less at ease in the urban culture of the capital. They might look to their wives, and their fathers or brothers-in-law, for guidance in doing business, acquiring property, and educating their children. When problems arose, they had fewer resources than did their wives. These factors contributed to women's position in the marriage and must have given them an enhanced role in family decision making. The fact that tailors displayed similar marriage patterns suggests that the Parisian guild family was frequently composed of a native-born wife and a provincial husband.

Choice of Mates

A number of historical studies—and at least one contemporary autobiographical account—demonstrate the importance of marriage for men in the urban trades.[8] Marriage presented a crucial opportunity to obtain resources to commence an independent professional career or to bolster an existing one. Men used matrimony to strengthen alliances in their trades and to forge new ties with related trade groups. Their wives' commercial or technical skills greatly affected their professional success. A charming presence behind the counter, a shrewd negotiator, or a careful bookkeeper could make the difference between a flourishing and a failing enterprise, while a spendthrift, drunken, or incompetent spouse could ruin a struggling craftsman.[9]

The relationship between marriage and career for women is much less clear. Historical studies of alliance patterns tend to focus on the groom, assuming that the woman had little choice in selecting her mate and that her career was subsumed by her husband's.[10] As a result, we know little about the role of women's work in creating unions or the potential for autonomous female occupations within married life. The particular considerations working women may have brought to matrimony, or the overall stakes at risk for women in the choice of a mate, also remain unclear, despite the fact that men and women of the working classes had considerable freedom in choosing their spouses. We may imagine, however, that marriage posed particular problems for women, especially for those who invested time and money in acquiring trade skills and guild membership. Matrimony required a woman to surrender her dowry, as well as her economic and legal independence, to a man who might or might not prove to be responsible, sober, fair-minded, and faithful. Because husbands held final authority over their wives' and children's lives, a prospective bride and her family had to choose very carefully.

The most obvious possibility for a seamstress was union with a tailor or another member of the garment trades. As husband and wife, these couples could pool their skills in a single workshop, working for both male and female clients or one sex exclusively. Through marriage, each would acquire a partner of professional expertise and experience. Despite the potential advantages, such alliances were unusual. Only 10 of the 159 seamstresses' husbands were tailors, including 7 master tailors and 3 journeymen. These figures suggest that the male and female sectors of the garment trades remained largely distinct. Tailors and seamstresses engaged in different forms of social and professional reproduction and forged alliances with different groups of people.[11] Members of other garment or textile trades were even less likely to wed seamstresses. In our sample of 159 unions, we find only 1 mercer groom and 1 clothmaker (*fabriquant d'étoffe*). Merchants and manufacturers thus did not marry seamstresses as a means of branching into the production of female garments. Instead, they must have sought brides at a higher socioprofessional level, among daughters of fellow merchants, bourgeois, or other local notables.

If they did not marry tailors or cloth dealers, whom did seamstresses marry and who chose to enter unions with them? In accord with the historical account, seamstresses often married men whose occupations met the professional interests of their own fathers, brothers, or cousins. For example, in 1751 Estienne André Guibert, a second-generation stonecutter, married Marie Jeanne Sauvageot, a mistress seamstress whose brother was also a stonecutter.[12] Jean-Baptiste Vatelier, a servant whose guardian was a master carpenter, married a building inspector's daughter.[13] A third contract involved Louis Greton, a master locksmith, and Marie Joseph Derly, a mistress seamstress whose cousin was a master locksmith. The groom's brother was also a journeyman locksmith.[14]

A master baker and his two daughters provide the most striking case of professional ties between a groom and his bride's family. In 1755, Charles Bassille, a master baker living on rue Saint-Honoré, gave his daughter in marriage to a second-generation master baker. Bassille and his wife awarded their daughter a dowry of 2,000 livres, composed of clothing, furniture, and cash. The bride supplemented this gift with another 450 livres worth of clothing and luxury items such as silverware and jewelry. According to their marriage contract, the bride had acquired these goods with income from her work as a seamstress.[15] A second daughter of the Bassille family married a master baker in 1761. Her father took advantage of this occasion to leave professional life. He sold his business to the new couple and subleased his living quarters and shop to them as well. For this daughter's dowry, Bassille deducted 538 livres from the price of his shop. The bride brought 1,000 livres in clothing and cash to the marriage, also earned from work as a seamstress. Their marriage contracts suggested that neither daughter planned to continue in the seamstresses' trade after marriage. They had done so to accumulate a dowry, but would now enter the family business. The future would undoubtedly see them installed behind the bakery counter, waiting on customers and keeping accounts, while their husbands supervised production.[16]

Marriage with seamstresses also furthered professional alliances among domestic servants. A number of the women who married servants had close relatives engaged in domestic service. Both parents of a mistress who married the servant of the "sub-tax-receiver of the King's domains" were servants. The marriage of the comte d'Aujan's butler in 1685 created a veritable dynasty of high-ranking service positions. The father of the bride was the butler of the marquis de la Farre, and a son born of this marriage would become the butler of the duc de Lorraine. Family and patronage networks thus ran through the world of domestic service in much the same way as they did in artisanal work.[17]

Despite the shared professional interests between the groom and the bride's family, we should not assume that these marriages resulted from male professional interests alone. Based on the contracts, it is impossible to distinguish the effects of simple trade sociability from professional strategy and self-interest. As they approached marrying age, around twenty-five or twenty-six years old, seamstresses' family and friends began to look for an appropriate candidate. It is hardly surprising that they found him among men they encountered in their daily working lives. Neighborhood sociability also played a role in bringing couples together. Forty percent of couples in this sample lived in the same parish, including 8 percent who lived on the same street. Women met their future husbands at the baker's shop, in the market, or at church. Their brothers befriended them in the workshop, bringing them home for dinner or to family outings. Brides performed needlework for their future grooms' mothers, worked alongside their sisters-in-law in the same workshop, or befriended them in a parish school or neighborhood clique. Ties of affection and perceived compatibility may have brought some of these modest working couples together in a manner that reinforced or undermined wider family interests.

A closer look at the husbands' occupations, moreover, suggests a second form of professional interest behind seamstresses' marriages. Rather than seeking a partner to share their occupations, it appears that many seamstresses' grooms chose their brides precisely because of the woman's independent trade. A man who had no work to offer his wife, such as a domestic servant or a municipal functionary, might well be attracted to a woman with her own occupation and income. Career women might also appeal to men in artisanal trades if they worked outside the home as journeymen or in a sector that did not employ female labor. Our sample includes a number of husbands from trades that may have offered little work to women, including men from the leather trades (a master currier and a saddlemaker), metal trades (a tinsmith, a smelter, an engraver, a mirrormaker, and two locksmiths), and the construction industry (a roofer, a mason, and a paver). In the same manner that fathers who did not require their daughters' assistance apprenticed them as seamstresses, husbands who could not use their wives' labor sought to marry needleworkers.

From the women's point of view, such unions could be particularly attractive, because they allowed them a measure of autonomy within marriage. They could continue to work in their own businesses and enjoy an independent source of income. They could also exercise authority in their own right as employers or instructors to apprentices. This living and working arrangement did not correspond to the household economy described in historical studies, where husband and wife joined forces in a family business. Nevertheless, it was a viable alternative and one that eighteenth-century Parisians appear to have acknowledged and accepted. In numerous households where the husband could not employ his wife, it offered a crucial supplementary income. For wives, it helped mitigate their husbands' legal, economic, and social authority.

The Relationship between Marriage and Mistress-ship

The weight of the seamstresses' career in alliance strategies is further underlined by the chronological relationship between marriage and guild membership. In contracts where information is available, entry to the guild usually predated marriage. In thirty-six cases, almost three-quarters of brides became mistresses before the contract, including half who did so during the three preceding years. In some cases, the two events were closely linked: one-fifth of the brides became mistresses within a year before or after the marriage. Historians have suggested that male artisans took advantage of their wives' dowries to acquire mastership. These figures suggest that seamstresses did the inverse, using guild membership—or impending entry to the guild—to acquire husbands. Their families viewed the acquisition of guild membership as a precursor to entry to the marriage market rather than a result of marital union.

The use of guild status to impress suitors is particularly evident in the dishonesty of a handful of brides who falsely claimed it. Anne Cabaille was probably in good faith when she called herself a mistress seamstress, for she was received into the guild only three weeks after her marriage. The same cannot be said of Elizabeth Charbonnet and Anne Michelle

Gérault, who did not attain this rank until five and six years respectively after their marriage contracts.[18] The value attached to guild membership is also emphasized by its monetary evaluation in seamstresses' dowries. Almost one-third of mistresses included their guild status as a component of their dowries. They ascribed it a worth ranging from 150 to 500 livres. The first figure corresponds to the fee for membership in the guild, while the second presumably included the costs of apprenticeship, reception, and establishment. On average, they evaluated their mistress status at 330 livres (median = 300). By contrast, male masters as a rule did not include mastership in their declarations of fortune at marriage.[19]

Bride and groom thus treated female guild membership as an unusual and attractive asset, sometimes going so far as to include it in the dowry. Women viewed their guild status as an integral part of their fortune and as a significant contribution to the future wealth of the family. Their grooms' acceptance of its inclusion in the dowry suggests that they agreed with this assessment. These mistresses planned to continue their independent careers after marriage; their grooms were not only aware of these plans, they approved them. Like the bakers' daughters, nonmistresses had less investment at stake and were more likely to shift their activities after marriage to aid in a husband's business.[20]

Marriage Capital

Following Parisian marriage custom, seamstresses' parents established dowries for their daughters at the time of marriage. This was not a free gift but represented all or part of the woman's share in her future inheritance from her parents. A benevolent third party or the bride herself could supplement this dowry, which generally consisted of household goods, clothing, and cash. The marriage contract assigned a monetary value to the various elements of the dowry to facilitate measurement against the groom's contribution and permit its recovery when one of the partners died.

The marriage contract not only stated the value of the bride's dowry, it also stipulated the precise portion that entered the couple's community of goods (*communauté de biens*). This "community of goods" was the common pool of wealth created between spouses by Parisian customary law. Although the parties shared ownership of the community, its control lay in the husband's hands. Any portion of the female dowry that did not enter the community, as well as any future real property such as real estate or perpetual annuities, remained in the wife's personal possession, if not under her authority. If a wife died without children, her estate reverted to her family of origin. Wives could also obtain complete financial independence, either at the outset of marriage by stipulating a separation of goods in the notarized contract, or after marriage by proving gross mismanagement on their husbands' part. Seamstresses and other women who conducted their own businesses automatically acquired the status of *marchande publique,* which gave them full legal authority over their commercial affairs.

Financial information in the contracts provides data on brides' and grooms' fortunes at marriage, but the contracts also pose severe obstacles to a precise calculation of wealth. The first problem is the lack of information regarding grooms' assets. Parisian law did not require grooms to declare their assets in marriage contracts or their contribution to the community of goods, and they often did not. Historians have offered varying interpretations of this silence, ranging from a tacit avowal of poverty to mere reticence on the groom's or the notary's part.[21] The contents of the contracts I examined argue for the latter hypothesis or, at the least, for a nonconclusive attitude. Accordingly, I have considered such cases as missing information rather than zero fortune. Even when grooms did provide this information, however, the documents do not offer a wholly transparent portrayal of either party's assets, because both sides' interests lay in inflating their declarations in order to evoke a greater contribution from the other. Despite these problems, the marriage contracts provide a rare and valuable impression of seamstresses' levels of fortune and, to a lesser extent, those of their grooms. The greater clarity required of brides in fact favors a study focusing on the female partner in marriage.

Aggregating mistresses and workers, the average value of seamstresses' dowries equaled 2,057 livres (median = 1,074), ranging from a low of 200 livres to a high of 16,604 livres. Most lay in a mid-range between 500 and 2000 livres (see table 8.1). Dowry values did not grow over the century. If we divide the sample into chronological groups, we find an average before 1750 of 2,670 livres, 1,575 livres during the 1750s, and 2,086 livres in the 1760s. A larger sample would be necessary to judge if the apparent decline from the 1750s to the 1760s resulted from a real drop in fortune among seamstresses or from a quirk of the sample.

Nonmistresses had smaller dowries than mistresses, with an average of 1,197 livres (median = 1,000) for the former versus 2,420 livres (median = 1,200) for the latter. Despite this discrepancy, nonmistress dowries were surprisingly substantial compared to other working men and women. A

TABLE 8.1 Range of dowry values among seamstresses

Dowry value (in livres)	Number of women
1–500	7
501–1,000	24
1,001–2,000	21
2,001–5,000	8
Above 5,000	4

study of marriage contracts from 1769 to 1804 revealed a median between 100 and 500 livres for male journeymen.[22] With regard to female workers, Olwen Hufton estimates that a woman who worked for fourteen to sixteen years prior to marriage could hope to save only 80 to 100 livres.[23] The nonmistress brides in our sample represent an elite among Parisian working people, closer in origins and fortune to mistresses than to poor workers. For their part, mistresses' fortune at marriage resembled those of other Parisian guild masters. The study of marriage contracts from 1769 to 1804 showed that in a group of 265 masters the median figure fell between 1,500 and 2,000 livres. Mistress seamstresses were slightly less affluent than masters, but shared the same overall socioeconomic level.[24]

Composition of Dowries

Parisian custom dictated that the bride's parents furnish her a dowry at the time of marriage. In a striking departure from this tradition, seamstresses in this sample provided more than half of the total value of their dowries themselves. On average, the brides contributed 872 livres (59 percent) and their parents 462 livres (32 percent). An average of 132 livres (9 percent) came from a third party, usually a relative. The brides' savings spanned a wide range, from 0 to 4,080 livres. On the whole, mistresses amassed more from their work than nonmistresses, with an average of 1,000 livres for the former versus 515 livres for the latter. These brides offer impressive testimony to the role of the trade in the accumulation of female dowries. In ten or fifteen years of work, seamstresses more than recuperated the money spent on apprenticeship and mistress-ship. Their contributions enhanced the fortunes they brought to marriage and, we may assume, their pool of potential husbands.

Unfortunately, notaries rarely specified the precise composition of the dowry, declaring merely that it consisted of cash, clothing, and household goods. A small number of punctilious brides shed light on dowry composition by drawing up detailed lists of the property they brought to marriage. When widowed mistress Jeanne Julie Vanse wedded the servant of an assistant royal tax collector in 1751, her trousseau consisted of five dresses, more than nine petticoats, seven corsets, six pairs of shoes, nine pairs of stockings, as well as household linen, jewelry, a watch, and miscellaneous items of clothing. She included in her list of assets 80 livres owed by a client, as well as 500 livres she claimed to have spent obtaining mistress-ship. Vanse estimated the total value of her fortune at 3,029 livres. Her widowed mother contributed an additional 2,513 livres in furniture and household linen, in return for which the couple agreed to lodge her and care for her until death.[25]

In 1749, mistress Quentine Souply possessed an almost equally lavish trousseau, including 1,459 livres worth of furniture, 401 livres in cooking utensils, 585 livres of household linen, 140 livres in jewelry, and an impressive 1,420 livres in clothing.[26] By contrast, mistress Anne Marguerite Bécart, married to a retired coach leaser in 1728, had a modest fortune. She owned cooking utensils, furniture, two beds — composed of canopied bed frames, mattresses, curtains, and other furnishings — and clothing, consisting chiefly of three satin dresses and four petticoats. These goods were evaluated together at only 668 livres.[27]

Remarriage and the Community of Goods

Despite the expectation of an ongoing career, the bride and her family apparently did not worry about the woman's financial constraints in marriage. Only four contracts rejected the customary financial community between the spouses. In each case, the union was a remarriage for one of the partners. Three of the brides married a widower with children, and each of their contracts explicitly established the husband's separate financial responsibility for himself and his children. In the fourth case, former *jurée* Elisabeth Lallemant wedded the poorer and younger Joseph Morard, also choosing to retain her financial autonomy. The marriage was Morard's first but Lallemant's third, and the only one in which she refused the financial community.[28]

Not all seamstresses who married widowers took such measures. An additional eleven seamstresses married widowers within the traditional arrangement; six of their grooms had children from previous marriages. Another three widowed brides took on a second husband. Unlike Lallemant, they all chose to marry within the financial community. Because these widows had children, while Lallemant did not, they may have judged that financial union with their future husbands offered them more security. Mistress seamstresses' status as *marchandes publiques* allowed them to conduct business-related financial affairs independently and without their husband's consent. This status alone seems to have guaranteed sufficient financial autonomy to the women involved.

Total Fortune at Marriage

Over half of the grooms in the sample did not provide information about their assets, and it is impossible to judge their fortunes. Among those who did offer information, their average worth was on the whole lower than their brides. For thirty-two cases, the grooms possessed 1,045 livres, compared to an average of 1,401 livres for their brides. Mistresses tended to marry slightly richer men than nonmistresses, with an average fortune of 1,136 livres for the former's grooms and 971 livres for the grooms of the latter. It is difficult to explain this discrepancy in male and female fortunes, which goes against common historical findings. One possible explanation is that men began apprenticeship later and spent more time in trade training, and thus had less time to acquire savings. Another possibility is that only poorer men could be pressured into stipulating the contents of their fortune in the contracts.

Grooms with fortunes smaller than their brides offered two measures to compensate for their relative poverty. The first was contained in the generous *douaire* they constituted for their brides. The *douaire* was a sort of widow's life insurance, a sum of money the groom pledged for her upkeep in the event of his death. Tradition called on grooms to provide a sum equal to one-half of their fortune at marriage. Among the thirty-two grooms who declared their assets, the *douaire* represented an average of 62 percent, surely an attempt to placate their brides for their financial weakness.[29] In addition to padding the *douaire,* grooms also allotted a greater share of their goods to the marriage community. In twenty-nine cases with information, we find an average contribution among brides of 527 livres (median = 400), or 42 percent of their average fortunes of 1,245 livres (median = 1,000). The grooms in these contracts accorded 505 livres (median = 300) to the community, or 50 percent of their average fortunes of 991 livres (median = 800). With this proportional discrepancy, husband and wife made roughly equal contributions to their future household despite their unequal assets.

The average value of bride and groom's combined fortunes in cases with full information was 2,236 livres, with a financial community worth 1,032 livres. These sums were modest in the scheme of Parisian society, but sufficient to establish a new professional and family life. Household goods and clothing provided the material necessities of life for the new couple, while liquid assets or professional tools could form the basis of a new commercial enterprise.

Permanent Celibacy

Many seamstresses followed a wholly different marriage strategy than in the cases discussed above, that of nonmarriage or permanent spinsterhood. A sample of almost eight hundred mistresses in apprenticeship contracts demonstrates the high proportion of single women in the trade. For 51 percent married mistresses and 12 percent widows, we find 37 percent unmarried women. Probate inventories offer similar statistics. In a sample of sixty-five cases, slightly over half (52 percent) of the women were either widowed or married, while the remainder (48 percent) had never married. Provincial seamstresses also numbered many single women. In 1768, a group of thirty-nine seamstresses in Caen included sixteen unmarried women (41 percent).[30]

These levels of spinsterhood significantly exceeded those of the general population. In a study of Old Regime marriage patterns, Louis Henry and Jacques Houdaille found that around 1675, only 6 or 7 percent of French women over the age of fifty had never married, a figure that rose a century later to 14 percent. Among three thousand probate inventories dating from the late seventeenth and eighteenth centuries, historian Annick Pardailhé-Galabrun found that 80 percent of Parisian men and women married at least once in their lifetime.[31]

Did seamstresses' high rates of spinsterhood represent an inability to marry or a conscious choice to remain single? A definite response is difficult. On the one hand, strong cultural pressure exhorted men and women to marry and establish a family in eighteenth-century Paris. Normative societal and cultural values made nonreligious celibacy an unusual and unattractive option for most women. Moreover, it was almost always in a woman's financial and practical self-interest to marry. Given the dangers of sickness and unemployment, and the difficulties of everyday life, women took a strong risk in refusing marriage. On the other hand, there is no obvious reason why these seamstresses could not have married. Poverty alone did not prevent the majority of eighteenth-century Parisian men and women from marrying and having children. With their trade skills and independent income—and their possible talents for dressing and self-presentation—these women should have been able to attract spouses as easily as other Parisian women.

Despite cultural prejudices, therefore, it would appear that a substantial group of Parisian seamstresses used their careers as an alternative to marriage. Relying on their skills and income to get by, they chose to forgo marriage and child rearing and live as single women. This may have been a conscious decision or one that emerged only with the passing of time. As the years passed and they managed to survive—or even thrive—financially, seamstresses may have put off marriage until it was too late. Resigned to, or contented with, a life without husband and children, they established their own households and conducted their own affairs, creating distinctive female living spaces within the Parisian population. Their numbers give credence to Louis-Sébastien Mercier's claims in the 1780s that the number of unmarried women in the capital was continually growing; the result, he said, of both poverty and choice. As he plaintively remarked: "The woman [who remains] unmarried by choice, is today no longer rare in the middling orders." [32]

Probate Inventories and Police Seals

If marriage contracts offer a glimpse of seamstresses as they began family life, two types of documents shed light on their activities in maturity and death. The first emanated from neighborhood police officials. When an individual died, those concerned with his or her estate could summon the police to apply protective seals within the deceased's apartment. As he did so, the *commissaire* drew up a report with the names and declarations of those present in the apartment, be they relatives, friends, workers, or creditors. Police officials also recorded—in more or less detail—the goods contained under their seals. A request for the application of seals was often a sign of distrust or suspicion among heirs, boding ill for peaceful division of the estate. In other cases, a sudden, unexplained death or the demise of an individual with no known heirs also prompted the application of protective seals and a police investigation.

Compared to probate inventories, police records offer limited information about fortune, because they make no attempt to assess the monetary value of household goods. Nevertheless, the records furnish significant details missing from the inventories. Compiled closer to the moment of death, these documents often contain traces of the deceased's life that had disappeared by the time of the inventory. Police documents also offer rare testimony of workers' modest belongings, which usually did not merit an expensive notarial inventory.

Once the seals were applied—or after a person's death if no seals were requested—the heirs addressed themselves to the lieutenant general of police for authorization to proceed with the probate inventory. After receiving this authorization, notaries brought an accredited appraiser to the deceased's home to list and evaluate all household goods, annuities, or other property belonging to the estate. Unlike police seals, the inventory was a legal requirement on the death of one spouse in a financial community. Given the cost and intrusion of the notary's services, however, many poor and even some well-to-do families chose to forgo the formal inventory. Indeed, because husband and wife did not normally inherit from each other, the surviving spouse had every interest in delaying the inventory.

The advantages and drawbacks of probate inventories as historical sources are well known. They provide unequalled access to the private and professional lives of ordinary historical actors, with invaluable information regarding the composition of households, size and distribution of apartments, ownership of material goods, display of cultural values and interests, extent of fortune and debt, and rare evidence regarding the conduct of professional affairs. Probate inventories also present numerous difficulties. Intended as a means to evaluate and safeguard an estate, these documents function imperfectly as tools for historians. Small fortunes usually did not merit a notarial inventory, resulting in a source biased toward the most successful individuals. Because notaries were exclusively interested in the worth of the estate, they listed only items with a discernible effect on it. Objects of little value or family records did not retain their notice. Notaries might also neglect to mention family members who had lost inheritance rights, either by dying or entering a religious order. Workers or servants who left the home after their employer's death similarly disappeared from the record. Finally, the inventories are limited by the circumstances of their creation. They offer a snapshot of life at the time of death, often accompanied by illness or old age. They cannot reveal the varied conditions of all ages and walks of life.[33]

My sample contains fifty-eight probate inventories supplemented in most cases by reports from the police seals, as well as seven police reports from estates where the inventory has disappeared or was not performed. The sample includes fifty-two mistresses and thirteen nonmistresses who died between the years 1714 and 1788. Although their age is usually not given, most were women of mature years and a long professional career. If we define a career as lasting between the acquisition of guild status and death, we find an average working life of twenty-two years (median = 20.5) for a group of twenty-six women. If we estimate that a woman was approximately twenty-five years old when she joined the guild, she would have died in her late forties or early fifties after a twenty-year career, a full lifespan by contemporary standards.

This average concealed, however, a wide range in careers and life expectancies. The shortest professional life lasted just one month. Jeanne Marie Alexandre died several weeks after she was admitted to the guild in 1762, joining in death a mistress sister who also passed away shortly after her guild reception. The longest careers lasted several decades, with the record going to the former guild official Elizabeth Lallemant, who was a mistress for over forty-eight years. The youngest mistress was probably in her mid-twenties when she died, while the oldest were in their late sixties and seventies. The dean of all the seamstresses was a nonmistress named Françoise Desloriers, who died in 1770 at eighty-one years of age.

Family Life

Be they old or young, our sample reveals a limited family life among mistress and nonmistress seamstresses. Their households were small, containing an average of just over two people each, including the seamstress herself (median = 2).[34] One-third apparently lived alone, managing the arduous daily tasks of cooking, cleaning, and shopping for provisions by themselves. In their final illness, they might have relied on relatives or hired nurses to care for them. When Cécile Barbier died in 1788, she owed nine livres to her nurse Marie Margueritte Beauvais. Nine months before her death, Françoise Desloriers took the wife Pasque as a lodger, giving the woman free housing in exchange for daily care.[35]

Another third of the seamstresses lived with one or more family members, but no workers or apprentices. This family member was usually not a husband, for only thirteen of the total group of sixty-five women were married at the time of their death. Given that two wives were estranged from their husbands, only eleven women (17 percent) lived in marital unions. Children were found more often than husbands in seamstresses' homes, but they too were uncommon. Among fifty-two widowed or married women, only sixteen had children who were mentioned in their probate inventories. On average, they had two children each, with a range from one to six living children.[36]

These findings confound once more the patterns discovered by demographic and social historians, who claim that natural fertility would have produced four or five children during a ten- or fifteen-year marriage. In her study of probate inventories, Pardailhé-Galabrun found a significantly higher incidence of child rearing than in our sample, with more than half of all households containing children. If our sample is representative, we may conclude that married seamstresses had significantly fewer children than the general population. This raises the question of what happened to the seamstresses' missing children. They may have fallen victim to the high mortality rates for infants sent from Paris to rural wet nurses, especially if their mothers routinely used wet nursing to free themselves from infant care. Alternatively, they may have never been born at all, if seamstresses followed the example of eighteenth-century domestic servants in their precocious adoption of contraception. Overall, these findings suggest that even among married seamstresses career commitments could outweigh family matters and lead to behavior that curtailed the birth or survival of children.[37]

To counter the risks of solitude and isolation, single and widowed seamstresses established alternate households based on their trade and employment of other women. These households accounted for the remaining one-third of the cases, and included women who lived in residences whose permanent or semipermanent members consisted of hired workers or apprentices, sometimes children, but no husbands. Sixteen out of sixty-three seamstresses lived with an annual worker, usually only one but sometimes two. Seven mistresses had apprentices. Five had one apprentice each, and two flagrantly violated guild statutes by engaging and housing three apprentices at once. The presence of an apprentice apparently signified high productivity, for in five of the seven cases the apprentice lived and worked alongside a live-in worker.

Workers could become semipermanent members of their employers' households. Marie Catherine Cardin lived with her mistress for sixteen years, until the latter's death in 1743. Cardin's only belongings in her employer's home consisted of her clothes and her bed. At the time of her death in 1754, Marie Germaine Pelée employed two sisters as yearly workers, one of whom had lived with Pelée for eleven years. Marie Thérèse Prempain lived with a "former" worker (*ancienne fille couturière*), suggesting that the relationship between mistress and worker could continue beyond active employment.[38]

In addition to these subordinate workers, one mistress, Marie Nicole Debuquant, formed a domestic and business association with a nonmistress seamstress, Marie Louise Frison. The two women jointly owned all of their household goods in addition to several annuities they had purchased together. Their partnership had endured at least seven years by the time of Debuquant's death in 1777. Frison was the executor of her partner's will as well as her sole heir. This pair is the only example in the inventories of a long-term, egalitarian domestic and professional association between seamstresses.[39] We do not know if their union included physical intimacy, but the fact that each woman had her own bed in the apartment suggests that they maintained at least the appearance of platonic friendship.

Five mistresses employed domestic servants, including one who employed her sister in this capacity at an annual salary of one hundred livres.[40] Like this case, the most complicated households consisted of a mixture of workers and family members. Widowed Laurence Ducouroy lived with her daughters, two workers, and an apprentice at her death in 1759. Marie Denise Delamaisonneuve lived with her two sisters, both of whom were seamstresses, and a hired worker. As these examples show, family relations frequently took on an economic cast in these households, as mothers, daughters, sisters, aunts, and nieces worked and lived together.[41]

In no case did the presence of a live-in worker coincide with that of a husband, and only one apprentice shared her mistresses' home with the woman's spouse. To a certain extent, space limitations must have discouraged married seamstresses from lodging workers. With a husband and one or two children present, there was little room left over to house hired employees. The mistresses' authority over adult workers may have also been incompatible with the husband's position as head of household.[42] She could not effectively supervise her own workers at the same time that she remained a docile and obedient wife. The husband's own trade commitments were not an issue for these households. In the total sample, only one seamstress's husband had an employee present in the home. In seamstresses' families, the household appears to have served as the site of female economic production, while the men worked outside the home. The ability to maintain female households was a prerogative of mistresses. Nonmistresses lived in greater solitude. In a sample of thirteen inventories and police seals, all nonmistresses lived alone or with one other person. Advanced age played an important role in their solitude, as did their subordinate economic status.

A number of mistress seamstresses thus distinguished themselves from other women by establishing and leading households based on their professional activities. Their status as employers gave them more than economic clout, it enabled them to create distinctive forms of gendered social relations. These mistresses' homes may have served as a refuge for women in the neighborhood when their husbands turned to drink, violence, or infidelity, or when their grown-up sons became abusive. Desperate women could find solace, temporary lodging, and even a new source of income from the mistress seamstress. For this reason, these unusual households may have attracted as much suspicion and hostility from male observers as they did respect. Living in unusual circumstances, with no male authority in the home, the mistress was accountable for the conduct of each member of her household, and perhaps was vulnerable to accusations of impropriety.

We might also expect distinctive modes of life and culture to arise in these households, revolving around the professional skills of cutting and sewing cloth and fitting garments, as well as competition over technical proficiency and knowledge of the latest fashions. Their inhabitants naturally accorded a great deal of importance to the female wardrobe and appearance. Conversations included animated debates about fashions in textiles, decorations, and sleeve lengths, as well as the comparative elegance of different ladies of the court nobility or the Parisian elite. Workers and apprentices exchanged stories of outfits worn or witnessed at marriages, balls, or in deliveries made to the fashionable quarters of the city. Another constant interest must have been the female body. Workers and apprentices scrutinized its mysteries, noting who had gained weight, lost it, had their first period, become pregnant, or entered menopause. Such discussions were probably accompanied by laughter, songs, or, when dealing with the most intimate personal secrets, a hushed whisper. Easygoing mistresses tolerated or participated in their workers' chatter, while stricter ones demanded silence during work.

In these homes religious piety coexisted with superstitions involving cutting cloth and sewing. In the late nineteenth century, seamstresses foresaw bad luck and disputes in a broken thread or spilled needles. They insisted that an apprentice had to prick herself at least seven times or draw blood before she began to assimilate her trade. They forecast a stranger's visit in a pair of dropped scissors, and they tried to attract suitors by leaving strands of hair in the hems of bridal gowns. Many superstitions revolved around love and sexuality, with the act of drawing a needle through cloth functioning as a veiled metaphor for copulation.[43] Like their nineteenth-century descendants, Old Regime seamstresses were women of the world, whose interests in clothing and fashion must have coincided with trade superstitions and strong religious sentiments.

The number of adult female relatives who chose to live and work together reveals the close emotional ties that could exist among female kin. Mistress Marie Denise Delamaisonneuve occupied two rooms and a small kitchen with her two sisters and a live-in worker. While the employee slept in a simple bed in the kitchen, the three sisters shared two rooms and two beds. When her daughter's marriage foundered, Laurence Ducouroy took the young woman back to live with her. A childless widow, Louise Blet resided with Marie Anne Brocard, her adult niece. As much as they fostered affection and solidarity, these living situations must have generated a certain degree of conflict. The enforced intimacy of everyday life, combined with workplace tensions and the double familial and economic authority the senior woman exercised over the junior, probably led to periodic explosions of anger and resentment. Nevertheless, in the absence of husband or child, these relationships constituted the central emotional and social ties of their adult lives.[44]

Over years of living together, mistresses also formed strong attachments to their workers. In 1767 Marie Thérèse Prempain purchased a five-hundred-livre annuity in the name of Marie Marguerite Michaux, the nonmistress seamstress who shared her home. Marie Germaine Pelée left a symbolic, if less valuable, bequest to her worker Marguerite Durant when she died in 1754. Pelée willed most of her belongings to her three sisters, but she also bequeathed the silver goblet in which "[she] always drank" to Durant. Apprentices might also win the affection of their mistresses. Jeanne Françoise Miller's will left a substantial bequest to her apprentice Jeanne Thérèse Rosalie Dubled. It included Miller's bed, two pairs of sheets, three pillowcases, her mantelpiece decoration, five chairs, a quilting frame, a worktable, a lace headdress, and six embroidered towels. Dubled also benefited from a one-fourth share of the residual estate.[45]

Even seamstresses who lived alone maintained close ties with neighbors, friends, and relatives. The childless widow Anne Malard left legacies to her nieces and nephews, including money and portraits of herself and her husband. In her will, spinster Edmée Boullet named an unrelated woman, Elizabeth Champion, as her universal heir "in recompense for the good care which [she and her husband] have taken of me in my illness." When Jeanne Pourcelet fell ill, her landlady sent word to the woman's only known relatives. These were her cousins, a cowherd who lived near the northern barrier of Paris and a daily laborer in Aubervilliers. Along with her neighbors, these relatives nursed Pourcelet until her death several days later.[46]

Living Space

All of the mistress seamstresses in the sample lived in rented apartments. Two were principal tenants of their buildings, responsible for subleasing, upkeep, and daily goings-on in the building; the remainder rented apartments. Their apartments were small on the whole, containing an average of only two and one quarter rooms. This average includes small ancillary rooms—which they described as *cabinets, antechambres* or *alcoves*—if they contained pieces of furniture indicating they were used as a distinct living space. The proliferation of these spaces after mid-century created new oases of privacy for seamstresses and other Parisians, who used them as dressing rooms, small bedrooms, workrooms, kitchens, or places of prayer, reading, and reflection. Mistresses may have used them to escape the intimacy of their workers and apprentices or to offer privacy to clients for fitting garments and discussing credit arrangements.[47]

The seamstresses paid an average of 162 livres in rent annually (median = 124), with a range from 30 to 550 livres. If we divide the overall average between pre-1760 and post-1760 figures, we find that mistresses' living space diminished after 1760 from almost three rooms to two rooms. Conversely, rents rose after 1760. Up to 1760, the women paid an average of 138 livres (median = 120) in rent, which increased after this date to 172 livres (median = 132). These findings concur with historians' observations of sharp rent inflation across the eighteenth century.[48]

At the cheapest end of the scale, Marie Anne Chemin, the widow of a corporal of the watch, paid 30 livres a year for one small room in 1773. It was accessible only through a room occupied by another widow. In the middle range, Marguerite Specq, widow of a *bourgeois de Paris,* spent 120 livres a year on her single room in 1743, which she occupied alone. Although the notaries did not indicate the dimensions of the rooms, Specq's more expensive rent must have provided her with a bigger and more comfortable space. Marie Anne Guichard, seamstress to two of Louis XV's daughters, paid the top price of 430 livres a year in 1777 for a three-room apartment that she shared with two employees. The apartment contained a kitchen, Guichard's bedroom, and another room that served as a combined workroom, entertaining space, and sleeping quarters for one of the workers. Although Guichard's apartment was not the largest in the sample, its location on the fashionable and expensive rue Saint-Honoré explains her elevated rent. With her royal clientele, Guichard had good reason to invest in an elegant apartment situated at the heart of the Parisian luxury district.[49] Another successful mistress, widowed Laurence Ducouroy, shared a four-room apartment with her daughter, two workers, and an apprentice for a rent of 300 livres. One room served as a kitchen and another as Ducouroy's bedroom, while the other two served combined purposes for sleeping, working, and entertaining. Ducouroy's grandson slept in a small side room when he was not in boarding school.[50] A seamstress's decision to rent lodgings spacious enough to house workers represented a conscious, and expensive, investment in her productive capacity, and thus a high commitment to the trade.

More likely to live alone, the thirteen nonmistresses occupied smaller apartments than the mistresses, with an average of between one and two rooms each (median = 1). Catherine Elisabeth Raffray, an unmarried worker seamstress, shared a one-room apartment with her niece.[51] Catherine de Beaumanoir, an unmarried corset worker, lived alone in a one-room apartment in 1764.[52] Journeywomen seamstresses who died while living with their mistresses usually did not merit a probate inventory. Their sole possessions might consist of their clothing and perhaps their bed in their mistresses' house.

Workers' ability to maintain permanent lodgings depended on full employment throughout the year and the provision of meals by their mistresses. Seasonal work cycles and high unemployment meant that many could not afford to sign a long-term lease. Police documents frequently reveal non-mistress seamstresses living together in cheap furnished rooms, rented by the night. They shared these rooms with other garment workers as well as laundresses, servants, or street vendors. On the night of December 7, 1766, a police official performed a series of raids on suspected prostitutes. Among lodgers in one room he discovered a thirty-two-year-old gold-thread embroiderer from Versailles; two linen seamstresses, aged nineteen and thirty-five; a twenty-year-old embroiderer from Reims; and a thirty-two-year-old Parisian fruit seller.[53] Seamstresses in these living

conditions constituted a large but marginal workforce, vulnerable to unemployment, homelessness, and destitution. Many had immigrated to
Paris and had limited connections in the city. Their lives were a distant remove from the settled and even modestly comfortable existence of more
privileged workers documented in the probate inventories.

The Inventory as an Indicator of Household Fortune

Assisted by professional appraisers, notaries assigned a monetary value to
all clothing, furniture, and other property present in the deceased's home,
unless owned by another person. These evaluations pose a series of problems for a reliable calculation of fortune. First, the appraiser's estimates
bore no certain relationship to the value the goods fetched at auction.
Second, family members sometimes redistributed or consumed elements
of the estate before the notary's arrival. Clothing could be taken and re-
adjusted to fit a newly orphaned child, wine might be drunk, and in
extreme cases, silverware or cash savings pilfered. Third, when the deceased was widowed, some notaries merely listed the presence or absence of items previously recorded in her husband's inventory, without
noting their value. Finally, the evaluation of paper holdings—annuities,
land, promissory notes, or accounts pending—is even more difficult, given
the vagueness and uncertainty surrounding their real value. Starting with
items of greatest clarity, my analysis of seamstresses' fortunes will begin
with household furnishings and personal possessions and follow with
other forms of property. We may assume that fortune rendered in notarial
inventories significantly underestimates its actual value.

For the purposes of this study, household possessions will include all
personal belongings recorded in the seamstresses' homes, including furniture, kitchen utensils, decorations and other furnishings, clothing, household linen, cash, silverware, and any business-related items. The total value
of the seamstresses' household possessions, as estimated in the inventories,
ranged from 22 livres to 3,363 livres. The average was 1,047 livres (median
= 774). Up to 1760, the average household fortune of nineteen seamstresses
was 1,159 livres (median = 1,117). After 1760, this average fell to 992 livres
(median = 636) for thirty-nine women. Combined with the decline in
dowry values over the eighteenth century, these figures suggest a drop in
real fortune among seamstresses at a time of rising inflation. The introduction of inexpensive consumer goods in the second half of the eighteenth

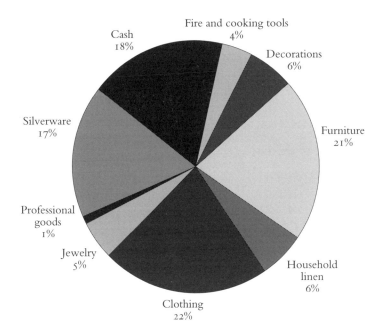

FIGURE 8.1 Average percentage composition of seamstresses' household possessions.

century, however, may have limited the perceptible decline in living standards.[54]

Furniture and furnishings constituted seamstresses' heaviest investment, accounting for 31 percent of household fortune on average. Clothing came next with 22 percent, followed closely by cash and silverware, with 17 percent and 18 percent, respectively. Household linen and jewelry were relatively minor investments worth 6 percent and 5 percent each. Finally, raw materials and specialized tools constituted only 1 percent of household fortune on average (see figure 8.1).

Nonmistresses accumulated fewer and less expensive goods than mistresses. Their average household fortune was only 627 livres (median = 401) compared to an average among mistresses of 1,187 livres (median = 958). This figure, moreover, represents the most successful workers, whose possessions were deemed worthy of a probate inventory. The most fortunate nonmistresses, nonetheless, were better off than the poorest mistresses, emphasizing the overlap that could exist between these two categories.

For a clearer view of the interior of seamstresses' homes, household possessions may be broken up into several categories. The first is that of furniture and furnishings, which I have further divided into three distinct groups: cooking and fire utensils, decorative objects, and furniture. The first group includes utensils used to store or cook food and liquids, along with those used to produce light or tend the fireplace, such as casseroles, frying pans, waterfountains, plates, bowls, cutlery, candlesticks, and snuffers. The second group consists of objects intended primarily for decorative or recreational purposes, such as paintings, engravings, religious objects, books, mirrors, and clocks. A third category encompasses all types of furniture and functional furnishings, such as chairs, tables, beds, and the tapestries and window curtains that helped to keep rooms warm and eliminate drafts. These distinctions did not formally exist in the inventories; I use them here to clarify the analysis.[55]

As we might expect, furniture represented the highest value among all household furnishings, with an average estimated worth of 231 livres, or 68 percent (median = 205). Decorations were a surprisingly substantial investment, evaluated at an average of 65 livres, or 19 percent (median = 45), of all furnishings. Most seamstresses, therefore, had enough surplus income to purchase decorative objects or items used in leisure activities. In doing so, they exercised their own taste and aesthetic sensibilities, as well as indulging intellectual or spiritual interests. The necessities of the kitchen, the fire, and lighting came last with an average worth of 45 livres, or 13 percent (median = 34).

Like other Parisians, seamstresses usually spent the most on their beds. These were complex constructions, usually canopied with heavy curtains to keep out cold air and to increase privacy. Underneath the canopy, the bed consisted of a wooden frame topped by a straw mattress, two woolen mattresses, various pillows, foot warmers, blankets, and counterpanes. The most expensive seamstresses' beds were worth two hundred livres, the simplest or oldest only thirty livres. Workers slept on even cheaper portable beds that could be folded and put aside during the work day or, if space permitted, in their own modest canopy beds. In addition to beds, the women's apartments contained numerous pieces of furniture, such as wardrobes, chests of drawers, trunks, and boxes, used for storing clothing or cooking utensils. The large number of chairs and tables the seamstresses owned testifies to their social lives as well as to the practical requirements of their trade. During the day, workers sat on chairs to sew garments; at night and on holidays friends and neighbors used the same chairs to eat, talk, and play games. Most seamstresses possessed a specialized worktable for cutting cloth, along with other tables for preparing food, eating, or writing accounts.

Seamstresses decorated their apartments with a diverse array of paintings, engravings, reliquaries, mirrors, and crucifixes. Using a crude counting system where every graphic image—painting, engraving, or print—equals one, regardless of its size or content, the seamstresses possessed an average of ten such images each, with a range from zero to seventy-one items. The majority of images was devotional in nature. Although notaries rarely noted their precise subject matter, a few cases offer an indication of the overall themes. Before she died, Marie Germaine Pelée had purchased a series of paintings and engravings depicting the life of Christ, including a portrait of Jesus and images of his descent from the cross and his meeting with the Good Samaritan along with a portrait of St. John the Baptist. Pelée's colleague Françoise Miller, who died in 1788, displayed her anti-Jesuitical sentiments with a picture depicting "the destruction of the Jesuits." In many cases, religious objects accompanied devotional images. Over 40 percent of the seamstresses owned a crucifix, a statuette of the Virgin Mary, and/or a crèche. Marie Thérèse Prempain owned thirty-one religious engravings, two shells transformed into reliquaries, two crucifixes, and a golden cross. Suzanne Faitout displayed her faith with seventeen small religious paintings and engravings, a wooden cross, a wooden statuette of the Virgin Mary, and a prayer stool. The prevalence of devotional images and objects among seamstresses testifies to their piety and the role of worship in their daily lives.[56]

A smaller number of seamstresses combined religious images with secular ones, such as portraits and landscapes. Portraits of French kings and members of the court nobility occupied a prominent place among nonreligious art works. Interest in their own families and faces also showed up on the seamstresses' walls. Fifteen percent of the sample possessed a family portrait, either of the woman herself, her husband, or members of an earlier generation. Antoinette Talbot demonstrated the coexistence of religious and worldly interests by juxtaposing her thirty-three devotional paintings and engravings with two landscapes, a picture of flowers, portraits of Louis XIV and Louis XV, and commissioned portraits of herself and her husband. The largest and most diverse collection belonged to Anne Catherine Patural and her journeyman printer husband. Their two-room apartment contained seventy-one paintings, including one seascape, a number of landscapes, and four devotional paintings. A large painting of the Virgin jostled for precedence with a painting of the Greek god Adonis, and two maps demonstrated an interest in geography.[57]

In addition to their cultural values, seamstresses' possessions also reveal something of their leisure activities and sociability. A twelve-hour workday left little time for leisure activities during the week. However, seamstresses took advantage of Sundays as well as the numerous Catholic holidays scattered throughout the year to practice religious devotion and to socialize with their friends. After attending church services or engaging in private prayer at home, they would have had spare time left to amuse themselves. Like other Parisians, they enjoyed playing card games, such as *piquet* or *cadrille,* sharing meals, and exchanging gossip. Seven seamstresses owned card tables or boxes to hold card sets. Some had purchased special sets of cups and saucers for entertaining friends. Others kept domestic pets like parrots, canaries, and squirrels to lighten their long hours of work.

Together, the furniture and decorations of their apartments created an environment that was both private and public, because seamstresses not only lived in their homes, they used them as workshops and places to receive clients and visitors. While the poorest members of the trade struggled from day to day with the barest necessities, the most successful had dwellings that reflected a concern for comfort and fashionable appearances. Marie Anne Guichard had outfitted her bedroom in a manner fitting for a seamstress to royal princesses. Her bed was the most expensive object in her bedroom, enclosed in its green damask canopy and curtains. A screen set up in the room afforded further privacy to her sleeping area and permitted clients to try on clothing in privacy. The room also included a veneered chest of drawers with a marble top, a similar night table, a stylish chiffonier chest of drawers, a small writing table, a wardrobe, four painted green chairs, and two *bergère*-style armchairs and four additional armchairs all covered in gray satin brocade. A drink tray contained cups and saucers for guests, while two landscapes and two family portraits provided decoration. Although royal princesses certainly never visited the apartment, their servants or more humble clients probably did, and Ducouroy must have hoped to make a favorable impression on them. On a smaller scale, widowed Laurence Ducouroy carefully outfitted a charming little room beside her bedroom. It contained two small tables, an antique walnut desk, four armchairs covered in flowered cotton, and a small drink tray with four cups, saucers, and a milk jug. The two-seat sofa and the two small varnished corner cupboards (*encoignures*) that completed the furnishings belonged to the latest fashions in home decor.[58]

The chiffoniers, corner cupboards, sofas, and ottomans found in the homes of successful seamstresses belonged to a class of furniture usually restricted to bourgeois Parisian households.[59] Other seamstresses demonstrated sophisticated tastes by serving coffee or tea to their guests. Coffee filtered through Parisian society after 1740, but tea remained an expensive and uncommon luxury product until the end of the eighteenth century.[60] Fifteen seamstresses had coffee mills, coffeepots, or boxes to hold coffee, and seven had a teapot or a box of tea (including three women who had paraphernalia for both coffee and tea). When they served these drinks to guests, in sets of matching china, seamstresses demonstrated familiarity with socially elite practices of living and entertaining. The cultivation of a lifestyle and home environment attuned to the latest styles reflected seamstresses' sense of occupying a distinctive place in the world of work. Elegance and fashion were not restricted to apparel; a seamstress wishing to project good taste, economic success, and civility had to frame her home environment accordingly. Apprentices and workers learned to emulate these practices, reproducing them in their own homes as best they could.

Reading and Writing

Even more than for their furnishings, seamstresses stand out from the Parisian working population for their virtuosity with the written word. Virtually all mistresses could write, a crucial skill in a trade that functioned on credit. In a sample of pre-1755 apprenticeship contracts, 140 out of 157 mistresses (or 89 percent) signed their names to the contract. In the same sample, 91 out of 121 apprentices (or 75 percent) were able to sign their apprenticeship contracts. Testifying to their frequent use of the written word, one third of seamstresses owned a specialized desk for writing. They would have used these pieces of furniture to keep accounts and write personal or commercial correspondence.

Apart from professional needs, literacy was also tied up in seamstresses' religious practices. Almost half of the women in probate inventories possessed books. Their libraries ranged from a small collection of four books to a maximum of eighty volumes. Reading as a pastime appears to have grown considerably over the eighteenth century, with only 25 percent of seamstresses owning books before 1760 compared with percent after this date. These figures may actually underestimate the number of readers among them, because six additional women possessed bookshelves with no mention of books. Like their decorations, most of the seamstresses' books were devotional in nature. They included the Bible, saints' lives, prayer books, such as the *Année chrétienne,* and titles such as *Essay de morale* by M. Nicole, *Meditations* by Père Avrillion, and the *Missile de Paris* and *Instruction sur la pénitence et sur la communion.* Only a small number of these women owned secular reading material. Seamstresses' books were generally inexpensive; for example, Françoise Jauhier's twelve volumes of devotional reading were evaluated at three livres. Marie Louise Souters owned thirty books on religion and history, estimated to be worth twenty livres.[61]

Mistresses' libraries were particularly impressive in comparison to other artisans. Among Steven Kaplan's master bakers, only 20 percent owned books compared to almost 50 percent of the total sample of mistress seamstresses. A sample of probate inventories encompassing all levels of Parisian society—including nobles, clerics, bourgeois, and working people—found books in 42 percent of the capital's households, a figure that rose to 51 percent for the second half of the eighteenth century. Seamstresses clearly occupied a distinctive cultural place within the world of work. Interest in the written word was not a function of marital status; wives and widows owned books at basically the same rate as unmarried women. Book ownership was, however, more common among mistresses than nonmistresses. Three-quarters of guild members owned books, but only half of non-mistresses did.[62]

Reading formed part of the private and working lives of seamstresses. They read devotional literature in their bedrooms by candlelight at night, or used their cabinets and alcoves as spaces for prayer and reflection. Reading aloud from devotional books may have constituted a regular part of the daily life of the seamstress household, with shared religious precepts and proverbs serving as a backbone to the discipline of work. One of the duties of the young apprentice may have involved reading aloud to her mistress and the workers in the shop.[63] If reading was bound up in the seamstresses' intimate life, however, it also belonged to a wider social and cultural world. Seamstresses' ability to read and write was not merely a prelude to religious devotion, it was a display of professional and cultural superiority and a means of demonstrating affiliation with a socially elite clientele. Their possession of bookshelves in which to hold their libraries and their specialized writing desks made this point clearly to all visitors. Neighbors and friends who were not so fortunate must have pestered mistresses to draft their letters and read the ones they received. Mistresses must have wielded literacy as a tool of professional and social authority over workers. Reading and writing constituted an essential distinguishing factor in the neighborhood, the workshop, and the labor market.

Seamstresses' Wardrobes and Household Linen

As professionals in the garment industry, seamstresses could be expected to award special time, skill, and money to their own wardrobes. Beyond learned or inherent fondness for clothing, commercial interest required them to present a well groomed and, as far as possible, fashionable exterior. Even more than other goods, it is difficult to use probate inventories to reconstruct the size and value of seamstresses' wardrobes. While members of the household might appropriate articles of clothing prior to the inventory, notaries made their own contribution to the ambiguity of the assessment by failing to separate items of clothing from articles of household linen. They often evaluated personal items such as undergarments, shirts, and bonnets together with sheets, tablecloths, napkins, or towels. To exclude personal linen altogether would have entailed further artificial reductions of the wardrobes; therefore I have included them in my calculations at the risk of inflating the totals slightly.

With these caveats, the average worth of seamstresses' wardrobes was 214 livres (median = 177).[64] At the abundant extreme of this scale stood Louise Blet, who died in 1767 with a wardrobe estimated at 907 livres. Blet owned eleven dresses, eight of which had matching skirts and three matching aprons, a stylish innovation found increasingly in the later inventories. Blet's dresses were made of satin, taffeta, damask, and cotton. They were colored white, gray, green, and brown, and decorated with stripes, checks, and fancy stitching. Blet possessed another thirteen skirts made of calico, silk, and damask, a green taffeta apron and a household apron. She had nineteen shirts with twenty-two pairs of decorated cuffs, as well as eight corsets, six camisoles, and eight pairs of stockings. She added decorative touches with a lace scarf, four headdresses, two neckerchiefs, and a satin-covered stomacher. For outerwear, she owned seven bonnets, two loose jackets, two fur muffs, a parasol, and one pair of shoes. For nightwear, Blet owned two dressing gowns, two night bonnets, and seven nightcaps.[65]

Although it did not equal the luxury found among the nobility or *haute bourgeoisie,* Blet's wardrobe contained considerably more items than possessed by most women of the artisanal trades. Blet's abundant dresses and skirts were of good material and attractive patterns. She could change garments every day, using some items for daily wear and saving others for important occasions. Blet apparently renewed her wardrobe with some frequency, because the notary described few of her garments as old or used. Variation in fabrics, as well as her possession of muffs and jackets, allowed her to adapt to seasonal weather conditions.

At the other extreme, Marie Jacqueline Ouvrard, a spinster who died in 1777, had a wardrobe barely exceeding the basics. It consisted of a brown striped dress and skirt, three additional cotton skirts, four shirts, two old mantles, three camisoles, two corsets, a loose cotton jacket with red stripes, three pairs of stockings, several old aprons, and three pairs of old shoes. Ouvrard's wardrobe was not only less abundant, her cycle of consumption was longer than Blet's. The notary described most of her garments as old and used. He estimated her wardrobe to be worth only sixty livres.[66]

Overall, however, seamstresses demonstrated a strong commitment to fashion as well as a precocious adoption of the major developments in French clothing styles of the eighteenth century. According to Daniel Roche, the chief characteristic of the eighteenth-century "clothing revolution" was the introduction of the dress as the centerpiece of the female wardrobe. During the second half of the eighteenth century, Roche claims, Parisian women rejected the customary two-piece ensemble in favor of the one-piece dress.[67] Appropriate to their role in producing and selling such garments, the seamstresses' inventories reveal an early adherence to the dress. A small number of pre-1760 inventories contain an average of almost five dresses for each woman, with a range from zero to seven. In 1735, mistress Françoise Battou and her colleague Jeanne Dollé each died with seven dresses in their wardrobes. The post-1760 figures represent only a fractional advance over the earlier period, with the average remaining at just under five dresses. The largest collections of dresses, however, belong to the latter period, with mistresses Antoinette Talbot, Marie Thérèse Turpin, and Louise Blet, who all died after 1760, owning ten dresses each.[68]

In addition to dresses, seamstresses in both periods also owned a large number of skirts and petticoats. Comparison of the pre-1760 and post-1760 periods shows an increase from an average of between eight and nine skirts and petticoats to between ten and eleven. Made of cotton or dimity, petticoats served as underwear for warmth and protection from the elements. Skirts were made of wool, silk, linen, or cotton and worn as outerwear with jackets or bodices. The fanciest skirts belonged to a matching dress ensemble.

In terms of color and fabric, the seamstresses also occupied the vanguard of the clothing revolution. Roche noted that somber colors and heavy woolen fabrics dominated nonnoble wardrobes in the first half of the century. By 1789, the palette had lightened to include bright colors and patterns, and woolen cloths had given way to lighter cottons and silks. The seamstresses' pre-1750 wardrobes included bright colors such as yellow, green, red, blue, and white, and patterns of stripes and flowers. Fabrics included cotton, *siamoise* (a blend of cotton and linen), taffeta, and muslin. In 1735, fifty-year old Françoise Battou's seven dresses included one of satin with red and green stripes, another of flowered satin, a black-and-white striped linen dress, and one of taffeta whose color changed in the light. In 1743, Charlotte Beroin owned three dresses, one of yellow damask with flowers, another of satin with white-and-purple stripes, and another of satin with purple-and-cinnamon colored stripes.[69]

Bright colors and patterns continued throughout the century, combined with a new interest in the calicoes that returned to the market after 1759. In 1762, the young mistress Jeanne Marie Alexandre died with seven dresses in her possession. Three were of satin, one with pink stripes, another of a crimson color, and the third with green-and-red stripes. Her other dresses were of golden-colored taffetas, white wool with light pink flowers, and checkered twill. At her death in 1771, forty-six-year-old spinster Marie Anne Godard Desmarets also owned seven dresses, the most notable of which were a satin dress with cherry-and-white stripes, another of taffeta with blue-and-white stripes, a third in blue satin with a floral pattern, a calico dress, and one of embroidered *siamoise* cloth. With their fashionable, brightly colored dresses, mistress seamstresses must have stood out among the Parisian working population.[70]

In general, the number of pieces in nonmistresses' wardrobes was smaller than those of the mistresses. Nonmistresses possessed an average of three to four dresses each, compared to an average of over five for the mistresses. They owned an average of eight skirts and petticoats each, compared to nearly eleven among mistresses. Nonmistresses also demonstrated slower cycles of renewal. Notaries or police officials frequently described their garments as old and used. However, the categories of mistress and nonmistress again overlapped at each extreme; the best-dressed nonmistresses equaled or surpassed their poorest mistress colleagues.

Cash and silverware comprised the most liquid portion of household goods. Cash holdings varied widely among my sample of seamstresses. Twenty-eight seamstresses had no money in their homes when they died, while the remaining thirty possessed sums ranging from 2 livres to 1,938 livres. On average, seamstresses who had money had 400 livres each (median = 129). They used it to satisfy daily expenses, to pay taxes and guild dues, and to purchase professional supplies. The cash on hand also represented a form of saving against seasonal work shortages. Silverware was another type of saving, which combined an ostentatious form of consumption with an investment that could be mortgaged in times of need. Seamstresses evidently preferred silverware to cash. Only twenty mistresses owned no silverware at all, compared to thirty-eight who did. On average, those who possessed it had 270 livres worth of silver (median = 269), with a range from 32 livres to 1,142 livres. These holdings show that many seamstresses did not live on the edge of poverty. They accumulated cash and exchangeable luxury items that offered security against work shortages and illness.

Professional tools or goods found in seamstresses' inventories were generally of little value. All seamstresses possessed chairs, worktables, candles, and clothes irons, essential accessories for their trade. Some conscientious notaries also noted the presence of scissors, thimbles, or needles, inexpensive objects that usually escaped the record. Four seamstresses owned tailors' mannequins, a practical tool for fitting and altering garments. Most seamstresses also had scraps of cloth in their possession when they died, but very few kept substantial stocks of cloth or other raw materials. Only thirteen seamstresses possessed cloth or tools that were appraised as distinct categories in their inventories; among these women were Marie Madeleine Bricon, who owned 120 livres worth of pins, needles, thread, and ribbons, and Marie Joseph Denizon, who had supplies evaluated at sixteen livres for making hoopskirts. When seamstresses did keep cloth or supplies, such goods represented only the necessary elements for a specific garment. They did not have stocks of cloth permanently available for prospective clients.[71]

After listing and evaluating all personal possessions, the notary moved on to examine the deceased's papers. Here his interest focused primarily on titles to property that might form part of the deceased's estate. Purely personal items merited scant attention. Indeed, family members often asked notaries to skip personal papers to avoid the expense of a prolonged inventory. Financial papers included titles to various types of property, such as real estate holdings and annuities (*rentes*), as well as account books and promissory notes. The greatest problems of all are encountered in assigning a monetary value to these forms of property. Notaries rarely indicated the value of real estate properties or the principal sums invested in lifetime annuities. It is also difficult to measure the validity of long-standing promissory notes or professional accounts. Given the difficulty of evaluating these forms of property, some historians concentrate solely on the evaluation of household goods. This solution is also unsatisfactory, because it rules out any possible estimation of total fortune. I have thus hazarded an estimation of paper wealth, while acknowledging the imprecision of the available data.

Rentes were a form of annuity that permitted investment and lending with interest, in a period when the Catholic Church's prohibition of usury remained theoretically in force. Institutions of the state or church were the most common creators of *rentes,* but individuals in need of a loan could constitute private annuities. The investor "purchased" an annuity by paying a principal sum to its creator, in exchange for which he or she received a yearly payment equivalent to 5 or 10 percent interest on the principal. At least two types of annuities existed: perpetual rents (*rentes perpetuelles*) and lifetime rents (*rentes viagères*). The perpetual rent was a form of real property that could not be alienated from the owner's estate, but rather passed across the generations within his or her family line. In theory, payment of the perpetual annuity terminated only when the lender "repurchased" the rent by refunding the principal. In practice, the government often devalued these investments by lowering their annual payments. Perpetual rents usually brought an initial return of *denier 20,* or 5 percent.

Rentes viagères endured only during the lifetime of the individual who purchased them. On the owner's death, the annuity ceased to exist and its capital disappeared. As with perpetual rents, public institutions or private individuals could issue lifetime annuities. The royal government issued public lifetime annuities, called *tontines,* at periodic intervals during the eighteenth century. *Tontines* were sold in different categories, based primarily on the age of the individual purchaser. Lifetime rents paid a higher rate than perpetual rents, usually 10 percent. In order to permit calculations of total fortune, lifetime annuities have been capitalized as if the annuity always represented the customary 10 percent of the principal.[72]

Perpetual rents were not widespread among seamstresses in our sample of probate inventories. Only eleven out of fifty-nine women possessed them, nine mistresses and two nonmistresses. The sums invested in perpetual annuities among those who owned them averaged 6,631 livres (median = 7,000), ranging from 1,000 to 12,082 livres. More seamstresses purchased lifetime annuities. Almost one-third of the women in our sample owned one or more at the time of their death, with an average investment among those who had them of 4,785 livres (median = 3,308), ranging from 400 to 16,100 livres. The most spectacular holdings in annuities usually accrued from inheritance from a husband or relative. Nevertheless, smaller investments could be the result of a successful career as a seamstress. Some needleworkers earned enough surplus income for modest investments, which cushioned the cyclical rise and fall of business. They did not, however, acquire investments substantial enough to forgo professional activity.

The popularity of lifetime annuities among seamstresses resulted in part from the small amount of capital the annuities required. While a perpetual annuity cost at least 1,000 livres, investors could purchase lifetime ones for sums as low as 200 or 300 livres. Lifetime annuities also offered a substantially higher rate of return, making them ideal for women with small incomes who worried about their old age. The two types of annuity also represented different views of the future and of family relations. Perpetual annuities were long-term investments intended to constitute a permanent addition to family patrimony. Lifetime annuities permitted the maximization and consumption of resources within one generation. They were a new form of investment, which grew rapidly during the eighteenth century. With their limited funds and their limited family lives, seamstresses were more concerned with their own futures than with family patrimony. They invested their money at a maximum rate of return to ensure survival during old age and forced retirement. Their patterns of annuity holding suggest that this was a typically female strategy, although further investigation will be necessary to determine gendered patterns of investment for the larger population.

Apart from perpetual or lifetime annuities, paper holding could also consist of promissory notes or bills of exchange. Promissory notes did not form a substantial element of seamstresses' fortunes. Roughly one-third of the sample had one or more in their possession when they died. Their value ranged from 23 livres to 5,250 livres, with an average of 689 livres (median = 91). In most cases, these notes appear to have been unrelated to the women's activities as a seamstress, but stemmed from personal transactions and money loaned to family members or friends.

Seamstresses' heirs learned of unsettled professional invoices by consulting the deceased woman's daily account books or through the verbal reports of workers or apprentices. Only one-third of seamstresses were recorded to have unsettled accounts when they died. They ranged from the 2 livres and 8 sous owed for the fabrication of two corsets to the almost 14,000 livres owed by the noble clients of a former seamstress to the queen. Like this case, noble clients generated the largest accounts among seamstresses. Noblewomen frequently owed accounts dating from fifteen or twenty years before the woman's deaths.[73] The average value of accounts outstanding was 1,167 livres among those who had them, but this figure was distorted a by few large cases (median = 333).

A final element of seamstresses' fortunes consisted of real estate properties. Although all of the mistresses in this sample rented their Parisian apartments, a handful owned real estate outside of Paris, which they had usually inherited from relatives. Laurence Ducouroy owned three houses in the village of Maison. Preferring to live in her rented four-room Parisian apartment, she leased the houses for 100, 170, and 500 livres annually.[74] Marie Barbe Monseignat inherited a house and adjacent land in Melun from her brother in 1747. She rented out this property for 470 livres in 1763, and 522 livres in 1768. Another mistress's husband held a share in a modest house and farmland in Normandy, which he rented for 7 livres annually. The value of each of these properties is unknown. Unlike her colleagues, Françoise LeClerc bought herself a house in Versailles for 3,700 livres in 1727, shortly after being awarded an official post as seamstress to the queen. It is not clear whether she still owned the house at her death in 1739. Apart from this house, LeClerc received rental income from an inherited house and land in the region of Marigny.[75]

Debt

More than half of seamstresses' inventories noted debts, ranging from 11 livres to 8,045 livres. Among those noted to owe money, the average amount was 757 livres, a figure inflated by one or two spectacular cases (median = 314). Probate inventories undoubtedly underestimated the extent of debt among seamstresses. Despite her best intentions, it is hard to imagine a sick or elderly woman dying without leaving any unpaid bills whatsoever. Mistresses owed money to their landlords, to the baker, the laundress, and almost always to the doctors and nurses who cared for them during their final illness. Laurence Ducouroy, the most heavily indebted mistress, had established three annuities: two for her children's dowries and another to an unrelated individual. These annuities amounted to a total yearly expense of 700 livres, but this sum was offset by the 770 livres she received in rent on her properties outside of Paris. In general, mistresses had little need to borrow heavily for professional reasons, given the small capital needed to function in the trade and the paltry stocks of raw materials they maintained.

Total Fortunes

For the purposes of this study, I have considered mistresses' total fortunes to be composed of household goods, investments, and other assets documented in their personal papers. Taking these elements together, the seamstresses' total fortunes averaged 4,545 livres (median = 1,880), ranging from 230 livres to 22,735 livres.[76] Twenty-five-year-old mistress Françoise Prud-homme was the poorest of all. Her belongings were restricted to 230 livres worth of furniture, kitchen utensils, linen goods, and clothing. Widowed mistress Marie Chemin had the second smallest fortune, with 173 livres of household possessions and 70 livres in cash.

At the other end of the scale, Louise Blet, the childless widow of a former guard at the Hôtel de Ville, was the richest seamstress, with 22,735 livres in her estate. This impressive fortune consisted for the most part of investments in perpetual and lifetime annuities that she had inherited from her husband. Unmarried mistress Marie Thérèse Prempain was the second richest, with 18,519 livres, again composed largely of annuities as well as substantial holdings in silverware, jewelry, and clothing. Closer to the norm, mistress Charlotte Beroin died in 1743, with a fortune evaluated at 2,213 livres. Along with 800 livres invested in lifetime annuities, she owned 327 livres in silver, 177 livres in clothes, and another 909 livres in household goods. In 1751, Marie Souters and her husband were worth 1,140 livres, which included 68 livres in cash, 467 livres in clothing, professional accounts outstanding worth 165 livres, and 440 livres in household goods. Unfortunately, the fortunes of mistresses with substantial real estate holdings are not accurately represented, because it was impossible to assign them a monetary value.[77]

Nonmistresses in general were less fortunate than their guild colleagues. The former had average total fortunes of 2,952 livres (median = 979) compared to 4,877 livres (median = 1,949) among the latter. Guild membership thus appears to have paid off in higher earnings across a woman's career. The division of mistresses' fortunes by marital status is also revealing. Widows possessed the largest holdings, with an average of 6,413 livres (median = 2,823). Wives came next, with an average of 4,262 livres each (median = 1,745). Spinsters had the smallest fortunes, with 3,612 livres on average (median = 1,220). They also, however, possessed the lowest levels of debt, with only 323 livres on average, compared to 1,058 livres among widows and 1,248 livres among wives. These figures suggest that men generated more income than women, but offset their earnings with significantly higher levels of debt.

Given the low debts reported among seamstresses, the values for net fortune differ little from those for gross fortune. Once debts have been subtracted, the average net fortune was 4,108 livres. Still some, seamstresses recorded a negative net fortune as a result of very high debts. After her death, the community between mistress Simmonet and her husband registered a negative fortune of 1,203 livres. This dire situation was counterbalanced by some 1,300 livres in professional merchandise that her husband owned.[78] The largest fortunes—Blet's 22,735 livres and Prempain's 18,519—remained untouched, because no debts were recorded to the estates. (Table 8.2 shows the breakdown of net fortune for the combined pool of workers and mistresses.)

Conclusion

In this chapter I have explored the social constraints and possibilities affecting seamstresses, as well as the function of guild membership in this play of constraint and choice. Like other women in Old Regime France, seamstresses most often married men who shared their origins, primarily in the guild trades or domestic service. Both the seamstresses and their husbands were better off than the majority of the people of Paris, but they did not attain the prosperity of prestigious masters and were far from the fortunes of merchant guildsmen. They belonged to the Parisian lower-middle class of modest masters, shopkeepers, and domestic servants. Mistresses

TABLE 8.2 Breakdown of seamstresses' net fortunes

Range of fortune (in livres)	Number of cases
less than zero	4
0–500	14
500–1,000	7
1,001–2,000	7
2,001–5,000	12
5,001–10,000	4
10,001–15,000	5
15,001–20,000	5
over 20,000	1

were nonetheless more prosperous than were workers, including skilled male journeymen. In economic terms, therefore, guild membership could trump the disadvantages of gender.

Seamstresses challenge existing notions of the "family economy" by demonstrating the importance of autonomous female careers in negotiations prior to marriage and in generating a supplementary income after it. One of the most important aspects of marriage among seamstresses, however, was the large number of unmarried women who belonged to the trade. The disproportionately high percentage of single seamstresses suggests that some women looked to the trade—and membership in the guild—as an alternative to marriage. The breakdown of mistresses' fortune by marital status reveals that marriage would have been the best financial choice for women, but it has also shown that not all unmarried working women lived in miserable poverty. Unmarried mistress seamstresses could generate enough income from their work to support themselves and pay salaries to one or more workers. They were sometimes able to pay high rents for lodging workers and make investments in silverware and annuities.

Important hierarchies of wealth and living standards existed among mistress seamstresses. A considerable gap separated the poorest mistress from the richest. The former possessed merely some old furniture and clothing, worth several hundred livres. She lived alone in a one-room apartment, where she performed all domestic chores by herself. The latter possessed up to twenty thousand livres in household goods, silverware, cash, and investments. She dressed almost as well as a bourgeois woman and employed two or three other women's labor on a permanent basis. The two may nevertheless have shared a common level of culture, including the reading habits and commercial practices that set them apart from other working women.

Overall, guild status made a tangible difference in these women's lives. Belonging to a guild affected women's marriage choices and the composition of their households. Mistresses' cultural sophistication and self-consciously elegant furnishings and dress also set them apart from the larger female population. Nonmistresses were generally poorer than guild members, living in smaller apartments with old clothes and scant furnishings. Most did not even possess fortunes worthy of notarial inventory. However, considerable overlap existed between the poorest mistresses and the most successful workers; little separated a poor and unsuccessful mistress from her nonguild colleague.

NINE

Making the New Century:

The Seamstresses, fin et suite

In 1776, the seamstresses' protest against the abolition of the guilds en-visioned a world where rapacious men seized control of female trades, leaving working women vulnerable to exploitation and abuse. Were these anxieties realized with the final abolition of the guilds in 1791? Did seam-stresses lose their dominance over women's clothing in the years following the revolution? The nineteenth-century garment industry has attracted considerable historical attention, on themes ranging from its structural transformation over time to labor organization to representations of the female needleworker. Although I will not attempt to provide an exhaus-tive account of this literature, it is worthwhile to reflect on the ways in which the past and the future were articulated in the seamstresses' trade. Attempts to draw continuities between the Old Regime and the nine-teenth century are fraught with difficulty, especially when dealing with concepts such as "corporatism" or "women's work."[1] Exploring the rela-tionship between the Old Regime past and the postrevolutionary future nonetheless serves valuable purposes. On the one hand, it offers crucial background to understanding the nineteenth-century experience, and on the other hand, it highlights both enduring and ephemeral achievements of the Old Regime. This examination of the experience of nineteenth-century seamstresses attempts to bridge the gap dividing the world we have lost from the world we have inherited.

The guilds staved off catastrophe in 1776, but they did not survive the first years of the French Revolution. In 1791, the National Assembly for-mally abolished trade corporations, ending a centuries-old tradition of guild organization in France. Despite the seamstresses' fears, this act did not immediately alter the structure or practice of work in the garment trades. After a period of crisis under the Revolution, the clothing trades enjoyed a "golden age" from 1800 to the mid-1820s, in which women continued to dominate the production of made-to-measure female apparel. In the 1830s and 1840s, however, the rise of a new ready-to-wear industry began to transform the production and sale of first male and then female clothing, ultimately leading to proletarianization of the workforce and a steady eclipse of female entrepreneurs. Women still comprised the majority of the workforce that made women's clothing, but they increasingly labored for male employers. As the seamstresses forecasted, a "free" market presented severe obstacles to female success in the garment trades.

These changes, however, did not wholly efface the legacy of the Old Regime guild. Strong continuities existed from the eighteenth to the nineteenth century, most obviously in the feminization of the garment trades. Divisions and hierarchies in the nineteenth-century garment trades also grew out of the Old Regime. Seamstresses, fashion workers, and linen-workers continued to constitute self-consciously distinct occupations and to regard each other with little sisterly solidarity. Traditions of trade organization and association persisted within the seamstresses' trade as well, flourishing in the political militancy of the 1830s and 1840s and after the legalization of trade unions in the 1880s. With one notable exception, however, seamstresses' organizations made no explicit use of their Old Regime institutional heritage. Nor were they drawing on "corporate" forms of thought somehow ingrained in their work practices or in their perceptions of labor. Instead, women inherited a strong practical and conceptual position in the needle trades, which encouraged both a moral legitimacy for their work in this sector and a trade-based female work identity. These factors were a product of the eighteenth-century experience, which left an ambivalent legacy for its heirs.

The Revolutionary Crisis

Fears and complaints about women's position in the garment trades appeared early in the Revolutionary process. In January 1789, a group of women calling themselves the "women of the Third-Estate" issued a petition to the king complaining about their restricted economic opportunities and the limited possibilities for female education. After a scant religious instruction, they were "taught to work" through vocational training that rendered them capable of earning only "five or six sous a day" at age fifteen or sixteen. In adulthood, unattractive women could hope only for marriage to simple artisans, while pretty ones were vulnerable to seduction and disgrace. To "prevent these evils," the petitioners demanded that men "not be allowed, under any pretext, to exercise trades that are the prerogative of women—such as seamstress, embroiderer, fashion merchant, etc., etc.; if we are left at least with the needle and the spindle, we promise never to handle the compass or the square." Echoing the functions of female guilds, they further asked that the king "assign us positions, which we alone will be able to fill, which we will occupy only after having passed a strict examination, after trustworthy inquiries concerning the purity of our morals."[2]

In 1790, the pamphlet *Motion de la pauvre Javotte, députée des pauvres femmes* (Motion of the poor Javotte, deputy of poor women) took the form of a spurious motion to the National Assembly. Speaking in the voice of a poor working woman, it called attention to increased female unemployment under the Revolution. "Poor Javotte" deplored the departure of aristocrats who previously provided vocational training and jobs to her family members. Now, she declared, Paris abounds with unemployed women who speak in "a thousand voices around me, in all the streets, at all the doors, along the avenues, in the districts, at the shows, before the National Assembly." Javotte catalogued the skills possessed by her mother and sisters, and described the economic viability of these skills under the Old Regime: "My mother does dressmaking [*fait la toilette*] and everything that relates to fashion; my sisters know how to do lacemaking and dressmaking. I can do cutting and embroidery."

In the social and economic conditions of the Revolution, these skills were useless. A poor old woman told her that "you can do everything . . . everything you have to do to end up at the Hôpital. The embroiderers are bankrupt, the fashion merchants close their shops, the seamstresses [*couturières*] lay off three-fourths of their workers, and soon ladies of quality won't have ladies' maids [*femmes de chambres*]. A poor seamstress, even in good times, didn't earn enough to buy shoes." Her protest that "I want to be honest and to work," met with the response "you will die of hunger." The pamphlet concluded by urging the Revolutionary government "to consider the fate of unfortunate women."[3] In calling attention to women's work, neither the "women of the Third-Estate" nor the poor Javotte mentioned the four female guilds that still existed in Paris or the male guild that controlled professional embroidery. They offered no indication that female work in sewing women's clothing was still protected by an all-female guild, which imposed its own tests of competency on potential members.

This silence may reflect the tenuous status of the corporate system in the new context of the Revolution. With the abolition of privilege on August 4, 1789, it must have seemed to observers that the guilds could not survive long. The royal procurator of the Châtelet of Paris seems to have ceased receiving new guild members by the end of that year, for there are no registers of admissions for 1790 or 1791. Among seamstresses, the last recorded admission of a new member took place on September 24, 1789. Only 60 mistresses joined the guild in 1789, compared to an annual average of 147 between 1780 and 1789. It is also revealing that the fresh-flower sellers referred to themselves in a 1789 petition as "the merchant flower sellers [*marchandes bouquetières*] formerly comprising the community of mistress flower sellers and merchants of floral garlands [*communauté des maîtresses bouquetières et marchandes chapelières en fleurs*] of the City and Faubourgs of Paris." By 1789, the flower sellers apparently no longer considered themselves to constitute a guild.[4]

Despite these early indications of weakness, formal legal measures to dismantle the corporations did not arrive until two years later. In March 1791, the National Assembly issued the d'Allarde law, abolishing guilds across France. Instead of joining corporations, artisans were obliged to purchase a work license from the government: "Beginning on the coming April first, it shall be free to every citizen to engage in whatever commerce, or to exercise whatever profession, art or trade he may wish, after having provided himself with a patent and paid its price, according to the rates hereafter determined."[5] Workers and employers would henceforth compete in a putatively free market, open to all men and women.

Unlike in 1776, this legislation sparked little protest from master artisans. Two years into the Revolution, it was perhaps clear to guild masters that their corporations could not survive the disavowal of privilege, not to mention new conceptions of economic liberty and the perceived need to remove intermediary institutions between the individual and the state. Some indeed may have been converted to revolutionary principles of free labor. For Revolutionary legislators, however, the removal of corporate restrictions did not equate with freedom of activity for workers. In June 1791, the National Assembly issued the Le Chapelier law, forbidding workers from associating in groups. This law remained in force until 1884, serving as the justification for official suppression of worker organization and unionization through much of the nineteenth century.

After 1791, the collapse of the luxury trades described by Javotte increased through wholesale noble emigration, disruption caused by war, and continuing economic crisis.[6] Many women formerly employed in these trades fell into unemployment, leading to increased hardship and fears of popular unrest. In response to these problems, and to meet the demands of war, the Revolutionary government undertook measures to provide men and women with useful work. In August 1793, the National Convention decreed the *levée en masse*, calling for all members of the population to join in the war effort: "Young men will go to battle; married men will forge arms and transport supplies; women will make tents, uniforms, and serve in the hospitals; children will pick rags; old men will have themselves carried to public squares, to inspire the courage of the warriors, and to preach the hatred of kings and the unity of the Republic."[7]

In accordance with this measure, the Convention began to distribute sewing work in the manufacture of army uniforms to unemployed Parisian women. By autumn of 1793, the women's grievances over the organization of this project, represented in a petition signed by more than 4,500 of them, resulted in its decentralization to individual sections of the city. Male commissioners in the sections now took responsibility for cutting cloth and distributing it to the needleworkers. By 1795, the distribution of work had passed to private contractors. Throughout the project's existence, participants complained continuously about the scanty pay and limited employment it offered. Given the lack of work in their own trades, seamstresses, linen-drapers, and other unemployed needleworkers must have been prominent among those who sought this form of employment. The fact that control of their work lay in the hands of male authorities or subcontractors must have rankled with former members of female guilds. These skilled artisans were not prevalent, apparently, in the public spinning workshops established for poor women between 1790 and 1795.[8]

The Parisian Garment Trades in the First Half of the Nineteenth Century: From "Golden Age" to Ready-to-Wear

The garment trades experienced a renewal under the more peaceful conditions of the Directory, which increased during the First Empire as members of the new imperial court and Parisian elites reinvested in fashion and ostentatious appearances. The luxurious fabrics of women's dresses and men's suits in the Napoleonic period belied the simplicity of their neoclassical style. This revival stretched from 1800 through the restoration of the Bourbon monarchy in 1814 and into the mid-1820s, a twenty-five-year period that one historian describes as the "golden age" of the garment trades.[9] During these years, skilled dressmakers continued to practice their trade much as they had done before the Revolution. Small workshops staffed and run by women dominated the sector of made-to-measure female apparel, which still comprised the most important source for new women's clothing. Men and women who wished to obtain good-quality new clothes had little choice but to hire a local seamstress or tailor. Some ready-to-wear clothes were sold, as they had been under the Old Regime, but these were mostly garments of cheap cloth destined for modest customers.[10]

Contemporary fashion journals describe the high-end of the clothing trades in the first decades of the nineteenth century as highly similar to the late-eighteenth-century situation. According to *L'Union des modes* of January 1837, for example, nuances in the decoration and length of sleeves remained in the hands of individual seamstresses. To see the season's new fashions they had to await the appearance of fashionable ladies on the Champs-Elysées dressed in their seamstress's or fashion merchant's latest creations. In the shops advertised in the journal, men and women bought finished accessories and decorations, but not dresses. Despite the fears of the "women of the Third-Estate" and the crisis described by "poor Javotte," the garment trades emerged from the Revolution with few apparent changes, apart from the loss of guild structures.[11]

Writing in 1837, however, *L'Union des modes* downplayed two important changes already underway in the garment trades. First, a slow process of consolidation had taken place in the first decades of the nineteenth century, as "merchant tailors" in the bespoke industry concentrated production in larger workshops, expanding practices begun in the late Old Regime. The depression of the late 1820s exacerbated this trend and encouraged reorganization and restructuring. Second, the 1830s and 1840s witnessed the gradual rise of a new industry in ready-to-wear clothing (*confection*) that would drastically transform the garment trades. Large-scale, dispersed production in ready-to-wear began in the sector of men's clothing and spread more slowly to women's wear. Manufacturers often kept skilled journeymen on their premises to cut cloth, but distributed the sewing work to less qualified male and female homeworkers. Unable to compete with this new industry or with larger manufacturers in the bespoke trade, many small male and female shop owners lost their businesses and entered the growing ranks of the working class.

The impact of these changes is much better established for men's clothing and male labor than for women workers and women's wear. A statistical survey of Parisian industry undertaken in 1847 and 1848 by the city's chamber of commerce counted over 230 men running *confection* enterprises, with those men employing more than 7,000 workers. By contrast, bespoke tailors numbered approximately 3,000 and employed almost 9,800 individuals. This represented an average of 30 workers each for the former and 3 for the latter. The average annual sales for a ready-to-wear shop was 125,000 livres versus 16,000 livres for the bespoke tailor.[12] Custom tailoring thus employed the largest workforce in the garment trades at mid-century, but reliance on low-paid homeworkers made *confection* a much more profitable sector. Most bespoke tailors were small producers, increasingly undercut and eliminated by large concerns in the ready-to-wear industry or by merchant tailors in their own sector of the trade. The introduction of the sewing machine in the mid-1850s heightened existing tendencies by increasing the scale of production and capital costs for manufacturers.[13]

Joan Scott raises important questions about the reality behind the 1847–1848 survey, particularly in terms of the classification of owners and laborers. As she points out, the situation is even more confused for female members of the garment industry.[14] The survey counted 225 *couturières/confectionneuses,* who employed 1,300 workers.[15] These women clearly did not represent all independent female needleworkers, and it is unclear how those included in the survey divided between ready-to-wear and bespoke production. Moreover, we do not know how many female workers the male entrepreneurs employed, nor how many of them made women's clothing. Nancy Green argues that the rapid change of women's fashion, along with the importance of domestic production of clothing, hindered the growth of ready-to-wear in this period. The continuing importance of small-scale custom-made production in turn slowed processes of consolidation and proletarianization.[16]

Closer examination of the garment industry would surely reveal that female entrepreneurs suffered the new conditions of production and distribution to an even greater extent than did men. They were particularly hampered by difficulties in acquiring credit, as well as by social and cultural constraints on their capacity to manage large manufacturing concerns. A study of Parisian bankruptcy records between 1818 and 1830 finds one-quarter of female bankruptcies occurring in the clothing trades. The largest group of bankrupt women entrepreneurs were dress shop owners. Women's difficulties in adapting to new circumstances allowed a gradual encroachment of male businessmen over female entrepreneurs.[17]

Changes underway in the organization of production were paralleled by the emergence of new forms of distribution to market finished garments. In the first half of the nineteenth century, *magasins de nouveautés,* heirs to the fashion merchants' boutiques, sold finished clothing and accessories, cloth, and other trinkets. Whereas the Old Regime shops had primarily sold luxury objects to elite customers, the new stores provided cheap imitations of fashionable styles aimed at consumers from the middling and lower classes. Advertising, which began to emerge in the Old Regime against the condemnation of the guilds, became more sophisticated and widespread. These changes culminated in the creation of the first department store (*grand magasin*), the Bon marché, in 1869. Over time, department stores began to organize production on their own, establishing large workshops to supply their racks of ready-to-wear clothing.[18]

Restructuring in the garment trades and the onset of proletarianization were not a direct result of the abolition of the guilds. The background for such changes lies in economic, commercial, and social transformations too broad to be fully described here. The removal of corporate institutional barriers did, however, facilitate the radical reorganization of the trade. For example, the elimination of guilds contributed to a deterioration of apprenticeship among male and female workers. Without the incentive of guild membership and the administrative support offered by corporations, apprenticeship gradually declined in the second half of the nineteenth century. Lack of formal training encouraged loss of skill among male and female workers, a crucial element of the proletarianization process. Removal of guild prohibitions against advertising, accumulating multiple workshops, putting-out work, or concentrating workers in one site also allowed merchant-manufacturers new liberty to exploit material and human capital. These practices had existed under the Old Regime, but they were hampered by explicit corporate regulation and fear of prosecution. Once guild controls disappeared, they began to emerge as new norms. The fact that the garment trades changed so little until the depression of the 1820s can be read as an indication of the strength of ingrained prohibitions and practices to this date.

Old Regime work practices survived into the 1830s and beyond in the high-end sectors of the garment trades, but the guild system did not. Despite sporadic interest from the time of Napoleon's First Empire to the Vichy government in World War II, guilds were never revived in France. This did not mean, however, that the Revolution eradicated the hundred-year tradition of association among needleworkers. In the 1830s and 1840s, Parisian seamstresses participated prominently in organized labor activism. They wrote for the Saint-Simonian newspaper *La Tribune des femmes,* which appeared between 1832 and 1834. In 1848, they sent female trade delegations to press claims before the new republican government. As we will see, organization accelerated in the 1880s and 1890s, with the removal of government prohibitions on unions and strikes.

To what extent were these forms of organization, or the professional claims they presented, related to the Old Regime corporation? Did "corporate" patterns of thinking and association survive the Revolution within this female trade? Studies of militant seamstresses and tailors in the 1830s and 1840s suggest that a number of striking continuities existed. One of the strongest links between the pre- and post-Revolutionary periods lay in the explicit articulation of a "female" work identity based on women's strong role in the production of clothing. As under the Old Regime, seamstresses coupled this work identity with sharp resistance to male encroachment in what they saw as innately female trades. In *La Tribune des femmes,* for example, seamstresses protested their work conditions and made claims for independence of their labor from male control. In 1848, seamstress delegates complained not only about the destruction of small producers, but about the loss of female enterprises to men.[19]

These parallels to the Old Regime, however, should not be interpreted as forms of direct inspiration from the past. Unlike the tailors of the 1830s and 1840s, seamstresses and other needleworkers did not even refer explicitly to their corporate past. Instead, they based their claims on their common practice of a female trade and their special interests as women.[20] Moreover, the contents of their claims in 1848 differed significantly from their Old Regime predecessors. According to Joan Scott, female garment workers complained primarily about low wages and the difficulties married women encountered in combining professional and domestic labor. These elements reveal a transition in the focus of activism from the autonomous guild mistress to the dependent worker, depicted as a mother charged with raising children and feeding a husband. This discursive shift derived from the increased proletarianization of the trade, and the parallel transition that had taken place in forms of trade association from guild structures composed exclusively of mistresses to militant organizations made up of workers and small owners.[21]

The discursive context of the 1830s and 1840s had also changed significantly since the Old Regime, forcing seamstress activists to struggle against increasingly negative perceptions of their work. Judith De Groat suggests that the Revolutionary government's failure to include garment workers among female craftswomen in the *Festival de la concorde* in 1848 reveals the low esteem into which the women workers had fallen. By this point, seamstresses and other needleworkers were known as the least skilled, lowest paid, and most sexually promiscuous of women workers. This reputation resulted from the inherent difficulties of their economic and social position, as well as from broader concerns about the nature and social role of "women's work." It was also a result of the disappearance of the Old Regime guild. Seamstresses had always been suspected of low standards of living and loose morals, but under the Old Regime their guild produced a counterdiscourse of female honor and corporate pride. Guild officials issued positive images of mistress seamstresses as respectable and responsible public figures, legally privileged interlocutors of the state and successful small entrepreneurs. Once the corporation disappeared, and with it many of the female businesswomen who comprised its membership, this discourse faded. Now seamstresses became the epitome of the degraded "woman worker," whose labor symbolized the tensions and dangers associated with economic transformation.[22]

Association in the 1830s and 1840s was sparked by changing labor conditions and by political circumstances that provided a forum for airing workers' grievances. The Old Regime inheritance did not take the form of a direct "corporate" legacy, inspiring seamstresses to envision their trade as a moral collectivity and to make demands based on this vision. Instead, it resided in the strong conceptual and practical "feminization" of the garment trades and the enhanced sense that needlework was the natural property of women. Seamstresses' numerical dominance of the trade provided them with visibility, a gender-specific work identity, and a perceived legitimacy in trade-based organizations. The corporate past of the seamstresses created the conditions for female labor activism, but it did not determine the forms of association or the contents of their demands. Mistress seamstresses' legal, social, and economic privilege had disappeared, and along with it the self-confident, proud, and exclusionist stance projected by its leaders.

The Parisian Garment Trades, 1880–1917:
Proletarianization and Unions

By the 1880s, the needle trades had expanded to contain some 85,000 female workers.[23] Proletarianization of the trade was now virtually complete. Most women involved in the garment trades were dependent workers employed by male bosses at home, in sweated workshops, or in large manufacturing sites. Driving these changes was the significant growth in the ready-to-wear industry for female clothing in the last decades of the nineteenth century. After years of resistance, premade clothing produced by large-scale manufacturers now took over the market for much of the female wardrobe. These changes were particularly important in the production of coats, blouses, and tailored suits.[24]

The custom-made sector, however, continued to occupy a crucial role in purveying its most traditional product: women's dresses. A significant number of small- and medium-sized custom shops still existed to provide female clients with made-to-measure dresses. Women dominated the less illustrious sectors of this trade—what Nancy Green terms *moyenne* and *petite* couture—working for individual clients from all social classes.[25] Some exceptional *couturières,* such as Madeleine Vionnet, Madame Paquin, and Jeanne Lanvin, succeeded in acquiring fame and prestige in the last years of the nineteenth and first decades of the twentieth century in the high-end sector of *haute couture.* They were increasingly surpassed, however, by male *couturiers.* Celebrated designers, such as Charles Frederick Worth and Jacques Doucet, prefigured the dominance of celebrity male *couturiers* in the twentieth century. Although a few women achieved success in *haute couture,* men were better situated to combine the cultural cachet of the artistic genius with the economic clout of the entrepreneur.[26]

The organized militancy of the 1840s reemerged in the 1870s and 1880s as labor associations gradually acquired legal status. In 1864, the government of Napoleon III repealed its prohibition on strikes, and in 1868 government ministers decided to tolerate labor associations, conditional on police registration and surveillance. Union activism took off after 1884, when the French government formally abrogated the d'Allarde law and allowed trade unions official sanction. The garment trades formed one of the earliest and most militant sites of labor organizing for both men and women. Originating in 1862, the Parisian Tailors' Union began to accept female members in 1868, although it did not allow them to speak in meetings until 1874. In 1889, the feminist newspaper *La Citoyenne* spoke of the creation of a new female sewing union. After 1892, Parisian seamstresses and other female needleworkers joined tailors in an umbrella organization called the Federation of Clothing Workers. The 1890s and 1910s witnessed the continued emergence of new female unions in France and the presence of female delegates at trade union congresses.[27]

Trade unions not only held meetings and made speeches, they also called strikes. Male and female members of the garment trades participated in strikes in 1901, 1910, and 1911. In the latter two movements, women composed the majority of members and occupied leadership positions among strike organizers.[28] This activism culminated in a general strike on May 19, 1917, when more than ten thousand Parisian seamstresses stopped work. They demanded the "English" week — meaning an end to work on Saturday afternoon — and an increase in wages. The strike lasted two weeks, meeting with official tolerance and a certain level of public support. The minister of the interior sponsored negotiations in the trade, which culminated in the acceptance of the English week and collective bargaining.[29]

Public response to the women's strike was bemused, mixing a degree of amused toleration with accusations of female hysteria and, above all, fear of contagion to the munitions industry. Observers were particularly struck by the apparent paradox of well-dressed working-class women participating in organized labor activism. Working in quintessentially female trades, many seamstresses, fashion workers, linenworkers, and flowermakers were young, unmarried women who went on strike in their best clothes and with flowers in their buttonholes. They seemed to onlookers the very emblem of frivolous, gay, and superficial femininity. Their strikes and demonstrations represented a world turned upside down, a carnivalesque street theater, which may have lightened the tensions of this difficult phase of World War I. What bemused observers did not realize was that this paradoxical combination of intrinsic femininity with organized militancy had a 150-year-old history. In the late seventeenth and eighteenth centuries, seamstresses drew on their feminine affiliation with needlework and clothing to establish legal rights over new garments such as hoopskirts and corsets. Observers in the 1720s reacted to their claims with a similar combination of puzzlement and humor, overlaid with indignation at shocking female fashions. The notion of "women's work" propagated by Old Regime seamstresses allowed their nineteenth- and early-twentieth-century descendants to claim labor rights, but it also contributed to essentialized and easily ridiculed images of the female needleworker.

The "Needle Union": The rebirth of the Seamstresses' Guild?

Left-wing labor organization in the 1880s drew an immediate response from the Catholic right. Galvanized by the growth of socialist political power, worker activism, secularization, and the centennial of the detested Revolution, Social Catholics resolved to take action to prove the capacity of organized religion to heal social discord. The Social Catholic association Oeuvre des cercles catholiques, led by Count Albert de Mun, resolved to address worker agitation by reuniting workers and employers in mixed trade associations. De Mun and other Social Catholic activists explicitly modeled these associations on Old Regime guilds, which they conceived in a nostalgic and highly idealized light. For Social Catholics, the attraction of the corporate model lay in the fact that it brought workers and owners together in a harmonious union. In their minds, guilds had served a range of social and economic needs, including protecting professional interests, sponsoring charity for poor masters and workers, and propagating religious faith. Women formed a significant target for Social Catholic organizers, because they believed women to be both more susceptible to religious influence and more vulnerable to corruption.[30]

In 1892, the lady patrons (*dames patronnesses*) of the Oeuvre des cercles catholiques initiated the establishment of the Parisian Union of the Needle (*Syndicat de l'aiguille*) after conducting an inquiry into the living conditions of female garment workers. Like other new "corporations," this was a mixed association that included workers, salaried employees, and owners. By 1896, it contained 241 members, among whom 70 were employers.[31] Social Catholic efforts to "incorporate" female garment and textile workers extended to the provinces as well. Between 1890 and 1894, new organizations came into being in many provincial cities, including Brest, Nantes, Orléans, Lyons, and Carcassonne. These were not cities that had contained independent female guilds under the Old Regime; Nantes was the only place where seamstresses had been members of tailors' guilds. Rather than resulting from local corporate traditions, the creation of new female "corporations" stemmed in many cases from the activities of a particularly zealous local priest.

Research into the garment trades undertaken by Social Catholics and their sympathizers, in combination with problems encountered by the leaders of the union, reveal ways in which some elements of the Old Regime trades persisted in the 1880s and 1890s, despite enormous structural changes. For example, the project of a Union of the Needle created to unite all female needleworkers quickly foundered on the resistance of female workers. Female needleworkers divided into seamstresses, linenworkers, fashionworkers, and artificial flowermakers and feathermakers. The hierarchy of female garment trades in the late nineteenth century also followed the Old Regime taxonomy. According to Social Catholic inquiries, those who worked for fashion merchants occupied the top of the scale, with seamstresses in the middle and linenworkers at the bottom. Needleworkers' loyalties and work identities continued to lie with their own trades, not the garment trades as a whole or their fellow women. Workers evinced pride in the female nature of their trades—as their Old Regime predecessors had done—but this pride did not overcome their "corporate" trade loyalties. As in 1675, a *couturière* in 1892 was a woman who made articles of clothing for other women, working alongside female colleagues. Trade definitions established in the Old Regime thus persisted more than one hundred years later, and indeed the word carries the same connotation in French today. [32]

Despite structural similarities in the garment trades and the persistence of trade loyalties, the Union of the Needle was a creature of the late nineteenth century, born of new economic, social, and political circumstances. The claims of its leaders notwithstanding, it functioned in entirely different ways and was intended to meet different needs than the Old Regime corporation. The seamstresses' guild was created by royal fiat and functioned as a branch of municipal police and administration, while the needleworkers' union had no ties with the state. It had no claim to intervene in the operation of the needle trades themselves, nor could it exclude nonmembers from working as seamstresses or linenworkers. Adherence to the union might bring charitable relief, but it did not alter women's legal or social status as membership in the Old Regime guilds had done. Moreover, rather than tying it to the Old Regime guild, as its founders claimed, the "mixed" composition of the union actually represented a sharp break with that tradition. In contradiction to the nostalgic views of Social Catholics, guilds were composed uniquely of masters and mistresses who fulfilled formal qualifications and paid heavy fees for the privilege of membership. Far from aping this exclusivity, the needleworkers' union struggled constantly and unsuccessfully to extend its membership. It posed no financial or technical obstacles to prospective members.

Old Regime forms of corporate organization thus played little role in shaping nineteenth-century seamstress associations, even among the groups that laid direct claim to the corporate inheritance. The purpose and functions of the Union of the Needle arose from the Social Catholic combat against the modern phenomena of secularization and organized worker agitation. Old Regime female guilds did influence the nineteenth century, however, by firmly establishing the "female" nature of certain garment trades and by outlining the particularistic trade definitions of seamstresses, linen-drapers, fashion workers, and other female workers. These foundations created the conditions for strong female work identities and encouraged workers—or concerned elite observers—to form female associations in these trades. The form and language of association changed, as did its rationale and purpose; however, the conditions of possibility for female trade militancy and organization were a direct legacy from the past.

Façons de dire *and* façons de faire: *An Old Regime in the Twentieth-Century Countryside?*

Seamstresses' ways of speaking and working thus changed enormously from the eighteenth century to the twentieth, along with ways of organizing and representing their labor. One pocket of resistance to these changes lay in the sector of *haute couture,* where highly skilled female needleworkers continued to make custom-made clothing. A second site lay in small towns and villages, where local seamstresses made—and continue to make— clothes for individual female clients. Ethnologist Yvonne Verdier offered a fascinating account of Emilienne, a village seamstress in the Côte d'Or whose career spanned the 1920s to the 1950s, with striking resonance with the Old Regime trade.

Emilienne's occupation consisted of making dresses, skirts, and other outfits for female customers affluent enough to pay for custom-made garments. She reported that she never worked for men and did not make undergarments or linen. Emilienne regularly accepted village girls as apprentices. Few learned to be professional seamstresses and most remained for only one year of female socialization. Those who did learn a trade from Emilienne stayed for three years, during which they learned to sew, make patterns, and fit garments. According to Verdier, village seamstresses often set themselves apart from other women through their elegance and cultivation. They were connected to Paris, spending their youth working there and later subscribing to Parisian fashion magazines.[33]

Was Emilienne a more direct inheritor of the Old Regime than her counterparts in Paris? Did change strike the big towns and cities, leaving an unbroken rural *longue durée* in female needlework? Certain aspects of Emilienne's work, indeed, appear close to the Old Regime. For example, the function of the trade as a vehicle for female socialization and for transmitting culturally normative modes of femininity had persisted across time. Like her Old Regime predecessor, Emilienne mastered a set of techniques and attitudes considered to be essential components of femininity, and she held specialized knowledge of new styles and sophisticated modes of dressing and living. In both eras, seamstresses served as intermediaries between fashionable and elegant elites and less privileged women. Where previously they bridged the great social divides of Paris and other cities, in the 1950s they spanned the geographic distance between urban capitals and the countryside. In both cases, they gave socially and culturally disadvantaged groups access to elite culture.

Seamstresses' role as a primary conduit from nature to culture also continued from the Old Regime to the twentieth century. On the one hand, they helped adolescent girls acquire the skills and comportment of adult femininity through an initiation into the discipline of the needle and female fashions. On the other hand, they endowed elite clients with socially accepted modes of female beauty. As in the Old Regime, the twentieth-century seamstress's responsibility was to help female clients attract male attention. When one client failed to find a suitor at a dance, Verdier reports, she vehemently laid the blame on the dress her seamstress made, leaving the artisan in tears.[34]

Like her eighteenth-century predecessors, Emilienne was set apart from other women by belonging to a female world in which men had little part. Verdier tells us that the village seamstress rarely married or formed a "normal" family, a finding in accord with Old Regime seamstresses' low rates of marriage and childbirth. With their nice clothes and elegant airs, the village seamstress attracted the attention of upper-class men, who dallied with them before marrying a suitable woman of their own milieu. As Verdier's sources told her, it was considered natural for such a woman to experience irregular love affairs and produce illegitimate children, as Emilienne did shortly after starting in business. The seamstress's reputation for light morals and an irregular lifestyle thus persisted for centuries.[35]

As much as the Old Regime can tell us about Emilienne, the village seamstress of the 1950s seems to offer a dim but precious glimpse of Old Regime ways of speaking and doing. It is tempting to see her small workshop and the female relations it embodied as a living model of the eighteenth-century trade. Of course, these continuities should not be exaggerated, nor should her marginal role be forgotten in a modern industry overwhelmingly dominated by ready-to-wear. Even Emilienne's best customers regularly bought dresses from shops in Paris and Dijon, and she was often asked to replicate styles offered there. Threatened in the 1950s, the village seamstress is increasingly rare today. For scholars trying to understand the production and reproduction of femininity and the transmission of gender ideologies over time, however, the continuing cultural and social importance of the seamstress from the eighteenth to the mid-twentieth century is an important source for reflection. With her economic weight drastically reduced from the Old Regime situation, the seamstress still played a distinctive role in the diffusion of models of femininity. As specialists in female taste, beauty, and skill, they helped to bridge gaps in society and culture to produce a shared vision of femininity, which in some ways transcended divisions of fortune and status.

Conclusion

The nineteenth century inherited from the Old Regime the idea that "women's work" was above all needlework, and that women had a privileged right to work in needle trades. Even more than under the Old Regime, this conception of women's work served both to give advantages to female labor in this sector and to restrict female economic opportunities to it. The nineteenth century also inherited the notion that women's work was an important and sensitive issue. One might express radically different opinions about it, but nobody felt that it was a trivial subject. Women's work acquired this importance not only because of concerns about the real suffering and difficulties of female workers, but because of the wider issues it raised, such as fears of female sexual promiscuity, the downfall of families, and ensuing social disorder.

A major transition from the Old Regime to the new, however, lay in the economic and social autonomy that women could acquire through their work. Old Regime administrators recognized that most women needed to work to help support their families, and they took various measures to encourage female employment. Creating guilds was merely one way they did so. Royal administrators could imagine women's inclusion in the guild system, because they thought that at least some forms of female labor were equivalent to male labor and they imagined women to be intrinsically capable of participating in corporate institutions. When they allowed women into the guild system, it was with all the legal, economic, and social privileges that men derived from corporate status. Women used these rights to conduct autonomous careers, acquire leverage over marriage negotiations, or evade marriage altogether.

During the second half of the nineteenth century, women's work was viewed more often as a problem and as a negative outcome of processes of industrialization and modernization. Needlework continued to be seen as the most "natural" form of female labor, but the site of this work and the means by which it took place became subjects of great controversy. There was little expectation or possibility for needleworkers to improve their economic or social position through participation in paid work. No guild existed to give them legal rights in business affairs, to represent their interests to the state, or to disseminate proud images of their labor. Even male trade unions were reluctant to allow women to participate in labor organizations on an equal footing with men. The loss of the guilds, combined with proletarianization and the decline of female entrepreneurship in the garment trades, meant that needlework increasingly became a ghetto for poor women workers.

These changes were part of a broader evolution in forms of social and economic distinction that seamstresses reflected and helped to produce. Before 1675, the tailors' guild ruled the production of clothing. The primary issue was therefore whether one belonged to their guild or not. With the creation of the seamstresses' guild, gender became a form of legal and institutional distinction in the garment trades. A needleworker's place in the trade increasingly had as much or more to do with gender than with guild status. After the abolition of the guilds in 1791, gender became a paramount concern in the division of labor.

In the late twentieth century, needle trades continue to be staffed by female hands. Since the late nineteenth century, however, new divisions and distinctions have emerged, complicating simple binaries between men and women or between owner and worker. As immigrant labor came to occupy an ever larger share of production in the late nineteenth century, race, ethnicity, and citizenship became new gauges of difference and inequality. In many cases, gender and ethnicity overlapped as immigrant women were put to work in urban sweatshops.[36] The relocation of production in the ready-to-wear industry to overseas sites adds another layer of complications to issues of economic, social, and cultural power in the garment trades. At this point, we have traveled far from the Old Regime world of work, too far perhaps to draw parallels or continuities. Conceptually and ideologically, the seamstresses' legacy lives on, but organization, practices, and structures of production and distribution in the garment trades have been almost entirely transformed. An eighteenth-century seamstress would have felt at home in certain ways in the 1890s; at the beginning of the twenty-first century, apart from the diminishing sector of *haute couture,* she would find the garment trades an utterly foreign country. With the survival of *haute couture* increasingly uncertain, the last vestiges of the Old Regime garment trades may disappear, leaving conceptual associations among femininity, fashion, and needlework as vivid but unique legacies of the guild.

Conclusion

Lucien Febure once declared that by analyzing a single button he could explain an entire society and culture. This book has taken a similar position in arguing for the broad insights to be gained about Old Regime France from a study of seamstresses and their trade. Indeed, my claims go even further, for I have suggested that seamstresses not only reflected the economic, social, and cultural world in which they lived, but also played a crucial role in shaping it. Their numbers, institutional organization, and the type of products they made allowed seamstresses an influence far beyond their humble status.

Seamstresses formed one of the largest male or female trades in Old Regime France, consistently outnumbering tailors in their independent or joint guilds. A major reason for the trade's success was the scarcity of alternatives given restrictions on female employment in many trades. It was particularly popular among families whose fathers could not use their daughters' labor at home. To fulfill their paternal duties—and profit from the supplemental income—these fathers looked outside the home for vocational training and employment. They discovered a series of benefits in the seamstresses' trade, including accessible training, low set-up costs, an all-female work environment, corporate regulatory mechanisms, and the potential for guild membership. Moreover, seamstresses' techniques belonged to a range of skills viewed as particularly appropriate for adolescent girls, even if they planned to abandon the trade at marriage. Until new opportunities emerged at the end of the century, this occupation was the choice of families from a surprisingly broad social scale.

Seamstresses were the largest group of apprentices in Paris, but most never became guild mistresses. They left the trade to make a new life outside of Paris or through marriage, illness, and premature death. Others continued as needleworkers, either in the employ of a mistress or as illegal, independent workers. Its great size, diversity, relative lack of guild supervision, and cyclical rhythms of production characterized the seamstresses' labor market. Hiring took place in an informal and dispersed manner, being highly dependent on personal contacts and networks of information exchange. The porous boundary between licit and illicit labor enabled women to pass in and out of legitimate employment, depending on the availability of jobs and clients.

Finished apprentices possessed the best chances for acquiring coveted annual positions guaranteeing lodging, food and full-time employment. Mistresses judged workers on their rapidity, range of techniques, and personal attributes of cleanliness, comportment, and literacy. Most workers held temporary jobs, lasting one to two days, several weeks or months, or many years in the luckiest cases. Day workers were more likely to be provincial immigrants without formal qualifications, burdened with low wages and constant under- or unemployment. Unlike men, they had no collective associations to fall back on and they did not travel outside of Paris in search of work. Begging and prostitution offered a precarious recourse in times of hardship.

Needleworkers were often poor and lacked formal training; their mistresses were usually modest artisans. Together, they formed an essential part of the urban economy. There must have been a seamstress living on every block of Paris, eager to alter and mend garments, or make new dresses, petticoats, and jackets. Women of virtually every social class hired seamstresses: a working girl bringing a second-hand garment for repairs, a shopkeeper's wife splurging on a new dress, or a noblewoman ordering a luxurious dress ensemble with expensive trimmings for her third or fourth new ensemble of the year. Across the eighteenth century, more women ordered more dresses as the amount and price of the fabric they required declined.

Not all seamstresses were alike. Their success depended on the social and economic standing of their clients, who chose them for their skill, imagination, and talent. Successful seamstresses commanded a range of techniques, including the ability to measure clients accurately, make patterns, cut cloth, and sew garments using a variety of stitches. Contemporary technical literature considered this a relatively low-skill trade, but surviving dresses reveal the experience and craftsmanship required to make the numerous pleats, elaborate decorations, and complex internal mechanisms of fancy dresses. In addition to technical proficiency, successful seamstresses mustered a variety of personal and commercial skills. They had to record expenses, purchase good quality supplies at low cost, and maintain written and personal relations with elite clients.

Through their success, seamstresses fostered conditions for their competitors. In the second half of the eighteenth century, the garment industry expanded to include a range of new trades, displacing seamstresses from their former dominance of the labor market. The greatest beneficiaries of women's revolution in consumption were fashion merchants, whose wares ranged from ribbons and trinkets to the luxurious decorations of court gowns. These astute merchants quickly surpassed needleworkers in prestige and economic success. Observers credited them with creating a new Parisian fashion system based on the public boutiques in which they displayed new styles.

Production, Consumption and the Creation of Modern Notions of Gender

As the seamstresses demonstrate, the women of eighteenth-century Paris were not merely parasitic consumers of new fashions; they were also the most important makers and sellers of female clothing and accessories. It was their labor, skill and innovation as much as their self-indulgent spending that drove the clothing revolution. Production and consumption existed in a mutually dynamic relationship, in which it is impossible to assign primary causality. From the mid-seventeenth century on, seamstresses' abundant and cheap labor encouraged women from wider social groups to consume more articles of clothing and renew their wardrobes more frequently. In turn, the growing market for women's clothing allowed seamstresses to flourish, first as an illegal trade group and then as a royally recognized female guild. Rising population across the eighteenth century contributed a great deal to this process, generating increased demand for clothing and a new supply of labor to meet it. With the emergence of the fashion merchants and the parallel rise of a fashion press, however, the relationship between production and consumption became more complex. From the 1750s on, the pace of fashion increased as commercialization and advertising provided new catalysts for consumption. These developments augmented demand for seamstresses' services, but further removed them from the most lucrative sectors of the garment trades.

The strong relationship between consumption and production was not merely part of seamstresses' practical experience, it was inscribed at the heart of their trade definition: a seamstress was a woman who made clothing for other women and children. This sexual division of production and consumption gained new significance in 1675. Guild status endowed seamstresses' trade practices with legal authority and strong normative connotations, which its numerous mistresses disseminated to a wide audience. The result was to enhance, and eventually essentialize, women's role in producing and consuming clothing.

The guild's creation thus had two principal consequences for gender ideologies: a new articulation of the difference between male and female work, and a redefinition of appearances as a uniquely and innately female sphere. In the seventeenth century, "women's work" was an ambiguous concept based on traditional and commonsense ideas about the skills women acquired in their daily lives. The female connotations of sewing allowed seamstresses to claim a moral legitimacy in the garment trades, which eventually won them incorporation as a guild. Over time, the guild's legal and institutional reification of existing notions of women's work contributed to a new level of rigidity in the sexual division of labor. From being a traditional aspect of femininity, needlework became an intrinsically female skill and eventually a biological characteristic of femininity. The primacy of needlework as a quintessential form of "women's work" in the nineteenth century drew directly from the Old Regime guild.

Seamstresses also contributed to changing gender ideologies by casting fashion and appearances as essentially female concerns. Linking women as producers and consumers of clothing, the seamstresses' trade encouraged observers to imagine an innately female sphere of appearances transcending distinctions of social and economic status. Across the eighteenth century, French women of distinct social groups came to share a common commitment to fashioning and displaying their self-identities and their femininity through clothing. In place of other material objects or forms of comportment, clothing became a privileged site of performing femininity. By the same token, French men renounced their centuries-old role in ostentatious sartorial display, giving up the bright colors and luscious fabrics they had previously used to manifest social status, power and virility.

At the same time as they fostered new ideas about femininity, seamstresses also created distinctive social relations among women. One way they did this was by serving as intermediaries between elite and working women. Needleworkers learned about new fashions and styles from their clients, and passed them on to their own workers and apprentices, family members, and neighbors. They also absorbed and transmitted broader patterns of elite behavior and lifestyle. Bonds between aristocratic and working women constituted specific forms of female patronage and mentoring. They were forged over decades of service and maintained through the universal practice of credit in the trade.

Within their own social milieus, the seamstresses' trade fostered distinctive living patterns and strategies. We have long believed that women's fathers and husbands wielded an overlapping legal, economic, and social authority over them, using this power to subsume female interests to those of the male family head. In the tailors' and seamstresses' case, the opposite was often true. Girls' fathers usually chose apprenticeship for them, but once they acquired trade skills seamstresses conducted their businesses independently. By contrast, men in the tailoring trade depended on their wives for access to their guild and for useful connections, advice, and technical skills. Ironically, these men were more dependent on marriage and family than their female counterparts in the needle trades.

These findings indicate the limitations of the historiographical account of the early modern "family economy." Instead of positing one patriarchal family economy, we must acknowledge that a range of different familial and economic strategies existed for men and women. These alternatives potentially reinforced, paralleled, or undermined the patriarchal family as a discrete unit of production and consumption. In many families, husband and wife pursued their own careers and made independent contributions to family wealth. Women's trades could be used not only to generate dowries, but for leverage in the marriage market. The low proportion of seamstresses whose daughters continued in the trade suggests that urban dwellers usually preferred the traditional model in which husband and wife cooperated in professional life. Nevertheless, alternatives were recognized and welcomed by both men and women.

More radically, professional women might establish their own female households, as widowed and single seamstresses created distinctive living units in which familial and professional bonds overlapped. Traces of the trade-specific culture they created survive in the superstitions recorded by late-nineteenth-century folklorists, and the story of Emilienne in the 1950s. The rest have disappeared, along with their daily gestures of work and most of the garments they created. Without romanticizing female social spaces, or exaggerating their cultural distinctiveness, historians need to adopt new methods to analyze them. We need to know more about the social networks women devised and the way professional bonds among women both transgressed recognized social categories and helped create them. To what extent did female trades create social connections among women and foster unusual or unexpected relations between men and women? Beyond trade activities, how did women's participation in credit networks, charitable foundations, and investment resemble or differ from men's, and to what extent did specifically female modes of behavior or interaction exist in these areas?

Along with other guildswomen, seamstresses demonstrate the important role women could play in the guild system of Old Regime France. Their participation ranged from hired female workers in male guild workshops to the ancillary privileges of masters' female kin to the secondary guild status of provincial seamstresses and, finally, to independent mistresses. Contrary to our historiographical impression, women and guilds were not incompatible entities. French women were avid adherents of the guild system when given the opportunity. Parisian seamstresses—like their provincial counterparts—evinced a persistent desire for formal vocational training and guild membership.

What did being a mistress seamstress offer women? First, it gave them concrete economic benefits. Archival sources reveal that guild mistresses fared better economically than nonmistresses. Second, it provided them with enhanced legal rights, to which their independent role in apprenticeship contracts and their trail of corporate lawsuits attest. Finally, although it is difficult to argue from legal briefs to lived experience, seamstresses seem to have derived a distinctive female corporate identity from their guild status. This identity was based on the female nature of the trade and the independence it allowed them vis-à-vis the patriarchal family. Over the eighteenth century, guild leaders forged a notion of female honor based on collective, public, corporate status, rather than a private, sexual purity.

Seamstresses' guild identity emerged largely in opposition to the tailors' preexisting conception of the corporation as a collection of patriarchal families. Behind tailors' defense of their wives' and daughters' privileges stood deeply rooted assumptions about male honor and pride and the interrelation of mastership and family leadership. For both men and women, therefore, guild membership signified not only economic advantages or even a distinct social status, but crucial notions of masculinity and femininity. Nevertheless, gender was clearly more important for seamstresses than for tailors. Their female gender profoundly shaped and constrained their guild practices and identity, generating remarkably similar patterns of trade privilege and guild reproduction in cities across France. For men, gender was merely one factor among many in producing modes of work and corporate membership.

It is also important to note that the categories of gender and guild status do not fully explain seamstresses' behavior or experience. Family ties and trade specialization—and perhaps adherence to other institutions, such as the parish or confraternity—also created loyalties and divisions among female artisans. Moreover, no consensus existed among needleworkers on whether corporate status was a positive or negative development. In Paris, the majority of seamstresses seem to have remained outside of the guild after it was formed in 1675. In Clermont-Ferrand after 1776, seamstresses proudly declared freedom from guild control and resisted tailors' attempts to bring them into their corporation. Were the seamstresses of Aix-en-Provence, Marseilles, and Caen disappointed or jubilant when they lost guild status in 1776?

While the sources do not permit us to answer that question definitely, it is clear that the seamstresses most committed to their guild identities were the acting and former officers that comprised the guild elite. These women hired lawyers, negotiated with state officials, and met regularly to deliberate guild affairs. Parisian guild leaders benefited personally from guild fees, and they appear to have been the sole candidates for its charity. In exchange for these benefits, officials and assembly members provided leadership that was, on the whole, competent, financially sound, and even benevolent. Guild leaders defended mistresses against illegal workers, their own errant colleagues, and outsiders who encroached on their privileges. Across the eighteenth century, they took action to increase the trade rights of the corporation and succeeded in acquiring significant new ones. As a result of their leadership, the guild maintained an impressive financial record and was relatively untouched by the conflict and dissension that divided other corporations. There were strong limits, however, to the guild's effectiveness in intervening in the daily life of the trade. Its most effective surveillance occurred at the signing of the apprenticeship contract, which usually took place in the guild's office. Beyond that point, the tremendous size of the guild's population sharply diminished the investigative or punitive capacity of the six-woman team of *jurées*.

Guild leaders maintained regular contact with public officials and offered their opinions on affairs related to their trade. Did these activities place them within an Old Regime public sphere? What kind of public and political role did guild membership convey to women? Following Jürgen Habermas's account of the public sphere, mistress seamstresses seem to belong to the private sphere of civil society in which commerce and labor take place. This characterization makes sense to the extent that guilds were by definition particularistic institutions, concerned not with universal, public issues, but with their own specific interests and privileges. From another point of view, however, guilds arguably did belong to a public sphere of a particularly Old Regime, corporate nature. Celebratory masses, funeral rites, and guild processions took place in the public eye and reasserted the corporation's position with the crowd who gathered to participate or observe. Moreover, guilds were seen and saw themselves as serving the public good. Their purpose was to ensure an adequate supply of goods for public consumption and to prevent disorder among workers. These public functions were voiced in the oaths of loyalty sworn by new masters and enacted in their police powers over the trade. Guilds were in some sense part of the state; one purpose of their assemblies was to deliberate on affairs pertinent to their trades and inform the king of their opinions.

When women joined guilds, therefore, they self-consciously entered an Old Regime corporate public sphere. The response described in chapter 5 by the bystanders at the seamstress's burial in Caen suggests, however, that contemporaries were less convinced of a legitimate, public role for women than were the guildswomen themselves. While they were long familiar with what I have described as a "corporate public sphere," city dwellers were less accustomed to viewing laywomen occupying a visible place within it. It is possible, however, that the seamstresses' status as junior partners in the only female guild of Caen rendered their public position ambivalent. In Paris or Rouen, where several independent women's guilds existed, gathered crowds may have accepted female assertions of a public identity more readily.

Did their experience in guilds politicize these women? Was membership in the seamstresses' guild a form of political apprenticeship that contributed to protofeminist claims for equal rights under the French Revolution? The answer depends on one's definition of "politics" and "feminism." Certainly, seamstresses learned to be effective actors within the Old Regime political realm, as their success in acquiring new privileges attests. They were especially adept at manipulating the status of their trade as a form of "women's work." Their guild leaders and lawyers used the feminine associations of their trade to argue that they should be allowed to make all garments for women, or, like the Caen seamstresses, that men should be prohibited from making any female garments. Within the limited parameters of their trade, they often succeeded in winning new ground. They did not, however, break free of the restrictions inherent in the notion of "women's work." It apparently never occurred to them to ask for rights to make men's clothing or to demand freedom to make any type of clothing for any client. Instead, they remained within the confines of their paradox, using the limitations of their trade as a source of protection and strength.

The seamstresses were therefore not "feminists" in the sense of demanding universal equality for all women. Old Regime seamstresses never based their claims on a principle of universal equality or equal female status before the law. Unlike Olympe de Gouges or Etta Palm d'Aelders, who demanded political and economic liberty for all women, the seamstresses forged particularistic arguments on behalf of a restricted group. Seamstresses' prerogatives did not ameliorate the legal, economic, or political situation of women in general. Indeed, their guild privileges arguably weakened women's status by erecting enclaves of female employment and lessening the potential for other activities to be seen as appropriate "women's work."

They may yet, however, be characterized as "feminist," to the extent that they made arguments based explicitly on their female sex that aimed to redress the particular limitations women faced in economic and social life. Seamstresses were self-conscious of the inequalities imposed on women in the labor market and therefore viewed their trade as a protected haven of female work and autonomy. Far from jeopardizing other women, they might have argued, their guild offered shelter to any woman who wished to join. Guild officers' vigilance in protecting their corporate privileges stemmed from the need to protect this rare haven, rather than from an exclusionary or antifeminist impulse.

The combination of privilege and constraint in the seamstresses' trade characterized other aspects of women's lives in early modern France. Other female guildswomen and members of female religious orders occupied a similar position. Widows and daughters also obtained exceptional legal and economic privileges as women, which were delimited by their femininity. After the French Revolution, these paradoxical forms of female privilege did not disappear. Throughout the nineteenth century, they persisted alongside the new inconsistency of a republicanism explicitly based on universal equality that excluded women from all forms of political participation. Unfulfilled promises of female equality coexisted with distinct and limited privileges accorded to women on the basis of their sex. Male and female resistance to feminism during the nineteenth and twentieth centuries was frequently justified on the basis of these particular forms of "female" privilege. Exploring the ambiguities of female rights in the pre-Revolutionary period thus provides a crucial perspective for assessing post-Revolutionary political and economic paradoxes of the female condition.

Stepping back from seamstresses' experience as women and guild members, how did this female guild fit into the trajectory of the French state from 1675 to 1791? What lessons do the seamstresses offer for understanding changes in the intentions and function of the Old Regime state and the corporate system it regulated? A first lesson involves the relationship between women's status and the growth of state power. Colbert's tenure as controller general arguably marked the apogee of royal intervention in the economy and society. Contrary to what one might expect, it did not result in the lowest period of female capacity, but the creation of a new independent female guild, with the array of legal, economic, and social advantages it offered. State rationalizing and centralizing impulses could thus endow women with new levels of equality, responsibility, and opportunity. There was no inherent relationship between the rise of state power and the decline of female status. No "compact" existed between the royal government and the patriarchal family. Indeed, by giving privileges to seamstresses, the crown ended up diminishing the status of the patriarchal family in favor of women's autonomous rights. This did not stem from an explicitly profeminist impulse on the royal government's part; in the same way, edicts whose result was to diminish women's rights were often not explicitly misogynistic. Instead, they were the local consequences of administrative efforts to solve specific economic, social, and legal problems. These efforts were, of course, guided by cultural notions of "appropriate" solutions, but over time innovative approaches to problem solving helped change cultural ideas.

Drawing on the first point, a second lesson involves the social and cultural consequences of state centralization and rationalization for ideas about gender. I have argued that seamstresses helped shape modern French gender ideologies by outlining a new sexual division of production and consumption. More broadly, the seamstresses' guild also raised the profile of sexual difference itself as a category for organizing society. Instead of family ties or gender-neutral corporate privileges, the seamstresses' guild was defined by the sex of its members. Although its privileges were defined by law, they had the effect of suggesting that the law itself was less important than were natural gender differences. The visibility and size of the guild helped disseminate the notion of distinguishing between men and women on a systematic basis and of segregating society on the basis of sex. Sexual difference as a principle for ordering society, in this case at least, grew out of royal efforts toward regularizing and rationalizing economic production. Before Enlightenment authors, such as Rousseau, identified essentialized characteristics of masculinity and femininity—and rationalized excluding women from public life based on their ascribed sexual characteristics—government administrative initiatives had fostered the idea of social segregation and policy making based on sexual difference. The use of sex as a tool of decision making helped some women, such as the seamstresses, who worked in "female" trades or occupied recognized feminine sectors of society. It disadvantaged others, who held prerogatives based on their family ties. These women, and their male kin, experienced the new principle of sexual difference as a corrosion of the traditional bonds and privileges they had enjoyed.

The multifaceted results of the guild's creation reveal a final lesson, that of the continuing significance of corporations as institutions and the the state's efficacy in shaping and influencing its subjects' lives through its influence on institutions. The accepted trajectory of corporate society—and by extension of the Old Regime state—cannot hold. Guilds were not dead institutions in eighteenth-century France. They continued to attract adherents, whether for self-interested or idealistic motives. Guild regulations regarding training, admissions, and work practices affected artisans' marital and family strategies, self-identities, and work lives. Corporate rules did not bring new trades or techniques into existence, but they did profoundly influence the social and cultural worlds of artisans and merchants. Behind guild organization stood the state, which ruled the creation of new guilds, their regulations, and the varieties of privilege among them. Through the commission to audit guild finances, the sale of offices, and the royal procurator at the Châtelet of Paris, the royal government continuously and effectively intervened in corporate affairs. Sometimes the effects of this intervention were purposeful and willed; more often they emerged as inadvertent or unconscious consequences.

Guilds did not disappear or dwindle away in the second half of the eighteenth century. They certainly changed in many ways, and public perceptions of them altered a great deal, but they continued to be crucial institutions for their members and for the state. Seamstresses' energetic engagement with guilds and state officials demonstrates that the politics of the absolutist monarchy had not withered away or radically transformed, but continued to operate and offer meaningful interaction to its subjects up to 1776 at least. The reforms of 1776 radically altered the guild system. Viewed by historians as the prolonged death spasm of the corporations, the period from 1776 to 1791 witnessed the emergence of a profoundly different system. The guilds were not ineluctably doomed to extinction in 1791, but their abolition makes it difficult to assess the impact of the 1776 reforms and the new system's potential for adaptation and survival. The use women would have made of their equal access to the guild system after 1776 must remain unknown. In the case of the seamstresses, at any rate, we may conclude that the inclusion of women in the guild system was as much a sign of its flexibility and ability to adapt to new circumstances as it was of its weakness.

The seamstresses' story was in many ways a triumphant one. They prove emphatically that women did not experience an absolute decline in status in seventeenth- or eighteenth-century France, but that, on the contrary, many women acquired new economic and social opportunities. Their story, however, also has darker undertones. In particular, their legacy in terms of the sexual division of labor and conceptions of femininity is fundamentally ambivalent. As an archetypal form of women's work, needlework was a source both of strength and of suffocation. Perhaps difficult to concede in the context of modern-day sweatshops, Old Regime seamstresses drew a considerable amount of power from the sexual division of labor they helped create. For a long time, needlework benefited these women, who had few other choices for obtaining autonomous careers or surviving outside of marriage. Its downfall resulted, as seamstresses feared, from the opening of the market, proletarianization, and the loss of control to men. The needleworkers' union of the 1890s throws into perspective the extent to which the eighteenth-century guild system offered a small group of privileged craftswomen a type of autonomy and self-organization almost impossible to imagine in the nineteenth century. Outside of the trade, female activists were not so sure of the benefits of needlework. Beginning in the late eighteenth century, feminists began to press claims for opening all economic activities to women. They insisted, quite rightly, that the strong association between women and needlework had done much to prevent women from entering other trades.

Another mixed legacy of the seamstresses has been the connection they helped establish between femininity and fashion. To this day, to be a woman is to be expected to express one's femininity through a special relationship to clothing and appearances. This is another aspect of womanhood that some women have experienced as empowering, but others have criticized as imposing external and restrictive conceptions of femininity. Being obliged to maintain appropriate female appearances, they point out, frequently makes it impossible for women to be taken seriously for anything else. The seamstresses and their clients reveal the extent to which women participated in creating these double binds. They reached out for the potential advantages of "women's work" and "female appearances"—in the form of guild status, economic autonomy, or informal sexual power— as much as they suffered in silence from them. Definitions of femininity were imposed from the outside, but they were also created and adopted by some women as strategies to negotiate the myriad restrictions they faced. Needlework has been a female ghetto of exhausting labor and low wages; it has also offered employment, sociability, and forms of creative expression. Maintaining female appearances required discomfort, pain, and sometimes physical mutilation, yet appearance has also been a site of the formation of female identity, of imagination and play, and of certain kinds of female power. The *maîtresses couturières* of Old Regime France have been replaced by celebrated male *couturiers,* and their workers by computerized machines and overseas sweatshops, yet the ambivalent legacy of needlework as women's work and the idea of fashion and appearances as a distinctly female concern remain vivid and contested aspects of French culture up to the present day. The fact that so many other societies share these concerns reveals that the seamstresses are one part of a story with much broader historical and geographical dimensions.

Notes

Introduction

1 Jean-Jacques Rousseau, *Emile ou de l'éducation,* ed. François Richard and Pierre Richard (1762; Paris: Editions Garnier Frères, 1961), 232.

2 The word *tailleur* comes from the late Latin verb *taliare* (to cut), while *couturier* and *couturière* derive from the Latin verb *consuere* (to sew). See *Le Robert Dictionnaire historique de la langue française,* vol. 1, ed. Alain Ray (Paris: Dictionnaires le Robert, 1992), vol. 1, 519.

3 René de Lespinasse and François Bonnardot, eds., *Le Livre des métiers d'Etienne Boileau* (Paris: Imprimerie nationale, 1879), 116.

4 *Couturier* is found in some sixteenth-century apprenticeship contracts and it is also used as a term for tailor in the late-fifteenth-century play *La Farce du cousturier,* published in Emmanuel Philipot, *Recherches sur l'ancien théâtre français, Trois farces du recueil de Londres, "Le Cousturier et Esopet, Le Cuvier, Maistre Mimin estudiant"* (Rennes: Plihon, 1931). On apprenticeship, see Carol Lee Loats, "Gender and Work in Sixteenth-Century Paris" (Ph.D. diss., University of Colorado, 1993).

5 Pierre Richelet, *Dictionnaire françois,* vol. 1 (1680; Genève: Slatkine, 1970), *couturier.* In 1690, Antoine Furetière echoed this definition, noting that the term was used for village tailors, or nonmaster tailors in the city, whose chief occupation was mending clothes for used-clothes dealers or for the poor. Antoine Furetière, *Dictionnaire universel,* vol. 1 (1690; Geneva: Slatkine, 1970), *couturier.*

6 *Le Dictionnaire de l'Académie françoise,* vol. 1 (1694; Lille: L. Danel, 1901), vol. 1, *couturier.*

7 *Le Robert Dictionnaire historique de la langue française* (519) gives the origins of *couturière* as follows: "D'abord costurere (v. 1150) et cousturère (v. 1200) désigne d'abord une femme qui fait de la couture professionnellement ou non."

8 Richelet, *Dictionnaire françois, couturière.*

9 *Le Dictionnaire de l'Académie françoise, couturière.*

10 *Encyclopédie, ou Dictionnaire raisonné des sciences, des arts et des métiers,* ed. Denis Diderot and Jean d'Alembert, vol. 4 (1751–1780; Stuttgard-Bad Cannstatt: From-

mann, 1966), 420, *couturière*. There was no entry for the male form, *couturier*, in the *Encyclopédie*.

11 Classic histories of the guilds in France include Emile Levasseur, *Histoire des classes ouvrières et de l'industrie en France avant 1789*, 2 vols. (1901; Geneva: Slatkine, 1981); Etienne Martin Saint-Léon, *Histoire des corporations de métiers depuis leurs origines jusqu'à leur suppression en 1791* (1909; Paris: Alcan, 1922); François Olivier-Martin, *L'Organisation corporative de la France d'Ancien Régime* (Paris: Librairie du Recueil Sirey, 1938); and Emile Coornaert, *Les corporations en France avant 1789* (Paris: Gallimard, 1941).

12 See, for example, Marcel Marion's account of guild defects and abuses in his *Dictionnaire des institutions de la France aux XVIIe et XVIIIe siècles* (1923; Paris: Picard, 1989), 144–52, *corporation*. This view of the guilds as "backward" and resistant to progress made its way into standard syntheses of French history in the 1960s and 1970s. See, for example, Robert Mandrou, *La France aux XVIIe et XVIIIe siècles* (1967; Paris: Presses universitaires de France, 1987), 92–95; Pierre Goubert, *Louis XIV et vingt millions de Français* (Paris: Fayard, 1966), 68–69, and *The Ancien Régime: French Society, 1600–1750*, trans. Steve Cox (New York: Harper and Row, 1973), 215; and Jacques Godechot, *Institutions de la France sous la Révolution et l'Empire* (Paris: Presses universitaires de France, 1968), 20. Among American historians, see William Reddy, *The Rise of Market Culture* (Cambridge, Eng.: Cambridge University Press, 1984), 34–38. Hilton Root has recently reinvigorated the liberal critique of guilds as one element of the overall blockage that state intervention and regulation imposed on the Old Regime economy. See Hilton L. Root, *La construction de l'Etat moderne en Europe: La France et l'Angleterre* (Paris: Presses universitaires de France, 1994), 139, 155 passim. See also the discussion of this historiography in Philippe Minard, "L'inspection des manufactures en France, de Colbert à la Révolution" (Ph.D. diss., Université Paris I-Panthéon-Sorbonne, 1994), 1–14; and Gail Bossenga, *The Politics of Privilege: Old Regime and Revolution in Lille* (Cambridge, Eng.: Cambridge University Press, 1991), 131, 166–67.

13 Steven Kaplan has published numerous articles and books on work and the regulation of trade in Old Regime France. These studies are too numerous to be listed here but are given in the bibliography. His most recent work is *The Bakers of Paris and the Bread Question* (Durham, N.C.: Duke University Press, 1996). See also Steven L. Kaplan and Cynthia Koepp, eds., *Work in France: Representations, Meaning, Organization, and Practice* (Ithaca: Cornell University Press, 1986); Michael Sonenscher, *Work and Wages: Natural Law, Politics, and the Eighteenth-Century French Trades* (Cambridge, Eng.: Cambridge University Press, 1989), and *The Hatters of Eighteenth-Century France* (Berkeley: University of California Press, 1987); James R. Farr, *Hands of Honor: Artisans and Their World in Dijon, 1550–1650* (Ithaca: Cornell University Press, 1988); Bossenga, *The Politics of Privilege;* William Sewell, *Work and Revolution in France: The Language of Labor from the Old Regime to 1848* (Cambridge, Eng.: Cambridge University Press, 1980); and Simona Cerutti, *La Ville et les métiers: Naissance d'un langage corporatif (Turin XVIIe–XVIIIe siècle)* (Paris: Editions de l'Ecole des hautes études en sciences sociales, 1990); and

Cynthia Truant, *The Rites of Labor: Brotherhoods of Compagnonnages in Old and New Regime France* (Ithaca: Cornell University Press, 1994).

14 On the relationship between state finances and privileged corps, see David Bien, "Offices, Corps, and a System of State Credit: The Uses of Privilege under the Ancien Régime," in *The Political Culture of the Old Regime,* vol. 1 of *The French Revolution and the Creation of Modern Political Culture,* ed. Keith Michael Baker (Oxford: Oxford University Press, 1987).

15 Steven L. Kaplan, "Les Corporations, les faux ouvriers et le faubourg Saint-Antoine," *Annales ESC* 40 (mars–avril 1988): 253–88, and "The Character and Implications of Strife among Masters Inside the Guilds of Eighteenth-Century Paris," *Journal of Social History* 19 (summer 1986): 631–48. See also Sonenscher, *Work and Wages,* 27.

16 Kaplan, "Social Classification and Representation in the Corporate World of Eighteenth-Century France: Turgot's Carnival," in *Work in France,* ed. Kaplan and Koepp.

17 See Sonenscher, *Work and Wages;* and Cerutti, *La Ville et les métiers.*

18 Jacques-Louis Ménétra, *Journal of My Life,* ed. Daniel Roche, trans. Arthur Goldhammer (New York: Columbia University Press, 1986).

19 So far, historians have largely limited themselves to noting the frequent presence of women in artisanal workshops. They have indicated the substantial role played by wives, daughters, and hired female employees. With few exceptions, however, they have not developed these observations with significant research or analysis. Studies of the guilds have barely explored the economic importance of female labor for incorporated trades, the difference these activities made to women's position in the family and the neighborhood, or the overall range of possibilities open to women in the corporate system as wives, widows, daughters, workers, or independent mistresses. For exceptions, see Maurice Garden on women in the silk-weaving industry in *Lyon et les lyonnais au XVIIIe siècle* (Paris: Les Belle Lettres, 1970); and Kaplan's account of the female elements of the bakers' trade in *The Bakers of Paris,* 105–9, 122–24.

20 On women in male guild trades, see Daryl Hafter, "Female Masters in the Ribbonmaking Guild of Eighteenth-Century Rouen," *French Historical Studies* 20, no. 1 (winter 1997): 1–14; and Elizabeth C. Musgrave, "Women in the Male World of Work: The Building Industries of Eighteenth-Century Brittany," *French History* 7, no. 1 (1989): 30–52. See also Daryl Hafter, "Women Who Wove in the Eighteenth-Century Silk Industry of Lyon," in *European Women and Preindustrial Craft,* ed. Daryl Hafter (Bloomington: Indiana University Press, 1995), and "Gender Formation from a Working-Class Viewpoint," in *Proceedings of the Annual Meeting of the Western Society for French History, 1988* 16 (1989): 415–22. On female apprentices, see Loats, "Gender and Work in Sixteenth-Century Paris," and "Gender, Guilds, and Work Identity: Perspectives from Sixteenth-Century Paris," *French Historical Studies* 20, no. 1 (winter 1997): 15–30. See also the response by William Sewell Jr., "Social and Cultural Perspectives on Women's Work: Comment on Loats, Hafter, and DeGroat," in the same issue, 49–54. Cynthia Truant's essays on women in the Parisian guilds emphasize the public role women ac-

quired through membership in guilds; see especially her "Parisian Guildswomen and the (Sexual) Politics of Privilege: Defending Their Patrimonies in Print," in *Going Public: Women and Publishing in Early Modern France*, ed. Elizabeth Goldsmith and Dena Goodman (Ithaca: Cornell University Press, 1995), and "The Guildswomen of Paris: Gender, Power, and Sociability in the Old Regime," in *Proceedings of the Annual Meeting of the Western Society for French History, 1987* 15 (1988): 130–38. See also Truant's essay "La maîtrise d'une identité? Corporations féminines à Paris aux XVIIe et XVIIIe siècles," and the companion essays in "Métiers, Corporations, Syndicalismes," a special issue of *Clio, Histoire, Femmes et Sociétés* 3 (1996). Finally, see Judith G. Coffin, "Gender and the Guild Order: The Garment Trades in Eighteenth-Century Paris," *The Journal of Economic History* 54, no. 4 (December 1994): 768–93.

21 The other three were the linen-drapers, the hemp merchants, and the fresh-flower sellers. See chapter 4 for an account of these guilds.

22 See Natalie Zemon Davis, *Society and Culture in Early Modern France* (Stanford: Stanford University Press, 1975), and "Women in the Crafts in Sixteenth-Century Lyon," in *Women and Work in Pre-Industrial Europe*, ed. Barbara A. Hanawalt (Bloomington: Indiana University Press, 1986). See also Louise A. Tilly and Joan W. Scott, *Women, Work, and Family* (New York: Holt, Rinehart and Winston, 1978); and works by Olwen Hufton, including *The Prospect before Her: A History of Women in Western Europe, 1500–1800* (New York: Vintage Books, 1998), "Women and the Family Economy in Eighteenth-Century France," *French Historical Studies* 9, no. 1 (spring 1975): 1–22, and "Women, Work, and Marriage in Eighteenth-Century France," in *Marriage and Society: Studies in the Social History of Marriage*, ed. R. B. Outhwaite (New York: St. Martin's Press, 1981). See also Gay Gullickson, *Spinners and Weavers of Auffay: Rural Industry and the Sexual Division of Labor in a French Village, 1750–1850* (Cambridge, Eng.: Cambridge University Press, 1986); Tessie Liu, *The Weavers' Knot: The Contradictions of Class Struggle and Family Solidarity in Western France, 1750–1914* (Ithaca: Cornell University Press, 1994); Hafter, ed., *European Women and Preindustrial Craft*; and James B. Collins, "The Economic Role of Women in Seventeenth-Century France," *French Historical Studies* 16, no. 2 (fall 1989): 436–70.

23 Joan Scott's work has been of tremendous importance for me, particularly her collections *Gender and the Politics of History* (New York: Columbia University Press, 1988) and, with Judith Butler, *Feminists Theorize the Political* (New York: Routledge, 1992). I have also relied on scholars offering their own visions of gender and gender history. See, for example, Isabel V. Hull, "Feminist and Gender History through the Literary Looking Glass: German Historiography in Post-modern Times," *Central European History* 22, no. 3 (1989): 279–300; Kathleen Canning, "Feminist History after the Linguistic Turn: Historicizing Discourse and Experience," *Signs* 19, no. 2 (1993): 368–404; and Laura L. Frader and Sonya O. Rose, "Introduction: Gender and the Reconstruction of European Working-Class History," in *Gender and Class in Modern Europe*, ed. Laura L. Frader and Sonya O. Rose (Ithaca: Cornell University Press, 1996), 1–36. See also Judith Butler, *Gender Trouble: Feminism and the Subversion of Identity* (New York: Routledge,

1990) and *Bodies that Matter: On the Discursive Limits of Sex* (New York: Routledge, 1993).

24 For these arguments, see Merry Wiesner, *Gender, Church, and State in Early Modern Germany* (London: Longman, 1998), and *Working Women in Renaissance Germany* (New Brunswick, N.J.: Rutgers University Press, 1986); Martha Howell, *Women, Production, and Patriarchy in Late Medieval Cities* (Chicago: University of Chicago Press, 1986), and "Women, the Family Economy, and the Structures of Market Production in Cities of Northern Europe during the Late Middle Ages," in *Women and Work in Preindustrial Europe,* ed. Hanawalt. See also Lyndal Roper, *The Holy Household: Women and Morals in Reformation Augusburg* (Oxford: Oxford University Press, 1989), 42–49; and Jean Quataert, "The Shaping of Women's Work in Manufacturing: Guilds, Households, and the State in Central Europe, 1648–1870," *American Historical Review* 90 (December 1985): 1122–48.

Although most of these studies concern Germany, their authors have often made European-wide claims, and English and French historians have largely accepted their arguments. See, for example, the comments of English historian Judith M. Bennett in " 'History that Stands Still': Women's Work in the European Past," *Feminist Studies* 14, no. 2 (summer 1988): 269–83. For a similar statement about French women's loss of guild status and overall economic and social opportunities across the sixteenth and seventeenth centuries, see Natalie Zemon Davis, "City Women and Religious Change," in *Society and Culture in Early Modern France,* 94. James Collins has argued that women faced increasing "institutional restrictions" in the seventeenth century, provoked by the fact that their practical choices and economic roles actually grew during this period. See "The Economic Role of Women in Seventeenth-Century France." Collins explicitly relies on the work of Sarah Hanley, who claims that a "family-state compact" increasingly placed women under the control of patriarchal families in the early modern period. According to Hanley, the centralizing state built its authority on families, rewarding male households for their compliance by guaranteeing them greater control over members of the household, including women. See Sarah Hanley, "Engendering the State: Family Formation and State Building in Early Modern France," *French Historical Studies* 16, no. 1 (spring 1989): 4–27, and more recently, "Social Sites of Political Practice in France: Lawsuits, Civil Rights, and the Separation of Powers in Domestic and State Government, 1500–1800," *American Historical Review* 102, no. 1 (February 1997): 27–52. My argument in this book is that in important ways women did not face new institutional restrictions across the early modern period but new institutional opportunities.

25 Scholars of eighteenth-century England pioneered the history of consumption. See Neil McKendrick, John Brewer, and J. H. Plumb, eds., *The Birth of a Consumer Society: The Commercialization of Eighteenth-Century England* (Bloomington: Indiana University Press, 1982); John Brewer and Roy Porter, eds., *Consumption and the World of Goods* (London: Routledge, 1993); Anne Bermingham and John Brewer, eds., *The Consumption of Culture, 1600–1800* (London: Routledge, 1995); John Brewer and Susan Staves, eds., *Early Modern Conceptions of Property* (London: Routledge, 1995); and Beverly Lemire, *Fashion's Favourite: The Cotton Trade*

and the Consumer in Britain, 1660–1800 (Oxford: Oxford University Press, 1991). For considerations of the "gendered" nature of consumer culture, see Victoria de Grazia, ed., *The Sex of Things: Gender and Consumption in Historical Perspective* (Berkeley: University of California Press, 1996); Whitney Walton, *France at the Crystal Palace: Bourgeois Taste and Artisan Manufacture* (Berkeley: University of California Press, 1992); and Leora Auslander, *Taste and Power: Furnishing Modern France* (Berkeley: University of California Press, 1996). The most important works on consumption in France under the Old Regime include Daniel Roche, *The Culture of Clothing: Dress and Fashion in the "Ancien Régime,"* trans. Jean Birrell (Cambridge, Eng.: Cambridge University Press, 1994), and *A History of Everyday Things: The Birth of Consumption in France, 1600–1800,* trans. Brian Pearce (Cambridge, Eng.: Cambridge University Press, 2000); Philippe Perrot, *Le luxe, une richesse entre faste et confort, XVIIIe–XIXe siècles* (Paris: Editions du Seuil, 1995), and *Les dessus et les dessous de la bourgeoisie, une histoire du vêtement au XIXe siècle* (Paris: Fayard, 1981); Annik Pardailhé-Galabrun, *The Birth of Intimacy: Privacy and Domestic Life in Early Modern Paris,* trans. Jocelyn Phelps (Philadelphia: University of Pennsylvania Press, 1991); Auslander, *Taste and Power;* and Fairchilds, "The Production and Marketing of Populuxe Goods in Eighteenth-Century Paris," in *Consumption and the World of Goods,* ed. Brewer and Porter.

26 Roche, *The Culture of Clothing,* chapter 5: "The Hierarchy of Appearances in Paris from Louis XIV to Louis XVI," 86–117.

27 A great deal has been written about the "crisis" of social history of the early and mid-1980s and the search for new methods and theoretical approaches. Critics pointed to social history's reliance on external, ostensibly objective, categories of analysis that seemed to reify social institutions and classes; they also insisted on the need to problematize the textual nature of historical sources. The crisis was international, but responses to it have varied, from the American "linguistic turn" and "new cultural history" to the Italian interest in microhistory. In France, a striking symptom of the crisis emerged in the reorientation of the *Annales* journal; see *Annales* editors, "Let's Try the Experiment," translated in *Histories: French Constructions of the Past,* ed. Jacques Revel and Lynn Hunt (New York: New Press, 1995). For insightful analyses of the problems associated with social history and potential solutions, see Jacques Revel, "Microanalysis and the Construction of the Social," and Roger Chartier, "The World as Representation," both translated in *Histories: French Constructions of the Past,* ed. Revel and Hunt. The emergence of gender, as opposed to women's, history was part of the larger move away from social history and toward cultural history; see in particular Scott, "Gender: A Useful Category of Historical Analysis," in *Gender and the Politics of History.* For recent perspectives on merging social and cultural history, see Victoria E. Bonnell and Lynn Hunt, eds., *Beyond the Cultural Turn* (Berkeley: University of California Press, 1999).

28 At the beginning of this project, Cynthia Truant very kindly furnished the names of the notaries who served the seamstresses' guild.

29 See Arlette Farge, *Fragile Lives: Violence, Power, and Solidarity in Eighteenth-Century Paris,* trans. Carol Shelton (Cambridge, Mass.: Harvard University Press, 1993) for

a gripping account of the tribulations of popular life in Paris in the eighteenth century.

ONE *Seamstresses and the Culture of Clothing in Old Regime France*

1 Roche, *The Culture of Clothing,* 86–117.
2 For Mary Wollstonecraft's critique of women's devotion to fashion and appearances, see Mary Wollstonecraft, *A Vindication of the Rights of Women,* ed. Carol H. Poston (1792; New York: Norton, 1988), 28–31, 43–52, 75–77. See also Jennifer Jones, " 'The Taste for Fashion and Frivolity': Gender, Clothing, and the Commercial Culture of the Old Regime" (Ph.D. diss., Princeton University, 1991), 1–4.
3 Thorstein Veblen, *The Theory of the Leisure Class: An Economic Study of Institutions* (1899: New York: Penguin Books, 1994), 80–85.
4 On consumption and gender identity, see Elizabeth Kowaleski-Wallace, *Consuming Subjects: Women, Shopping, and Business in the Eighteenth Century* (New York: Columbia University Press, 1997), 5. For gendered analyses of consumption, see de Grazia, ed., *The Sex of Things;* and Vickery, "Women and the World of Goods: A Lancashire Consumer and Her Possessions, 1751–81," in *Consumption and the World of Goods,* ed. Brewer and Porter.
5 For one attempt to reconcile production and consumption, see de Vries, "Purchasing Power and the World of Goods: Understanding the Household Economy in Early Modern Europe," in *Consumption and the World of Goods,* ed. Brewer and Porter.
6 For anthropological discussions of the significance of dress and textiles, see Ruth Barnes and Joanne B. Eicher, eds., *Dress and Gender: Making and Meaning* (Providence, R.I.: Berg Publishers, 1992); Annette B. Weiner and Jane Schneider, eds., *Cloth and Human Experience* (Washington, D.C.: Smithsonian Institution Press, 1989); J. Cordwell and R. A. Schwarz, eds., *The Fabrics of Culture* (The Hague: Mouton Press, 1979); and J. A. Hamilton and J. W. Hamilton, "Dress as a Reflection and Sustainer of Social Reality: A Cross-Cultural Perspective," *Clothing and Textiles Research Journal* 7, no. 2 (1989): 16–22. On the relationship between clothing and gender in the American context, see Claudia Brush Kidwell and Valerie Steele, eds., *Men and Women: Dressing the Part* (Washington, D.C.: Smithsonian Institution Press, 1989).
7 Georg Simmel, "Fashion," *American Journal of Sociology* 62 (1904; May 1957), 541–88.
8 The "bourgeois gentleman" is Monsieur Jourdan, the antihero of Molière's comedy by that name. See Molière, *Le Bourgeois gentilhomme, Les Femmes savantes, Le Malade imaginaire,* ed. Georges Couton (Paris: Gallimard, 1973). For an analysis of one story about cross-class dressing, see Nicole Pellegrin, "L'être et le paraître au XVIIe siècle: Les apparences vestimentaires dans l'*Histoire comique de Francion* de Charles Sorel," in *La France d'Ancien régime: Etudes réunies en l'honneur de Pierre Goubert,* vol. 2 (Toulouse: Privat 1984): 519–29. See also Daniel Roche's analysis of *Le Bourgeois gentilhomme* in *The Culture of Clothing,* 91–93.

9　On the limitations of the "emulation" model, see Colin Campbell, "Understanding Traditional and Modern Patterns of Consumption in Eighteenth-Century England: A Character-Action Approach," in *Consumption and the World of Goods,* ed. Brewer and Porter, and *The Romantic Ethic and the Spirit of Modern Consumerism* (Oxford: Basil Blackwell, 1987). On the relationship between language and clothing, see Alan Hunt, *Governance of the Consuming Passions: A History of Sumptuary Law* (New York: St. Martin's Press, 1996), 64, where he states: "Dress allows us to make 'statements' in our presentation of self that would involve much higher risks if they were made in the more explicit medium of spoken language." See also Grant McCracken, *Culture and Consumption: New Approaches to the Symbolic Character of Consumer Goods and Activities* (Bloomington: Indiana University Press, 1988), 57–70.

10　An enormous literature exists on the history of fashion in France during the seventeenth and eighteenth centuries. See J. Quicherat, *Histoire du costume en France depuis les temps les plus reculés jusqu'à la fin du XVIIIe siècle* (Paris: Hachette, 1875); Maurice Leloir, *Dictionnaire du costume et de ses accessoires* (Paris: Grund, 1951), and *Histoire du costume de l'antiquité à 1914,* vol. 9: *Epoque Louis XIV (Première partie) de 1643 à 1678* (Paris: H. Ernst, 1934); Carl Kohler, *A History of Costume,* trans. Alexander K. Dallas (1928; New York: Dover Publications, 1963); François Boucher, *Histoire du costume en Occident, de l'Antiquité à nos jours* (Paris: Flammarion, 1965); Yvonne Deslandres, *Le Costume, image de l'homme* (Paris: Albin Michel, 1976); Madeleine Delpierre, *Dress in France in the Eighteenth Century,* trans. Caroline Beamish (New Haven: Yale University Press, 1997); James Laver, *L'Histoire de la mode et du costume,* trans. Michèle Hechter (Paris: Thames & Hudson, 1990); Aileen Ribeiro, *The Art of Dress: Fashion in England and France 1750–1820* (New Haven: Yale University Press, 1995), and *Dress in Eighteenth-Century Europe* (London: B. T. Batsford, 1984). See also the numerous museum exhibition catalogues, including *Costumes français du XVIIIe siècle, 1715–1789* (Paris: Musée Carnavalet, November 1954–January 1955); *Elégances du XVIIIe siècle, costumes français, 1730–1794* (Paris: Musée de la mode et du costume, December 1963–April 1964); Madeleine Delpierre, *La mode et ses métiers du XVIIIe siècle à nos jours* (Paris: Musée de la mode et du costume, 1981), and *Modes enfantines, 1750–1950* (Paris: Musée de la mode et du costume, 1979).

11　Jean-Jacques Rousseau, "Lettre à d'Alembert," in *Discours sur les sciences et les arts: Lettre à d'Alembert,* ed. Jean Varloot (Paris: Gallimard, 1987), 213.

12　Sumptuary laws imposing distinctions between noble and nonnoble attire remained in force to the end of the Old Regime. In 1629, Louis XIII reiterated prohibitions against nonnoble use of precious stones and gold embroidery in clothing. The wearing of a sword also remained—at least in theory—an exclusive privilege of the Second Estate up to the French Revolution.

13　Historians have long pointed out the special emphasis on the king's body in French monarchical ideology. Classics include Ernst H. Kantorowicz, *The King's Two Bodies: A Study in Mediaeval Political Theology* (Princeton: Princeton University Press, 1957); Marc Bloch, *The Royal Touch: Sacred Monarchy and Scrofula in England and France,* trans. J. E. Anderson (London: Routledge, 1973); and Norbert

Elias, *The Court Society,* trans. Edmund Jephcott (New York: Pantheon Books, 1983). With recent historiographical interest in "political culture" a new literature has emerged on the role of the body in the political symbolism of Old Regime and Revolutionary France. See Lynn Hunt, ed., *The Invention of Pornography: Obscenity and the Origins of Modernity, 1500–1800* (New York: Zone Books, 1993); Antoine de Baecque, *Le Corps de l'histoire: Métaphores et politique (1770–1800)* (Paris: Calmann-Lévy, 1993); Dorinda Outram, *The Body and the French Revolution: Sex, Class, and Political Culture* (New Haven: Yale University Press, 1989); and Sara E. Melzer and Kathryn Norberg, eds., *From the Royal to the Republican Body: Incorporating the Political in Seventeenth- and Eighteenth-Century France* (Berkeley: University of California Press, 1998).

14 Nicolas Faret, *L'honneste homme ou l'art de plaire à la court* (1636; Geneva: Slatkine, 1970), 91. The visual markers of elite status did not end with the exterior layer of cloth. By the time of Louis XIV, the French aristocracy had undergone a century of training in controlling and disciplining their bodies. The notion of *civilité,* propagated in etiquette manuals from the sixteenth century on, taught not only correct manners and discourse but proper bodily comportment as well. These lessons included prohibitions against spitting, eating with one's fingers, and urinating in public, as well as positive commandments to hold oneself upright and restrain bodily movements. The ideal body of Old Regime France was a highly schooled and cultivated entity, which carefully regulated its exchanges with the outside world and moved in deliberate, studied, and graceful gestures. This model endured until the second half of the eighteenth century, when Rousseau and others insisted on a return to the "natural" body, liberated from such false restraints. On the "civilizing process," see Norbert Elias, *The Civilizing Process,* trans. Edmund Jephcott (New York: Pantheon Books, 1978). See also Georges Vigarello, *Le Corps redressé: Histoire d'un pouvoir pédagogique* (Paris: Jean-Pierre Delarge, 1978). On perceptions of beauty in eighteenth-century France, see Marie-Claude Phan, " 'A faire belle', à faire femme," 67–78, and Véronique Nahoum-Grappe, "Briller à Paris au XVIIIe siècle," (135–56), both in *Parure, pudeur, étiquette,* a special issue of *Communications* 46 (1987). On clothing and changing breast shape, see Ribeiro, *Dress in Eighteenth-Century Europe,* 118.

15 *Le Mercure galant,* 23 avril 1672, 306–7.

16 On clothing in the French Revolution, see Nicole Pellegrin, *Les Vêtements de la liberté: Abécédaire des pratiques vestimentaires en France de 1780 à 1800* (Aix-en-Provence: Alinéa, 1989); Madeleine Delpierre, ed., *Modes et révolutions, 1780–1804* (Paris: Delpierre Editions Paris-Musées, 1989); Lynn Hunt, *Politics, Culture, and Class in the French Revolution* (Berkeley: University of California Press, 1984), and "Freedom of Dress in Revolutionary France," in *From the Royal to the Republican Body,* ed. Melzer and Norberg, 224–49.

17 On criticisms of women and informal female power in the prerevolutionary period, see Sarah Maza, *Private Lives and Public Affairs: The Causes Célèbres of Pre-Revolutionary France* (Berkeley: University of California Press, 1993); and Joan Landes, *Women in the Public Sphere in the Age of Revolution* (Ithaca: Cornell University Press, 1988). On Marie-Antoinette, see Chantal Thomas, *The Wicked Queen:*

The Origins of the Myth of Marie Antoinette, trans. Julie Rose (New York: Zone Books, 1999); Lynn Hunt, "The Many Bodies of Marie Antoinette: Political Pornography and the Problem of the Feminine in the French Revolution," and Sarah Maza, "The Diamond Necklace Affair Revisited (1785–86): The Case of the Missing Queen," both in *Eroticism and the Body Politic,* ed. Lynn Hunt (Baltimore: Johns Hopkins University Press, 1991); Jacques Revel, "Marie-Antoinette in Her Fictions: The Staging of Hatred," trans. Terri Nelson and Bernadette Fort, in *Fictions of the French Revolution,* ed. Bernadette Fort (Evanston, Ill.: Northwestern University Press, 1991); and Lynn Hunt, *The Family Romance of the French Revolution* (Berkeley: University of California Press, 1992), 89–123.

18   AN AD XI 16, "Statuts, ordonnances et déclaration du Roy, confirmative d'iceux, pour la Communauté des Couturières de la Ville, Fauxbourgs et Banlieue de Paris" (Paris: Veuve G. Paulus Du-Mesnil, 1734).

19   Furetière, *Dictionnaire universel, "hongreline."*

20   Furetière, *Dictionnaire universel, "robbe de chambre."*

21   The phrase is from D'Offemont, *Avis trés important au public: Sur différentes espéces de Corps et de Bottines d'une nouvelle invention* (Paris: Chez la Veuve Delaguette, 1758).

22   Marie de Rabutin-Chantal, marquise de Sévigné, *Lettres de Madame Sévigné,* ed. Bernard Raffalli, 16 mai 1676 (Paris: Garnier-Flammarion, 1976), 194.

23   Delpierre, *Modes enfantines, 1750–1950,* 17.

24   A strict hierarchy dictated the length of skirt trains at court: "The queen's train measured ten meters seventy [centimeters], those of the Daughters of France seven, the princesses of the blood five, the duchesses three." Leloir, *Dictionnaire du costume,* 299.

25   According to fashion historian Aileen Ribeiro, until 1783 "the 'grand habit' was not only worn for court presentations, but for ceremonial occasions such as the chapters of the order of the Saint-Esprit, baptisms and marriages of members of the royal family, and the 'grands bals parés,' the court balls." Ribeiro, *Dress in Eighteenth-Century Europe,* 128.

26   This intention was attributed by a critic of stays. See Alphonse Leroy, *Recherches sur les habillemens des femmes et des enfans, ou Examen de la manière dont il faut vêtir l'un et l'autre sèxe* (Paris: Le Boucher, 1772), 239.

27   *Le Dictionnaire de l'Académie française, "manteau."*

28   For the pattern of a mantua owned by the Metropolitan Museum in New York, see Nora Waugh, *The Cut of Women's Clothes, 1600–1930* (London: Faber and Faber, 1968), diagram 6.

29   *L'Extraordinaire du Mercure galant,* janvier 1678, 508–9.

30   I have not found an entirely satisfactory reason for the adoption of this dress; as noted earlier, it was a European phenomenon rather than a French one, so the explanation must surpass national boundaries. Fashion operates here, as in later examples, as an autonomous variable that introduces unexpected changes, thereby disrupting markets for production and distribution and challenging existing regulations.

31   *Le Mercure galant,* 23 avril 1672.

32 The adoption of the *manteau* in the 1670s thus challenges the periodization of the "clothing revolution" identified by Daniel Roche. Roche used 1700 as a starting date, showing major changes up to 1789, with the most important aspect of change being the widespread dissemination of the dress, or *robe*. If we accept, however, that the *manteau* was in fact a type of dress, and not an overcoat as he suggests, then it is clear that very large numbers of women wore dresses before 1700. Significant shifts in women's dress, with strong ramifications for consumption, had thus already taken place by the 1670s. See Roche, *The Culture of Clothing,* 120–22.

33 *L'Extraordinaire du Mercure galant,* janvier 1678, 541.

34 Women usually wore the *robe à la française* open down the front, pinning or hooking the sides of the dress to the stays. The underskirt, which showed between the two sides of the dress, was made from the same material as the dress or in a complementary fabric, and the stays were covered by a stomacher. The two front sides of the dress were often trimmed with a folded border running from the neck to the floor, while the skirt could be decorated with tiers of ruffles, known as *volantes.* The sleeves were three-quarter length, ending usually in another two tiers of ruffles. Women frequently pinned a lace or linen cuff of three additional tiers at the end of the sleeves, called *engageantes.* See Deslandres, *Le Costume, image de l'homme,* 130–34; and Delpierre, *Dress in France in the Eighteenth Century,* 10

35 Ribeiro, *Dress in Eighteenth Century Europe,* 128.

36 On developments in fashion during the 1770s and 1780s, see Ribeiro, *Dress in Eighteenth-Century Europe,* 148–59; and Delpierre, *Dress in France in the Eighteenth Century.*

37 On women's fashions during the Revolution and First Empire, see Ribeiro, *The Art of Dress,* and *Fashion in the French Revolution* (New York: Holmes and Meier, 1988); and Delpierre, ed., *Modes et révolutions, 1780–1804.*

38 Furetière, *Dictionnaire universel,* "*mode.*"

39 For one scholar's account of the court's role in creating fashion, see Hélène Himelfarb, "Versailles, source ou miroir des modes Louis-quatoriziennes? Sourches et Dangeau, 1684–1685," *Cahiers de l'association internationale des études françaises,* no. 38 (1986): 121–43.

40 By the time of Louis XIII in the early seventeenth century, the word fashion (*mode*) had acquired the basic significance it still holds today, referring to innovations in styles of clothing or other goods and practices, produced through a constant process of change and renewal. See Louise Godard de Donville, *La Signification de la mode sous Louis XIII* (Aix-en-Provence: EDISUD, 1978).

41 *Le Mercure galant,* 22–29 juillet 1672, 312–13.

42 *Le Mercure galant,* 23 avril 1672, 283–84.

43 *Le Mercure galant,* 22–29 juillet 1672, 313.

44 *Le Mercure galant,* 15 mai 1678, 545. From the beginning of the eighteenth century, dolls were dressed in the latest Paris fashions and sent to various European capitals as a means to disseminate these fashions. However, their circulation was limited to a small elite. See McKendrick, "The Commercialization

of Fashion," in *The Birth of a Consumer Society,* ed. McKendrick, Brewer, and Plumb, 43–47. McKendrick does not explain who manufactured and sent these dolls, but they were probably sent by merchant mercers to advertise fabric and decoration designs, not by individual seamstresses or tailors. On fashion in the *Mercure,* see Jones, " 'The Taste for Fashion and Frivolity,' " chapter 3. See also Reed Benhamou, "Fashion in the *Mercure:* From Human Foible to Female Failing," *Eighteenth-Century Studies* 31, no. 1 (1997): 27–43. Colin Campbell makes the important point that imitation does not necessarily imply emulation, as contemporary observers themselves were inclined to assume it did. He adds that "since most of these observers of the social scene were themselves either members or representatives of the superior classes, their jealous regard for their own privileges, combined with an intense anxiety about the stability of the social order (especially after 1789), meant that they were prone to see imitative consumption as inherently threatening." "Traditional and Modern Consumption," in *Consumption and the World of Goods,* ed. Brewer and Porter, 41.

45 By the eighteenth century, the term had come to signify a poor woman who worked in the garment trades. The changing meanings of this term emphasize the close connections drawn between women's clothing and their work in the clothing trades.

46 Antoine de Courtin, *Nouveau traité de la civilité qui se pratique en France, parmi les honnestes gens* (Paris: H. Josset, 1672), 76.

47 In keeping with this tendency, the *Mercure galant* journal focused its fashion reporting on new ways of ornamenting dresses and men's suits or on the latest inventions of the silk manufacturers of Lyons. The January 1678 issue of the quarterly supplement, *L'Extraordinaire du Mercure galant,* for example, listed no less than twenty-three new fabrics that had been introduced for the season. In October of that year, Donneau de Visé reported the recent invention of two new colors by silk manufacturers: "*paille*" and "*prince.*" Rumors of a third color had reached his ears, but he was unable to offer further details until Sieur Gaultier, a Parisian merchant mercer, had unveiled them. *L'Extraordinaire du Mercure galant,* janvier 1678, 537–38; *Le Mercure galant,* octobre 1678, 367.

48 See for example, Jacques Joseph Duguet [attributed], *Cas de conscience, décidé, par l'auteur de la prière publique: On demande s'il est permis de suivre les modes, et en particulier, si l'usage des paniers peut être souffert? avec les réponses aux objections* (1728). On reactions to the hoopskirt in England, see Erin Mackie, *Market à la Mode: Fashion, Commodity, and Gender in "The Tatler" and "The Spectator"* (Baltimore: Johns Hopkins University Press, 1997), 104–12.

49 D'Henissart [attributed], *Satyre sur les cerceaux, paniers, criardes et manteaux-volans des Femmes, et sur leurs autres ajustemens* (Paris: C.-C. Thiboust, 1727), 21: "Des corps de Robes de la Cour/Il faut imiter la Noblesse./ Il n'est rien de si gracieux,/Que cette charmante methode;/Et par cet air majestueux/La femme est toûjours à la mode."

50 From *Réponse à la critique des femmes sur leurs manteaux-volans, paniers criardes ou cerceaux dont elles font enfler leurs jupes* published at the end of the *Satyre sur les cerceaux.*

51 *Ordonnance burlesque de la reine des modes, au sujet des paniers, des cerceaux, des vertu-gadins et autres ajustemens des femmes* (Paris: Imprimerie de Imbert de Bats, [1719]).

52 *Lettres patentes en faveur du royaume des modes et provinces en dépendant* [1719].

53 *L'Apologie ou la défense des paniers* (Paris: Imprimerie de Valleyre père [1727]).

54 BN MSS Joly de Fleury 2000, f. 91, "Mémoire signifié pour la communauté des marchandes-maîtresses couturières de la ville de Paris."

55 Ibid.

56 See, for example, BN MSS Joly de Fleury 2000 f. 81, "A Nosseigneurs de Parlement, suplient humblement les jurez en charge de la communauté des maîtres-marchands tailleurs d'habits de Paris"; f. 84, "Mémoire pour les maîtres jurez et gardes des marchands-maîtres tailleurs d'habits et pourpointiers de la ville, faux-bourgs et banlieue de Paris"; and f. 86, "Addition de mémoire signifié servant de réponse au mémoire signifiée le 22 février 1727, pour la communauté des maîtres tailleurs à Paris."

57 BN MSS Joly de Fleury 2000, f. 81 "A Nosseigneurs de Parlement."

58 In contrast to the tailors' assertion, see François-Antoine de Garsault, *L'Art du tailleur, contenant le tailleur d'habits d'hommes, les culottes de peau, le tailleur de corps de femmes et enfants, la couturière et la marchande de modes* (Paris: Imprimerie de L. F. Delatour, 1769), 41.

59 BN MSS Joly de Fleury 2000, f. 91 "Mémoire signifié pour la communauté des marchandes-maîtresses couturières."

60 BN MSS Joly de Fleury 2000, f. 84, "Mémoire pour les maîtres jurez et gardes des marchands-maîtres tailleurs d'habits et pourpointiers de la ville, fauxbourgs et banlieue de Paris."

61 AN AD XI 26, "Arrest de la cour de Parlement, portant règlement entre la communauté des maîtres tailleurs d'habits, et celle des maîtresses coûturieres," 7 août 1727.

62 Jacques-Bénigne Winslow, "Sur les mauvais effets de l'usage des Corps à baleine," in *Histoire de l'Académie royale des sciences, année 1741.* (Paris: L'imprimerie royale, 1744). Previous discussions of the "medicalization" of discourses on women's apparel have ignored Winslow's contribution. See Nicole Pellegrin, "L'uniforme de la santé: Les médecins et la réforme du costume," *Dix-huitième siècle,* no. 23 (1991): 129–40; and Roche, *The Culture of Clothing,* chapter 15. Winslow lived from 1669 to 1760.

63 Winslow, "Sur les mauvais effets de l'usage des Corps à baleine," 176.

64 Ibid., 176–77.

65 LeRoy, *Recherches sur les habillemens des femmes et des enfans,* 241.

66 D'Offemont, *Avis très important au public,* 4.

67 Reisser, *Avis important au sexe, ou essai sur les corps baleinés pour former et conserver la taille aux jeunes personnes* (Lyon: Chez V. Reguilliat, 1770), 51–52.

68 Rousseau, *Emile,* 458.

69 Ibid., 456. Although he believed in women's natural tendency to care for their appearances, Rousseau spoke out strongly against the fashion system. Instead of following the whims of fashion, he argued, a woman should learn what clothes suited her and remain faithful to them. Expensive clothing and decorations were

usually the mark of an unattractive woman, he claimed, while real beauty clothed itself in simplicity and natural elegance (458). On women and appearances in Rousseau, see Landes, *Women in the Public Sphere in the Age of Revolution*, 66–89.

70 Rousseau, *Emile*, 459.

71 Ibid., 232. For a range of political and social reasons—in which Rousseau's arguments were influential—men would indeed begin to abandon ostentatious and colorful dress from the end of the eighteenth century. The wide range of social and cultural strategies and messages they had deployed through extravagant dress were recodified in much subtler shades and nuances. As courtly and royal politics were increasingly criticized, the visual presentation of masculinity that they had nurtured was rejected as well. On the "masculine renunciation" of ostentatious dress in England, see J. C. Flügel, *The Psychology of Clothes* (New York: Hogarth Press, 1969); and David Kuchta, "The Making of the Self-Made Man: Class, Clothing, and English Masculinity, 1688–1832," in *The Sex of Things*, ed. de Grazia, 54–78.

72 Rousseau, *Emile*, 232.

73 On the tailor as eunuch, see ibid.

74 Ibid. For arguments about women's exclusion from the public sphere in Rousseau, see Landes, *Women in the Public Sphere in the Age of Revolution*, 66–89. I follow Landes' analysis of the sexual foundations of Rousseau's notions of male and female roles in society, without accepting her contention that the public sphere from which Rousseau wished to eliminate women included the markets or the world of work.

75 AN AD XI 16, "Lettres patentes du Roi, portant nouveaux statuts pour la communauté des maitresses couturières-découpeuses de la ville de Paris" (Paris: P. G. Simon, 1782).

76 Ibid.

77 In 1769, François de Garsault noted in his *L'Art du tailleur* (2) that "for the past several years some Merchant Mercers' wives have been giving themselves the title of Fashion Merchants." See Delpierre, *La Mode et ses métiers du XVIIIe siècle à nos jours*, 13–14; Roche, *The Culture of Clothing*, 308; Jones, " 'The Taste for Fashion and Frivolity,' " 63–76, and "*Coquettes* and *Grisettes:* Women Buying and Selling in Ancien Régime Paris," in *The Sex of Things*, ed. de Grazia, 25–53.

78 Louis-Sébastien Mercier, *Tableau de Paris*, vol. 1, ed. Jean-Claude Bonnet (Paris: Mercure de France, 1994), 409.

79 Garsault, *L'Art du tailleur*, 54.

80 The almanac of Roze de Chantoiseau offered plentiful information about the specific items that some of the most reputed fashion merchants and mercers sold. For example, Sieur Collard of the rue Grénétat sold lace, Marly gauze, ribbons, and other articles of fashion at the Sign of the Holy Spirit. Sieur Fortin, of the rue Montmartre, sold "*modes*"—the term used for the latest women's accessories— and enjoyed a high reputation for the fabrication of mantillas and court finery. The widow Denis was said to "make and sell everything concerning fashion." She also rented bonnets, veils, and mantles for mourning dress. None of these merchants advertised a specialty in supplying women's dresses, confirming that

the seamstresses' control over dressmaking largely persisted in the second half of the eighteenth century. Roze de Chantoiseau, *Tablettes royales de renommée ou almanach général d'indication de négocians, artistes célèbres et fabricans des Six Corps, arts et métiers de la ville de Paris et autres villes du royaume* (Paris: Desnos et la Veuve Duchesne, 1773).

81 On the emergence of a fashion press, see Evelyne Sullerot, *Histoire de la presse féminine en France, des origines à 1848* (Paris: Librairie Armand Colin, 1966); Caroline Rimbault, "La Presse féminine de langue française au XVIIIe siècle" (Thèse de 3e cycle, EHESS, Paris I, 1981); Nina Rattner Gelbart, *Feminine and Opposition Journalism in Old Regime France: "Le Journal des dames"* (Berkeley: University of California Press, 1987); Roche, *The Culture of Clothing*, 470–500; and Françoise Vittu, "Presse et diffusion des modes françaises," in *Modes et révolutions: 1780–1804* (Paris: Musée Galliera, 1989), 129–36.

82 On the use of noble patronage in advertising, see Natacha Coquery, "De l'hôtel aristocratique aux ministères: Habitat, mouvement, espace à Paris au XVIIIe siècle" (Ph.D. diss., Université de Paris I, 1995), 126.

83 For a constrasting reading of this journal, see Jennifer Jones, "Repackaging Rousseau: Femininity and Fashion in Old Regime France," *French Historical Studies* 18 (fall 1994): 939–61.

84 *Le Cabinet des Modes ou les Modes Nouvelles,* 4 octobre 1785.

85 See, for example, *Le Cabinet des Modes,* 1 avril 1786, which offers a long discussion of fashions in men's suits.

TWO *From Mending to* Modes: *Trade Hierarchies and the Labor Market*

1 See Roche, *The Culture of Clothing*, 257–92; and Delpierre, *La mode et ses métiers,* for a discussion of the network of textile, garment, and accessories trades in eighteenth-century Paris. On relations between related guilds in the Bolognese leather industry, see Carlo Poni, "Local Market Rules and Practices: Three Guilds in the Same Line of Production in Early Modern Bologna," in *Domestic Strategies: Work and Family in France and Italy, 1600–1800,* ed. Stuart Woolf (Cambridge, Eng.: Cambridge University Press, 1991).

2 On ties between the faubourg Saint-Antoine and the Parisian guilds, see Kaplan, "Les Corporations, les faux ouvriers et le faubourg Saint-Antoine"; Alain Thillay, "Le Faubourg Saint-Antoine et la liberté du travail sous l'Ancien Régime," *Histoire, économie et société,* 11, no. 2 (1992), and "La liberté du travail au Faubourg Saint-Antoine à l'épreuve des saisies des jurandes parisiennes, (1642–1778)," *Revue d'histoire moderne et contemporaine* 44, no. 4 (octobre–décembre 1997): 634–49; and Raymonde Monnier, *Le Faubourg Saint-Antoine, 1789–1815* (Paris: Société des Etudes Robespierristes, 1981).

3 BN MSS Joly de Fleury 1728.

4 Jacques Savary des Bruslons, *Dictionnaire universel de commerce,* 3 vols. (Paris: Veuve Estienne, 1741). Michael Sonenscher reproduces Savary des Bruslon's figures for the population of the Parisian guilds in *Work and Wages,* 8.

5 Estimates of the Parisian population in this and the following paragraph are

based on Daniel Roche, *The People of Paris: An Essay in Popular Culture in the 18th Century,* trans. Marie Evans (Berkeley: University of California Press, 1987), 20; and Raymonde Monnier, "Le Travail des femmes sous l'Empire," *Bulletin d'histoire économique et sociale de la Révolution française,* (1979), 48.

6 BN MSS Joly de Fleury 596, "Obsérvations pour les marchandes et maîtresses couturières au sujet de l'Edit de rétablissement des corps."

7 BN MSS Joly de Fleury 1427.

8 Chapter 7 includes a full discussion of apprenticeship practices in the trade.

9 On the numerical composition of the seamstresses and other garment trades, see Roche, *The Culture of Clothing,* 293–312. The first contemporary evaluation of the total population of *couturières* dates from the First Empire. Daniel Roche reports that records from the Prefecture of Police indicate that twelve thousand *couturières* obtained a work license (*livret*) by 1807.

10 On the social composition of Parisian neighborhoods, see Adeline Daumard and François Furet, *Structures et relations sociales à Paris au XVIIIe siècle. Cahiers des Annales,* no. 18 (Paris: Armand Colin, 1961).

11 Abraham du Pradel [Nicolas de Blegny, pseud.], *Livre commode des adresses de Paris,* 2 vols., ed. Edouard Fournier (1692; Paris: P. Daffis, 1878); and Roze de Chantoiseau, *Tablettes royales de renommée.*

12 BN MSS Joly de Fleury 596. This manuscript, written sometime between 1773 and 1776 by an anonymous author, consisted of revised statutes for the guild accompanied by a second author's commentary on them. The two authors were most likely the royal procurator at the Châtelet of Paris and the lieutenant general of police, the two officials responsible for supervising the guild system.

13 In his *Dictionnaire raisonné universel des arts et métiers,* the abbé Jaubert gave the following account of specialization in the seamstresses' trade: "There are seamstresses for dress and skirt ensembles [*habits*], seamstresses for children's stays, linen seamstresses, and seamstresses for decorations [*agréments*]." As this description demonstrates, contemporary observers did not always acknowledge the formal taxonomies of the guild system and might lump into the same category all female needleworkers who worked for female employers. Abbé Pierre Jaubert, *Dictionnaire raisonné universel des arts et métiers* (Paris: P. F. Didot jeune, 1773), *couturière.*

14 AC Aix-en-Provence HH 145. See chapter 5 for a discussion of the Marseilles dispute.

15 AN AD XI 16, "Lettres patentes du roi, portant nouveaux statuts pour la Communauté des maitresses couturieres-découpeuses de la ville de Paris."

16 AD Calvados 1 B 2042. The lieutenant general of police granted the woman's request and she was subsequently accepted into the guild.

17 du Pradel, *Livre commode des adresses de Paris.*

18 BN MSS Joly de Fleury 2000. f. 86, "Addition de mémoire signifié servant de réponse au mémoire signifié le 22 février 1727."

19 Roze de Chantoiseau, *Tablettes royales de renommée.* Two of the twenty-six seamstresses specialized in hoopskirts.

20 AN MC Etude XLVI 285, 23 décembre 1739.

21 AN MC Etude LVIII 483, 1 août 1777.

22 For Dollé, see AN MC Etude XXVI 425, 10 novembre 1735. For Môlé, see AN MC Etude CXVIII 288, 19 mars 1714.

23 AN MC Etude LXXII 333, 14 janvier 1755.

24 AN MC Etude CXVIII 467, 6 novembre 1751.

25 AN MC Etude LXXXIX 555, 22 août 1754.

26 AD Calvados C 5901, 20 avril 1774.

27 AD Calvados C 4579, Capitation des arts et métiers 1757. For more details on this assessment, see chapter 6.

28 BA 80 J 4710. "Statuts et ordonnances des marchands-maîtres tailleurs-d'habits, pourpointiers-chaussetiers de la ville, fauxbourgs et banlieue de Paris," (Paris: Veuve d'André Knapen, 1742).

29 Ibid.

30 AN AD XI 16. "Statuts, ordonnances et déclaration du Roy, confirmative d'iceux, pour la communauté des couturières de la ville, fauxbourgs et banlieue de Paris."

31 For a discussion of Old Regime labor markets in general, including wage rates, types of employment, and the role of corporate regulation, see Steven L. Kaplan, "La lutte pour le contrôle du marché du travail à Paris au XVIIIe siècle," *Revue d'histoire moderne et contemporaine* 36 (juillet-septembre 1989): 361–412; and Jean-Yves Grenier, *L'économie d'Ancien Régime: Un monde de l'échange et de l'incertitude* (Paris: A. Michel, 1996), 241–68.

32 Seamstress guild assembly records can be found in the archives of their notary. See chapter 6 for further discussion of assembly meetings and minutes.

33 Grenier discusses these two extremes of labor qualifications and their ramifications for the labor market in *L'économie d'Ancien Régime,* 247–48.

34 Nicolas-Edmé Restif de la Bretonne, *Les Contemporaines communes, ou Aventures des belles Marchandes, Ouvrières, etc. de l'âge-présent* (1786; Geneva: Slatkine, 1988), vols. 21–22, "La Jolie Couturière," 171.

35 AN Y 15201, 24 septembre 1774.

36 For Cardin, see AN Y 11673, 4 mars 1743; for Pelée, see AN MC Etude LXXXIX 555, 22 août 1754.

37 Michael Sonenscher has postulated very short periods of employment among journeymen tailors in Rouen, based on registers from the guild employment office from 1778 to 1780. Based on these figures, he hypothesizes that journeymen's mobility was the result of unemployment rather than an inherent or traditional pattern of itinerancy. Sonenscher acknowledges, but probably underestimates, the fact that these registers tend to efface long periods of employment among more stable journeymen. See Sonenscher, *Work and Wages,* 87.

38 AN Y 14048, 19 janvier 1713.

39 In the city of Rouen, Michael Sonenscher found that "masters expected to take on additional labour immediately after Easter and just before the Feast of All Saints, and that journeymen timed their movements to coincide with the additional demand for labour." Sonenscher, *Work and Wages,* 162–63.

40 Erica-Marie Benabou, *La prostitution et la police des moeurs* (Paris: Perrin, 1987), 313. Jean-Yves Grenier discusses the problem of endemic underemployment in the

Old Regime, emphasizing the almost constant shortage of jobs as a continuing concern for royal and municipal authorities. Grenier, *L'économie d'Ancien Régime,* 250–51.

41 AN MC Etude CVIII 500, 22 août 1752.

42 Respectively, AN Y 14850; AN Y 14336, 24 janvier 1773; AN Y 13112, 3 novembre 1760.

43 Roche, *The Culture of Clothing,* 313–14. The overall average was calculated by Steven Kaplan in "Réflexions sur la police du monde du travail, 1700–1815," *Revue historique* 261 (janvier–mars 1979): 19.

44 Respectively, AN Y 11496, 13 mars 1776; AN MC Etude XCVIII 587, 20 juin 1770; AN MC Etude LVIII 483, 1 août 1777.

45 AN MC Etude XXVI 425, 10 novembre 1735. Ducouroy may have fallen ill in the last months of her life, leading her to hire additional live-in workers.

46 AN MC Etude CXII 573, 23 mai 1759.

47 See Grenier, *L'économie d'Ancien Régime,* 257–68. Using wage rates from the building trades, Ernest Labrousse calculated that over the eighteenth century, wages rose only 24 percent compared to an increase in the price of grain close to 70 percent. See Ernest Labrousse, *Esquisse du mouvement des prix et des revenus en France au XVIIIᵉ siècle,* 2 vols. (Paris: Dalloz, 1933).

48 For Ducouroy, see AN MC Etude CXII, 3 mai 1759. For Briard des Coutures, see AN MC Etude XCVIII 587, 20 juin 1770.

49 AN Y 12989, 16 mars 1771.

50 AN MC Etude CVIII 500, 22 août 1752.

51 Cited in Benabou, *La prostitution et la police des moeurs,* 299.

52 Restif de la Bretonne, *Les Contemporaines communes,* 166–67, 181.

53 For Denizon, see AN MC Etude XC 489, 12 mai 1781. For Guelorget, see AN MC Etude X 693, 30 juin 1781. For Ducasble, see AN MC Etude XCII 845, 9 juillet 1782.

54 Respectively, AN MC Etude XXXVIII 387, 18 février 1751; AN MC Etude C 654, 23 mars 1761; AN MC Etude C 656, 30 juillet 1761. Agreements to pay any salary at all were rare in apprenticeship contracts, where as a rule the apprentice paid for his or her training rather than being paid.

55 Sonenscher, *Work and Wages,* 175.

56 AD Calvados 1 B 2000, 30 octobre 1778.

57 See Christopher Johnson, "Patterns of Proletarianization: Parisian Tailors and Lodève Woolens Workers," in *Consciousness and Class Experience Explained,* ed. John M. Merriman (New York: Holmes and Meier, 1979), and "Economic Change and Artisan Discontent: The Tailors' History, 1800–1848," in *Revolution and Reaction: 1848 and the Second French Republic,* ed. Roger Price (London: Croom Helm, 1975). See also Scott, "Work Identities for Men and Women: The Politics of Work and Family in the Parisian Garment Trades in 1848," in *Gender and the Politics of History,* 93–112; and Sewell, *Work and Revolution in France,* 175–76.

58 AN Y 9363, 23 mai 1749.

59 AN MC Etude XXI 454, 25 avril 1770.

60 AN MC Etude XCVIII 587, 20 juin 1770.

61 AN Y 13306, 7 mai 1781.

62 AN MC Etude LVIII 483, 1 août 1777.

63 AN MC Etude CXVIII 288, 1714. The *Encyclopédie* contains descriptions of the *découpeurs'* work and engravings of their tools. For images of *piqueurs'* and *découpeurs'* work in seventeenth- and eighteenth-century garments, see Avril Hart and Susan North, *Fashion in Detail: From the 17th and 18th Centuries* (New York: Rizzoli International Publications, Inc., 1998), 27–31, 174–181.

64 For Mademoiselle Eloffe's accounts, see records published in Comte Gustave-Armand Henri de Reiset, ed., *Modes et usages au temps de Marie-Antoinette: Livre journal de Madame Eloffe. Marchande de modes, couturière, lingère ordinaire de la Reine et des dames de sa cour* (Paris: Firmin-Didot, 1885), which contains reproductions of Mademoiselle Eloffe's account book. For Rose Bertin's accounts, see Emile Langlade, *La Marchande de modes de Marie-Antoinette, Rose Bertin* (Paris: A. Michel, 1911); and Pierre de Nouvion and Emil Liez, *Un Ministre de modes sous Louis XVI, Mademoiselle Bertin, marchande de modes de la reine, 1747–1813* (Paris: Henri Leclerc, 1911).

65 AD Calvados 1 B 1974, 13 juin 1731.

66 AN Y 13112, 23 octobre 1760. Other mistresses may have developed ties to production in the faubourg Saint-Antoine, although I have found no evidence of such associations.

67 See Johnson, "Patterns of Proletarianization," 68; Scott, "Work Identities for Men and Women," and " 'L'Ouvrière! Mot impie sordide . . .': Women Workers in the Discourse of French Political Economy, 1840–1860," in *Gender and the Politics of History,* 139–63; and Judith Coffin, *The Politics of Women's Work: The Parisian Garment Trades* (Princeton: Princeton University Press, 1996), 58–60. For the English case, see Barbara Taylor, "Socialism, Feminism, and Sexual Antagonism in the London Tailoring Trade in the Early 1830s," *Feminist Studies* 5 (spring 1979).

68 Garsault, *L'Art du tailleur.*

69 AN Y 11338, 10 janvier 1759.

70 AN Y 9363, 23 mai 1749.

71 AN Y 9363, 25 janvier 1744.

72 AN Y 13112, 31 octobre 1760.

73 AC Aix-en-Provence HH 135.

74 AD Calvados C 5901, 20 avril 1774.

75 AN Y 13766, 2 mars 1758.

76 AN MC Etude LXV 486, 25 avril 1787.

77 AN Y 13112, 4 juillet 1760.

78 AN Y 12803, 26 janvier 1781. Nonmistresses who worked for their own clients, rather than for another seamstress, generally referred to themselves simply as "seamstress" (*couturière*) instead of "seamstress worker" (*ouvrière couturière*) or "girl seamstress" (*fille couturière*). Although these documents do not raise the issue, seamstresses who went to work in clients' homes must have been more vulnerable to charges of improper sexual conduct than were those who remained in their own homes and brought an apprentice along on visits to clients.

79 AD Calvados 1 B 1974, 27 avril 1731.

80 AN Y 9363, 7 avril 1747.

81 AN Y 9363, 23 mai 1749.

82 AN Y 9363, 20 mai 1749.

83 Jacques-Louis Ménétra offered accounts of his own *compagnonnage* experiences in the late-eighteenth century, as did Agricol Perdiguier in the first half of the nineteenth century. See Ménétra, *Journal of My Life;* and Agricol Perdiguier, *Le Livre du compagnonnage* (Paris: Pagnerre, 1841), and *Mémoires d'un compagnon* (1854–55; Paris: Librairie du compagnonnage, 1964). George Sand's *Le Compagnon du Tour de France* (Paris: Perrotin 1841) was directly inspired by Perdiguier. In the historical literature, see Emile Coornaert, *Les Compagnonnages en France du Moyen age à nos jours* (Paris: les Editions ouvrières, 1966); Germain Martin, *Les associations ouvrières au XVIIIe siècle (1700–1792)* (Paris: A. Rousseau, 1900); Henri Hauser, *Le compagnonnage d'arts et métiers à Dijon aux XVIIe et XVIIe siècles* (1907; Marseille: Lafitte, 1979); Etienne Martin Saint-Léon, *Le Compagnonnage: Son histoire, ses coutumes, ses règlements et ses rites* (1901; Paris: Imprimerie du compagnonnage, 1977); Hippolyte Blanc, *Le Compagnon des corporations de métiers et l'organisation ouvrière du XIIIe au XVIIe siècle* (Paris: Secrétariat de l'Assocation Catholique, 1883). More recently, see Cynthia Truant, *The Rites of Labor.*

84 See Kaplan, "La lutte pour le contrôle du marché du travail," and "Réflexions sur la police du monde du travail, 1700–1815."

85 AC Aix-en-Provence HH 135.

86 Michael Sonenscher argues that Parisian tailors also failed to form labor associations: "Paris, with its vast corporation of master tailors and highly developed division of labor, was simply too large for any association of journeymen to be able to exercise effective control over the supply of labor in the eighteenth-century." "Journeymen's Migrations and Workshop Organization in Eighteenth-Century France," in *Work in France,* ed. Kaplan and Koepp, 91.

87 AN Y 14512, 23 août 1712.

88 AN Y 9376, 16 février 1723.

89 The seamstresses therefore do not seem to support Michael Sonenscher's contention that law courts, and in particular the Parlements, played a primary role in distributing justice in the world of work. See Sonenscher, *Work and Wages,* 55 passim.

90 AN Y 11496, 13 août 1776.

91 AN Y 13766, 16 septembre 1758.

92 AN Y 14551, 11 décembre 1766.

93 Sonenscher, *Work and Wages,* 83.

94 AC Aix-en-Provence HH 144, "Registre des réceptions des maîtres tailleurs."

95 For information regarding general immigration patterns to Paris, see Roche, *The People of Paris,* 21–31. See chapters 7 and 8 for the origins of apprentices and mistresses.

96 Respectively, BN MSS Fr. 11358, f. 96, 9 mai 1760 and BN MSS Fr. 11358, f. 104, 23 mai 1760.

97 Benabou, *La prostitution et la police des moeurs,* 313.

98 BN MSS Fr. 11358, f. 301, 31 août 1759.

99 BN MSS Fr. 11358, f. 96, 9 mai 1760.

100 AN Y 12055, 13 septembre 1768.

101 AN Y 12989, 12 mai 1771.

102 AN Y 12216, 19 novembre and 28 décembre 1788.

103 See also the hierarchy of prostitution described by Louis-Sébastien Mercier in *Tableau de Paris*, vol. 1, 220–21.

104 AN Y 9475, 5 février 1772, "Rolle des prisonniers détenus de police es prisons de Paris arrêté par Monsieur le Lieutenant Général de Police." In *La prostitution et la police des moeurs*, Benabou demonstrated the close ties between the worlds of work and prostitution. Her study of women arrested for prostitution entering Saint Martin prison during the years 1765, 1766, and 1770 revealed that 940 of the 2,069 women arrested (45.5 percent) declared an occupation in the making of clothing or decorations, or in textile production. Among them were an "overwhelming majority" of seamstresses and linenworkers. Other professions included fashion workers (*ouvrières en modes*), tailors' employees, and cloth cutters (*découpeuses*) (281).

105 AN Y 11388, 9 mai 1772.

106 Benabou, *La Prostitution et la police des moeurs*, 308. Benabou points out that if the women were inventing their professions, they would have been more likely to choose a vague term, such as *laboureur* or *gagne denier*, rather than a profession that could be verified.

107 BN MSS Fr. 11358, f. 301, 31 août 1759.

108 BN MSS Fr. 11358, f. 108, 30 mai 1760.

109 BN MSS Fr. 11360, f. 397, 6 fevrier 1768.

110 See, for example, BN MSS Fr. 11359, f. 694, 17 mai 1765.

111 BN MSS Fr. 11358, f. 313, 7 décembre 1759.

112 BA MSS 10238, f. 237, 28 avril 1754.

113 BN MSS Fr. 11360, f. 398, 6 février 1768.

114 BN MSS Fr. 11358, f. 13, 18 janvier 1760.

115 BN MSS Fr. 11358, f. 96, 9 mai 1760.

116 BN MSS Fr. 11358, f. 124, 20 juin 1760.

117 BN MSS Fr. 11359, f. 285, 8 janvier 1764.

THREE *Tools, Techniques, and Commercial Practices*

1 See Coffin, *The Politics of Women's Work;* and Scott, "Work Identities for Men and Women," and "'*L'Ouvrière, mot impie . . .*'" both in *Gender and the Politics of History.* See also Judith A. DeGroat, "The Public Nature of Women's Work: Definitions and Debates during the Revolution of 1848," *French Historical Studies* 20, no. 1 (winter 1997): 31–47; Victoria E. Thompson, *The Virtuous Marketplace: Women and Men, Money and Politics in Paris, 1830–1870* (Baltimore: Johns Hopkins University Press, 2000); Lorraine Coons, "'Neglected Sisters' of the Women's Movement: The Perception and Experience of Working Mothers in the Parisian Garment Industry, 1860–1915," *Journal of Women's History* 5, no. 2 (fall 1993): 50–74, and *Women Home Workers in the Parisian Garment Industry, 1860–1915* (New

York: Garland, 1987); Karen Offen, " 'Powered by a Woman's Foot': A Documentary Introduction to the Sexual Politics of the Sewing Machine in Nineteenth-Century France," *Women's Studies International Forum* 11, no. 2 (1988): 93–101.

2 A study of seamstresses' techniques of production has implications beyond clarifying labor practices. By permitting an assessment of the extent to which representations corresponded to practices, it supplies a crucial complement to discourses about the female needleworker. This is not to argue for an evaluation of discursive texts based on their truth value, but to insist on the need to establish as fully as possible the contexts in which historical documents are produced and distributed. Comparison between practice and discourse opens up the rhetorical and strategic possibilities of texts, which we cannot recognize without knowledge of the divergent resources available to social actors, of individuals' adherence to different groups or institutions, and of the power relations operating in the concrete situations in which they wrote or spoke.

3 Deslandres, *Le Costume, image de l'homme*, 81.

4 Roslin, *Le Tarif des marchands fripiers, tailleurs, tapissiers, couturiers et autres personnes qui veulent se faire faire des habits ou meubles* (Paris: A. de Heuqueville 1734).

5 On Enlightenment attitudes toward work, see Cynthia J. Koepp, "The Alphabetical Order: Work in Diderot's Encyclopédie," 229–57, and William H. Sewell, "Visions of Labor: Illustrations of the Mechanical Arts Before, In, and After Diderot's *Encyclopédie*," 258–96, both in *Work in France,* ed. Kaplan and Koepp.

6 Garsault, *L'Art du tailleur.*

7 On clothing in the *Encyclopédie,* see Roche, *The Culture of Clothing,* 435–69.

8 Garsault, *L'Art du tailleur,* 48.

9 For an assessment of images of labor in the *Encyclopédie,* see Sewell, "Visions of Labor," 258–96. Sewell suggests that images of women at work were usually little more than "a pretext for depicting a pretty girl" (260). I believe that the engravings are in fact useful tools for assessing gender roles, because they reveal the trades in which informed contemporaries believed women were regularly employed. The specific tasks women perform in the engravings also provide clues to contemporary perceptions—and even realities—of the sexual division of labor in these trades.

10 AN MC Etude CXI 301, 4 mai 1770.

11 AN MC Etude XC 489, 12 mai 1781. Another mistress also possessed a caged parrot and a caged squirrel. The impression of financial ease created by Denizon's specialized work space—as well as the 300 livres the couple paid for their three rooms—was misleading. Denizon's inventory revealed debts totaling 1,925 livres. The importance of her contribution to their "family economy" surfaces in the debt her husband contracted subsequent to her illness and death. In addition to 614 livres borrowed from his mother for daily expenses, he borrowed another 192 livres to pay for Denizon's burial.

12 AN MC Etude LXXXIX 555, 22 août 1754.

13 AN MC Etude XLVI 388, 13 mars 1762.

14 Restif de la Bretonne, *Les Contemporaines communes,* 170.

15 Martine Sonnet, *L'Education des filles au temps des Lumières* (Paris: Cerf, 1987).

16 In her ethnological study of a village in the Côte d'Or in the 1970s, Yvonne Verdier offered a fascinating account of local girls' apprenticeship with a village seamstress. According to her account, apprentices paid for their first year, but not their second, and received wages in their third year. See Yvonne Verdier, *Façons de dire, façons de faire: La laveuse, la couturière, la cuisinière* (Paris: Gallimard, 1979).

17 AC Aix-en-Provence HH 134.

18 From Tobias Smollet, *Travels*, cited in Ribeiro, *Dress in Eighteenth-Century Europe*, 60.

19 Reiset, *Modes et usages au temps de Marie-Antoinette*, 15.

20 AD de la Seine 5B6, registre 4882.

21 Roche, *The Culture of Clothing*, 284–85.

22 AN MC Etude LXXXIX 555, 22 août 1754.

23 Thérèse de Dillmont, *Encyclopédie des ouvrages des dames* (1851; Paris: Librairie Ch. Delagrave, 1993).

24 AN MC Etude XXXIV 678, 10 décembre 1770.

25 AN MC Etude XXXVI 425, 2 septembre 1735.

26 Mercier, *Tableau de Paris*, vol. 1, 450–51. See also the scene in *Le Bourgeois gentilhomme* where Monsieur Jourdain recognizes the cloth of his latest suit in the suit worn by his tailor. Molière, *Le Bourgeois gentilhomme*, 54.

27 AN AD XI 16, "Lettres patentes du roi, portant nouveaux statuts pour la communauté des maîtresses couturières-découpeuses de la ville de Paris."

28 AN MC ET XLVI 285, 23 décembre 1739.

29 AN MC Etude CXI 301, 4 mai 1770.

30 AN MC Etude XC 489, 12 mai 1781.

31 Roze de Chantoiseau, *Tablettes royales de renommée,* "merciers." See also Carolyn Sargentson, *Merchants and Luxury Markets: The Marchands Merciers of Eighteenth-Century Paris* (London: The Victoria and Albert Museum, 1996), 30–31.

32 AN Y 11942, 1 juillet 1758.

33 AN Y 11338, 10 janvier 1759.

34 For Bridet-Clément's business records, see AD de la Seine D5B6 registre 4882.

35 Molière, *Le Bourgeois gentilhomme*, 53.

36 AN Y 12984 15 juin 1768.

37 AN Y 12984, 17 juin 1768.

38 On female insults and slander, see David Garrioch, "Verbal Insults in Eighteenth-Century Paris," in *The Social History of Language*, ed. Peter Burke and Roy Porter (Cambridge, Eng.: Cambridge University Press, 1987); and Arlette Farge, *Vivre dans la rue à Paris au XVIIIe siècle* (Paris: Gallimard 1979). For the English case, see Laura Gowing, *Domestic Dangers: Women, Words, and Sex in Early Modern London* (Oxford: Oxford University Press, 1996).

39 AN Y 9500, 28 novembre 1760.

40 "D'ouvrier en fût il jamais plus habile/Je donne le bon air à mes habillemens/ Paroissez à la Cour ou Restez à la Ville/Madame et vous allez faire nombre d'Amans."

41 "Je me plais d'habiller une aussi belle fille/ Que vous aymable Iris, dont l'esprit est bien fait/Pour faire votre corps et votre habit parfait/Souffrez que l'on vous fasse un ou deux points d'éguille [sic]."

42 "Décolte cet habit ma fille/Tu me caches tous mes appas/On est si peu de tems gentille/Hé pour quoy n'en profiter pas?"

43 See Véronique Nahoum-Grappe, "The Beautiful Woman," in *Renaissance and Enlightenment Paradoxes,* ed. Natalie Zemon Davis and Arlette Farge, vol. 3 of *A History of Women in the West,* ed. Georges Duby and Michelle Perrot (Cambridge, Mass.: Harvard University Press, 1993), 95. As Nahoum-Grappe writes: "In other words, beauty was a tactical mask, which women more or less deliberately and elaborately chose to wear. . . . The goal was not simply sexual seduction, although it was usually interpreted as such. Beauty was also an unreliable but effective tool for social action, especially when women were prevented from using other tools (whether legal, cultural, economic or political)."

44 For a modern perspective on seamstresses' sexual aura, see Yvonne Verdier, *Façons de dire, façons de faire,* 229–41.

45 "Il est honeste, Il est discret/Il cache adroitement un défaut de Nature/et d'une amoureuse adventure/il sçait bien garder le secret."

46 For measurements for the *robe à la française,* see Garsault, *L'Art du tailleur,* 48.

47 From *The Taylor's Complete Guide* (1796), cited in Janet Arnold, *Patterns of Fashion: Englishwomen's Dresses and their Construction* (London: Macmillan, 1977), 8.

48 *Encyclopédie,* "*tailleur.*"

49 See chapter 4 for an explanation of the origins of the guild.

50 Garsault, *L'Art du tailleur.* Garsault estimated that a *robe à la française* worn without hoopskirts was one and a third aunes (1.39 meters) long. The back of the dress was two aunes wide, the equivalent of four full widths of silk cloth (2.36 meters). Each of the two front pieces was half an aune in width, each taking up a full width of silk cloth (1.18 meters). The sleeves used one-third of a square aunes each (approximately 40 square centimeters), the sleeve flounces an additional three-quarters of an aune (90 centimeters). The matching skirt was two-thirds of an aune long (30 inches, or 79 centimeters) and two-and-a-half aunes wide (1 yard, or 3 meters).

51 Madame de Genlis, *De l'esprit des étiquettes de l'ancienne cour et des usages du monde de ce temps* (Paris: Mercure de France, 1996), 26. Genlis wrote between 1812 and 1813, recalling her life at the French court under Louis XVI.

52 Natalie Rothstein, ed., *A Lady of Fashion: Barbara Johnson's Album of Styles and Fabrics* (London: Thames and Hudson, 1987). Other negligees required only eighteen or nineteen yards (between fourteen and fifteen aunes) and Johnson may have worn them over smaller hoops.

53 Garsault, *L'Art du tailleur,* 50.

54 See Waugh, *The Cut of Women's Clothes,* diagrams 13, 18, and 19. See Arnold, *Patterns of Fashion,* 32–35, 38–39.

55 See for example, Waugh, *The Cut of Women's Clothes,* diagrams 19 and 20; and Arnold, *Patterns of Fashion,* 22–23, 28, 32–34.

56 For a closer look at the details of seventeenth- and eighteenth-century dress con-

struction and decorations, see Hart and North, *Fashion in Detail from the 17th and 18th Centuries.*

57   See, for example, Arnold, *Patterns of Fashion,* 6, 44.

58   Reiset, *Modes et usages du temps de Marie-Antoinette,* 47, 59.

59   AN AD XI 16, "Lettres patentes du roi, portant nouveaux statuts pour la communauté des maîtresses couturières-découpeuses de la ville de Paris."

60   Garsault, *L'Art du tailleur,* 38.

61   Roze de Chantoiseau, *Tablettes royales de renommée,* "*merciers.*"

62   A number of variations existed on this basic pattern. The *corps à l'anglaise* and the *corps à la duchesse* were laced in the front, rather than the back. The former had side seams that curved in toward the waist, creating a more comfortable fit. Stays for pregnant women opened on the sides and in the front. Stays worn on horseback were more lightly whaleboned and were shorter in the front to allow the woman to lean forward in the saddle. Because young boys' bodies' had slender hips, their stays descended further over the hips than those for women.

63   AC Aix-en-Provence HH 135, 18 août 1726.

64   Cited in Arnold, *Patterns of Fashion,* 9.

65   AD de la Seine D5B5, registre 3597.

66   This information is from a collection of eighteenth-century bills held at the Musée Galliera, Paris under "dossier de Bercy".

67   AD de la Seine, D5B6, registre 205.

68   AN MC Etude XII 582, 26 janvier 1763.

69   AC Aix-en-Provence HH 135, 18 août 1726.

70   AD de la Seine D5B6, registre 205.

71   Reiset, *Modes et usages au temps de Marie-Antoinette,* 40. This book contains reproductions of Mademoiselle Eloffe's account book.

72   Ibid., 84.

73   Daniel Roche's analysis of a Parisian noble family's spending habits confirms that even outside of the highest court aristocracy, noblewomen spent more for the services of fashion merchants than for their seamstresses. Roche found that between 1769 and 1788 baron Schomberg's family paid 1,056 livres (3.64 percent of their clothing expenditure) to seamstresses, and 2,442 livres (8.42 percent of clothing expenditure) to fashion merchants. See Roche, *The Culture of Clothing,* 211, table 21. The fact that fashion merchants figure much more prominently than seamstresses in bankruptcy records indicates the high risks involved in purveying expensive luxury products on credit.

74   Reiset, *Modes et usages au temps de Marie-Antoinette,* 68.

75   See, for example, the memoirs of Marie-Antoinette's first lady-in-waiting, Madame Campan. Campan recounts the court's consternation at Bertin's access to Marie-Antoinette's private chambers and blames the merchant for inciting Marie-Antoinette to extravagant expenses on clothing, an example followed by women at court and beyond. Madame Campan, *Mémoires de Madame Campan, première femme de chambre de Marie-Antoinette,* ed. Jean Chalon (Paris: Mercure de France, 1988), 73. See also the baronne d'Oberkirch's account of her visit to Bertin's Paris boutique. Baronne Henriette Louise de Waldner de Freundstein

d'Oberkirch, *Mémoires de la Baronne d'Oberkirch sur la cour de Louis XVI et la société française avant 1789,* ed. Suzanne Burkard (Paris: Mercure de France, 1989), 145–46.

76 Bertin's accounts may be consulted in the Bibliothèque Doucet, Manuscrits Microfilm, 1. This collection consists of outstanding bills that her heirs sought to recoup in the first decades of the nineteenth century, several years after Bertin's death in 1813.

77 AN MC Etude XCII 845, 9 juillet 1782. Only one seamstress in the inventories did not work for credit, Marie Josephe Denizon. Her husband stated that "son épouse ne tenoit aucun registre pour raison de sa profession attendu qu'elle ne travaillait qu'au comptant." See AN MC Etude XC 489, 12 mai 1781.

78 AN MC Etude LXXXI 460, 12 avril 1777.

79 AD de la Seine, D5B6, registre 205.

80 Ibid.

81 AN MC Etude LXXXIX 555, 22 août 1754.

82 Musée Galliera, dossier de Bercy, no. 47.

83 AN MC Etude XXVI 425, 10 novembre 1735.

84 For an account of the credit practices of Parisian nobles, see Coquery, "De l'hôtel aristocratique aux ministères," 20–21.

85 AN MC Etude XLVI 285, 23 décembre 1739.

86 AN MC Etude XVI 781, 24 décembre 1762.

87 AN Y 11665, 8 décembre 1735.

88 AN Y 13112, 4 juillet 1760.

89 AN Y 13112, 2 mai 1760.

90 BA MSS 11 479.

91 BN MSS Joly de Fleury 596, 16 novembre 1776.

FOUR *The Royal Government, Guilds, and the Seamstresses of Paris, Normandy, and Provence*

1 Davis, "City Women and Religious Change," 94. This passage is cited in Collins, "The Economic Role of Women in Seventeenth-Century France," 437. For early and influential versions of this argument, see Alice Clark, *The Life of Working Women in the Seventeenth Century* (1919; London: Routledge and K. Paul, 1982); and Ivy Pinchbeck, *Women Workers and the Industrial Revolution, 1750–1850* (New York: Routledge, 1930). More recently, see Merry Wiesner, *Working Women in Renaissance Germany,* and *Gender, Church, and State in Early Modern Germany;* Martha Howell, *Women, Production, and Patriarchy in Late Medieval Cities,* and *The Marriage Exchange: Property, Social Place, and Gender in Cities of the Low Countries, 1300–1550* (Chicago: University of Chicago Press, 1998); Jean H. Quataert, "The Shaping of Women's Work in Manufacturing: Guilds, Households, and the State in Central Europe, 1648–1870"; and Lindsey Charles and Lorna Duffin, eds., *Women and Work in Preindustrial England* (London: Croom Helm, 1985). These historians have challenged Clark's idealized view of female economic opportunities in the Middle Ages, but agreed that a significant decline in the scope and autonomy of female labor occurred through the early modern period. For a provocative

argument about the "compact" between the patriarchal family and monarchical power in this period, see Sarah Hanley, "Social Sites of Political Practice in France," and "Engendering the State: Family Formation and State Building in Early Modern France."

2 This figure is based on the membership figures that Parisian guilds furnished in the 1720s to Jacques Savary des Bruslons. See Roche, *The People of Paris,* 71 and Sonenscher, *Work and Wages,* 8.

3 On privilege in the corporate society of Old Regime France, see Roland Mousnier, *Les Institutions de la France sous la monarchie absolue* (Paris: Presses universitaires de France, 1980); and François Olivier-Martin's *L'Organisation corporative de la France d'Ancien Régime.* More recently, see Bien, "Offices, Corps, and a System of State Credit," and "The Secrétaires du Roi: Absolutism, Corps, and Privilege under the Ancien Régime," in *Vom Ancien Régime zur Französischen Revolution,* ed. Ernst Hinrichs, Eberhard Schmitt, and Rudolf Vierhaus (Göttingen: Vandenhoeck and Ruprecht, 1978). See also Bossenga, *The Politics of Privilege;* Jacques Revel, "Les Corps et communautés," in *The Political Culture of the Old Regime,* vol. 1 of *The French Revolution and the Creation of Modern Political Culture,* ed. Keith Michael Baker (Oxford: Oxford University Press, 1987); and Alain Guéry and Robert Descimon, "Privilèges: La légalisation de la société," in *L'Etat et les pouvoirs,* ed. Jacques Revel and André Burguière, vol. 2 of *Histoire de la France* (Paris: Seuil, 1989), 326–33.

4 Georges-Claudius Lavergne, *Archives des corporations des arts et métiers* (Paris: Charavay frères, 1879), 14. On the corporations and the Great Chain of Being, see Kaplan, "Social Classification and Representation in the Corporate World of Eighteenth-Century France" in *Work in France,* ed. Kaplan and Koepp.

5 In Paris, two of four municipal officers, or *échevins,* were appointed from the Six Corps, as was one member of the royal Conseil de Commerce created in 1700. See Sargentson, *Merchants and Luxury Markets: The Marchands Merciers of Eighteenth-Century Paris,* 8.

6 The phrase belongs to Bien, "Offices, Corps, and a System of State Credit," 92: "In brief, privilege existed in a kind of symbiotic relationship with the state."

7 The edict is reproduced in René de Lespinasse, ed., *Les Métiers et corporations de la ville de Paris,* vol. 1 (Paris: Imprimerie nationale, 1886), 123–28.

8 For the text of royal edicts suppressing suburban guilds, see Lespinasse, *Les Métiers et corporations de la ville de Paris,* vol. 1, 119–21. On the Faubourg Saint-Antoine see chapter 2, note 2.

9 See for example, Jean-Claude Perrot, *Genèse d'une ville moderne: Caen au XVIIIe siècle,* vol. 1 (Paris: Mouton, 1975), 321–22. As Perrot writes: "Le lieutenant de police déclarait en 1731, à propos de tels ou tels artisans-commerçants libres: 'Ils sont censés, si l'on veut, faire corps et communauté à l'égard de Sa Majesté, et cette communauté quoique non existante, est sujette aux mêmes impositions qu'une véritable communauté.' "

10 Maurice Agulhon, *La Sociabilité méridionale: Confréries et associations dans la vie collective en Provence orientale à la fin du XVIIIe siècle,* 2 vols. (Aix-en-Provence: La Pensée universitaire, 1966).

11 For numerical evaluations of female domestic servants in Paris, see Roche, *The People of Paris*, 65–69; Fairchilds, *Domestic Enemies: Servants and Their Masters in Old Regime France* (Baltimore: Johns Hopkins University Press, 1984), 2; and Sarah Maza, *Servants and Their Masters in Eighteenth-Century France: The Uses of Loyalty* (Princeton: Princeton University Press, 1983), 26–28.

12 At first glance, women's place in the early modern guild world appears to have declined significantly from the Middle Ages. Etienne Boileau's thirteenth-century catalogue of Parisian guilds, the *Livre des Métiers,* listed at least four guilds dominated by women: two silk-spinning trades, the silk ribbonmakers, and the makers of silk headdresses (*coiffures*). Boileau also listed trades composed of both men and women, including the makers of flower garlands and the makers of silk wimples (*coiffes*). The comparison between the medieval and the early modern situations, however, is deceptive. First, medieval women's guilds were less autonomous than their seventeenth-century counterparts. The statutes transcribed by Boileau show they were administered by male overseers (*prud'hommes*), rather than their own mistresses. Second, if women had lost this handful of medieval corporations by the end of the fifteenth century, they had also established control over two new trades. The linen-drapers' guild was created in 1485, after the female practitioners of the trade successfully eradicated a male guild of linen and canvas merchants. By 1645, their privileges included the sale of linen cloth as well as the manufacture and retail sale of finished linen goods. A similar process took place among hemp merchants, where women took over the guild's membership and administrative structures in the fifteenth and sixteenth centuries. For the medieval period, see Etienne Boileau, *Le livre des métiers d'Etienne Boileau.* For the hemp merchants, see Lespinasse, *Les Métiers et corporations de la ville de Paris,* vol. 3, 45. Useful review essays on European women and guilds include Olwen Hufton's review article in *Signs,* 14, no. 1 (autumn 1988): 223–34; Bennett, "'History that Stands Still'"; and Maryanne Kowaleski and Judith M. Bennett, "Crafts, Guilds, and Women in the Middle Ages: Fifty Years after Marian K. Dale," *Signs* 14, no. 2 (winter 1989): 474–87.

13 AN AD XI 20, "Statuts, ordonnances et articles que les marchandes maîtresses toilières, lingères, canevassières . . ." (Paris, 1645). See the articles pertaining to the *lingères* in Lespinasse, *Les Métiers et Corporations de la ville de Paris,* vol. 3; and Jaubert, *Dictionnaire raisonné universel des arts et métiers,* vol. 2. Cynthia Truant is currently completing a book-length study of the Parisian linen-drapers.

14 BN MSS Delamare 2179 f. 58, "Estat des corps de marchands et des arts et métiers de la ville de Paris." A branch of the mercers' guild traded in wholesale linen cloth in competition with the linen-drapers, although they had no rights to sell in the Halle aux Toiles.

15 BN MSS Joly de Fleury 1728, fols. 186–99.

16 Ibid.

17 Lespinasse, *Les métiers et corporations de la Ville de Paris,* vol. 1, 228–39.

18 Martin Saint-Léon, *Histoire des corporations de métier,* 495. See also Lespinasse, *Les métiers et corporations de la ville de Paris,* vol. 3, 622–36. Administratively tied to the Parisian Faculty of Medicine and royal medical officers, the barber-surgeons'

corps was not a guild in the strict sense of the word. It did, however, possess statutes similar to those of the Parisian guilds and was included along with them in many acts of royal legislation. For an account of the most famous eighteenth-century midwife, see Nina Rattner Gelbart, *The King's Midwife: A History and Mystery of Madame du Coudray* (Berkeley: University of California Press, 1998).

19 Lespinasse, *Les métiers et corporations de la ville de Paris*, vol. 2, 187–223. In 1648, the royal government created a royal academy for painting and sculpture, which merged with the existing painter-sculptors' guild in 1652. In 1663, the monarchy granted the academy a monopoly over instruction in painting and sculpture.

20 Martin Saint-Léon, *Histoire des corporations de métier*, 73: "Mais entre toutes les villes du nord de la France et de la Belgique, c'est peut-être à Rouen que la corporation professionnelle ou plus exactement le guilde d'artisans apparaît pour la première fois avec les caractères de la plus indiscutable authenticité."

21 See Ouin-Lacroix, *Histoire des anciennes corporations et des confréries réligieuses de la capitale de la Normandie;* and Hafter, "Métiers féminins à Rouen au XVIIIe siècle."

22 Molière, *Le Bourgeois gentilhomme*, 164–65.

23 Letter from the royal procurator at the Châtelet of Paris to the controller general, April 4, 1692, Arthur-Michel de Boislisle, ed., *Correspondance des contrôleurs généraux des finances avec les intendants des provinces*, vol. 2, no. 1069 (Paris: Imprimerie nationale, 1874–97).

24 See *Encyclopédie, ou Dictionnaire raisonné des sciences, des arts et des métiers*, vols. 23–26, 29–32.

25 BN MSS Delamare 2179. The text was written anonymously in 1688.

26 BA 80 J 4710, "Statuts et ordonnances des marchands-maîtres tailleurs d'habits, pourpointiers-chaussetiers de la ville, fauxbourgs et banlieue de Paris," article 4. Despite the tailors' claim to a monopoly on ready-to-wear clothing, the *fripiers'* guild also possessed the right to sell ready-to-wear garments, if made from cloth beneath a specified value.

27 BA 80 J 4710, "Statuts et ordonnances des marchands-maîtres tailleurs d'habits, pourpointiers-chaussetiers de la ville, fauxbourgs et banlieue de Paris."

28 The contracts are held in the Minutier Central at the Archives nationales in Paris. A card catalogue in the Salle des Inventaires contains references to several hundred of these contracts.

29 Loats, "Gender and Work in Sixteenth-Century Paris."

30 See de Vries, "Between Purchasing Power and the World of Goods," in *Consumption and the World of Goods,* ed. Brewer and Porter. With regard to the timing of the female trade's emergence, several factors were probably involved. One might posit the rise of seamstresses as an indirect result of the growth of the French army in the second half of the seventeenth century. If tailors shifted their activities to meet the tremendous demand for new army uniforms, the lack of adequate suppliers of women's clothing may have opened a niche for female artisans. One might also consider the possible effects of an "industriousness" revolution, which Jan de Vries claims preceded the consumer and industrial revolutions. According to de Vries, seventeenth-century European families began to reorient their labor toward the market, leading to a new intensity and frequency of em-

ployment for women and children. The growth of seamstresses in this case would represent a redeployment of female labor away from the household economy toward an additional and independent source of remuneration.

31 A vast literature exists on Colbert and mercantilism. Classics include Pierre Clément, *Histoire de Colbert et de son administration*, 2 vols. (1874; Geneva: Slatkine, 1981); Charles W. Cole, *Colbert and a Century of French Mercantilism*, 2 vols. (New York, 1939); Eli F. Heckscher, *Mercantilism*, 2 vols. trans. Mendel Shapiro (London: G. Allen and Unwin, 1935); and Henri Sée, "Que faut-il penser de l'oeuvre economique de Colbert?" *Revue historique* 152 (1926): 181–94. More recently, see Philippe Minard, *La Fortune du colbertisme* (Paris: Fayard, 1997); Roland Mousnier, ed., *Un Nouveau Colbert: Actes du colloque pour le tricentaire de la mort de Colbert* (Paris: S.E.D.E.S., 1985); and Julian Dent, *Crisis in Finance: Crown, Financiers, and Society in Seventeenth-Century France* (Newton Abbot, Eng.: David and Charles, 1973).

32 Lespinasse, *Les Métiers et corporations de la ville de Paris*, vol. 1, 117.

33 Ibid.

34 For a highly skeptical reading of the 1673 edict, see Jean-Louis Bourgeon, "Colbert et les corporations," in *Un nouveau Colbert*. In this article, Bourgeon attacks the "general false idea" that Colbert's aim was to generalize the guild system, insisting that Colbert deliberately established separate spheres of production to compete with the guild system. While Bourgeon's argument usefully underlines Colbert's openness to variation and experimentation in economic organization, I believe he overstates his case in denying any administrative intent whatsoever to the 1673 edict.

35 BN MSS Delamare 21 791, "Table des arts et mestiers à etablir en communauté en la ville et faubourgs de Paris suivant l'édit du mois du Mars 1673."

36 Jean-Claude Perrot cites a Caen lieutenant general of police who suggested that desire from the trade was the most important criterion for incorporation: "Pour avoir les prérogatives de communauté et acquérir ou conserver à l'exclusion des autres ou concurremment avec elles, une portion de commerce, il faut une volonté actuelle de composer une communauté, une espèce d'association, des réglements autorisés, une prestation de serment, des préposés du corps pour veiller à l'observation du bon ordre." Perrot, *Genèse d'une ville moderne*, 322.

37 Levasseur, *Histoire des classes ouvrières et de l'industrie en France avant 1789*, 184.

38 AN AD XI 16, "Statuts, ordonnances et declaration du Roy, confirmative d'iceux, pour la communauté des couturières de la ville, fauxbourgs et banlieue de Paris."

39 Ibid.

40 Ibid.

41 The royal government's care to protect the tailors' preexisting privileges echoed clearly in the seamstresses' letters patent, which ordered that the women's new statutes be enforced: "Sans néanmoins que lesdits. Statuts ni l'érection des Couturières en Corps de Métier puissent faire préjudice au droit et à la faculté qu'ont eu jusqu'ici les Maîtres Tailleurs de faire des Jupes, Robes de Chambre, toutes sortes d'habits de Femmes et d'Enfans, que Nous voulons leur être conservés en son entier, ainsi qu'ils en ont joui jusqu'à présent." See "Statuts, ordonnances et déclaration du Roy, confirmative d'iceux, pour la communauté des couturières

de la ville, fauxbourgs et banlieue de Paris." See chapter 1 for a full discussion of the types of garments permitted to seamstresses.

42 M. de Marillac, intendant of Rouen, to the controller general, 9 juin 1685, *Correspondance des contrôleurs généraux,* vol. 2, no. 185.

43 BA 80 J 4729, "Statuts et ordonnances des maîtresses bouquetières chapelières en fleurs de cette ville et fauxbourgs de Paris," (Paris, 1678).

44 BN MSS Joly de Fleury 1728, fols. 186–99.

45 BA 80 J 4729, "Statuts et ordonnances des maîtresses bouquetières chapelières en fleurs de cette ville et fauxbourgs de Paris."

46 BN MSS de la Mare 21 792, f. 393.

47 Thomas Schaeper in his work on the Council of Commerce, formed in 1700, argues that this view is overly pessimistic. He cites revisionist historians who have "noted that Louis XIV's foreign policy, like the king himself, became more subdued and that several royal ministers and bureaucrats of this period were quite competent, imaginative, and eager to grapple with the difficulties besetting the government." See Thomas J. Schaeper, *The French Council of Commerce, 1700–1715: A Study of Mercantilism after Colbert* (Columbus: Ohio State University Press, 1983), 3.

48 See the lengthy description of these offices in chapter 6.

49 BN MSS Joly de Fleury 1728, fols. 109–14. Twenty-three trades were included in the original list. A supplement added another seven and divided the projected joint community of *aubergistes, garottiers,* and *loueurs de chambres garnies* into three separate guilds.

50 Ibid.

51 Ibid. René Marion offers an extended reading of this document and marketwomen's relationship to the corporate system in her dissertation, "The *Dames de la Halle:* Community and Authority in Early Modern Paris," (Ph.D. diss., Johns Hopkins University, 1994), 90–154.

52 The edict of 1691 specifically referred to some of these female vendors. Instead of ordering their incorporation it ruled that "female fruit-sellers and hucksteresses [*regrattières*]" who held a fixed shop would pay only thirty sous to practice their trades, while ambulatory merchants could do so free of charge. See Lespinasse, *Les Métiers et corporations de la ville de Paris,* vol. 1, 127.

53 According to their letters patent, registered by the Parlement of Rouen on August 5, 1722, the Le Havre seamstresses were granted the same trade rights as seamstresses in Paris and Rouen. They could make all women's and children's clothing, with the exception of the *corps de robe* and *bas de robe.* They were prohibited from making men's clothing. See Alphonse Martin, *Anciennes communautés d'arts et métiers du Havre* (Fécamp: Imprimerie de L. Durand, 1880), 169.

54 On Nevers, see Martin Saint-Léon, *Histoire des corporations des métiers,* 106.

55 Olivier-Martin, *L'Organisation corporative de la France d'Ancíen Régime,* 164.

56 AN K 1032.

57 For example, see the Aix tailors' assembly minutes, AC Aix-en-Provence HH 133–39.

58 Perrot, *Genèse d'une ville moderne,* vol. 1, 109, 145.

59 AD Calvados 1 B 1971. These women were subject to standard requirements for corporate membership, including formal apprenticeship with a female guild member. In August 1693, the acting officials of the tailors' guild made several complaints to the lieutenant general of police, in which they accused their predecessors of failing to record new masters' and mistresses' names in the official register. They demanded that each woman be obliged to produce "sa lettre de réception à ladite maîtrise si aucune elle a ensemble sa lettre de jurande et marché d'apprentissage."

60 AD Calvados C 2924, "Règlemens et statuts donnez par sa majesté pour les maîtres et maîtresses tailleurs d'habits de la ville, fauxbourgs et banlieue de Caen" (Caen: Veuve Rudeval, 1738).

61 AD Calvados C2924, "Arrest du donseil d'estat du roy portant reglement entre les maîtresses couturières de la ville de Caen, et les maîtres tailleurs de la même ville" (Caen: Veuve Rudeval, 1738).

62 Ibid.

63 Ibid.

64 A. Bourde, "La Provence au Grand Siècle," in *Histoire de la Provence,* ed. Edouard Baratier (Toulouse: Edouart Privat, 1969), 319.

65 AD Bouches-du-Rhône C2400, "Statuts et réglements que les maîtres marchands tailleurs d'habits de cette ville de Marseille, fauxbourgs et son terroir, ont résolus d'observer entr'eux" (Marseille: Veuve Boy et fils, 1733).

66 See Agulhon, *La Sociabilité méridionale,* vol. 1, 140, 153, 170.

67 AD Bouches-du-Rhône C2400, "Statuts et réglements que les Maîtres Marchands Tailleurs d'Habits de cette Ville de Marseille, Fauxbourgs et son Terroir, ont résolus d'observer entr'eux." According to the text of the statutes, a previous deliberation of the guild had authorized the syndics to draft new statutes "in conformity with those of the Sworn Master Tailors of the City of Paris." This directive testifies to the growing importance of the Parisian example in guild affairs across France.

68 AD Bouches-du-Rhône C2400.

69 Ibid.

70 Ibid.

71 Ibid.

72 Ibid. While it is unclear whether these recommendations came into effect, the Marseilles seamstresses remained within the tailors' guild until the abolition of the guilds in 1791.

73 Perrot, *Genèse d'une ville moderne,* vol. 1, 323.

74 BN MSS Joly de Fleury 1729, 23 août 1767. An earlier piece of legislation from 1767 also reflected an ambivalent attitude toward the guilds. In May 1767, the royal government created a set of twelve mastership letters, or *lettres de maîtrise,* for all guilds across France. The purchase of a *lettre de maîtrise* automatically bestowed guild membership on its owner without the requirements of apprenticeship or guild fees. By creating these letters, as it had done before, the royal government sought to garner new income from prospective guild members. In 1767, it also used this measure to respond to growing attacks on the guilds' exclu-

sive membership policies. The edict thus served as a summons to the corporate system to accept more outsiders, at the same time as it generated fiscal revenue.

75 Ibid.

76 BN MSS Joly de Fleury 1729, 13 septembre 1767.

77 Lespinasse, *Les métiers et corporations de la ville de Paris,* vol. 1, 104. On the 1776 abolition of the guilds, their restoration, and their ultimate destruction in 1791, see Steven L. Kaplan, *La fin des corporations.* Trans. Béatrice Vierne (Paris: Fayard, 2001).

78 Ibid., 165–66.

79 Lavergne, ed. *Archives des corporations des arts et métiers,* 24.

80 Lespinasse, *Les métiers et corporations de la ville de Paris,* vol. 1, 176.

81 The August edict directly addressed the status of the small female vending trades that figured in the series of projects examined above. It prohibited ambulatory vending (*colportage*) among guild masters and mistresses, although it permitted small fruit, vegetable, and other food vendors to sell in this fashion. The edict also suppressed the trade titles (*lettres domaniales*) that had previously been sold to these vendors. Henceforth, the sale of fruit, beer, eau de vie, and other foodstuffs could be undertaken freely.

82 Lespinasse, *Les métiers et corporations de la ville de Paris,* vol. 1.

83 AN Y 9333. These figures do not include masters and mistresses who had belonged to the guild before 1776 and who were required by the edict of August 1776 to pay fees to renew their membership. Returning masters do not appear in the records of the royal procurator of the Châtelet, but may be found in AN series P, which recorded *revenus casuels.*

84 For the seamstresses' complaints about the *découpeuses,* see BN MSS Joly de Fleury 596. Despite these fears, records from the reception of mistresses show that no more than a handful of men were accepted to the joint seamstress-*découpeuses'* guild between 1776 and 1791. *Découpeurs* formed a very small trade and men apparently had little taste for joining a guild that had been exclusively female for one hundred years. We must imagine that many tailors continued to work for women, despite the seamstresses' new monopoly. For post-1776 receptions, see AN Y 9333 and 9334.

85 AN AD XI 16, "Lettres patentes du roi, portant nouveaux statuts pour la communauté des maîtresses couturières-découpeuses de la ville de Paris." See chapter 1 for a more complete discussion of the 1781 statutes.

86 Revel, "Corps et communautés," 237. The edict of February 1778 reestablished guilds in the city of Rouen, while an edict of April 1779 did so for the rest of the province of Normandy.

87 BN MSS Joly de Fleury 1728.

88 BN MSS Joly de Fleury 1730.

FIVE *The Tailors and the Seamstresses: Corporate Privilege, Gender, and the Law*

1 This case is located in AD Calvados 1 B 1978, 16 août 1741. The police report blends the seamstresses' account of the tailors' words and deeds with explanatory inter-

jections from the police scribe: "Allez allez mesdames vous deshabiller vous avez perdu vostre étalage si vous voulez vous deshabiller et presenter vos habits à des filles qui par curiosité étoient présentes nous leur souffrirons plus tôt porter les coins du drap qu'à vous autres pour vous néan."

2 See Robert Darnton's well-known explanation of the joke behind another group of artisans' seemingly incomprehensible laughter in *The Great Cat Massacre and Other Episodes in French Cultural History* (New York: Vintage Books, 1985), ch. 2. See also reactions to Darnton's analysis in Roger Chartier, "Texts, Symbols, and Frenchness," in his *Cultural History Between Practices and Representations* (Ithaca: Cornell University Press, 1988); and Dominick La Capra, "Chartier, Darnton, and the Great Symbol Massacre," *Journal of Modern History* 60 (1988): 95–112.

3 On the crown's reliance on privilege for revenue, and the social and political consequences of this system, see Bien, "The Secretaires du Roi," 159–68, and "Offices, Corps, and a System of State Credit". On privilege itself, see also Revel, "Les Corps et communautés"; Bossenga, *The Politics of Privilege;* and Cerutti, *La Ville et les métiers,* 82–85.

4 AN Y 9500, 6 mars 1759. This document is a police transcription of the May 1756 assembly meeting, of which the original notes are lost. The assembly members resolved to fund an immediate investigation into the loss and possible replacement of the guild's papers.

5 See references to royal declarations forbidding tailors from making cloth buttons on September 25, 1694; January 26, 1726; May 15, 1736; and April 21, 1751 in Lespinasse, *Les Métiers et corporations de la ville de Paris,* vol. 3, 202, 204. See also the letter on this subject from the lieutenant general of police Nicholas de la Reynie to the controller general, June 17, 1696, in Boislisle, ed., *Correspondance des contrôleurs généraux des finances avec les intendants des provinces,* vol. 1, no. 1543, 426.

6 The phrase is from William Beik, *Absolutism and Society in Seventeenth-Century France: State Power and Provincial Aristocracy in Languedoc* (Cambridge, Eng.: Cambridge University Press, 1985), 225. On this subject see also David Bell, *Lawyers and Citizens: The Making of a Political Elite in Old Regime France* (Oxford: Oxford University Press, 1994). Reliance on the law did not mean that artisans habitually fought out through the Parlements their individual conflicts with workers or other masters, as Michael Sonenscher suggests in *Work and Wages.* Nor does it mean they were inspired by some notion of natural law, a notion that remains somewhat hazy in Sonenscher's use of it.

7 Anette Smedley-Weill, *Les intendants de Louis XIV* (Paris: Fayard, 1995), 337.

8 Together, the Parlements exercised sovereign judicial authority within France, judging cases on appeal from lower tribunals and in the first instance for churchmen, nobles, and some members of the Third Estate. The Parlements' judgments, or *arrêts de règlement,* held the force of law unless overturned by the royal council. Parlements also exercised legislative powers, because royal edicts held no force until they had been registered by the magistrates of the local Parlement. This legislative authority was reinforced by the Parlements' claimed capacity to delay registering new laws until their magistrates had examined them and submitted any disagreements to the king. The right of "remonstrance" gave them a certain

political power, which they increasingly exploited across the eighteenth century. Classics on the Parlements include Jean Egret, *Louis XV et l'opposition parlementaire* (Paris: A. Colin 1970); J.-François Bluche, *Les magistrats du Parlement de Paris au XVIIIe siècle* (Paris: impr. Jacques et Demontrond, 1960); William Doyle, *The Parlement of Bordeaux and the End of the Old Regime 1771–1790* (London: Ernest Benn, 1974); and J. H. Shennan, *The Parlement of Paris* (Ithaca: Cornell University Press, 1968). More recently, see Bailey Stone, *The French Parlements and the Crisis of the Old Regime* (Chapel Hill: University of North Carolina Press, 1986); John Rogister, *Louis XV and the Parlement de Paris, 1737–1754* (Cambridge, Eng.: Cambridge University Press, 1995); and Dale Van Kley, *The Damiens Affairs and the Unraveling of the Ancien Régime, 1750–1770* (Princeton: Princeton University Press, 1984). See also Doyle, "The Parlements," in *The Political Culture of the Old Regime*, 157–67.

9 See Revel, "Les Corps et communautés," 228–29. Revel suggests that the attack against the guilds in 1776 represented in fact a disguised political attack against the entire corporate system, and thus ultimately against the Parlements themselves. According to Revel, this explains why the Parlement in turn would speak so strongly in defense of the guilds. See chapter 4 for a discussion of the Parisian Parlement's defense of the guild system.

10 This title appears in the minutes of the seamstresses' guild assembly. See, for example, AN MC Etude CVIII 336, 13 mars 1719. On this office, see Olivier-Martin, *L'Organisation corporative de la France d'Ancien Régime,* 226.

11 Valuable information on the structure of the Parisian police is contained in Henri Berbaud and Michèle Bimbinet-Privat, *Le Châtelet de Paris, Répertoire numérique de la Série Y* (Paris: Archives nationales, 1993).

12 On the relationship between the Parisian people and the police, see Kaplan, "Réflexions sur la police du monde du travail, 1700–1815," 17–77; Farge, *Fragile Lives,* 19–30; David Garrioch, *Neighbourhood and Community in Paris, 1740–1790* (Cambridge, Eng.: Cambridge University Press, 1986), and "The People of Paris in the Eighteenth Century: Reflections on the Introduction of a 'Modern' Police Force," *European History Quarterly* 24 (1994): 511–35; Roche, *The People of Paris,* 271–77; and Alan Williams, "The Police and the Administration of Eighteenth-Century Paris," *Journal of Urban History* 4, no. 2 (February 1978): 157–82.

13 The next level of justice above the local police officials was the lieutenant general of police, who presided over the *bailliage* court in the north and the *sénéchaussée* in the south. A Parlement might be located in the same town as the guilds it judged, as in Aix-en-Provence, or in a neighboring capital, as was the case in Caen where the Parlement of Normandy sat in nearby Rouen. On the intendants, see Smedley-Weill, *Les intendants de Louis XIV;* and Vivian R. Gruder, *The Royal Provincial Intendants: A Governing Elite in Eighteenth-Century France* (Ithaca: Cornell University Press, 1968). Each intendant was assigned to a particular *intendance,* also known as a *généralité,* which constituted an administrative and, above all, fiscal jurisdiction.

14 In general, southern France relied on written law codes inherited from the Romans, while northern France used customary laws that varied from region to region and even village to village.

15 Léon Abensour, *La femme et le féminisme avant 1789* (1923; Geneva: Slatkine, 1977), 17.

16 *L'Encyclopédie, ou Dictionnaire raisonné des sciences, des arts et des métiers,* vol. 6, 475.

17 Even in Normandy, families found means to bypass restrictions on female inheritance rights, for example by drawing up contracts outside of the jurisdiction of Norman law. See Perrot, "Note sur les Contrats de mariage normands," in *Structures et relations sociales à Paris au XVIIIe siècle,* ed. Daumard and Furet.

18 A series of provisions protected wives' interests within marriage. In Parisian customary law, widows recuperated their dowries and any other property they had acquired since marriage. They could also renounce the couple's financial community and thereby escape responsibility for debt. Women could even retain financial independence after marriage by stipulating a separation of goods in their marriage contracts or reclaim it subsequently by demonstrating their husbands' gross financial mismanagement. They could obtain a physical separation as well, but only if they proved that their husbands' abuse placed their lives at risk, or if he installed his mistress within the family home. Similar stipulations existed in provincial law codes. On women's legal status and marriage law, see James F. Traer, *Marriage and the Family in Eighteenth-Century France* (Ithaca: Cornell University Press, 1980); Ralph E. Giesey, "Rules of Inheritance and Strategies of Mobility in Prerevolutionary France," *American Historical Review* 82, no. 2 (April 1977): 271–89; Jacques Lelièvre, *La Pratique des contrats de mariage chez les notaires au Châtelet de Paris de 1769 à 1804* (Paris: Editions Cujas, 1959); and Abensour, *La femme et le féminisme.*

19 Pothier, *Traité de la puissance maritale.*

20 Sonenscher, *Work and Wages,* 44. See also Hafter, "Gender Formation from a Working-Class Viewpoint," and "Female Masters in the Ribbonmaking Guild of Eighteenth-Century Rouen"; and the comment on her article by William Sewell, titled "Social and Cultural Perspectives on Women's Work: Comment on Loats, Hafter, and DeGroat."

21 AN AD XI 16, "Arrest du conseil d'estat du Roy qui ordonne l'exécution des statuts," 9 février 1675.

22 BN MSS Joly de Fleury 1728. According to the records of the royal procurator at the Châtelet, eighty-two new mistresses entered the guild between May and December 1675; these pioneers were followed by another seventy-five women in 1676.

23 AN AD XI 16, "Arrest du conseil d'estat du Roy qui ordonne l'exécution des statuts." The edict's failure to mention the faubourg Saint-Antoine, the largest island of freedom near Paris, is puzzling. It suggests that few seamstresses worked in the suburb, or that the crown tacitly accepted the freedom of women working there.

24 AN AD XI 16, "Arrest du conseil d'estat du Roy," 31 mai 1675. The ruling underlined the fiscal interests of the royal government, stating that renegade seamstresses would "deprive His Majesty of the aid he could hope for from the establishment of the said Community."

25 AN AD XI 16, "Extrait des registres du conseil d'estat," 11 avril 1676.

26 BA 80 J 4710, "Statuts et ordonnances des marchands-maîtres tailleurs-d'habits, pourpointiers-chaussetiers de la ville, fauxbourgs et banlieue de Paris."

27 In addition to the tailors, several other Parisian guilds formally enshrined the capacity of masters' daughters to work in the trade. These guilds included, for example, the embroiderers, the used-clothing and furniture dealers, and the makers of gold and silver buttons and *passementerie* (*passementiers-boutonniers d'or et d'argent*). See Lespinasse, *Les Métiers et corporations de la ville de Paris,* vol. 2, 181 n. 14, 154–55; vol. 3, 432 n. 14.

28 AN AD XI 16, "Arrests notables de la cour de parlement, rendus au profit de la communauté des maîtresses couturières de la ville et faux-bourgs de Paris," avril 22 1678.

29 AN AD XI 16, "Arrests notables de la cour de parlement, rendus au profit de la communauté des maîtresses couturières."

30 See chapter 4 for a fuller account of developments in Caen from 1712 to 1719.

31 AD Calvados 6E 89.

32 Minutes of these hearings provided much of the background information and the citations for this section. They are located in AD Calvados 6E 89. The *sub-délégué*'s name was Vobain Desplanches de Clouille.

33 AD Calvados, 6E 89. The tailors' use of Domat's comments on venal officehold-ers to discuss their own situation may reflect the absence of legal commentary on the status of guild masters.

34 Ibid.

35 Ibid.

36 Ibid.

37 Ibid.

38 Ibid.

39 Ibid.

40 On sexual insults to women, see Garrioch, "Verbal Insults in Eighteenth-Century Paris," in *The Social History of Language.*

41 AD Bouches-du-Rhône C 2400, "Statuts et règlemens que les maîtres marchands tailleurs d'habits de cette ville de Marseille ont résolus d'observer entr'eux."

42 See chapter 4 for a full discussion of developments in Marseilles.

43 AD Bouches-du-Rhône C 2400.

44 AD Bouches-du-Rhône C 2400. Municipal officers raised similar suspicions about a document seamstresses had supposedly signed in 1732 to approve a raise in their guild fees. Once again, municipal officers claimed, the tailors had used their own female relatives to foster an illusion of consent from seamstresses. Questioned on these points, the tailors denied the accusations of collusion with the "seamstresses." According to the intendant, the tailors asserted they could prove that only two of the signatories in 1732 were their own wives or daughters. In contrast to the *échevins'* version, they claimed that the reason the Parlement allowed them to raise the fees was that they had paid almost six hundred livres in fees to confirm the seamstresses privileges.

45 Ibid. Unfortunately, no information is offered regarding the "set price" of stays in Marseilles.

46 Ibid.

47 Ibid.

48 Ibid.

49 Ibid.

50 Steven Kaplan has used these documents to demonstrate the social and cultural weight of mastership for guild masters. See Kaplan, "Social Classification and Representation in the Corporate World of Eighteenth-Century France." Other historians have raised doubts about the representative value of the *mémoires*, suggesting, for example, a political interpretation of the struggle over the guilds' existence. See Revel, "Corps and Communautés."

51 Two recent articles treat these sources in a rather different fashion than I do. See Coffin, "Gender and the Guild Order"; and Truant, "Parisian Guildswomen and the (Sexual) Politics of Privilege." Unlike Coffin and Truant, I am skeptical of the relationship between the melodramatic rhetoric of the seamstresses' *mémoires* and the actual perceptions of guild members. I also find it problematic to derive evidence of trade structures and practices from these documents, as Coffin does.

52 This biographical information is from Maza, *Private Lives, Public Affairs.*

53 BN MSS Joly de Fleury 462, f. 117. "Supplément au mémoire à consulter des Six Corps, pour la communauté des couturières."

54 Ibid.

55 Ibid.

56 For the appeals to Marie-Antoinette and Joly de Fleury, see BN MSS Joly de Fleury 596.

57 Ibid. "Obsérvations pour les Marchandes et maîtresses couturières au sujet de l'Edit de rétablissement des corps et communautés."

58 BN MSS Joly de Fleury 462, f. 173, "Réflexions des maîtres tailleurs de Paris, sur le projet de supprimer les jurandes."

59 Ibid.

60 Ibid. "Un père bon ouvrier, est un Citoyen estimable; son exemple, son talent, son nom, deviennent pour ses enfans la partie la plus interessant de sa succession."

61 Ibid.

62 These cases also provide material for reflection on recent debates about the role of law in the guild system and in particular about the claims of Michael Sonenscher in *Work and Wages.* Was it, as Sonenscher argues, a conception of natural rights that endowed guild members with their understanding of corporate privilege? I would argue that it was not the tabula rasa of natural law that gave them such rights, but the positive laws and legal traditions associated with both marriage and guild statutes. Marriage law permitted widows the right to inherit corporate privileges in usufruct from their husbands, as did the officers' widows discussed by Domat. Daughters' prerogatives were not automatic natural rights, but privileges written into guild statutes. The guild family operated as a miniature corporation within the corporation, and membership in it conveyed a set of particular privileges regulated by legal documents.

1 For examples of contemporary critiques of the guild system, see Jean-Marie Roland de la Platière, "Règlement," in *Manufactures, arts et métiers*, vol. 13 of the *Encyclopédie méthodique* (Paris: Panckoucke, 1785); and Turgot's edict abolishing the guilds, reproduced in Lespinasse, ed., *Les métiers et corporations de la ville de Paris*, vol. 1, 104. Marcel Marion offers an account of royal fiscal exploitation of the guilds and an indignant list of their defects and abuses in his *Dictionnaire des institutions de la France XVIIe-XVIIIe siècle*, "Corporation," 144–52. See also Mandrou, *La France aux XVIIe et XVIIIe siècles*, 92–95; Goubert, *Louis XIV et vingt millions de Français*, 68–69, and *The Ancien Régime: French Society, 1600–1750*, 215; and Godechot, *Institutions de la France sous la Révolution et l'Empire*, 20. See Reddy, *The Rise of Market Culture*, 34–38; and Root, *La construction de l'Etat moderne en Europe*, 139, 155. For a critical discussion of this historiography, see Minard, "L'inspection des manufactures en France, de Colbert à la Révolution," 1–14; and Bossenga, *The Politics of Privilege*, 131, 166–67. Both authors question the opposition between state-imposed "regulation" and the "real" needs or interests of merchants and manufacturers.

2 Kaplan, *The Bakers of Paris*, 191.

3 Bossenga, *The Politics of Privilege*, 7.

4 For the bakers, see Kaplan, *The Bakers of Paris*, 162. Information on tailors comes from their 1660 statutes, "Statuts et ordonnances des marchands-maîtres tailleurs d'habits, pourpointiers-chaussetiers de la ville, fauxbourgs et banlieue de Paris."

5 AN AD XI 16, "Statuts, ordonnances et déclaration du Roy, confirmative d'iceux, pour la communauté des couturières de la ville, fauxbourgs et banlieue de Paris."

6 The registers of the royal procurator at the Châtelet of Paris recorded guild elections from the late-seventeenth century, noting the names of candidates and, in most cases, the number of votes they received. Existing registers cover the period from the creation of the guild in 1675 to 1684 and from 1736 to 1791. My estimate of the electoral pool is based on the highest number of votes received by a candidate in any given year.

7 BN MSS Joly de Fleury 596. Similar initiatives were undertaken in other guilds during the eighteenth century. See Kaplan, "The Character and Implications of Strife among Masters inside the Guilds of Eighteenth-Century Paris."

8 AN Y 9393, 23 juillet 1771.

9 This information is taken from a sample of almost eight hundred apprenticeship contracts dated between 1713 and 1761. See chapter 7 for a full account of apprenticeship in the trade.

10 Nicole Jacqueline Fourgault, a mistress's daughter, entered the guild in 1739 and was elected as a *jurée* thirty-four years later in 1773. Her colleague Marie Jeanne Forest was a newcomer to the trade. She became a mistress in 1740 and a *jurée* in 1774. Like many officials elected in the 1770s, Forest was called on to lead the guild again during the uncertain years following the 1776 reforms.

11 AN AD XI 16, "Lettres patentes du roi, portant nouveaux statuts pour la communauté des maîtresses couturières-découpeuses de la ville de Paris."

12 Roze de Chantoiseau, *Tablettes royales de renommée*, "*couturières*."

13 Family ties between mothers and daughters have been deduced by matching last names and also, where possible, by the fact that the younger woman entered the guild as a mistress's daughter. Overly common family names have been excluded from this list. Another sixteen *jurées* had daughters who joined the guild but did not serve as *jurées*. Many entered the guild immediately following their mothers' elections to benefit from the favorable entry conditions for *jurées'* daughters. In 1763, for example, the guild elected Marie Françoise LeRoy, wife of Duplessis, as a *jurée*. The same year, three women—probably her daughters—joined the guild as mistresses' daughters: Françoise Marie Duplessis, Madeleine Henriette Duplessis, and Marie Françoise Duplessis. While Madeleine Henriette attained the post of *jurée* in 1788, her two sisters never did.

14 AN MC Etude V 373, 14 mai 1734. Chollet received a fee of seventy-five livres for each child from the charitable foundation of the parish of Saint-Jean-en-Grève, the parish in which the guild offices were located.

15 AN MC Etude XXI 446, 19 mai 1768.

16 The seamstresses' corporate status endowed them with an implicit right to hold assembly meetings to debate group interests and formulate collective policy. In Caen, as revealed in chapter 5, a key element of the seamstresses' claim to independent guild status was their possession of an autonomous assembly after 1719. The dispute between tailors and seamstresses in Marseilles also demonstrates the central role played by collective meetings and collectively signed documents in legal decision making, even for trade groups that did not possess formal administrative institutions. Initiatives taken on behalf of a trade group held little legitimacy unless backed by the explicit authorization of an assembly, however undemocratically constituted.

17 AN MC Etude CVIII 332, 18 juin 1718.

18 See, for example, AN V7 428, 14 mars 1756, and 25 avril 1760. In the financial year 1750–1751, the guild spent 1,041 livres and 5 sous for tokens distributed at twelve assemblies. In the financial year 1754–1755, the guild paid 1,065 livres for assembly tokens. The custom of distributing sugar dated from 1676. In 1731, the *jurées* refused to continue this practice, lacking the assembly's explicit authorization for the expense. In 1735, the acting *jurées* protested that this refusal had led to a decline in attendance at assemblies. The assembly unanimously voted to approve the distribution of the sugar. In the fiscal year 1750–1751, the guild spent 958 livres and 16 sous on the sugar, and in 1754–1755 they spent 702 livres. See V 7 428, 14 mars 1756, and 25 avril 1760.

19 In the financial year 1773–1774, the guild distributed 352 livres to *jurées* and *anciennes* who attended the drawing up of accounts. If each woman received her four livres for attendance a total of 88 women were present. See AN V7 428, 2 mai 1776.

20 The chairing of the assembly itself shifted during the course of the eighteenth century from the senior *anciennes* to the acting officials. A meeting on August 10,

1719, was chaired by the dean, or *doyenne,* of the guild. The doyenne was presumably the most senior among the *anciennes,* although the guild's statutes did not mention this position. In subsequent years, the *jurées* assumed authority over assembly meetings, and after the 1750s the term "doyenne" did not reappear. In 1781, the new statutes gave acting officers explicit authority over the assembly: "The syndics and adjuncts will be responsible for ensuring that all takes place, in the said assemblies, with appropriate order, decency and tranquillity." See AN AD XI 16, "Lettres patentes du roi, portant nouveaux statuts pour la communauté des maîtresses couturières-découpeuses de la ville de Paris."

21 See, for example, the police investigation into fraudulent administrative practices on the part of the *bacheliers* found in AN Y9363, 20 mai 1749. Complaints regarding the *bacheliers'* financial extortion on this date were accompanied by complaints from the guild's clerks regarding a violent assault in the guild offices by the same men. See AN Y 9363, 25 mai 1747. The deliberations of the tailors' guild in Aix also reveal numerous cases of contestation, particularly regarding guild finances and elections. See AC Aix-en-Provence HH 133–39 for registers covering the period 1674 to 1784. For other trades, see Kaplan, "The Character and Implications of Strife among Masters inside the Guilds of Eighteenth-Century Paris," and *The Bakers of Paris,* 183–87.

22 AN MC Etude CVIII 337, 10 août 1719.

23 AN MC Etude CVIII 336, 31 mars 1719. The building has since disappeared.

24 In 1716, John Law was authorized by the Regency government to set up the first bank in French history. The large number of banknotes issued by Law's bank resulted in a sharp decrease in interest rates, creating ideal conditions for debtors to reimburse debts. The bank crashed in 1720, but not before many debtors—including the state—had shed significant debt at the expense of the lending institutions. See Emmanuel LeRoy Ladurie, *The Ancien Régime: A History of France, 1610–1774,* trans. Mark Greengrass (Oxford: Blackwell Publishers, 1996), 286–95. See also Jacques Cellard, *John Law et la Régence, 1715–1729* (Paris: Plon, 1996) and Antoin E. Murphy, *John Law: Economic Theorist and Policy-Maker* (Oxford: Clarendon Press, 1997).

25 AN MC Etude CVIII 336, 31 mars 1719.

26 AN Y 9509.

27 For the first two leases, see AN MC Etude CVIII 413, 4 juillet 1733; for Grosset's second renewal, see AN MC Etude CVIII 445, 28 décembre 1740. For Rogier, see AN MC Etude CVIII 536, 4 mars 1760.

28 AN Y 9509.

29 See Boullet's probate inventory, AN MC Etude XXXIII 475, 26 novembre 1735.

30 AN MC Etude CVIII 427, 27 septembre 1736.

31 AN MC Etude CVIII 445, 6 octobre 1740.

32 AN MC Etude CVIII 433, 8 november 1738.

33 AN MC Etude CVIII 505, 5 juillet 1753.

34 AN MC Etude CVIII 510, 21 septembre 1754.

35 AN MC Etude CVIII 512, 15 mai 1755.

36 AN Y 9509.

37 AN AD XI 16, "Lettres patentes du roi, portant nouveaux statuts pour la communauté des maîtresses couturières-découpeuses de la ville de Paris."

38 See audits of guild finances performed by the royal commission to liquidate guild debt, held in AN V7 428. A later section of this chapter discusses the audits in greater detail.

39 AN MC Etude CVIII, 10 mars 1744. On Jacques-Vincent Delacroix, see chapter 5.

40 AN Y 9380, 20 mai 1740.

41 AN Y 9372, 16 janvier 1682.

42 AN Y 12803, 26 janvier 1781.

43 AN Y 12984, 19 mars 1768.

44 AN Y 12985, 10 et 11 mai 1769.

45 The material rewards for their efforts could also, however, lead them into corruption and scandal. See the discussion of one such scandal in chapter 2.

46 Other merchants caught selling *dominos* on the rue Saint-Honoré in February 1747 included a fashion merchant, a master beltmaker, another hatter, and another buttonmaker. They all claimed to have leased shop space either to a mistress seamstress, a master tailor, or a *fripier*. See AN Y 9363, 10 février 1747.

47 AN Y 13112, 18 février 1760.

48 AN AD XI 16, "Lettres patentes du roi, rortant nouveaux statuts pour la communauté des maitresses couturieres-découpeuses de la ville de Paris."

49 AN MC Etude CVIII 479, 1 août 1748.

50 AN AD XI 16, "Statuts et reglements de la confrérie de Saint-Louis érigée en l'église paroissiale de Saint-Gervais de Paris," published with "Statuts, ordonnances et déclaration du roy, confirmative d'iceux pour la communauté des couturières." (Paris: Veuve G. Paulus Du-Mesnil, 1734).

51 AN MC Etude CVIII 490, 6 septembre 1750. The records of the church of Saint-Gervais do not offer any additional information regarding this confraternity.

52 Complaints filed by acting officials before the royal procurator at the Châtelet indicate that these were indeed levied—and that mistresses often failed to pay them.

53 AN MC Etude CVIII 513, 25 avril 1756.

54 AN MC Etude CVIII, 413, 10 août 1733.

55 BN MS Joly de Fleury 596, "Observations pour les marchandes maîtresses couturières au sujet de l'Edit de rétablissement des corporations."

56 On the subject of royal taxation see Marcel Marion, *L'impôt sur le revenu au XVIIIe siècle* (Toulouse: E. Privat, 1901), and *Les impôts directs sous l'Ancien régime* (Paris: E. Cornély 1910).

57 In assessing its members for the tax, the seamstresses' officers acted independently of the tailors, with whom they formed a single guild. I thank Michael Kwass for information on the Caen *capitation* of 1757.

58 AD Calvados C 4579, Capitation des arts et métiers 1757.

59 AN V7 428.

60 AN MC Etude CVIII 464, 29 mars 1745. For a discussion of royal guild offices, see René Nigeon, *Etat financier des corporations parisiennes d'arts et métiers an XVIIIe siècle* (Paris: Les Editions Reider, 1934); and Bossenga, *The Politics of Privilege*, 120–30.

61 Nigeon, *Etat financier des corporations parisiennes,* 17.

62 AN H2 2120.

63 AN AD XI 16, "Declaration du roy, pour unir et incorporer au corps et communauté des maîtresses cousturières de la ville de Paris, les offices de jurées, créez par edit du mois de mars 1691," 28 avril 1693. The source of the remaining six thousand livres is unknown.

64 The guild claimed this figure of 27,500 livres; government sources put the price at 25,000 livres. Both prices were comparable to the 21,000 and 22,000 livres paid, respectively, by the bonnetmakers and the candlemakers. See Nigeon, *Etat financier des corporations parisiennes,* 18.

65 As an assembly meeting of 1718 would note: "In execution of the said [edict] the *anciennes jurées* had imposed on themselves a voluntary assessment to compose part of the sum of 27,500 livres." AN MC Etude CVIII 332, 10 août 1718.

66 The *droit royal* had been imposed on all Parisian guilds as a result of the 1691 edict; it would appear that the royal government cancelled it in the aftermath of the 1693 offices.

67 AN MC Etude CVIII 332, 10 août 1718. In a 1718 assembly meeting, the *anciennes* recalled this sacrifice: "Au lieu de recevoir tous les droits à elles attribués [elles] se sont contentées de recevoir très peu de chose afin de remplir le prix des dites finances."

68 AN H2 2120, see the receipt from the "conseiller secrétaire du roi, garde des registres du conseiller général des finances" of 2 mai 1714.

69 AN MC Etude CVIII 332, 10 août 1718.

70 AN MC Etude CVIII 464, 29 mars 1745.

71 AN MC Etude CVIII 432, 16 août 1738.

72 These were the annual payments attached to the different offices the guild had purchased since 1691. They included 250 livres a year from the office of auditor of guild accounts, 250 livres for the treasurer, payer, and receiver of the guilds (which the guild had since repurchased from Sieur Hamel), 150 livres for the controller of weights and measures, and 150 livres for the guild clerk.

73 As in their previous experiences of borrowing, the guild reimbursed the loan quickly. On May 9, 1749, Guenisey signed a declaration before the guild's notary acknowledging his receipt of 15,000 livres plus 787 livres and 10 sous in unpaid annuities. For the original loan, see AN MC Etude CVIII 467, 21 Octobre 1745. For the guild's reimbursement, see AN MC Etude CVIII 483, 9 mai 1749.

74 AN V 7 428, 22 mars 1762.

75 AN MC Etude CVIII 531, 5 mai 1759. This was a common technique for royal fundraising, applied to many different officeholders apart from the guilds. The use of this tactic did not prevent the royal government from continually diminishing the stipends it paid for the guild offices. For example, the 750-livre annual stipend for the office of *greffier héréditaire* was reduced to 600 livres in 1716 and to 300 in January 1720. Stipends were thus liable to contradictory forms of manipulation by the royal government, which did not fulfill its tacit promise to reimburse the guilds at least partially for their purchase of the offices through the yearly fees associated with them. See AN H2 2120 for the receipt from the "con-

seiller secrétaire du roi, garde des registres du conseiller général des finances" of 2 mai 1714.

76 AN MC Etude CVIII 531, 5 mai 1759.

77 AC Aix-en-Provence HH 133; AD Bouches-du-Rhône CD 2400.

78 AN V7 428, 19 février 1756.

79 On this commission, see Nigeon, *Etat financier des corporations parisiennes*. Nigeon's analysis is limited, but it remains the only full-length treatment of the audit commission.

80 AN V 7 428, 4 juillet 1736.

81 AN V7 428, 18 juillet 1736.

82 The guild's fiscal year was determined by the election of new *jurées* and the promotion of a new senior official to the post of guild accountant. The outgoing accountant's term ended with the naming of her successor, at which point she prepared the accounts of her year in office. Because guild elections took place each year in late May or early June, the fiscal year ran from May of one year through April of the next.

83 AN V7 428, 1 février 1770.

84 See, for example, AN V7 428, 19 février 1756.

85 AN V7 428, 1 février 1770.

86 AN V7 428, 14 mars 1756.

87 The guild's notary received a total of four livres for each contract. See chapter 7 for a discussion of the notary's role in apprenticeship.

88 AN V7 428, 8 décembre 1761.

89 AN V7 428, 22 mars 1762.

90 AN V7 428: "Je n'empêche pour le Roy que par le jugement à intervenir les jurées qui ont successivement passé les charges de jurande dans leur communauté depuis 1745 jusq'en 1761 soient déchargées de tous forcemens de recette relativement aux 16 sous 6 deniers."

91 AN V7 428, 25 avril 1768.

92 AN V7 428, 1 février 1770.

93 AN V7 428, 28 avril 1774.

94 Indeed, the commission seems to have supervised the seamstresses much less tightly than it did the bakers' guild, to judge by Kaplan's findings in *The Bakers of Paris,* 174–83.

SEVEN *Career Paths in the Seamstresses' Trade: From Apprenticeship to Mistress-ship*

1 For studies of apprenticeship in France, see Nicole Pellegrin, ed., *Apprentissages XVIe–XXe siècles,* a special issue of *Revue d'histoire moderne et contemporaine* 40, no. 3 (juillet-septembre 1993). For eighteenth-century Paris, see, in particular, Kaplan, "L'Apprentissage au XVIIIe siècle." The literature on English apprenticeship is more extensive. See Ilana Krausman Ben-Amos, *Adolescence and Youth in Early Modern England* (New Haven, Conn.: Yale University Press, 1994), and "Women Apprentices in the Trades and Crafts of Early Modern Bristol," *Conti-*

nuity and Change 6, no. 2 (1991): 227–52; Graham Mayhew, "Life-Cycle Service and the Family Unit in Early Modern Rye," *Continuity and Change,* 6, no. 2 (1991): 201–26; and Pamela Sharpe, "Poor Children as Apprentices in Colyton, 1598–1830," *Continuity and Change* 6, no. 2 (1991): 253–70. For journeymen's paths to mastership, see Edward J. Shephard Jr., "Social and Geographic Mobility of the Eighteenth-Century Guild Artisan: An Analysis of Guild Receptions in Dijon, 1700–1790," in *Work in France,* ed. Kaplan and Koepp; and Michael Sonenscher, "Journeymen's Migrations and Workshop Organization in Eighteenth-Century France", and *Work and Wages.* Carol Loats has written the most extensive study of female apprenticeship, in which she stresses the large number of female apprentices in sixteenth-century Paris. See Loats, "Gender and Work in Sixteenth-Century Paris."

2 See, for example, works by Olwen Hufton, including *The Prospect Before Her,* 62–101, "Women and the Family Economy in Eighteenth-Century France," and "Women, Work, and Marriage in Eighteenth-Century France." See also Tilly and Scott, *Women Work and Family;* and Davis, "Women in the Crafts in Sixteenth-Century Lyon."

3 See chapter 4 for a discussion of seventeenth-century apprenticeship contracts.

4 For these contracts, see AN MC Etude CVIII 324.

5 This information is contained in the audits performed on the seamstresses' guild by the royal commission set up for this purpose. See AN V7 428.

6 An index of all Parisian notarial contracts for the year 1761 revealed a total of approximately 1,800 apprenticeship contracts in Paris.

7 AN LL 801, "Registre servant de tables aux matières contenues dans les livres des délibérations du bureau de l'oeuvre et fabrique de la paroisse de Saint-Jean-en-Grève"; AN LL 802, "Deuxième registre servant de tables aux matières contenues dans les livres des délibérations du bureau de l'oeuvre et fabrique de la paroisse de Saint-Jean-en-Grève."

8 AN H5 3782, "Comptes de la fabrique de la paroisse de Saint-Jean-en-Grève."

9 Claude-Joseph Ferrière, chapter 3, "Des Brevets d'apprentissage," in *La Science parfaite des notaires ou le moyen de faire un parfait notaire,* vol. 2 (Paris: C. Osmont, 1728).

10 Drawn from an exhaustive archival index, the samples from 1751 and 1761 should represent all apprenticeship contracts for those two years. Unfortunately, the contracts drawn up by the guild's notary are missing. For the year 1760–1761, the guild recorded almost three hundred new apprentices. The 1761 archival index contains only sixty-one. The fate of the missing contracts remains unclear, but their loss significantly distorts the sample. We have one large sample from the early-eighteenth century furnished exclusively by the guild notary, and a smaller group of contracts from the second half of the century furnished by every notary except the guild notary. This discrepancy carries obvious problems of representativity, but the use of both sources together helps mitigate the inevitable distortions.

11 See AN MC Etude CVIII 325, 326, 440, and 632, for seamstress apprenticeship contracts drawn up by the guild notary.

12 For an example, see AN CM Etude CXII 556, 14 mai 1751: "Elle promet pendant

ledit temps montrer et enseigner sondit métier de couturière et tout ce dont elle se mesle et entremet en iceluy sans luy en rien cacher."

13 MC Etude CVXVII 818, 22 septembre 1761: "De répondre aux bonnes intentions de ses père et mère, d'écouter en tout les salutaires avis de sa maîtresse."

14 For one example, see AN MC CXV 592, 21 juin 1751.

15 A large portion of this sample was drawn from AN MC Etude XVI 685, février–mai 1733.

16 This suggestion is made in Roche, *The Culture of Clothing*, 305–6.

17 It should be noted that in some cases the apprentices' Parisian roots did not sink very deep. Five mothers—four widows and one wife—gave a Parisian address for themselves while also declaring that their husbands had lived outside of the capital.

18 I have included only cases where fathers were still alive.

19 A *garçon* could either be an apprentice or, more likely in these cases, a journeyman.

20 I have enumerated some fathers who performed similar forms of labor in different categories when they were employed by municipal or royal institutions, rather than by a specific individual or family. Different forms of employment created different relationships to the labor market and to other social groups.

21 On this point, see Daumard and Furet, *Structures et relations sociales à Paris au XVIIIe siècle*, 32.

22 As Louise Tilly and Joan Scott have remarked: "Family labor was differentiated by age and sex. So, if a family had no need for a daughter's labor, she would be sent to a job somewhere else." Tilly and Scott, *Women, Work, and Family*, 33.

23 Kaplan, "L'Apprentissage au XVIIIe siècle," 450.

24 Ibid., 452. The real average among seamstresses was probably slightly higher than 14.4 years, because an additional twenty-five apprentices claimed to be majors, or at least 25 years old. Another fifteen were married women and two were widows. If we assign these forty-one women an age of 25 years each, the average age rises to 15.1 years. The comparison still holds, however, because Kaplan's average similarly excluded "major" apprentices.

25 Kaplan, "L'Apprentissage au XVIIIe siècle," 452. See also Jean-Pierre Hardy and David-Thierry Ruddel, *Les Apprentis artisans à Ouébec, 1660–1815*, (Québec: Les presses de l'université du Québec, 1977), 37.

26 These included two widowed mothers, one of whom had since remarried; two mothers whose husbands were still alive but apparently absent; and a girl presented by an unrelated guardian.

27 Kaplan, "L'Apprentissage au XVIIIe siècle," 450.

28 Prominent in this group were apprentices who engaged in apprenticeship without a parent or guardian. Out of a total of 55 women, 48 chose the form of instruction-only apprenticeship. They accounted for almost half of the 102 apprentices who would receive only instruction.

29 See AN MC Etude LXXIX 115, 11 octobre 1761.

30 AN AD XI 16, "Declaration du roy, pour unir et incorporer au corps et commu-

nauté des maîtresses cousturières de la ville de Paris, les offices de jurées, créez par édit du mois de mars 1691," 28 avril 1693.

31 The guild's allocation of these twenty livres, as we have seen, would create serious financial difficulties for subsequent *jurées*. See chapter 6 for this discussion.

32 See AN V7 428, 22 mai 1762. The sample of apprenticeship contracts taken from 1761 seems to confirm the guild's claim, showing that most notaries charged six livres for drafting the contract.

33 AN MC Etude CVIII 326, 22 décembre 1716.

34 AN MC Etude XII 582, 26 janvier 1763.

35 AN Y 14850, 22 janvier 1788.

36 AN MC Etude CVIII 325, 21 avril 1716.

37 AN MC Etude CVIII 632, 16 juin 1739.

38 AN V7 428, 22 mars 1762.

39 AN LL 802, "Deuxième registre servant de tables aux matières." Thus far virtually ignored by historians, the parish foundations were crucial grassroots institutions. They not only distributed a variety of forms of aid to needy parishioners, but also served as a source of influence and patronage for the notable laymen who administered them.

40 AN LL 802, "Deuxième registre servant de tables aux matières."

41 Limited scholarship exists on charitable apprenticeship. The English system functioned quite differently, with masters being obliged to take charity apprentices, for low fees, as a way to ease the burden of poor relief. Those who refused could be fined. See Mary B. Rose, "Social Policy and Business: Parish Apprenticeship and the Early Factory System, 1750–1834," *Business History* 31, no. 4 (October 1989): 5–32. For the French case, see A. Garnier, "La Fondation Charmolue et autres fondations charitables pour la mise en apprentissage des orphelins et des enfants pauvres," *Bulletin de la société historique et archéologique de Langres* 11, no. 159 (1955): 197–232, and "La Fondation Charmolue et autres fondations charitables pour la mise en apprentissage des orphelins et des enfants pauvres," (part 2), *Bulletin de la société historique et archéologique de Langres* 13, no. 166 (1957): 37–52.

42 There is no evidence that the foundation administrators imposed this preference; indeed the varying terms used to stipulate these services indicate that there were no fixed terms required by the charity.

43 The procedures followed in choosing apprentices varied from parish to parish and bequest to bequest. Sometimes the parish administrators selected children themselves, in other cases the benefactor named his or her own kin to this role.

44 The term *alloué* was also sometimes used for journeymen who were engaged for fixed periods by their masters. See the discussion on *alloués* by Kaplan in "L'Apprentissage au XVIIIe siècle," 459–66.

45 AN MC Etude I 452, 6 juillet 1751.

46 AN MC Etude XLIV 398, 6 juillet 1751.

47 AN L 643, no. 2.

48 For the community of Sainte Agnès, see LL 1659, f. 79. On charitable vocational institutions in general, see Sonnet, *L'éducation des filles au temps des Lumières.* Son-

net places these institutions in the wider context of female schools in eighteenth-century Paris, but does not indicate the impact of this type of vocational training on the labor market. She does state that graduates of free parish schools that were not dedicated to vocational training often went on to perform apprenticeship.

49 For conflicts between mistresses and apprentices and their families, see, for example, AN Y 9376, 7 décembre 1723; Y 9378, 10 juillet 1731, 1 août 1732, 9 juillet 1734; Y 9388, 31 janvier 1758; Y 9392, 1 mars 1765, 26 août 1766.

50 AN V7 428, 22 mars 1762.

51 The Archives nationales holds these records in Y 9323 through Y 9334. It should be noted that these records are not infallible. There are numerous cases of mistaken first names or of reception dates being off by a few days or weeks. Apart from such errors, the records lack an unknown number of individuals. For example, those who purchased letters of mastership in 1767 and other years are recorded in a separate register held in the P series at the Archives nationales. New masters may have also been ascribed to the wrong trades, or guild officials may have hidden them to avoid sharing mastership fees. Despite these potential lacunae, the records are on the whole trustworthy. Swearing in new guild members before the king's procurator was a solemn moment, taken seriously by police officials, corporate leaders, and the masters and mistresses themselves. Mistaken attribution is particularly unlikely in the case of the seamstresses, because they composed one of only four women's guilds.

52 AN Y 9323, 9330.

53 Edward Shephard analyzed guild admissions in Dijon over the eighteenth century, finding a similar drop in admissions during the 1740s. Shephard, "Social and Geographic Mobility of the Eighteenth-Century Guild Artisan," 113.

54 "Edit du roi portant nouvelle création de six corps de marchands et de quarante-quatre communautés d'arts et métiers," 11 août 1776.

55 I use "unqualified" here and subsequently to indicate the lack of formal qualifications. I do not mean that they had no skill or experience in the trade. Many masters and mistresses who entered through this path received trade training, perhaps in the provinces or through *allouage*. The actual skills they possessed, however, presents a perplexing—and unsolved—problem.

56 After 1776, no path of entry was recorded for incoming masters and mistresses.

57 In these figures I have excluded as statistically insignificant the mistresses entering through *lettres de maîtrise* and the Hôpital de la Trinité.

58 Mistresses' daughters and *sans qualité* mistresses were both quite volatile groups, with a standard deviation of 4.2 for an annual average of 11.4 in the first case, and a deviation of 9.2 for an average of 22.5 in the second. By contrast, apprentices were considerably more stable, with a standard deviation of 21 for an annual average of 102.4 mistresses. Across the period, the correlation between apprentices and *sans qualités* was 0.32 and between apprentices and mistresses' daughters 0.41. The figure for daughters and *sans qualités* was 0.0. I thank Vivek Singh, Benhamine Hafele, Rung-Ching Tsai, and Professor Douglas Simpson of the University of Illinois at Urbana-Champaign for providing correlation data.

59 AN Y 9323–9334.

60 Between 1736 and 1789, the correlation was only 0.32.

61 The fee of 420 livres was stated in the "Edit du roi portant nouvelle création de six corps de marchands et de quarante-quatre communautés d'arts et métiers." This edict lowered the charges for individuals entering the new tailors-*fripiers'* guild to 400 livres.

62 Most of these were recorded to have entered "by marriage," with no indication if the wife was a daughter or widow of a master.

63 Compared to other Parisian guilds, this level of generational continuity was probably on the lower end of the scale. Michael Sonenscher in *Work and Wages* (116), found that 34 percent of Parisian master locksmiths were sons of masters from 1742 to 1776. Sonenscher notes the important role of marriage in the transmission of mastership, but interprets this only as "a source of tension between journeymen who had served an apprenticeship in a particular city and journeymen who had been apprenticed elsewhere." He does not speculate on the significance of this finding for women's role in the family. Sonenscher, *Work and Wages,* 110.

64 Jacques Rancière has argued that the tailors' trade was the preserve of poor men and youngest sons, describing training in the trade as "a poor man's apprenticeship." Rancière, "The Myth of the Artisans," in *Work in France,* ed. Kaplan and Koepp, 319. For a similar account of patterns of upward mobility for sons, and maintenance of the status quo for daughters, see Liu, *The Weavers' Knot,* 238–49.

65 Lespinasse, *Les Corporations d'arts et métiers de la ville de Paris,* vol. 3, "*Tailleurs d'habits.*"

66 See BN MSS Joly de Fleury 1249 for records of artisans who worked at the Hôpital de la Trinité.

67 In Caen, the lieutenant general of police presided over the admission of new guild masters and apprenticeship agreements. Records of these events are available in the departmental archives for the period 1719 to 1791. This study is based on a sample of guild admissions every five years from 1724 to 1789, as well during the hardship years of 1740–1741, 1766–1768, 1775–1791. See AD Calvados 1 B 2006, 2016–2021, 2026, 2032, 2037–2039, 2042, 2047, 2052, 2057–2058, 2063, 2065, 2069, 2073–2078, 2080.

68 AD Calvados, Dépôt de AC Caen 615 EDT 610. Unfortunately, it is not known how this number divided among new masters, reconfirmed old ones, and *agregés.*

69 AD Calvados C 4610.

70 From 1745 to 1790, the guild recorded a total of 140 masters entering the guild. AC Aix-en-Provence HH 144, "Registre des réceptions des maîtres tailleurs."

71 The post-1776 reforms eliminated apprenticeship as a requirement for mastership, but the Aix tailors continued to record it as a path to entry to the guild.

EIGHT *Marriage, Fortune, and Family: The World of the Mistress Seamstress*

1 AN Y 11946, 7 juin 1749.

2 See, for example, Hufton, "Women and the Family Economy in Eighteenth-Century France," and "Women, Work, and Marriage in Eighteenth-Century

France." See also Tilly and Scott, *Women, Work, and Family;* and Davis, "Women in the Crafts in Sixteenth-Century Lyon." More recently, see Hafter, ed., *European Women and Pre-Industrial Craft;* Gullickson, *The Spinners and Weavers of Auffay;* and Liu, *The Weavers' Knot.*

3 In their study of marriage contracts, Adeline Daumard and François Furet claimed that 60 percent of marriages in 1749 were preceded by a marriage contract. Daumard and Furet, *Structures et relations sociales à Paris,* 23. François Lebrun has estimated that 60 to 75 percent of Parisian marriages were preceded by a notarized marriage contract. François Lebrun, "Amour et mariage," in *Histoire de la population française,* vol. 2, ed. J. Dupâquier (Paris: Presses universitaires de France, 1988), 308.

4 Among twenty-three nonmistresses, nineteen called themselves simply "seamstresses" (*couturières*), and one used the term *ouvrière en couture.* In three cases I have included marriage contracts with no information on profession, when I knew from supplementary information that the bride apprenticed as a seamstress and later became a mistress.

5 Of 159 cases, 136 were mistresses and 23 nonmistresses.

6 For the marriage contract, see AN MC Etude XXXIII 358, 2 janvier 1685, and for the probate inventory, AN MC Etude CXVIII 288, 19 mars 1714.

7 These are not necessarily the same couples, because sometimes information was available only for the bride or the groom.

8 See Garden, *Lyon et les lyonnais au XVIIIe siècle;* Kaplan, *The Bakers of Paris;* Roche, *The People of Paris;* and the memoirs of Ménétra, *Journal de ma vie.*

9 Véronique Nahoum-Grappe offers a reading of a fascinating case held in the Parisian police archives that appears to be a merchant mercer's diary, in which he recounts the story of his wife's increasing rejection of married life and of participation in his trade, as she discovered the joys of fine food, entertaining, and going out on walks alone and with other men. See Nahoum-Grappe, "Briller à Paris," 143–46. Arlette Farge originally discussed the document in her *Fragile Lives,* 85–100. The document itself is held in AN Y 11741.

10 This is the case, for example, in Daumard and Furet, *Structures et relations sociales à Paris au milieu du XVIIIe siècle,* the most important work on marriage patterns in eighteenth-century Paris.

11 In some cases it is also clear that wider family interests were involved in these marriages. The brother of one mistress who married a tailor was himself a master tailor. The father of another groom used his children's marriages to establish a network of family alliances within the garment trades. In 1751, Pierre Chauvin, a *bourgeois de Paris,* gave his twenty-year-old son André, a journeyman tailor, in marriage to a twenty-five-year-old mistress seamstress. On the same day, the groom's sister also married a journeyman tailor. Under his title of *bourgeois de Paris,* this father may have been himself a master tailor or otherwise active in the production and sale of clothing. By accumulating skilled workers in the family, as well as acquiring the mistress status of his daughter-in-law, he may have been attempting to augment or diversify his production. See AN MC Etude XXI 446, 16 avril 1768.

12 AN MC Etude LXI 450, 30 juin 1751.

13 AN MC Etude XXXVIII 392, 7 novembre 1751.

14 AN MC Etude XXX 321, 12 avril 1751.

15 AN MC Etude VII 297, 1 juin 1755. I am grateful to Steven Kaplan for providing this and the following archival references.

16 AN MC Etude VII 329, 17 décembre 1760.

17 For the marriage contract, see AN MC Etude XXXIII 358, 2 janvier 1685. The information regarding the son comes from his mother's after-death inventory, AN MC Etude CXVIII 288, 19 mars 1714.

18 For Cabaille, see AN MC Etude XXXV 708, 2 avril 1761; for Charbonnet, see AN MC Etude LXXII 355, 3 novembre 1761; for Gérault, see AN MC Etude XXXV 707, 22 janvier 1761.

19 Fourteen out of forty-seven mistresses included the *maîtrise* in the dowry.

20 The value ascribed to female guild privileges is also underlined by a master tailor who included in his daughter's dowry the privilege that she would bestow on her new husband to be received into the guild as a master's son-in-law. Her 1,200-livre dowry thus included 300 livres for the "droit de maîtrise à la profession de tailleur qui réside en la personne de ladite future comme fille de maître." AN MC Etude LXXXI 292, 17 décembre 1741.

21 Adeline Daumard and François Furet put forward the poverty thesis in their *Structures et relations sociales à Paris,* 20–21, which Steven Kaplan refuted in his study *The Bakers of Paris,* 307–8.

22 Lelièvre, *La Pratique des contrats de mariage chez les notaires au Châtelet de Paris de 1769 à 1804,* 43.

23 Hufton, "Women, Work, and Marriage in Eighteenth-Century France," 195.

24 Lelièvre, *La Pratique des contrats de mariage,* 42. At marriage, mistress seamstresses were poorer than master bakers. Steven Kaplan has found marriage contributions among master bakers ranging from 2,337 to 3,783 livres across the eighteenth-century. Kaplan, *The Bakers of Paris,* 310.

25 Using available information, cash and investments accounted on average for 30 percent of the dowry, clothing and household goods for 22.4 percent, a mixture of cash and household goods for 45 percent, and mistress-ship for only 3.2 percent of the total dowry. For Vanse, see AN MC Etude LI 970, 12 mai 1751.

26 AN MC Etude I 439, 11 février 1749.

27 AN MC Etude XX 491, 21 novembre 1728.

28 AN MC Etude XXXVI 503, 14 mars 1762.

29 In the total sample, grooms stipulated an average *douaire* of 845 livres (median = 500). If these sums represented 50 percent of their fortune, the grooms would have possessed an average of 1,690 livres, a figure substantially lower than the seamstresses' overall average of 2,057 livres.

30 Figures taken from the collection of the *dixième de l'industrie* tax in 1768. AD Calvados C 5532.

31 Louis Henry and Jacques Houdaille, "Célibat et age au mariage aux XVIIIe et XIXe siècles en France," *Population* 1 (1978), 43–44. Pardailhé-Galabrun, *The Birth of Intimacy,* 34.

32 Mercier, *Le Tableau de Paris*, vol. 1, 796.

33 For a discussion of the use of probate inventories in French history, see Pardailhé-Galabrun, *The Birth of Intimacy*, 2–7; Daniel Roche, *The People of Paris*, 59–63; Françoise Lehoux, *Le cadre de vie des médecins parisiens aux XVIe et XVIIe siècles* (Paris: A. et J. Picard, 1976); Michel Marion, *Recherches sur les bibliothèques privées à Paris au milieu du XVIIIe siècle* (Paris: Bibliothèque nationale, 1978); and Maurice Garden, "Les Inventaires après décès: Source globale de l'histoire sociale lyonnaise ou juxtaposition de monographies familiales?" *Cahiers d'histoire* 12 (1967): 153–73. See also the collection entitled *Les actes notariés: source de l'histoire sociale, XVIe–XIXe siècles: Actes du colloque de Strasbourg, mars 1978*, ed. Bernard Vogler (Strasbourg, 1979).

34 This is, however, a minimum figure, because the notary noted more beds than people in six cases.

35 For Barbier, see AN MC Etude IX 818, 1 juillet 1788; for Desloriers, see AN Y 10784 A, 17 janvier 1770.

36 They also did not have grandchildren, except in a small number of cases, so this is not just a question of elderly women outliving their own offspring.

37 Pardailhé-Galabrun, *The Birth of Intimacy*, 36. For figures regarding childbirth see Lebrun, "Amour et mariage."

38 Respectively, AN Y 11673, 4 mars 1743; AN MC Etude VII 449, 2 mars 1781; and AN MC Etude LXXXIX 555, 22 août 1754.

39 AN MC Etude XVI 824, 27 août 1777.

40 AN MC Etude XXXVI 425, 10 novembre 1735.

41 For Ducouroy, see AN MC Etude CXII 573, 23 mai 1759; for Dollé, see AN MC Etude XXXVI 425, 10 novembre 1735; for Delamaisonneuve, see AN MC Etude VIII 1233, 7 avril 1788.

42 The mistresses formed a disproportionately large number of female household heads compared to the female population in general. François Lebrun has claimed that only 30 percent of women were household heads at age fifty-five, and only 40 percent at age seventy. In this sample, thirty-eight out of forty-two women or 90 percent were household heads. Lebrun, "Amour et mariage," 331.

43 For nineteenth-century superstitions, see Paul Sébillot, *Légendes et curiosités des métiers* (1894–1895; Marseille: Lafitte, 1981), 227–34.

44 Respectively, AN MC Etude VIII 1233, 7 avril 1788; AN MC Etude CXII 573, 23 mai 1759; and AN MC Etude IX 741, 16 septembre 1767.

45 Respectively, AN MC Etude VII 449, 2 mars 1781; AN MC Etude LXXXIX 555, 16 juillet 1754; and AN MC Etude XLIV 604, 5 juillet 1788.

46 Respectively, AN MC Etude XLVI 388, 12 février 1762; AN MC Etude XXXIII 475, 21 novembre 1735; and AN MC Etude XVI 810, 25 février 1774.

47 For a description of Parisian interiors and the growth of private spaces within the home, see Pardailhé-Galabrun, *The Birth of Intimacy*, 40–72.

48 Roche, *The People of Paris*, 107. I have established the break at 1760 instead of the more logical date of 1750, because of the small number of pre-1750 inventories. Divided this way, the total sample includes twenty inventories up to 1760 and forty-five post-1760 ones.

49 Respectively, AN MC Etude I 551, 24 mars 1773; AN MC Etude V 373, 28 mai 1734; and AN MC Etude LVIII 483, 1 août 1777.

50 AN MC Etude CXII 573, 23 mai 1759.

51 AN MC Etude LXXXI 331, 13 août 1751.

52 AN MC Etude CVIII 568, 22 septembre 1764.

53 AN Y 14511, 7 décembre, 1766.

54 Nonmistress Jeanne Gabrielle Haguenier was the poorest seamstress in terms of household goods, with only 22.2 livres in clothing and furnishings. The second poorest was mistress Marie Forestier, who died in 1728 with 176.4 livres of household goods. Marie Anne Guichard occupied the highest rank, with 3,363 livres. On the proliferation of inexpensive goods in Paris, see Roche, *History of Everday Things;* and Fairchilds, "The Production and Marketing of Populuxe Goods in Eighteenth-Century Paris."

55 Of course, tapestries and window curtains also fulfilled aesthetic functions. My decision to place them with furniture stems from the fact that notaries usually evaluated them with items of furniture.

56 For Pelée, see AN MC Etude LXXXIX 555, 22 août 1754; for Miller, see AN MC Etude XLIV 604, 5 juillet 1788; for Prempain, see AN MC Etude VII 449, 2 mars 1781; and for Faitout, see AN MC Etude LXXVI 380, 11 août 1761.

57 For Talbot, see AN MC Etude XXI 454, 25 avril 1770; and for Patural, see AN MC Etude XLIV 520, 6 avril 1776.

58 For Guichard, see AN MC Etude LVIII 483, 1 août 1777; for Ducouroy, see AN MC Etude CXII 573, 23 mai 1759.

59 For a discussion of fashions in home decor, see Pardailhé-Galabrun, *The Birth of Intimacy,* 110; and Auslander, *Taste and Power: Furnishing Modern France.*

60 Pardailhé-Galabrun, *The Birth of Intimacy,* 93–94.

61 For Jauhier, see AN MC Etude I 576, 23 janvier 1779; for Souters, see AN MC Etude CXVIII 467, 6 novembre 1751.

62 Pardailhé-Galabrun, *The Birth of Intimacy,* 175; Kaplan, *The Bakers of Paris,* 351–52.

63 For a discussion of reading in the eighteenth century, see Orest Ranum's essay "The Refuges of Intimacy," in *Passions of the Renaissance,* ed. Roger Chartier, vol. 3 of *A History of Private Life,* eds. Philippe Ariès and Georges Duby (Cambridge, Mass.: Harvard University Press, 1989), 259.

64 These figures include the actual seamstress's clothing only; if we include the husband's, from five cases containing information, the average rises to 221 livres. The lowest wardrobe value, 4 livres, demonstrates the weakness of the inventories as a source. Françoise Môlé, widow of a bourgeois de Paris, possessed 160 livres in silverware and 322 livres in household belongings; she certainly possessed more than 4 livres worth of clothing.

  Daniel Roche gives average wardrobe values of 344 livres for "artisans and shopkeepers," 42 for "wage-earners," and 115 for domestic servants, based on 100 probate inventories for each category from 1700. For the year 1789, the averages for these categories rise to 587, 115, and 293 livres respectively. These averages appear to include the wardrobes of both husband and wife. Roche, *The Culture of Clothing,* 94.

65 AN MC Etude IX 741, 16 septembre 1767.

66 AN MC Etude LXXXI 460, 12 avril 1777.

67 Roche, *The Culture of Clothing*, 121–22.

68 For Battou, see AN MC Etude XXXVI 425, 2 septembre 1735; for Dollé, see AN MC Etude XXXVI 425, 10 novembre 1735; for Talbot, see AN MC Etude XXI 454, 25 avril 1770; for Turpin, see AN MC Etude LXXXVI 667, 30 janvier 1756; and for Blet, see AN MC Etude IX 741, 16 septembre 1767.

69 For Battou, see AN MC Etude XXXVI 425, 2 septembre 1735; for Beroin, see AN MC Etude LXIX 631, 10 mai 1743.

70 For Alexandre, see AN MC Etude LX 345, 4 juin 1762; for Godard, see LVIII 440, 8 mai 1771.

71 For Bricon, see AN MC Etude CXI 301, 4 mai 1770; and for Denizon, see AN MC Etude XC 489, 12 mai 1781. See chapter 3 for a lengthier account of the acquisition of professional supplies.

72 See Philip T. Hoffman, Gilles Postel-Vinay, and Jean Laurent Rosenthal, "Private Credit Markets in Paris, 1690–1849," *The Journal of Economic History* 52, no. 2 (1992): 293–306. See also David R. Weir, "Tontines, Public Finance, and Revolution in France and England, 1688–1789," *The Journal of Economic History* 55, no. 1 (March 1989): 95–124.

73 Chapter 3 examines the function of credit in the trade in greater detail. For this chapter, I simply added up the value of outstanding accounts as part of mistresses' total fortunes. I included accounts in the estimation of total fortune only in cases where payment appeared to be a real possibility. I excluded accounts dating ten years prior to the seamstresses' death, unless the notary offered some evidence of the client's intention to settle the account.

74 AN MC Etude CXII 573, 23 mai 1759. Her inventory does not specify the origin of this property; she most likely inherited it from a relative.

75 For Monseignat, see AN MC Etude XXXIV 678, 10 décembre 1770; for LeClerc, see AN MC Etude XLVI 282, 23 décembre 1739.

76 The inventories suggest a drop in absolute holdings over the eighteenth century, with an average prior to 1760 of 4,614 livres (median = 2,704), and a post-1760 average of only 4,512 livres (median = 1,057). These figures, however, may represent an increased availability of notarial inventories to modest fortunes over the period, rather than a real drop in living standards. The relative scarcity of pre-1750 inventories would certainly strengthen this hypothesis.

77 Respectively, AN MC Etude IX 741, 16 septembre 1767; AN MC Etude VII 449, 2 mars 1781; AN MC Etude LXIX 631, 10 may 1743; and AN MC Etude CXVIII 467, 6 novembre 1751. Daniel Roche gives averages for total moveable wealth in 1700 of 4,100 livres for artisans and shopkeepers, 776 for wage earners, and 4,200 for servants, based on one hundred probate inventories for each category. These figures rose in 1789 to 8,457; 1,776; and 8,251, respectively. Roche, *The Culture of Clothing*, 94.

78 AN MC Etude LIX 355, 13 septembre 1779.

1 Pioneering work on the post-revolutionary legacy of corporatism was done by Sewell in *Work and Revolution in France.*

2 Document reproduced in Darline Gay Levy, Harriet Branson Applewhite, and Mary Durham Johnson, eds., *Women in Revolutionary Paris, 1789–1795* (Urbana: University of Illinois Press, 1979), 18–21. I have used their translation of the French text.

3 Document reproduced in Levy, Applewhite, and Johnson, eds., *Women in Revolutionary Paris, 1789–1795,* 58–60. I have used the editors' translation of the French text, but have substituted "seamstress" for "dressmaker" in their translation of the word *couturière.*

4 Document reproduced in ibid., 22. See chapter 7 for membership statistics.

5 Cited in Sewell, *Work and Revolution in France,* 87.

6 For women's work in Revolutionary Paris, see Dominique Godineau, *The Women of Paris and Their French Revolution,* trans. Katherine Streip (1988; Berkeley: University of California Press, 1998); and Angela Groppi, "Le Travail des femmes à Paris à l'époque de la Révolution française," *Bulletin de l'histoire économique et sociale de la Révolution française* (1979): 27–46.

7 Cited in John Lynn, *The Bayonets of the Republic,* (Boulder, Colo.: Westview, 1996), 56. I am grateful to John Lynn for this reference.

8 The sewing project is described in Godineau, *The Women of Paris and Their French Revolution,* 72–75. Godineau also describes the creation of charitable spinning workshops, examined in greater detail by Lisa DiCaprio, "The Enterprise of Welfare: State-Sponsored Work for Women in Revolutionary Paris" (Ph.D. diss., Rutgers University, 1996). According to Godineau, few women "of the artisan class" sought employment in these workshops (78).

9 Johnson, "Patterns of Proletarianization," 68.

10 Christopher Johnson suggests that bespoke production in the tailoring trade was increasingly dominated by large-scale merchant manufacturers in the late Old Regime and the first decades of the eighteenth century. It is not clear if a similar transition occurred in the production of women's clothing. See Johnson, "Patterns of Proletarianization," 68.

11 See *L'Union des modes,* no. 7, 12 janvier 1837; and no. 14, 22 mars 1837.

12 Johnson, "Economic Change and Artisan Discontent," 93.

13 On the introduction of the sewing machine, see Judith Coffin, "Credit, Consumption, and Images of Women's Desires: Selling the Sewing Machine in Late Nineteenth-Century France," *French Historical Studies* 18, no. 3 (spring 1994): 749–83, and *The Politics of Women's Work,* chs. 2 and 3; Monique Peyrière, "L'industrie de la machine à coudre en France, 1830–1914," in *La Révolution des aiguilles: Habiller les Français et les Américains, 19e-20e siècles,* ed. Louis Bergeron (Paris: Editions de L'Ecole des hautes études en sciences sociales, 1996), 95–114; Nicole Pellegrin, "Femmes et machines à coudre: Remarques sur un objet technique et ses usages," *Pénélope* 9 (automne 1983): 64–71; and Grace Rogers Cooper, *The Sewing Ma-*

chine: Its Invention and Development (Washington, D.C.: Smithsonian Institution Press, 1968).

14 Joan Scott, "Statistical Representations of Work: *La Statistique de l'industrie à Paris, 1847–1848,*" in *Gender and the Politics of History*, 113–38.

15 These figures are given by Nancy L. Green in *Ready-to-Wear and Ready-to-Work: A Century of Industry and Immigrants in Paris and New York* (Durham, N.C.: Duke University Press, 1997), 78.

16 Green, *Ready-to-Wear and Ready-to-Work*, 78–80.

17 See Charles Crouch, "The Petite Bourgeoisie of Paris during the Bourbon Restoration, 1814–1830: A Prosopographical Inquiry into the Political and Economic Integration of the Parisian Lower Middle Class" (Ph.D. diss., University of Illinois at Urbana-Champaign, 1991), 142. Crouch reports 177 female bankruptcies, with 44 in the clothing industry. The latter figure includes 11 dress-shop owners. Altogether, women comprised only 8 percent of over 5,000 bankruptcies occurring from 1818 to 1830. Crouch also finds that merchant tailors represented 5.1 percent of the total bankruptcies in this period, a result he interprets as evidence of a process of consolidation of production and proletarianization.

18 On the *magasins de nouveautés*, see Michael B. Miller, *The Bon Marché: Bourgeois Culture and the Department Store, 1869–1920* (Princeton: Princeton University Press, 1981), 19–28. On department stores, see Miller, *The Bon Marché*; and Rosalind Williams, *Dream Worlds: Mass Consumption in Late Nineteenth-Century France* (Berkeley: University of California Press, 1982).

19 See Scott, "Work Identities for Men and Women," in her *Gender and the Politics of History*; and DeGroat, "The Public Nature of Women's Work."

20 Scott, "Work Identities for Men and Women," 103.

21 Scott, "Work Identities for Men and Women," 102–8. On women's homework in the garment trades, see Lorraine Coons, " 'Neglected Sisters' of the Women's Movement"; and Coffin, *The Politics of Women's Work*, 121–40.

22 DeGroat, "The Public Nature of Women's Work," 41–42.

23 See Charles Benoist, *Les Ouvrières de l'aiguille: Notes pour l'étude de la question sociale* (Paris: L. Chailley 1895), 254.

24 Green, *Ready-to-Wear and Ready-to-Work*, 20–23, 40–42, 78–80.

25 Ibid., 79.

26 François Boucher, *20,000 Years of Fashion: The History of Costume and Personal Adornment* (New York: Harry N. Abrams, 1987), 391–93.

27 On women and unions in the Second Empire and Third Republic, see Madeleine Guilbert, *Les Femmes et les organisations syndicales avant 1914: Présentation et commentaires de documents pour une étude du syndicalisme féminin* (Paris: Centre national de la recherche scientifique, 1966); Marie-Hélène Zylberberg-Hocquard, *Féminisme et syndicalisme en France* (Paris: Editions Anthropos, 1978); Michelle Perrot, "Les Femmes et le syndicalisme au temps de la naissance de la CGT," *Cahiers d'Histoire de l'Institut de Recherches Marxistes* 61 (1995): 47–53; Patricia Hilden, "Women and the Labour Movement in France, 1869–1914," *Historical Journal* 29, no. 4 (1986): 809–932; and Charles Sowerwine, *Sisters or Citizens? Women and Socialism in France since 1876* (New York: Cambridge University Press, 1982). On labor movements in

the nineteenth-century garment trades, see Coffin, *The Politics of Women's Work,* 175–90. For general works on French syndicalism, see, among others, Lenard Berlanstein, *The Working People of Paris, 1871–1914* (Baltimore: Johns Hopkins University Press, 1984); Michelle Perrot, *Les Ouvriers en grève: France, 1871–1890* (Paris: Mouton, 1973); and Bernard Moss, *The Origins of the French Labor Movement, 1830–1914: The Socialism of Skilled Workers* (Berkeley: University of California Press, 1976).

28 Coffin, *The Politics of Women's Work,* 185–86.

29 Françoise Thébaud, *La femme au temps de la guerre de 14* (Paris: Editions Stock, 1986), 258–64; and Jean-Jacques Becker, "Les midinettes en grève à Paris," in *Le Monde,* 13 août 1994.

30 On Social Catholicism, see Henri Rollet, *L'Action sociale des catholiques en France, 1871–1901* (Paris: Editions contemporaines, 1947); Jean-Baptiste Duroselle, *Les débuts du catholicisme social en France* (Paris, 1951); Jean-Marie Mayeur, "Les Eglises dans la société," in *L'Histoire religieuse de la France, 19–20 siècle,* ed. Jean-Marie Mayeur (Paris: Editions Beauchesne, 1975); Pierre Pierrard, *L'Eglise et les ouvriers* (Paris: Hachette littérature, 1984); and Gérard Cholvy, *L'Histoire religieuse de la France contemporaine,* 2 vols. (Toulouse: Privat, 1985).

31 For a contemporary account of the Union of the Needle, see Gabriel Levasnier, *Papiers de famille professionnelle: L'ancienne "communauté" des couturières de Paris et le syndicat actuel de l'aiguille, 1675–1896* (Paris: Imprimerie de C. Rivière, 1896). On women in the Christian union movement in the early-twentieth century, see Joceline Chabot, "Les Syndicats féminins chrétiens et la formation militante de 1913 à 1936: 'Propagandistes idéales' et 'héroine identitielle,'" *Mouvement social* 165 (1993): 7–21.

32 See Benoist, *Les Ouvrières de l'aiguille,* 257: "Après avoir commencé par réunir toutes les ouvrières ensemble, on s'était aperçu qu'il valait mieux les réunir par métiers, couturières ensemble, modistes ensemble." For further information on the Union of the Needle, see its published journal, *Le Bulletin de l'aiguille.* See also Henri Rollet, *L'Action sociale des catholiques en France.*

33 Verdier, *Façons de dire, façons de faire,* 198–202, 231–32.

34 Ibid., 205.

35 Ibid., 233–35.

36 On immigrant labor in the garment trades, see Green, *Ready-to-Wear and Ready-to-Work,* and *The Pletzl of Paris: Jewish Immigrant Workers in the "Belle Époque"* (New York: Holmes and Meier, 1986).

Bibliography

PRIMARY SOURCES

MANUSCRIPT AND ARCHIVAL SOURCES

Manuscript and archival sources for this volume were too numerous and scattered to be listed individually. Throughout the book, I have provided precise archival references for documents cited. Here, I will indicate only the series and subseries that I used in different archives and manuscript collections.

1. *Archives nationales* (Paris)

AD. This subseries consists of printed documents, for the most part laws and regulations. It includes statutes of the Parisian guilds as well as printed copies of judgments from the royal council or the Parisian Parlement regarding the guilds.

F. This series contains documents deposited by the different ministries of the French government. Subseries F12 pertains to commerce and industry in Paris and the provinces and contains correspondence between the royal controller general and provincial intendants.

H2. This subseries contains documents on the municipal government of Paris and its finances. I used it for information about the financial affairs of the seamstresses' guild.

K and KK. This series and subseries are composed of diverse materials, including documents issuing from the royal government, the king's household, and the administration of Paris and provincial cities.

L and LL. This series and subseries hold records regarding the French Catholic Church, its relations with the Vatican, and the administration of different ecclesiastical institutions, including the Parisian parishes. It furnished records of the sponsorship of apprenticeship by the parish of Saint-Jean-en-Grève.

Minutier Central. The Minutier Central constitutes the Parisian notarial archives. It contains a wide variety of notarized contracts, such as probate inventories, marriage contracts, apprenticeship contracts, and financial contracts. I made extensive use of notarial archives from the seventeenth and eighteenth centuries, particularly Etude CVIII, the office that serviced the seamstresses' guild during the eighteenth century. I also made use of the indexes for the Minutier central that have been completed for the years 1751 and 1761.

V7. This subseries contains records of extraordinary royal commissions, including the commission established in 1716 to audit the guilds' debts. It provided audits of the seamstresses' guild from the 1730s to the 1770s.

Y. This series contains the archives of the police of Paris, including minutes and registers from the king's procurator at the Châtelet and the papers of the Parisian police *commissaires*. It constituted one of the most important sources for this book. The office of the king's procurator supplied records of entries to the seamstresses' and tailors' guilds as well as judgments on guild-related complaints. The papers of the *commissaires* provided records from police seals on seamstresses' apartments, as well as myriad complaints from or about seamstresses that involved work-related conflicts, theft, prostitution and vagrancy arrests, and sexual assault.

2. *Bibliothèque nationale* (Paris)
Manuscript Collections:
Collection Joly de Fleury. This manuscript collection contains a large variety of administrative documents, including correspondence between Attorney General Joly de Fleury and other royal administrators, along with guild-related documents.

Collection de la Mare. The documents in this manuscript collection, created by the police inspector Delamare, address the administration and police of Paris in the eighteenth century.

Manuscrits français. This enormous collection includes reports from Paris inspectors of police on prostitution in the city.

Cabinet des Estampes.
The print and engraving collection of the Bibliothèque nationale contains numerous fashion engravings from the late seventeenth and eighteenth centuries. Many of the illustrations for this volume came from this source.

3. *Archives de Paris et de l'ancien département de la Seine* (Paris)
Subseries 4B6 and 5B6. These subseries contain bankruptcy records from the commercial tribunal, known as the consular court (*jurisdiction consulaire*). The records include dossiers on individual bankruptcy cases and account books belonging to artisans or merchants who declared bankruptcy.

4. *Archives départementales du Calvados* (Caen) and *Archives departementales des Bouches-du-Rhone* (Marseilles)
French departmental archives make use of a standard classification system. I thus made use of the same series in each of the departmental archives I used.

B. Courts and Jurisdictions. This series contains registers of entries to provincial guilds and apprenticeship contracts held by provincial police officials. It also includes the archives of provincial police courts and police inquiries.

C. Provincial Administration. This series contains documents emanating from the administration of the provinces prior to 1789. It includes information about a diverse range of matters including the military, justice, agriculture, commerce, industry, taxation, and public construction. It also contains the papers and correspondence of the intendants of the districts that composed each province.

E. This series usually contains, among other materials, the papers of the guilds in provincial cities and towns.

5. *Archives municipales d'Aix-en-Provence* (Aix-en-Provence)

HH. This subseries contains the papers of the city's guilds, when they have not been deposited in departmental archives. In Aix, one finds minutes of the tailors' guild assembly meetings (HH 132–HH 139), as well as other documents produced by this guild.

6. *Bibliothèque de l'Arsenal* (Paris)

This library holds a large and varied collection of manuscript documents in addition to its printed sources. I used the manuscript collection for Parisian police inspectors' reports on prostitution as well as records of the surveillance and interrogation of members of the Jansenist movement.

7. *Bibliothèque Doucet* (Paris)

Microfilm Manuscrit 1. Succession de Rose Bertin. This source contains records from the efforts undertaken by Rose Bertin's heirs in the early nineteenth century to recover outstanding debts owed to the fashion merchants. The documents include copies of Bertin's bills and correspondence between her heirs' lawyers and her former clients.

PRINTED PRIMARY SOURCES

L'Apologie ou la défense des Paniers. Paris, 1727.

Benoist, Charles. *Les ouvrières de l'aiguille: Notes pour l'étude de la question sociale.* Paris: L. Chailley, 1985.

Le Cabinet des Modes. (1785–1786).

Campan, Madame. *Mémoires de Madame Campan, première femme de chambre de Marie-Antoinette.* Ed. Jean Chalon, notes by Carlos De Angulo. Paris: Mercure de France, 1988.

Clément, Pierre. *Colbert: Lettres, instructions et mémoires.* 10 vols. Paris: Imprimerie impériale, 1861–1882.

Corneille, Pierre. "La Galérie du palais," in *Oeuvres de P. Corneille,* vol. 2. Ed. Ch. Marty-Laveaux. Paris: Hachette, 1862.

Boislisle, Arthur-Michel de, ed. *Correspondance des contrôleurs généraux des finances avec les intendants des provinces.* 3 vols. Paris: Imprimerie nationale, 1874–97.

Bridaine, P. *L'indignité et l'extravagance des paniers pour les femmes chrétiennes.* Paris, 1757.

Burtel. *Art de la Couturière en Robes: Guide des Dames et des Damoiselles*. Paris: Audot, 1828.

Courtin, Antoine de. *Nouveau traité de la civilité qui se pratique en France, parmi les honnestes gens*. 1671; Paris: H. Josset, 1672.

Dancourt. *Les Bourgeoises à la mode*. Paris, 1693.

Dillmont, Thérèse de. *Encyclopédie des ouvrages des dames*. 1851; Paris: Librairie Ch. Delagrave, 1993.

D'Offemont. *Avis très important au public: Sur différentes espèces de Corps et de Bottines d'une nouvelle invention*. Paris: Chez la Veuve Delaguette, 1758.

Donneau de Visé, Jean, ed. *Le Mercure galant*. 1672–1710.

Duguet, Jacques Joseph [attributed]. *Cas de conscience décidé, par l'auteur de la Prière Publique: On demande s'il est permis de suivre le mode, et en particulier si l'usage des paniers peut être souffert?* 1728.

L'Encyclopédie méthodique: Manufactures, arts et métiers. Paris: Chez Panckoucke, 1782–1791.

L'Encyclopédie, ou Dictionnaire raisonné des sciences, des arts et des métiers. Ed. Denis Diderot and Jean d'Alembert. 35 vols. 1751–1780; Stuttgart-Bad Cannstatt: Frommann, 1966.

Faret, Nicolas. *L'honneste homme ou l'art de plaire à la court*. 1636; Geneva: Slatkine, 1970.

Ferrière, Claude-Joseph. *La Science parfaite des notaires ou le moyen de faire un parfait notaire*, 2 vols. Paris: C. Osmont, 1728.

Furetière, Antoine. *Dictionnaire universel*. 3 vols. 1690; Geneva: Slatkine, 1970.

Garsault, François-Antoine de. *L'Art du tailleur, contenant le tailleur d'habits d'hommes, les culottes de peau, le tailleur de corps de femmes et enfants, la couturière, et la marchande de modes*. Paris: Imprimerie de L. F. Delatour, 1769.

Genlis, Madame de. *De l'esprit des étiquettes de l'ancienne cour et des usages du monde de ce temps*. Paris: Mercure de France, 1996.

Henissart, Chevalier d' [attributed]. *Satyre sur les cerceaux, paniers, criardes et manteaux-volans des femmes, et sur leurs autres ajustemens*. Paris: Thiboust, 1727.

Isambert, François-André, ed., *Recueil général des anciennes lois françaises*. 29 vols. Paris: Belin-LePrieur, 1821–1833.

Jaubert, Abbé Pierre. *Dictionnaire raisonné universel des arts et métiers*. Paris: P. F. Didot jeune, 1773.

Lavergne, Georges Claudius, ed. *Archives des corporations des arts et métiers*. Paris: Charavay frères, 1879.

LeRoy, Alphonse. *Recherches sur les habillemens des femmes et des enfans, ou Examen de la manière dont il faut vêtir l'un et l'autre sexe*. Paris: LeBoucher, 1772.

Levasnier, Gabriel. *Papiers de famille professionnelle: L'Ancienne "communauté" des couturières de Paris et le syndicat actuel de l'aiguille, 1675–1896*. Paris: Imprimerie de C. Rivière, 1896.

Levy, Darline Gay, Harriet Branson Applewhite, and Mary Durham Johnson, eds. *Women in Revolutionary Paris, 1789–1795*. Urbana: University of Illinois Press, 1979.

Lespinasse, René de, ed. *Les Métiers et corporations de la ville de Paris*. 3 vols. Paris: Imprimerie nationale, 1886.

Lespinasse, René de, and François Bonnardot, eds. *Le Livre des métiers d'Etienne Boileau*. Paris: Imprimerie nationale, 1879.

Magasin des modes nouvelles francoises et angloises. 1786–1787.

Ménétra, Jacques-Louis. *Journal of My Life*. Ed. Daniel Roche, trans. Arthur Goldhammer. New York: Columbia University Press, 1986.

Mercier, Louis-Sébastien. *Tableau de Paris*. 2 vols. Ed. Jean-Claude Bonnet. Paris: Mercure de France, 1994.

Molière. *Le Bourgeois gentilhomme, Les Femmes savantes, Le Malade imaginaire*. Ed. Georges Couton. Paris: Gallimard, 1971.

———. *Les Précieuses ridicules*. In *Oeuvres complètes de Molière*. Ed. Georges Mongredien. Paris: Garnier-Flammarion, 1964.

Murger, Henri. *Scènes de la vie de Bohème*. Paris, 1851.

Oberkirch, Henriette-Louise de Waldner de Freundstein, baronne d'. *Mémoires de la Baronne d'Oberkirch sur la cour de Louis XVI et la société française avant 1789*. Ed. Suzanne Burkard. Paris: Mercure de France, 1989.

Pradel, Abraham du [pseudonym Nicolas de Blegny]. *Livre commode des adresses de Paris*. 2 vols. Ed. Edouard Fournier. 1692; Paris: P. Daffis, 1878.

Ramazzini, Bernardino. *Diseases of Workers*. Trans. W. C. Wright. New York: Hafner Publishing, 1964.

Reiset, Gustave-Armand Henri, Comte de, ed. *Modes et usages au temps de Marie-Antoinette. Livre journal de Madame Eloffe. Marchande de modes, couturière, lingère ordinaire de la Reine et des dames de sa cour*. Paris: Firmin-Didot, 1885.

Reisser. *Avis important au sexe, ou essai sur les corps baleinés pour former et conserver la taille aux jeunes personnes*. Lyon: Chez V. Reguilliat, 1770.

Restif de la Bretonne, Nicolas-Edmé. "Les Nuits de Paris." In *Paris le jour, Paris la nuit*, ed. Michel Delon. Paris: Robert Laffont, 1990.

———. *Les Contemporaines communes, ou Aventures des belles Marchandes, Ouvrières, etc. de l'âge-présent*, vols. 21–22. 1786; Geneva: Slatkine, 1988.

Roslin, M. *Le Tarif des Marchands Fripiers, Tailleurs, Tapissiers, Couturiers et autres personnes qui veulent se faire faire des Habits ou Meubles*. Paris: A. de Heuqueville, 1734.

Rothstein, Natalie, ed. *A Lady of Fashion: Barbara Johnson's Album of Styles and Fabrics*. London: Thames and Hudson, 1987.

Rousseau, Jean-Jacques. *Discours sur les sciences et les arts: Lettre à d'Alembert*. Ed. Jean Varloot. Paris: Gallimard, 1987.

———. *Emile ou de l'éducation*. Ed. François Richard and Pierre Richard. 1762; Paris: Editions Garnier Frères, 1961.

Roze de Chantoiseau. *Tablettes royales de renommée ou almanach général d'indication des négocians, artistes célèbres et fabricans des Six Corps, arts et métiers de la ville de Paris et autres villes du royaume*. Paris: Desnos et la Veuve Duchesne, 1773.

Satyre nouvelle contre le luxe des femmes: Pour la réformation des modes, Nompareilles, Rubans, Falbalas, Abattans, Raions, Maris, Colinettes, Cremones, Sourcils de Haneton, Mousquetairs, Souris, Battanpouce, Assassins, Suffoquans, Favoris, Stinquerques et Prétintailles. Paris, 1703.

Savary des Bruslons, Jacques. *Dictionnaire universel de commerce*. 3 vols. Paris: Veuve Estienne, 1741.

Sévigné, Marie de Rabutin-Chantal, marquise de. *Lettres de Madame de Sévigné*. Ed. Bernard Raffalli. Paris: Garnier-Flammarion, 1976.

Winslow, Jacques-Bénigne. "Sur les mauvais effets de l'usage des Corps à baleine." *Histoire de l'Académie royal des sciences* (1741): 172–83.

Wollstonecraft, Mary. *A Vindication of the Rights of Women*. Ed. Carol H. Poston. 1792; New York: Norton, 1988.

SELECTED SECONDARY SOURCES

Abensour, Léon. *La Femme et le féminisme avant 1789*. 1923; Geneva: Slatkine, 1977.

Acloque, Geneviève. *Les Corporations, l'industrie et le commerce à Chartres du XIe siècle à la Révolution*. 1917; Paris: Slatkine, 1967.

Adams, Christine. "A Choice Not to Wed? Unmarried Women in Eighteenth-Century France." *Journal of Social History* 29, no. 4 (1996): 883–94.

Agulhon, Maurice. *La Sociabilité méridionale: Confréries et associations dans la vie collective en Provence orientale à la fin du XVIIIe siècle*. 2 vols. Aix-en-Provence: La Pensée universitaire, 1966.

Amussen, Susan Dwyer. *An Ordered Society: Gender and Class in Early Modern England*. Oxford: Basil Blackwell, 1988.

Andress, David. "Economic Dislocation and Social Discontent in the French Revolution: Survival in Paris in the Era of the Flight to Varennes." *French History* 10, no. 1 (March 1996): 30–55.

Applewhite, Harriet B., and Darline G. Levy, eds. *Women and Politics in the Age of the Democratic Revolution*. Ann Arbor: University of Michigan Press, 1990.

Arnold, Janet. *Patterns of Fashion: Englishwomen's Dresses and Their Construction*. London: Macmillan, 1977.

Auslander, Leora. *Taste and Power: Furnishing Modern France*. Berkeley: University of California Press, 1996.

Badiou, D. "Les Couturières parisiennes." Mémoire de maîtrise, Université de Paris I, 1981.

Baker, Keith Michael, ed. *The French Revolution and the Creation of Modern Political Culture*. 3 vols. Oxford: Oxford University Press, 1987.

Baratier, Edouard, ed. *Histoire de la Provence*. Toulouse: Privat, 1969.

Barnes, Ruth, and Joanne B. Eicher, eds. *Dress and Gender: Making and Meaning*. Providence, R.I.: Berg Publishers Inc., 1992.

Beik, William. *Absolutism and Society in Seventeenth-Century France: State Power and Provincial Aristocracy in Languedoc*. Cambridge, Eng.: Cambridge University Press, 1985.

Bell, David. "The 'Public Sphere,' the State, and the World of Law in Eighteenth-Century France." *French Historical Studies* 17 (fall 1992): 912–34.

Benabou, Erica-Marie. *La prostitution et la police des moeurs au XVIIIe siècle*. Ed. Pierre Goubert. Paris: Perrin, 1987.

Benedict, Philip, ed. *Cities and Social Change in Early Modern France*. London: Unwin Hyman, 1989.

Benhamou, Reed. "Fashion in the *Mercure:* From Human Foible to Female Failing." *Eighteenth-Century Studies* 31, no. 1 (1997): 27–43.

Bennett, Judith M. " 'History that Stands Still': Women's Work in the European Past." *Feminist Studies* 14 (summer 1988): 269–83.

Berg, Maxine. "What Difference Did Women's Work Make to the Industrial Revolution?" *History Workshop Journal* 35 (spring 1993): 22–44.

———. *Markets and Manufactures in Early Industrial Europe.* London: Routledge, 1991.

Berg, Maxine, Pat Hudson, and Michael Sonenscher, eds. *Manufacture in Town and Country before the Factory.* Cambridge, Eng.: Cambridge University Press, 1983.

Bergeron, Louis, ed. *La Revolution des aiguilles: Habiller les Français et les Américains, 19e–20e siècles.* Paris: Editions de l'ecole des hautes etudes en sciences sociales, 1996.

Biehn, Michel. *En jupon piqué et robe d'indienne: Costumes provençaux.* Marseille: J. Lafitte, 1987.

Bien, David. "Offices, Corps, and a System of State Credit: The Uses of Privilege under the Ancien Regime." In *The Political Culture of the Old Regime,* vol. 1 of *The French Revolution and the Creation of Modern Political Culture,* ed. Keith Michael Baker. Oxford: Oxford University Press, 1987.

———. "The Secretaires du Roi: Absolutism, Corps, and Privilege under the Ancien Regime." In *Vom Ancien Régime zur Französischen Revolution,* ed. Ernst Hinrichs, Eberhard Schmitt, and Rudolf Vierhaus. Gottingen: Vandenhoeck and Ruprecht, 1978.

Blanc, Hippolyte. *Le Compagnon des corporations de métiers et l'organisation ouvrière du XIIIe au XVIIe siècle.* Paris: Secrétariat de l'Association catholique, 1883.

Boissonnade, P. *Colbert, le triumphe de l'etatisme.* Paris: M. Rivière, 1932.

Boltanski, Luc. *The Making of a Class: Cadres in French Society.* Trans. Arthur Goldhammer. Cambridge, Eng.: Cambridge University Press, 1987.

Bondois, Paul-M. *Colbert et l'industrie de la dentelle.* Paris: M. Riviere, 1926.

Bossenga, Gail. *The Politics of Privilege: Old Regime and Revolution in Lille.* Cambridge, Eng.: Cambridge University Press, 1991.

———. "Protecting Merchants: Guilds and Commercial Capitalism in Eighteenth-Century France." *French Historical Studies* 15 (fall 1988): 693–703.

Boucher, François. *Twenty Thousand Years of Fashion: The History of Costume and Personal Adornment.* New York: Harry N. Abrams, 1987.

———. *Histoire du costume en Occident, de l'Antiquité à nos jours.* Paris: Flammarion, 1965.

Bourdieu, Pierre. *Distinction: A Social Critique of the Judgment of Taste.* Trans. Richard Nice. Cambridge, Mass.: Harvard University Press, 1984.

Bourgeon, Jean-Louis. "Colbert et les corporations: l'Exemple de Paris." In *Un Nouveau Colbert: Actes du colloque pour le tricentenaire de la mort de Colbert,* ed. Roland Mousnier. Paris: SEDES, 1985.

Bouvier-Ajam, Maurice. *Histoire du travail en France, des origines à la Révolution.* Paris: R. Pichon and R. Durand-Auzias, 1957.

Braesch, Frédéric. "Essai de statistique de la population ouvrière de Paris vers 1791." *La Révolution française* 63 (1912–1913): 289–321.

Braudel, Fernand. *Les structures du quotidien*, vol. 1 of *Civilisation matérielle, économie et capitalisme, XVe–XVIIIe siècle*. Paris: Librarie Armand Colin, 1979.

Breward, Christopher. *The Culture of Fashion: A New History of Fashionable Dress*. Manchester: Manchester University Press, 1995.

Brewer, John and Roy Porter, eds. *Consumption and the World of Goods*. London: Routledge, 1993.

Bridenthal, Renate, Claudia Koonz, and Susan Stuard, eds. *Becoming Visible: Women in European History*. Boston: Houghton Mifflin, 1987.

Campbell, Colin. *The Romantic Ethic and the Spirit of Modern Consumerism*. Oxford: Basil Blackwell, 1987.

Carrière, Jacqueline. "La Population d'Aix-en-Provence à la fin du XVIIe siècle, étude de démographie historique d'après le registre de capitation de 1695." D.E.S. Faculté de lettres d'Aix-en-Provence, 1957.

Cerutti, Simona. *La Ville et les métiers: Naissance d'un langage corporatif (Turin XVIIe-XVIIIe siècle)*. Paris: Editions de l'ecole des hautes études en sciences sociales, 1990.

Charles, Lindsey, and Lorna Duffin, eds. *Women and Work in Preindustrial England*. London: Croom Helm, 1985.

Chartier, Roger. "Le Monde comme représentation." *Annales* 44 (November–December 1989): 1505–20.

———, ed. *Passions of the Renaissance*. Vol. 3 of *A History of Private Life*. Ed. Philippe Ariès and Georges Duby. Cambridge, Mass.: Harvard University Press, 1989.

Chassagne, Serge. *Oberkampf: Un Entrepreneur capitaliste au siècle des lumières*. Paris: Aubier Montaigne, 1980.

Chassaigne, Marc. *La lieutenance générale de police de Paris*. 1906; Geneva: Slatkine-Megariotis, 1975.

Chauvin, Jacques, Nicole Pellegrin, and Marie-Christine Planchard. *L'Aiguille et le sabaron: Techniques et productions du vêtement en Poitou, 1880–1950*. Poitiers: Centre d'archéologie et d'éthnologie poitevine, Musée de la Ville de Poitiers et de la Société des antiquaires de l'Ouest, 1983.

Clark, Alice. *Working Life of Women in the Seventeenth Century*. 1919; London: Routledge and K. Paul, 1982.

Coffin, Judith. *The Politics of Women's Work: The Parisian Garment Trades, 1750–1914*. Princeton: Princeton University Press, 1996.

———. "Gender and the Guild Order: The Garment Trades in Eighteenth-Century Paris." *The Journal of Economic History* 54 (December 1994): 768–93.

———. "Credit, Consumption, and Images of Women's Desires: Selling the Sewing Machine in Late Nineteenth-Century France." *French Historical Studies* 18, no. 3 (spring 1993): 49–83.

Cole, Charles W. *Colbert and a Century of French Mercantilism*. 2 vols. New York: Columbia University Press, 1939.

Collins, James B. "The Economic Role of Women in Seventeenth-Century France." *French Historical Studies* 16, no. 2 (fall 1989): 436–70.

Coons, Lorraine. " 'Neglected Sisters' of the Women's Movement: The Perception and Experience of Working Mothers in the Parisian Garment Industry, 1860–1915." *Journal of Women's History* 5, no. 2 (fall 1993): 50–74.

———. *Women Homeworkers in the Parisian Garment Industry, 1860–1915.* New York: Garland, 1987.

Coornaert, Emile. *Les Compagnonnages en France, du Moyen age à nos jours.* Paris: Les Editions ouvrières, 1966.

———. *Les Corporations en France avant 1789.* Paris: Gallimard, 1941.

Coquery, Natacha. "De l'hôtel aristocratique aux ministères: Habitat, mouvement, espace à Paris au XVIIIe siècle." Ph.D. diss., Université de Paris I, 1995.

Le Costume en Normandie du XVIIIe au XXe siècle. Luneray: Bertout, 1989.

Crouch, Charles. "The Petite Bourgeoisie of Paris during the Bourbon Restoration, 1814–1830: A Prosopographical Inquiry into the Political and Economic Integration of the Parisian Lower Middle Class." Ph.D. diss., University of Illinois at Urbana-Champaign, 1991.

Crowston, Clare. "Engendering the Guilds: Seamstresses, Tailors, and the Clash of Corporate Identities in Old Regime France." *French Historical Studies* 23, no. 2 (spring 2000): 339–71.

Cubells, Monique. *La Provence des lumières: Les parlementaires d'Aix au XVIIIe siècle.* Paris: Maloine, 1984.

Dardel, Pierre. *Commerce, industrie et navigation à Rouen et au Havre au XVIIIe siècle, rivalité croissante entre ces deux ports, la conjoncture.* Rouen: Société libre d'émulation de la Seine-Maritime, 1966.

Daumard, Adeline, and François Furet. *Structures et relations sociales à Paris au XVIIIe siècle. Cahiers des Annales,* no. 18. Paris: Armand Colin, 1961.

Davis, Natalie Zemon. "Women in the Crafts in Sixteenth-Century Lyon." In *Women and Work in Preindustrial Europe.* Ed. Barbara Hanawalt. Bloomington: Indiana University Press, 1986.

———. *Society and Culture in Early Modern France.* Stanford: Stanford University Press, 1975.

Davis, Natalie Zemon, and Arlette Farge, eds. *Renaissance and Enlightenment Paradoxes,* vol. 3 of *A History of Women in the West.* Ed. Georges Duby and Michelle Perrot. Cambridge, Mass.: Harvard University Press, 1993.

de Grazia, Victoria, ed. *The Sex of Things: Gender and Consumption in Historical Perspective.* Berkeley: University of California Press, 1996.

DeGroat, Judith A. "The Public Nature of Women's Work: Definitions and Debates during the Revolution of 1848." *French Historical Studies* 20, no. 1 (winter 1997): 31–47.

Delpierre, Madeleine. *Dress in France in the Eighteenth Century.* Trans. Caroline Beamish. New Haven: Yale University Press, 1997.

———. *Modes et révolutions, 1780–1804.* Paris: Delpierre Editions Paris-Musées, 1989.

———. *La mode et ses métiers du XVIIIe siècle da nos jours.* Paris: Musée de la mode et du costume, 1981.

———. *Modes enfantines, 1750–1950.* Paris: Musée de la mode et du costume, 1979.

Deslandres, Yvonne. *Le Costume, image de l'homme.* Paris: Albin Michel, 1976.

Deyon, Pierre. "Variations de la production textile aux XVIe et XVIIe siècles: sources et premiers résultats." *Annales. Économies, sociétés et civilisations* 18 (September–October 1963): 939–55.

Dupâquier, Jacques, ed. *Histoire de la population française.* 2 vols. Paris: Presses universitaires de France, 1988.

Elias, Norbert. *The Civilizing Process.* Trans. Edmund Jephcott. New York: Pantheon Books, 1978.

Erickson, Amy Louise. *Women and Property in Early Modern England.* London: Routledge, 1993.

Fairchilds, Cissie. *Domestic Enemies: Servants and Their Masters in Old Regime France.* Baltimore: Johns Hopkins University Press, 1984.

Farge, Arlette. *Fragile Lives: Violence, Power, and Solidarity in Eighteenth-Century.* Trans. Carol Shelton. Cambridge, Mass.: Harvard University Press, 1993.

Farge, Arlette, and Christiane Klapisch-Zuber, eds. *Madame ou Mademoiselle? Itinéraires de la solitude féminine, XVIIIe–XXe siècles.* Paris: Montalba, 1984.

Farge, Arlette, and Jacques Revel. *Logiques de la foule: L'affaire des enlèvements d'enfants, Paris, 1750.* Paris: Hachette, 1988.

Farr, James. *Hands of Honor: Artisans and their World in Dijon, 1550–1650.* Ithaca: Cornell University Press, 1988.

Faure, Alain. "Petit atelier et modernisme économique: La production en miettes au XIXe siècle." *Histoire, économie et société* 5, no. 4 (1986): 531–57.

La Femme en Normandie. Actes du XIXe congrès des sociétés historiques et archéologiques de Normandie. Caen: Archives départementales du Calvados, 1986.

Forster, Robert, and Orest Ranum, eds. *Family and Society: Selections from Annales, économies, sociétés, civilisations.* Trans. Elborg Forster and Patricia Ranum. Baltimore: Johns Hopkins University Press, 1976.

Fox-Genovese, Elizabeth. *The Origins of Physiocracy: Economic Revolution and Social Order in Eighteenth-Century France.* Ithaca: Cornell University Press, 1976.

Franklin, Alfred. *Dictionnaire historique des arts, métiers et professions exercés dans Paris depuis le XIIIe siècle.* Paris: H. Welter, 1906.

Gaines, Jane, and Charlotte Herzog, eds. *Fabrications: Costume and The Female Body.* New York: Routledge, 1990.

Gallinato, Bernard. *Les Corporations à Bordeaux à la fin de l'Ancien régime: Vie et mort d'un mode d'organisation du travail.* Bordeaux: Presses universitaire de Bordeaux, 1992.

Garden, Maurice. *Lyon et les lyonnais au XVIIIe siècle.* Paris: Les Belles lettres, 1970.

———. "Les Inventaires après décès: Source globale de l'histoire sociale lyonnaise ou juxtaposition de monographies familiales?" *Cahiers d'histoire* 12 (1967): 153–73.

Garrioch, David. "Verbal Insults in Eighteenth-Century Paris." In *The Social History of Language.* Ed. Peter Burke and Roy Porter. Cambridge, Eng.: Cambridge University Press, 1987.

———. *Neighbourhood and Community in Paris, 1740–1790.* Cambridge, Eng.: Cambridge University Press, 1986.

Gayot, Gérard, and Jean-Pierre Hirsch, eds. *La Révolution française et le développement du capitalisme. Actes du colloque de Lille, 19–21 novembre 1987.* Villeneuve d'Ascq: Revue du Nord, 1989.

Gelbert, Nina Rattner. *Feminine and Opposition Journalism in Old Regime France: "Le Journal des dames."* Berkeley: University of California Press, 1987.

Giesey, Ralph E. "Rules of Inheritance and Strategies of Mobility in Prerevolutionary France." *American Historical Review* 82, no. 2 (April 1977): 271–89.

Godard de Donville, Louise. *Signification de la mode sous Louis XIII.* Aix-en-Provence: EDISUD, 1978.

Godineau, Dominique. *The Women of Paris and Their French Revolution.* Trans. Katherine Streip. 1988; Berkeley: University of California Press, 1998.

Goody, Jack, Joan Thirsk, and E. P. Thompson, eds. *Family and Inheritance: Rural Society in Western Europe, 1200–1800.* Cambridge, Eng.: Cambridge University Press, 1976.

Goubert, Pierre. *The Ancien Régime: French Society, 1600–1750.* Trans. Steve Cox. New York: Weidenfeld and Nicolson, 1973.

———. *Louis XIV et vingt millions de Français.* Paris: Fayard, 1966.

Gowing, Laura. *Domestic Dangers: Women, Words, and Sex in Early Modern London.* Oxford: Oxford University Press, 1996.

Green, Nancy L. *Ready-to-Wear and Ready-to-Work: A Century of Industry and Immigrants in Paris and New York.* Durham, N.C.: Duke University Press, 1997.

———. *The Pletzl of Paris: Jewish Immigrant Workers in the "Belle Époque."* New York: Holmes and Meier, 1986.

Grenier, Jean-Yves. *L'économie d'Ancien Régime: Un monde de l'échange et de l'incertitude.* Paris: A. Michel, 1996.

Groppi, Angela. "Le Travail des femmes à Paris à l'époque de la Révolution française." *Bulletin d'histoire économique et sociale de la Révolution française* (1979): 27–46.

Guéry, Alain, and Robert Descimon. "Privilèges: La légalisation de la société." In *L'Etat et les pouvoirs,* ed. Jacques Revel and André Burguière. Vol. 2 of *Histoire de la France.* Paris: Seuil, 1989.

Guilbert, Madeleine. *Les Femmes et les organisations syndicales avant 1914: Présentation et commentaires de documents pour une étude du syndicalisme féminin.* Paris: Centre national de la recherche scientifique, 1966.

———. *Les fonctions des femmes dans l'industrie.* Paris: Mouton, 1966.

Gullickson, Gay. *Spinners and Weavers of Auffay: Rural Industry and the Sexual Division of Labor in a French Village, 1750–1850.* Cambridge, Eng.: Cambridge University Press, 1986.

Hafter, Daryl. "Female Masters in the Ribbonmaking Guild of Eighteenth-Century Rouen." In the "Forum on Women and Work," *French Historical Studies* 20, no. 1 (winter 1997): 1–14.

———, ed. *European Women and Preindustrial Craft.* Bloomington: Indiana University Press, 1995.

———. "Gender Formation from a Working-Class Viewpoint: Guildswomen in Eighteenth-Century Rouen." *Proceedings of the Annual Meeting of the Western Society for French History* 16 (1989): 415–22.

Hall, Gaston. "La Comédie classique devant les phénomènes de la mode." *Cahiers de l'association internationale des études françaises,* no. 38 (1986): 105–19.

Hamilton, J. A., and J. W. Hamilton. "Dress as a Reflection and Sustainer of Social

Reality: A Cross-Cultural Perspective." *Clothing and Textiles Research Journal* 7 (1989): 16–22.

Hanawalt, Barbara A., ed. *Women and Work in Preindustrial Europe.* Bloomington: Indiana University Press, 1986.

Hanley, Sarah. "Social Sites of Political Practice in France: Lawsuits, Civil Rights, and the Separation of Powers in Domestic and State Government, 1500–1800." *American Historical Review* 102, no. 1 (February 1997): 27–52.

———. "Engendering the State: Family Formation and State Building in Early Modern France." *French Historical Studies* 16, no. 1 (spring 1989): 4–27.

Hardy, Jean-Pierre, and David-Thierry Ruddel. *Les Apprentis artisans à Québec, 1660–1815.* Québec: Les presses de l'université du Québec, 1977.

Hart, Avril, and Susan North. *Fashion in Detail: From the 17th and 18th Centuries.* New York: Rizzoli International Publications, 1998.

Hauser, Henri. *Le Compagnonnage d'arts et métiers à Dijon aux XVIIe et XVIIIe siècles.* 1907; Marseille: Lafitte, 1979.

Heckscher, Eli. *Mercantilism.* 2 vols. Trans. Mendel Shapiro. London: G. Allen and Unwin, 1935.

Henry, Louis, and Jacques Houdaille. "Célibat et âge au mariage aux XVIIIe et XIXe siècles, vol. 1: Célibat définitif." *Population* 1 (1978): 43–84.

Himelfarb, Hélène. "Versailles, source ou miroir des modes Louis-quatoriziennes? Sourches et Dangeau, 1684–1685." *Cahiers de l'association internationale des études françaises,* no. 38 (1986): 121–43.

———. *La Fin des corporations.* Trans. Béatrice Vierne. Paris: Fayard, 2001. "Private Credit Markets in Paris, 1690–1849." *The Journal of Economic History* 52, no. 2 (1992): 293–306.

Howell, Martha. *Women, Production, and Patriarchy in Late Medieval Cities.* Chicago: University of Chicago Press, 1986.

Hudson, Pat, and W. R. Lee, eds. *Women's Work and the Family Economy in Historical Perspective.* Manchester: Manchester University Press, 1990.

Hufton, Olwen. *The Prospect before Her: A History of Women in Western Europe, 1500–1800,* vol. 1. New York: Vintage Books, 1998.

———. "Women without Men: Widows and Spinsters in Britain and France in the Eighteenth Century." *Journal of Family History* 9, no. 4 (winter 1984): 355–76.

———. "Women, Work, and Marriage in Eighteenth-Century France." In *Marriage and Society: Studies in the Social History of Marriage,* ed. R. B. Outhwaite. New York: St. Martin's Press, 1981.

———. "Women and the Family Economy in Eighteenth-Century France." *French Historical Studies* 9, no. 1 (spring 1975): 1–22.

———. *The Poor of Eighteenth-Century France, 1750–1789.* Oxford: The Clarendon Press, 1974.

Hunt, Alan. *Governance of the Consuming Passions: A History of Sumptuary Law.* New York: St. Martin's Press, 1996.

Hunt, Lynn. *The Family Romance of the French Revolution.* Berkeley: University of California Press, 1992.

—. *Politics, Culture, and Class in the French Revolution.* Berkeley: University of California Press, 1984.

Hunt, Lynn, and Jacques Revel, eds. *Histories: French Constructions of the Past.* New York: The New Press, 1995.

Hurpin, Georges. "Les corps de métiers rouennais au commencement du XVIIIe siècle." *Cahiers Léopold Delisle* 21–22 (1982).

Inventaires après-décès et ventes de meubles: Apports à une histoire de la vie économique et qutodienne (XIVe–XIXe siècles). Louvain-la-Neuve: Academia, 1988.

Jaton, Anne Marie. "Du corps paré au corps lavé: Une morale du costume et de la cosmétique." *Dix-huitième siècle* 18 (1986): 215–26.

Johnson, Christopher H. "Patterns of Proletarianization: Parisian Tailors and Lodève Woolens Workers." In *Consciousness and Class Experience in Nineteenth-Century Europe,* ed. John M. Merriman. New York: Holmes and Meier, 1979.

—. "Economic Change and Artisan Discontent: The Tailors' History, 1800–1848." In *Revolution and Reaction: 1848 and the Second French Republic,* ed. Roger Price. London: Croom Helm, 1975.

Jones, Eric L. "The Fashion Manipulators: Consumer Tastes and British Industries, 1660–1800." In *Business Enterprise and Economic Change, Essays in Honor of Harold F. Williamson.* Ed. Louis P Cain and Paul J. Uselding. Kent, Ohio: Kent State University Press, 1973.

Jones, Jennifer. "*Coquettes* and *Grisettes:* Women Buying and Selling in Ancien Régime Paris." In *The Sex of Things: Gender and Consumption in Historical Perspective,* ed. Victoria de Grazia and Ellen Furlough. Berkeley: University of California Press, 1996.

—. "Repackaging Rousseau: Femininity and Fashion in Old Regime France." *French Historical Studies* 18 (fall 1994): 939–61.

—. "'The Taste for Fashion and Frivolity': Gender, Clothing, and the Commercial Culture of the Old Regime." Ph.D. diss., Princeton University, 1991.

Kaplan, Steven Laurence. *The Bakers of Paris and the Bread Question, 1700–1775.* Durham: Duke University Press, 1996.

—. "L'apprentissage au XVIIIe siècle: Le cas de Paris." *Revue d'histoire moderne et contemporaine* 40 (juillet–septembre 1993): 436–79.

Hoffman, Philip T., Gilles Postel-Vinay, and Jean-Laurent Rosenthal. *Priceless Markets: The Political Economy of Credit in Paris, 1660–1870.* Chicago: University of Chicago Press, 2000.

—. "La lutte pour le contrôle du marché du travail à Paris au XVIIIe siècle." *Revue d'histoire moderne et contemporaine* 36 (juillet–septembre 1989): 361–412.

—. "Les Corporations, les faux ouvriers et le faubourg Saint-Antoine." *Annales. Economics Sociétés, Civilisations* (mars–avril 1988): 253–88.

—. "The Character and Implications of Strife among Masters inside the Guilds of Eighteenth-Century Paris." *Journal of Social History* 19 (summer 1986): 631–48.

—. "The Luxury Guilds of Eighteenth-Century Paris." *Francia* 9 (1982): 257–98.

—. "Réflexions sur la police du monde du travail, 1700–1815." *Revue historique* 261 (janvier–mars 1979): 17–77.

Kaplan, Steven Laurence, and Cynthia Koepp, eds. *Work in France: Representations, Meaning, Organization, and Practice.* Ithaca: Cornell University Press, 1986.

Kaplow, Jeffrey. *The Names of Kings: The Parisian Laboring Poor in the Eighteenth-Century.* New York: Basic Books, 1972.

Kidwell, Claudia Brush, and Valerie Steele, eds. *Men and Women: Dressing the Part.* Washington, D.C.: Smithsonian Institution Press, 1989.

Kohler, Carl. *A History of Costume.* Ed. Emma von Sichart, trans. Alexander K. Dallas. 1928; New York: Dover, 1963.

Kowaleski, Maryanne, and Judith M. Bennett. "Crafts, Guilds, and Women in the Middle Ages: Fifty Years after Marian K. Dale." *Signs* 14, no. 2 (winter 1989): 474–88.

Kowaleski-Wallace, Elizabeth. *Consuming Subjects: Women, Shopping, and Business in the Eighteenth Century.* New York: Columbia University Press, 1997.

Labrousse, Ernest. *Esquisse du mouvement des prix et des revenus en France au XVIIIe siècle.* 2 vols. Paris: Dalloz, 1933.

———— et al. *Histoire économique et sociale de la France,* vol. 2, 1660–1789. Paris: Presses universitaires de France, 1977.

Lacombe, F. "Les Tailleurs d'habits à Paris, 1700–1789." Mémoire de maîtrise, Université de Paris I, 1985.

Laffont, Jean L., ed. *Notaires, notariat et société sous l'Ancien Régime. Actes du colloque de Toulouse, 15 et 16 décembre 1989.* Toulouse: Presses universitaires du MIRAIL, 1990.

Landes, Joan. *Women and the Public Sphere in the Age of the French Revolution.* Ithaca: Cornell University Press, 1988.

Langlade, Emile. *La Marchande de modes de Marie-Antoinette, Rose Bertin.* Paris: A. Michel, 1911.

Laqueur, Thomas. *Making Sex: Body and Gender from the Greeks to Freud.* Cambridge, Mass.: Harvard University Press, 1990.

Laver, James. *L'Histoire de la mode et du costume.* Trans. Michèle Hechter. Paris: Thames & Hudson, 1990.

Lelièvre, Jacques. *La Pratique des contrats de mariage chez les notaires au Châtelet de Paris de 1769 à 1804.* Paris: Editions Cujas, 1959.

Leloir, Maurice. *Dictionnaire du costume et de ses accessoires, des armes et des étoffes, des origines a nos jours.* Paris: Grund, 1951.

————. *Histoire du costume de l'antiquité à 1914,* vol. 9. Paris: H. Ernst, 1934.

Lemire, Beverly. *Dress, Culture, and Commerce: The English Clothing Trade before the Factory, 1660–1800.* London: St. Martin's Press, 1997.

————. *Fashion's Favourite: The Cotton Trade and the Consumer in Britain, 1660–1800.* Oxford: Oxford University Press, 1991.

Levasseur, Emile. *Histoire des classes ouvrières et de l'industrie en France avant 1789.* 2 vols. 1901; Geneva: Slatkine, 1981.

Libron, Fernand, and Henri Clouzot. *Le Corset dans l'art et les moeurs du XIIIe au XXe siècle.* Paris: F. Libron, 1933.

Liu, Tessie. *The Weavers' Knot: The Contradictions of Class Struggle and Family Solidarity in Western France, 1750–1914.* Ithaca: Cornell University Press, 1994.

Loats, Carol Lee. "Gender, Guilds, and Work Identity: Perspectives from Sixteenth-Century Paris." In the "Forum on Women and Work," *French Historical Studies* 20, no. 1 (winter 1997): 15–30.

———. "Gender and Work in Sixteenth-Century Paris." Ph.D. diss., University of Colorado, 1993.

Mackie, Erin. *Market à la Mode: Fashion, Commodity, and Gender in The Tatler and The Spectator.* Baltimore: Johns Hopkins University Press, 1997.

Marchand, Joseph. *Un Intendant sous Louis XIV: Etude sur l'administration de Lebret en Provence (1687–1704).* Paris: Hachette, 1889.

Marion, Marcel. *Dictionnaire des institutions de la France aux XVIIe et XVIIIe siècles.* 1923; Paris: Picard, 1989.

Marion, René Sue. "The *Dames de la halle*: Community and Authority in Early Modern Paris." Ph.D. diss., John Hopkins University, 1995.

Markovitch, Tihomir. *Les industries lainières de Colbert à la Révolution.* Geneva: Droz, 1976.

Martin, Alphonse. *Anciennes communautés d'arts et métiers du Havre.* Fécamp: Imprimerie de L. Durand, 1880.

Martin, Germain. *Les Associations ouvrières au XVIIIe siècle (1700–1792).* Paris: A. Rousseau, 1900.

Martin Saint-Léon, Etienne. *Le Compagnonnage: Son histoire, ses coutumes, ses règlements et ses rites.* 1901; Paris: Imprimerie du compagnonnage, 1977.

———. *Histoire des corporations des métiers depuis leurs origines jusqu'a leur supression en 1791.* 1909; Paris: Alcan, 1922.

Maza, Sarah. *Private Lives and Public Affairs: The Causes Célèbres of Pre-Revolutionary France.* Berkeley: University of California Press, 1993.

———. "Women, the Bourgeoisie, and the Public Sphere." *French Historical Studies* 17, no. 4 (fall 1992): 935–50.

———. *Servants and Their Masters in Eighteenth-Century France: The Uses of Loyalty.* Princeton: Princeton University Press, 1983.

McCracken, Grant. *Culture and Consumption: New Approaches to the Symbolic Character of Consumer Goods and Activities.* Bloomington: Indiana University Press, 1988.

McKendrick, Neil, John Brewer, and J. H. Plumb. *The Birth of a Consumer Society: The Commercialization of Eighteenth-Century England.* Bloomington: Indiana University Press, 1982.

Melzer, Sara E., and Kathryn Norberg, eds. *From the Royal to the Republican Body: Incorporating the Political in Seventeenth- and Eighteenth-Century France.* Berkeley: University of California Press, 1998.

"Métiers, corporations, syndicalismes." Special issue of *Clio, Histoire, Femmes et Sociétés* 3 (1996).

Miller, Michael B. *The Bon Marché: Bourgeois Culture and the Department Store, 1869–1920.* Princeton: Princeton University Press, 1981.

Milliot, Vincent. "Le Travail sans le geste: Les représentations iconographiques des petits métiers parisiens, XVI–XVIIIe siècles." *Revue d'histoire moderne et contemporaine* 41, no. 1 (1994): 5–28.

Minard, Philippe. *La Fortune du colbertisme*. Paris: Fayard, 1998.

———. "L'Inspection des manufactures en France de Colbert à la Révolution." 2 vols. Ph.D. diss., Université Paris-I Panthéon Sorbonne, 1994.

Mollat, Michel, ed. *Histoire de Rouen*. Toulouse: Privat, 1979.

Monnier, Raymonde. "L'Evolution de l'industrie et le travail des femmes à Paris sous l'Empire." *Bulletin d'histoire économique et sociale de la Révolution française* (1979): 47–60.

Moreau, François. *Le Mercure galant de Dufresny*. Oxford: J. Touzot, 1982.

Mousnier, Roland, ed. *Un Nouveau Colbert: Actes du colloque pour le tricentaire de la mort de Colbert*. Paris: Editions SEDES, 1985.

———. *Les Institutions de la France sous la monarchie absolue*. 2 vols. Paris: Presses universitaires de France, 1980.

Muir, Edward, and Guido Ruggiero, eds. *Sex and Gender in Historical Perspective*. Trans. Margaret A. Gallucci, with Mary M. Gallucci and Carole C. Gallucci. Baltimore: Johns Hopkins University Press, 1990.

Musée de la mode et du costume. *Modes et révolutions: 1780–1804*. Paris: Musée Galliera, 1989.

Musset, Jacqueline. *L'Intendance de Caen: Structure, fonctionnement et administration sous l'intendant Esmangart, 1775–1783*. Condé-sur-Noireau: C. Corlet, 1985.

Nigeon, René. *Etat financier des corporations parisiennes d'arts et métiers au XVIIIe siècle*. Paris: Les Editions Rieder, 1934.

Nahoum-Grappe, Véronique. "Briller à Paris au XVIIe siècle." In "Pareur, Pudeur, étiquette," special issue of *Communications* 46 (1987): 135–56.

Nouvion, Pierre de, and Emile Liez. *Un ministre de modes sous Louis XVI, Mademoiselle Bertin, marchande de modes de la Reine, 1747–1813*. Paris: Henri Leclerc, 1911.

Offen, Karen. " 'Powered by a Woman's Foot': A Documentary Introduction to the Sexual Politics of the Sewing Machine in Nineteenth-Century France." *Women's Studies International Forum* 11, no. 2 (1988): 93–101.

Olivier-Martin, François. *L'Organisation corporative de la France d'Ancien Régime*. Paris: Librairie du Recueil Sirey, 1938.

Ouin-Lacroix, Charles Abbé. *Histoire des anciennes corporations d'arts et métiers et des confréries religieuses de la capitale de la Normandie*. Rouen: Imprimerie Lecointe frères, 1850.

Pardailhé-Galabrun, Annik. *The Birth of Intimacy: Privacy and Domestic Life in Early Modern Paris*. Trans. Jocelyn Phelps. Philadelphia: University of Pennsylvania Press, 1991.

Parker, Rozsika. *The Subversive Stitch: Embroidery and the Making of the Feminine*. London: Routledge, 1984.

Pellegrin, Nicole, ed. "Apprentissages (XVIe–XXe siècles)." Special issue of *Revue d'histoire moderne et contemporaine* 40, no. 3 (juillet-septembre 1993).

———. "L'uniforme de la santé: Les médecins et la réforme du costume." *Dix-huitième siècle* 23 (1991): 129–40.

———. *Les vetements de la liberté: Abécédaire des pratiques vestimentaires en France de 1780 à 1800*. Aix-en-Provence: Alinéa, 1989.

———. "L'être et le paraître au XVIIe siècle: Les apparences vestimentaires dans *l'Histoire comique de Francion* de Charles Sorel." In *La France d'Ancien régime: Études réunies en l'honneur de Pierre Goubert.* v. 2 Toulouse: Privat, 1984.

―――. "Femmes et machines à coudre: Remarques sur un objet technique et ses usages." *Pénélope* 9 (automne 1983): 64–71.

Peristiany, J. G., and Julian Pitt-Rivers, eds. *Honor and Grace in Anthropology.* Cambridge, Eng.: Cambridge University Press, 1992.

Perrot, Jean-Claude. *Genèse d'une ville moderne: Caen au XVIIIe siècle.* 2 vols. Paris: Mouton, 1975.

Perrot, Michèlle. "L'éloge de la ménagère dans le discours des ouvriers français au XIXe siècle." *Romantisme* 13–14 (1976): 105–21.

Perrot, Michèlle. *Les Ouvriers en grève, 1871–1890.* Paris: Mouton, 1973.

Perrot, Philippe. *Le luxe, une richesse entre faste et confort, XVIIIe–XIXe siècles.* Paris: Editions du Seuil, 1995.

―――. *Le Travail des apparences ou les transformations du corps féminin, XVIIIe–XIXe siècles.* Paris: Seuil, 1984.

―――. *Les dessus et dessous de la bourgeoisie, une histoire du vêtement au XIXe siècle.* Paris: Fayard, 1981.

Phan, Marie-Claude. "'A faire belle,' à faire femme." In "Parure, pudeur, étiquette," special issue of *Communications* 46 (1987): 67–78.

Pied, E. *Les Anciens corps d'arts et métiers de Nantes.* 3 vols. Nantes: Imprimerie de A. Dugas, 1903.

Pinchbeck, Ivy. *Women Workers and the Industrial Revolution, 1750–1850.* New York: Routledge, 1930.

Pitt-Rivers, Julian. *The Fate of Shechem or the Politics of Sex: Essays in the Anthropology of the Mediterranean.* Cambridge, Eng.: Cambridge University Press, 1977.

Poni, Carlo. "Local Market Rules and Practices. Three Guilds in the Same Line of Production in Early Modern Bologna." In *Domestic Strategies: Work and Family in France and Italy, 1600–1800.* Ed. Stuart Woolf. Cambridge, Eng.: Cambridge University Press, 1991.

Quataert, Jean H. "The Shaping of Women's Work in Manufacturing: Guilds, Households, and the State in Central Europe, 1648–1870." *American Historical Review* 90 (December 1985): 1122–48.

Quicherat, J. *Histoire du costume en France depuis les temps les plus reculés jusqu'à la fin du XVIIIe siècle.* Paris: Hachette, 1875.

Reddy, William. *The Rise of Market Culture: The Textile Trade and French Society, 1750–1900.* Cambridge, Eng.: Cambridge University Press, 1984.

Rétat, Pierre. "Luxe." *Dix-huitième siècle* 26 (1994): 79–88.

Revel, Jacques. "Les Corps et communautés." In *The Political Culture of the Old Regime,* vol. 1 of *The French Revolution and the Creation of Modern Political Culture,* ed. Keith Michael Baker. Oxford: Oxford University Press, 1987.

Ribbe, Charles de. *Les Corporations ouvrières de l'Ancien régime en Provence.* Aix-en-Provence: Imprimerie de Illy, 1865.

Ribeiro, Aileen. *The Art of Dress: Fashion in England and France, 1750–1820.* New Haven, Conn.: Yale University Press, 1995.

―――. *Fashion in the French Revolution.* New York: Holmes and Meier, 1988.

———. *Dress in Eighteenth-Century Europe, 1715–1789.* London: B. T. Batsford, 1984.

Roach, Mary Ellen, and Joanne Bubolz Eicher. *Dress, Adornment, and the Social Order.* New York: Wiley, 1965.

Roche, Daniel. *History of Everday Things: The Birth of Consumption in France.* Trans. Brian Pearce. Cambridge, Eng.: Cambridge University Press, 2000.

———. *The Culture of Clothing: Dress and Fashion in the Ancien Régime.* Trans. Jean Birrell. Cambridge, Eng.: Cambridge University Press, 1994.

———. *The People of Paris: An Essay in Popular Culture in the 18th Century.* Trans. Marie Evans. Berkeley: University of California Press, 1987.

Root, Hilton. *La Construction de l'Etat moderne en Europe.* Paris: Presses universitaires de France, 1994.

Ruhlmann, Georges. *Les Corporations, les manufactures et le travail libre à Abbeville au XVIIIe siècle.* Paris: Recueil Sirey, 1948.

Sargentson, Carolyn. *Merchants and Luxury Markets: The Marchands Merciers of Eighteenth-Century Paris.* London: The Victoria and Albert Museum, 1996.

Schaeper, Thomas J. *The French Council of Commerce, 1700–1715: A Study of Mercantilism after Colbert.* Columbus: Ohio State University Press, 1983.

Schwarz, R. A., "Uncovering the Secret Vice: Toward an Anthropology of Clothing and Andornment." In *The Fabrics of Culture: The Anthropology of Clothing and Adornment.* Ed. Justine M. Cordwell and Ronald A. Schwarz. The Hague: Mouton, 1979.

Scott, Joan. *Gender and the Politics of History.* New York: Columbia University Press, 1988.

Sebillot, Paul. *Légendes et curiosités des métiers.* 1894–1895; Marseille: Lafitte, 1981.

Sewell, William H. *Work and Revolution in France: The Language of Labor from the Old Regime to 1848.* Cambridge, Eng.: Cambridge University Press, 1980.

Simmel, Georg. "Fashion." *International Quarterly* 10 (1904): 130–55.

Smedley-Weill, Anette. *Les Intendants de Louis XIV.* Paris: Fayard, 1995.

Soboul, Albert. *La société française dans la seconde moitié du XVIIIe siècle: Structures sociales, cultures et modes de vie.* Paris: Centre de documentation universitaire, 1969.

Sonenscher, Michael. *Work and Wages: Natural Law, Politics, and the Eighteenth-Century French Trades.* Cambridge, Eng.: Cambridge University Press, 1989.

———. *The Hatters of Eighteenth-Century France.* Berkeley: University of California Press, 1987.

Sonnet, Martine. *L'Education des filles au temps des Lumières.* Paris: Cerf, 1987.

Spencer, Samia, ed. *French Women and the Age of Enlightenment.* Bloomington: Indiana University Press, 1984.

Sullerot, Evelyne. *Histoire et sociologie du travail féminin.* Paris: Gonthier, 1968.

———. *Histoire de la presse féminine en France, des origines à 1848.* Paris: Librairie Armand Colin, 1966.

Sussman, George. *Selling Mother's Milk: The Wet-Nursing Business in France, 1715–1914.* Urbana: University of Illinois Press, 1982.

Thompson, Victoria. *The Virtuous Marketplace: Women and Men, Money and Politics in Paris, 1830–1870.* Baltimore: Johns Hopkins University Press, 2000.

Tilly, Louise A., and Joan W. Scott. *Women, Work, and Family.* New York: Holt, Rinehart and Winston, 1978.

Traer, James F. *Marriage and the Family in Eighteenth-Century France.* Ithaca: Cornell University Press, 1980.

"Travail, métiers et professions en Normandie." Special issue of *Cahiers Léopold Delisle* 31–32 (1982–1983).

Truant, Cynthia. "La maîtrise d'une identité? Corporations féminines à Paris aux XVIIe et XVIIIe siècles." *Clio, Histoire, Femmes et Sociétés* 3 (1996).

———. "Parisian Guildswomen and the (Sexual) Politics of Privilege: Defending their Patrimonies in Print." In *Going Public: Women and Publishing in Early Modern France,* ed. Dena Goodman and Elizabeth C. Goldsmith. Ithaca: Cornell University Press, 1995.

———. *The Rites of Labor: The Brotherhoods of Compagnonnage in Old and New Regime France.* Ithaca: Cornell University Press, 1994.

———. "The Guildswomen of Paris: Gender, Power, and Sociability in the Old Regime." *Proceedings of the Annual Meeting of the Western Society for French History* 15 (1988): 130–38.

Veblen, Thorstein. *The Theory of the Leisure Class: An Economic Study of Institutions.* 1899; New York: Penguin Books, 1994.

Verdier, Yvonne. *Façons de dire, façons de faire: La laveuse, la couturière, la cuisinière.* Paris: Gallimard, 1979.

Vidal, Pierre. *Histoire de la corporation des tailleurs d'habits, pourpointiers, chaussetiers de la ville de Paris.* Paris, 1923.

Vigarello, Georges. *Le Corps redressé: Histoire d'un pouvoir pédagogique.* Paris: Jean-Pierre Delarge, 1978.

Waquet, Françoise. "La Mode au XVIIe siècle: De la folie à l'usage." *Cahiers de l'association internationale des études françaises,* 38 (1986): 91–104.

Waugh, Nora. *The Cut of Women's Clothes, 1600–1930.* London: Faber, 1968.

Weir, David R. "Tontines, Public Finance, and Revolution in France and England, 1688–1789." *The Journal of Economic History* 55, no. 1 (March 1989): 95–124.

Weiner, Annette B., and Jane Schneider, eds. *Cloth and Human Experience.* Washington, D.C.: Smithsonian Institution Press, 1989.

Wiesner, Merry. *Gender, Church, and State in Early Modern Germany.* London: Longman, 1998.

———. *Working Women in Renaissance Germany.* New Brunswick, N.J.: Rutgers University Press, 1986.

———. "Spinsters and Seamstresses: Women in Cloth and Clothing Production." In *Rewriting the Renaissance: The Discourses of Sexual Difference in Early Modern Europe,* ed. Margaret W. Ferguson, Maureen Quilligan, and Nancy J. Vickers. Chicago: University of Chicago Press, 1986.

Williams, Alan. *The Police of Paris, 1718–1789.* Baton Rouge: Louisiana State University Press, 1979.

———. "The Police and the Administration of Eighteenth-Century Paris." *Journal of Urban History* 4, no. 2 (February 1978): 157–82.

Williams, Rosalind. *Dream Worlds: Mass Consumption in Late Nineteenth-Century France.* Berkeley: University of California Press, 1982.

Woolf, Stuart, ed. *Domestic Strategies: Work and Family in France and Italy, 1600–1800.* Cambridge: Cambridge University Press, 1991.

Zylberberg-Hocquard, Marie-Hélène. *Féminisme et syndicalisme en France.* Paris: Editions Anthropos, 1978.

Index

(Page numbers in italics refer to pages with an image of the index entry.)

women's, 30, 25–26, 51–55, 59–63, 64;
during French Revolution, 30; as a
marker of femininity, 406; owned by
seamstresses, 373–75; political functions of, 29–30; seasonal changes in,
127; as a social and cultural signifying
system, 27–29. *See also* Dress bodice; Dresses; Fashion; *Manteau* dress;
Men's suits; *Robe à l'anglaise; Robe à la
française;* Skirt Bodice; Skirts; Stays
"Clothing revolution," 12, 23, 41, 71,
374–75, 405
Code du commerce, 187, 189
Coffee, 371
Colbert, Jean-Baptiste, 174, 187–89, 191,
203, 214, 222
Compagnonnage, 101–2
Confection. See Ready-to-wear industry
Confraternity, 204; of seamstresses'
guild, 266, 275–77
Congé system, 86
Consular court (*juridiction consulaire*),
102, 222
Consumer culture, 12, 23–24, 72
Consumption, of clothing, 12, 23–25,
405–6; impact of *manteau* dress on,
37–40; relation to production of,
24–25. *See also* "Clothing revolution"
Contraception, 360
Corporate identity, notions of, 219;
seamstresses', 225, 243, 248, 253–
54, 408; tailors', 251–52; women's,
224. *See also* Corporate organization; Guild membership; Mastership;
Trade identity
Corporate organization, 256–57; expansion of, 187–90; nineteenth-
century legacy of, 392–94, 396–98;
principles of, 84–85, 175–79, 202–
3, 221, 258, 286, 333–34; women's
relation to, 10–11, 173, 180–82, 183–
84, 195–97, 209–10, 211–12, 218–19,
232. *See also* Corporate privilege;
Corporatism; Corps; Guilds
Corporate privilege, 175–77, 219–20;

conceptions of, 235–36; family basis
of, 232; in garment trades, 218. *See
also* Corporate organization; Corps;
Guilds
Corporations. *See* Guilds
Corporatism, 384
Corps, 175, 177
Corsets, 47
Cotton cloth, 161–62, 375
Council of Commerce, 202
Court: dresses worn for presentation at,
162–63; influence over fashion of, 36,
47, 48–51, 69–70. *See also* Court dress
Court dress (*grand habit*), 33, *34, 35,* 43,
162–63
Courtin, Antoine de, 50
Coutances, 198
Couturier, 2, 186, 394
Couturière, 2–3, 186, 397
Credit, 133, 164–68, 169, 250, 379, 390
Cutting cloth, 150–52

d'Allarde law, 387, 394
Daughters: legal rights of, 223–24,
411; of master tailors, 227–32, 237–
39, 242, 251, 333–35, 338; of mistress
seamstresses, 281, 329–31, 338; of
seamstress guild officers, 261–62
Davis, Natalie Zemon, 174
Découpeurs, 95, 212
Debt, 379–80
De Groat, Judith, 393
Delacroix, Jacques-Vincent (lawyer),
245–50, 271
Demography, 356, 360
Department stores, 391
Dillmont, Thérèse de, 130
Division of labor, 117–19, 124–26
Dixième de l'industrie, 278–79, 286
D'Offemont (tailor), 61–62
Domestic servants, 10, 119, 179–80,
307–8, 343, 345–46, 349, 361
Dominos. See Ball costumes
Donneau de Visé, Jean. *See Le Mercure
galant*

Fashion workers, 79; apprenticeship with, 301; as prostitutes, 108–10

Fathers: of apprentice seamstressses, 307–9; guild masters as, 311; of seamstresses, 307–9, 403; tailors as, 229–30, 251, 253, 335. *See also* Family

Female apparel. *See* Women's clothing

Female body, 362. *See also* Appearances; Female modesty; Fitting; Health; Puberty; Sexuality; Stays

Female modesty, 57–58, 59, 119, 191, 236, 246

Femininity, 310; biological grounding of, 73; clothing as display of, 12, 406, 415; guild membership and notions of, 408; seamstresses as embodiment of, 143–44; seamstresses' influence on notions of, 11–12, 24–25, 72, 414–15; and sexual division of labor, 11, 174; transmission of, 342, 399–400; and women's work, 182–83, 184. *See also* Gender; Honor; Masculinity; Sexuality

Feminism, 410–12

Ferrière, Claude-Joseph, 301

Filassières' guild. *See* Hemp merchants' guild

Fitting, 138, *140, 141,* 158–59, 247

Fortune: guild status as part of, 351; of seamstresses at death, 380–81; of seamstresses at marriage, 352–54, 355–56

Free markets, 385, 387; Turgot's vision of, 209, 216

French Revolution, 384, 385–88; projects for clothing reform during, 30

Fresh-flower sellers' guild, 189, 211, 300, 387; exclusion of male members by, 193; fears of prostitution in, 194

Friendship, 87, 136–37

Fripiers' guild, 74, 274. *See also* Used-clothes dealers

Fruit sellers, 195–97

Funeral ceremonies, 217–18, 275

Furetière, Antoine: on fashion, 48; on *hongrelin,* 32; on *manteau,* 36

Furniture: seamstresses', 119–23, 367, 368–71

Garment trades: cycles of production in, 89; guild divisions within, 74–75, 112, 397; in nineteenth century, 94, 385, 388–95; prostitution among workers of, 107–10; sexual division of labor in, 11–12, 67, 73, 85–86, 174, 192–93, 203, 214, 216, 228–29, 254–55, 414. *See also* Homeworkers; Needleworkers; Seamstresses; Tailors

Garsault, François-Antoine de, 116. *See also L'Art du tailleur*

Gender: and corporate identity, 219, 408–9; consequences of seamstresses' guild for, 11–12, 24–25, 72, 406, 412–13; and consumer culture, 24; in debates over production rights, 57–58; definition of, 9–10; and division of garment trades, 11–12, 112, 174, 192, 254–55, 401; historiography on, 8, 10–11, 113–14; and nature, 73; and patterns of guild recruitment, 339–40; role of apprenticeship in transmission of, 341–42; role of seamstresses' trade in creation of, 11–12, 400. *See also* Femininity; Masculinity

Grain and seed dealers' guild, 181

Great Chain of Being, 176–77, 209

Green, Nancy, 390, 394

Grisettes, 40, 48, 49

Guild membership: advantages of, 225–26, 298, 408; conceptions of meaning of, 219, 229, 235–36, 253; effects on fortune of, 381, 382–83; relationship between marriage and, 15, 184, 347, 350–51; social and cultural weight of, 6–7. *See also* Corporate identity; Corporate privilege; Guilds; Mastership

Guilds: 1776 abolition of, 67, 208–10, 244, 328, 413; 1791 abolition of, 26,

Marie-Antoinette, 28, 81, 161, 285; alteration of garments of, 155–56; appeal by seamstresses' guild to, 245, 247; criticism of extravagance of, 30; influence on fashion of, 70; relations with fashion merchants of, 163–64

Marriage, 251; choice of mates for, 347–50; effects on fortune of, 381; importance for male artisans of, 347; as interruption of seamstresses' careers, 326; notarial contracts for, 15, 344–45, 352; as path of entry to tailors' guilds, 333–35, 337, 338; role of female occupations in, 344, 345, 382, 407; seamstresses' patterns of, 347–50, 356–57; strategies for, 329–30

Marseilles, 14, 198; relations between seamstresses and tailors of, 203–7, 237–44; trade specialization among seamstresses of, 78

Masculinity, 10, 11, 342, 408–9; clothing and, 70–71; and male work in the garment trades, 144; Rousseau on, 65. *See also* Femininity; Gender; Honor

Masterpieces (*chefs d'oeuvre*), 79, 125–26, 205–6, 258, 267, 270

Masters of guilds, 307–8, 345; dowry values among, 353; and relations with faubourg Saint-Antoine, 6; relations with guilds of, 7, 112; relations with illegal workers of, 100–101; use of putting-out system by, 94–95

Mastership: tailors' definition of, 225, 235–36. *See also* Corporate identity; Corporate privilege; Guild membership; Guilds

Material culture, 14

Maza, Sarah, 249

Measuring, 138, *139*, 147–48

Medicine: in debates on fashion, 59–63

Mendicancy, 106–7

Mending, 67, 83, 99, 155; price of, 166

Ménétra, Jacques-Louis, 7

Mercers' guild, 67–68, 74; entry to, 327; purchase of guild offices by, 280; size

of, 75; as suppliers of seamstresses, 134–35; women's entry to, 211. *See also* Merchant mercers

Merchant mercers, 50–51, 79, 156, 348. *See also* Mercers' guild

Mercier, Louis-Sébastien, 17, 68, 131–32, 357

Le Mercure galant, 30; on fashion, 48–50; on the manteau dress, 37, 40–41

Midwives, 181–82

Migration: to Paris from provinces, 89, 104–6, 306–7, 366

Militia, 280, 286

Mistresses: corporate rights of families of, 201–2; household formation by, 360; legal rights of, 218, 224, 226, 253, 302–3. *See also* Corporate identity; Guild membership; Seamstresses' guild; Women's guilds

Mixed-sex guilds, 181

Mobility: of journeymen tailors, 104; of seamstresses, 86, 102

Molière, 27–28, 182

Morality, 386. *See also* Female modesty; Sexuality

Mourning dress, 127–29, 136

Mun, Count Albert de, 396

Murger, Henri, 113

Muslin, 46, 47, 161, 375

Nantes, 198

Napoleon Bonaparte, 46

National Assembly, 387

National Convention, 388

Natural law, 67

Natural rights, 209

Nature: and gender, 73; as ruling principle for fashion, 46, 63, 71–72; as standard for judging society and culture, 26, 73

Needles, 129–30. *See also* Needlework; Sewing

Needlework: as a feminine activity, 11–12, 64–66, 73, 182, 187, 216, 311, 395–96, 400–401, 406, 414–15; male guilds' domination of, 183. *See also* Needleworkers; Sewing; Stitches

Needleworkers: divisions among, 397; historiography on, 113–14; nineteenth-century images of, 113. *See also* Seamstresses; Seamstress workers

Neighborhood, 316, 320, 349

Nevers, 198

Noblewomen: as clients for seamstresses, 81–83

Nonguild trades, 178–79, 189, 195–97, 207–8

Normandy, 14, 200, 215; customary law of, 223, 232. *See also* Caen; Rouen

Numeracy, 165

Old-stockings menders, 196

Ouvriers sans qualité. See Illegal workers

Palais-Royal, 68

Pardailhé-Galabrun, Annick, 356, 360

Paris: as center for tailoring, 81; distribution of seamstresses in, 76–77; division of garment trades of, 74–75; labor markets of, 86–87; migration of garment workers to, 104–6; as model for provincial guilds, 179, 204, 206–7, 238, 244; number of guilds in, 189–90; Parlement of, 58, 192, 228–29

Parlements, 221; as defenders of the guilds, 209–10

Patronage: for charitable apprenticeship, 320–21; among seamstresses, 262–63; between seamstresses and clients, 168–69, 407

Patterns, *115, 150–52, 151,* 156, *157*

Perrot, Jean-Claude, 207

Petticoats: owned by seamstresses, 374–75. *See also* Skirts

Piecework, 94–95, 97

Pins, 130–31

Pleats: for the *robe à la francaise,* 152–53

Police *commissaires,* 16, 222, 272, 357

Police seals, 357–58

Polonaise dress, 43, *44,* 118

Postures of work, 117, 119

Poverty: caused by French Revolution, 385; among seamstresses, 83–84, 93–94, 284–86, 290, 292, 344

Prices: among seamstresses, 91–92, 159–62, 240; among tailors, 159, 160–62

Privacy, 364

Privilege, 219–20. *See also* Corporate privilege

Privileged areas, 178, 226

Probate inventories, 15–16, 40–41, 82, 166, 358–59, 365, 366, 372, 377

Production cycles, 89, 127–29

Proletarianization, 385, 390, 391, 394

Promissory notes, 379

Prostitution, 10, 16, 92–93, 103, 104, 105, 107–10, 137, 163, 194, 210, 246–47, 249

Provence, 14, 179, 200, 215; Parlement of, 159, 204, 238, 243–44. *See also* Aix-en-Provence; Marseilles

Puberty, 310, 342

Public space: women in, 54, 55, 236

Public sphere, 410

Putting-out system, 94–96

Quilting, 78, 95, 160

Reading: by Parisians, 372; by seamstresses, 371–73

Ready-to-wear industry, 94, 385, 389–91, 394

Real estate property, 379

Rédingote dress, 43

Reisser (tailor), 62–63

Religion, 204, 233–34, 369–70, 371

Remarriage, 354–55

Reputation, 80, 250, 261, 315, 316

Rennes, 198

Rent, 364–65

Rentes. See Annuities

Restif de la Brétonne, Nicolas-Edmé, 17, 88, 91, 92–93, 113, 124

Riding jackets, 43, 147

Robe à l'anglaise, 43, 150, 154, 155
Robe à la française, 32, 42–43, 61; alterations of, 155; amount of cloth used in, 148–49; steps for making, 150–54
Robe volante, 25, 41, 42, 52
Roche, Daniel, 12, 23, 41, 90, 374–75
Roper, Lyndal, 10
Rouen, 201; creation of seamstresses' guild in, 193; migration of tailors to, 104; women's guilds of, 182
Rousseau, Jean-Jacques: on association between women and appearances, 64–65, 73; as critic of stays, 64; on sewing as a feminine activity, 1; on women as fashion merchants, 65–66, 69. See also Emile
Royal Academy of Science, 59, 115
Royal commission to audit guild debts, 16, 284, 287–91
Royal council, 202, 221, 226–28, 231
Royal government, 56, 174, 177, 189–90; and archival sources about guilds, 16; attitudes toward guilds of, 207–8; after Colbert's death, 194–96; creation of guild offices by, 194–95, 280–86; interaction with women of, 412; intervention in guild affairs of, 286–91, 292–93, 413; relationship to privilege of, 219–20
Royal procurator of the Châtelet of Paris: admission of guild members by, 192, 326–28, 331, 333, 387; as judge in apprenticeship disputes, 305, 324–25; as judge for internal guild conflicts, 265, 276; jurisdiction over guilds of, 16, 221–22, 258; judgments of, 56, 102, 260; oversight of seamstress officials by, 266, 268; report on Parisian seamstresses by, 190–91; seamstresses' use of court of, 271–73; payments by seamstresses' guild to, 288
Rue Saint-Honoré, 68, 77, 79, 135, 273, 274

Sack dress. See Robe volante
Saint-Antoine: faubourg of, 6, 75, 178
Saint-Dominique, 99
Sainte-Eustache: parish of, 320, 323
Saintes, 198
Saint-Gervais: parish church of, 266, 275–76
Saint-Jean-en-Grève, parish of, 77, 300–301, 319–20
Saint-Louis, 275
Saint-Malo, 198
Saint-Martin: prison of, 107
Sainte-Agnès: community of, 323
Salaries, 91–92, 93. See also Wages
Sand, George, 101
Sans-culottes, 29
Savary des Bruslons, Jacques, 75, 331
Schools, 124; as sources of vocational training, 323
Scissors, 129
Scott, Joan, 390, 392
Seamstress guild officials, 227, 242, 291–92; daily administration by, 270–71; elections of, 258–60; idealization of, 246; participation in apprenticeship of, 316; as recipients of guild fees, 281–82; recruitment of, 263; responsibilities of, 257–58, 264–65, 289; self-perception of, 248, 265–66. See also Seamstresses' guild
Seamstress workers, 111, 404, 409–10; on annual contracts, 88–89; conflicts between mistresses and, 102–4; on daily contracts, 89–91; failure to achieve guild membership of, 298, 325; "first" workers, 91; fortunes of, 381, 383; lack of organization among, 86, 102–3; literacy of, 165; living conditions of, 365–66; as members of employers' households, 88–89, 359–61, 363, 365; migration of, 104–6; numbers of, 76; participation in allouage by, 322; regulations for employment of, 85–86; salaries and

wages of, 91–92, 102–3; sexuality of, 85–86, 103–4, 105, 247; specialization among, 79–80; tasks in workshop of, 125–26; wardrobes of, 375. *See also* Fashion workers; Journeymen; Seamstresses; Seamstresses' guild

Seamstresses: attractions of trade for, 168, 299–300, 340, 403; as conduits from nature to culture, 4, 399; credit relations of, 164–68; criteria for success among, 404–5; distribution of piecework by, 95, 96; distribution within Paris of, 76–77; entry to guild system of, 173–74; existence prior to incorporation of, 185–87, 190, 213; family ties between tailors and, 186, 237–39, 242–44; fortunes of, 380–81; guild membership as source of honor for, 236–37; hierarchies among, 80–84, 382–83; husbands of, 345–46; informal labor market of, 86–87, 111; as intermediaries for prostitution, 108–9; and the *manteau* dress, 40; marriage choices of, 347–50, 356–57; nineteenth-century experience of, 384–85, 388–98; numbers of, 75–76; place in garment trades of, 169; prices charged by, 159–62; in provincial tailors' guilds, 198–207, 212–13, 215, 230–44; relations with clients of, 136–44; religion among, 204, 233–34, 369–70, 371; sexualization of, 143–44, 246–47, 393; as social intermediaries, 4, 399, 406–7; socioeconomic origins of, 306–9; symbolic meanings attached to, 112; in technical literature, 116; trade identity of, 229, 234; trade specialization among, 78–80, 186, 242–43; wardrobes of, 373–75; work patterns of, 126; workshop size among, 90. *See also* Needleworkers; Seamstress guild officials; Seamstresses' guild; Seamstress workers

Seamstresses' guild (Caen), 83, 100; entry to, 325, 337–38; payment of *capitation* tax by, 279; raids on illegal workers by, 231; relations between tailors' guild and, 201–3, 217–18, 230–37; size of, 337

Seamstresses' guild (Le Havre), 198

Seamstresses' guild (Paris): administration of, 257–58, 263–66, 270–73; almanac of, 119, *120;* assembly of, 14, 258, 260, 263–66, 287, 291; charity in, 275, 277–78; conflict between tailors' guild and, 55–59, 226–44; confraternity of, 266, 275–77; creation of, 190–93, 214, 225–27; elections of, 259–60; entry fees of, 225, 227, 271–72, 281, 328–29; entry to, 297–98, 325–31, 387; impact on gender ideologies of, 406, 412–13; impact on provinces of, 174–75, 214; notary of, 14, 103, 270–71, 288, 302–3, 315–16; offices of, 266–70; post-1776 reestablishment of, 212; production rights of, 31–36, 274–75; protest against 1776 abolition by, 245–50, 384; purchase of guild offices by, 280–87; raids on illegal workers by, 99, 272–73; regulation of apprenticeship by, 87, 298–300, 305, 311, 315; and royal declaration of 1693, 273, 276, 278, 281–82, 299, 328–29; 1781 statutes of, 66–67, 133, 156, 212, 259, 261; 1675 statutes of, 31, 192, 259, 298; size of, 75–76, 110, 225, 331; as source of fiscal revenue, 189, 191, 278–80; supervision of labor market by, 85–86, 87, 111; work experience required by, 125. *See also* Seamstresses; Seamstress guild officials; Seamstress workers

Seamstresses' guild (Rouen), 193

Séguier, Antoine-Louis, 176–77, 209–10, 249

Sevigné, Madame de, 33

Sewing machine, 94, 390

charged by, 98, 285; entry to, 338–40; labor shortage in, 102; price scale of, 159, 161; regulation of female homeworkers by, 98; relation between seamstresses and, 197, 241; rules on cutting cloth of, 150–51; size of, 338–39

Tailors' guild (Caen): dues charged by, 201; entry to, 336–37; relations between seamstresses and, 198–203, 217–18, 230–37; rights to women's clothing of, 234–37; size of, 337

Tailors' guild (Marseilles): dues charged by, 285; relations between seamstresses and, 203–7, 237–44

Tailors' guild (Paris): admission of *sans qualité* masters by, 335–36; corruption in, 100–101; electorate of, 259; entry to, 331–36; internal conflicts of, 265; loss of letters patent by, 220; officials of, 100–101, 250; place in garment trades of, 74; protest against 1776 abolition by, 245, 250–52; raids on illegal workers by, 96, 97, 100–101, 226, 273–74; regulation of employment by, 84–85; relations between seamstresses' guild and, 55–59, 66–67, 190–91, 192, 226–30; role of family in, 227–30, 251, 253, 333–35; rules on cutting cloth of, 150; sale of property of, 269; size of, 75–76, 331; trade rights of, 79, 36, 185–86, 192, 274; women's entry to, 211. *See also* Journeymen; Tailors

Taste, 125, 246, 371

Te deums, 276–77

Tea, 371

Technical literature, 114–18

Tontines, 378

Tools, 116–17, 129–31, 168, 367, 376

Trade sociability, 233–34, 349, 370

Trade specialization: among seamstresses, 78–80; among tailors' female workers, 97

Trade unions, 385, 394–98

La Tribune des femmes, 392

Turgot, Anne-Robert-Jacques, abolition of guilds by, 208–10, 244, 249; views on free market of, 209, 216; views on women's work of, 209

Unemployment, 89–90, 105, 106–8, 365–66, 388

Union of the Needle, 396–98

Unmarried women: fortunes of, 381, 382; households of, 88–89; 262, 306, 344, 356–57, 360, 364, 407; legal rights of, 223, 224; terms for, 80. *See also* Marriage; Widows; Wives; Women

Used-clothes dealers, 79, 96, 241. See also *Fripiers'* guild

Veblen, Thorstein, 23–24

Verdier, Yvonne, 398–400

Victoria and Albert Museum, 154

Vigée Lebrun, Elizabeth-Louise, 46

Vingtième de l'industrie, 83. See also *Capitation; Dixième de l'industrie*

Violence, 107, 137, 167–68

Vocational training, 323, 385–86. See also *Allouage;* Apprentices; Apprenticeship

Wages: conflict over payment of, 102–3; for prostitutes, 109; among seamstress workers, 92–93; in skilled male trades, 93–94; among tailors, 94; wage scale of tailors' guild, 84. *See also* Salaries

War, 188, 280, 283, 285, 328

Whalebone, 31, 33–34, 37, 42, 55, 56–58, 156, 238–44

Widows: fortunes of, 381; legal rights of, 224, 411; mourning period for, 127; of officeholders, 231–32; rights of, in male guilds, 84, 184, 211, 228; among seamstresses, 89, 356, 360, 363–64, 407; in tailors' guilds, 230–37, 251, 333–35. *See also* Marriage; Unmarried women; Wives; Women

Wiesner, Merry, 10
Winslow, Jacques-Bénigne (anatomist),
    59–63
Wives: autonomy in marriage of, 350;
    legal rights of, 223–24, 234; prop-
    erty rights of, 351–52; role in family
    businesses of, 347; of master tailors,
    251, 233, 234, 334–35. *See also* Mar-
    riage; Unmarried women; Widows;
    Women
Wollstonecraft, Mary, 23
Women: as consumers of clothing, 12,
    23; illnesses of, from wearing stays,
    60–61; in guild families, 227–28;
    legal rights of, 223–25, 234, 253; place
    in guild world of, 10–11, 173, 180–
    82, 183–84, 195–97, 209–10, 211–12,
    218–19, 232; in public spaces, 54, 236;
    Rousseau's views on, 64–66. *See also*
    Unmarried women; Wives; Women's
    guilds
Women's clothing: breakdown in social
    distinctions in, 41; changing styles of,
    25–26, 31–47; growing diversity of,
    43; tailors' right to fabricate, 234–37
Women's guilds, 247, 386; creation of,
    190–94; in late seventeenth-century

Paris, 180–82; men's rights in, 211;
    nineteenth-century legacy of, 398;
    proposals for creation of, 189, 195–97,
    205, 207–8, 215–16. *See also* Fresh-
    flower-sellers' guild; Hemp mer-
    chants' guild; Linen-drapers' guild;
    Mixed-sex guilds; Seamstresses'
    guild
Women's work, 179–80; historiog-
    raphy on, 10, 173, 297, 343; in late
    seventeenth-century Paris, 195–97,
    323; in male guilds, 183–84; and mar-
    riage strategies, 345, 347–50, 407;
    nineteenth-century debates about,
    113–14; official attitudes toward, 215,
    393, 400–401; Old Regime notions
    of, 174, 182–85, 395–96, 400, 406,
    410–11, 414–15; Turgot's views on,
    209. *See also* Femininity; Sexual
    division of labor
Workday: length of, 90; typical, 135
Work identities: among female
    workers, 108; among seamstresses,
    190, 392–93. *See also* Corporate iden-
    tity
Workshops, 117–23; size of, 90

Clare Haru Crowston is Assistant Professor of History
at the University of Illinois at Urbana-Campaign

Library of Congress Cataloging-in-Publication Data
Crowston, Clare Haru.
Fabricating women : the seamstresses of Old Regime France,
1675–1791 / Clare Haru Crowston.
p. cm.
Includes bibliographical references and index.
ISBN 0–8223–2662–0 (cloth : alk. paper)
ISBN 0–8223–2666–3 (pbk. : alk. paper)
1. Women tailors—France—History.   2. Women
dressmakers—France—History.   3. Women in guilds—
France—History.   4. Sexual division of labor—France—
History.   5. Clothing industry—France—History.
HD6073.C62 F7334   2001
331.4'87'0944—dc21   2001023936